Lecture Notes in Artificial Intelligence 2922

Edited by J. G. Carbonell and J. Siekmann

Subseries of Lecture Notes in Computer Science

T0226313

Springer

Berlin
Heidelberg
New York
Hong Kong
London
Milan
Paris
Tokyo

Frank Dignum (Ed.)

Advances in Agent Communication

International Workshop on
Agent Communication Languages, ACL 2003
Melbourne, Australia, July 14, 2003
Revised and Invited Papers

 Springer

Series Editors

Jaime G. Carbonell, Carnegie Mellon University, Pittsburgh, PA, USA
Jörg Siekmann, University of Saarland, Saarbrücken, Germany

Volume Editor

Frank Dignum
Utrecht University
Institute of Information and Computing Sciences
P.O.Box 80.089, 3508 TB Utrecht, The Netherlands
E-mail: dignum@cs.uu.nl

Cataloging-in-Publication Data applied for

A catalog record for this book is available from the Library of Congress.

Bibliographic information published by Die Deutsche Bibliothek
Die Deutsche Bibliothek lists this publication in the Deutsche Nationalbibliografie;
detailed bibliographic data is available in the Internet at <http://dnb.ddb.de>.

CR Subject Classification (1998): I.2.11, I.2, C.2.4, C.2, D.2, F.3

ISSN 0302-9743
ISBN 3-540-20769-4 Springer-Verlag Berlin Heidelberg New York

Springer-Verlag is a part of Springer Science+Business Media

springeronline.com

© Springer-Verlag Berlin Heidelberg 2004
Printed in Germany

Typesetting: Camera-ready by author, data conversion by Olgun Computergrafik
Printed on acid-free paper   SPIN: 10976029   06/3142   5 4 3 2 1 0

Preface

In this book we present a collection of papers around the topic of Agent Communication. The communication between agents has been one of the major topics of research in multi-agent systems. The current work can therefore build on a number of previous workshops, the proceedings of which have been published in earlier volumes in this series. The basis of this collection is the accepted submissions of the workshop on Agent Communication Languages which was held in conjunction with the AAMAS conference in July 2003 in Melbourne. The workshop received 15 submissions of which 12 were selected for publication in this volume. Although the number of submissions was less than expected for an important area like Agent Communication there is no reason to worry that this area does not get enough attention from the agent community. First of all, the 12 selected papers are all of high quality. The high acceptance rate is only due to this high quality and not to the necessity to select a certain number of papers. Besides the high-quality workshop papers, we noticed that many papers on Agent Communication found their way to the main conference. We decided therefore to invite a number of authors to revise and extend their papers from this conference and to combine them with the workshop papers. We believe that the current collection comprises a very good and quite complete overview of the state of the art in this area of research and gives a good indication of the topics that are of major interest at the moment.

The papers can roughly be divided over the following four topics:

- Fundamentals of agent communication
- Agent communication and commitments
- Communication within groups of agents
- Dialogues

Although the topics are of course not mutually exclusive they indicate some main directions of research. We therefore have arranged the papers in the book according to the topics indicated above.

The first six papers focus on some fundamental issues in agent communication. The paper of *A. Jones and X. Parent* explains how the semantics of messages can be given in terms of the institutional context in which they are sent. *M. Rovatsos, M. Nickles and G. Weiss* go one step further and pose the thesis that the interaction itself provides the meaning of the messages. The use of cognitive coherence theory is explored in the paper of *P. Pasquier, N. Andrillon, B. Chaib-draa and M.-A. Labrie*. This theory is used to explain why certain utterances are used and why some effects are achieved. In the paper of *R. Kremer, R. Flores and C. La Fournie* the performatives that are used in the messages are discussed and a hierarchy of performative types is proposed. The last two papers in this section deal with the verification of agent communication. In the paper of *M.-P. Huget and M. Wooldridge* model checking is used as a method to check the compliance of agent communication to some properties. *U. Endriss, N. Maudet, F. Sadri and F. Toni* propose a logical formalism to describe communication protocols. The use of this formalism makes it possible to verify the communication protocols against some properties such as guaranteed termination, answers when you expect them, etc.

The concept of "commitment" is used by a growing number of researchers in agent communication and therefore is given a separate section in this book. The first paper of this section is by *N. Fornara and M. Colombetti* and discusses how protocols can be specified when the ACL is based on a semantics of commitments. A logical model to describe the commitments themselves as a basis for agent communication is discussed in the paper of *M. Verdicchio and M. Colombetti. J. Bentahar, B. Moulin and B. Chaib-draa* argue that commitments can be combined into a commitment and argument network to formalize agent communication. When commitments are used to model agent communication some issues arise in how to create and dissolve them. In the paper of *A. U. Mallya, P. Yolum and M. Singh* some of the issues around resolving commitments are discussed. In the paper of *A. Chopra and M. Singh* especially some nonmonotonic properties of commitments are handled.

A relatively new topic that arose at this year's workshop is that of multi-party dialogues. Many issues come up in this setting that do not play a role in dialogues between only two agents. The main issues are discussed in the first two papers of this section. The paper of *D. Traum* focuses on the complete setting of the dialogues, including the focus of attention, etc. The second paper of *F. Dignum and G. Vreeswijk* discusses the issues from the dialogue perspective. The latter paper also gives a first attempt to create a test bed in which one can check the properties of multi-party dialogues. This is of particular interest because it will be hard to formally prove some of these properties given the complex settings and many parameters that play a role.

In the papers of *P. Busetta, M. Merzi, S. Rossi and F. Legras* and of *F. Legras and C. Tessier* some practical applications and implications of multiparty dialogues are discussed. Finally, in the paper of *J. Yen, X. Fan and R. A. Volz* the importance of proactive communication in teamwork is discussed.

The last section of the book is centered around the concept of dialogues in agent communication. The first two papers discuss some fundamental issues concerning dialogues while the other three papers describe some applications of dialogue theory in negotiation and resolving discrepancies. The paper of *P.E. Dunne and P. McBurney* handles some issues around the selection of optimal utterances within a dialogue. In the paper of *S. Parsons, P. McBurney and M. Wooldridge* the mechanics of the dialogues themselves are discussed.

In the paper of *R.J. Beun and R.M. van Eijk* we see the application of dialogue games in resolving discrepancies between the ontologies of the agents. A topic that will certainly become more and more relevant in open agent systems!

The paper of *P. McBurney and S. Parsons* describes how the idea of "posit spaces" can be exploited to describe protocols for negotiation between agents. In the final paper by *I. Rahwan, L. Sonenberg and F. Dignum* a first attempt is made to describe how negotiation dialogues can be modeled using the interests of the agents as a basis.

We want to conclude this preface by extending our thanks to the members of the program committee of the ACL workshop who were willing to review the papers in a very short time span, and also of course to the authors who were willing to submit their papers to our workshop and the authors who revised their papers for this book.

October 2003   Frank Dignum
                                                        Utrecht, The Netherlands

Workshop Organization

Organizing Committee

Frank Dignum	Utrecht University, Utrecht, The Netherlands
Marc-Philippe Huget	University of Liverpool, UK

Program Committee

Brahim Chaib-draa	Laval University (Canada)
Phil Cohen	Oregon Health and Science University (USA)
Marc d'Inverno	Westminster University (UK)
Frank Dignum	Utrecht University (The Netherlands)
Rogier van Eijk	Utrecht University (The Netherlands)
Tim Finin	University of Maryland (USA)
Marc-Philippe Huget	University of Liverpool (UK)
Andrew Jones	King's College London (UK)
Jean-Luc Koning	Leibniz-ESISAR (France)
Yannis Labrou	Fujitsu Laboratories (USA)
Alessio Lomuscio	King's College London (UK)
Abe Mamdani	Imperial College (UK)
Peter McBurney	University of Liverpool (UK)
Simon Parsons	City University of New York (USA)
Carles Sierra	AI Research Institute (Spain)
Munindar Singh	North Carolina State University (USA)
David Traum	USC Institute of Creative Technology (USA)
Hans Weigand	Tilburg University (The Netherlands)
Mike Wooldridge	University of Liverpool (UK)

Table of Contents

Section III: Communication within Groups of Agents

Section IV: Dialogues

Author Index

Conventional Signalling Acts and Conversation

Andrew J.I. Jones and Xavier Parent

Department of Computer Science, King's College London
The Strand, London WC2R 2LS, UK
{ajijones,xavier}@dcs.kcl.ac.uk

Abstract. This article aims to provide foundations for a new approach to Agent Communication Languages (ACLs). First, we outline the theory of signalling acts. In contrast to current approaches to communication, this account is neither intention-based nor commitment-based, but convention-based. Next, we outline one way of embedding that theory within an account of conversation. We move here from an account of the basic types of communicative act (the statics of communication) to an account of their role in sequences of exchanges in communicative interaction (the dynamics of communication). Finally, we apply the framework to the analysis of a conversational protocol.

1 Introduction

Current approaches to conversation can be divided into two basic categories:

- those that are intention-based or mentalistic. Inspired by Grice [14], these approaches focus on the effects communicative acts have on participants' mental states (see e.g. [30, 20]);
- those that are commitment-based, in that they assign a key role to the notion of commitment (see e.g. [36, 29, 9]).

What the relative merits are of intention-based and convention-based approaches to communication is a question that has been much debated within the Philosophy of Language [14, 22, 26, 3]. We cannot here enter into the details of this debate. Suffice it to say that it has become increasingly clear that the role played by the Gricean recognition-of-intention mechanism is not as important as one might think. Indeed, as far as literal speech acts are concerned, it is necessary to assume such a mechanism only for those cases where communicative acts are performed in the absence of established conventional rules. On the other hand, as some researchers working on Agent Communication Language (ACL) have also observed, the intention-based account takes for granted a rather controversial assumption, according to which agents' mental states are verifiable. This last observation is in fact one of the starting points of the commitment-based account as proposed by Singh [29] and Colombetti [9]. However, there are also some strong reasons to believe that that account too is fundamentally problematic. The most obvious reason has to do with the fact that it is not entirely clear what it means for speaker j to commit himself to an assertion of p. Should not

F. Dignum (Ed.): ACL 2003, LNAI 2922, pp. 1–17, 2004.

the propositional content of a commitment be a future act of the speaker? If so, to what action is j preparing to commit himself, when asserting p? A natural reaction is to say that, in asserting p, speaker j in fact commits himself to defend p if p is challenged by k. This is the view defended by Walton and Krabbe [36], and by Brandom [4, 5]. However, in line with Levi [21], we believe that this defence does not stand up to close scrutiny. What counts as an assertion in a language-game may correlate very poorly with j's beliefs. For instance, j can say that p without being able to defend p[1]. Does that mean that j is not making an assertion? If not, what is he doing? As we shall see, to focus exclusively on agents' commitments amounts, ultimately, to confusing two kinds of norms, which have been called "preservative" and "constitutive". The first are the kind that control antecedently existing activities, e.g. traffic regulation, while the second are the kind that create or constitute the activity itself, e.g. the rules of the game.

Objections of these kinds, we believe, indicate the need for an account of signalling acts based not on *intentions*, or *commitments*, but on *public conventions*.

The paper is structured as follows. Section 2 outlines the basic assumptions and intuitions which motivate the theory of conventional signalling acts. Section 3 outlines one way of embedding that theory within an account of conversation. We move here from an account of the basic types of communicative act (the statics of communication) to an account of their role in sequences of exchanges in communicative interaction (the dynamics of communication). The proposed framework is applied to the analysis of a conversational protocol.

2   Conventional Signalling Acts

The account of signalling acts outlined in this section bases the characterisation of communicative action neither on the intentions of communicators, nor on their commitments, but rather on the publically accessible conventions the use of which makes possible the performance of meaningful signalling acts. Consideration, first, of the communicative act of asserting will serve as a means of presenting the basic assumptions and intuitions which guide this approach.

2.1   Indicative Signalling Systems

The term 'indicative signalling system' is here used to refer to a signalling system in which acts of asserting can be performed. Such systems are constituted by conventions which grant that the performance, in particular circumstances, of instances of a given class of act-types *count as* assertions, and which also specify what the assertions mean. For example, the utterance with a particular intonation pattern of a token of the sentence "The ship is carrying explosives" will count, in an ordinary communication situation, as an assertion that the ship is carrying explosives. The raising, on board the ship, of a specific sequence of flags, will also count as an assertion that the ship is carrying explosives. In the

---

[1] For instance, Levi gives the example of a teacher explaining a thesis to a group of students.

first case the signal takes the form of a linguistic utterance, and in the second it takes the form of an act of showing flags. These are just two of a number of different types of media employed in signalling systems. For present purposes, it is irrelevant which medium of communication is employed. But for both of these signalling systems there are conventions determining that particular acts count as assertions with particular meanings.

According to Searle [26], if the performance by agent j of a given communicative act counts as an assertion of the truth of A, then j's performance *counts as an undertaking to the effect that A is true*. What lies behind that claim, surely, is that when j asserts that A what he says *ought* to be true, in some sense or other of 'ought'. The problem is to specify what sense of 'ought' this is. (Cf. Stenius [31].) The view adopted here is that the relevant sense of 'ought' pertains to the specification of the conditions under which an indicative signalling system is in an optimal state: given that the prime function of an indicative signalling system is to facilitate the transmission of reliable information, the system is in a less than optimal state, relative to that function, when a false signal is transmitted. The relevant sense of 'ought' is like that employed in "The meat ought to be ready by now, since it has been in the oven for 90 minutes". The system, in this case the oven with meat in it, is in a sub-optimal state if the meat is not ready – things are not then as they ought to be, something has gone wrong. The fact that the principles on which the functioning of the oven depends are physical laws, whereas the principles on which the signalling system depends are man-made conventions, is beside the point: in both cases the optimal functioning of the system will be defined relative to the main purpose the system is meant to achieve, and thus in both cases failure to satisfy the main purpose will represent a less-than-optimal situation.

Suppose that agents j and k are users of an indicative signalling system s, and that they are mutually aware that, according to the signalling conventions governing s, the performance by one of them of the act of seeing to it that C is meant to indicate that the state of affairs described by A obtains. The question of just what kind of act 'seeing to it that C' is will be left quite open. All that matters is that, by convention (in s), seeing to it that C counts as a means of indicating that A obtains. The content of the convention which specifies the meaning, in s, of j's seeing to it that C will be expressed using a relativised 'counts as' conditional (see, for a detailed formal account, [19]), relativised to s, with the sentence E_jC as its antecedent, where E_jC is read 'j sees to it that C' or 'j brings it about that C'[2]. How, then, is the form of the consequent to be represented? The communicative act is an act of asserting that A, and thus counts as an undertaking to the effect that the state of affairs described by A obtains. As proposed in the previous paragraph, this is interpreted as meaning that, when the communicative act E_jC is performed, s's being in an optimal state would require that the sentence A be true. So the form of the signalling convention according to which, in s, j's seeing to it that C counts as an undertaking to the effect that A, is given by

---

[2] The logic of the relativised action operator is given in [19] and [17]. The best available introduction to this kind of approach to the logic of agency is to be found in [11].

$$\text{(sc-assert)} \qquad E_j C \Rightarrow_s I_s^\star A \tag{1}$$

where $I_s^\star$ is a relativised optimality, or ideality, operator (a normative operator of the evaluative kind[3]), $I_s^\star A$ expresses the proposition that, were s to be in an optimal state relative to the function s is meant to fulfil, A would have to be true, and $\Rightarrow_s$ is the relativised 'counts as' conditional.

We state informally some assumptions we associate with (sc-assert). First, signalling system s is likely to contain a number of other conventions of the same form, according to which j's seeing to it that C' counts as an undertaking to the effect that A', j's seeing to it that C'' counts as an undertaking to the effect that A'', ... and so on. So the conventions expressed by conditionals of form (sc-assert) may be said to contain the *code* associated with indicative signalling system s – the code that shows what particular kinds of assertive signalling acts in s are meant to indicate. We might then also say that s itself is *constituted* by this code. Secondly, we assume that the (sc-assert) conditionals constituting s hold true for *any* agent j in the group U of agents who use s; that is, each agent in U may play the role of communicator. Thirdly, we assume that the members of U are all mutually aware of the (sc-assert) conditionals associated with s[4].

2.2   Communicator and Audience

Suppose that j and k are both users of signalling system s, and that (sc-assert) is any of the signalling conventions in s. Then we adopt the following schema:

$$((E_j C \Rightarrow_s I_s^\star A) \wedge B_k E_j C) \rightarrow B_k I_s^\star A \tag{2}$$

The import of the schema is essentially this: if k (the audience) believes that j performs the communicative act specified in the antecedent of (sc-assert), then k will accept that the consequent of (sc-assert) holds. He believes, then, that were signalling system s to be in an optimal state, A would be true. Another way of expressing the main point here is as follows: since k is familiar with the signalling conventions governing s, he is aware of what j's doing C is meant to indicate, and so, when k believes that j has performed this act, k is also aware of what would then have to be the case if the reliability of j's assertion could be *trusted*. This is not of course to say that k will necessarily trust j's reliability, but *if* he does so he will then also go on to form the belief that A. In summary, assuming (sc-assert) and (2), and supposing that

$$B_k E_j C \tag{3}$$

it now follows that

$$B_k I_s^\star A \tag{4}$$

---

[3] On the distinction between *evaluative* and *directive* normative modalities, see [17]. For the logic of the $I_s^\star$ operator we adopt a (relativised) classical modal system of type EMCN. As is shown in [8], a classical system of this type is identical to the smallest normal system K. For details, see [17].

[4] See [17] for some remarks on the analysis of mutual belief.

If k now also *trusts the reliability of j's assertion,* k goes on to form the belief

$$B_k A \tag{5}$$

This type of trust is to be distinguished from 'trust-in-sincerity'. For we may say that, in this same communication situation, *if k also trusts the sincerity of j's assertion*, k goes on to form the belief:

$$B_k B_j A \tag{6}$$

Note the various possibilities here: k might trust neither the reliability nor the sincerity of j's assertion, in which case neither (5) nor (6) holds. Alternatively, k might trust j's sincerity without trusting the reliability of his assertion ((6), but not (5)), or k might trust the reliability of j's assertion without trusting j's sincerity ((5) but not (6)). The latter case may arise if, for instance, k believes that the source of information supplying j is indeed reliable, even though he (k) also believes that j does not think the source is reliable. Finally, of course, k might trust both the reliability and the sincerity of j's assertion.

Note, furthermore, that the set of four *trust positions* we have just indicated may be expanded into a larger set of positions, depending on whether or not j is *in fact* reliable and *in fact* sincere[5].

It can readily be seen that, in contrast to the approach advocated in the FIPA COMMUNICATIVE ACT LIBRARY SPECIFICATION [XC00037G, 29.01. 2001][6], the present account of asserting makes no assumptions about the sincerity of the communicator. Furthermore, there is no assumption to the effect that j, when performing the act $E_j C$, intends thereby to produce in k one or both of the beliefs (5) and (6). Indeed the only background assumption about the communicator's intention that is implicit in this account is that k, when forming the belief represented by (4), supposes that j's communicative act is to be taken as a serious, *literal* implementation of the governing convention (sc-assert); i.e., k does not think that j is play-acting, communicating ironically, talking in his sleep, etc. In such *non*-literal communication situations there are good reasons (which will not be developed here) for supposing that (2) does not hold for a rational audience k. One distinctive feature of the present approach is that this background assumption about the communicator's intention can *remain* implicit, since the mechanism by means of which assertoric signalling is effected turns essentially on the governing signalling conventions – the publically accessible rules which show what particular types of communicative acts

---

[5] The use of the term 'position' here is quite deliberate, alluding to the theory of normative positions, and in particular to some well studied techniques for generating an exhaustive characterisation of the class of logically possible situations which may arise for a given type of modality (or combination of modalities), for a given set of agents, vis-à-vis some state(s) of affairs. See, e.g., [18] and [28] for illustrations of the development and application of the generation procedure. A more comprehensive account of the concept of trust, which incorporates the notion of 'trusting what someone says', is presented in [16].

[6] See http://www.fipa.org/

are taken to indicate − rather than on the intentions of agents who employ those conventions[7].

It might also be observed that it is very natural indeed to adopt this background assumption in the contexts for which the theory of ACLs is currently being developed. For the primary interest there is certainly not in *non*-literal communication, or in 'communicating one thing but meaning another', but in the *literal* (albeit quite possibly *deceitful*) usage of signals with *public, conventional meanings*.

2.3   Commitment

Some recent approaches to ACLs have assigned a key role to the notion of *commitment* (e.g., Singh in [29] and Colombetti in [9]), and it might be suggested that when an agent j asserts that A, his act counts as an *undertaking* to the effect that A is true in the sense that j *commits* himself to the truth of A. So it might be supposed that there is here an alternative way of understanding the essential rule governing asserting to that offered above in terms of the $I_s^\star$ operator.

However, this suggestion raises a number of difficulties. First, just what is meant by saying that an agent commits himself to the truth of some sentence A ? Does it mean that j is under some kind of obligation to accept that A is true ? If so, in relation to which other agents is this obligation held, i.e., who is it that requires of j that j shall accept the truth of A ? Everyone to whom he addresses his assertion ? Surely not, for there may well be members of the audience who do not care whether j is being sincere, and there may also be others who require j to be insincere: perhaps j is their designated 'spokesman' whom they have instructed to engage in deception when that strategy appears to meet their interests. Furthermore, since the current concern with ACLs is related to the design of *electronic* agents, it has to be said that there is very little agreement on what it might mean for an electronic agent to enter into a commitment.

The view taken here is that the move towards agent *commitment* (as the basis for understanding the *undertaking* involved in an act of asserting) is the result of a confusion − a confusion which was already indicated by Føllesdal [13] in his discussion of Stenius. The point is this: the reason why it is very commonly required of communicators that they shall tell the truth, or at least attempt to tell the truth as they see it, is that conformity to that requirement (that norm) will help to *preserve* the practice of asserting *qua* practice whose prime function is to facilitate the transmission of reliable information. But norms designed to *preserve* the practice should not be confused with the rules or conventions which

---

[7] Within the Philosophy of Language there has been a good deal of discussion of the relative merits of intention-based and convention-based approaches to the characterisation of communicative acts. This is not the place to enter into that discussion. Suffice it to say that FIPA's approach to ACLs seems to have been heavily, perhaps one-sidedly, influenced by theories deriving in large mesure from the Gricean, intention-based theory of meaning.

themselves *constitute* the practice — the conventions whose very existence makes possible the game of asserting, and which determine that the performance of an instance of a given act-type counts as a means of saying that such-and-such a state of affairs obtains. An attempt to use the notion of communicator's commitment to characterise the nature of asserting confuses preservative norms with constitutive conventions. To be sure, those conventions will eventually become de-valued, relative to the function they were designed to meet, if there is continual violation of the preservative norms. But this should not be allowed to obscure the fact that it is the conventions, and not the preservative norms, that create the very possibility of playing the asserting game, in an honest way, or deceitfully.

2.4 Some Other Types of Communicative Acts

Asserting is of course just one type of communicative act among many. This section provides just a sketch of some other types, and certainly does not pretend to give anything like an exhaustive characterisation of communicative act-types. But it does illustrate the flexibility and expressive power of the logical framework here employed. We consider four types:

- Commands
- Commissives (placing oneself under an obligation, e.g., promising)
- Requests
- Declaratives (in the sense of Searle & Vanderveken, [27])

In each case, the governing signalling convention will take the form of (sc-assert) with, crucially, some further elaboration of the scope-formula A in the consequent. This means that each of these signalling act-types is a sub-species of the act of asserting — a consequence which is harmless, and which simply reflects the fact that all communicative acts are acts of transmitting information — information which may, or may not, be true. However, as will be suggested in section 2.5, there is nevertheless one very important difference between pure assertives and these sub-species.

Commands
Let j be the agent issuing the command, and let k be the agent who is commanded to see to it that A. Then the form of the governing signalling convention is:

$$\text{(sc-command)} \qquad E_j C \Rightarrow_s I_s^\star OE_k A \qquad (7)$$

where the 'O' operator is a directive normative modality representing *obligation*. So, according to (sc-command), if j sees to it that C, s would then be in an optimal state, relative to its function of facilitating the transmission of reliable information, if there were an obligation on k to see to it that A.

Commissives
Let j be the agent issuing the commissive. Then the form of the governing signalling convention is:

$$(\text{sc-commit}) \qquad E_j C \Rightarrow_s I_s^\star O E_j A \qquad (8)$$

So, according to (sc-commit), if j sees to it that C, s would then be in an optimal state, relative to its function of facilitating the transmission of reliable information, if j were himself under an obligation to see to it that A [8].

Requests

Let j be the agent making the request, and let the aim of the request be to get agent k to see to it that A. Then the form of the governing signalling convention is:

$$(\text{sc-request}) \qquad E_j C \Rightarrow_s I_s^\star H_j E_k A \qquad (9)$$

where the relativised 'H' operator represents the modality 'attempts to see to it that...'. So, according to (sc-request), if j sees to it that C, s would then be in an optimal state, relative to its function of facilitating the transmission of reliable information, if j were attempting to see to it that k sees to it that A [9].

Declaratives

These are the kinds of signalling acts that are performed by, for instance, the utterance of such sentences as:

- 'I pronounce you man and wife'
- 'I name this ship *Generalissimo Stalin*'
- 'I pronounce this meeting open'

The point of declaratives is to create a new state of affairs, which will itself often carry particular normative consequences concerning rights and obligations, as when two persons become married, or a meeting is declared open. In the spirit of the approach developed in [19], we may say that declaratives are used by designated agents within institutions as a means of generating institutional facts: facts which, when recognised by the institution as established, are deemed to have particular kinds of normative consequences.

Let j be the agent issuing the declarative, and let A describe the state of affairs to be created by the declarative. Then the form of the governing signalling convention is:

$$(\text{sc-declare}) \qquad E_j C \Rightarrow_s I_s^\star E_j A \qquad (10)$$

So, according to (sc-declare), if j sees to it that C, s would then be in an optimal state, relative to its function of facilitating the transmission of reliable information, if j sees to it that A. For instance, j utters the words 'I pronounce you man and wife', and then s's being in an optimal state would require that j has indeed seen to it that the couple are married.

---

[8] On the logic of the directive normative modality, see [17].
[9] On the logic of the 'attempts to see to it that...' modality, see [17].

2.5   Being Empowered

For each of the four types just considered, if j is an empowered/authorised agent, then the *mere performance* by j of the act of seeing to it that C will be sufficient in itself to *guarantee* the truth of the respective formula to the right of the $I_s^\star$ operator[10]. For instance, if j is empowered/authorised to command k, then his seeing to it that C will indeed create an obligation on k to do A. Likewise, if j is empowered/authorised to commit himself, then performing the appropriate communicative act will be enough to place himself under an obligation. And if j is empowered/authorised to make a request to k, then his communicative act will constitute an attempt to get k to do the requested act. And so on.

Here lies the key to the crucial difference, alluded to above, between pure assertions and the other types of communicative act. For pure assertions, there is no notion of empowerment or authorisation which will license the inference of A from the truth of $I_s^\star A$. The closest one could get to such a notion would be the case where j is deemed to be an authority on the subject about which he is making an assertion: but even then, his *saying* that A does not *make it the case that* A [11].

We have now outlined a new formal approach to the theory of ACLs, in which a class of signalling conventions, governing some distinct types of communicative acts, can be represented. Other types of communicative act remain to be characterised. But we now turn to the task of embedding this 'static' account of communication within a theory of *conversation*, in which sequences of inter-related signalling acts are transmitted.

3   Modelling Conversations

Conversations are essentially dynamic in nature. In this section, we outline one possible way of adding a dynamic dimension to the theory of signalling acts, by combining it with the arrow logic of van Benthem [32–34] and colleagues [35, 24].

Our proposal is twofold. First, we suggest giving a compact expression to conversation protocols, by means of a formula of the object-language. Second, we suggest using this kind of representation to provide the beginning of a procedure for keeping a record of the conventional effects achieved in a conversation[12].

---

[10] We leave implicit here the obvious point that, in many cases, the communicative act has to be performed in a particular context − e.g., in the presence of witnesses − if it is to achieve its conventional effect.

[11] This is an old idea in a new guise. A number of early contributors to the literature on performatives (Lemmon, Åqvist and Lewis, among them) suggested that the characteristic feature of performatives, in contrast to constatives, was 'verifiability by use', or the fact that 'saying makes it so'. See [15] for references.

[12] Of course, the account outlined in this paper can only be suggestive of how future work should proceed. For instance, the account says nothing about the specific criterion the agent should apply in choosing which utterance will constitute its next contribution. For a discussion of this issue, see P.E. Dunne and P. McBurney's contribution to this volume ([10]).

The reason why we do not use dynamic logic in its traditional form (see Pratt [25]), is that it presupposes a kind of approach to the logic of agency that is very different from the treatment provided in the theory of signalling acts. As indicated in section 2.1, the present framework treats agency as a modal operator, with some reading such as 'agent j sees to it that'. Dynamic logic has explicit labels for action terms. These are not propositions but (to put it in Castañeda's terms) practitions.

It might well be the case that temporal logic provides a better account than arrow logic. Exploration of this second possibility is the main focus of our current investigations. The reason why we have chosen to concentrate first on arrow logic is that, when moving to the dynamics, we do not have to redefine the main ingredients of the semantics used for the static account. Indeed all we need to do is to interpret the points in a model as transitions. The completeness problem for the integrated framework is, then, relatively easy.

3.1   Embedding the Static Account within Arrow Logic

The syntax of arrow logic has in general the following three building blocks:

- a binary connective denoted by ∘ referred to as "composition" (or "circle");
- a unary connective denoted by ˘ referred to as "reverse" (or "cap");
- a propositional constant denoted by Id referred to as "identity".

The sentences that replace $A, B, ...$, that the first two connectives take as arguments, are supposed to describe an event, an action, etc. More expressive modal operators can be added into the vocabulary of the logic. For present purposes, we need not introduce them. Suffice it to observe that this way of turning the static account into a dynamic account is very natural, because a frame in arrow logic is no more than an ordinary Kripke frame. The only difference is that the universe W is viewed as consisting of arrows. These are not links between possible worlds. In fact they are treated themselves as the possible worlds[13]. As far as the 'dynamification' of the static framework is concerned, it then suffices to keep the package of truth-clauses already employed in the static framework, and to introduce those usually used for the three new building blocks.

The full account of the framework will be the focus of attention in a longer report on this work. Here we will characterise the arrow formalism only in terms of its proof-theory, and in terms of the graphics which help to give an intuitive account of the three new building blocks. Semantically, the introduction of these modalities is straightforward, by adding relations between arrows.

For instance, the evaluation rule for ∘ ("circle") states that $A \circ B$ is true at an arrow α iff it can be decomposed into two arrows at which A and B hold, respectively. This can be pictured as in figure 1:

---

[13] In this approach, arrows are not required to have some particular internal structure (to be "ordered pairs", for instance).

In $\beta : A$ In $\gamma : B$

In $\alpha : A \circ B$

Fig. 1. Composition

The intended meaning of this connective is relatively transparent. A sentence of the form $A \circ B$ can be read as meaning that the event described by A is followed by the event described by B. The two arrows at which A and B are evaluated can be seen as two intervals (periods of time).

Next, the evaluation rule for Id ("identity") says that, for Id to be true at α, α must be a transition that does not lead to a different state. This can be pictured as follows:

In α : Id

Fig. 2. Identity

Finally, the truth-clause for $\check{}$ ("reverse") says that, for $A^{\check{}}$ to be true at α, there must be an arrow β that is the reversal of α and at which A holds:

In $\alpha : A^{\check{}}$

In $\beta : A$

Fig. 3. Reverse

It is natural to say that such an operator has the meaning of 'undo-ing' an action. In figure 3, arrow β, at which A is true, leads from one state to another. Intuitively, the endpoint of β contains the effects of the performance of A in β. Arrow α, at which $A^{\check{}}$ is true, goes in the opposite direction, so that the effects of the performance of A in transition β are cancelled. Of course, we give this model for heuristic purposes only, since the formalism is not expressive enough to allow us to reason about states as well. However, it is possible (at least in principle) to remove this limitation, by switching to so-called two-sorted arrow logics. Introduced in van Benthem [33], these are designed for reasoning about both states and transitions. It seems very natural to try to refine the formalism in such a way that what obtains within states is also taken into account. We shall explore this issue in future research.

We now turn to the axiomatic characterization of the framework. When no particular constraints are imposed on the semantical counterparts of the dynamic operators, the proof theory of the integrated framework can in fact be obtained by adding the following rules of inference and axiom schemata to the basic logic:

Rules of inference

$$\frac{\vdash B \rightarrow C}{\vdash (A \circ B) \rightarrow (A \circ C)} \text{(r1)} \qquad \frac{\vdash A \rightarrow C}{\vdash (A \circ B) \rightarrow (C \circ B)} \text{(r2)} \qquad \frac{\vdash A \rightarrow B}{\vdash (A)^{\smile} \rightarrow (B)^{\smile}} \text{(r3)}$$

$$\frac{\vdash A}{\vdash \neg(\neg A \circ B)} \text{(r4)} \qquad \frac{\vdash A}{\vdash \neg(B \circ \neg A)} \text{(r5)} \qquad \frac{\vdash A}{\vdash \neg((\neg A)^{\smile})} \text{(r6)}$$

Axiom schemata

$$\vdash (A \vee B) \circ C \rightarrow (A \circ C) \vee (B \circ C) \tag{a1}$$
$$\vdash A \circ (B \vee C) \rightarrow (A \circ B) \vee (A \circ C) \tag{a2}$$
$$\vdash (A \vee B)^{\smile} \rightarrow A^{\smile} \vee B^{\smile}. \tag{a3}$$

The first three rules express a principle of closure under logical consequence. The next three are the arrow counterparts of the necessitation rule. Axioms (a1)-(a3) say that $\circ$ and $^{\smile}$ distribute over $\vee$. The converse of implication (a1) can easily be derived by using (r2), and similarly for (a2) and (a3).

A proof of soundness and (strong) completeness for the extended framework will be included in a longer report on our work, in preparation. The proof is based on the standard technique of canonical model construction.

3.2   The English Auction Protocol

In this section, we illustrate the expressive capacity of the logic, by showing how it can be applied to the analysis of a conversational protocol. We focus on what are called English auctions, at least as a starting point. We here give the basic idea of the treatment.

Figure 4 below depicts the English Auction Protocol used between an auctioneer agent a and each agent buyers b. The nodes (circles) represent states of the conversation, and the arcs (lines) represent speech acts that cause transition from state to state in the conversation. The circles with a double-line represent the final states of the conversation.

The propositional letters attached to the arcs are notational shorthand for the following speech acts:

- A: a puts item c up for auction;
- B: b makes a bid;
- C: a informs b that the item is sold to another buyer;
- D: a declares that the auction is at an end;
- E: a informs b that another buyer overbids;
- F: a informs b that his bid wins.

We use propositional letters for clarity's sake only. In fact, A corresponds to the antecedent of a conventional signalling rule of type (sc-declare), and likewise

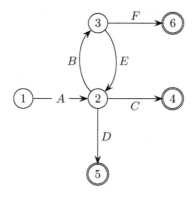

Fig. 4. English Auction Protocol

for D. B is to be replaced by the antecedent of a signalling convention taking the form of (sc-commit). The scope formula in the consequent uses a conditional obligation, $O(E_b A_2/A_1)$, according to which b is under the obligation to pay if his offer is accepted. We leave aside discussion of the problem of how to analyse the conditional obligation operator $O(/)$ (an elaborate formal treatment is available in [6])[14]. C, E and F each correspond to the antecedent of a signalling convention taking the form of (sc-assert).

The main function of a protocol is to define the sequences of speech acts that are permissible during a conversation. The basic idea is to assume that such sequences can be expressed in a compact way, by means of a disjunction containing $\circ$, $\breve{} $ and/or Id. For instance, the English Auction Protocol is an instantiation of the formula

$$(A \circ D) \vee (A \circ C) \vee (A \circ (B \circ F)) \vee (A \circ (B \circ (E \circ C))) \tag{11}$$

where (as we have just indicated) A, B, C, D, E and F stand for the antecedents of the appropriate signalling conventions. Since $\circ$ distributes over $\vee$, (11) can be simplified into

$$A \circ (D \vee C \vee (B \circ (F \vee (E \circ C)))) \tag{12}$$

(11) considers in isolation the sequences of acts that are allowed by the protocol. The first disjunct in (11), $A \circ D$, translates the path 1-2-5. The second disjunct, $A \circ C$, translates the path 1-2-4. The third disjunct, $A \circ (B \circ F)$ translates the paths 1-2-3-6. The fourth and last disjunct, $A \circ (B \circ (E \circ C))$, translates the

---

[14] The formalization of contrary-to-duty (CTD) scenarios raises a problem that is usually considered as a hard one by deontic logicians. We note in passing that the concept of norm violation has an obvious counterpart in commitment-based approaches to conversation. In particular, Mallya et. al.'s contribution to this volume (see [23]) puts some emphasis on the notion of breach of a commitment in a conversation. It would be interesting to investigate what such frameworks have to say about CTD scenarios.

path 1-2-3-2-4. Formula (12) puts the sequences of speech acts together, and indicates the points when interactants have the opportunity to choose between two or more speech acts. (12) can be read as follows. Once A has been done, then we can have either D, C or B. And once B has been done, we can have either F or E-followed-by-C. For simplicity's sake, we assume here that auctioneer a receives at most two bids. The fact that auctioneer a can receive more than two bids might be captured by an operator expressing iteration.

As the auction evolves, there is a shift in focus from the whole disjunction (11) to one specific disjunct. The latter records the acts (which are not necessarily verbal) performed in a conversation. It seems reasonable to expect a formal language for ACLs to also provide a way of keeping a record of the conventional effects achieved by these acts. As a further refinement, the recording might take into account the fact that users of signalling system s are empowered agents, or the fact that one agent j trusts some other agent k. Although we need to subject this issue to further investigation, we can already give some hint of how such a record can be achieved in the present framework. It consists in using a construction proposed by Fitting [12]

$$S \models U \rightarrow X \tag{13}$$

which exploits the idea that the local and the global consequence relations used in modal logic can be subsumed under one more general relation. The formal definition of this notion can easily be adapted to the present framework. Intuitively, S expresses global assumptions, holding at all arrows. In contrast, U enumerates local assumptions, holding at particular arrows. In line with our previous analysis — see section 2.1 — we assume that S contains the signalling conventions adopted by institution s. These are mutually believed by the agents who use s. Here, S plays the role of a black box that takes U (a sequence of communicative acts) as input and gives X (a list of conventional effects) as output. For instance, if the focus is on the sequence $A \circ (B \circ F)$, then S is the set having the following three elements:

$$E_a A_1 \Rightarrow_s I_s^\star E_a A_4 \tag{14}$$
$$E_b A_2 \Rightarrow_s I_s^\star O(E_b A_6 / A_5) \tag{15}$$
$$E_a A_3 \Rightarrow_s I_s^\star A_7 \tag{16}$$

Now let us adopt the point of view of an external observer x. This means that we can specify U in (13) as

$$B_x E_a A_1 \circ (B_x E_b A_2 \circ B_x E_a A_3) \tag{17}$$

As can easily be verified, the doxastic form of modus ponens (2) used in the 'static' framework allows us to specify X in (13) as

$$B_x I_s^\star E_a A_4 \circ (B_x I_s^\star O(E_b A_6 / A_5) \circ B_x I_s^\star A_7), \tag{18}$$

which represents a record of the conventional effects achieved in the conversation.

Depending on x's beliefs about the empowerment and trustworthiness of the communicators a and b, the record will include some further features. For instance, if x believes that a and b are empowered to declare and commit, respectively, and if x also believes that a's assertion of A_7 is trustworthy (reliable), then the record will also show:

$$B_x E_a A_4 \circ (B_x O(E_b A_6/A_5) \circ B_x A_7). \qquad (19)$$

One last remark is to be made. So far we have used only the operator $\circ$, in order not to distract the reader from the main point we wish to make in this paper. It is possible to use the other two operators, Id and $^\smile$, so as to capture further aspects of the protocol. The modal constant Id can be used to capture the obvious fact that, once a has suggested a starting-price for the goods, it may happen that another agent, call it b', opens the bid. (In this case, all b sees is the new announcement.). Operator $^\smile$ can be used to express the fact that, once E has been performed, the conversation returns to the prior state 2. Finally, it should be mentioned that the presence of a potential cycle might easily be captured by using the unary connective usually denoted by * and referred to as "iteration" (also "Kleene star"). We defer the full discussion of this issue to another occasion.

4   Concluding Remarks

Although the 'dynamic' account outlined in this paper is preliminary, we believe it points the way to a comprehensive theory of conversation, providing guidance to protocol designers. At the dynamic level, we have basically proposed a compact expression of conversation protocols, by using arrow logic. Although we need to subject this point to further investigation, we are inclined to think that this kind of representation will be able to facilitate the systematic comparison of protocols.

In closing, let us add one further remark in connection with the second suggestion we have made. It is that the record process should take into account questions about whether users of signalling system s are empowered agents, or questions about whether one agent j trusts some other agent k. Considerations of the first type become particularly relevant when, for instance, we focus on those situations where agents buy and sell goods on *behalf of* some other agents. In recent years, we have seen the development of a number of systems that make it possible to advertise and search for goods and services electronically. Let us take the case of the MIT's Kasbah prototype [7]. It is a Web-based system where users create autonomous agents to buy and sell goods on their behalf. Each of these agents is autonomous in that, once released into the marketplace, it negotiates and makes decisions on its own, without requiring user intervention. Suppose agent k makes a bid on behalf of user j. The background signalling convention (governing k's communicative act) takes the form

$$(E_k C \Rightarrow_s I_s^\star E_k E_j A) \wedge (E_j A \Rightarrow_s I_s^\star E_j B) \qquad (20)$$

If k is empowered to make an offer (if, for instance, a time-out has not taken place), then the truth of $E_k E_j A$ (and, hence, the truth of $E_j A$) is guaranteed. If user j is empowered as buyer (if j is not under age, or if j's credit is greater than or equal to the price of the good), then the truth of $E_j B$ also obtains. Here the idea is to classify the performance of a communicative act as valid or invalid according to whether or not the agent that performed the action was institutionally empowered. Some work along these lines has already been conducted in the context of the study of the Contract-Net-Protocol (see Artikis et al. [1, 2]). A thorough investigation of the relation between that account and the one outlined in this paper remains to be done.

References

1. A. Artikis, J. Pitt, and M. Sergot. Animated specifications of computational societies. In C. Castelfranchi and L. Johnson, editors, *Proceedings of Conference on Autonomous Agents and Multi-Agent Systems (AAMAS)*, pages 1053–1062, 2002.
2. A. Artikis, M. Sergot, and J. Pitt. Specifying electronic societies with the Causal Calculator. In F. Giunchiglia, J. Odell, and G. Weiss, editors, *Proceedings of Workshop on Agent-Oriented Software Engineering III (AOSE)*. Springer, 2003.
3. J. Bennett. *Linguistic Behavior*. Cambridge, 1976.
4. R. Brandom. Asserting. *Nous*, 17:637–650, 1983.
5. R. B. Brandom. *Making it Explicit - Reasoning, Representing, and Discursive Commitment*. Harvard University Press, London, England, 1994.
6. J. Carmo and A.J.I. Jones. Deontic logic and contrary-to-duties. In D. Gabbay and F. Guenthner, editors, *Handbook of Philosophical Logic*, volume 8, pages 265–343. Kluwer Academic Publishers, Dordrecht, Holland, 2nd edition, 2002.
7. A. Chavez and P. Maes. Kasbah: an agent marketplace for buying and selling goods. In *Proceedings of the 1st International Conference on the Practical Application of Intelligent Agents and Multi-Agent Technology (PAAM-96)*, pages 76–90, London, 1996. UK.
8. B.F. Chellas. *Modal Logic - an introduction*. Cambridge University Press, Cambridge, 1980.
9. M. Colombetti. A commitment-based approach to agent speech acts and conversations. In *Proceedings of the Workshop on Agent Languages and Conversation Policies*, pages 21–29, Barcelona, 2000. (Held at the *'Agents 2000'* conference).
10. P.E. Dunne and P. McBurney. Concepts of optimal utterance in dialogue: Selection and complexity. In F. Dignum, editor, *Advances in Agent Communication*, LNAI, page in this volume. Springer Verlag.
11. D. Elgesem. *Action Theory and Modal Logic*. PhD thesis, Institutt for filosofi. Det historik-filosofiske fakultetet. Universitetet Oslo, 1993. See also Elgesem's paper 'The modal logic of agency'. In *The Nordic Journal of Philosophical Logic*, vol. 2, 1997, pp. 1-46.
12. M. Fitting. Basic modal logic. In Hogger C. Gabbay D.M. and Robinson J., editors, *Handbook of logic in Artificial Intelligence and Logic Programming*. Oxford University Press, Oxford, 1983. Volume 1.
13. D. Follesdal. Comments on Stenius's 'Mood and language game'. *Synthese*, 17:275–280, 1967.
14. H.P. Grice. Meaning. *The Philosophical Review*, 66:377–388, 1957.

15. A.J.I. Jones. *Communication and Meaning - an essay in applied modal logic.* D. Reidel, Dordrecht - Holland, 1983.
16. A.J.I. Jones. On the concept of trust. *Decision Support Systems*, 33:225–232, 2002.
17. A.J.I. Jones. A logical framework. In J. Pitt, editor, *The Open Agent Society*, chapter 3. John Wiley and Sons, Chichester, UK, 2003. To appear.
18. A.J.I. Jones and M. Sergot. Formal specification of security requirements using the theory of normative positions. In Y. Deswarte, G. Eizenberg, and J.-J Quisquater, editors, *Computer Security - ESORICS 92*, Lecture Notes in Computer Science 648, pages 103–121. Springer-Verlag, 1992.
19. A.J.I. Jones and M. Sergot. A formal characterisation of institutionalised power. *Journal of the Interest Group in Pure and Applied Logic*, 4:427–443, 1996. Reprinted in E. Garzón Valdés et al., eds., *Normative Systems in Legal and Moral Theory - Festschrift for Carlos E. Alchourrón and Eugenio Bulygin*, Duncker & Humblot, Berlin, Germany, 1997, pages 349-367.
20. Y. Labrou and T. Finin. Semantics and conversations for an agent communication language. In Martha E. Pollack, editor, *Proceedings of the Fifteenth International Joint Conference on Artifical Intelligence (IJCAI-97)*, pages 584–591, Nagoya, Japan, 1997. Morgan Kaufmann publishers.
21. I. Levi. Review of: Making it explicit. *Journal of Philosophy*, 93:145–158, 1996.
22. D.K. Lewis. *Convention: a Philosophical Study.* Harvard University Press, Cambridge, 1969.
23. A.U. Mallya, P. Yolum, and M.P. Singh. Resolving commitments among autonomous agents. In F. Dignum, editor, *Advances in Agent Communication*, LNAI, page in this volume. Springer Verlag.
24. M. Marx. Dynamic arrow logic. In M. Marx, M. Masuch, and P. Polos, editors, *Arrow Logic and Multi-Modal Logic*, pages 109–129. CSLI Publications, 1996.
25. V.R. Pratt. Semantical considerations on Floyd-Hoare logic. In *Proc. 17th IEEE Symp. on Foundations of Computer Science*, pages 109–121, 1976.
26. J.R. Searle. *Speech Acts - an essay in the philosophy of language.* Cambridge University Press, Cambridge, 1969.
27. J.R. Searle and D. Vanderveken. *Foundations of illocutionary logic.* Cambridge University Press, Cambridge, 1985.
28. M. Sergot. Normative positions. In P. McNamara and H. Prakken, editors, *Norms, Logic and Information Systems*, pages 289–308. IOS Press, Amsterdam, 1999.
29. M.P. Singh. Agent communication languages: rethinking the principles. *IEEE Computer*, 31(12):40–47, 1998.
30. I. A. Smith, P. R. Cohen, J. M. Bradshaw, M. Greaves, and H. Holmback. Designing conversation policies using joint intention theory. In *Proceedings of the Third International Conference on Multi-Agent Systems (ICMAS98)*, 1998.
31. E. Stenius. Mood and language game. *Synthese*, 17:254–274, 1967.
32. J. van Benthem. *Language in Action.* The MIT Press, Amsterdam, 1991.
33. J. van Benthem. A note on dynamic arrow logics. In J. van Eijck and A. Visser, editors, *Logic and Information Flow*, pages 15–29. MIT Press, Cambridge, 1994.
34. J. van Benthem. *Exploring Logical Dynamics.* CSLI Publications, Stanford, California, 1996.
35. Y. Venema. A crash course in arrow logic. In M. Marx, M. Masuch, and P. Polos, editors, *Arrow Logic and Multi-Modal Logic*, pages 3–34. CSLI Publications, 1994.
36. D.N. Walton and E.C.W. Krabbe. *Commitment in Dialogue.* State University of New York Press, 1995.

An Empirical Model of Communication in Multiagent Systems*

Michael Rovatsos, Matthias Nickles, and Gerhard Weiss

Department of Informatics
Technical University of Munich
85748 Garching bei München, Germany
{rovatsos,nickles,weissg}@cs.tum.edu

Abstract. This paper proposes a new model of communication in multiagent systems according to which the *semantics* of communication depends on their *pragmatics*. Since these pragmatics are seen to result from the consequences of communicative actions as these have been empirically observed by a particular agent in the past, the model is radically *empirical, consequentialist* and *constructivist*. A formal framework for analysing such evolving semantics is defined, and we present an extensive analysis of several properties of different interaction processes based on our model. Among the main advantages of this model over traditional ACL semantics frameworks is that it allows agents to reason about the *effects* of their communicative behaviour on the structure of communicative expectations as a whole when making strategic decisions. Also, it leads to a very interesting domain-independent and non-mentalistic notion of conflict.

1 Introduction

One of the main challenges in the definition of speech-act based [1] agent communication language (ACL) semantics is explaining the link between *illocution* and *perlocution*, i.e. describing the *effects* of utterances (those desired by the sender and those brought about by the recipient of the message) solely in terms of the speech acts used. Various proposed semantics suggest that it is necessary to either resort to the mental states of agents [4, 3, 20] or to publicly visible commitments [5, 6, 8, 15, 19, 10, 21] in order to capture the semantics of speech acts, i.e. to aspects of the system that are *external* to communication itself.

In the context of *open* large-scale multiagent systems (MAS) characterised by dynamically changing populations of self-interested agents whose internal design is not accessible to others, it is not clear how specifications of mental attitudes or systems of commitments can be linked to the observed interactions. How can we make predictions about agents' future actions, if the semantics of their

* This work is supported by Deutsche Forschungsgemeinschaft (German Research Foundation) under contract No. Br 609/11-2. An earlier version of this paper has appeared in [17].

F. Dignum (Ed.): ACL 2003, LNAI 2922, pp. 18–36, 2004.

communication is defined in terms of mental states or commitments not related
to the design of these agents?

In this paper, we suggest a view of communication that is a possible response to this problem. This view is based on abandoning the classical notion
of "meaning" of utterances (in terms of "denotation") and the distinction between illocution and perlocution altogether in favour of defining the meaning of
illocutions solely *in terms of* their perlocutions.

Our view of communication is

1. *consequentialist*, i.e. any utterance bears the meaning of its consequences
   (other observable utterances or physical actions),
2. *empirical*, since this meaning is derived from empirical observation, and
3. *constructivist*, because meaning is always regarded from the standpoint of a
   self-interested, locally reasoning and (boundedly) rational agent.

By grounding meaning in interaction practice and viewing semantics as an emergent and evolving phenomenon, this model of communication has the capacity
to provide a basis for talking about agent communication that will prove useful
as more and more MAS applications move from closed to open systems. Its practical use lies in the possibilities it offers for analysing agent interactions and for
deriving desiderata for agent and protocol design. At a more theoretical level,
our framework provides a very simple link between autonomy and control and
introduces a new, powerful notion of conflict defined in purely communicative
terms, which contrasts mentalistic or resource-level conflict definitions such as
those suggested in [12]. As a central conclusion, "good" protocols are proven
to be both autonomy-respecting and contingency-reducing interaction patterns,
which is shown through an analysis of example protocols with our framework.

The remainder of this paper is structured as follows: section 2 presents the
assumptions underlying our view of communication, and in section 3 we lay
out requirements for agents our model is suitable for. Sections 4 and 5 describe
the model itself which is defined in terms of simple consequentialist semantics
and entropy measures. An analysis of several interaction scenarios follows in
section 6, and we round up with some conclusions in section 7.

2   Basics

To develop our model of communication, we should first explain the most important underlying assumptions.

Firstly, we will assume that agents are situated in an environment that is co-
inhabited by other agents they can communicate with. Agents have preferences
regarding different states of the world, and they strive to achieve those states
that are most desirable to them. To to this end they *deliberate*, i.e. they take
action to achieve their goals. Also, agents' actions have effects on each other's
goal attainment – agents are *inter-dependent*.

Secondly, we will assume that agents employ causal models of communicative behaviour in a goal-oriented fashion. In open, dynamic and unpredictable

systems, it is useful to organise experience into cause-and-effect models (which will depend much more on statistical correlation rather than on "real" causality) of the behaviour of their environment in order to take rational action (in a "planning" sense of means-ends reasoning). This is not only true of the physical environment, but also of other agents.

In the context of this paper, we will consider the foremost function of communication to be *to provide such a causal model for the behaviour of agents in communication*. These *communicative expectations* can be used by an agent in a similar way as rules that it discovers regarding the physical environment.

Thirdly, there are some important differences between physical action executed to manipulate the environment and communicative interaction, i.e. messages exchanged between agents:

1. The *autonomy* of agents stands in contrast to the rules that govern physical environments – agents receive messages but are free to fulfil or disappoint the expectations [2] associated with them. An agent can expect his fellow agents to have a model of these expectations, so he can presume that they are deliberately violating them whenever they are deviating from expectations. This stands in clear contrast to the physical environment which may appear highly non-deterministic but is normally not assumed to reason about whether it should behave the way we expect it to behave.
2. Communication *postpones* "real" physical action[1]: it allows for the establishment of causal relationships between messages and subsequent messages or physical actions.

   This enables communicating agents to use messages as *symbols* that "stand for" real[2] action without actually executing it. Hence, agents can talk about future courses of action and coordinate their activities in a *projective* fashion before these activities actually occur. This can be seen as a fundamental property of communication endowing it with the ability to facilitate cooperation.

With this in mind, we make the following claims:

1. Past communication experience creates expectations for the future.
2. Agents employ information about such expectations strategically.
3. Communicative expectations generalise over individual observations.
4. Uncertainty regarding expectations should be reduced in the long run.
5. Expectations that hinder the achievement of agent goals have to be broken.

Claim 1 states that causal models can be built by agents from experience and used for predicting future behaviour. Many representations for these models can

---

[1] Of course, communication takes place in physical terms and hence *is* physical action. Usually, though, exchanging messages is not supposed to have a strong impact on goal achievement since it leaves the physical environment virtually unmodified.

[2] Note that "real" action can include changes of mental states, e.g. when an agent provides some piece of information to another and expects that agent to believe him. For reasons of simplicity, we will restrict the analysis in this paper to communicative patterns that have observable effects in the physical environment.

be conceived of, like, for example, *expectation networks* which we have suggested in [13]. Statement 2 is a consequence of 1 and the above assumptions regarding agent rationality: we can expect agents to use *any* information they have to achieve their goals, so this should include communicative expectations.

The first claim that is not entirely obvious is statement 3 which points at a very distinct property of communicative symbols. It implies that in contrast to other causal models, the meaning of symbols used in communication is supposed to hold across different interactions. Usually, it is even considered to be identical for *all* agents in the society (cf. sociological models of communication [9, 11]). The fact that illocutions (which usually mark certain paths of interactions) represented by performatives in speech act theory are parametrised with "sender" and "recipient" roles conforms with this intuition. Without this generalisation (which is ultimately based on a certain homogeneity assumption among agents [11]), utterances would degenerate to "signals" that spawn particular reactions in particular agents. Of course, agents may maintain rich models of individual partners with whom they have frequent interactions and which specialise the general meaning of certain symbols with respect to these particular agents. However, since we are assuming agents to operate in large agent societies, this level of specificity of symbol meaning cannot be maintained if the number of constructed models is to be kept realistically small – agents are simply forced to abstract from the reactions of an individual agent and to coerce experiences with different agents into a single model.

Claims 4 and 5 provide a basis for the design criteria applied when building agents that are to communicate effectively. Unfortunately, though, the goals they describe may be conflicting. Item 4 states that the uncertainty associated with expectations should be kept to a minimum. From a "control" point of view, ideally, an agent's peers would react to a message in a mechanised, fully predictable way so that any contingency about their behaviour can be ruled out. At the same time, the agent himself wants to be free to take any decision at any time to achieve his own goals. Since his plans might not conform with existing expectations, he may have to break them as stated by statement 5. Or he might even desire some *other* peer to break an existing expectation, if, for example, the existing "habit" does not seem profitable anymore. We can summarise these considerations by viewing any utterance as a *request*, and asking *what* is requested by the utterance: the confirmation, modification or novel creation of an expectation.

These considerations lead to several desiderata for semantic models of communication:

– The meaning of a message can only be defined in terms of its *consequences*, i.e. the messages and actions that are likely to follow it. Two levels of effects can be distinguished:
  1. The immediate reactions of other agents and oneself to the message.
  2. The "second-order" impact of the message on the expectation structures of any observer, i.e. the way the utterance alters the causal model of communicative behaviour.

- Any knowledge about the effects of messages must be derived from *empirical* observation. In particular, a semantics of protocols cannot be established without taking into account how the protocols are *used* in practice.
- Meaning can only be *constructed* through the eyes of an agent involved in the interaction, it strongly relies on relating the ongoing communication to the agent's own goals.

Following these principles, we have developed a framework to describe and analyse communication in open systems that will be introduced in the following sections.

3 Assumptions on Agent Design

3.1 The InFFrA Social Reasoning Architecture

In order to present the view of communication that we propose in this paper, we first need to make certain assumptions regarding the type of agents it is appropriate for. For this purpose, we shall briefly introduce the abstract social reasoning architecture InFFrA that has previously been described in full detail in [18]. We choose InFFrA to describe this view of communication, because it realises the principles laid out in the previous section, while making only fairly general assumptions about the kind of agents our models are suitable for.

InFFrA is based on the idea that agents organise the interaction situations they find themselves into so-called *interaction frames* [7], i.e. knowledge structures that represent certain categories of interactions. These frames contain information about

- the possible interaction *trajectories* (i.e. the courses the interaction may take in terms of sequences of actions/messages),
- *roles and relationships* between the parties involved in an interaction of this type,
- *contexts* within which the interaction may take place (states of affairs before, during, and after an interaction is carried out) and
- *beliefs*, i.e. epistemic states of the interacting parties.

While certain attributes of the above must be assumed to be shared knowledge among interactants (so-called *common attributes*) for the frame to be carried out properly, agents may also store their personal experience in a frame (in the form of *private attributes*), e.g. utilities associated with previous frame enactments, etc. What makes interaction frames distinct from interaction protocols and conversation policies is that

(i) they provide comprehensive characterisations of an interaction situation (rather than mere restrictions on the range of admissible message sequences),
(ii) they always include information about experience with some interaction pattern, rather than just rules for interaction.

Apart from the interaction frame abstraction, InFFrA also offers a control flow model for social reasoning and social adaptation based on interaction frames, through which an InFFrA agent performs the following steps in each reasoning cycle:

1. *Matching:* Compare the current interaction situation with the currently activated frame.
2. *Assessment:* Assess the usability of the current frame.
3. *Framing decision:* If the current frame seems appropriate, continue with 6. Else, proceed with 4.
4. *Re-framing:* Search the frame repository for more suitable frames. If candidates are found, "mock-activate" one of them and go back to 1; else, proceed with 5.
5. *Adaptation:* Iteratively modify frames in the repository and continue with 4.
6. *Enactment:* Influence action decisions by applying the current frame. Return to 1.

This core reasoning mechanism called *framing* that is supposed to be performed by InFFrA agents in addition to their local goal-oriented reasoning processes (e.g., a BDI [16] planning and plan monitoring unit) is reasonably generic to cater for almost any kind of "socio-empirically adaptive" agent design.

Using the InFFrA architecture, we can specify a "minimal" set of properties for agent design to be in accordance with the principles laid out for our framework in section 2.

3.2 "Minimal" InFFrA Agents

The simplest InFFrA-compliant agent design that can be conceived of is as follows: we consider agents that engage in two-party turn-taking interactions that occur in discrete time and whose delimiting messages/actions can always be determined unambiguously. This means that agents always interact only with one peer at a time, that these encounters consist of a message exchange in which agents always take turns, and that an agent can always identify the beginning and end of such an encounter (e.g. by applying some message timeout after which no further message from the other agent is expected anymore).

We also assume the existence of some special "deictic" message performative $do(A, X)$ that can be sent by agent A to indicate it is executing a physical (i.e. non-communicative) action X in the environment. More precisely, $do(A, X)$ is actually a shortcut for an observation action of the "recipient" of this message by which he can unambiguously verify whether A just executed X and which he interprets as part of the encounter; it need *not* be some distinguished symbol that has been agreed upon.

Further, we assume that agents store these encounters as "interaction frames" $F = (C, w, h)$ in a (local) frame repository $\mathcal{F}$ where C is a condition, w is a message sequence and h is a vector of message counters.

The message sequence of a frame is a simple kind of trajectory that can be seen as a word $w \in \Sigma^*$ from some alphabet of message symbols Σ (which include the do-symbols that refer to physical actions). Although agents may invent new symbols and the content language of messages (e.g. first-order logic) may allow for an infinite number of expressions, Σ is finite, since it always only contains symbols that have already occurred in previous interactions.

Since specific encounters are relevant/possible under particular circumstances only, we assume that the agent has some knowledge base KB the contents of which are, at any point in time, a subset of some logical language L, i.e. $KB \in 2^L$. Then, provided that the agent has a sound inference procedure for L at its disposal, it can use a condition (expressed by a logical formula $C \in L$) to restrict the scope of a message sequence to only those situations in which C holds:

$$(C, w, h) \in \mathcal{F} \Leftrightarrow (KB \models C \Rightarrow w \text{ can occur })$$

In practice, C is used to encode any information about roles and relationships, contexts and beliefs associated with a frames as described in section 3.1.

As a last element of the frame format we use, agents employ "usage counters" $h \in \mathbb{N}^{|w|}$ for each message in a frame trajectory. The counter values for all messages in some prefix trajectory sequence $w \in \Sigma^*$ is incremented in all frames who share this prefix word whenever w occurs, i.e.

$$(w \text{ has occurred } n \text{ times} \wedge |w| = i) \Rightarrow$$
$$\forall (C, wv, h) \in \mathcal{F}.\forall i \leq |w|.h_i = n$$

(for some $v \in \Sigma^*$). This means that h is an integer-valued vector that records, for each frame, how often an encounter has occurred that started with the same prefix w (note that during encounters, h_i is incremented in *all* frames that have shared prefixes w if this is the message sequence just perceived until the ith message). Therefore, $count(F)[i] \geq count(F)[i + 1]$ for any frame F and any $i \leq |traj(F)|$ (we use functions $cond(F)$, $traj(F)$ and $count(F)$ to obtain the values of C, w and h in a frame, respectively). To keep F concise, no trajectory occurs twice, i.e.

$$\forall F, G \in \mathcal{F}.traj(F) \neq traj(G)$$

and if a message sequence $w = traj(F)$ that has been experienced before occurs (describing an *entire* encounter) under conditions C' that are not compatible with $cond(F)$ under any circumstances (i.e. $cond(C) \wedge C' \models \text{false}$), F is modified to obtain $F' = (cond(F) \vee C', w, h)$.

As a final element in this agent architecture, we assume the existence of a utility function

$$u : 2^L \times \Sigma^* \to \mathbb{R}$$

which will provide to the agent an assessment of the utility $u(KB, w)$ of any message/action sequence w and any knowledge base content KB. Note that while it appears to be a rather strong assumption that the utility of any message sequence can be numerically assessed in any state of belief, this is *not* intended as a measure for how good certain messages are in a "social" sense. Rather, it suffices if u returns estimates of the "goodness" of physical do-messages with respect to goal achievement and assigns a small negative utility to all non-physical messages that corresponds to the cost incurred by communication.

Minimal InFFrA agents who construct frame repositories in this way can use them to record their interaction experience: In any given situation, they can filter out those frames that are irrelevant under current belief and compute probabilities for other agents' actions and for the expectations others towards them given their own previous behaviour. They can assess the usability of certain frames by consulting their utility function, and they use the trajectories in $\mathcal{F}$ both to determine the frames that are applicable and to pick their next actions.

4   Empirical Semantics

As mentioned before, the semantic model we want to propose is purely *consequentialist* in that it defines the meaning of utterances in terms of their effects.

Let $2 \cdot H \in \mathbb{N}$ be some upper bound on the possible length of encounters, and let $\Delta(\Sigma^H)$ be the set of all discrete probability distributions over all words from Σ^* no longer than H.

We define the interpretation $I_{\mathcal{F}}$ induced by some frame repository $\mathcal{F}$ as a mapping from knowledge base states and current encounter sequence prefixes to the posterior probability distributions over all possible postfixes (conclusions) of the encounter. Formally, $I_{\mathcal{F}} \in (2^L \times \Sigma^H \to \Delta(\Sigma^H))$ with

$$I_{\mathcal{F}}(KB, w) = \lambda w'.P(w'|w)$$

where

$$P(w'|w) = \alpha \cdot \sum_{\substack{F \in \mathcal{F},\, traj(F)\,=\,ww', \\ KB\, \models\, cond(F)}} count(F)[|traj(F)|]$$

for any $w, w' \in \Sigma^H$ and some normalisation constant α.

This means that, considering those frames only whose conditions hold under KB, we compute the ratio of experienced conclusions w' to the already perceived prefix encounter w and the number of all potential conclusions to w.

The intuition behind this definition is that during an interaction encounter, if the encounter started with the initial sub-sequence w, the interpretation function $I_{\mathcal{F}}$ will yield a probability distribution over all possible continuations w' that may occur in the remainder of the current interaction sequence.

Finally, given this probability distribution, we can also compute the expected "future utility" of any message sequence w by computing

$$\bar{u}(w) = \sum_{w' \in \Sigma^H} I_{\mathcal{F}}(KB, w)(w') \cdot u(KB', w')$$

if KB' is the state of the knowledge base after w' has occurred[3].

The definitions in this section resemble the framework of Markov Decision Processes (MDPs) very much, and to capture the fact that probabilities of communication effects are *affected* by the decision-making agent herself, the MDP model would have to be modified appropriately. For the purposes of the present analysis, though, defining some simple measures on expectation structures will suffice.

5   Entropy Measures

With the above definitions at hand, we can now return to the principles of communication laid out in section 2. There, we claimed that an agent strives to

---

[3] This is because w' might involve actions that change the state of the environment. Unfortunately, this definition requires that the agent be able to predict these changes to the knowledge base *a priori*.

reduce the uncertainty about others' communicative behaviour, and at the same time to increase his own autonomy.

We can express these objectives in terms of the *expectation entropy EE* and the *utility deviation UD* that can be computed as follows:

$$EE_{\mathcal{F}}(w, KB) = \sum_{w' \in \Sigma^H} -P(w'|w) \log_2 P(w'|w)$$

$$UD_{\mathcal{F}}(w, KB) = \sqrt{\sum_{w' \in \Sigma^H} (u(w', KB) - \bar{u}(w', KB))^2}$$

Total *entropy* $\mathcal{E}_{\mathcal{F}}(w, KB)$ of message sequence w is defined as follows:

$$\mathcal{E}_{\mathcal{F}}(w, KB) = EE_{\mathcal{F}}(w, KB) \cdot UD_{\mathcal{F}}(w, KB)$$

How can these entropy measures be interpreted? The expectation entropy assesses the information-theoretic value of having performed/perceived a certain sequence w of messages. By computing the information value of all potential continuations, EE (again, we drop subscripts and arguments whenever they are obvious from the context) expresses the entropy that is induced by w in terms of potential continuations of this encounter prefix: the lower EE, the higher the value of w with respect to its ability of reducing the uncertainty of upcoming messages/actions. Thus, by comparing expectation entropies for different messages in the process of selecting which message to utter, the agent can compare their values or regard the system of all possible messages as an "encoding" for future reactions.

Utility deviation, on the other hand, is defined as the standard deviation between the utilities of all possible continuations of the encounter given w so that the importance of the potential consequences of w can be assessed. Its power lies in being closely related to the expected utility of the encounter, while at the same time providing a measure for the *risk* associated with the encounter sequence perceived so far.

Returning to the observation we made regarding the "request" nature of any communicative action in section 2, we can now rephrase this view in terms of the mathematical tools introduced in the above paragraphs: Any message $v \in \Sigma$ considered in the context of an encounter has an expectation entropy associated with it, so that $EE(wv, KB)$ can be used to predict how much using v will help to "settle" the communication situation, i.e. to reduce the number of potential outcomes of the entire encounter. At the same time $UD(wv, KB)$ can be used to check how "grave" the effects of different outcomes would be.

By combining these two measures into $\mathcal{E}$, the agent can trade off the reduction of uncertainty against sustainment of autonomy depending on its willingness to conform with existing expectations or to deviate in order to pursue goals that contradict the expectations held towards the agent.

6   Analysis

To see how the above framework may help interpret the meaning of utterances and guide the agent's behaviour, we will compare three different interaction scenarios, in which the frame repositories of some agent a_1 have been compiled into the trees shown in figures 1, 2 and 3, respectively (we use trees of interaction trajectories as defined in [2] instead of sets of sequences as a more compact representation). The nodes which represent messages are connected by edges that are labelled with transition probabilities in *italics* (computed using $count(F)$). We use variables A, B, X etc. to capture several "ground" situations by a single tree. The substitutions that are needed to reconstruct past interactions using the tree are not displayed in the examples, but form part of the private attributes (cf. section 3.1).

Where the direct utility associated with an action is not zero, the increase/decrease in total utility is printed on top of the action in **bold** face in square brackets [] (if communication preceding these "utility nodes" comes at a cost, this has been already considered in the utility of the leaf node). For simplicity, we also assume the trees presented here to be the result of combining all frames that are consistent with the current knowledge base, i.e. frame conditions have already been checked.

6.1   Interaction Scenarios

The repository shown in figure 1 summarises experience with a "simple-request" protocol (SRP) where one agent starts by requesting an action X and the other may simply execute the requested action or end the encounter (the $\perp$ symbol is used to denote encounter termination whenever termination probability is below 1.0) – in a sense, this is the most "minimal" protocol one can think of. So far, only 30% out of all requests have been fulfilled, all others went unanswered.

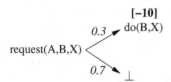

Fig. 1. SRP (simple-request protocol) frame repository tree.

We now picture a situation in which agent a_1 is requested by agent a_2 to execute some action, but this action has a utility of -10 for a_1. Note that the probabilities in the tree are derived from observing *different* interactions where a_1 may have held both participating parties' roles in different instances, but the utility decrease of 10 units is computed on the grounds of the current situation, by instantiating variable values with agent and action names (e.g. $A = a_2$, $B = a_1$ and $X = deliver(quantity = 100)$).

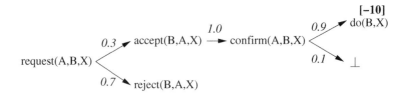

Fig. 2. RAP (request-accept protocol) frame repository tree.

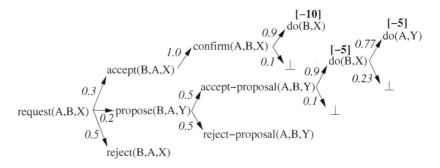

Fig. 3. RCOP (request-counter-offer protocol) frame repository tree.

Figure 2 shows a "request-accept" protocol (RAP) that leaves some more options to the requestee as he may accept or reject the request. After confirmation of the requesting agent (which is certain), the requestee executes the request with a probability of 90%; in 10% of the cases, the agent who agreed to fulfil the request is unreliable.

The "request-counter-offer" protocol (RCOP) in figure 3 offers more possibilities still: it includes "accept" and "reject" options, but it also allows for making a proposal Y that the other agent may accept or reject in turn, and if this proposal is accepted, that other agent is expected to execute action Y if the first agent executes X. The distribution between `accept`/`propose`/`reject` is now $0.3/0.2/0.5$, because it is realistic to assume that in 20% of the cases in which the initial offer would have been rejected in the RAP, the requestee was able to propose a compromise in the RCOP. As before, the requestee fails to perform X with probability 0.1, and this unreliability is even larger (23%) for the other agent. This is realistic, because the second agent is tempted to "cheat" once his opponent has done his duty. In the aforementioned scenario, we assume that the "compromise" actions X and Y (e.g. $X = deliver(quantity = 50)$, $Y = pay\_bonus$) both have utility -5.0, i.e. the compromise is not better than the original option $deliver(quantity = 100)$.

Now let us assume a_1 received the message

$$\mathtt{request}(a_2, a_1, deliver(quantity = 100))$$

from a_2 who starts the encounter. The question that a_1 finds herself in is whether he should perform the requested action despite the negative utility just for the sake of improving the reliability of the frame set or not[4].

6.2 Entropy Decrease vs. Utility

First, consider the case where he chooses to perform the action. In the SRP, this would decrease $UD(\texttt{request})$ from 5.39 to 5.36 [5], but it would increase $EE(\texttt{request})$ from 0.8812 to 0.8895. The total entropy $\mathcal{E}(\texttt{request})$ would increase from 4.74 to 4.76. In case of not executing the requested action utility deviation would rise to 5.40, expectation entropy would decrease to 0.8776, and the resulting total entropy would be 4.73.

How can we interpret these changes? They imply that choosing the more probable option $\bot$ reduces entropy while performing the action increases it. Thus, since most requests go unanswered, doing nothing reassures this expectation. Yet, this increases the risk (utility deviation) of $\texttt{request}$, so a_1's choice should depend on whether he thinks it is probable that he will *herself* be in the position of requesting an action from someone else in the future (if e.g., the utility of $\texttt{do}$ becomes +10.0 in a future situation and a_1 is requesting that action). But since the difference in $\Delta\mathcal{E}$ (the difference between entropies after and before the encounter) is small (0.02 vs. -0.01), the agent should only consider sacrificing the immediate payoff if it is *highly* probable that the roles will be switched in the future.

Let us look at the same situation in the RAP case. The first difference to note here is that

$$UD(\texttt{accept}) = UD(\texttt{confirm}) = 6.40 > 4.76 = UD(\texttt{request})$$

This nicely illustrates that the "closer" messages are to utility-relevant actions, the greater the potential risk, unless occurrence of the utility-relevant action is absolutely certain. This means that the 0.9/0.1 distribution of $\texttt{do}/\bot$ constitutes a greater risk than the 0.7/0.3 distribution of $\texttt{reject}/\texttt{accept}$, even though $EE(\texttt{confirm}) < EE(\texttt{request})$!

If a_1 performs the requested action, the total entropy of $\texttt{request}$ increases from 4.86 to 4.89, if he doesn't (by sending a $\texttt{reject}$), it decreases to 4.84. Since this resembles the entropy effects in the SRP very much, what is the advantage of having such a protocol that is more complex?

6.3 External Paths and Path Criticality

The advantages of the RAP become evident when looking at the entropies of $\texttt{accept}$ and $\texttt{confirm}$ after a $\texttt{reject}$, which remain unaffected (since they are

---

[4] Ultimately, this depends on the design of the agent, i.e. in which way this reliability is integrated in utility computation.

[5] The small changes are due to the fact that the frame repository is the product of 100 encounters – a single new encounter induces only small changes to the numerical values.

located on different paths than `reject`). So RAP is, in a sense, superior to SRP, because it does allow for deviating from a certain expectation by *deferring* the expectations partly to messages on unaffected *external paths*. Effectively this means that after a `reject`, a `request` becomes riskier in future encounters, but if the agent waits until the `accept` message in a future interaction, he can be as certain of the consequences as he was before. Of course, in the long run this would render `request` almost useless, but if used cautiously, this is precisely the case where autonomy and predictability can be combined to serve the needs of the agents.

The most dramatic changes to entropy values will be witnessed if the agent doesn't perform the action, but promises to do so by uttering an `accept` message: $\mathcal{E}(\texttt{request})$ increases from 4.86 to 5.05, $\mathcal{E}(\texttt{accept})$ and $\mathcal{E}(\texttt{confirm})$ both increase from 3.00 to 3.45. This is an example of how our analysis method can provide information about *path criticality*: it shows that the normative content of `accept` is very fragile, both because it is closer to the utility-relevant action and because it has been highly reliable so far.

6.4   Trajectory Entropy Shapes

Let us now look at the RCOP and, once more, consider the two alternatives of executing the request right away or rejecting the request. Now, the total entropy decreases from 14.41 to 14.38 and 14.35 in the case of `accept`/`reject`, respectively. This is similar to the SRP and the RAP, even though the effects of different options are now less clearly visible (which due to the fact that refusal and acceptance are now more evenly distributed). Also, the total entropy of `request` that is more than three times higher than before (with comparable utility values). This suggests that it might be a good idea to split the RCOP into two frames that start with different performatives, e.g. `request-action` and `request-proposal`.

Of course, the `propose` option is what is actually interesting about the RCOP, and the final step in our analysis will deal with this case. If a_1 analyses the possible runs that include a `propose` message, he will compare the effects of the following encounters on the frame tree with each other:

Short name	Encounter
"success":	$\texttt{request}(A, B, X) \ldots \rightarrow \texttt{do}(A, Y)$
"A cheats":	$\texttt{request}(A, B, X) \ldots \rightarrow \texttt{do}(B, X)$
"B cheats":	$\texttt{request}(A, B, X) \ldots \rightarrow \texttt{accept-proposal}(A, B, Y)$
"rejection":	$\texttt{request}(A, B, X) \rightarrow \texttt{reject-proposal}(B, A, X)$

Figures 4 and 5 show the values of $\mathcal{E}(w)$ and $\Delta\mathcal{E}(w)$ (the change in total entropy before and after the encounter) computed for the messages along the path

$$w = \texttt{propose}(A, B, X) \rightarrow \ldots \rightarrow \texttt{do}(A, Y)$$

A first thing to note is the shape of the entropy curve in figure 4 which is typical of meaningful trajectories. As illustrated by the boxed "perfect" entropy curve,

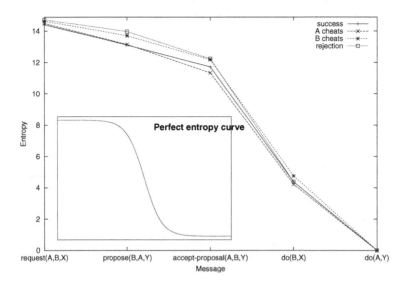

Fig. 4. RCOP entropies along "success" path for all four interaction cases.

reasonable trajectories should start with an "autonomy" part with high entropy which gives agents several choices, and then continue with a "commitment" part in which entropy decreases rapidly to make sure there is little uncertainty in the consequences of the interaction further on.

Secondly, figure 5 which shows the changes to the node entropies before and after the respective interaction proves that as in the RAP, cheating has a negative impact on entropies. Moreover, the effects of "A cheats" appear to be much worse than those of "B cheats" which reassures our intuition that the closer utterances are to the final outcome of the encounter, the more critical will the expectations about them be.

Thirdly, as before, the "rejection" dialogue and the "success" dialogue are acceptable in the sense of decreasing entropies of propose and accept-proposal (note that the small entropy increase of request is due to the 0.1/0.23 probabilities of cheating after accept-proposal and $do(B, X)$). The fact that "success" is even better than "rejection" suggests that, in a situation like this, there is considerable incentive to compromise, if the agent is willing to sacrifice current payoff for low future entropies.

6.5   Conflict Potential

Looking at the plots in figure 5, a more general property of communication becomes evident: we can imagine an agent reckoning what to do in an ongoing encounter who evaluates the potential entropy changes to relevant paths after each message.

For this purpose, let $\mathcal{F}'$ be the result of adding a new encounter w' to the current repository $\mathcal{F}$ (we assume $count(w)$ and $cond(w)$ are computed as described

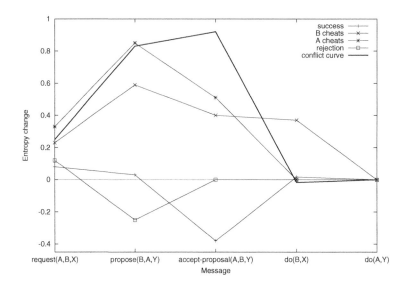

Fig. 5. RCOP entropy changes $\Delta\mathcal{E}$ along $\texttt{propose}(A, B, X) \rightarrow \ldots \rightarrow \texttt{do}(A, Y)$.

in section 3). The *entropy change* induced on trajectory $w \in \Sigma^*$ by performing encounter $w' \in \Sigma^*$ is defined as

$$\Delta\mathcal{E}_{\mathcal{F}}(w, w') = \mathcal{E}_{\mathcal{F}'}(w) - \mathcal{E}_{\mathcal{F}}(w)$$

This quantity provides a measure of the *expectation-affirmative* or *expectation-negating* character of an utterance. In other words, it expresses to which degree the agents are saying "yes" or "no" to an existing expectation.

The *conflict potential* of an encounter can be derived by comparing the *expected* entropy change to the *occurred* entropy change, and thus revealing to which degree the agents exceeded the expected change to expectation structures. We can define the conflict potential exerted by the occurred encounter w'' on encounter w if the expected encounter was w' as

$$\mathcal{CP}_{\mathcal{F}}(w'', w', w) = \int_{w[1]}^{w[\|w\|]} \Delta\mathcal{E}_{\mathcal{F}}(w, w'') - \Delta\mathcal{E}_{\mathcal{F}}(w, w')dw_i$$

This is the area under the "conflict curve" in figure 5, that computes

$$\Delta\mathcal{E}(\text{"success"}, \text{"A cheats"}) - \Delta\mathcal{E}(\text{"success"}, \text{"success"})$$

This curve shows how the difference between expected and actual entropy change grows larger and larger, until the encounter is terminated unsuccessfully. This increases the probability that the participating agents will stop trusting the expectation structures, and that this will inhibit the normal flow of interaction, especially if $\mathcal{CP}$ is large for several paths w.

A noteworthy property of this view of conflict is that in cases where, for example, entirely new performatives are tried out, the conflict potential is 0 because the expected entropy change (which is very large, because the agents know nothing about the consequences of the new performative) is identical to that actually experienced. So what matters about conflict is not whether the expectations associated with a message are clear, but rather whether the effect of uttering them comes close to our expectations about that effect on the expectation structures – a property we might call *second-order expectability*.

7   Conclusions

This paper presented a novel model for defining and analysing the semantics of agent communication that is radically *empirical, consequentialist* and *constructivist*. Essentially, it is based on the idea that the meaning of communication lies in the expectations associated with communicative actions in terms of their consequences. This expectations always depend on the perspective of an observer who has derived them from his own interaction experience.

By relying on a simple statistical analysis of observed communication that makes no domain-dependent assumptions, the proposed model is very generic. It does impose some restrictions on the design of the agents by assuming them to be capable of recording and statistically analysing observed interaction sequences.

A common critique of such "functionalist" semantics of agent communication that has to be taken seriously is that there is more to communication than statistical correlations between messages and actions, because the purpose of communication is not always physical action (but also, e.g., exchange of information) and that many (in particular, normative) aspects of communication are neglected by reducing semantics to an empirical view. We still believe that such empirical semantics can serve as a "greatest common denominator" for divergent semantic models of different agents, if no other reliable knowledge about the meaning of messages is available. If, on the other hand, such knowledge is available, our framework can still be used "on top" of other (mentalistic, commitment-based) semantics.

Using very general entropy-based measures for probabilistic expectation structures, we performed an analysis of different empirically observed interaction patterns. This analysis proved that useful expectation structures are structures that leave enough room for autonomy but are at the same time reliable once certain paths are chosen by interactants – they are *autonomy-respecting* and *contingency-reducing* at the same time.

Such structures are characterised by the following features:

- *external paths* whose entropies remain fairly unaffected by agent's choices in the early phases of an encounter;
- *low expectation entropy* where *utility deviation* is high – the higher the potential loss or gain of a path, the more predictable it should be (esp. towards the end of an encounter);

- *alternatives* for different utility configurations; paths that are likely to have a wider range of acceptable outcomes for the partners (e.g. by containing do-actions for all parties, cf. RCOP) are more likely to become stable interaction procedures, as they will be used more often.

One of the strengths of our framework is that empirical semantics suggest including considerations regarding the usefulness of "having" a certain semantics in the utility-guided decision processes of agents. Agents can compute entropy measures of message trajectories prior to engaging in actual communication and assess the first- and second-order effects of their actions under current utility conditions or using some long-term estimate of how the utility function might change (i.e. which messages they will want to be reliable in the future). The fact that agents consider themselves being in the position of someone else (when computing entropy changes) links the protocol character of communication to the self-interested decision-making processes of the participating agents, thus making communication truly meaningful.

As yet, we have not formalised an integrated decision-theoretic framework that allows these long-term considerations to be included in social "message-to-message" reasoning, but our model clearly provides a foundation for further investigation in this direction. Also, we have not yet dealt with the question of how an agent can optimally *explore* existing communicative conventions in a society so as to obtain a good expectation model as quickly as possible and how to balance this *exploration* with the *exploitation* in the sense of utility maximisation. Our use of information-theoretic measures suggests that *information value* considerations might be useful with this respect.

Another novelty of our framework is the definition of conflict potential as a "decrease in trust towards the communication system". Sudden, unexpected "jumps" in entropies that become bigger and bigger render the expectation structures questionable, the meaning of communicative acts becomes more and more ambiguous. This definition of computational conflict is very powerful because it does not resort to domain-dependent resource or goal configurations and is defined solely in terms of communicative processes. However, we have not yet suggested resolution mechanisms for such conflict interactions. We believe that reifying conflict in communication (i.e. making it the subject of communication) is of paramount importance when it comes to conflict resolution and are currently working in this direction.

Future work will also focus on observing and influencing evolving expectations at different levels. In [13], we have recently proposed the formalism of *expectation networks* that is suitable for constructing large-scale "communication systems" from observation of an entire MAS (or at least of large agent sub-populations) through a global system observer. There, we have also analysed to which degree the frame repositories of locally reasoning InFFrA agents can be converted to global expectation networks and vice versa. This paves the way for developing methods that combine (i) *a priori* designer expectations that are represented through expectation structures [2] with (ii) emergent global communication patterns at the system level and (iii) agent rationality, creativity and adaptation through strategic application of communicative expectations.

We strongly believe that this approach has the capacity to unify the different levels addressed in the process of engineering open MAS via the concept of empirical semantics. The material presented in this paper can be seen as a first step in this direction.

References

1. J. L. Austin. *How to do things with Words.* Clarendon Press, 1962.
2. W. Brauer, M. Nickles, M. Rovatsos, G. Weiß, and K. F. Lorentzen. Expectation-Oriented Analysis and Design. In *Proceedings of the 2nd Workshop on Agent-Oriented Software Engineering,* volume 2222 of *LNAI,* 2001. Springer-Verlag.
3. P. R. Cohen and H. J. Levesque. Communicative actions for artificial agents. In *Proceedings of the First International Conference on Multi-Agent Systems (ICMAS-95),* pages 65–72, 1995.
4. P. R. Cohen and C. R. Perrault. Elements of a Plan-Based Theory of Speech Acts. *Cognitive Science,* 3:177–212, 1979.
5. N. Fornara and M. Colombetti. Operational specification of a commitment-based agent communication language. In *Proceedings of the First International Joint Conference on Autonomous Agents and Multiagent Systems (AAMAS'02),* pages 536–542, 2002. ACM Press.
6. N. Fornara and M. Colombetti. Protocol specification using a commitment-based ACL. In this volume.
7. E. Goffman. *Frame Analysis: An Essay on the Organisation of Experience.* Harper and Row, New York, NY, 1974.
8. F. Guerin and J. Pitt. Denotational Semantics for Agent Communication Languages. In *Proceedings of the Fifth International Conference on Autonomous Agents (Agents'01),* pages 497–504. ACM Press, 2001.
9. N. Luhmann. *Social Systems.* Stanford University Press, Palo Alto, CA, 1995.
10. A. U. Mallya, P. Yolum, and M. Singh. Resolving commitments among autonomous agents. In this volume.
11. G. H. Mead. *Mind, Self, and Society.* University of Chicago Press, Chicago, IL, 1934.
12. H.-J. Müller and R. Dieng, editors. *Computational Conflicts – Conflict Modeling for Distributed Intelligent Systems.* Springer-Verlag, Berlin, 2000.
13. M. Nickles, M. Rovatsos, W. Brauer, G. Weiß. Communication Systems: A Unified Model of Socially Intelligent Systems. In K. Fischer, M. Florian, editors, *Socionics: Its Contributions to the Scalability of Complex Social Systems.* LNAI, Springer-Verlag, 2003. To appear.
14. J. Pitt and A. Mamdani. Designing agent communication languages for multi-agent systems. In *Proceedings of the Ninth European Workshop on Modelling Autonomous Agents in a Multi-Agent World (MAAMAW-99),* volume 1647 of LNAI, pages 102–114. Springer-Verlag, 1999.
15. J. Pitt and A. Mamdani. A protocol-based semantics for an agent communication language. In *Proceedings of the 16th International Joint Conference on Artificial Intelligence (IJCAI-99),* 1999.
16. A. S. Rao and M. P. Georgeff. BDI agents: From theory to practice. In *Proceedings of the First International Conference on Multi-Agent Systems (ICMAS-95),* pages 312–319, 1995.

17. M. Rovatsos, M. Nickles, and G. Weiß. Interaction is Meaning: A New Model for Communication in Open Systems. In *Proceedings of the Second International Joint Conference on Autonomous Agents and Multi-Agent Systems (AAMAS'03)*, 2003.
18. M. Rovatsos, G. Weiß, and M. Wolf. An Approach to the Analysis and Design of Multiagent Systems based on Interaction Frames. In *Proceedings of the First International Joint Conference on Autonomous Agents and Multiagent Systems (AAMAS'02)*, 2002.
19. M. Singh. A social semantics for agent communication languages. In *Proceedings of the IJCAI Workshop on Agent Communication Languages*, 2000.
20. M. P. Singh. A semantics for speech acts. *Annals of Mathematics and AI*, 8(1–2):47–71, 1993.
21. M. Verdicchio and M. Colombetti. A logical model of social commitment for agent communication. In this volume.

An Exploration in Using Cognitive Coherence Theory to Automate BDI Agents' Communicational Behavior

Philippe Pasquier, Nicolas Andrillon,
Marc-André Labrie, and Brahim Chaib-draa

DAMAS (Dialogue, Agents and MultiAgents Systems) Laboratory
Laval University, Computer Science & Software Engineering Dept Pavillon Pouliot
Ste-Foy, PQ, G1K 7P4, Canada
{pasquier,andrillon,chaib,labrie}@iad.ift.ulaval.ca
http://www.damas.ift.ulaval.ca/~pasquier/

Abstract. The cognitive coherence theory for agent communication pragmatics allows modelling a great number of agent communication aspects while being computational. This paper describes our exploration in applying the cognitive coherence pragmatics theory for BDI agents communication. The presented practical framework rely on our dialogue games based agent communication language (DIAGAL) and our dialogue game simulator toolbox (DGS). It provides the necessary theoretical and practical elements for implementing the theory as a new layer over classical BDI agents. In doing so, it brought a general scheme for automatizing agents' communicational behavior. Finally, we give an example of the resulting system execution.

1 Introduction

Agents and multi-agents technologies allow the conception and development of complex applications. In the current distributed data processing paradigm, the fundamental characteristic of these systems is the agents skill in communicating with each other in a useful way regarding to their individual and collective goals. If numerous works have aimed to define agents communication languages, few have concentrated on their dynamic and automatic use by agents. This last task is left to the system designers, who analyse and specify manually the agent communicational behavior, usually by means of rules or by designing ad hoc protocols and static procedures to use them. In this paper, we introduce our investigation toward a theoretical and practical framework for the pragmatics of agent communication, i.e. the automation of agents' communicational behaviors.

In this paper, we first summarize our approach for agent communications pragmatics, the cognitive coherence theory (section 2). This conceptual framework is based on a unification of the cognitive dissonance theory which is one of main motivational theories in social psychology and Thagard's philosophy of mind theory: the coherence theory. After detailing our dialogue games based

F. Dignum (Ed.): ACL 2003, LNAI 2922, pp. 37–58, 2004.

agent communication language (DIAGAL, section 3), we briefly present our dialogue game simulator (DGS, section 4), a practical framework to experience dialogue games. We indicate then, how our coherence pragmatics approach was implemented to automate conversations using DIAGAL games, among BDI agents (section 5). Finally, we give an example of automatic conversation between agents to illustrate our "complete" automatic communication framework (section 6).

2   Dialogue Pragmatics

2.1   The Cognitive Coherence Framework

In cognitive sciences, cognitions gather all cognitive elements: perceptions, propositional attitudes such as beliefs, desires and intentions, feelings and emotional constituents as well as social commitments. From the set of all cognitions result attitudes which are positive or negative psychological dispositions towards a concrete or abstract object or behavior. All attitudes theories, also called cognitive coherence theories appeal to the concept of homeostasis, i.e. the human faculty to maintain or restore some physiological or psychological constants despite the outside environment variations. All these theories share as a premise the *coherence principle* which puts coherence as the main organizing mechanism: *the individual is more satisfied with coherence than with incoherence.* The individual forms an opened system whose purpose is to maintain coherence as much as possible (one also speaks about balance or about equilibrium). Attitude changes result from this principle in incoherence cases.

Our pragmatics theory follows from those principles by unifying and extending the cognitive dissonance theory, initially presented in 1957 by Festinger [6] with the coherence in thought and action theory of the computational philosopher Thagard [20]. This last theory allows us to directly link the cognitive dissonance theory with notions, common in AI and MAS, of elements and constraints.

In our theory, elements are both private and public agent's cognitions: beliefs, desires, intentions and social commitments. Elements are divided in two sets: the set A of accepted elements (which are interpreted as true, activated or valid according to the elements type) and the set R of rejected elements (which are interpreted as false, inactivated or not valid according to the type of elements). Every non-explicitly accepted element is rejected. Two types of non-ordered binary constraints on these elements are inferred from the pre-existing relations that hold between them in the agent's cognitive model:

- *Positive constraints*: positive constraints are inferred from positive relations which can be: explanation relations, deduction relations, facilitation relations and all other positive associations considered.
- *Negative constraints*: negative constraints are inferred from negative relations: mutual exclusion, incompatibility, inconsistency and all the negative relations considered.

For each of these constraints a weight reflecting the importance and validity degree for the underlying relation is attributed. These constraints can be satisfied or not: a positive constraint is satisfied if and only if the two elements that it binds are both accepted or both rejected. On the contrary, a negative constraint is satisfied if and only if one of the two elements that it binds is accepted and the other one rejected. So, two elements are said to be *coherent* if they are connected by a relation to which a satisfied constraint corresponds. And conversely, two elements are said to be *incoherent* if and only if they are connected by a relation to which a non-satisfied constraint corresponds. Given a partition of elements among A and R, one can measure the *coherence degree* of a non-empty set of elements by adding the weights of constraints connected to this set (the constraints of which at least a pole is an element of the considered set) which are satisfied divided by the total number of concerned constraints. Symmetrically, the incoherence of a set of cognitions can be measured by adding the weights of non-satisfied constraints concerned with this set and dividing by the total number of concerned constraints.

In this frame, the basic hypothesis of the cognitive dissonance theory is that incoherence (what Festinger names dissonance [6]) produces for the agent a tension which incites him to change. The more intense the incoherence, the stronger are the insatisfaction and the motivation to reduce it. A cognition incoherence degree can be reduced by: (1) abolishing or reducing the importance of incoherent cognitions (2) adding or increasing the importance of coherent cognitions.

Festinger's second hypothesis is that in case of incoherence, the individual is not only going to change his cognitions or to try to change others's ones to try to reduce it, he is also going to avoid all the situations which risk increasing it. Those two hypotheses were verified by a large amount of cognitive and social psychology studies and experiences [25].

One of the major advantages of the cognitive dissonance theory captured by our formulation is to supply incoherence (that is dissonance in Festinger's terminology) measures, i.e. a metric for cognitive coherence. This metric is available at every level of the system: for a cognitive element, for a set of elements, for an agent, for a group of agents or even for the whole MAS system. These measures match exactly the dissonance intensity measures first defined by Festinger (because a dissonance link in Festinger's model corresponds to a non-satisfied constraint in Thagard's model and a consonance link corresponds to a satisfied constraint). Festinger's hypothesis, along with those measures give us a very general motivational scheme for our agents.

2.2   Dialogue as Coherence Seeking

As we argue elsewhere [12, 13], using coherence as a motivational motor allows us to model a great number of expected features for dialogue pragmatics. In particular, it allows us to answer (even partially) the following questions:

1. *Why agents should dialogue?* Agents dialogue in order to reduce incoherences they cannot reduce alone. We distinguish internal (or personal) incoherence from external (or collective) incoherence depending on whose elements are involved in the incoherence[1].

---

[1] In the presented system, external elements are social commitments.

2. *When should an agent take a dialogue initiative, on which subject and with whom?* An agent engages in a dialogue when an incoherence magnitude exceeds a fixed level[2] and he cannot reduce it alone. Whether because it is an external incoherence and he cannot accept or reject external cognitions on his own, or because it is an internal incoherence he fails to reduce alone. The subject of this dialogue should thus focus on the elements which constitute the incoherence. The dialogue partners are the other agents involved in the incoherence if it is an external one or an agent he thinks could help him in the case of a merely internal incoherence.

3. *By which type of dialogue?* Even if we gave a general mapping of incoherence types toward dialogue types [13], the theory is generic enough for being applied to any conventional communicational framework. Hereafter (section 5), we gave the procedural scheme for this choice using DIAGAL dialogue games as primitive dialogue types.

4. *How to define and measure the utility of a conversation?* As we state in [12], following the coherence principle and the classical definition of utility functions, the utility of a dialogue is the difference between the incoherence before and after this dialogue. Furthermore, we define the expected utility of a dialogue as the incoherence reduction in case of success of the dialogue, i.e. the expected dialogue results are reached. As dialogues are attempts to reduce incoherence, expected utility is used to choose between different competing dialogues types (dialogue games in our case).

5. *When to stop dialogue or else, how to pursue it?* The dialogue stops when the incoherence is reduced or else either it continues with a structuration according to the incoherence reductions chain or it stops because things cannot be re-discussed anymore (this case where incoherence persists often leads to attitude change as described in section 5).

6. *What are the impacts of the dialogue on agents' private cognitions?* In cases where dialogue, considered as an attempt to reduce an incoherence by working on the external world, definitively fails, the agent reduces the incoherence by changing his attitudes in order to recover coherence (this is the attitude change process described in section 5).

7. *Which intensity to give to illocutionary forces of dialogue acts?* Evidently, the intensities of the illocutionary forces of dialogue/speech acts generated are influenced[3] by the incoherence magnitude. The more important the incoherence magnitude is, the more intense the illocutionary forces are.

8. *What are the impacts of the dialogue on agents' mood?* The general scheme is that: following the coherence principle, coherence is a source of satisfaction and incoherence is a source of dissatisfaction. We decline emotional attitudes from internal coherence dynamic (happiness arises from successful reduction, sadness from failed attempt of reduction, fear from a future important reduction attempt, stress and anxiety from an incoherence persistence,...).

---

[2] This level or a "Should I dialogue?" function allows us to model different strategies of dialogue initiative.

[3] Actually, this is not the only factor, as we exemplify elsewhere, other factors could also matter: social role, hierarchical positions,...

9. *What are the consequences of the dialogue on social relations between agents?*
Since agents can compute and store dialogue utility, they can build and
modify their relations with others agents in regard to their past dialogues.
For example, they can strengthen relations with agents with whom past
dialogues were efficient and useful, according to their utility measures, ...

All those dimensions of our theory - except 7, 8 and 9 - will be exemplified
in section 6. But before implementing our pragmatics theory, we need an agent
communication language.

3   A Dialogue Game Language Based on Commitments: DIAGAL

DIAGAL[DIAlogue Games Agent Language] is our commitment-based agent
language in which we define semantics of the communicative acts in terms of
public notions, e.g. social commitments [3]. The use of those public cognitions
allows us to overcome classical difficulties of "intentional" agent communication
approaches: the sincerity hypothesis does not hold anymore and the semantic
verification problem is solved (see [14] for explanations).

3.1   Social Commitments

As our approach is based on commitments, we start with some details about the
notion of commitment. The notion of commitment is a social one, and should
not be confused with the notion of individual commitment used to emphasize
individual intention persistance. Conceptually, social commitments model the
obligations agents contract toward one another. Crucially, commitments are oriented responsibilities contracted towards a partner or a group. In the line of [24],
we distinguish action commitments from propositional commitments.

Commitments are expressed as predicates with an arity of 6. An accepted
action commitment thus take the form:

$$C(x, y, \alpha, t, s_x, s_y)$$

meaning that x is committed towards y to α at time t, under the sanctions s_x
and s_y. The first sanction specifies conditions under which x reneges its commitment, and the second specifies conditions under which y can withdraw from
the considered commitment. Those sanctions[4] could be social sanctions (trust,
reputation,...) as well as material sanctions (economical sanctions, repairing actions, ...). An accepted propositional commitment would be have propositional
content p instead α. Rejected commitments take the form $\neg C(x, y, \alpha, t, s_x, s_y)$
meaning that x is not committed toward y to α

This notation for commitments is inspired from [18], and allows us to com-
pose the actions or propositions involved in the commitments: $\alpha_1 | \alpha_2$ classically

---

[4] Since we did not investigate a whole agent architecture in this paper, we leave
sanctions as a realistic conceptual abstraction.

stands for the choice, and $\alpha_1 \Rightarrow \alpha_2$ for the conditional statement that α_2 will occur in case of the occurrence of the event α_1. Finally, the operations on the commitments are just creation and cancellation.

Now, we need to describe the mechanism by which the commitments are discussed and created during the dialogue. This mechanism is precisely modelled within our game structure. To account for the fact that some commitments are established within the contexts of some games *and only make sense within this context* [9, 11], we make explicit the fact that those *dialogical commitments* are particular to game g (by indicating g as a subscript). This will typically be the case of the dialogue rules involved in the games, as we will see below.

3.2   Game Structure

We share with others [4, 7, 11] the view of dialogue games as structures regulating the mechanism under which some commitments are discussed through the dialogue. Unlike [4, 11] however, we adopt a strict commitment-based approach within game structure and express the dialogue rules in terms of dialogical commitments. Unlike [7] on the other hand, we consider different ways to combine the structures of the games.

In our approach, games are considered as bilateral structures defined by:

- *entry conditions, (E):* conditions which must be fulfilled at the beginning of the game, possibly by some accommodation mechanism;
- *success conditions, (S):* conditions defining the goal of the initiator participant when engaged in the game;
- *failure conditions, (F):* conditions under which the initiator can consider that the game reached a state of failure;
- *dialogue rules, (R):* rules specifying what the conversing agents are "dialogically" committed to do.

As previously explained, all these notions, even dialogue rules, are defined in terms of (possibly conditional, possibly dialogical) commitments. Within games, conversational actions are time-stamped as "turns" (t_0 being the first turn of dialogue within this game, t_f the last).

3.3   Grounding and Composing the Games

The specific question of how games are grounded through the dialogue is certainly one of the most delicate [10]. Following [16], we assume that the agents can use some meta-acts of dialogue to handle games structure and thus propose to enter in a game, propose to quit the game, and so on. Games can have different status: they can be *open, closed,* or simply *proposed.* How this status is discussed in practice is described in a *contextualization* game which regulates this meta-level communication. Figure 1 indicates the current contextualisation moves and their effects in terms of commitments. For example, when a proposition to enter a game j ($prop.in(x, y, j)$) is played by the agent x, y is committed

Move	Operations
$prop.in(x, y, j)$	$create(y, C_j(y, x, acc.in(y, x, j)$
	$\|ref.in(y, x, j)\|prop.in(y, x, j')))$
$prop.out(x, y, j)$	$create(y, C_j(y, x, acc.out(y, x, j)$
	$\|ref.out(y, x, j)))$
$acc.in(x, y, j)$	create dialogical commitments for game j
$acc.out(x, y, j)$	suppress dialogical commitments for game j
$ref.in(x, y, j)$	no effect on the public layer
$ref.out(x, y, j)$	no effect on the public layer

Fig. 1. DIAGAL contextualisation game.

to accept ($acc.in$), to refuse ($acc.in$) or to propose entering another game j' ($prop.in(y, x, j')$), which would lead to a presequencing type of dialogue games structuration.

Concerning the possibility of combining the games, the seminal work of [24] and the follow-up formalisation of [16] have focused on the classical notions of *embedding* and *sequencing*. Even if, recent works, including ours, extend this to other combinations [11, 3], in our present simulation framework, we only consider the three games' compositions allowed by the previous contextualisation game.

– *Sequencing* noted $g_1; g_2$, which means that g_2 is proposed after the termination of g_1.
– *Pre-sequencing* noted $g_2 \rightsquigarrow g_1$, which means that g_2 is opened while g_1 is proposed. Pre-sequencing is used to establish, to enable some of g_1 entry conditions or to explicit some information prior to the entrance in g_1.
– *Embedding* noted $g_1 < g_2$, which means that g_1 is opened while g_2 was already opened.

A game stack captures that commitments of the embedded games are considered as having priority over those of the embedding game.

3.4   Basic Games

Up to now we have introduced four basic building dialogue games, which are exactly those which lead (in case of success) to the four types of commitments which can hold between two agents X and Y, namely:

1. for an attempt to have an action commitment from Y toward X accepted, agent X can use a "request" game (rg);
2. for an attempt to have an action commitment from X toward Y accepted, agent X can use an "offer" game (og);
3. for an attempt to have a propositional commitment from X toward Y accepted, agent X can use an "inform" game (ig);
4. for an attempt to have a propositional commitment from Y toward X accepted, agent X can use an "ask" game (ag).

Next subsections detail those four games. Sanctions were omitted in our games specifications just for better readability.

Request Game (*rg*). This game captures the idea that the initiator (x) "request" the partner (y) for an action α and this latter can "accept" or "reject". The conditions and rules are:

$$
\begin{array}{l|l}
E_{rg} & \neg C(y, x, \alpha, t_0) \text{ and } \neg C(y, x, \neg\alpha, t_0) \\
S_{rg} & C(y, x, \alpha, t_f) \\
F_{rg} & \neg C(y, x, \alpha, t_f) \\
R_{rg} & C_g(x, y, request(x, y, \alpha), t_0) \\
& C_g(y, x, request(x, y, \alpha)) \Rightarrow \\
& C_g(y, x, accept(y, x, \alpha) | refuse(y, x, \alpha), t_1), t_0) \\
& C_g(y, x, accept(y, x, \alpha) \Rightarrow C(y, x, \alpha, t_2), t_0) \\
& C_g(y, x, refuse(y, x, \alpha) \Rightarrow \neg C(y, x, \alpha, t_2), t_0)
\end{array}
$$

Offer Game (*og*). An offer is a promise that is conditional upon the partner's acceptance. To make an offer is to put something forward for another's choice (of acceptance or refusal). To offer then, is to perform a conditional commissive. Precisely, to offer α is to perform a commissive under the condition that the partner accept α. Conditions and rules are in this case:

$$
\begin{array}{l|l}
E_{og} & \neg C(x, y, \alpha, t_0) \text{ and } \neg C(x, y, \neg\alpha, t_0) \\
S_{og} & C(x, y, \alpha, t_f) \\
F_{og} & \neg C(x, y, \alpha, t_f) \\
R_{og} & C_g(x, y, offer(x, y, \alpha), t_0) \\
& C_g(y, x, offer(x, y, \alpha)) \Rightarrow \\
& C_g(y, x, accept(y, x, \alpha) | refuse(y, x, \alpha), t_1), t_0) \\
& C_g(x, y, accept(y, x, \alpha) \Rightarrow C(x, y, \alpha, t_2), t_0) \\
& C_g(x, y, refuse(y, x, \alpha) \Rightarrow \neg C(x, y, \alpha, t_2), t_0)
\end{array}
$$

Inform Game (*ig*). Notice that a human partner can be disposed to be in accord or agreement with someone without uttering any word. He can also agree by doing an explicit speech act. In this case - required for agents since they do not support implicit communication - the partner can agree or disagree. The conditions and rules for this couple is the following:

$$
\begin{array}{l|l}
E_{ig} & \neg C(x, y, p, t_0) \text{ and } \neg C(x, y, \neg p, t_0) \\
S_{ig} & C(x, y, p, t_f) \\
F_{ig} & \neg C(x, y, p, t_f) \\
R_{ig} & C_g(x, y, assert(x, y, p), t_0) \\
& C_g(y, x, assert(x, y, p)) \Rightarrow \\
& C_g(y, x, agree(y, x, p) | disagree(y, x, p), t_1), t_0) \\
& C_g(x, y, agree(y, x, p) \Rightarrow C(x, y, p, t_1), t_0) \\
& C_g(y, x, disagree(y, x, p) \Rightarrow \neg C(x, y, p, t_2), t_0)
\end{array}
$$

Ask Game (*ag*). We use "ask" in the sense of asking a closed question, which consists of requesting the partner to agree or disagree with a proposition p. According to these remarks, we propose the following structure for the *ask* game:

$$
\begin{array}{l|l}
E_{ag} & \neg C(y,x,p,t_f) \text{ and } \neg C(y,x,\neg p,t_f) \\
S_{ag} & C(y,x,p,t_f) \\
F_{ag} & \neg C(y,x,p,t_f) \\
R_{ag} & C_g(x,y,question(x,y,p),t_0) \\
& C_g(y,x,question(x,y,p)) \Rightarrow \\
& C_g(y,agree(y,x,p)|disagree(y,x,p),t_1),t_0) \\
& C_g(y,x,agree(y,x,p)) \Rightarrow C(y,x,p,t_2),t_0) \\
& C_g(y,x,disagree(y,x,p)) \Rightarrow \neg C(y,x,p,t_2),t_0)
\end{array}
$$

Notice that in those games, the included speech acts are labelled with a relative integer (not shown on the Figures) indicating the illocutionary force intensity degree relatively to the default basic illocutionary force degree. For example, in the request game the request stands for the directive category for action which is mapped to: suggest: -2, direct: -1, request: 0, demand: 1, order: 2. Allowing agents to use the appropriate illocutionary forces intensity degree for each dialogue/speech act leads to many variations of those basic games.

4   The Dialogue Game Simulator

We have developed a toolbox, the dialogue game simulator, in order to simulate and visualize games-based dialogue as presented in the previous section while allowing the integration of some future concepts. The dialogue games simulator (DGS) aims to be an effective tool for games testing and validation as well as a means of exploring different agent architectures concerning dialogue pragmatics. DGS main interface allows managing connected agents, loading dialogue games and visualizing synthetic dialogue diagrams. DGS was developed in JAVA using JACK[TM] agent technology [8]. In this section, we briefly present the various components of DGS.

4.1   Game Files

As mentioned previously, a game is composed of entry conditions, success conditions, failure conditions and rules. In DGS, each of these game components is defined in its own file, adding to the possible information re-use while facilitating the maintainability of the files. All those files are written in XML. Using XML has the advantage of being easily manageable in liaison with JAVA while offering a good way of describing information. The DTD (Document Type Definition), associated with XML files, describes the precise way in which the game designer must create his files. That gives designers and users a mean of knowing if a game conforms to the specifications and if it is manageable by the simulator.

The games are loaded when the simulator starts and are placed in a list where agents can charge them when connecting.

4.2   Agenda and Dialogue Manager

The *agenda* and *dialogue manager* are the principal tools provided by DGS. Those tools should be included/embedded in all agents who aim to use loaded

DIAGAL Dialogue Games. The agenda is a kind of individual "commitment store" where commitments are classified according to the time they were contracted. This structure contains commitments in action and propositional commitments that hold as well as dialogical commitments in action deduced from the current dialogue game(s) rules. Each agent has his own agenda which does not contain commitments of all agents which are connected to the simulator, but only those for which he is debtor or creditor.

The agenda is managed by the agent's dialogue manager module which adds or removes commitments according to current dialogue games rules and external events. A commitment in action is fulfilled when an action (perceived as an external event) that corresponds exactly to its description occurs. The dialogue manager also checks that every agent's operations conforms to the current contextualisation and opened dialogue games.

4.3   Action Board and Game Stack

The *action board* stores the actions which were played during simulation. It is modelled as an UML sequence diagram. Each workspace has its own action board where users can observe the exchanges of messages between agents as well as the time which is attached to these actions. It is represented as a history of the actions carried out relating to each initiated dialogue. The action board aims to help the simulator user understand and analyze what occurred in a dialogue between two agents.

The *game stack* is a common structure used by dialogue managers of conversing agents to keep track of the embedded games during a conversation. Each time a new game is opened, it is placed on the top of the stack inside the related workspace and it becomes the current game of this workspace. The stack makes it possible to know which game will become active when the top one will be closed and withdrawn from the stack. This stack is also used to manage the priority between the games: the top element having more priority over the bottom element.

4.4   Dialogue Workspace

The *dialogue workspace* is an environment which contains all the data which are specific to a dialogue between two agents: games stack, actions board and some information about hierarchical relations between conversing agents.

In Figure 2, we present a simplified overview of the DGS framework. This figure presents two agents interacting through a dialogue workspace. They communicate by sending each other messages (communicative actions) and as such messages are produced, the simulator places them into the actions board. In accordance with the current game on the game stack, the dialogue managers of the sender and receiver agents deduce the appropriate commitments from the game files and places them into their agendas.

In its current form, DGS allows simulating conversations between pairs of software agents (three agents resulting in three pairs). The next section focuses

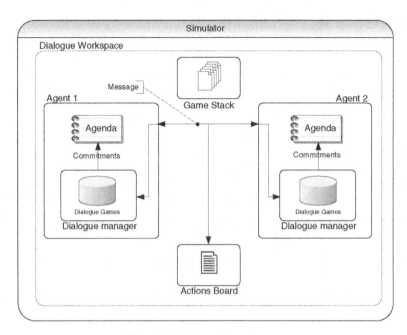

Fig. 2. Simulator overview.

on our first attempt to implement the coherence theory for automatizing dialogues between BDI agents. Those dialogues would take place in the DGS framework using precisely DIAGAL dialogue games presented in the previous sections.

5   Integrating Coherence Theory to BDI Agents

5.1   Linking Private and Social Cognitions

In this section, we describe our first attempt at the complex task of integrating the concepts of the coherence theory in BDI agents practical reasoning. More precisely, we implemented our coherence pragmatics as a new layer above the existing BDI architectures. Since we do not propose a whole coherentist approach for agent modelling, we will have to extend the classical BDI framework so that it can fit with our approach. In particular, traditional BDI frameworks do not involve social commitments treatments.

Choosing a conventional approach for agent communication leads us to extend the intentional paradigm for agent practical reasoning issued from rational interaction theories: *cognitive agent should not reason solely about his and others intentions, he should also reason about potential and already existing social commitments* (coming from held dialogues or system's conventions). In order to use our pragmatics theory to automatize the communication level of the traditional BDI abstract architecture, we need to connect private cognitions (mental states) with public ones (social commitments).

Prior to those links, we assume that our intentional layer is filtered from the BDI agent's whole intentions set. We assume that the intention we receive are either *social individual intentions* or failed individual intentions[5]. Social individual intentions are intentions concerning goals which require social aspects to be worked on. For example, an employee which has an intention about something his boss would be responsible for would have to make some social commitments socially accepted before achieving it. More generally, any intention that is embedded in a somewhat collective activity would have to be a social individual intention except if it is part of an already socially accepted collective plan. Those social intentions are intentions about a (even indirectly) collective state of affairs indicating that those intentions will be part of an external incoherence. Finally, individual intentions concerning goals which do not match any individual plan or whose associated plan failed could be included in this layer (this matches the case where the agent faces an internal incoherence he cannot reduce alone). This phase of identifying intentions which could have a social impact appears to be crucial for integrating conventional approaches to existing cognitive agent architectures.

In this context, we can return to the general question: what are the links between social commitments and private mental states? As a first answer, we propose linking private and public cognitions as follows[6]:

- According to the classic practical reasoning scheme, private cognitions finally end in intentions through deliberation and we make the usual distinction between *intention to* (do something or make someone do something) and *intention that* (a proposition holds) [1];
- Regarding public cognitions, we distinguish *commitments in action* from *propositional commitments* [24];
- An accepted commitment is the socially accepted counterpart of an intention, commitments in action are the counterparts of "intentions to" and propositional commitments are the counterparts of "intentions that".

Those relations are not completely new since many authors have already considered individual intentions as a special kind of individual commitment [1, 23]. Our links extend this to reach the social level in the appropriate cases (social individual intentions or failed individual intentions). Constraints between the intentional private layer and the social commitments layer would be inferred from those links as well as any other logical links between intentions and social commitments.

5.2   BDI Formulation of the Attitude Change Process

In our model, *any agent tries to maximize his coherence*, i.e. tries to reduce his incoherences beginning with the most intense one. To reduce an incoherence, the

---

[5] With the "individual" qualifier in both, we mean that we do not refer to notions of we-intention or collective intentions such as those developed by Searle [17] or Tuomela [22]. Here, intentions are classical private intentions.

[6] Although, we give a first account here, much more work should be done on this point.

agent has to accept or reject cognitions to better satisfy the constraints which connect them. These cognitions can be private or public. To be able to integrate communication into our model, it is now necessary to introduce the fundamental link which exists between our formulation of the cognitive dissonance theory and the notion of resistance to change.

All the cognitions are not equally modifiable. This is what Festinger names the resistance to change of cognitions. The resistance to change of a cognition is a function of the number and the importance of the elements with which it is coherent, also depending on its type, age, as well as the way by which it was acquired: perception, reasoning or communication. Social commitments are particular cognitions which are not individually modifiable but must be socially established and dialogue games are tools for attempting to establish collectively accepted commitments. That is, in order to get a social commitment accepted, an agent has to have a dialogue. Dialogues are the only means for agents to try to establish social commitments coherent with their private cognitions. However, after those dialogues, some commitments can remain incoherent with private intentions.

After any dialogue game, the discussed commitment is either accepted or rejected. As we saw before, an accepted commitment is not modifiable anymore without facing the associated sanctions. And we assume that a discussed commitment which is still rejected will gain in resistance to change. The point here is that an agent could not make attempts to have the desired commitment accepted indefinitely.

This resistance to change and associated sanctions would partially forbid the agent to gain coherence by changing the commitment acceptance state. We could simplify by saying that the discussed commitments usually stand for social obligations and fix one of the poles of the constraints which are connected to them. To reduce possible incoherence while conforming to discussed commitments, agents should then change their private cognitions to restore the coherence. This is the spring of the *attitude change* in our system and it formalizes the vision of the psychologists Brehm and Cohen on this subject [2], supported by a great number of experiments.

In the present simplified framework, the only private cognitions we consider are the intentions, but we assume that the underlying BDI layer would spread the attitude change among all the private cognitions. An example of this attitude change mechanism is supplied in section 6.

In MAS, knowing when an agent should try to modify the environment (the public social commitments layer, among others) to satisfy his intentions, and when the agent has to modify his mental states to be coherent with his environment is a crucial question. In practical reasoning, this question take the form: when an agent should reconsider his intention and deliberate again and when should he persist in acting in the previous deliberated way? As we have just seen, within our approach, agents face the same problem and different strategies toward the modification of already discussed commitments (including reasoning about sanctions and resistance to change in order to know if the agent should

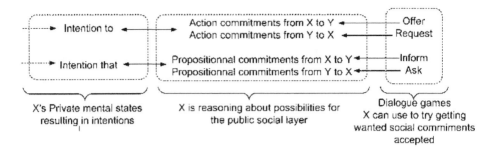

Fig. 3. Links between private cognitions, public cognitions and DIAGAL dialogue games.

persist or not) would lead to different individual commitment types in a way analogous with that of Rao and Georgeff [15]. The main difference is that this choice, like others, would be dynamically based on expected utility, i.e. expected coherence gain.

In Figure 3, we sum up (hiding the quantitative level of calculus) the means by which we link intentions, social commitments and DIAGAL dialogue games. From the left to right we have two types of intentions linked with the four possible corresponding commitments types (the four ones seen in section 3.4). Notice that until they have been really discussed, those commitments are only potential commitments generated by the agent to reason with. To cohere with one of its accepted intentions, an agent will usually (according to the expected utility calculus) consider trying to get the corresponding commitment accepted. To make such an attempt, the agent will choose a DIAGAL dialogue game whose success condition unifies with the wanted commitment.

5.3   The Expected Utility Function

As we have seen in section 2.1, the whole agent cognitive coherence is expressed as the sum of weights of satisfied constraints divided by the sum of weights of all constraints[7]. At each step of his reasoning, an agent will search for a cognition acceptance state change which maximizes the coherence increase, taking into account the resistance to change of that cognition (technically a 1-optimal move). If this attitude is a commitment, the agent will attempt to change it through dialogue and if it is an intention, it will be changed through attitude change. In that last case, we call the underlying architecture of the agents to spread the attitude change and re-deliberate.

In our implementation, an agent determines which is the most useful cognition acceptance state change by exploring all states reachable from its current state and select the cognition which can *in case of a successful change* be the

---

[7] Notice that the general coherence problem: to give the elements partition between A and R that maximize coherence is NP-complete. A formal demonstration could be found in [21].

most useful to change. A state is said to be reachable if it can be obtained from the current state by modifying only one cognition. Since all cognitions cannot be equally modified, we introduced a notion of cost to take into account resistance to change or sanctions associated to cognitions. All explored states are so evaluated through an *expected utility function* expressed as below:

$$g(exploredState) = coherence(exploredState) - cost(cognitionChanged)$$

where *exploredState* is the evaluated state, *cognitionChanged* is the cognition we are examining the change, and *cost* is a cost function expressed as:

1. if *cognitionChanged* is an intention, its cost of change equals its resistance to change;
2. if *cognitionChanged* is a rejected commitment, its cost of change equals its resistance to change, which is initially low but which could be increased at each unfruitful attempt to establish it (depending on the agent's commitment strategy as we will see in the next section);
3. if *cognitionChanged* is an accepted commitment, its cost of change is provided by its associate sanction (which could be null).

5.4   The Treatment Algorithm

Our agents behavior is guided by their coherence and their social commitments. At each step of the simulation, our agents consult their agendas and behave in order to fulfill the commitments which have been deduced from previous actions of agents and rules of dialogue games. When agents must determine the actions they have to produce, they apply the following algorithm:

Procedure CommunicationPragmatics()
1: List commitments=agenda.getCommitments();
2: List dialogCommitments=agenda.getDialogCommitments();
3: treatCommitments();
4: **if** dialogCommitments.isEmpty() **then**
5:    initiateDialogue();
6: **else**
7:    treatDialogCommitments();
8: **end if**

As we have seen in section 3.1, we distinguish between two types of commitments: the dialogical ones and the extra-dialogical ones. The procedure for treating the extra-dialogical commitments (line 3) consists in updating the cognitive model of the agent by browsing extra-dialogical commitments in the agenda and operate as follows. (1) Each time an accepted commitment is encountered, the corresponding commitment in the agent's cognitive model is marked as accepted. If the corresponding intention in the cognitive model of the agent is rejected, then the agent call the underlying BDI architecture for a possible attitude change process. (2) Each time a rejected commitment is encountered, the resistance to change of the corresponding potential commitment in his cognitive model is increased, so that after eventually several unsuccessful attempts, this commitment will be so expensive to establish that it will not constitute a useful change of cognition[8]. This last case would lead to attitude change. This operation is performed before treating the dialogical commitments in order that as soon as a commitment is established, it is taken into account in the rest of the dialogue.

The procedure of initiating a dialogue (line 5) consists in searching for the most useful cognition to change[9]. If it is a commitment, the agent initiates a dialogue with the appropriate dialogue game, or begins an attitude change process if it is an intention. The choice of the appropriate dialogue game is made by unifying the commitment the agent wants to establish with the conditions of success of the games loaded in the simulator.

Treating dialogical commitments (line 7) consists in exploring all the possible actions that are determined by dialogue games and selecting the one which has the best consequences for coherence. If the extra-dialogical commitment which is concerned by the current game is not the most useful change for the agent, it will embed a game by proposing the entrance in a new, subjectively more appropriate, dialogue game.

Notice that coordination of dialogue turns is ensured by the dialogue games rules and the resulting dialogical commitments order in the agents' agendas. Finally, this algorithm is called each time:

- the underlying BDI architecture finishes a deliberation process (or a re-deliberation process after a call initiated by our algorithm for an attitude change process). We assume that the produced intentions are either social individual intentions or individual intentions that the agent could not realize alone.
- the agent has something in his agenda. This ensures, that the agent re-execute this algorithm until all dialogs are closed and that the agent will treat dialogue initiated by others. For example, when the agent receives a *prop.in* message for entering a particular dialogue game, the corresponding dialogical commitment given by the contextualisation game is added to his agenda. Notice that, we assume as a first simplification that the agent is dialogically cooperative and that he systematically accept entering the game (in the treatDialogCommitments() procedure).

Finally, we implement JACK[TM] BDI[10] agents using this pragmatics framework to manipulate DIAGAL dialogue games within the DGS.

---

[8] Notice that following Rao and Georgeff vocabulary [15] the amount of the increase in resistance to change will lead to the different commitment strategies: if this increase in the resistance to change is null the agent will be blindly committed in trying to get this social commitment accepted, if the increase is drastically important this individual commitment will be an open-minded one and in between, we would get a wild range of single minded commitment strategies. Notice that those commitment strategies could dynamically depend on: the incoherence magnitude, the dialogue topic, the partner, the social context,...

[9] There could be none, for example if the coherence is already maximal.

[10] JACK is a commercial JAVA agent framework due to Agent Oriented Systems (AOS) which implements PRS (Procedural Reasoning System) and dMars (Distributed Multi Agent Reasoning System) concepts [8].

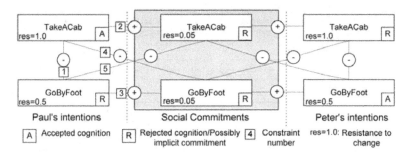

Fig. 4. Cognitive models of Paul and Peter.

6   Example

Let's assume that we have two agents, Paul and Peter, who have agreed on a common plan to go to the concert of their favorite band and split the bill. A subtask of this plan is to go to buy the tickets at the store. Paul has been assigned this task and is now about to deliberate about the way he will go to the store. He has to choose between two mutually exclusive intentions: the one of taking a cab and the one of going by foot. We assume that Paul's underlying BDI architecture has accepted the first one and rejected the second one (perhaps in order to save time). As they will split the bill (and that taking a cab costs money), Peter would rather that Paul went by foot. Thus, he has the rejected intention that Paul take a cab and the accepted one that Paul go by foot.

Both intentions may be associated with two corresponding potential commitments (according to links established in section 5.1): the social commitment from Paul toward Peter to take a cab and the social commitment from Paul toward Peter to go by foot. In addition, the commitment to take a cab and the intention of taking a walk are incompatible, as well as the commitment of taking a walk and the intention of taking a cab. From this initial state, according to our model, a positive constraint between intention and pending commitment is induced from the correspondance relation and negative constraints are induced from the the mutually exclusive relation and the incompatibility relations. Figure 4 presents the network of intentions of both Paul (on the left side) and Peter (on the right) as well as the pending rejected commitments. Notice that the commitments represented are potential commitments used by agents to reason. At this stage, they are not real social commitments since they have not been established by dialogue. In this example, a weight of 1 has been affected to all constraints as a simplification[11].

In DGS, we can decide which agent has the acting initiative, thus determining on whom incoherence dialogue will be taken. We will assume that Paul has the initiative. Initially, as shown by Figure 4, Paul has three satisfied constraints

---

[11] Considerations about the hybrid symbolic connectionist knowledge representation techniques would get us out of the scope of this article. We refer the interested reader to Sun's work [19].

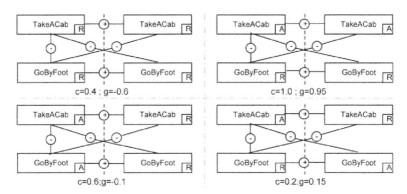

Fig. 5. Sates explored by Paul

(number 1, 3 and 4) in an amount of five constraints so it has a coherence of 0.6. Paul will therefore try to increase it by localizing the most useful cognition to change. The Figure 5 shows the different states that can be reached by Paul from its initial situation. Below each is indicated the coherence c obtained in this state as well as the value of the expected utility function g. According to those results, Paul will make an attempt to get the commitment $C(Paul, Peter, take\_a\_Cab)$ accepted. Since it is a social commitment, Paul will use one of the dialogue games which are tools to attempt establishing commitments. Since this commitment is a commitment toward Peter, Peter will be the dialogue partner. Paul will then choose between the available dialogue games whose success conditions unify with the desired commitment. The only DIAGAL dialogue game which has a success condition of the form $C(initiator, partner, action)$ is the offer game.

Paul will thus propose to Peter to play this game, we suppose that Peter is dialogically cooperative and would accept to play the game. Then, according to the request game rules, Paul will produce a directive speech act with an appropriate illocutionary force intensity degree[12].

Before replying, Peter will check if he does not have a higher incoherence to reduce by searching its own most useful change of cognition and locate the commitment from Paul toward him to go by foot, as shown on figure 6.

Thus, Peter will embed a DIAGAL request dialogue game concerning this commitment. Paul will answer Peter according to its coherence (which would decrease in case of acceptance) and deny the proposition and the resistance to change of the still rejected commitment will increase. The embedded request game is then closed. To illustrate the attitude change, we have drastically increased the resistance of change of the commitment of taking a cab in order that Peter's expected utility function will select the intention that Paul went by foot

---

[12] We illustrate our example with the use of basic illocutionary forces intensity degree for the speech/dialogue acts (here the "offer"), but DIAGAL allows us to choose a specific strength degree for each speech act. Thus, the strength degree could have been linked to: (1) Paul's current incoherence magnitude, (2) Paul's expected increase of coherence, that is the expected utility and (3) social positions of Peter and Paul, . . .

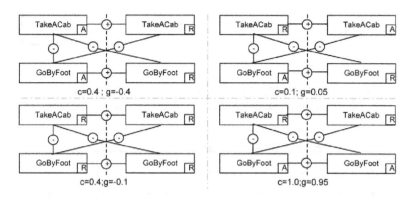

Fig. 6. States explored by Peter before replying.

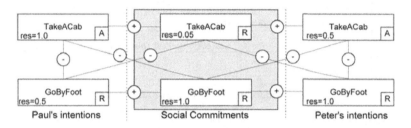

Fig. 7. Cognitive models of Paul and Peter.

as the most potentially useful change. At the end of this embedded dialogue game, Peter's treatCommitments() procedure will recall the underlying BDI architecture for a re-deliberation which would at least include the rejection of the "intention to" that Paul went by foot.

Propagating attitude change and re-deliberation (which would normally be processed by the underlying architecture) is simulated in our present system by systematically revising as many intentions as possible as long as it increases whole coherence. The new cognitive models of the agents after this dialogue are those of Figure 7. Paul's intentions remains unchanged since no social commitment conflicts with its intentions while Peter's ones have been reevaluated. Peter, according to his new set of intentions will then accept Paul's offer to take a cab and they will finally quit the embedding dialogue offer game. After this dialogue, both agents will have all their constraints satisfied (i.e. a coherence of 1).

Resulting Dialogues. The diagram of sequence shown on Figure 8 illustrates the messages exchanged between Paul and Peter as detailed above. This diagram is actually part of the action board which DGS fills during the execution so that the user can see what the agents are doing.

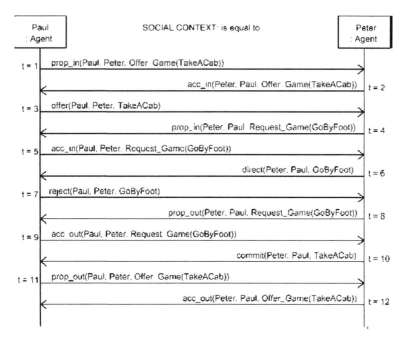

Fig. 8. Dialogues between Paul and Peter.

The two dialogue games initiated by Paul and Peter are presented as well as speech-acts used by both agents. Notice that all those steps were held automatically by the agents implementing our coherence theory for communication pragmatics in the way described earlier.

In the case where Peter is given the initiative at the beginning, the symmetrical dialogue would have happened, Peter trying to establish the commitment of going by foot, Paul imbricating a game on the commitment of taking a cab, denied by Peter and both finally agreeing on Paul going by foot. In that case the dialog result in the opposite situation. This is normal since we consider that the commitments socially rejected by dialogue gain a very high resistance to change. It results in a non-persistence of intentions in case of refusal (i.e. an highly influenceable open-minded commitment strategy). In that particular case (chosen in order to simplify the exemple), dialogue initiative plays a crucial role.

7   Conclusion and Prospects

The cognitive coherence theory for agent communication pragmatics allows modelling a great number of agent communication dimensions while being computational. This paper describes our exploration in applying the cognitive coherence pragmatics theory for BDI agents communication. The presented practical framework relies on our dialogue games based agent communication language (DIAGAL) and our dialogue game simulator toolbox (DGS). It provides the necessary theoretical and practical elements for implementing the theory as a new layer over classical BDI agents. In doing so, it brought a general scheme for automatizing agents communicational behavior.

Classically, practical reasoning equals deliberation plus means-ends reasoning. Deliberation is about deciding what states of affairs the agent wants to achieve whereas means-ends reasoning is about deciding how to achieve these states of affairs. Within our model, coherence gain evaluation trough the expected utility function extend the deliberation process to take into account the social level whereas selecting a dialogue games by unifying its success conditions with the wanted social result is part of the mean-end reasoning. We also insist on the dialogue effect on agent's private mental states through the attitude change process. This process is activated by a kind of reconsider() function (see [15]) which has been modelled and integrated in our expected utility function and which results depends on the chosen individual commitment strategy (which is taken into account when the resistance to change of explicitly rejected commitments are updated).

Although the architecture presented in this paper is efficient, much more work remains to be done. In particular we want to: (1) work more profoundly on the links between private and public cognitions (2) provide a well-founded theory for sanction and social relations dynamic management[13] (3) extend the current framework with argumentation seen as constraints propagation allowing agents to reason about others' cognitive constraints and thus taking them into account, introducing cooperation.

In this article we choose to apply our theory as a new layer above the existing BDI architectures. But, a long term work would be to propose a pure coherentist approach for the whole cognitive agents architecture. This would permit to take more advantage of the power of coherentist approaches [20], using the powerful hybrid symbolic-connexionist formalisms attached with them.

References

1. M. E. Bratman. What is intention? In P. R. Cohen, J. L. Morgan, and M. E. Pollack, editors, *Intentions in Communication*, pages 15–32. The MIT Press: Cambridge, MA, 1990.
2. J. Brehm and A. Cohen. *Explorations in Cognitive Dissonance*. John Wiley and Sons, inc, 1962.
3. B. Chaib-draa, N. Maudet, and M.A. Labrie. DIAGAL, a tool for analysing and modelling commitment-based dialogues between agents. In *Proceedings of Canadian AI 2003*, 2003.
4. M. Dastani, J. Hulstijn, and L. V. der Torre. Negotiation protocols and dialogue games. In *Proceedings of the BNAIC*, 2000.
5. F. Dignum and M. Greaves, editors. *Issues in agent communication*. LNAI, Vol. 1916, Springer-Verlag, 2000.

---

[13] Memorizing dialogue utility measures defined in our coherence theory could be of great help for this purpose.

6. L. Festinger. *A Theory of Cognitive Dissonance*. CA: Stanford University Press, 1957.

7. R. F. Flores and R. C. Kremer. A formal theory for agent conversations for actions. *Computational intelligence*, 18(2), 2002.

8. N. Howden, R. Rönnquist, A. Hodgson, and A. Lucas. Jack intelligent agents summary of an agent infrastructure. In *5th International Conference on Autonomous Agents*, 2001.

9. N. Maudet. *Modéliser les conventions des interactions langagières: la contribution des jeux de dialogue*. PhD thesis, Université Paul Sabatier, Toulouse, 2001.

10. N. Maudet. Negociating games — a research note. *Journal of autonoumous agents and multi-agent systems*, 2002. (Submitted).

11. P. McBurney, S. Parsons, and M. Wooldridge. Desiderata for agent argumentation protocols. In *Procceedings of the First International Conference on Autonomous Agents and Multi-Agents*, 2002.

12. P. Pasquier and B. Chaib-draa. The cognitive coherence approach for agent communication pragmatics. In *Proceedings of the second international joint conference on autonomous agents and multiagents systems, AAMAS'03*. ACM Press, 2003.

13. P. Pasquier and B. Chaib-draa. Cohérence et conversations entre agents: vers un modèle basé sur la consonance cognitive. In J.P. Müller and P. Mathieu, editors, *Systèmes multi-agents et systèmes complexes, actes des JFIADSMA'02*, pages 188–203, Hermes Science Publication, Paris, 2002.

14. P. Pasquier and B. Chaib-draa. Engagements, intentions et jeux de dialogue. In *Actes des Secondes Journées Francophones des Modèles Formels de l'Interaction (MFI'03)*, Cépaduès, 2003.

15. A. S. Rao and M. P. Georgeff. An abstract architecture for rational agents. In C. Rich, W. Swartout, and B. Nebel, editors, *Proceedings of Knowledge Representation and Reasoning (KR&R-92)*, pages 439–449, 1992.

16. C. Reed. Dialogue frames in agent communication. In *Proceedings of the Third International Conference on MultiAgent Systems (ICMAS)*, 1998.

17. J. R. Searle. Collective intentions and actions. In P. R. Cohen, J. Morgan, and M. E. Pollack, editors, *Intentions in Communication*, pages 401–416. The MIT Press: Cambridge, MA, 1990.

18. M. P. Singh. A social semantics for agent communication language. In *[5]*, pages 31–45. 2000.

19. R. Sun. *Connectionist-Symbolic Integration*, chapter An introduction to hybrid connectionist-symbolic models. Lawrence Erlbaum Associates., 1997.

20. P. Thagard. *Coherence in Thought and Action*. The MIT Press, 2000.

21. P. Thagard and K. Verbeurgt. Coherence as constraint satisfaction. *Cognitive Science*, 22:1–24, 1998.

22. R. Tuomela and K. Miller. We-intentions. *Philosophical Studies*, 53:367–389, 1988.

23. G.H. von Wright. *Freedom and determination*. North Holland Publishing Co., 1980.

24. D. Walton and E. Krabbe. *Commitment in dialogue*. State University of New York Press, 1995.

25. R. Wickland and J. Brehm. *Perspectives on Cognitive Dissonance*. NY: Halsted Press, 1976.

A Performative Type Hierarchy
and Other Interesting Considerations in the Design
of the CASA Agent Architecture

Rob Kremer[1], Roberto Flores[2], and Chad La Fournie[1]

[1] Department of Computer Science, University of Calgary
2500 University Dr. N.W., Calgary, Canada, T2N-1N4
{kremer,laf}@cpsc.ucalgary.ca
http://sern.ucalgary.ca/~kremer/
[2] Institute of Cognitive Sciences and Technologies, National Research Council
Viale Marx 15, 00137 Rome, Italy
robertof@cpsc.ucalgary.ca

Abstract. In this paper, we describe several interesting design decisions we
have taken (with respect to inter-agent messaging) in the re-engineered CASA
architecture for agent communication and services. CASA is a new architecture
designed from the ground up; it is influenced by the major agent architectures
such as FIPA, CORBA, and KQML but is intended to be independent (which
doesn't imply incompatible). The primary goals are flexibility, extendibility,
simplicity, and ease of use. The lessons learned in the earlier implementation
have fed the current design of the system. Among the most interesting of the
design issues are the use of performatives that form a type lattice, which allows
for observers, who do not necessarily understand all the performatives, to none-
theless understand a conversation at an appropriate semantic level. The new design considerations add a great deal of flexibility and integrity to an agent
communications architecture.

1 Introduction

We have been working on an infrastructure for agent-based system that would easily
support experimentation and development of agent-based systems. We implemented
the first-cut system, and began work on the analysis of what we could learn from our
experience.

We had gained enough knowledge to formalize our theory of agent conversations
based on social commitments [5], but the CASA infrastructure itself, although seemingly quite adequate, seemed rather ad-hoc, and lacking in solid theoretical foundation.

The various types of service agents in the CASA system each sent and received
what seemed to be a set of ad-hoc messages, which did the job, but still seemed unsat-
isfying in that there seemed to be no apparent pattern to them. We had more-or-less
followed the FIPA [8] performative model (the CASA message structure closely
follows the FIPA structure, which, in turn borrows heavily from KQML [1]).

F. Dignum (Ed.): ACL 2003, LNAI 2922, pp. 59–74, 2004.
© Springer-Verlag Berlin Heidelberg 2004

We decided to take a hard look at the system with an eye to looking for patterns to modify our design to a more satisfying structure. This paper describes some of our analysis that lead to the current design.

In the remainder of this section we give a brief introduction to the CASA infrastructure. In Section 2, we describe various problems and solutions (a.k.a. design decisions) we have encountered in our building and using the CASA system. These include the arranging of performatives in a type lattice, specification of some relational constraints, and the resulting compositional properties of some messages, the addition of several new fields in messages, and the removal of some performatives into a separate type lattice called *acts*. In Section 3 focus on conversations, rather than messages, and describe how CASA can support either conversation protocols, or social commitments as a basis for inter-agent communication, and weigh some of the merits of the two different approaches. In sections 4 and 5 we discuss our future work and conclusions.

1.1 Background: CASA

The fundamental objective of CASA is to support communication among agents and related services. Therefore, CASA offers a generic communication and cooperation infrastructure for message passing, archiving (data, knowledge bases, and transaction histories), agent lookup, and remote agent access. It is an open system infrastructure that may be easily extended as the future need for services becomes apparent. CASA makes no demands on *intra*-agent architecture (internal agent architecture), however, agent templates are provided in the form of classes that one can inherit from and specialize (in Java and C++). Currently, generic class-templates are provided and conversation-protocol and social-commitment specialized class-templates are under development.

As shown in Figure 1, *Cooperation Domains* (CDs) acts as a central "hub" for multi-agent conversations such that all participants may send messages directly to the Cooperation Domain for point-to-point, multi-cast, type-cast[1], and broadcast communication within the Cooperation Domain (a group of agents working together on some task). Agents within a cooperation domain may also use the cooperation domain to store persistent data that will permanently be associated with the conversation, giving the conversation a lifetime beyond the transient participation of the agents, as is often required. Cooperation Domains may also store transaction histories for future playback of the chronological development of the conversation artifacts. Cooperation Domains may perform all these tasks because all messages use a standard "envelope" format (currently either KQML [1] or XML [15])[2], which flexibly provides a basic

---

[1] Type-cast is similar to multi-cast, but the destination specification describes agent types (rather than individuals), and the cooperation domain forwards the message to agents known to conform to the type(s).

[2] Actually, the envelope formats can be either KQML or XML (mixed) as we can dynamically switch between the two owing to our employing the Chain of Command pattern [10] to interpret messages.

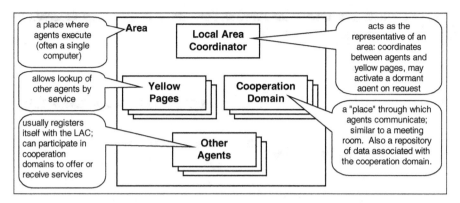

Fig. 1. Basic Communication and Cooperation Services in CASA.

semantic "wrapper" on messages that may be otherwise domain specific: both the utility of generic services and the efficiency of domain specific languages are therefore provided.

Yellow page servers (also called Yellow Page Agents, Yellow Pages, or YPs) allow agents to look up other agents by the services they offer. An *area* is defined nominally as a single computer (but could be a cluster of several computers, or a partition on a single computer). There is exactly one *local area coordinator* (LAC) per area, which is responsible for local coordination and tasks such as "waking up" a local agent on behalf of a remote agent. All application agents reside in one or more areas. See Figure 2 for a screen dump of a LAC interface showing several agents running.

Messages are needed to support interactions among agents. Messages are generically defined either as *Request*, *Reply* or *Inform* messages; where *Requests* are used to ask for the provision of a service, *Replies* to answer requests, and *Informs* to notify agents without requiring the receiving agent to perform any action. Since these messages are too ambiguous for the definition of interaction protocols, other, more meaningful, message subtypes are derived from these general definitions of messages. For example, *Refuse* is derived from *Reply*; an agent can *Refuse* a earlier *Request* of another agent as a special type of *Reply* (as *Agree* would be another special type of reply).

2 Messages

In our analysis of the system we first looked at the performatives in the messages, and existing FIPA performatives. These include:

Accept Proposal	*Agree*	*Cancel*
Call for Proposal	*Confirm*	*Disconfirm*
Failure	*Inform*	*Inform If*
Inform Ref	*Not Understood*	*Propagate*
Propose	*Proxy*	*Query If*
Query Ref	*Refuse*	*Reject Proposal*
Request	*Request When*	*Request Whenever*
Subscribe		

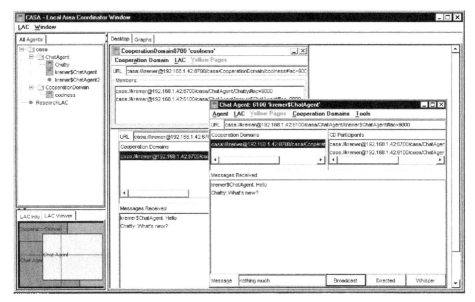

Fig. 2. A screen dump of a CASA LAC interface with a Cooperation Domain and two simple 'chat' agents communicating with one another. All three agents are running in the same process here, but they may all run in independent processes or on different machines.

2.1   The Problem

The FIPA performatives seem rather awkward when one tries to use them in a real application such as this. The meaning of each and its relationship to the others is not always clear. In some cases, it seems they have overlapping meaning. For example, *Refuse* and *Reject Proposal* can occur under the same circumstances, and the former would seem to be a subtype of the latter. Thus, it they should be arranged in a type lattice. Furthermore, our use of them (in developing the CASA infrastructure) seemed to indicate that *Inform*, *Request*, and *Reply* were somehow much more fundamental than the others.

A common technique used in communication protocols (especially in the face of unreliable communication channels) is to always have the receiver return a confirmation (an *acknowledge* message) to the sender so that the sender can verify that the message was received (and resend if necessary). Such an *Ack* message is conspicuously missing from the FIPA performatives, so we chose to extend FIPA's protocol[3], and go with an *Ack* (acknowledgement) to an *Inform* to allow us to check on transmission of a message in the event we are using an unreliable communication channel.

---

[3]   In fact, we're not sure if we really are extending FIPA's protocol, since we could find no protocol for a simple *Inform*. So we aren't sure if a FIPA agent would expect an *Ack* after an *Inform* or not.

(Note that we do not *require* agents to use the *Ack* protocol, but agents may agree to use it if so desired.[4])

When we tried to draw a type hierarchy of all the messages required in CASA, we found it looked something like this[5]:

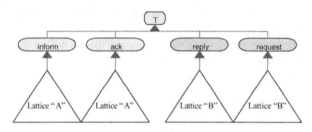

Fig. 3.

For example, when an agent wishs to join a cooperation domain, it sends a *joinCD* (lattice B) request to the cooperation domain, and the cooperation domain responds with a *joinCD* (lattice B) reply.

2.2 Rearranging Performatives

It seems interesting that for each specific *Request*, we have a mirrored *Reply* and, similarly, for each specific *Inform* we have a mirrored *Ack*. It seems to us that *Request/Reply* and *Inform/Ack* are more fundamental than their subtypes. It appears we should keep *Request/Reply* and *Inform/Ack* as "fundamental message types", and then put all the other things in a separate type lattice of "ACTs". We extend our message headers to include a new field *act*. This more-or-less turns *performatives* into speech acts, and *acts* into physical acts.

Thus, our message header looks like this:

```
performative:  request
act:           inviteToJoinCD
to:            Bob
from:          Alice
receiver:      CDagent1
sender:        Alice
...
```

Getting back to acknowledging protocols, we can write down a very simple conversation protocol: that of an *Inform/Ack* pair (here we use diamond-shaped arrowheads to indicate sequence):

---

[4] Actually, an agent who *isn't* using the *Ack* protocol *will Ack* if it receives a message marked with a request-ack field – see Figure 13 and Section 2.7.

[5] This type hierarchy is a simplification of the hierarchy we built containing all the performatives in the FIPA Communicative Act Repository Specification (FIPA00037) [7], which ended up being fairly complex. Although simplified, the above diagram captures the essence of the original.

Fig. 4.

This adds a certain sense of reliability to the message transmission: Alice will always know (by the *Ack*) that Bob received her *Inform*[6]. In the case of a *Request/Reply*, if Bob received a *Request* from Alice, and *Replies*, then Alice will know that Bob received the *Request*, so there is no need for an *Ack* in this case. But Bob (the receiver of the request) has no way of knowing if Alice received the *Reply*. It would be appropriate for Alice to send an *Ack* to Bob:

Fig. 5.

If this is the case, then *Reply* looks a lot like inform. It's a specialization (subtype) of *Inform*:

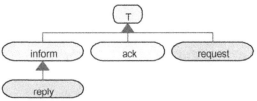

Fig. 6.

This makes sense: after all, if I'm *replying* to you, I'm *informing* you of what I'm doing with your request.

Furthermore, it would be consistent to think of a *Reply* as being a kind of *Ack* to a *Request*. After all, if we reply to a request, the reply certainly carries all the functionality of an *Ack*. Therefore, *Reply* would be a subtype of both *Inform* and *Ack*:

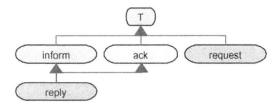

Fig. 7.

By the same reasoning as a reply is an inform, we can derive that a request must also be in an form. After all, if I'm *requesting* something of you, I'm *informing* you that I want you to do something for me:

---

[6] But Alice won't know if Bob *didn't* receive the *Inform*, since the *Ack* could have been lost. This is a well known problem in the literature.

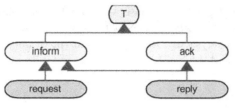

Fig. 8.

This seems to be a rather satisfying configuration, although slightly asymmetrical.

2.3 Adding Constraints

We will overload the last diagram by adding a sequence relation to indicate that an *Inform* is followed by an *Ack*:

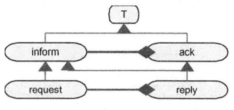

Fig. 9.

One can observe that an *Inform* must be followed by an *Ack*, and a *Request* must be followed by a *Reply* (and not an *Ack*). This does not violate the *Inform/Ack* constraint since *Reply* is a subtype of *Ack* anyway. In addition, the above diagram says that one can't *Ack* a *Request*, because it's not a *Reply*[7]. Just what we want.

2.4 Composing Messages

All this has interesting consequences in implementation. Nothing in the CASA message exchange changes, but it does tell us that a *request* protocol is a composition of two *inform* protocols (where the [overloaded] middle message is a specialized *Ack*):

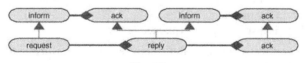

Fig. 10.

---

[7] One might argue that a request might be followed by *both* an *Ack* and a *Request*, and conform to this diagram, but this cannot be because in a proper conversation thread, speech acts are well ordered: one message cannot be followed by more than one other message.

This composition is legal only because we had previously observed that a *Reply* is a subtype of both *Ack* and *Inform*. The fact that we can do this composition lends support to our earlier analysis that *Request* is a subtype of *Inform* and *Reply* is a subtype of both *Inform* and *Ack*.

2.5 When Things Go Wrong

All this is fine when the world is unfolding as it should. But sometimes things don't go as planned and errors happen. An agent may want to negatively acknowledge (*Nack*) an inform ("I don't believe you", "I don't understand the message"). Or an agent may be unable (or unwilling) to perform a request ("Sorry, can't do it"). Or a message may simply not be returned for whatever reason.

Since these forms of failure can be regarded as being speech acts (as opposed to physical acts), we can simply add them as subtypes of *replies* (which also makes them subtypes of *acks* as well):

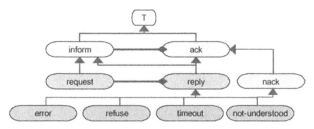

Fig. 11.

Thus, conversation specifications (protocols), don't need to worry about error conditions: since an error is just a specialization of a *reply* or an *ack*, it is a "normal" part of a regular conversation, at least at the speech-act level. Agents may and will alter their behaviour when errors occur, but there is no reason to unduly complicate a protocol description if the circumstances do not warrant it.

The errors defined in Figure 11 are:

– *error*, which is general catch-all for some exceptional error that may occur.
– *refuse,* which is used when an agent explicitly refuses a request (or possibly to deny an inform, similar to the FIPA *disconfirm*).
– *not-understood,* which is used to inform the sending agent that the receiving agent cannot interpret the message.
– *timeout*, which is a special case explained below.

There are several ways to handle the case where an acknowledge to an inform or a reply to a request is not returned. We find it very convenient to make use of a timeout message, which, in fact, are not ordinary messages in that they are not normally sent between agents. But rather, agents "send" timeout messages to themselves as a simple "bookkeeping" technique: Whenever a message is sent it includes a timeout field which specifies by when an acknowledge/reply is expected. If no acknowledge/reply

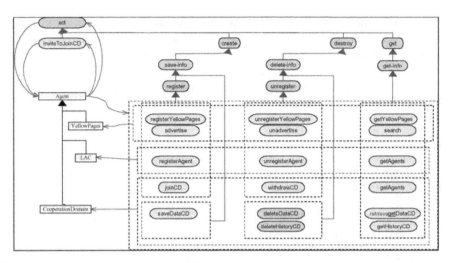

Fig. 12. Partial ontology of messages. This diagram describes this ontology in terms of typing (the solid arrows represent the *is-a* relationship), sequence (the V-arrows represent the direction of the message, as in "from-agent → message → to-agent"), and grouping (the messages in the dotted boxes all conform the to relationships impinging on the dotted box). Thus, we may read the *advertise* message as being a subtype of *register*, and being sent by an *AbstractAgent* and received by either a *AbstractYellowPages* agent or an *AbstractLAC* agent.

is received by the time the timeout expires, the agent merely "sends" a matching timeout message to itself. This technique greatly simplifies agent logic because agents are always guaranteed to receive a reply (even if it may only be a timeout). In addition, since overworked receiving agents also are aware of the timeout encoded in the message header, they may safely ignore expired messages without further processing.

2.6 Acts

Now we turn our attention the type lattice of *act*s we had mentioned in Section 2.2. We have created a separate type lattice of *acts* that is somewhat subservient to the smaller type lattice of performatives. We attempted this type lattice for the fundamental messages necessary to manage the CASA infrastructure (see Figure 12)[8].

The figure shows remarkable regularity. There are three fundamental (but not necessarily exclusive) types of acts: *create*, *destroy*, and *get*, corresponding to the three fundamental things one can do with data: write, delete, and read. For each of the agent types, there is a corresponding triplet of messages that represent it's functionality. For example, an agent may request of a YellowPages agent to be advertised (*ad-*

---

[8] The initial formulation of the ACT type lattice, of course, was not so clean. The process of building this diagram caused us to tweak our design by renaming a few messages, combining similar functions into single more powerful functions, and adding a few messages that had remained missing.

vertise), to be removed from the list of advertised agents (*unadvertised*), or to search for some other agent among the YellowPages agent's registered advertisers (*search*). This otherwise perfect symmetry is broken only in one case: An agent may delete a history list (*deleteHistoryCD*) and read the history list (*getHistoryCD*), but it may not write into the history list (the history list is written to as the Cooperation Domain records all the messages it processes).

```
<!DOCTYPE CASAmessage [
  <!ELEMENT CASAmessage (version, performative, act?, sender,
    receiver, from?, to?, timeout?, reply-with?, in-reply-to?,
    request-ack?, language?, language-version?, ontology?,
    ontology-version?, content?)>
  <!ELEMENT version           (#PCDATA)>
  <!ELEMENT performative      (#PCDATA)>
  <!ELEMENT act               (#PCDATA)>
  <!ELEMENT sender            (#PCDATA)>
  <!ELEMENT receiver          (#PCDATA)>
  <!ELEMENT from              (#PCDATA)>
  <!ELEMENT to                (#PCDATA)>
  <!ELEMENT timeout           (#PCDATA)>
  <!ELEMENT reply-with        (#PCDATA)>
  <!ELEMENT in-reply-to       (#PCDATA)>
  <!ELEMENT request-ack       (#PCDATA)>
  <!ELEMENT language          (#PCDATA)>
  <!ELEMENT language-version  (#PCDATA)>
  <!ELEMENT ontology          (#PCDATA)>
  <!ELEMENT ontology-version  (#PCDATA)>
  <!ELEMENT content           ANY      >
]>
```

Fig. 13. A CASA message DTD (there are additional elements for thematic roles and semantic modifiers, but these have be omitted in the interests of brevity.

2.7   A More Powerful Message

As already mentioned, CASA exchanges messages with headers in either KQML format or XML format. Both of these formats contain exactly the same information, so it matters little (except that XML is more verbose) which is used. The XML DTD in Figure 13 describes our message format.

Most of the fields in the message are either described above or are standard to FIPA [8].

Why did we extend the FIPA message header format? Largely, this is because we are concerned with the observable properties (as opposed to the internal, private properties) of agent interaction. We want an external observer to be able to judge the soundness (conformance to social conventions or protocols) of a conversation without necessarily understanding all of the subtleties and details of the conversation. That is, an external observer should be able "understand" a conversation even though the observer does not understand the language and ontology used in the *content* section of the message. FIPA's message format is a very good foundation for such understanding. For example, the ideas of the *performative* label to enable an observer to superficially understand the message type; the idea of the separate *sender/receiver* and *to/from* labels to enable an observer to understand when a message is merely be forwarded as opposed to being actually addressed to the recipient agent; the idea of the *language* label to enable the observer to judge whether the observer can understand the *content*; and the *reply-with* and *in-reply-to* labels to enable the observer to disambiguate multiple concurrent conversational threads. However, our experience with strict reliance on observable properties motivated us to put more "semantic" information in the message. These include:

- We have arranged the performatives in a type lattice to enable an external observer, not conversant in the details of some specialized conversational domain, to understand the conversation based on being able to follow a particular foreign performative (or act) up the type lattice until the observer finds a performative (or act) that *is* understood (see section 2.2).

- We have added a separate *act* label, motivated by our observation that the more fundamental performative, such as inform, request, and reply, are qualitatively different from the lower-level "performatives" (see section 2.6). We have therefore taken out some of FIPA's (and or own) "performatives", and placed them in a separate type lattice under the message label *act*.

- We have added an ontology label, which is intended to extend the FIPA language label, since an observer may understand a certain language (e.g. prolog) but not understand the ontology used (e.g. the prolog predicate library used).

- We have also qualified the message and language and ontology labels with version numbers to support the evolution of these definitions. The version numbers allow observers (and conversation participants) to recognize when they have an older version of the message/language/ontology definition, and may not understand the entire contents, or when they are dealing with a conversation participant who has an older definition, and may be able to adjust their interpretations and utterances to match.

All of these extensions are optional, and allow us to still be compliant with FIPA message, so long as the FIPA agents are willing to ignore foreign labels in incoming messages. Figure 14 shows an example of a CASA request/reply message pair.

These extensions allow an external observer to monitor messages and make sense of them without having the omniscient and gaze into the internal "thought process" of the participating agents. While the original FIPA definition of the agent allows this to some extent, our extensions support further semantic interpretation of messages, and offer pragmatic solutions to some of practical problems that occur in real-life, evolving situations.

All of this is useful, but must be extended to the *composition* of messages, which is described in the next section.

```
( :request
  :act          register.instance
  :sender       casa://kremer@192.168.1.42:8700/casa/CooperationDomain/coolness
  :receiver     casa://kremer@192.168.1.42:9000
  :timeout      1066456360438
  :reply-with   casa://kremer@192.168.1.42:8700/casa/CooperationDomain/coolness--0
  :language     casa.URLDescriptor
  :content      "casa://kremer@192.168.1.42:8700/casa/CooperationDomain/coolness true"
)

( :reply
  :act          register.instance
  :sender       casa://kremer@192.168.1.42:9000/casa/LAC/ResearchLAC
  :receiver     casa://kremer@192.168.1.42:8700/casa/CooperationDomain/coolness
  :timeout      1066456360438
  :reply-with   casa://kremer@192.168.1.42:9000/casa/LAC/ResearchLAC--1
  :in-reply-to  casa://kremer@192.168.1.42:8700/casa/CooperationDomain/coolness--0
  :language     casa.StatusURLandFile
  :content      "( 0 \"Success\"
                casa://kremer@192.168.1.42:8700/casa/CooperationDomain/coolness#lac=9000
                \"/casaNew/root/casa/CooperationDomain/coolness.casa\" )"
)
```

Fig. 14. An example of a CASA request/reply message pair using the KQML message format. In this case, a Cooperation Domain is registering with a LAC (to let the LAC know it is running). The LAC responds with a success status together with the Cooperation Domain's fully-qualified URL and the file it should use to use to store any persistent data. (Backslashes are used as escape characters in the content part.)

3   Conversations

In our work with CASA, we are aiming a high degree of flexibility with respect to the construction of agents. We therefore choose to design in enough flexibility to allow agents that are based on either conversation protocols or on social commitments [4].

3.1   Conversation Protocols

When in conversation protocols mode, CASA conversations are modeled by using conversation protocols (CPs) to define the possible utterances and responses that can be exchanged between agents. Following FIPA standards for interaction protocols [8], we define a variety of patterns in which initiators and participants interact. This model is flexible in that any new interaction or conversation can be added by simply defining the possible messages (such as INFORM/REQUEST), and their counterparts (ACK/REPLY). For example, suppose a very simple interaction was needed to model two agents: one with the role of requesting a service, and another that may or may not agree to provide the service. This can be done by adding the following to each of the agents' list of possible messages:

Agent 1	Agent 2
performative: *Request* act: *service X*	performative: *Reply* act: *service X*
	performative: *Reject* act: *service X*

In addition, the agents' library of reactive protocols in updated (which is consulted when a CP agent receive a message "out of the blue" starting a new conversation), and a pattern is written to handle the particular protocol. In this fashion, more complex interactions can be added.

The internal mechanisms, which determine how an agent will decide what (if any) message to send, are implementation dependant. In fact, we leave such details out since we wish to concentrate on the way in which agents communicate and on observable agent behaviour. We leave the matter of how agents should behave and their internal workings to the individual agent developer. The key is that agents involved in the interaction require the protocol to be pre-defined.

3.2 Social Commitments

The social commitment (SC) model is an alternative to the CP model described above, and provides a mechanism by which agents can negotiate obligations among one another. A social commitment is an obligation that is negotiated between potential debtor and creditor agents (see [5], [4], [11], [6], [2] & [14]). Such negotiation of obligations mimics the behaviour of agents using CPs, but in more flexible manner. For example, suppose an agent (agent A) were to issue a proposal to another agent (agent B). Figure 15 shows the sequence of events and the possibilities agent B can reply with. If the *debtor* agent (agent B) accepts the proposal by responding with an *accept* reply to agent A, it adopts the obligation to provide the *creditor* agent (agent A) with some service. It should also be noted that the commitment is not imposed on the debtor agent; it is negotiated. A more complex example might allow for agent B to refuse the proposal and make a counterproposal which would, in turn, be evaluated by agent A.

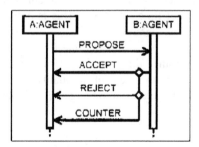

Fig. 15. A simple proposal.

The possible replies that might be issued by the receiving agent include acceptance, rejection or counterproposal, and the sending agent may at any time issue a withdrawal its own proposal.

The value of using the social commitments model is twofold. First, it allows for linking the external world (including interactions with other agents) with the internal agent mechanisms. An agent maintains a list of the current and past obligations both owed to other agents and to itself. This information could be used to "rationally" influence the agent's future actions. Thus, a conversation is never rigidly "scripted" as in conversation protocols, but flows naturally from an agent disposing its current obligations. Second, it provides a degree of autonomy (through the negotiation process) for adopting commitments. An agent is free to accept or reject proposals as described above.

3.3 Observer Agent

One aspect that enhances the flexibility of the CASA model is that agents can be used in various capacities other than being directly involved in conversations. A sufficiently privileged agent may join a cooperation domain and observe the communication between other agents. This agent, which may simply be a "plug-in agent" for the cooperation domain, could perform various functions. It could perform the role of a conversation manager, tracking and organizing the messages sent between agents; it could perform the role of janitor, cleaning up obsolete conversations and connections; or it could perform the role of a translator, resending messages broadcast in one language in another language. An agent may also observe conversations between other agents in order to gather information about how it can best proceed toward its goals. Note that, it is owing to the arrangement of the performatives and acts into a type lattice that there is sufficient information in the message "envelope" to allow an "outside" agent to "understand" a conversation even if it does not understand the domain-specific performatives, acts, content language, and ontology of the participating agents.

In the context of the social commitments model, it might be useful to have a judging or policing agent observing interactions between agents, checking on their conformance to social norms, such as whether or not agents discharge their obligations within an acceptable period of time (or at all). This is only possible because the SC model relies only on *observable* behaviour.

The above examples are meant to illustrate the flexibility of CASA, in that it can be extended in many ways other than adding additional conversation protocols. It supports future developments in the areas of rationality and social knowledge as they relate to conversations and interactions among agents in a society.

4 Future Work

Although the work in CASA and social commitment theory is progressing well, there is still much to do. We have several projects underway in various related research fields. We are working on further extending the CASA message "envelope" to include more formal reference objects and relationships based on theories from linguistics (e.g. [12], [13]). For example, we can add fields such as *agent* (initiator of an act), *patient* (the entity undergoing the effects of an act), *theme* (the entity that is changed by the act), *experiencer* (the entity that is a aware, but not in control of, the act), and *beneficiary* (the entity for who's benefit the act is preformed.

The detailed semantics of messages, as described here, has not yet been worked out. Some of our future work involves the formal specification of message semantics, at least as it relates to the services offered within CASA. Some formal specification of the social commitment model has been done (see [4] & [5]), but the formal specification of CASA services has hardly been touched so far.

Furthermore there a several pragmatic areas that need to be worked out if CASA, or a CASA-like system is to be used in real settings (such as what we are working for manufacturing systems). For example, security will be an issue, and we are currently undertaking research to determine an appropriate approach to protecting stored data, messages themselves, and cooperation membership in such a dynamic and distributed environment.

5 Conclusions

In this paper, we have described some of our design decisions in the CASA infrastructure primarily with respect to the structure of inter-agent messages. Most of the discussion contrasts our structure with that of the FIPA model. We differ from FIPA's viewpoint primarily in that we concern ourselves more with the *observable* behaviour of agents, and the ability of an outside observer to understand the meaning of a conversation. Minimally, we would like the outside observer to be able to deduce if the agents are participating in logical conversation and conforming to a set of social norms.

To this end, we have conformed to the FIPA message structure with a few changes (primarily ordering the performatives in a type lattice), and extending it in several ways. We have extended the message structure by adding the fields such as *act*, and *ontology*. In addition, we have added version numbers as attributes to the message language itself, and to the language and ontology fields.

We also briefly discussed conversations, which are composed of messages, and discussed CASA's support for agents based on either conversational protocols or social commitments.

Acknowledgements

We are grateful to the Natural Sciences and Engineering Council of Canada (NSERC), Smart Technologies, Inc., the Alberta Software Engineering Research Consortium (ASERC) and the Alberta Informatics Circle of Research Excellence (iCORE) for their financial support throughout the realization of this work.

References

1. Becerra, G. "A Security Pattern for Multi-Agent Systems". In Proceedings of Agent Based Technologies and Systems, Far, B.H., Rochefort, S. and Moussavi, M. (eds.), Calgary, Canada, August, 2003, pp 142-153.
2. Chopra, A. and Singh, M.P. "Nonmonotonic Commitment Machines". In Dignum, F. (ed.), Advances in Agent Communication, LNAI, Springer Verlag. In this volume.

3. Finin, T. and Labrou, Y. "KQML as an Agent Communication Language". In Bradshaw, J.M. (ed.), Software Agents, MIT Press, Cambridge, 1997. pp. 291-316.

4. Flores, R.A. "Modelling Agent Conversations for Action". Ph.D. Thesis, Department of Computer Science, University of Calgary, Canada. 2002.

5. Flores, R.A. and Kremer, R.C. "To Commit or Not To Commit: Modelling Agent Conversations for Action". In B. Chaib-draa and F. Dignum (eds.), Computational Intelligence, Special Issue on Agent Communication Languages, Blackwell Publishing, 18:2, May 2002, pp. 120-173.

6. Fornara, N. and Colombetti, M. "Protocol Specification using a Commitment-based ACL". In Dignum, F. (ed.), Advances in Agent Communication, LNAI, Springer Verlag. In this volume.

7. Foundation for Intelligent Physical Agents (FIPA). FIPA Communicative Act Repository Specification. Foundation for Intelligent Physical Agents. Oct. 18, 2002. http://www.fipa.org/specs/fipa00037/

8. Foundation for Intelligent Physical Agents (FIPA). FIPA Interaction Protocol Library Specification. Foundation for Intelligent Physical Agents. Aug. 10, 2001. http://www.fipa.org/specs/fipa00025/XC00025E.html#_Toc505480198

9. Foundation for Intelligent Physical Agents (FIPA). FIPA Specifications, Version 1. 1997.

10. Gamma, E., Helm, R., Johnson, R., and Vlissides, J. "Design Patterns: Elements of Reusable Object-Oriented Software". Addison-Wesley Professional Computing Series, Addison-Wesley, Reading Mass., 1994.

11. Mallya, A.U., Yolum, P. and Singh, M. "Resolving Commitments Among Autonomous Agents". In Dignum, F. (ed.), Advances in Agent Communication, LNAI, Springer Verlag. In this volume.

12. Saeed, J.I. "Semantics". Blackwell Publishers Ltd., Oxford, UK, 1997.

13. Thurgood, G. "English 222: Pedagogical Grammar". Chapter 9. English Department, California State University, Chico. Aug, 2002. http://www.csuchico.edu/~gt18/222/Ch%2009.pdf

14. Verdicchio, M. and Colombetti, M. "A logical model of social commitment for agent communication". In Dignum, F. (ed.), Advances in Agent Communication, LNAI, Springer Verlag. In this volume.

15. World Wide Web Consortium (W3C) "Extensible Markup Language (XML)". Architecture Domain, World Wide Web Consortium, Oct. 14, 2002. http://www.w3.org/XML/

Model Checking
for ACL Compliance Verification

Marc-Philippe Huget and Michael Wooldridge

Department of Computer Science
University of Liverpool
Liverpool L69 7ZF, UK
{mph,mjw}@csc.liv.ac.uk

Abstract. The problem of checking that agents correctly implement the semantics of an agent communication language has become increasingly important as agent technology makes its transition from the research laboratory to field-tested applications. In this paper, we show how model checking techniques can be applied to this problem. Model checking is a technique developed within the formal methods community for automatically verifying that finite-state concurrent systems implement temporal logic specifications. We first describe a variation of the MABLE multiagent BDI programming language, which permits the semantics (pre- and post-conditions) of ACL performatives to be defined separately from a system where these semantics are used. We then show how assertions defining compliance to the semantics of an ACL can be captured as claims about MABLE agents, expressed using MABLE's associated assertion language. In this way, compliance to ACL semantics reduces to a conventional model checking problem. We illustrate our approach with a number of short case studies.

1 Introduction

The problem of checking that agents correctly implement the semantics of an agent communication language has become increasingly important as agent technology makes its transition from the research laboratory to field-tested applications. In this paper, we show how *model checking techniques* can be applied this problem, by making use of our MABLE language for the automatic verification of multiagent systems [19].

Model checking is a technique that was developed within the formal methods community for automatically verifying that finite-state systems implement temporal logic specifications [1]. The name "model checking" arises from the fact that verification can be viewed as a process of checking that the system is a model that validates the specification. The principle underpinning the approach is that the possible computations of given a system S can be understood as a directed graph, in which the nodes of the graph correspond to possible states of S, and arcs in the graph correspond to state transitions. Such directed graphs are essentially *Kripke structures* — the models used to give a semantics to temporal

F. Dignum (Ed.): ACL 2003, LNAI 2922, pp. 75–90, 2004.

logics. Crudely, the model checking verification process can then be understood as follows: Given a system $\mathcal{S}$, which we wish to verify satisfies some property φ expressed in a temporal logic L, generate the Kripke structure $M_{\mathcal{S}}$ corresponding to $\mathcal{S}$, and then check whether $M_{\mathcal{S}} \models_L \varphi$, i.e., whether φ is L-valid in the Kripke structure $M_{\mathcal{S}}$. If the answer is "yes", then the system satisfies the specification; otherwise it does not.

Our approach to model checking for the ACL compliance problem is as follows. In a previous paper [19], we described our first implementation of the MABLE language. MABLE is a language intended for the design and automatic verification of multi-agent systems; it is essentially an imperative programming language, augmented by some features from Shoham's agent-oriented programming paradigm [15]: in particular, agents in MABLE possess data structures corresponding to their *beliefs*, *desires*, and *intentions* [18]. A MABLE system may be augmented by a number of *claims* about the system, expressed in a simplified form of the $\mathcal{LORA}$ language given in [18]. Our MABLE compiler translates the MABLE system into processes in PROMELA, the input language for the SPIN model checking system [7–9]; claims are translated into SPIN-format LTL formulae. The SPIN system can then be directly invoked to determine whether or not the original system satisfied the original claim.

In this paper, we show how MABLE has been extended in two ways to support ACL compliance testing. First, we have added a feature to allow programmers to define the semantics of ACL performatives separately from a program that makes use of these performatives, thus making it possible for the same program to exhibit different behaviours with different semantics. Second, we have extended the MABLE claims language to support a dynamic logic-style "happens" construct: we can thus write a claim that expresses that (for example) whenever an agent performs action α, property φ eventually follows. By combining these two features, we can automatically verify whether or not an agent respects ACL semantics.

The remainder of the paper is structured as follows. We begin with an overview of the ACL compliance checking problem. We then describe a variation of the MABLE multiagent BDI programming language, which permits the semantics (pre- and post-conditions) of ACL performatives to be defined separately from a system where these semantics are used. We then show how assertions defining compliance to the semantics of an ACL can be captured as claims about MABLE agents, expressed using MABLE's associated assertion language. In this way, compliance to ACL semantics reduces to a conventional model checking problem. We illustrate our approach with a number of short case studies, and conclude with a discussion of future work.

2   ACL Compliance Verification

One of the main reasons why multi-agent systems are currently a major area of research and development activity is that they are seen as a key enabling technology for the Internet-wide electronic commerce systems that are widely predicted to emerge in the near future [5]. If this vision of large-scale, open multi-agent systems is to be realised, then the fundamental problem of *inter-operability* must be addressed. It must be possible for agents built by different organisations using different hardware and software platforms to safely communicate with one-another via a common language with a universally agreed semantics. The inter-operability requirement has led to the development of several standardised *agent communication languages* (ACLs) [11, 4]. The development of these languages has had significant input from industry, and particularly from European telecommunications companies.

However, in order to gain acceptance, particularly for sensitive applications such as electronic commerce, it must be possible to determine whether or not any system that claims to *conform* to an ACL standard actually does so. We say that an ACL standard is *verifiable* if it enjoys this property. FIPA — currently the main standardisation body for agent communication languages — recognise that "demonstrating in an unambiguous way that a given agent implementation is correct with respect to [the semantics] is not a problem which has been solved" [4], and identify it as an area of future work. (Checking that an implementation respects the *syntax* of an ACL such as that proposed by FIPA is, of course, trivial.) If an agent communication language such as FIPA's is ever to be widely used — particularly for such sensitive applications as electronic commerce — then such compliance testing is important. However, the problem of compliance testing (*verification*) is not actually given a concrete definition by FIPA, and no indication is given of how it might be done.

In [17], the verification problem for agent communication languages was formally defined for the first time. It was shown that verifying compliance to some agent communication language reduced to a verification problem in exactly the sense that the term in used in theoretical computer science. To see what is meant by this, consider the semantics of FIPA's `inform` performative [4, p25]:

$$
\begin{aligned}
&\langle i, inform(j, \varphi) \rangle \\
&\quad \text{FP:} \quad B_i\varphi \wedge \neg B_i(Bif_j\varphi \vee U_j\varphi) \\
&\quad \text{RE:} \quad B_j\varphi
\end{aligned}
\tag{1}
$$

Here $\langle i, inform(j, \varphi) \rangle$ is a FIPA message: the message type (performative) is `inform`, the content of the message is φ, and the message is being sent from i to j. The intuition is that agent i is attempting to convince (inform) agent j of the truth of φ. The FP and RE define the semantics of the message: FP is the *feasibility pre-condition*, which states the conditions that must hold in order for the sender of the message to be considered as sincere; RE is the *rational effect* of the message, which defines what a sender of the message is attempting to achieve. The B_i is a modal logic connective for referring to the beliefs of agents (see e.g., [6]); Bif is a modal logic connective that allows us to express whether an agent has a definite opinion one way or the other about the truth or falsity of its parameter; and U is a modal connective that allows us to represent the fact that an agent is "uncertain" about its parameter. Thus an agent i sending an *inform* message with content φ to agent j will be respecting the semantics of the FIPA ACL if it believes φ, and it it not the case that it believes of j either that j believes whether φ is true or false, or that j is uncertain of the truth or falsity of φ.

It was noted in [17] that the FP acts in effect as a *specification* or *contract* that the sender of the message must satisfy if it is to be considered as respecting the semantics of the message: an agent respects the semantics of the ACL if, when it sends the message, it satisfies the specification. Although this idea has been understood in principle for some time, no serious attempts have been made until now to adopt this idea for ACL compliance testing.

We note that a number of other approaches to ACL compliance testing have been proposed in the literature. Although it is not the purpose of this paper to contribute to this debate, we mention some of the key alternatives. Pitt and Mamdani defined a *protocol-based semantics* for ACLs [12]: the idea is that the semantics of an ACL are defined in terms of the way that they may be used in the context of larger structures, i.e., protocols. Singh championed the idea of *social* semantics: the idea that an ACL semantics should be understood in terms of the observable, verifiable changes in social state (the relationships between agents) that using a performative causes [16].

3   MABLE

MABLE is a language intended for the design and automatic verification of multi-agent systems. The language was introduced in [19]; here, we give a high-level summary of the language, and focus in detail on features new to the language since [19].

Agents in MABLE are programmed using what is essentially a conventional imperative programming language, enriched with some features from agent-oriented programming languages such as AGENT0 [15], GOLOG [10], and AGENTS-PEAK [13]. Thus, although the control structures (iteration, sequence, and selection) resemble (and indeed are closely modelled on) those found in languages such as C, agents in MABLE have a *mental state*, consisting of data structures that represent the agent's beliefs, desires, and intentions (cf. [18]). The semantics of MABLE program constructs are defined with respect to the mental states of the agents that perform these statements. For example, when an agent executes an assignment operation such as

```
x = 5
```

then we can characterise the semantics of this operation by saying that it causes the agent executing the instruction to subsequently believe that the value of x is 5.

In addition, MABLE systems may be augmented by the addition of formal *claims* made about the system. Claims are expressed using a (simplified) version of the belief-desire-intention logic $\mathcal{LORA}$ [18], known as $\mathcal{MORA}$ [19]; we decsribe this language in more detail below.

The MABLE language has been fully implemented. The implementation makes use of the SPIN system [7–9], a freely available model-checking system for finite state systems. Developed at AT&T Bell Labs, SPIN has been used to formally verify the correctness of a wide range of finite state distributed and concurrent systems, from protocols for train signalling to autonomous space-craft control systems [8]. SPIN allows claims about a system to be expressed in propositional Linear Temporal Logic (LTL): SPIN is capable of automatically checking whether or not such claims are true or false.

The MABLE compiler takes as input a MABLE system and associated claims (in $\mathcal{MORA}$) about this system (see Figure 1). MABLE generates as output a description of the MABLE system in PROMELA, the system description language for finite-state systems used by the SPIN model checker, and a translation of the claims into the LTL form used by SPIN for model checking. SPIN can then be used to automatically verify the truth (or otherwise) of the claims, and simulate the execution of the MABLE system, using the PROMELA interpreter provided as part of SPIN.

Communication in MABLE. In the version of MABLE described in [19], communication was restricted to `inform` and `request` performatives, the semantics of which were modelled on the corresponding FIPA performatives. However, this communication scheme rapidly proved to be too limiting, and has been significantly extended in the current version of MABLE. In particular, a user may use any kind of performative required: MABLE provides generic `send` and `receive` program instructions.

The structure of MABLE's message sending statement is as follows:

$$\texttt{send(CA } j \texttt{ of } \varphi)$$

where `CA` is a communicative act (i.e., a performative name), j is the intended recipient of the message, and φ is the content. The sender of this message is not represented here, but is the agent executing the statement. The basic meaning of the statement is that a message is sent to agent j using the communicative act CA: the content of the message is φ. (The keyword `of` is syntactic sugar only; it can be replaced by any identifier, and has no effect on the semantics of the program.)

Here is a concrete example of a MABLE `send` statement.

```
send(inform agent2 of (a == 10))
```

This means that the sender informs `agent2` that `a == 10`. For the moment, we will postpone the issue of the semantics of this statement; as we shall see below, it is possible for a programmer to define their own semantics, separately from the program itself.

The structure of the `receive` statement is as follows.

$$\texttt{receive(CA } i \texttt{ of } \varphi)$$

As might be guessed, this means that the receiver receives a message from i for which the communicative act is CA and the message content is φ. Communication is synchronous in the current version of MABLE, and so for this statement to succeed there must be a corresponding `send` by agent i.

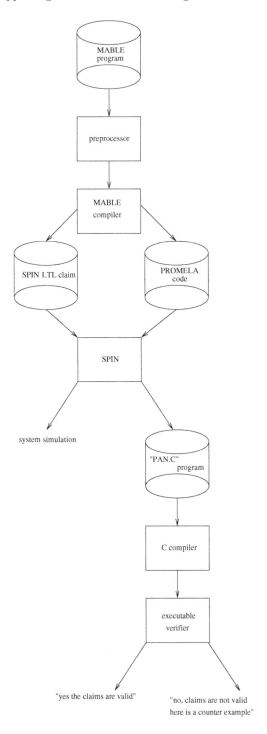

Fig. 1. Operation of MABLE

A key component of the current instantiation of MABLE is that programmers can define their *own* semantics for communicative acts, separately from a program. Thus it is possible to explore the behaviour of the same program with a range of different semantics, and thus to investigate the implications of different semantics.

The basic model we use for defining semantics is a STRIPS-style pre-/post-condition formalism, in the way pioneered for the semantics of speech acts by Cohen and Perrault [2], and subsequently applied to the semantics of the KQML [3] and FIPA [4] languages. Thus, to give a semantics to performatives in MABLE, a user must define for every such communicative act a pre-condition and a post-condition. Formally, the semantics for a communicative act CA are defined as a pair $\langle CA_{pre}, CA_{post} \rangle$, where CA_{pre} is a condition (a MABLE predicate), and CA_{post} is an assertion. The basic idea is that, when an agent executes a send statement with performative CA, this message will not be sent until CA_{pre} is true. When an agent executes a receive statement with performative CA, then when the message is received, the assertion CA_{post} will be made true.

The MABLE compiler looks for performative semantic definitions in a file that is by convention named `mable.sem`. A `mable.sem` file contains a number of performative definitions, where each performative definition has the following structure:

```
i: CA(j, phi)
pre-condition
post-condition
```

where `i`, `j` and `phi` are the sender, recipient, and content of the message respectively, and `CA` is the name of the performative. The following lines define the pre-condition and post-condition associated with the communicative act CA. It is worth commenting on how these semantics are dealt with by the MABLE compiler when it generates PROMELA code.

With respect to the pre-condition, the above performative definition is translated into a PROMELA *guarded command* with the following structure.

```
pre-condition -> send the message
```

The "->" is PROMELA's guarded command structure: to the left of -> is a condition, and to the right is a program statement (an action). The semantics of the construct are that the process executing this statement will *suspend* (in effect, go to sleep) until the condition on the left hand side is true. When (more accurately, if) the condition becomes true, then the right hand side is "enabled": that is, it is ready to be executed, and assuming a fair process scheduler, will indeed be executed.

Notice that it is possible to define the pre-condition of a performative simply as "1", i.e., a logical constant for truth, which is always true; in this case, the send message part of the performative will always be enabled.

With respect to the post-condition, MABLE translates receive messages into PROMELA code with the following structure:

```
receive message;
make post-condition true
```

Thus once a message is received, the post-condition will be made true. Notice that post-conditions in a `mable.sem` file *do not* correspond to the "rational effect" parts of messages in FIPA semantics [4]; we elaborate on the distinction below.

Here is a concrete example of a `mable.sem` performative semantic definition:

```
i:inform(j,phi)
1
(believe j (intend i (believe j phi)))
```

This says that the sender of a message will always send an `inform` message directly; it will not wait to check whether any condition is true. It also says that when an agent receives an `inform` message, it will subsequently believe that the sender intends that the receiver believes the content.

Several examples of pre-conditions and post-conditions are given in Section 4. The use of semantics during the translation process is shown in Figure 2.

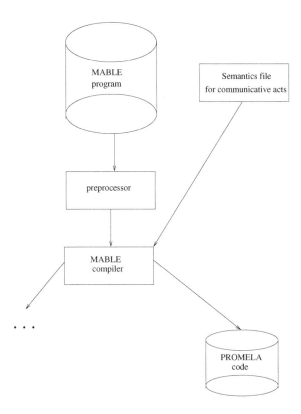

Fig. 2. Operation of the MABLE system with the semantics file

```
formula ::=
    forall IDEN ":" domain formula  /* universal quantification */
  | exists IDEN : domain formula    /* existential quantification */
  | any primitive MABLE condition   /* primitive conditions */
  | ( formula )                     /* parentheses */
  | (happens Ag stmt)               /* statement is executed by agent */
  | (believe Ag formula)            /* agent believes formula */
  | (desire Ag formula)             /* agent desires formula */
  | (intend Ag formula)             /* agent intends formula */
  | [] formula                      /* always in the future */
  | <> formula                      /* sometime in the future */
  | formula U formula               /* until */
  | ! formula                       /* negation */
  | formula && formula              /* conjunction */
  | formula || formula              /* disjunction */
  | formula -> formula              /* implication */


domain ::=
    agent                           /* set of all agents */
  | NUMERIC .. NUMERIC              /* number range */
  | { IDEN, ..., IDEN }             /* a set of names */
```

Fig. 3. The syntax of $\mathcal{MORA}$ claims

In summary, by disconnecting the semantics of a communicative act from a program that carries out such an act, we can experiment to see the effect that different kinds of semantics can have on the same agent. In the following section, we will see how this may be done in practice.

Claims. A key component of MABLE is that programs may be interspersed with *claims* about the behaviour of agents, expressed in $\mathcal{MORA}$, a subset of the $\mathcal{LORA}$ language introduced in [18]. These claims can then be *automatically* checked, by making use of the underlying SPIN model checker. If the claim is disproved, then a counter example is provided, illustrating why the claim is false.

A claim is introduced outside the scope of an agent, with the keyword claim followed by a $\mathcal{MORA}$ formula, and terminated by a semi-colon. The formal syntax of $\mathcal{MORA}$ claims is given in Figure 3. The language of claims is thus that of quantified linear temporal BDI logic, with the dynamic logic style happens operator, similar in intent and role to that in $\mathcal{LORA}$ [18]. Quantification is only allowed over finite domains, and in particular, over: agents (e.g., "every agent believes φ"); finite sets of objects (e.g., enumeration types); and integer number ranges. We will here give an overview of the main constructs of the claim language, focussing on those that are new since [19].

The goal of $\mathcal{MORA}$ (and also in fact of the whole MABLE framework) is that we should be able to verify whether programs satisfy properties of the kind expressed in BDI logics [14,18]. To illustrate how $\mathcal{MORA}$ claims work, we here give some informal examples.

Consider the following $\mathcal{LORA}$ formula, which says that if agent a_1 believes the reactor failed, then a_1 intends that whenever a_2 believes the reactor failed (i.e., a_1 wants to communicate this to a_2).

$$(\mathsf{Bel}\ a_1\ \mathit{reactorFailed}) \Rightarrow (\mathsf{Int}\ a_1\ (\mathsf{Bel}\ a_2\ \mathit{reactorFailed}))$$

We can translate such a formula more or less directly into a $\mathcal{MORA}$ claim, suitable for use by MABLE. Consider the following:

```
claim []
  ((believe a1 reactorFailed) ->
  (intend a1 (believe a2 reactorFailed)));
```

The only noticeable difference is that, in the $\mathcal{LORA}$ formula, the intended interpretation is that we need to make the "whenever" explicit with the use of the temporal [] ("always") connective. The following $\mathcal{LORA}$ formula says that if some agent wants agent a_2 to believe that the reactor has failed, then eventually, a_2 will believe it has failed.

$$\forall i \cdot (\mathsf{Int}\ i\ (\mathsf{Bel}\ a_2\ \mathit{reactorFailed})) \Rightarrow \Diamond(\mathsf{Bel}\ a_2\ \mathit{reactorFailed})$$

This translates directly into the following $\mathcal{MORA}$ claim.

```
claim
 forall i : agent
 []((intend i (believe a2 reactorFailed))
   -> <>(believe a2 reactorFailed));
```

Thus far, the examples we have given illustrate features that were present in the version of MABLE documented in [19]; we now describe the main new feature of $\mathcal{MORA}$ claims, modelled on $\mathcal{LORA}$'s Happens construct [18, p.62]. In $\mathcal{LORA}$, there is a path expression of the form

$$(\mathsf{Happens}\ i\ \alpha)$$

which intuitively means "the next thing that happens is that agent i does α". Thus, for example, the following $\mathcal{LORA}$ formula says that if agent a_1 performs the action of flicking the switch, then the reactor eventually hot.

$$(\mathsf{Happens}\ a_1\ \mathit{flickSwitch}) \Rightarrow \Diamond\mathit{reactorHot}$$

The current version of MABLE provides such a facility. We have a $\mathcal{MORA}$ construct

$$(\mathsf{happens}\ \mathit{ag}\ \mathit{stmt})$$

where ag is the name of an agent and stmt is a MABLE program statement. This predicate will be true in a state whenever the next statement enabled for execution by agent ag is stmt. Consider the following concrete example.

```
claim
  []((happens a1 x = 10;)
    -> <>(believe a1 x==10));
```

This claim says that, whenever the next statement to be enabled for execution by agent a1 is the assignment x=10; (notice that the semi-colon is part of the program statement, and must therefore be included in the **happens** construct), then eventually, a1 believes that variable x has the value 10. (A single equals sign in MABLE is an assignment, while a double equals sign is the equality predicate.) As we will see below, the **happens** construct plays a key role in our approach to ACL compliance verification.

Before leaving this section, a note on how the **happens** construct is implemented by the MABLE compiler. The idea is to *annotate the model* that MABLE generates, with new propositions that will be set to be true in a given state whenever the corresponding agent is about to execute the corresponding action. To do this, the MABLE compiler passes over the parse tree of the MABLE program, looking for program statements matching those that occur in **happens** claims. Whenever it finds one, it inserts a program instruction setting the corresponding new proposition to true; when the program statement is executed, the proposition is set to false. The toggling of the proposition value is wrapped within PROMELA **atomic** constructs, to ensure that the toggling process itself does not alter the control flow of the generated system.

Although this process increases the size of the generated model, it does so only linearly with the number of **happens** constructs, and does not appear to affect performance significantly. Similarly, the pre-processing time required to insert new propositions into the model is polynomial in the size of the model and the number of **happens** claims.

4   Verifying ACL Compliance

We now demonstrate how MABLE can be used to verify compliance with ACL semantics. We begin with a running example that we will use in the following sections. The MABLE code is given in Figure 4. In this example, two agents have several beliefs and they simply send a message among themselves containing this belief. The selection of the message to be sent is done non deterministically through the **choose** statement. The insertion of these beliefs in agents' mental state is done through the **assert** statements. Beliefs correspond to conditions on values and differ from one agent to another one. After sending messages, agents wait for a message from the other agent. (Due to space restrictions, we do not give the PROMELA code that is generated by these examples.)

Verifying Pre-conditions. Verifying pre-conditions means verifying that agents satisfy the pre-condition part of an ACL performative's semantics whenever they send the corresponding message. We will focus in this paper only on the **inform** performative; the cases for **request** and the like are similar.

Two approaches are possible for the pre-conditions: either agents are *sincere* (they only ever send an **inform** message if they believe its content), or else they are not (in which case they can send a message without checking to see whether

```
int selection-agent1;
int selection-agent2;
agent agent1 {
  int inform-agent2;
  inform-agent2 = 0;

  selection-agent1 = 0;
  assert((believe agent1 (a == 10)));
  assert((believe agent1 (b == 2)));
  assert((believe agent1 (c == 5)));

  choose(selection-agent1, 1, 2, 3);
  if (selection-agent1 == 1) {
    print("agent1 -> a = 10\n ");
    send(inform agent2 of (a == 10));
  }
  if (selection-agent1 == 2) {
    print("agent1 -> b = 2\n ");
    send(inform agent2 of (b == 2));
  }
  if (selection-agent1 == 3) {
    print("agent1 -> c = 5\n ");
    send(inform agent2 of (c == 5));
  }

  receive(inform agent2 of inform-agent2);
  print("agent1 receives %d\n ", inform-agent2);

}

agent agent2 {

  int inform-agent1;
  inform-agent1 = 0;

  selection-agent2 = 0;
  assert((believe agent2 (d == 3)));
  assert((believe agent2 (e == 1)));
  assert((believe agent2 (f == 7)));

  choose(selection-agent2, 1, 2, 3);
  if (selection-agent2 == 1) {
    print("agent2 -> d = 3\n ");
    send(inform agent1 of (d == 3));
  }
  if (selection-agent2 == 2) {
    print("agent2 -> e = 1\n ");
    send(inform agent1 of (e == 1));
  }
  if (selection-agent2 == 3) {
    print("agent2 -> f = 7\n ");
    send(inform agent1 of (f == 7));
  }

  receive(inform agent1 of inform-agent1);
  print("agent2 receives %d\n", inform-agent1);

}
```

Fig. 4. The base example

they believe it). We can use MABLE's ACL semantics to define these two types of agents. Consider first the following `mable.sem` definition.

```
i:inform(j,phi)
(believe i phi)
(believe j (intend i (believe j phi)))
```

This says that the pre-condition for an `inform` performative is that the agent believes the content (`phi`) of the message. By defining the semantics in this way, an agent will only send the message if it believes it. (If the sender *never* believes the content, then its execution is indefinitely postponed.)

By way of contrast, consider the following `mable.sem` definition of the `inform` performative.

```
i:inform(j,phi)
1
(believe j (intend i (believe j phi)))
```

Here, the guard to the `send` statement is 1, which, as in languages such as C, is interpreted as a logical constant for truth. Hence the guard will *always* succeed, and the message send statement will always be enabled, irrespective of whether or not the agent actually believes the message content. Notice that this second case is actually the more general one, which we would expect to find in most applications.

The next stage is to consider the process of actually checking whether or not agents respect the semantics of the language; of course, if we enforce compliance by way of the `mable.sem` file, then we would hope that our agents will always satisfy the semantics. But it is of course also possible that an agent will respect the semantics even though they are not enforced by the definition in `mable.sem`. (Again, this is in fact the most general case.)

For inform performatives, we can express the property to be checked in $\mathcal{LORA}$ [18] as follows:

$$A \,\square\,(\text{Happens } i \; inform(j, \varphi)) \Rightarrow (\text{Bel } i\varphi)$$

This formula simply says that, whenever agent i sends an "inform" message to agent j with content φ, then i believes φ. Now, given the enriched form of MABLE claims that we described above, we can directly encode this formula in $\mathcal{MORA}$, as follows:

```
claim
  []
  (
    (happens agent1
      send(inform agent2 of (a == 10));)
    ->
    (believe agent1 (a == 10))
  );
```

This claim will hold of a system if, whenever the program statement

```
send(inform agent2 of (a == 10));
```

is executed by `agent1`, then in the system state from which the `send` statement is executed, `agent1` believes that `a == 10`.

We can insert this claim into the system in Figure 4, and use MABLE to check whether it is valid. If we do this, then we find that the claim is indeed valid; inspection of the code suggests that this it what we expect.

Verifying pre-conditions implies as well that we check agents do not inform other agents about facts that they do not believe. Given the MABLE code presented in Figure 4, we have just to remove the line

```
assert((believe agent1 (a == 10)));
```

and then set the pre-condition of the `inform` to 1 (i.e., true) in the `mable.sem` file, and check the previous claim. Obviously, the claim is not valid since `agent1` informs `agent2` about something it does not believe.

Verifying Rational Effects. We consider an agent to be respecting the semantics of an ACL if it satisfies the specification defined by the pre-condition part of a message whenever it sends the message [17]. The rational effect part of a performative semantics define what the sender of the message wants to achieve by sending it; but of course, this does not imply that sending the message is sufficient to ensure that the rational effect is achieved. This is because the agents that receive messages are assumed to be autonomous, exhibiting control over their own mental state. Nevertheless, it is useful to be able to determine in principle whether an agent respects the rational effect part of an ACL semantics or not, and this is the issue we discuss in this section.

We will consider two cases in this section: *credulous* agents and *sceptical* agents. Credulous agents correspond to agents that always believe the information sent by other agents. We can directly define credulous agents in the following `mable.sem` file.

```
i:inform(j, phi)
(believe i  phi)
(believe j  phi)
```

This says that the recipient (j) of an `inform` message will always come to believe the contents of an `inform` message.

Sceptical agents are those that believe that the sender intends that they believe the information; they do not necessarily come to directly believe the contents of the message.

```
i:inform(j, phi)
(believe i  phi)
(believe j (intend i (believe j phi)))
```

We can directly define a $\mathcal{MORA}$ claim to determine whether or not an agent that is sent a message eventually comes to believe it.

```
claim []
 (
  (happens agent1
    send(inform agent2 of (a == 10));)
  ->
  <>(believe agent2 (a == 10))
 );
```

This claim is clearly valid for credulous agents, as defined in the `mable.sem` file given above; running MABLE with the example system immediately confirms this.

Of course, the claim may also be true for sceptical agents, depending on how their program is defined. We can directly check whether or not a particular sceptical agent comes to believe the message it has been sent, with the following claim:

```
claim
  []
 (
  (believe agent2
    (intend agent1
      (believe agent2 (a == 10))))
  ->
  <>(believe agent2 (a == 10))
 );
```

5   Conclusion

We have described extensions to the MABLE multiagent programming language and its associated logical claim language that make it possible to verify whether MABLE agents satisfy the semantics of ACLs. We illustrated the approach with a number of case studies. A key issue for future work is that of moving from the design level (which is what MABLE represents) to the implementation level, in the form of, for example, JAVA code. One possibility we are currently investigating is to enable MABLE to automatically generate JAVA code once a design has been satisfactorily debugged. Another interesting avenue for future work is investigating whether the MABLE framework might be used in the verification of other ACL semantics, such as Pitt's protocol-based semantics [12], or Singh's social semantics [16].

Acknowledgments

This work was supported by the EC under project IST-1999-10948 (SLIE) and by the EPSRC under project GR/R27518.

References

1. E. M. Clarke, O. Grumberg, and D. A. Peled. *Model Checking*. The MIT Press: Cambridge, MA, 2000.
2. P. R. Cohen and C. R. Perrault. Elements of a plan based theory of speech acts. *Cognitive Science*, 3:177–212, 1979.
3. T. Finin and R. Fritzson. KQML — a language and protocol for knowledge and information exchange. In *Proceedings of the Thirteenth International Workshop on Distributed Artificial Intelligence*, pages 126–136, Lake Quinalt, WA, July 1994.
4. FIPA. Specification part 2 — Agent communication language, 1999. The text refers to the specification dated 16 April 1999.
5. C. Guilfoyle, J. Jeffcoate, and H. Stark. *Agents on the Web: Catalyst for E-Commerce*. Ovum Ltd, London, April 1997.
6. J. Y. Halpern and Y. Moses. A guide to completeness and complexity for modal logics of knowledge and belief. *Artificial Intelligence*, 54:319–379, 1992.
7. G. Holzmann. *Design and Validation of Computer Protocols*. Prentice Hall International: Hemel Hempstead, England, 1991.
8. G. Holzmann. The Spin model checker. *IEEE Transactions on Software Engineering*, 23(5):279–295, May 1997.
9. G. J. Holzmann. *The SPIN Model Checker: Primer and Reference Manual*. Addison-Wesley: Reading, MA, 2003.
10. H. Levesque, R. Reiter, Y. Lespérance, F. Lin, and R. Scherl. Golog: A logic programming language for dynamic domains. *Journal of Logic Programming*, 31:59–84, 1996.
11. J. Mayfield, Y. Labrou, and T. Finin. Evaluating KQML as an agent communication language. In M. Wooldridge, J. P. Müller, and M. Tambe, editors, *Intelligent Agents II (LNAI Volume 1037)*, pages 347–360. Springer-Verlag: Berlin, Germany, 1996.
12. J. Pitt and E. H. Mamdani. A protocol-based semantics for an agent communication language. In *Proceedings of the Sixteenth International Joint Conference on Artificial Intelligence (IJCAI-99)*, Stockholm, Sweden, August 1999.
13. A. S. Rao. AgentSpeak(L): BDI agents speak out in a logical computable language. In W. Van de Velde and J. W. Perram, editors, *Agents Breaking Away: Proceedings of the Seventh European Workshop on Modelling Autonomous Agents in a Multi-Agent World, (LNAI Volume 1038)*, pages 42–55. Springer-Verlag: Berlin, Germany, 1996.
14. A. S. Rao and M. Georgeff. Decision procedures for BDI logics. *Journal of Logic and Computation*, 8(3):293–344, 1998.
15. Y. Shoham. Agent-oriented programming. *Artificial Intelligence*, 60(1):51–92, 1993.
16. M. Singh. Agent communication languages: Rethinking the principles. *IEEE Computer*, pages 40–49, December 1998.
17. M. Wooldridge. Verifiable semantics for agent communication languages. In *Proceedings of the Third International Conference on Multi-Agent Systems (ICMAS-98)*, pages 349–365, Paris, France, 1998.
18. M. Wooldridge. *Reasoning about Rational Agents*. The MIT Press: Cambridge, MA, 2000.
19. M. Wooldridge, M. Fisher, M.-P. Huget, and S. Parsons. Model checking multiagent systems with MABLE. In *Proceedings of the First International Joint Conference on Autonomous Agents and Multiagent Systems (AAMAS-2002)*, pages 952–959, Bologna, Italy, 2002.

Logic-Based Agent Communication Protocols

Ulle Endriss[1], Nicolas Maudet[2], Fariba Sadri[1], and Francesca Toni[1,3]

[1] Department of Computing, Imperial College London
180 Queen's Gate, London SW7 2AZ, UK
{ue,fs,ft}@doc.ic.ac.uk
[2] LAMSADE, Université Paris 9 Dauphine
75775 Paris Cedex 16, France
maudet@lamsade.dauphine.fr
[3] Dipartimento di Informatica, Università di Pisa
Via F. Buonarroti 2, 56127 Pisa, Italy
toni@di.unipi.it

Abstract. An agent communication protocol specifies the rules of interaction governing a dialogue between agents in a multiagent system. In non-cooperative interactions (such as negotiation dialogues) occurring in open societies, the problem of checking an agent's conformance to such a protocol is a central issue. We identify different levels of conformance (weak, exhaustive, and robust conformance) and explore, for a specific class of logic-based agents and an appropriate class of protocols, how to check an agent's conformance to a protocol *a priori*, purely on the basis of the agent's specification.

1 Introduction

Protocols play a central role in agent communication. A protocol specifies the rules of interaction between two or more communicating agents by restricting the range of allowed follow-up utterances for each agent at any stage during a communicative interaction (dialogue). Such a protocol may be imposed by the designer of a particular system or it may have been agreed upon by the agents taking part in a particular communicative interaction before that interaction takes place.

Protocol are *public*, i.e. they are (at least in principle) known to all participating agents (and possibly also to any outside observers). As several authors have pointed out, some form of public protocol is a necessary requirement for the definition of a suitable semantics of an agent communication language [13, 16]. Without public conventions (as specified by a protocol), it would not be possible to assign meaning to an agent's utterances.

This *"conventionalist"* view stands in contrast to the *"mentalistic"* approach taken, for instance, in the definition of FIPA-ACL [8], where the legality of utterances is specified in terms of the mental states of the agents participating in an interaction. This is not to say that an agent's mental state is not relevant to communication. On the contrary, an agent's goals and beliefs will strongly influence that agent's communicative behaviour. However, these mental attitudes

F. Dignum (Ed.): ACL 2003, LNAI 2922, pp. 91–107, 2004.

should not have to be taken into account when we define what constitutes a *legal* utterance at a given point in time. We therefore distinguish an agent's communication *strategy*, which may be *private* and will be determined by the agent's goals and beliefs, from the public protocol which lays down the conventions of communication in a given multiagent system in terms of publicly observable events (i.e., in particular, previous utterances) alone.

By the very nature of protocols as public conventions, it is desirable to use a formal language to represent them. In particular, when used in connection with agents that are specified or even implemented using some form of executable logic, a logic-based representation language for communication protocols has many advantages. This paper summarises some of our recent work in the field of logic-based agent communication protocols, which has been initiated in [4] and further developed in [5]. It extends [4,5] in that it discusses possible avenues for future work and it provides a more detailed comparison between our approach and related work in the area. In particular, Sections 5 and 6 are new.

Paper Overview. In Section 2, we discuss two options for representing interaction protocols: finite automata and our logic-based language. In Section 3 we then introduce three different levels of conformance to such a protocol: weak, exhaustive, and robust conformance. In Section 4 we show that our logic-based representation greatly facilities checking whether a given agent is guaranteed to always behave in conformance to a particular protocol. We briefly recall the definition of a class of logic-based agents introduced in [14] and present sufficient criteria for such agents to be either weakly or exhaustively conformant to a protocol. Section 5 discusses potential generalisations of our protocol language and Section 6 discusses related work. Section 7 concludes.

2   Representing Agent Communication Protocols

In this section we present a logic-based representation formalism for a simple yet expressive class of interaction protocols. We assume some restrictions on the kind of interactions that we want to model. The dialogues we consider only involve *two agents* which *sequentially alternate* dialogue moves (utterances). These restrictions (notably avoiding concurrency) allow us to concentrate on a particular class of protocols, namely those representable by means of *deterministic finite automata* (DFAs), of which there are numerous examples in the literature.

Deterministic Finite Automata-Based Protocols. A DFA consists of (i) a set of states (including an initial state and a set of final states), (ii) an input alphabet, and (iii) a transition function δ which maps pairs of states and elements of the input alphabet to states [12]. In the context of communication protocols, elements of the input alphabet are dialogue moves and states are the possible stages of the interaction.

A protocol based on such a DFA representation determines a class of well-formed dialogues where each and every dialogue move is a *legal* continuation of the interaction that has taken place so far:

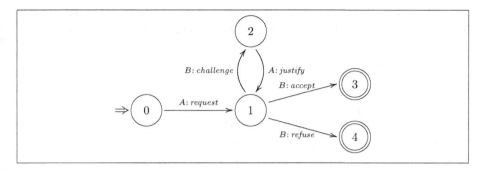

Fig. 1. A simple negotiation protocol

Given a protocol based on a DFA with transition function δ, a dialogue move P is a legal continuation (or simply a legal move) with respect to a state S iff there exists a state S' such that $S' = \delta(S, P)$.

Example. Fig. 1 shows a simple example of a DFA-based protocol which regulates a class of negotiation dialogues between two agents A and B. It specifies that after a *request* made by A (in an initial state 0), B may either *accept* that request, *refuse* it, or choose to *challenge* it. Either one of the first two options would end the negotiation dialogue (bringing the dialogue into a final state). In case agent B decides to *challenge*, agent A has to reply with a *justify* move, which takes the dialogue back to the state where B can either *accept*, *refuse*, or *challenge*.

Logic-Based Protocols. Protocols such as that of Fig. 1 can alternatively be represented as sets of if-then-rules which specify the set of correct responses for a particular incoming dialogue move. For example, to express that agent B could react to a *request* move sent by A either by accepting, refusing, or challenging the request, we may use the following if-then rule:

$$tell(A, B, request, D, T) \Rightarrow tell(B, A, accept, D, T+1) \vee$$
$$tell(B, A, refuse, D, T+1) \vee$$
$$tell(B, A, challenge, D, T+1)$$

Here, the variable B refers to the name of the agent whose communicative behaviour is restricted by the rule and A represents the agent sending a message to B. Note that variables in the above formula are implicitly universally quantified over the whole formula[1]. In general, in this logic-based representation, dialogue moves are instances of the following schema:

$$tell(X, Y, Subject, D, T)$$

---

[1] In our chosen representation, in cases where there are variables that only appear on the righthand side of an implication, these variables are understood to be existentially quantified.

Here, X is the utterer, Y is the receiver $(X \neq Y)$, D is the identifier of the dialogue[2], and T the time when the move is uttered. *Subject* is the type of the dialogue move, i.e. a performative (such as *request*) of the communication language, possibly together with a content (as in *request(item$_{17}$)*). For most of this paper, we are going to omit the content of dialogue moves, as it is usually not relevant to the definition of legality conditions for automata-based protocols and similar formalisms. Also, we shall mostly use the abbreviated form $P(T)$ for dialogue moves (where P stands for the performative of the respective move and T stands for the time of the move), thereby omitting the parameters not relevant to our discussion. For example, our earlier concrete rule could be represented in short as

$$request(T) \Rightarrow accept(T+1) \vee$$
$$refuse(T+1) \vee$$
$$challenge(T+1)$$

For the sake of simplicity, we will assume that the start of the protocol is triggered by some external event $START$ – it is possible to conceive this as the result of some meta-level negotiation process to agree on a particular protocol. The start signal $START(X, Y, D, T)$ is sent by the system to agent Y to sanction at time T the beginning of a dialogue with identifier D amongst agent Y and agent X. We will assume that the system sends such a signal exactly once and exactly to one agent during a dialogue. We will also assume that each time this signal is sent to an agent, it has a new dialogue identifier. Similarly, a dialogue ends once one of the agents sends the signal $STOP$ to the system. $STOP(X, Y, D, T)$ is sent by agent X to the system at time T to sanction the end of a dialogue with identifier D between X and Y. Dialogue inputs for an agent are either dialogue moves sent by other agents or a $START$ signal sent by the system.

   Going back to the example of Fig. 1, we observe that this automaton in fact represents two subprotocols, one for the *initiator* of a dialogue, and one for its *partner* (naturally, each agent can serve as initiator and as partner of a dialogue, at different times). We will refer to these two subprotocols as $\mathcal{P}_i$ and $\mathcal{P}_p$. They can be translated into a set (composed of two subsets) of if-then-rules. Here is the subprotocol for the initiator:

$$\mathcal{P}_i : \begin{cases} START(X, Y, D, T) & \Rightarrow tell(Y, X, request, D, T+1) \\ tell(X, Y, accept, D, T) & \Rightarrow STOP(Y, X, D, T+1) \\ tell(X, Y, refuse, D, T) & \Rightarrow STOP(Y, X, D, T+1) \\ tell(X, Y, challenge, D, T) & \Rightarrow tell(Y, X, justify, D, T+1) \end{cases}$$

Note that agent Y does not have any choices when replying to messages received from agent X (at least not as far as the performatives of the dialogue moves are concerned). Also note that agent Y is responsible for transmitting the $STOP$ signal to the system after having received either one of the terminating moves from X. The subprotocol for the partner in a dialogue consists of two rules:

---

[2] In general, the identifier might be a function of a protocol name.

$$\mathcal{P}_p : \begin{cases} tell(X, Y, request, D, T) \Rightarrow tell(Y, X, accept, D, T{+}1) \lor \\ \qquad\qquad tell(Y, X, refuse, D, T{+}1) \lor \\ \qquad\qquad tell(Y, X, challenge, D, T{+}1) \\ tell(X, Y, justify, D, T) \Rightarrow tell(Y, X, accept, D, T{+}1) \lor \\ \qquad\qquad tell(Y, X, refuse, D, T{+}1) \lor \\ \qquad\qquad tell(Y, X, challenge, D, T{+}1) \end{cases}$$

Note that agent Y have multiple choices when replying to messages received from agent X.

Shallowness. In our example we have simply translated an automata-based protocol into if-then-rules where we have a single performative on the lefthand side. We call protocols that permit such a straightforward translation *shallow*. Shallow protocols correspond to DFAs where it is possible to determine the next state of the dialogue on the sole basis of the previous move. Of course, this is not always the case for all protocols, since in some protocols it may be necessary to refer to the current state of the dialogue to determine the new state (think of two transitions with the same label leaving two different states and leading to two different states).

In principle, any automata-based protocol can be transformed into a protocol that is shallow in this sense (by simply renaming any duplicate transitions). In fact, many of the automata-based protocols proposed in the multiagent systems literature happen to be shallow already or could at least be made shallow by renaming only a small number of transitions.

Well-Formedness Requirements. In the light of the above remarks, we will generally represent shallow protocols as two sets of rules of the following form:

$$P(T) \Rightarrow P_1'(T{+}1) \lor P_2'(T{+}1) \lor \cdots \lor P_k'(T{+}1)$$

We will call these rules *protocol rules*. The righthand side of a protocol rule defines the possible continuations with respect to the protocol after the input P (which we will sometimes refer to as the *trigger* of the rule). The set of all triggers appearing in a subprotocol for a given agent is called the set of *expected inputs* for that agent. To ensure that this protocol is *well-formed* we will require that the two sets of rules meet a number of requirements (R1–R5):

- (R1, *initiation*): there is at least one rule with $START$ on the lefthand side in the protocol, and $START$ may never occur on the righthand side of a rule;
- (R2, *matching*): any dialogue move except $STOP$ occurring on the righthand side of one subprotocol also occurs on the lefthand side of the other, and vice versa;
- (R3, *non-concurrency*): every subprotocol includes the following additional rule to avoid concurrent moves ($\bot$ stands for *false*):

$$tell(X, Y, S_1, T, D) \land tell(X, Y, S_2, T, D) \land S_1 \neq S_2 \Rightarrow \bot;$$

- (R4, *alternating*): for each rule occurring in a subprotocol, if X is the receiver and Y the utterer of the dialogue move occurring on the lefthand side, it must be the case that X is the utterer and Y the receiver of every dialogue move occurring on the righthand side (except for *START* and *STOP*);
- (R5, *distinct triggers*): in each subprotocol, all dialogue moves occurring on the lefthand side of the rules are distinct from each other.

We note here that these are very simple requirements. Any protocol that is well-formed in this sense will provide a *complete* description of what constitutes a sequence of legal dialogue moves. R2 (matching) is the central requirement here; it ensures that for any move that is itself a legal continuation of the dialogue that has taken place so far, there will be a protocol rule that determines the range of legal follow-ups for that move. Ensuring this property in non-shallow protocols is more complicated as we shall see in Section 5.

3   Levels of Conformance

Broadly speaking, an agent is *conformant* to a given protocol if its behaviour is legal with respect to that protocol. We have found it useful to distinguish three *levels* of conformance to a protocol, which we are going to discuss next. Note that we are going to define these notions on the basis of the *observable* conversational behaviour of the agents (i.e. what they utter or not) alone, without making further assumptions on how they actually come to generate these utterances.

Weak Conformance. We start with the notion of *weak conformance*:

> An agent is *weakly conformant* to a protocol $\mathcal{P}$ iff it never utters any dialogue move which is not a legal continuation (with respect to $\mathcal{P}$) of any state of the dialogue the agent might be in.

It is clear that any application governed by a protocol at least requires the level of weak conformance – otherwise it would not make sense to define a protocol in the first place. This is true at least if, as in this paper, we perceive protocols as (syntactic) rules that define the legality of an utterance as a follow-up in a given dialogue. If we adopt a broader notion of protocols, however, levels of conformance that are less restrictive than our weak conformance may also be considered. Yolum and Singh [18], for instance, advocate a *flexible* approach to interaction protocols in which agents may skip steps in a protocol as long as this does not render the interaction as a whole meaningless. Such protocols cannot be specified purely syntactically any more, but have to capture the "intrinsic meanings of actions" [18] for us to be able to decide which "shortcuts" are admissible and which are not.

Exhaustive Conformance. The notion of weak conformance captures that the agent does *not* utter any illegal moves, but does not actually require that the agent utters any dialogue move at all. For interactions where "silent moves" are undesirable, a stronger version of conformance is usually required. We make this idea precise with the notion of *exhaustive conformance*:

An agent is exhaustively conformant to a protocol $\mathcal{P}$ iff it is weakly conformant to $\mathcal{P}$ and it will utter at least one dialogue move which is a legal continuation of any legal input of $\mathcal{P}$ it receives.

Exhaustive conformance is certainly what is intuitively expected in *most* interactions – it is indeed often preferred to avoid considering silent moves as part of a protocol, at least to avoid confusion with lost messages. One may then argue that exhaustive conformance should be the minimum requirement for any interaction.

We believe, however, it is worth making the distinction between weak and exhaustive conformance. The first reason is that there are examples where the lack of response can be considered to be part of the protocol. In such circumstances, it can be sufficient to design a weakly conformant agent, provided that silent moves will not have undesirable consequences. For instance, in a Dutch auction process "when there is no signal of acceptance from the other parties in the auction (other agents in the negotiation) the auctioneer makes a new offer which he believes more acceptable (by reducing the price). Here, because of the convention (protocol) under which the auction operates, a lack of response is sufficient feedback for the auctioneer to infer a lack of acceptance." [10]. In this case, the agent can safely be designed to react appropriately only to the proposals it is ready to accept. But if we consider recent argumentation-based protocols inspired by dialectical models it is sometimes assumed that "silence means consent" [2]. In this case, a lack of response can commit the receiver to some propositions – this is a typical case where it is crucial that agents are exhaustively conformant. The second reason for our distinction of weak and exhaustive conformance is that they are *conceptually* different since weak conformance only involves *not* uttering (any illegal moves), while exhaustive conformance involves uttering (some legal move). This implies substantially different approaches when the issues of checking and enforcing conformance are raised, as we shall see later.

Robust Conformance. Another important problem of agent communication is the need to deal with illegal incoming messages, and to react appropriately to recover from such violations. For instance, any FIPA-compliant communicative agent has to integrate a performative **not-understood** as part of its language [8]. This motivates us to introduce the following notion of *robust conformance:*

*An agent is robustly conformant to a protocol $\mathcal{P}$ iff it is exhaustively conformant to $\mathcal{P}$ and for any illegal input move received from the other agent it will utter a special dialogue move (such as **not-understood***) indicating this violation.*

Robust conformance goes a step further than exhaustive conformance since it requires that an appropriate response is uttered also in reply to illegal input moves. Technically, this necessitates that the agent is able to identify the legality of an incoming dialogue move, i.e. it needs to be able to check conformance with respect to the *other* agent's subprotocol.

Note also that in the case where all agents in the society are known to be weakly conformant, it is theoretically unnecessary to deal with robust conformance (since no agent will ever utter an illegal move). The same applies to systems that are "policed" in the sense that messages not conforming to the protocol will simply not be delivered to the intended recipient. Such an assumption would, however, somewhat contradict the "spirit" of an open society. We should also point out that in dialogues with a very high contingent of illegal utterances the additional `not-understood` moves may in fact burden communication channels unnecessarily, and, therefore, simply ignoring illegal moves would in fact be a better strategy.

4   Checking Conformance

When *checking* an agent's conformance to a publicly agreed interaction protocol we can distinguish two cases: checking conformance *at runtime* and checking conformance *a priori*[3]. The former means checking the legality of the moves as they occur in a dialogue. This would enable a society of agents or a particular agent to determine the legality of an observed dialogue move. Checking conformance *a priori* means checking the legality of an agent's communicative behaviour on the basis of its specification. In other words, *a priori* conformance allows us to guarantee in advance that a computee will be conformant to a given protocol.

In general, checking *a priori* whether an agent will always behave in conformance to a given set of protocols is difficult, if not impossible. Firstly, the *privacy* requirement of a society of agents makes it problematic for the society to access the agent's private specification, and secondly the *complexity* of the specifications makes it hard – even when access to that specification is granted (for the agent itself, for instance) – to actually decide whether the agent will be conformant or not. In particular, the behaviour of the agent will typically depend on some hardly tractable notions, such as beliefs and intentions. As we shall see in this section, for a particular class of logic-based agents and for our shallow protocols we can overcome these difficulties, at least in the case of weak conformance. We are also going to discuss how to extend these results to checking exhaustive conformance, although – as far as our privacy requirements are concerned – our results will necessarily be less satisfying in this case.

Logic-Based Agents. We are now going to consider the case of a specific class of agents based on abductive logic programming that have recently been used in the context of negotiation scenarios [14]. The communication *strategy* S of such an agent (which forms part of its *knowledge base* K) is represented as a set of if-then rules of the following form:

$$P(T) \wedge C \;\Rightarrow\; P'(T{+}1)$$

On receiving dialogue move P at time T [4], an agent implementing this rule would utter P' at time $T{+}1$, provided condition C is entailed by its (*private*)

---

[3] Guerin and Pitt [9] refer to the latter as *compliance at design time.*

[4] As earlier in the paper, we represent dialogue moves in short simply by referring to the performative in the move and to the time of the move.

knowledge base. Again, variables are understood to be implicitly quantified in the same way as our protocol-rules. The dialogue moves P and P' will be based on the agent's communication language. Below, we refer to if-then rules as the above as *strategy rules*.

Response Spaces. In preparation for defining a suitable criterion for guaranteed weak conformance to a given protocol, we introduce the notion of *response space* for a logic-based agent. Intuitively, the response space of an agent specifies the possible moves that the agent can make when using a given strategy S, *without* considering the specific conditions relating to its private knowledge base. This abstraction from an agent's communicative behaviour is related to the idea of an agent automaton proposed by Singh [15].

The response space S^* of an agent with strategy S based on the communication language $\mathcal{L}$ is defined as follows:

$$\{P(T) \Rightarrow \bigvee\{P'(T+1) \mid [P(T) \wedge C \Rightarrow P'(T+1)] \in S\} \mid P \in \mathcal{L}\} \text{ with } \bigvee\{\} = \bot$$

That is, the response space is, essentially, the set of protocol rules we get by first dropping all private conditions C and then conjoining implications with identical antecedents by collecting the corresponding consequents into a single disjunction. For example, the strategy

$$S = \{request(T) \wedge happy \Rightarrow accept(T+1),$$
$$request(T) \wedge unhappy \Rightarrow refuse(T+1)\}$$

determines the following response space:

$$S^* = \{request(T) \Rightarrow accept(T+1) \vee refuse(T+1)\}$$

Checking Weak Conformance. We are now going to state a simple criterion that offers an elegant way of checking weak conformance *a priori* for a logic-based agent. In particular, it avoids dealing with the dialogue history, and it does not make any assumptions on the content of the agent's knowledge base (except to require that it is possible to extract the response space, as previously described). The following is a sufficient criterion for weak conformance:

> An agent is weakly conformant to a protocol $\mathcal{P}$ whenever that protocol is a logical consequence of the agent's response space.

This result is proved in [5]. Observe, however, this is not a necessary criterion for weak conformance, because, looking at the form of strategies, it is clear that *private* conditions may prevent the agent from uttering a particular dialogue move. In other words, it could be the case that S^* does not entail $\mathcal{P}$ but that the agent is still weakly conformant to $\mathcal{P}$ because of its specific knowledge base.

The above result shows that, in the case of weak conformance, it is possible to check conformance *a priori* by inspecting only a relatively small part of an agent's specification (namely, what we could call its "communication module" or communication strategy). In particular, we are *not* required to make any judgements based on the content of its (probably dynamically changing) knowledge base in general.

Checking Exhaustive Conformance. In the case of exhaustive conformance, the situation is rather different. To understand why, recall that as well as requiring weak conformance, exhaustive conformance requires the property of uttering at least one legal move for any legal input. The latter property, which we shall simply refer to as *exhaustiveness* (of an agent) may be considered independently from a particular protocol. In [14], for instance, the authors define a notion of exhaustiveness with respect to a given communication language (as being able to utter a response for any incoming move belonging to that language). Even for our agents, whose communicative behaviour is determined by if-then rules of the form $P(T) \wedge C \Rightarrow P'(T+1)$, it is not generally possible to guarantee exhaustiveness (be it with respect to a given protocol, language, or in general). We cannot generally ensure that one of these rules will indeed "fire" for an incoming move $P(T)$, because none of the additional conditions C may be entailed by the current state of the agent's knowledge base.

As shown in [3], one way of ensuring exhaustive conformance would be to rely on logical truths that are independent from the (possibly dynamic) knowledge base of the agent. For a strategy S and any performative P in a given communication language, let $\mathrm{COND}_S(P)$ denote the disjunction of all the private conditions that appear in a strategy rule in S together with the trigger $P(T)$, i.e.:

$$\mathrm{COND}_S(P) = \bigvee \{C \mid [P(T) \wedge C \Rightarrow P'(T+1)] \in S\} \text{ with } \bigvee \{\} = \bot$$

Now, if $\mathrm{COND}_S(P)$ is a tautology for every performative P appearing on the lefthand side of the relevant subprotocol of a protocol $\mathcal{P}$, then any agent implementing the strategy S is guaranteed to utter *some* move for any input expected in $\mathcal{P}$. Hence, we obtain a useful sufficient criterion for exhaustive conformance (again, with respect to our shallow protocols):

> An agent with strategy S is exhaustively conformant to a protocol $\mathcal{P}$ whenever it is weakly conformant to $\mathcal{P}$ and $\mathrm{COND}_S(P)$ is a tautology for every expected input P (for that agent, with respect to $\mathcal{P}$).

Of course, generally speaking, checking this condition is an undecidable problem because verifying theoremhood in first-order logic is. In practice, however, we would not expect this to be an issue given the simplicity of typical cases. As an example, consider a protocol consisting of only the following rule stipulating that any request by another agent X should be either accepted or refused:

$$request(X, T) \Rightarrow accept(T+1) \vee refuse(T+1)$$

An agent may implement the following simple strategy:

$$request(X, T) \wedge friend(X) \quad \Rightarrow accept(T+1)$$
$$request(X, T) \wedge \neg friend(X) \Rightarrow refuse(T+1)$$

The disjunction $\neg friend(X) \vee friend(X)$, with X being implicitly universally quantified, is a theorem. Hence, our agent would be exhaustively conformant (note that the agent is certainly going to be weakly conformant, because the protocol is a consequence of its response space – in fact, the two are actually identical here). A similar idea is also present in [14], although not in the context of issues pertaining to protocol conformance. Fulfilling the above criterion is not an unreasonable requirement for a well-designed communication strategy S that is intended to be used for interactions governed by a given protocol P.

We continue our discussion of exhaustiveness by observing that, in cases where we can identify a *static* part of an agent's knowledge base (beyond the set of rules making up its communication strategy), we can give an even more general sufficiency criterion that guarantees exhaustive conformance:

> *An agent with strategy S is exhaustively conformant to a protocol P whenever it is weakly conformant to P and* $\text{COND}_S(P)$ *is a logical consequence of the static part of the agent's knowledge base for every expected input P.*

To illustrate the idea, we slightly change our earlier example and replace the agent's second strategy rule with the following strategy rule:

$$request(X, T) \land enemy(X) \Rightarrow refuse(T+1)$$

That is, our agent will refuse any request by X if it considers X to be an enemy. Now our first criterion does not apply anymore; we cannot ensure exhaustive conformance. However, if the agent's knowledge base includes a formula such as $\neg enemy(X) \Rightarrow friend(X)$, expressing that anyone who is not an enemy should be considered a friend, then we can show that $friend(X) \lor enemy(X)$ is a logical consequence of that knowledge base and, thereby, that our agent will be exhaustively conformant to the protocol. Note that this agent may generate two responses for a single input, namely in cases where both $friend(X)$ and $enemy(X)$ are true, which would conflict with the non-concurrency requirement of our protocols (see well-formedness requirement R3).

Enforcing Conformance. Finally, even when an agent cannot be shown to be conformant *a priori*, it may still be possible to constrain its behaviour at runtime by simply forcing it to comply to the rules of the protocol. The problem of *enforcing* conformance (referred to as *regimentation* by Jones and Sergot [11]) is then to try to find easy (and hopefully automatic) ways to ensure that an agent will always be conformant to a given protocol. As shown in [5], for any shallow protocol P, a logic-based agent generating its dialogue moves from a knowledge base of the form $K \cup P$ will be weakly conformant to P.

That is, the agent could simply "download" the appropriate protocol when entering a society and thereby guarantee conformance (and avoid possible penalties) *without* requiring any additional reasoning machinery. The intuition behind the proof of this result is that the additional protocol rules given by P (together with the non-concurrency rule of well-formedness requirement R3) would render any branches in the agent's internal derivation tree corresponding to illegal dialogue moves inconsistent and thereby actively prevent the agent from uttering such moves.

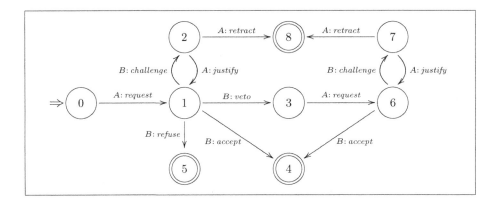

Fig. 2. A protocol that is problematic for n-triggers rules

5   Beyond Shallow Protocols

In this section, we are going to highlight a number of ways in which our logic-based representation language for protocols may be extended to describe a wider class of communication protocols.

Protocols with Several Triggers. Shallow protocols can be seen as a special case of what could be called *n-triggers protocols*, which can be represented by if-then rules whose lefthand side may refer to any of the n previous utterances (both the agent's and its partner's) rather than just the very last utterance. Such if-then rules (referred to below as *n-trigger protocol rules* have the form:

$$P_1(T-1) \vee \cdots \vee P_n(T-n) \;\Rightarrow\; P_1'(T) \vee \cdots \vee P_k'(T)$$

For this class of protocols, we may or may not require a trigger to be present for *every* time point from $T-n$ to $T-1$. The latter seems to be more convenient for most examples. However, if the range of time points referred to in the list of triggers on the lefthand side is not always the same, then it becomes more difficult to formulate appropriate well-formedness conditions for this class of protocols. It is more complicated to determine if a given set of protocol rules is contradictory in the sense of forcing different responses in the same situation, and whether it is complete, in the sense of providing a rule for every possible state a dialogue following these rules may end up in.

Using n-trigger protocol rules, we can describe protocols where the last n moves matter. However, a DFA can express more complicated features. To illustrate this point, consider the automaton of Fig. 2. This is an example for a two phase negotiation protocol. Starting in state 0, agent A sends a first *request* which takes us into state 1. In this state, agent B may *challenge* the other agent, *accept* or *refuse* the request, or use its right to *veto*. In the case of a challenge, we enter a justification loop until either A *retracts* the request or B stops challenging. In state 6 the situation is very similar to state 1, but in state 6 agent

B is not allowed to veto , nor is it allowed to refuse the request (but it can still challenge or accept the request). So it is a bit of a gamble for B to veto A's request and ask for a new request by A, as B can never refuse or veto the new request. Now, after receiving either a *request* or a *justify* move, it is crucial to be able to determine whether one is in state 1 or in state 6, because these states are different, as we have just seen. Intuitively, it is easy to see that in order to be in the state 6, B must have sent a *veto* move at some point during the dialogue. But because of the loops, it is not possible to specify when this dialogue move has occurred. So, this protocol cannot be represented as a set of n-trigger protocol rules.

If we allow for arbitrary time references (rather than merely specific time points in the past) together with temporal constraints on the lefthand side of a rule then we *can* express that *veto* must have occurred at some point. In such an enriched language, we would be able to write protocol rules for state 6:

$$request(T-1) \wedge veto(T') \wedge (T' < T) \Rightarrow accept(T) \vee challenge(T)$$
$$justify(T-1) \wedge veto(T') \wedge (T' < T) \Rightarrow accept(T) \vee challenge(T)$$

However, writing similar rules for state 1 is still not possible, as we cannot express that *veto* has *not* occurred in the past.

Of course, we could further enrich our language and allow for negation and explicit quantification in protocol constraints to also capture this kind of situation. However, the more we enrich our language the more difficult it will be to actually work with protocols expressed in that language. One major problem would be to formulate appropriate well-formedness conditions to ensure that protocols are non-contradictory and complete.

Logical State-Based Representation of DFAs. An alternative avenue of research would be to adopt a state-based representation in logic, encoding straightforwardly DFAs into two kinds of rules: *state maintenance rules* representing the transition function (that is, given a state and a move, determining the next state), of the form

$$state(N, T) \wedge P(T) \Rightarrow state(N', T+1)$$

and *legality rules* determining the set of legal continuations from this state of the dialogue, of the form

$$state(N, T) \Rightarrow \bigvee_{i \in I} P_i(T+1)$$

Conceptually however, if we want to be able to check conformance using the techniques described earlier in this paper, all agents should be required to express their own communication strategies in terms of the same DFA. This, we believe, is quite a strong restriction that we would like to avoid in open agent societies (in comparison, the only assumption so far has been that strategy rules refer at least to the latest move on the lefthand side of the protocol rules).

Other Extensions. The protocols we have discussed so far all refer only to the performatives (such as *request*) of utterances when evaluating legality conditions. In some situations, we may also wish to refer to the *content* of an utterance (for instance, to prevent an agent from proposing a price lower than the previous proposed price in the course of an auction, to deal with deadlines, etc.). This content is expressed in a content language which may be infinite. To permit explicit reference to this content, protocols should be augmented with data structures allowing to keep track of this information (or at least of those contents deemed relevant to contrain the legal follow-ups of the interaction). Examples of such protocols can be found in argumentation-based approach to agent interaction [2], where it is often assumed that agents have access to so-called *commitment stores* to record each others arguments throughout the dialogue. In general, such protocols will be more expressive than the protocols described via DFAs[5].

In [7], a number of abstract models for protocols where content items influence the range of legal follow-ups have been studied in terms of abstract machine models (such as pushdown automata). It would be interesting to combine these ideas with our approach and to design logic-based protocol representation languages that allow for the explicit reference to an utterance's content.

6   Related Work and Discussion

In this section we briefly discuss two related approaches to logic-based protocols for agent communication, namely the "social integrity constraints" of Alberti *et al.* [1] and the set-based protocol description language for the specification of logic-based electronic institutions introduced by Vasconcelos [17].

Social Integrity Constraints. Alberti *et al.* [1] put forward a logic-based representation formalism for communication protocols that is closely related to ours. Their "social integrity constraints" are similar to our protocol rules; however, they explicitly introduce operators to refer to events (such as agents uttering particular dialogue moves) that *happen* in an agent society and those that are *expected* to happen in the future (or, indeed, that should have happened in the past). In our system, these notions are implicit: the lefthand side of a protocol rule such as $request(T) \Rightarrow accept(T+1) \vee refuse(T+1)$ refers to events that have just happened, while those on the righthand side specify the expectations put on the agent whose turn it is next.

Another difference is that the integrity constraints of Alberti *et al.* may include temporal constraints over the time parameters of the social events (i.e. dialogue moves) occurring in a rule. This allows for the representation of a wider class of protocols than just shallow protocols. On the downside, this added expressive power makes the design of well-formed protocols more difficult a task.

---

[5] Note however that adding only a *set* recording contents of a *finite* language is not more expressive than a DFA (even if, practically, it can soon turn out to be tedious to use the automaton-like design).

Given a set of protocol rules in a rich description language, how do we check whether this protocol really covers every possible dialogue state[6]?

Similarly, the more expressive a protocol representation language, the more difficult will it be to check an agent's conformance to such a protocol. While in the case of automata-based protocols (and certainly shallow protocols) checking conformance *at runtime* is essentially a trivial problem, this becomes a major issue for systems where the legality of a given move at a given time cannot be decided once and for all at the time it occurs. Indeed, much of [1] is devoted to this issue for the case of social integrity constraints. Of course, checking conformance *a priori* is considerably more difficult. It firstly requires an abstraction from the agent's specification, expressed in the same language used to express protocols (in the case of our system, this abstraction is given by the very simple notion of response space). This abstraction then needs to be related to the actual protocol in order to define a suitable criterion for guaranteed conformance.

Logic-Based Electronic Institutions. Vasconcelos [17] puts forward another logic-based system for specifying protocols in the context of developing electronic institutions [6]. Electronic institutions are an attempt to provide an "institutional" framework for the development of open agent societies. This includes, in particular, the provision of institutional rules that govern dialogue between agents inhabiting such a society, i.e. communication protocols.

The language proposed in [17] is based on first-order logic, but enriched with sets. This allows for the representation of relevant events in the past, which may influence the legality of follow-up moves. From a computation-theoretic point of view, Vasconcelos'system is related to the class of "protocols with a blackboard" described in [7]. As discussed before, protocols of this class extend automata-based protocols by allowing for utterances to be stored in a set (the blackboard) and for legality conditions that make reference to the elements of that set.

7   Conclusion

We have discussed conformance as the basic notion of ensuring that the behaviour of an agent is adapted to a public protocol regulating the interaction in a multiagent system. Our approach starts from on an alternative representation formalism for communication protocols based on if-then-rules for the kinds of protocols that can be represented as deterministic finite automata. In particular, we have restricted ourselves to a class of protocols where it is not necessary to consider the history of the dialogue besides the latest move to determine the possible legal dialogue continuations (shallowness). We have then discussed the

---

[6] It should be noted that, in fact, this is only a problematic issue if one requires a protocol to provide a *complete* specification of what constitutes legal behaviour in a communicative interaction. While we take the view that a protocol should provide such a complete specification in order to facilitate a complete interpretation of the dialogues actually taking place, Alberti *et al.* "tend to constrain agents' interaction a little as possible, only when needed" [1].

distinction of three levels of conformance: weak conformance which requires that an agent never makes an illegal move, exhaustive conformance which in addition requires an agent to actually make a (legal) move whenever it is his turn in a dialogue, and robust conformance which also requires an appropriate reaction to illegal incoming moves. In the case of weak and exhaustive conformance, we have provided sufficient criteria that can be used to determine whether an agent can be guaranteed to behave in conformance to a given protocol.

Competence. In this paper we have studied the concept of conformance to a communication protocol, which is undoubtedly one of the very central notion to be considered when working with protocols. However, the ability to merely *conform* to a protocol is not not sufficient to be a *competent* user of that protocol. Intuitively, we understand competence with respect to a protocol as the capacity of an agent to "deal adequately" with that protocol. Take, for instance, our negotiation protocol shown in Figure 1. Now assume an agent (supposed to take the role of agent B in that protocol) is engaging in a dialogue regulated by this protocol using the following response space:

$$\mathcal{S}^* = \{ request(T) \Rightarrow refuse(T+1),$$
$$justify(T) \Rightarrow refuse(T+1)\}$$

Even if this agent was exhaustively conformant to the protocol, it would intuitively not be competent as it could never reach either state 2 or 3 (and consequently the interaction could never terminate with an accepted request). A notion of competence that takes into account such issues is studied in [3].

Acknowledgements

This research has been funded by the European Union as part of the SOCS project (IST-2001-32530). The last author has been partially supported by the MIUR (Italian Ministery of Eduction, University, and Research) programme "Rientro dei Cervelli".

References

1. M. Alberti, M. Gavanelli, E. Lamma, P. Mello, and P. Torroni. Specification and Verification of Agent Interactions using Social Integrity Constraints. In W. van der Hoek et al., editors, *Proceedings of the Workshop on Logic and Communication in Multi-Agent Systems (LCMAS-2003)*, 2003.
2. L. Amgoud, N. Maudet, and S. Parsons. Modelling Dialogues using Argumentation. In *Proceedings of 4th International Conference on MultiAgent Systems (ICMAS-2000)*. IEEE, 2000.
3. U. Endriss, W. Lu, N. Maudet, and K. Stathis. Competent Agents and Customising Protocols. In A. Omicini et al., editors, *Proceedings of the 4th International Workshop on Engineering Societies in the Agents World (ESAW-2003)*, 2003.

4. U. Endriss, N. Maudet, F. Sadri, and F. Toni. Aspects of Protocol Conformance in Inter-agent Dialogue. In J. S. Rosenschein et al., editors, *Proceedings of the 2nd International Joint Conference on Autonomous Agents and Multiagent Systems (AAMAS-2003)*. ACM Press, 2003. Extended Abstract.
5. U. Endriss, N. Maudet, F. Sadri, and F. Toni. Protocol Conformance for Logic-based Agents. In G. Gottlob and T. Walsh, editors, *Proceedings of the 18th International Joint Conference on Artificial Intelligence (IJCAI-2003)*. Morgan Kaufmann Publishers, 2003.
6. M. Esteva, J.-A. Rodríguez-Aguilar, C. Sierra, P. Garcia, and J. L. Arcos. On the Formal Specification of Electronic Institutions. In F. Dignum and C. Sierra, editors, *Agent Mediated Electronic Commerce: The European AgentLink Perspective*. Springer-Verlag, 2001.
7. R. Fernández and U. Endriss. Abstract Models for Dialogue Protocols. In M. Marx, editor, *Proceedings of the 5th International Tbilisi Symposium on Language, Logic and Computation*, 2003.
8. Foundation for Intelligent Physical Agents (FIPA). *Communicative Act Library Specification*, 2002. http://www.fipa.org/specs/fipa00037/.
9. F. Guerin and J. Pitt. Guaranteeing Properties for E-commerce Systems. In J. Padget et al., editors, *Agent-Mediated Electronic Commerce IV: Designing Mechanisms and Systems*. Springer-Verlag, 2002.
10. N. Jennings, S. Parsons, P. Noriega, and C. Sierra. On Argumentation-based Negotiation. In *Proceedings of the International Workshop on Multi-Agent Systems (IWMAS-1998)*, 1998.
11. A. Jones and M. Sergot. On the Characterisation of Law and Computer Systems: The Normative Systems Perspective. In *Deontic Logic in Computer Science: Normative System Specification*. John Wiley and Sons, 1993.
12. H. R. Lewis and C. H. Papadimitriou. *Elements of the Theory of Computation*. Prentice-Hall International, 2nd edition, 1998.
13. J. Pitt and A. Mamdani. A Protocol-based Semantics for an Agent Communication Language. In *Proceedings of the 16th International Joint Conference on Artificial Intelligence (IJCAI-1999)*. Morgan Kaufmann Publishers, 1999.
14. F. Sadri, F. Toni, and P. Torroni. Dialogues for Negotiation: Agent Varieties and Dialogue Sequences. In *Proceedings of the 8th International Workshop on Agent Theories, Architectures and Languages (ATAL-2001)*. Springer-Verlag, 2001.
15. M. P. Singh. A Customizable Coordination Service for Autonomous Agents. In *Proceedings of the 4th International Workshop on Agent Theories, Architectures and Languages (ATAL-1997)*, 1997.
16. M. P. Singh. Agent Communication Languages: Rethinking the Principles. *IEEE Computer*, 31(12):40–47, 1998.
17. W. W. Vasconcelos. Expressive Global Protocols via Logic-based Electronic Institutions. In J. S. Rosenschein et al., editors, *Proceedings of the 2nd International Joint Conference on Autonomous Agents and Multiagent Systems (AAMAS-2003)*. ACM Press, 2003. Extended Abstract.
18. P. Yolum and M. P. Singh. Flexible Protocol Specification and Execution: Applying Event Calculus Planning Using Commitments. In *Proceedings of the 1st International Joint Conference on Autonomous Agents and Multiagent Systems (AAMAS-2002)*. ACM Press, 2002.

Protocol Specification
Using a Commitment Based ACL[*],[**]

Nicoletta Fornara[1] and Marco Colombetti[1,2]

[1] Universitá della Svizzera italiana, via Buffi 13, 6900 Lugano, Switzerland
nicoletta.fornara@lu.unisi.ch
[2] Politecnico di Milano, Piazza L. Da Vinci 32, I-20133 Milano, Italy
marco.colombetti@lu.unisi.ch

Abstract. We propose a method for the definition of *interaction proto-cols* to be used in open multiagent systems. Starting from the assumption that *language* is the fundamental component of every interaction, we first propose a semantics for Agent Communication Languages based on the notion of *social commitment*, and then use it to define the meaning of a set of basic communicative acts. Second, we propose a verifiable and application-independent method for the definition of interaction proto-cols, whose main component is the specification of an *interaction diagram* specifying which actions may be performed by agents under given con-ditions. Interaction protocols fully rely on the application-independent meaning of communicative acts. We also propose a set of *soundness con-ditions* that can be used to verify whether a protocol is reasonable. Fi-nally, our approach is exemplified by the definition of an interaction protocol for English auctions.

1 Introduction

Interaction Protocols are patterns of behavior that agents have to follow to engage in a communicative interaction with other agents within a multiagent system (MAS). The specification of interaction protocols is crucial for the de-velopment of a MAS: the advent of Internet makes it urgent to develop general, application-independent methods for the definition of interaction protocols, to be used as components of open, dynamic, heterogeneous, and distributed inter-action frameworks for artificial agents. Indeed, the definition of new interaction protocols is a critical task, because a badly designed protocol may lead to un-successful interactions; thus there is a need for general methods, criteria, and tools for protocol design. We think that there are some important properties that interaction protocols for open frameworks have to satisfy. In particular, an interaction protocol should:

---

[*] This paper is a revision of the paper [7] ACM copyright.
[**] Partially supported by Swiss National Science Foundation project 200021-100260, "An Open Interaction Framework for Communicative Agents".

F. Dignum (Ed.): ACL 2003, LNAI 2922, pp. 108–127, 2004.
© Springer-Verlag Berlin Heidelberg 2004

- Specify legal sequences of communicative acts that form a complete interaction within a system. Every communicative act used in a protocol should maintain its meaning, as defined in a general, application-independent communicative act library of a standard Agent Communication Language (ACL).
- Enable interactions among purely reactive agents, that blindly follow a given protocol, and deliberative agents, that are able to reason about the consequences of actions, and decide whether to take or not to take part in an interaction.
- Allow for effective verification that agents behave in accordance to the specifications of the interaction protocol.

Moreover, a general method for the development of interaction protocols should allow a designer to verify whether a protocol is "sound" with respect to general, application-independent soundness criteria.

So far, several approaches to the definition of interaction protocols have been proposed. Some authors define interaction protocols as finite state machines or Petri nets (see for example [4] and [10]), but do not take into account the meaning of the exchanged messages, which in our opinion is crucial to obtain the properties listed above. Other approaches take into account the meaning of the exchanged messages, but do not rely on a standard ACL with application-independent semantics; for instance Esteva *et al.* [5] specify the protocols available in an electronic institution using finite state machines, but define the meaning of only some of the message types using *ad-hoc* rules. An example of interaction protocol specification which fully takes into account the meaning of the exchanged messages is proposed by Yolum and Singh [18], who introduce a method based on event calculus to define protocols that may be used by artificial agents to determine flexible paths of interaction complying with the specifications. The main difference between Yolum and Singh's proposal and the one put forward in this paper is that with the method described in this paper all the preconditions and effects of the performance of communicative acts on the state of the interaction are completely specified; we also propose a method through which protocol designers may verify if a protocol is sound with respect to a number of general, application-independent soundness criteria related also to the meaning of the exchanged messages.

Our approach to agent interaction presupposes the definition of a standard ACL with unambiguous semantics. In a previous paper [6] we have shown how the semantics of an ACL can be defined in terms of (social) commitments. Our definitions set the rules for the execution of communicative acts, which are regarded as commitment-manipulation actions. Starting from such an analysis, which will be briefly summarized in Section 2, we show how an interaction protocol can be defined. It is important to remark that our protocols are defined starting from the communicative act library of a predefined ACL, and that all communicative acts preserve their general meaning when used within a protocol. As we shall see, an interaction protocol mainly consists of a set of rules that regulate the performance of certain communicative acts; part of these rules are expressed in terms of an *interaction diagram* that specifies which actions can be performed by the agents at every stage of the interaction. Of course, an arbitrary collection of rules does not necessarily define a reasonable interaction protocol. We therefore propose a set of application-independent and verifiable *soundness conditions*, which guarantee that protocols possess certain properties that are crucial for a successful interaction. Such conditions are expressed in terms of the content of the system state at each stage of the interaction, as consequence of the performance of communicative acts.

The paper is organized as follows. Section 2 introduces a commitment-based framework for the definition of an ACL, and a minimal communicative act library that we consider essential to describe communicative interactions in an open MAS. In Section 3 we define a general method for the definition of interaction protocols, and introduce a set of soundness conditions, related to the meaning of the messages exchanged by the agents, which may be used to validate interaction protocols. In Section 4 we present a specification of a form of English auction, an interaction protocol widely used in electronic commerce applications, based on the formalism presented in the paper. Finally, in Section 6 we draw some conclusions.

2   A Commitment-Based Agent Communication Language

A complete operational specification of a commitment-based ACL and a discussion of its motivations can be found in [6]. The semantics proposed in that paper is given by describing the effects that sending a message has on the social relationship between the sender and the receiver of the message using an unambiguous, objective, and public concept, that is, *social commitment*. We assume that the open system in which artificial agents interact consists of the following components:

- A group of registered agents $\{a, b, ...\}$.
- A variable set of *commitment objects* $\{C_1, C_2, ...\}$, which are instances of the commitment class discussed below.
- A variable set of *temporal proposition objects* $\{P, Q, ...\}$, which are instances of the corresponding class discussed below, and are used to express propositions about the application domain and the interaction process.
- A fixed set of actions that agents may perform, including both communicative acts belonging to a communicative act library and application domain actions.
- A fixed set of event-driven routines that automatically update the state of commitment objects on the basis of the truth value of its content and condition. These routines are represented by *update rules* as described in Table 1.
- A set of domain-specific objects $\{O_1, O_2, ...\}$, which represent entities of the application world. Such entities may possess both "natural" or and "institutional" attributes; for example, the color of a product being sold is a natural attribute, while the price of the same product is an institutional attribute. Natural attributes are assumed to reflect the physical properties of the corresponding entities of the real world, and typically cannot be changed during

Table 1. Update Rules.

event	action	rule
$P.truth\_value() = 1$	$C_i(a, a, b, P|T) \rightarrow C_i(f, a, b, P|T)$	1
$P.truth\_value() = 0$	$C_i(a, a, b, P|T) \rightarrow C_i(v, a, b, P|T)$	2
$Q.truth\_value() = 1$	$C_i(p, a, b, P|Q) \rightarrow C_i(a, a, b, P|T)$	3
$Q.truth\_value() = 0$	$C_i(p, a, b, P|Q) \rightarrow C_i(c, a, b, P|Q)$	4
$P.truth\_value() = 1$	$C_i(u, a, b, P|T) \rightarrow C_i(a, a, b, P|T)$	5
$P.truth\_value() = 1$	$C_i(p, a, b, P|Q) \rightarrow C_i(f, a, b, P|Q)$	6
$curr\_time > t$	$C_i(u, a, b, P|Q, t) \rightarrow C_i(c, a, b, P|Q)$	7
legend: $u = unset$, $p = pending$, $c = cancelled$,		
$a = active$, $f = fullfilled$, $v = violated$, $T = TRUE$		

an interaction (of course, they might be changed if some of the interacting agents were assumed to be physical robots). On the contrary, institutional attributes can be affected by the performance of certain communicative acts, in particular by declarations (as discussed below). We assume that each domain-specific object has a value-setting method for each of its institutional properties; for example the method "setState()" can be invoked to set the "state" property.

- A fixed set of *roles* $\{role_1, role_2, ...\}$. This concept is introduced to abstract from the specific agents that take part in an interaction.
- A fixed set of *authorizations* associated to roles, that specify which agent is authorized to perform a particular declaration (see Section 2.1 for details).

Commitment objects are used to represent the network of commitments binding the interacting agents; they have an internal structure, a life cycle, and a set of methods available for manipulation. The internal structure of a commitment object consists of the following fields:

- a unique commitment *identifier* (*id*);
- a reference to the commitment's *debtor*, that is, the agent that has the commitment;
- a reference to the *creditor*, that is, the agent relative to which the debtor is committed;
- the commitment's *content*, that is, the representation of the proposition (describing a state of affairs or a course of action) to which the debtor is committed relative to the creditor;
- the commitment's *conditions*, that is, a list of propositions that have to be satisfied in order for the commitment to become active;
- a *state*, taken from the finite set $\{unset, cancelled, pending, active, fulfilled, violated\}$, used to keep track of the dynamic evolution of the commitment; and
- a *timeout*, which is relevant only in the case of unset commitments, and will therefore be treated as an optional parameter. It represents the time limit for the debtor of an unset commitment to accept, fulfill or reject it. After it is elapsed the activation of rule 7 transforms the commitment to cancelled.

Commitment objects will be represented with the following notation:

$$C_{id}(state, debtor, creditor, content|conditions[, timeout]).$$

We use *temporal proposition* objects to represent the content and the conditions of a commitment. A temporal proposition object consists of the following fields:

- a *statement* in a suitable language which may state that: (i) a certain state of affairs holds; (ii) an action has been performed; (iii) a specific commitment with certain specific attributes holds;
- the *truth_value* of the statement, which may be true (1), false (0) or undefined ($\bot$);
- a *time interval*, which may go from a single instant to the entire life of the system, relative to which the statement is considered;
- and a temporal *mode*, either ($\forall$) or ($\exists$), which specifies whether the statement should be true for the whole time interval or on at least an instant of the time interval.

We assume that the truth value of temporal proposition objects is updated by a suitable "notifier". In particular: if the mode is '$\exists$' the notifier sets the truth-value to true if the statement becomes true at any point of the time interval, otherwise sets it to false when the time interval expires; if the mode is '$\forall$' the notifier sets the truth-value to false if the statement becomes false at any point of the time interval, otherwise sets it to true when the time interval expires. It is important to remark that the truth value of a temporal proposition object can switch from $\bot$ to 1 or 0, but then cannot change any more. In particular cases, as we shall see, it is possible to infer in advance that the statement of a temporal proposition object can no longer become true (false) within the associated time interval. In this case the notifier may set the truth value to false (true) before the time interval expires. To do so, the notifier may exploit specific inference rules (more on this later).

Temporal proposition objects are represented with the following notation:

$$P_{identifier}(statement, time\ interval, mode, truth\_value).$$

As we have already said, temporal proposition objects are used to represent content and conditions of a commitment. In particular the conditions of a commitment consist of a list $[P, Q, ...]$ of temporal proposition objects that have to be satisfied in order for the commitment to become active. The truth value of a list of temporal proposition objects is computed as follows: (i) an empty list of temporal proposition objects is true; (ii) a true temporal proposition object is removed from the list; (iii) a list containing a false proposition object is false.

To make the notation simpler, when the list of conditions contains one temporal proposition object the square brackets are dropped. We also remark that a temporal proposition object, used to express the content or a condition of a commitment object, may in turn represent another commitment object. In particular temporal proposition objects can be used to represent conditions on the temporal evolution of commitments. An example of this is given in Subsection 2.1.

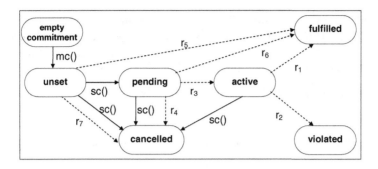

Fig. 1. The life-cycle of commitments.

The life cycle of a commitment object is described by the finite state machine in Figure 1. The state of a commitment can change as an effect of the invocation of its basic methods (solid lines) or of environmental events (represented by dotted lines labelled with the name of the related update rule described in Table 1), that is, of events that change the truth-value of a commitment's conditions or content. We assume that when a commitment object is declared, the constructor of the class creates an empty commitment object, $C_i()$. We represent the invocation of a method by the name of the object followed by a dot and by the name of the method with its parameter list. Commitments are created and manipulated through the following basic operations:

- *Make commitment.* By invoking the method
  $mc(a, b, P, Q)$ with arbitrary debtor a, creditor b, content P, and condition list Q, a new unset commitment object is created:

$$C_i().mc(a, b, P, Q[, to]) \rightarrow C_i(unset, a, b, P|Q[, to])$$

- *Set commitment.* The method $sc(s)$ changes the current state of an existing commitment object to s:

$$C_i(-, a, b, P|Q).sc(s) \rightarrow C_i(s, a, b, P|Q)$$

- *Add condition.* The method $ac(R)$ adds a new temporal proposition object R to the conditions of the commitment:

$$C_i(s, a, b, P|Q).ac(R) \rightarrow C_i(s, a, b, P|R \bullet Q),$$

where the symbol $\bullet$ denotes the operation of inserting a new element in a list.

Basic operations should not be viewed as actions that are directly performed by agents. Rather, they are low-level primitives used to implement operations on commitment objects, more specifically, agents manipulate commitments through a communicative act library.

In this paper we do not tackle the crucial problem of completely formalizing the electronic institution [5] where interactions among communicative agents take place. However regarding the complete definition of the ontology of the commitment we think that it is possible to list a reasonable set of basic authorizations that have to be taken into account when new communicative acts are defined using operation on commitment objects. Such basic authorizations are:

- any agent can create an *unset* commitment with arbitrary debtor and creditor;
- the debtor of an *unset* commitment can set is to either *pending* or *cancelled*;
- the creditor of an *unset, pending,* or *active* commitment can set it to *cancelled*.

These basic authorizations may be modified or new ones may be introduced on the basis of the particular electronic institution where the interaction actually takes place.

Finally note that we defined the conditions under which commitments are fulfilled or violated, but we are not concerned with the management of violations e.g. in terms of sanctions, because this aspect lies beyond the use of commitments for the definition of ACL semantics.

2.1   Library of Communicative Acts

We shall now define the meaning of the basic types of communicative acts as identified by Speech Act Theory [14]. We extend the definitions of [6] by introducing the definition of a new commissive act, the *conditional accept* act, and a treatment of *declarations*; both will be used in the example of Section 4. In the following definitions the sign "$=_{def}$" means that performing the action represented on the left-hand side is the same as performing the action represented on the right-hand side, and the symbol ":=" means that the act represented on the left-hand side is actually performed through the invocation of the methods listed on the right-hand side.

Assertives. According to Speech Act Theory, the point of an assertive act is to commit the sender, relative to the receiver, to the truth of what is asserted. We consider the **inform** act as our prototypical assertive act. This act is used by agent a to inform agent b that P is the case. In a commitment-based approach, an act of informing can be defined as follows ($TRUE$ is the identically true temporal propositional object):

$$\mathbf{inform}(a, b, P) := \{C_i().mc(a, b, P, TRUE);$$
$$C_i(unset, a, b, P|TRUE).sc(pending)\}.$$

The final result is an active commitment, thanks to the intervention of Update Rule 3.

Directives. As defined in Speech Act theory, the point of a directive act is to get the receiver to perform an action (possibly a speech act). We treat **request**

as our basic directive act, and define it as the creation of an unset commitment with the sender as the creditor and the receiver as the debtor. The request by agent a to agent b to bring about P if condition list Q is satisfied is defined as:

$$\textbf{request}(a, b, P, Q[, to]) := \{C_i().mc(b, a, P, Q[, to])\}.$$

The receiver of a request can react in three different ways: it can perform the requested action, accept the request, or refuse it. Questions (or queries) are requests to be informed about something. Here we deal with only wh-questions; for a definition of yes-no-questions see [6]. In wh-questions the requested act of informing cannot be completely described by the sender (otherwise, why should it ask the question?). In this cases the sender provides a "template" for the answer, that is, a temporal proposition object $S(\mathbf{x})$ containing a meta-variable $\mathbf{x}$ that the receiver has to replace with a constant value c. A query has therefore the form:

$$\textbf{request}(a, b, P, TRUE)$$
$$where\ P.statement() = \textbf{inform}(b, a, S(\mathbf{x}))$$
$$\textbf{inform}(b, a, S(\mathbf{x})) =_{def} \textbf{inform}(b, a, S(c))$$
$$for\ some\ constant\ value\ c.$$

This definition implies that the performance of the requested inform act with the temporal proposition $S(c)$ as a parameter makes the temporal proposition P true. Indeed, as remarked by Searle [15] the concept of a question is more general: by a question, an agent may request the execution of a non-assertive communicative act (like a directive, or a commissive). However, our definition above easily generalizes to such cases (an example can be found in Section 4).

Commissives. The point of a commissive act, as defined by Speech Act theory, is to commit the debtor, relative to the creditor, to the execution of an action of a given type. Here we define the basic commissive act of *promising*:

$$\textbf{promise}(a, b, P, Q) := \{C_i().mc(a, b, P, Q);\ C_i(unset, a, b, P|Q).sc(pending)\}.$$

To make an unconditional promise the constant proposition object $TRUE$ is used as the condition, and thus the pending commitment created by the promise is immediately turned into an active commitment by Update Rule 3. Three types of commissive acts can be performed only in connection with an unset commitment, namely **accept**, **conditional accept** and **reject**. Accepting and rejecting are defined as follows:

$$preconditions:\ \exists\ C_i(unset, b, a, P|Q[, to]))$$
$$\textbf{accept}(b, a, C_i(unset, b, a, P|Q[, to])) := \{C_i(unset, b, a, P|Q[, to]).sc(pending)\}$$

$$preconditions:\ \exists\ C_i(unset, b, a, P|Q[, to]))$$
$$\textbf{reject}(b, a, C_i(unset, b, a, P|Q[, to])) := \{C_i(unset, b, a, P|Q[, to]).sc(cancelled)\}$$

Another useful commissive act is "conditional accept", which may be used by agents to negotiate the condition of an unset commitment. In particular, conditional acceptance will appear in the example proposed in Section 4. In fact, in the English Auction Protocol at every round of the bidding process the auctioneer accepts the currently highest bid on condition that no higher bids will be accepted later. In general, the debtor of an unset conditional commitment C_i can accept it provided that an additional condition, represented by a temporal proposition object, holds. Conditional acceptance transforms an unset commitment into a pending commitment, and adds a new condition to the original condition list of the unset commitment:

$$preconditions : \; \exists \, C_i(unset, b, a, P|Q[, to]))$$
$$\textbf{condAccept}(b, a, C_i(unset, b, a, P|Q[, to]), R) :=$$
$$\{C_i(unset, b, a, P|Q[, to]).ac(R); C_i(unset, b, a, P|R \bullet Q[, to]).sc(pending)\}$$

Note that when condition R becomes true, the debtor is left with a pending conditional commitment of the form $C_i(pending, b, a, P|Q)$.

Proposals. A proposal is a combination of a directive and a commissive act. Even if proposals are not basic acts, they deserve special attention because they are crucial in many interesting application fields, like for example electronic commerce. A **propose** act can be defined as the parallel execution of a request and a promise, as denoted by the symbol $||$:

$$\textbf{propose}(a, b, P, Q[, to]) =_{def} \textbf{request}(a, b, P, Q[, to]) \; || \; \textbf{promise}(a, b, Q, S)$$
$$where \; S.statement() = C_i(pending, b, a, P|Q)$$

Note that in the above definition the statement of temporal object S represents the commitment object $C_i(pending, b, a, P|Q)$.

Declarations. Declarations are a special type of communicative acts. Examples of declarations are "I pronounce you man and wife" or "I declare the auction open". The point of a declaration is to bring about a change in the world, obviously not in the physical or natural world but in an institutional world [16, 2], that is, a conventional world relying on common agreement of the interacting agents (or, more precisely, of their designers). Declarations actually change the institutional world simply in virtue of their successful performance. In our interaction framework, to treat declarations we introduce objects with *institutional properties*, that is, conventional properties that result from common agreement, like for example the ownership of a product. Such properties can be affected by declaration acts. It is however necessary to identify which agents are *authorized* or *empowered* to perform a given declaration act in the system. Typically, authorizations are granted to agents in virtue of the *role* they play in an interaction, and thus authorizations are naturally associated to roles. To do so, we need to

introduce a construct to express that an agent having a given role in the interaction system is empowered to bring about an institutional change of a given
kind:

$$precondition s : empowered(role_i, O_k.setProp_j()) \land a.role() = role_i$$
$$\mathbf{declare}(a, O_k.prop_j = x) := \{O_k.setProp_j(x)\}.$$

3   Interaction Protocols

Having defined an essential Communicative Act Library we can now proceed to
the specification of interaction protocols. An interaction protocol is defined by an
environment and an *interaction diagram*. In particular, a protocol's environment
defines:

- A nonempty set of *roles* that agents can play in the interaction. To each role,
  a set of specific authorizations may be associated.
- A nonempty set of *participants*, which are the agents interacting by using the
  protocol. Every participant must play a well-defined role in the interaction.
  The set of participants may vary during the execution of the protocol, but
  is always finite.
- A possibly empty set of global *constants* and *variables*, that may be subject
  to global *constraints*.
- A collection of commitment objects, temporal proposition objects, and
  domain-specific entities used to represent all concepts involved in the interaction.
- A set of *authorizations*, associated to roles, to perform certain institutional
  actions, in particular declarations.

A protocol's interaction diagram specifies which actions may be performed
by each agent at each stage of the interaction. More precisely, an interaction
diagram (see for example Figure 2) is defined by a finite graph in which:

- Every node represents a state of the interaction. To every state we can associate a representational content, that is, the set of all facts that hold at the
  state, expressed in terms of: protocol variable values, commitment objects,
  temporal proposition objects, and domain-specific objects.
- There is a single distinguished *initial node*, with no incoming edge, and a set
  of distinguished *final nodes*, with no outgoing edge. The interaction starts
  from the initial node and ends when a final node is reached.
- Every edge describes a transition from a state to another state. A transition
  may correspond to the execution of a communicative act or to the occurrence
  of a relevant environmental event; when the transition occurs, the content of
  the target state can be completely computed from the content of the source
  state, and from the semantics of the communicative act or a description of
  the environmental event responsible for the transition.

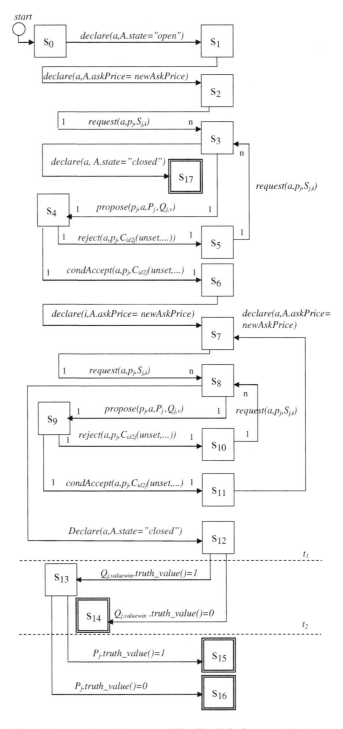

Fig. 2. Interaction diagram of the English Auction Protocol.

- When more than one communicative-act edge goes out of a given node, it is possible to specify the conditions (defined as arbitrary Boolean expressions) under which each act may be executed. As a whole, the set of condition-action pairs going out of a node behaves like a *guarded command* [3]: at least one of the actions must be executed, but the agent specified as the actor of the action is free to choose which action to perform among those whose *guard* is true. If all guards are mutually exclusive, the guarded command is equivalent to a sequence of if-then statements.
- It is possible to associate a cardinality to communicative act edges. In particular cardinality "1 to n" means that the same message is sent by one agent to n agents, and cardinality "1 to 1" means that a message is send by one agent to another agent.

3.1   Soundness Conditions

To describe a sensible interaction pattern, an interaction protocol must satisfy a number of general, application-independent *soundness conditions*. A first, fairly trivial, set of conditions concerns the topology of the interaction diagram:

- Every node of the interaction diagram must be reachable from the initial node.
- There must be at least a final node.

Another, less trivial, set of soundness conditions concerns the content of states. Such conditions, express constraints related to the meaning of the exchanged messages, as defined by the communicative act library adopted.

- All communicative acts that are allowed by a protocol at state s must have their preconditions satisfied by the content associated to s when their guard is true. This condition guarantees that all communicative acts allowed by the interaction protocol may actually be executed.
- All commitments included in the content of a final state must be cancelled, fulfilled, or violated. This condition guarantees that the whole interaction has been completed.

An interesting problem is raised by the fact that during the execution of a protocol, the same state may be reached from the start state following different paths (i.e., performing different chains of actions). For example, a certain state of an interaction could be reached because an agent has autonomously made a promise or because the agent was requested to make a promise, accepted the request, and then fulfilled the resulting commitment by actually making the promise. If we abstract from the different paths, we intuitively feel that the interaction has reached the same state; however, if we compute the content of the state we get different results. The point is that these results, although different, are equivalent from the point of view of the interaction, in that they have the same "commissive import". More precisely, we say that state s is *equivalent* to state s' if and only if the contents of s and s' are identical, with the only exception of commitments that are fulfilled, violated, or cancelled. We can therefore formulate another soundness condition:

– If a state of an interaction can be reached through different paths, the contents of the state computed along the different paths must be equivalent.

The situation is even more complex when the definition of an interaction protocol has a loop, that is, a cycle in the interaction diagram. Interaction loops naturally appear when a sequence of communication acts can be repeated several times, like for example in the English Auction Protocol (Section 4). The existence of loops makes it possible to reach the same state following different paths in the interaction diagram. In this case, however, the notion of equivalence discussed above is still necessary but no longer sufficient. This problem is well known in computer programming, and it can be solved by introducing the concept of a *loop invariant*. For example, consider again the protocol for an English Auction. At a generic iteration, the auctioneer is committed to selling the product currently under the hammer to a specific agent for a specific price, on condition that no higher price will be offered. Of course, the specific agent that made the highest offer, as well as the associated price, will change from one iteration to another one. However, we can describe the situation in terms of loop invariants, by saying that the auctioneer is committed to selling the product to *the agent that made the highest offer*, for *the price defined by such an offer*, on condition that no higher offer will be made. The soundness condition given above can now be reformulated as follows:

– If a state of an interaction can be reached through different paths, the contents of the state computed along the different paths, expressed in terms of suitable invariants, must be equivalent.

4   The English Auction Protocol

In this section we present a specification of a form of English auction protocol using the framework proposed so far. We chose this protocol as an example because it is used in many electronic commerce applications on the web, and because it is fairly complex: in particular, it is an interesting example of iterative interaction protocol. In this example we consider the interaction process needed to sell a single product o, which can obviously be repeated to sell several products.

4.1   The Environment

The environment of the English Auction Protocol includes the following elements:

– **Roles.** *Auctioneer* and *Client*.

– **Participants.** One agent, a, in the role of *Auctioneer* and n agents, $\{p_1, ..., p_n\}$, in the role of *Client*.

– **Constants and Constraints.** t_{max}, the maximum duration of the auction; t_1, the deadline for the payment; t_2, the deadline for the delivery. $t_{max} < t_1 < t_2$.

- **Domain-specific entities.**
  Object o, representing the product on sale, with a *resPrice* field for the reservation price.
  Object A, representing the auction, with fields for the following variables (initialized as indicated): *state* = *"closed"*; *askPrice* = 0; t_{end} automatically set to t_{system} when *state* is set to "closed"; $t_{inactivity}$ i.e. the maximum time of inactivity between two subsequent bids.
  The action of transferring the ownership of an object or of a sum of money to another agent is an institutional action involving the institutional notions of ownership and money. For the sake of simplicity, we treat here this action as a primitive domain action. The fact that agent a transfers to agent b the ownership of x (an object or a sum of money) is represented by $give(a, b, x)$.

- **Variables.** The environment has the following variables (initialized as indicated): $newAskPrice$ =
  $o.resPrice()$; $value_{win}$ = 0; t_{system}, a global clock accessible to all participants; t_{bid} = 0, the time of the last accepted bid; i a counter that is automatically incremented every time the bidding process is iterated.

- **Authorizations.** The auctioneer is empowered to open and close the auction and to set the ask price of the product on sale:
  $empowered(Auctioneer, A.setState())$,
  $empowered(Auctioneer, A.setAskPrice())$.

Scheme of Temporal Proposition Objects. In the interaction framework proposed so far the *content language* used to express the content and the condition fields of commitment objects is based on the use of temporal proposition objects. Given that in complex interactions like the ones that follow the English Auction Protocol many temporal proposition objects are involved, we concisely describe them through *schemes*, that represent possible temporal proposition object in parametric form. Parameters will be bound to specific values when the interaction actually takes place and an instance of the temporal proposition object is created (truth values are always initialized to $\perp$, and therefore are not indicated in schemes). In our example, parameter *now* is initialized at t_{system} when the temporal proposition object is created; and parameter v and v' are used to indicate an amount of money.

- Scheme P_j represents the proposition "the auctioneer gives product o to client p_j, in the time interval from the end of the auction to t_2":
  $P_j(give(a, p_j, o), t_{end}...t_2, \exists)$;

- Scheme $Q_{j,v}$ represents the proposition "client p_j gives the amount v of money to the auction house represented by the auctioneer, in the time interval from the end of the auction to t_1": $Q_{j,v}(give(p_j, a, v), t_{end}...t_1, \exists)$;

- Scheme $S_{j,i}$ represents the proposition "client p_j makes a proposal during iteration i":
  $S_{j,i}(propose(p_j, a, P_j, Q_j(\mathbf{x})), now...now + t_{inactivity}, \exists)$;

- Scheme $U_{j,v}$ represents the proposition "the auctioneer is committed, relative to client p_j, to proposition P_j under condition $Q_{j,v}$, in the time interval from now to the end of the auction":

$$U_{j,v}(C_{id2j}(pending, a, p_j, P_j|Q_{j,v}), now...t_{end}, \exists);$$

- Scheme $W_{v'}$ represents the proposition "the auctioneer does not accept any proposal with value greater than v' in the time interval from now to the end of the auction":

$$W_{v'}(\neg \exists j \ (condAccept(a, p_j, C_{id2j}(unset, a, p_j, P_j|Q_{j,v}), W_v) \wedge \ v > v')),$$
$$now...t_{end}, \exists);$$

Communicative Acts. In this section specific conditions (guards) for the performance of the communicative acts used in the English Auction Protocol are given. Obviously in order that the communicative act is successfully performed also the preconditions defined in the Library of Communicative Acts have to be satisfied. Some of these acts have to be repeated at every round i of the bidding process. In order to be able to refer to commitment objects created by previously preformed communicative acts we report also the effects of the performance of communicative acts: they can also be computed from the definitions given in the library of communicative acts. Therefore in the protocol communicative acts retain the semantics defined in the library of communicative acts, this contrasts with the approaches in which the semantics of communicative acts is affected by the protocol [12]. Moreover the performance of certain communicative acts changes the value of some environmental variables.

- The auctioneer declares the auction open (state s_0).

$$guards : A.state() = "closed"$$
$$\textbf{declare}(a, A.state = "open")$$

- The auctioneer declares the current ask-price of the ongoing auction (state s_1, s_6, s_{11}).

$$guards : A.askPrice() < newAskPrice$$
$$\textbf{declare}(a, A.askPrice() = newAskPrice)$$

- The auctioneer makes the "call for proposals" (state s_2, s_5, s_7, s_{10}).

$$\textbf{request}(a, p_j, S_{j,i}, TRUE, t_{inactivity})$$
$$effects : C_{id1j}(unset, p_j, a, S_{j,i}, TRUE, t_{inactivity})$$

- One participant makes its proposal (state s_3, s_8).

$$guards : \{(t_{system} < t_{max}), (t_{system} - t_{bid} < t_{inactivity})\}$$
$$\textbf{propose}(p_j, a, P_j, Q_{j,v})$$
$$effects : \{C_{id2j}(unset, a, p_j, P_j|Q_{j,v}[, to]), C_{id3j}(pending, p_j, a, Q_{j,v}|U_{j,v}),$$
$$S_{j,v}.truth\_value() = 1\}$$

- If the value of the proposal is greater than the current ask-price the auctioneer has to accept it (state s_4, s_9).

  $guards : v > A.askPrice()$;

  $\mathbf{condAccept}(a, p_j, C_{id2j}(unset, a, p_j, P_j|Q_{j,v}), W_v)$

  $effects : \{C_{id2j}(pending, a, p_j, P_j|[Q_{j,v}, W_v]), \forall\ v' < v\ W_{v'}.truth\_value() = 0\}$

  $variable\ updates : \{newAskPrice = v,\ t_{bid} = t_{system}\}$

- If the value of the proposal is less than or equal to the current ask-price the auctioneer has to reject it (state s_4, s_9).

  $guards : v \leq A.askPrice()$;

  $\mathbf{reject}(a, p_j, C_{id2j}(unset, a, p_j, P_j|Q_{j,v}))$

  $effects : \{C_{id2j}(cancelled, a, p_j, P_j|Q_{j,v}), U_{j,v}.truth\_value() = 0\}$

- The auctioneer can declare closed the auction only if the time of inactivity is equal to the constant value defined at the beginning of the auction or when the fixed end time of the auction is reached (state s_3, s_8).

  $guards : \{(t_{system} \geq t_{max}) \vee (t_{system} - t_{bid} > t_{inactivity}), A.state() = "open"\}$

  $\mathbf{declare}(a, A.state = "closed")$

  $effects : \{W_{value_{win}}.truth\_value() = 1, U_{j,value_{win}}.truth\_value() = 1\}$

  $variable\ updates : \{t_{end} = t_{system}, value_{win} = newAskPrice\}$

4.2   Interaction Diagram

The interaction diagram that specifies the English auction Protocol is reported in Figure 2. It is possible to verify that an actual interaction complies with the protocol by checking that the sequence of communicative acts bring from the unique start state to one of the final states. Moreover it is possible to prove the soundness of this protocol specification. In particular the contents of each state accessible through different paths results equivalent. For states s_9, s_{10}, s_{11}, that are in the loop of the protocol, it is necessary to identify a loop invariant describing p_j as the client who made the highest offer.

5   Discussion

Both in this paper and in [6] our main research focus has been on the definition of an operational semantic for an agent communication language based on the notion of social commitment. In particular in this paper we tried to show the potentialities of this approach to define application independent and verifiable interaction protocols for multiagent systems and to verify whether a given protocol is sound with respect to general soundness criteria.

Given that the definition of an agent communication language is strictly related to the definition of a *content language*, in our formalization we introduced the notion of temporal propositions to express the content of communicative acts. We do not think that the proposed structure for temporal propositions is enough expressive to cover all the interesting situations where agents need to interact, but it has proved enough expressive for the formalization of some crucial examples like the protocol of the proposals and the English auction. The complete investigation of how to operationally define a content language with some specific characteristics is beyond the scope of these papers.

Whatever the structure of the content language may be, a crucial requirement of our approach is that the events that have to happen in order to make the content and the condition of commitment objects (formalized through temporal proposition objects) true or false have to be *observable*. In our model there are mainly two types of events that are relevant for interaction systems:

- the events that happen in the real world external to the interaction system and which are signaled to the system through suitable "sensors", for example a change in the balance of a bank account;
- the events that happen directly in the interaction system, for example the exchange of a message.

In a real application there may be observable and unobservable events, for example because some events could be too expensive to be observed, or because it is impossible to ascertain who is the actor of the action that caused the event, or because its observation would violate the law in force about privacy, etc. In order for the proposed model to be actually adopted it is necessary that each application defines which are the types of events that can be observed and consequently can change the truth value of temporal propositions in the systems. This is not a limitation of the model but reflects objective limitations of any computational system.

Another critical aspect of this approach could be the problem of how artificial agents can become aware that a certain event has actually happened, that the information received is truthful, and consequently that the corresponding temporal proposition becomes true or false and the related commitment is therefore fulfilled or violated. We think that this is mainly a problem of *trust* in the source of information. In fact in our everyday life we may have: *non-certified* interactions, like when we speak with our friends, and *certified* interaction, for example when we buy a house. In the same way in artificial interaction systems we can recognize a similar distinction: situations where agents interact without a certified mediator and situations where a certified mediator is required. In non-certified interactions agents can get information about events by trusted informers, like for example a bank or an electronic sensor. In case of violation of a commitment an agent can for example decide to reduce its level of trust in the defaulting agent. In certified interactions an "above parties" entity, trusted by all the participant and able to listen all the exchanged messages, provides the information about the state of affair and about the performed actions and in case of violation of commitments undertaken by one of the interacting agents takes certain legal proceedings. Regarding this point and in contrast to what is asserted in [8] by Jones and Parent, it is important to remark that in the commitment approach to the definition of the semantics of ACLs the fact to be committed to some state of affairs described by proposition p is not a commitment to defend p if challenged by other agents, but it is a commitment to the truth of p. Such commitment could become violated if its content turns out to be false. A more complete discussion about the commitment approach and the conventional signals approach can be found in [17].

Keeping on with the discussion about other approaches, in [11] McBurney and Parsons propose a computational model of e-commerce called Posit Spaces based on the notion of joint commitments. In their ontology of commitment the available locutions are propose, accept and delete which are equivalent to our creation of an unset commitment, acceptance of the commitment and its cancellation; in our proposal we defined also the rejection of a commitment that is important to avoid that a proposed commitment remains in the system forever. In Posit Spaces the dynamic evolution of the state of commitments and the basic authorizations on their manipulation are not explicit, what is said is that they follow the rules of the electronic institution. In our approach (see Section 2) we give a basic set of rules for the evolution of the commitment from unset to fulfilled, violated, or cancelled and basic authorizations on the manipulation of commitments that we think are the basic rules that every interaction system has to follow even if specific institution can change them or add new ones. Moreover the absence of any description of the structure of posits (one or more commitments) and of their meaning makes from our point of view the proposed operational model incomplete. An interesting aspect of Posit Spaces is the utilization of tuple spaces, a model of communication between computational entities, and the introduction of an operational model to treat multi-party commitments.

In [13] Rovatsos et al. propose a model of communication for open systems based on the notion of expected utility and on the idea that the meaning of communicative acts lies in their experienced consequences. This approach has the limitation to make some assumptions regarding the type of interacting agents in particular that they have a utility to maximize. Furthermore from our point of view the empirical semantics proposed can be an interesting model of how the human system of social rules and the meaning of speech acts have evolved during centuries, but it is hard to apply to open artificial agents interactions where the agents are heterogeneous and developed by different designers and where the interaction with the same set of agents usually is very short.

Mallya et al. in [9] propose a content language, similar to the one proposed in our approach, where temporal aspects of the content of commitments are taken into account. In particular they enhance the expressive power of the language by introducing the possibility to nest multiple levels of time intervals and propose some results for the detection of commitment violation before the occurrence of the events to which the commitment is referred.

In [1] Bentahar et al. present a formal framework to represent conversations between agents based on the notion of social commitment and argumentation. Regarding to their treatment of the notion of commitment, they distinguish, like us, between proposed commitment, accepted commitment and conditional commitment. The two approaches differ in the possible states of the commitment and in the set of allowed operations on commitments. However their approach, like also the approach presented in [9], provides for agents an action to fulfill and violate commitments, therefore is deeply different from our proposal where commitments become fulfilled or violated on the basis of the truth value of the temporal proposition and not for an action actively performed by an agent.

In [17] Verdicchio and Colombetti give a logical model of the notion of commitment which is close even if not completely compatible with the one presented here. We plan to make the two models compatible in the near future.

6   Conclusions

In this paper we presented an application independent method for the definition of interaction protocols, based on the meaning of the exchanged messages, that can be used to define patterns of interaction in open, dynamic, and heterogeneous agent systems. The method proposed is based on a general ACL, whose semantics is defined in terms of commitments, and on a further component defining protocol-specific interaction rules. The resulting interaction protocols are verifiable, in the sense that is possible to test whether an agent is behaving in accordance to it. Moreover, soundness condition are proposed to verify if a the structure of a given interaction protocol is reasonable. We also show how our method can be used to define a complex and common interaction protocol, the English Auction.

With respect to our previous operational proposal [6] of a commitment-based ACL semantics, in this paper we introduce a treatment of conditional acceptance and of declarations.

Our method for the definition of interaction protocols differs from most existing proposals, in that it is based on the use of an application-independent library of communicative acts, whose meaning is fully preserved when they occur in a protocol. With respect to the proposal put forward by Yolum and Singh in [18], our approach is focussed on the protocol design phase more than on the possibility of shortcutting predefined interaction patterns at run time. Indeed, we expect that agents used in practical application will mostly be simple reactive agents; if this idea is correct, proving the soundness of a protocol at design time is more important than allowing agents to plan intelligent variations of existing protocols. In principle, however, a deliberative agent with reasoning capabilities could understand our protocols on the basis of an ontology of commitment, linguistic knowledge (i.e., knowledge of a Communicative Act Library with semantics), and the ability to reason on interaction diagrams (i.e., a version of finite state machines).

References

1. J. Bentahar, B. Moulin, and B. Chaib-draa. Commitment and argument network: a new formalism for agent communication. In F. Dignum, editor, *Advances in Agent Communication*, LNAI, page in this volume. Springer Verlag.

2. M. Colombetti and M. Verdicchio. An analysis of agent speech acts as institutional actions. In *Proc. First International Joint Conference on Autonomous Agents and MultiAgent Systems AAMAS 2002*, pages 1157–1164, New York, 2002. ACM Press.
3. E. W. Dijkstra. *A Discipline of Programming*. Prentice-Hall International, 1976.
4. M. d'Inverno, D. Kinny, and M. Luck. Interaction protocols in agentis. In *Proceedings of the Third International Conference on Multi-Agent Systems*, pages 112–119. IEEE Press, 1998.
5. M. Esteva, J. Rodríguez-Aguilar, C. Sierra, P. Garcia, and J. L. Arcos. On the formal specification of electronic institutions. *Lecture Notes in Computer Science*, 1991:126–147, 2001.
6. N. Fornara and M. Colombetti. Operational specification of a commitment-based agent communication language. In *Proc. First International Joint Conference on Autonomous Agents and MultiAgent Systems AAMAS 2002*, pages 535–542. ACM Press, 2002.
7. N. Fornara and M. Colombetti. Defining interaction protocols using a commitment-based agent communication language. In *Proc. Second International Joint Conference on Autonomous Agents and MultiAgent Systems AAMAS 2003*, pages 520–527. ACM Press, 2003.
8. A. Jones and X. Parent. Conventional signalling acts and conversation. In F. Dignum, editor, *Advances in Agent Communication*, LNAI, page in this volume. Springer Verlag.
9. A. Mallya, P. Yolum, and M. Singh. Resolving commitments among autonomous agents. In F. Dignum, editor, *Advances in Agent Communication*, LNAI, page in this volume. Springer Verlag.
10. H. Mazouzi, A. E. Fallah, and S. Haddad. Open protocol design for complex interactions in multi-agent systems. In *Proc. First International Joint Conference on Autonomous Agents and MultiAgent Systems AAMAS 2002*, pages 517–526, New York, 2002. ACM Press.
11. P. McBurney and S. Parsons. The posit spaces protocol for multi-agent negotiation. In F. Dignum, editor, *Advances in Agent Communication*, LNAI, page in this volume. Springer Verlag.
12. J. Pitt and A. Mamdani. A protocol-based semantics for an agent communication language. In D. Thomas, editor, *Proceedings of the 16th International Joint Conference on Artificial Intelligence (IJCAI-99-Vol1)*, pages 486–491, S.F., 1999. Morgan Kaufmann Publishers.
13. M. Rovatsos, M. Nickles, and G. Weiss. Interaction is meaning: a new model for communication in open systems. In F. Dignum, editor, *Advances in Agent Communication*, LNAI, page in this volume. Springer Verlag.
14. J. R. Searle. *Speech Acts: An Essay in the Philosophy of Language*. Cambridge University Press, Cambridge, United Kingdom, 1969.
15. J. R. Searle. Conversation. In H. Parret and J. Verschueren, editors, *(On) Searle on Conversation*, pages 7–29. J. Benjamins Publishing Company, Amsterdam, 1991.
16. J. R. Searle. *The construction of social reality*. Free Press, New York, 1995.
17. M. Verdicchio and M. Colombetti. A logical model of social commitment for agent communication. In F. Dignum, editor, *Advances in Agent Communication*, LNAI, page in this volume. Springer Verlag.
18. P. Yolum and M. P. Sing. Flexible protocol specification and execution: Applying event calculus planning using commitments. In *Proc. First International Joint Conference on Autonomous Agents and MultiAgent Systems AAMAS 2002*, pages 527–534, New York, 2002. ACM Press.

A Logical Model of Social Commitment
for Agent Communication*

Mario Verdicchio[1] and Marco Colombetti[1,2]

[1] Politecnico di Milano, Dipartimento di elettronica e informazione
Piazza Leonardo da Vinci 32, 20133 Milano, Italy
Phone: +39-02-2399-3686
Fax: +39-02-2399-3411
{Mario.Verdicchio,Marco.Colombetti}@Elet.PoliMi.It
[2] University of Lugano
Via Buffi 13, 6904 Lugano, Switzerland
Phone: +41-91-912-4773
Marco.Colombetti@Lu.UniSi.CH

Abstract. As part of the goal of developing a genuinely open multiagent system, many efforts are devoted to the definition of a standard Agent Communication Language (ACL). The aim of this paper is to propose a logical framework for the definition of ACL semantics based upon the concept of (social) commitment. We assume that agent communication should be analyzed in terms of communicative acts, by means of which agents create and manipulate commitments, provided certain contextual conditions hold. We propose formal definitions of such actions in the context of a temporal logic that extends CTL* with past-directed temporal operators. In the system we propose, called $CTL^{\pm}$, time is assumed to be discrete, with no start or end point, and branching in the future. $CTL^{\pm}$ is then extended to represent actions and commitments; in particular, we formally define the conditions under which a commitment is fulfilled or violated. Finally, we show how our logic of commitment can be used to define the semantics of an ACL.

1 Introduction

One of the main goals in the field of autonomous agents is the development of genuinely open multiagent systems. As part of this enterprise, many efforts are devoted to the definition of a standard Agent Communication Language (ACL). So far, two ACLs have been widely discussed in the literature: KQML [4] and FIPA ACL [5], but we do not yet have a universally accepted standard. In particular, there is no general agreement on the definition of ACL semantics.

The aim of this paper is to propose a framework for the definition of ACL semantics based upon the concept of (social) commitment, thus adopting an approach that has already been proposed and discussed by some authors [12,2]. In our view, a commitment-based approach to semantics has remarkable advantages over the more traditional proposals based on mental states (see for example [1,8]). In particular, commitments, contrary to mental states, are public and observable, thus they do not

---

* This work extends a paper with the same title that is included in the Proceedings of the 2nd International Joint Conference on Autonomous Agents and Multi-Agent Systems (AAMAS 03)

F. Dignum (Ed.): ACL 2003, LNAI 2922, pp. 128–145, 2004.
© Springer-Verlag Berlin Heidelberg 2004

need to be attributed to other agents by means of inference processes, and can be stored in public records for further reference.

Our framework, like all major proposals in the field of ACLs, relies on the assumption that agent communication should be analyzed in terms of communicative acts. In our view, communicative acts are performed by agents to create and manipulate commitments. That is, agents modify the social state of a multiagent system by carrying out speech acts that affect the network of commitments binding agents to one another. For instance, when agent a informs agent b that p, then a becomes committed, relative to b, to the fact that p holds. As we shall show in the rest of this paper, we can similarly model other kinds of communicative acts from the perspective of commitments.

Previous versions of our model have been published elsewhere [2,6]. However, we try here for the first time to delineate a full logical model of commitment, including the aspects related to time. In Section 2 we illustrate some aspects of our model of time and action. In Section 3 we present a formal model of commitment. In Section 4 we investigate on the relations between message exchanges, communicative acts and the creation and manipulation of commitments. Finally, in Section 5, we draw our conclusions and illustrate some future work.

2 Time and Action

2.1 Time

For the treatment of time, we adopt a framework close to the CTL^* temporal logic [3]. As is well known, CTL^* is a powerful logic of branching time, developed to prove properties of computational processes. In the context of agent interaction, we found it necessary to extend CTL^* with past-directed temporal operators. In the system we propose, called $CTL^\pm$ and essentially equivalent to $PCTL^*$ [9], time is assumed to be discrete, with no start or end point, and branching in the future.

The formal language L of $CTL^\pm$ is the smallest set such that:

$A \subseteq L$, where A is a suitable set of atomic formulae;
$\neg L \subseteq L$, $(L \wedge L) \subseteq L$;
$X^+L \subseteq L$, $X^-L \subseteq L$, $(LU^+L) \subseteq L$, $(LU^-L) \subseteq L$;
$AL \subseteq L$, $EL \subseteq L$.

The intuitive meaning of the temporal operators is the same as in CTL^*, with the additional stipulation that:

X^+ means *at the next instant* (in the future);
X^- means *at the previous instant* (in the past);
U^+ means *until* (in the future);
U^- means *since* (in the past).

A and E are *path quantifiers*, respectively meaning *for all paths* and *for some path*.

To define the formal semantics of L, let S be a set of *states*. A $CTL^\pm$ *frame* F on S is an infinite tree-like structure on S, where every state has exactly one *predecessor* and a nonempty set of *successors*.

A *path* in frame F is an infinite sequence $p = \langle p_0,...,p_n,...\rangle$ of states, such that for every element p_n in the sequence, element p_{n+1} is one of the successors of p_n in F. The subsequence of p starting from element p_n is itself a path, and will be denoted by p^n. The set of all paths starting from state s will be denoted by $Paths(s)$. Paths allow us to formalize the concepts of being "in the past" or "in the future" of some state. More precisely, we say that state s' *is in the future of* s (in frame F) iff there is a path p such that $s = p_0$ and, for some n, $s' = p_n$. Symmetrically, we say that s' *is in the past of* s (in frame F) iff there is a path p such that $s' = p_0$ and, for some n, $s = p_n$.

A $\text{CTL}^{\pm}$ *model* is a pair $M = \langle F,v\rangle$, where F is a $\text{CTL}^{\pm}$ frame and v is an evaluation function assigning a Boolean truth value to every atomic formula at every state. We are now ready to define the truth conditions of an **L** formula in model M on path p:

$M,p \models \varphi$, where φ is an atomic formula, iff $v(\varphi,p_0) = 1$;

$M,p \models \neg\varphi$	iff	$M,p \not\models \varphi$;
$M,p \models (\varphi \wedge \psi)$	iff	$M,p \models \varphi$ and $M,p \models \psi$;
$M,p \models X^+\varphi$	iff	$M,p^1 \models \varphi$;
$M,p \models X^-\varphi$	iff	for some path q, $(q^1 = p$ and $M,q \models \varphi)$;
$M,p \models (\varphi U^+ \psi)$	iff	for some n, $(M,p^n \models \psi$ and for all m s.t. $0 \leq m < n$, $M,p^m \models \varphi)$;
$M,p \models (\varphi U^- \psi)$	iff	for some path q and for some n, $(q^n = p$ and $M,q \models \psi$ and for all m s.t. $0 \leq m < n$, $M,q^m \models \varphi)$;
$M,p \models A\varphi$	iff	for all $q \in Paths(p_0)$, $M,q \models \varphi$;
$M,p \models E\varphi$	iff	for some $q \in Paths(p_0)$, $M,q \models \varphi$.

We define an **L** formula to be *true in model M at state* s iff it is true in M on all paths starting from s:

$M,s \models \varphi$	iff	for all $p \in Paths(s)$, $M,p \models \varphi$.

Finally, we define a formula to be *valid* iff it is true on all paths of every model:

$\models \varphi$	iff	for all M and all p, $M,p \models \varphi$.

Taking the temporal operators X^+, X^-, U^+, and U^- as primitives, we can introduce the following operators as abbreviations: F^+ (sometimes in the future), F^- (sometimes in the past), G^+ (always in the future), G^- (always in the past):

$F^+\varphi =_{def} true\, U^+\varphi,$
$F^-\varphi =_{def} true\, U^-\varphi,$
$G^+\varphi =_{def} \neg F^+\neg\varphi,$
$G^-\varphi =_{def} \neg F^-\neg\varphi.$

We also define a "weak until" and a "weak since" temporal operators:

$\varphi W^+\psi =_{def} G^+\varphi \vee \varphi U^+\psi,$
$\varphi W^-\psi =_{def} G^-\varphi \vee \varphi U^-\psi.$

Later on we shall use another derived operator, representing the intuitive concept of "until-and-no-longer". This operator is defined as follows:

$\varphi Z^+\psi =_{def} \varphi W^+\psi \wedge G^+(\psi \rightarrow G^+\neg\varphi).$

In other words, $\varphi \, Z^+ \psi$ is true iff in the future: ψ never becomes true and φ is true forever, or ψ eventually becomes true and since then φ is no longer true. More derived temporal operators will be defined later on to treat specific examples.

2.2 Events and Actions

We now extend the temporal language **L** of CTL$^\pm$ in order to represent events and actions. We do this by introducing a number of predicates on sorted arguments.

We reify events, that is, we treat them as a sort of individuals, called *event tokens*. Every event token belongs to at least one *event type*, and takes place (*happens*) at exactly one time instant. We focus on a special kind of events, *actions*, which are brought about by an agent, called the *actor* of the action.

In the following, variables e, e', ..., will range on event tokens; variables x, y, ..., will range on agents; and variables t, t', ..., will range on event types. We take $Happ(e)$, $Type(e,t)$ and $Actor(e,x)$ as primitive predicates, and define:

$$Done(e,x,t) =_{\text{def}} Happ(e) \wedge Type(e,t) \wedge Actor(e,x).$$

The formula $Done(e,x,t)$ expresses the fact that event e of type t is brought about by agent x. For the sake of convenience, at times we shall use the "m-dash" character to express existential quantification, as in the example below:

$$Done(e,-,t) =_{\text{def}} \exists x \, Done(e,x,t).$$

The semantics of **L** has now to be enriched to account for the interpretation of the extended language. This can be done by: adding a typed domain D of individuals to every model M; defining an interpretation of first-order terms into D; defining an interpretation of primitive predicates in D; and defining the semantics of the first-order quantifiers $\forall$ and $\exists$. In this paper we do not develop these technical aspects in details, and thus rely on the reader's intuition for the interpretation of first-order expressions.

As usual, we now need to introduce a number of axioms to constrain the interpretation of primitive predicates. It should be noted that such axioms do not alter the structure of temporal frames, but reduce the set of allowable models by putting constraints on the interpretation of terms and predicates. Validity of formulae must then be understood with respect to the class of CTL$^\pm$ models that satisfy such constraints.

As we already said, the instant at which an event takes place on a path is unique. We therefore adopt the axiom

$$Happ(e) \rightarrow \mathsf{X}^- \mathsf{G}^- \neg Happ(e) \wedge \mathsf{AX}^+ \mathsf{G}^+ \neg Happ(e). \tag{UH}$$

3 Commitment

3.1 Representing Commitments

We define a commitment as a social state between agents including three components:

- the *debtor*, that is, the agent that is committed;
- the *creditor*, that is, the agent relative to which the debtor is committed,
- the *content*, that is, the state of affairs to which the debtor is committed relative to the creditor.

A commitment is said to be a *precommitment* when it has been proposed, but not yet accepted or refused. In such a case, we say that the (potential) debtor is precommitted to the (potential) creditor. In our treatment, both precommitments and actual commitments arise from the performance of communicative acts.

We view (social) commitment as a deontic state, akin to obligation. For such a reason, it is essential to define when a commitment is *fulfilled* and when it is *violated*. We shall give the relevant formal definitions in the following subsections. However, in this paper we do not investigate what is going to happen when a commitment is fulfilled or violated (e.g., in terms of agent reputation, sanctions, etc.). These are important aspects of multiagent systems management, but go beyond the conceptual definition of commitment.

We now extend our formal language to accommodate for the treatment of commitments. The resulting language will be called *Semantic Language*, given that its purpose is to define the semantics of ACL messages. To represent a commitment, we need to represent a debtor, a creditor, and a content. Debtors and creditors are agents, and shall be represented by first-order terms of sort *agent* like we already did in Subsection 2.2. The representation of content is more critical. It seems to us that there are basically two possibilities:

- The content can be represented by a formula of the Semantic Language. In this case, commitment can be represented through a modal operator, analogously to the deontic logic representation of obligation.
- The content can be represented as a first-order term. In this case, a commitment can be represented by a first-order formula.

We believe there are at least two reasons to adopt the latter solution. The first, obvious reason is that the technicalities required by a predicative representation are simpler than the ones required by a modal representation. The second, more important, reason is that in the context of agent communication the content of a commitment, as we shall see later on, is always derived from an agent message. More precisely, a commitment's content derives from a statement in some Content Language (CL): think for example of the value of the :content parameter in KQML or FIPA ACL messages. With respect to a CL, the Semantic Language we are presently defining can be viewed as a meta-language. It is therefore feasible to represent a CL statement by a first-order term of the Semantic Language. Such a first-order term may be viewed as the representation of the abstract syntax of a concrete CL statement. Of course, in the Semantic Language it is not sufficient to represent the syntax of a CL statement: we also need to represent its semantics. To do so, we shall assume that:

- The abstract syntax of any CL statement can be represented by a first-order term of the Semantic Language.
- If u is such a term, then the meaning of the corresponding statement is represented by a formula of the Semantic Language, which we shall denote by $\lfloor u \rfloor$. In other words, $\lfloor u \rfloor$ is a truth-preserving translation of u into a formula of the Semantic Language. For such a translation to be possible the Semantic Language will have to include enough predicate, function, and constant symbols to represent the meaning of CL statements.

We introduce two predicates, *Comm* and *Prec*, to represent commitments and pre-commitments. In particular,

$Comm(e,x,y,u)$

will mean that event e has brought about a commitment for agent x, relative to agent y, to the truth of $\lfloor u \rfloor$. When the above formula is true, we shall say that e is a *commitment-inducing event*. Precommitments are represented analogously:

$Prec(e,x,y,u)$

will mean that event e has brought about a precommitment for agent x, relative to agent y, to the truth of $\lfloor u \rfloor$.

Under given conditions, that we shall analyze later on, commitments can be *made* or *cancelled*, and precommitments can be *made*, *cancelled* or *accepted* (i.e., turned into actual commitments). This is possible thanks to the performance of tokens of suitable action types, formally defined in the next subsection: make commitment (*mc*), make precommitment (*mp*), cancel commitment (*cc*), cancel precommitment (*cp*), and accept precommitment (*ap*). Such actions, as we shall see later on, are performed by exchanging messages in an ACL.

3.2 A Logical Model of Commitment

The action types for commitment manipulation are defined by axioms describing their *constitutive effects*, that is, by describing the state of affairs that necessarily hold if a token of a given action type is successfully performed.

Make Commitment

$$Done(e,-,mc(x,y,u)) \rightarrow \mathbf{A}\,(Comm(e,x,y,u)\,\mathbf{Z}^{+}\,Done(-,-,cc(e,x,y,u))). \qquad \text{(MC)}$$

Axiom MC says that:
if an agent (not necessarily x or y) successfully performs an action of making a commitment with x as the debtor, y as the creditor, and u as the content,

then on all paths x is committed, relative to y, to content u,

until an agent possibly cancels such a commitment, after which the commitment no longer exists.

It is important to remark that Axiom MC only defines what making a commitment means. It does not establish in what way, and under what conditions, an agent may actually make or cancel a commitment in a concrete situation. This aspect will be dealt with in Section 4.

Make Precommitment

$$Done(e,-,mp(x,y,u)) \rightarrow \mathbf{A}\,(Prec(e,x,y,u)\,\mathbf{Z}^{+}\,(Done(-,-,ap(e,x,y,u)) \qquad \text{(MP)}$$
$$\vee\,Done(-,-,cp(e,x,y,u)))).$$

Axiom MP is analogous to MC.

Accept Precommitment

$$Done(e',-,ap(e,x,y,u)) \wedge \neg Done(-,-,cp(e,x,y,u)) \rightarrow \qquad \text{(AP)}$$
$$\mathbf{A}\,(Comm(e',x,y,u)\,\mathbf{Z}^{+}\,Done(-,-,cc(e',x,y,u))).$$

Axioms AP says that:

if an agent successfully performs an action of accepting a precommitment brought about by event e, with debtor x, creditor y, and content u,

and no agent has just cancelled such a precommitment,

then the action of acceptance brings about on all paths a commitment for x, relative to y, to content u, which will stand until it is possibly cancelled.

Again, this axiom does not say by what means or under what conditions an agent may actually accept a precommitment in a concrete situation.

The next axiom assures that an event, which takes place at a certain instant, can (pre)commit agents only from that moment on. No (pre)commitment is retroactive:

$Happ(e) \rightarrow \mathsf{X}\mathsf{G}^-(\neg Prec(e,x,y,u) \wedge \neg Comm(e,x,y,u))$.

Finally, the next axiom states that all (pre)commitments are necessarily brought about by some event:

$Prec(e,x,y,u) \vee Comm(e,x,y,u) \rightarrow \mathsf{F}^- Happ(e)$.

3.3 Fulfillment and Violation

Intuitively, a commitment is fulfilled when its content is true, and is violated when its content is false. However, given that we are working in the context of branching-time logic, the formal definitions are not trivial.

Let us start with an informal example. Suppose that thanks to event e_1, agent a is committed, relative to agent b, to the content expressed by CL sentence u_1, whose intuitive meaning is "it will rain until midnight." Suppose further that e_1 takes place at 4:00 pm, and that it persistently rains from that time to 6:00 pm, inclusive. Intuitively, at 6:00 the commitment induced by e_1 is neither fulfilled nor violated (we shall say that the commitment is *pending*). Now consider two possible developments:

- It goes on raining until midnight. In this case, the commitment induced by e1 is fulfilled at time 0:00 am.
- At 6:01 pm it suddenly stops raining. In this case, the commitment induced by e1 is violated at 6:01 pm.

In order to formalize these intuitions, two problems must be solved. The first problem has to do with the *temporal indexicality* of content sentences. By this we mean that the truth of the sentence "it will rain until midnight" has to be evaluated with respect to the state at which the commitment is made (the *point of speech*, in Reichenbach's terminology[1] [11]). On the other hand, to know whether the commitment is fulfilled or violated we have to wait until something relevant happens, that is, until the first state at which it stops raining, or the first state at which it is midnight (Reichenbach's *point of event*). But then, and this is the second problem, what is the truth value of the content at a generic state (Reichenbach's *point of reference*) lying between the point of speech and the point of event?

---

[1] The German philosopher Hans Reichenbach proposed a famous model of verb tenses in Chapter 7 of his book *Elements of Symbolic Logic*. We adopt his terminology, but reinterpret it with some freedom.

We propose a solution in which:

- content sentences are temporally de-indexicalized in a simple and uniform way, by conjoining their translation into the Semantic Language with an atomic formula setting the point of speech;
- the truth value of a content sentence at a given point of reference is evaluated with respect to all paths starting from the point of reference.

Fulfillment

On the basis of our previous considerations, fulfillment can be formally defined as follows:

$$Fulf(e,x,y,u) =_{\text{def}} Comm(e,x,y,u) \wedge AF^-(Happ(e) \wedge \lfloor u \rfloor). \tag{FC}$$

To understand this definition correctly, it is helpful to go back to our previous example. Let us assume that

$$[u_1] = (rain\ U^+\ midnight),$$

and suppose that the commitment-inducing event e_1 takes place in model M at state s:

$M,s \models Happ(e_1)$,

$M,s \models A\ (Comm(e_1,a,b,u_1)\ Z^+ Done(-,-,cc(e_1,a,b,u_1)))$.

Now consider an arbitrary state s' in the future of s. We have

$M,s' \models Fulf(e_1,a,b,u_1)$ iff $M,s' \models Comm(e_1,a,b,u_1) \wedge AF^-(Happ(e_1) \wedge \lfloor u_1 \rfloor)$.

Let us assume that the commitment made at s has not been cancelled until s' (inclusive). This implies that

$M,s' \models Comm(e_1,a,b,u_1)$.

Under such conditions, the commitment is fulfilled at s' iff

$M,s' \models AF^-(Happ(e_1) \wedge \lfloor u_1 \rfloor)$,

that is, iff for all $p \in Paths(s')$,

$M,p \models F^-(Happ(e_1) \wedge \lfloor u_1 \rfloor)$.

Therefore, for the commitment to be fulfilled at s', the formula

$Happ(e_1) \wedge (rain\ U^+\ midnight)$

must be true at some state in the past of s'. Now, thanks to Axiom UH (Section 2.2) we know that on every path the state at which an event takes place is unique. Thus, for the commitment to be fulfilled at s', the formula

$(rain\ U^+\ midnight)$

must be true, for all $p \in Paths(s)$ going through s'. A model satisfying these requirements is depicted in Figure 1.

This example shows how statement u_1 is de-indexicalized by evaluating it in the state s at which event e_1 took place.

Moreover, the definition of fulfillment at s' considers the truth value of s_1 on all paths starting from s and going through s'. The set of such paths typically becomes smaller when s' is moved further in the future of s. As a consequence, a commitment that is not yet fulfilled at s may be fulfilled at some state s' in the future of s.

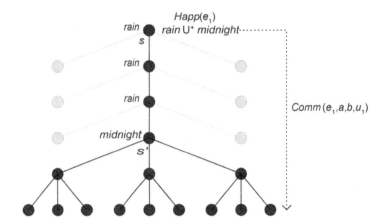

Fig. 1. Formula *rain* U⁺ *midnight* is true on all paths starting from *s* and going through *s'*.

Violation

Analogously to fulfillment, we can define violation as follows:

$$Viol(e,x,y,u) =_{def} Comm(e,x,y,u) \wedge \mathsf{AF}^- (Happ(e) \wedge \neg \lfloor u \rfloor). \tag{VC}$$

Pending commitments

A commitment is pending iff it is neither fulfilled nor violated:

$$Pend(e,x,y,u) =_{def} Comm(e,x,y,u) \wedge \neg Fulf(e,x,y,u) \wedge \neg Viol(e,x,y,u). \tag{PC}$$

Thanks to Axiom UH (Section 2.2), from the above definition we can derive:

$$\models Pend(e,x,y,u) \leftrightarrow Comm(e,x,y,u) \wedge \mathsf{EF}^-(Happ(e) \wedge \lfloor u \rfloor) \wedge \mathsf{EF}^-(Happ(e) \wedge \neg \lfloor u \rfloor).$$

However, Definition PC raises a fairly subtle formal problem, which we shall analyze in the next subsection.

3.4   Some Properties of Commitment

We shall now try to show that the axioms and definitions given in the previous subsections determine a satisfactory "logic of commitment."

Let us start with a few notes on fulfillment and violation. It is easy to see that if a commitment is introduced through a *make commitment* or *accept precommitment* action and later cancelled, it can no longer be fulfilled or violated. This is a direct consequence of Axioms MC and AP, and of Definitions FC and VC. Even if a commitment has already been fulfilled or violated in the past, it is no longer fulfilled or violated after it is cancelled. It is possible, however, to express the idea that a commitment has been fulfilled or violated in the past, by using the F⁻ operator. It would also be possible to constrain *cancel commitment* actions so that commitments that have already been fulfilled or violated can no longer be cancelled.

Some commitments can be fulfilled, but can never be violated in a finite period of time. An example is a commitment whose content, translated into the Semantic Language, is F^+rain. Analogously, some commitments can be violated but never fulfilled in finite time. Consider for example a commitment to G^+rain.

All commitments whose content is logically valid are immediately fulfilled. Dually, all commitments whose content is logically contradictory are immediately violated. Moreover, all commitments whose point of event is in the past of the point of speech are immediately fulfilled or violated.

From the definitions of Section 3.3, every commitment is either fulfilled, or violated, or pending, and these three states are mutually exclusive. In fact it is possible to prove that

$\models Comm(e,x,y,u) \rightarrow \mathbf{xor}(Fulf(e,x,y,u), Viol(e,x,y,u), Pend(e,x,y,u))$;

that is, exactly one of $Fulf(e,x,y,u)$, $Viol(e,x,y,u)$, or $Pend(e,x,y,u)$ is true in all models at every state at which $Comm(e,x,y,u)$ holds.

This result, however, should be interpreted with some care. To show why, let us go back again to our example of Section 3.3. Suppose that thanks to event e_1, agent a is committed, relative to agent b, to the fact that it will rain until midnight; that e_1 takes place at 4:00 pm; and that it persistently rains from that time to 6:00 pm, inclusive. As we have remarked in the previous subsection, at 6:00 the commitment induced by e_1 is intuitively *pending*.

However, without further assumptions it is not possible to prove this. The reason is that there are models of the Semantic Language in which the commitment is not pending, but fulfilled. Consider for example a one-path frame, and assume that the atomic formula *rain* is true at every state. In such a model, the commitment to the fact that it will rain until midnight is fulfilled as soon as it is made. Given that in some models the commitment is fulfilled, it is not possible to prove that it is pending.

The problem has nothing to do with our definitions. Rather, it derives from the fact that certain intuitions about the world are not represented in the Semantic Language. In this case, the intuition is that rain is *contingent*, in the sense that it is always logically possible that it rains or that it does not rain at the next state. If we want to carry this intuition into the Semantic Language, we need to exclude all models that do not meet it. This can be done by assuming the following *contingency axiom* for rain:

$EX^+rain \wedge EX^+\neg rain$.

Of course, this axiom does not belong to a logical model of commitment, but represents a fragment of domain knowledge. Such knowledge has to be expressed in terms of suitable axioms if we want to derive properties of commitments that square with our intuitions about the world.

So far we said nothing about the behaviour of the commitment predicate with respect to the structure of content. To do so, however, we must make some assumptions about the abstract syntax of the CL. Let us assume that the CL allows for the Boolean connectives, quantifiers and temporal operators that, for the sake of simplicity, we will represent by the same symbols we use in the Semantic Language.

Now consider the formula

$Comm(e,x,y, u \wedge v)$.

The question is: if e commits x, relative to y, to $u \wedge v$, does it also separately commit x to u and to v? In fact, our logic does not allow us to derive $Comm(e,x,y,u)$ or $Comm(e,x,y,v)$ from $Comm(e,x,y, u \wedge v)$. It turns out, however, that we do not need to add anything to our axioms and definitions to obtain a satisfactory behavior of commitment with respect to conjunction. Indeed, it is easy to see that

$\models Comm(e,x,y, u \wedge v) \wedge AF^-(Happ(e) \wedge \neg \lfloor u \rfloor) \rightarrow Viol(e,x,y, u \wedge v),$

$\models Comm(e,x,y, u \wedge v) \wedge AF^-(Happ(e) \wedge \neg \lfloor v \rfloor) \rightarrow Viol(e,x,y, u \wedge v).$

The validity of these formulae allows one to say, in informal speech, that

if a debtor is committed, relative to a creditor, to the conjunction of u and v,

then the debtor is committed, relative to the creditor, to both u and v,

in the sense that the falsity of either u or v implies a violation of the original commitment.

Another interesting problem is given by the treatment of *conditional commitments*, that is, commitments that become active provided some condition holds. Conditional commitments are not trivial to define in terms of the material conditional, and are often given an *ad hoc* treatment (see for example [6,13]), not dissimilar from the treatment of conditional obligation in deontic logic. To see where difficulties come from, let us see what happens if a conditional commitment is simply defined as a commitment with a conditional content. Suppose for example that event e_1 commits agent a, relative to agent b, to the fact that if a lightning is seen, a thunder will be heard immediately after. Further suppose that event e_1 takes place in model M at state s (i.e., s is the point of speech), and let formula

$$Comm(e_1,a,b, lightning \rightarrow X^+ thunder) \tag{1}$$

express such a commitment. The obvious problem is that the commitment expressed by Formula 1 is immediately fulfilled if no lightning is seen at the point of speech, because

$$AF^-(Happ(e_1) \wedge (lightning \rightarrow X^+ thunder))$$

is true at s if *lightning* is false at s. This problem, however, is not due to a limitation of material conditional, but to the fact that Formula 1 does not correctly represent the content of the commitment. In fact, the statement to which a commits may be interpreted in two ways: (i), "always in the future, a thunder will be heard immediately after a lightning is seen;" or (ii), "as soon as a lightning will be seen, a thunder will be heard immediately after." With the first interpretation, a's commitment is represented by

$$Comm(e_1,a,b, G^+(lightning \rightarrow X^+ thunder)). \tag{2}$$

The commitment of Formula 2 can never be fulfilled in finite time, and is violated at state s', in the future of s, iff

$$AF^-(Happ(e_1) \wedge \neg G^+(lightning \rightarrow X^+ thunder))$$

holds at s', that is, iff

$$AF^-(Happ(e_1) \wedge F^+(lightning \wedge \neg X^+ thunder))$$

holds at s'. In other words, the commitment of Formula 2 is violated in the future of s as soon as on all paths starting from s and going through the current state it is the case that a lightning will be seen that is not immediately followed by a thunder.

With the second interpretation, the commitment is expressed by

$$Comm(e_1,a,b, lightning\ S^+ X^+ thunder), \tag{3}$$

where the "as soon as" operator S^+ is defined as below:

$$\lfloor u\ S^+ v \rfloor =_{def} (\lfloor u \rfloor \rightarrow \lfloor v \rfloor) \wedge (X^+(\lfloor u \rfloor \rightarrow \lfloor v \rfloor)\ W^+ \lfloor u \rfloor).$$

The commitment of Formula 3 is fulfilled at a state s', in the future of s, iff

$$\mathsf{AF}^- (Happ(e_1) \wedge ((lightning \rightarrow \mathsf{X}^+ thunder)$$
$$\wedge (\mathsf{X}^+(lightning \rightarrow \mathsf{X}^+ thunder) \mathsf{W}^+ lightning))$$

holds at s'. This formula becomes true at state s' if, and only if, for all paths starting from s and going through s' the first occurrence of a thunder after s is immediately followed by a lightning. Moreover, as it can easily be checked, the commitment of Formula 3 is violated at a state in the future of s as soon as it is the case that a lightning will be seen that is not immediately followed by a thunder.

These examples suggest that a satisfactory logic of commitment is induced by Definitions FC and VC, which specify the conditions under which a commitment is fulfilled or violated.

4 Communicative Acts and ACL Messages

In the previous section we have defined the results of a number of commitment-manipulation actions, but we have not yet explained how these actions can be performed. The idea is the following: agents can perform commitment-manipulation actions by exchanging ACL messages, provided certain contextual conditions hold.

We consider as the fundamental unit of agent communication the *exchange of a message*. By this we mean that a message is sent by an agent, the *sender*, and received by another agent, the *receiver*. In turn, a message is viewed as a pair made up by a *type indicator* and a *body*. Type indicators (corresponding to KQML's *performatives*) are constant symbols taken from a finite set, whose definition is part of the ACL specification. The body can be a sentence in some CL, whose abstract syntax is represented in our Semantic Language by a first-order term (see Section 3), or a more complex structure (for example a tuple of elements), typically including a CL sentence. When event e is an exchange of a message of type τ and body σ, sent by agent x to agent y, we write:

$Done(e,x,exch(y,\tau,\sigma))$.

Under given conditions, such an event implies a valid performance of a commitment-manipulation action. It is important to note that by associating commitment manipulation actions to messages, we formally specify a commitment-based semantics for an ACL. More precisely, the meaning of message $\langle \tau,\sigma \rangle$ is defined as the effect that exchanging $\langle \tau,\sigma \rangle$ has on the network of commitments binding the sender and the receiver. By defining a coherent set of message types in this way, it is possible to specify a Communicative Act Library with its associated semantics.

Below we analyze a few examples.

Informing

We assume that the body of an *inform* message is an arbitrary CL sentence. Informing is then defined as committing to the truth of the message body. More precisely, when agent x exchanges with agent y a message of type *inform* with an arbitrary CL sentence s as the body, agent x commits, relative to y, to the truth of s:

$$Done(e,x,exch(y,inform,s)) \rightarrow Done(e,x,mc(x,y,s)). \hfill \text{(Inf)}$$

Requesting

We assume that the body of a request message is an *action expression*, which describes the requested action by indicating its type, its actor, and possibly a temporal constraint. Concrete action expressions belonging to a specific CL should not be confused with the first-order term representing the abstract syntax of the expression in the Semantic Language. For example, here is an example of a possible concrete action expression describing the action type of actor `ag-1` moving object `obj-1` from location `loc-1` to location `loc-2` before `end-of-turn`:

```
(action :actor ag-1
        :type (move :object obj-1
                    :from   loc-1
                    :to     loc-2)
        :deadline end-of-turn)
```

The abstract syntax of this expression is given by the first-order term

$$u_1 = before(done(ag_1,move(obj_1,loc_1,loc_2)),end\text{-}of\text{-}turn),$$

which in turn can be translated into the Semantic Language formula

$$\lfloor u_1 \rfloor \models Done(\text{-},ag_1,move(obj_1,loc_1,loc_2))\ \mathsf{B}^+\ end\text{-}of\text{-}turn,$$

where

$$\varphi\,\mathsf{B}^+\psi =_{def} \neg(\neg\varphi\mathsf{U}^+\psi).$$

With these assumptions, if term s represents the abstract syntax of an action expression, the semantics of a *request* message is defined by:

$$Done(e,x,exch(y,request,s)) \rightarrow Done(e,x,mp(y,x,s)). \tag{Req}$$

Accepting

We define *accepting* not only with respect to requests, but with respect to precommitments in general. We assume that the body of an acceptation message is a tuple including all the elements that uniquely identify the accepted precommitment:

$$Done(e',y,exch(x,accept,\langle e,y,x,s\rangle))\wedge Prec(e,y,x,s) \rightarrow Done(e',y,ap(e,y,x,s)). \tag{Acc}$$

Ordering

The difference between a request and an order is that while requests can be accepted or refused, orders cannot. In the terms of our approach, a request brings about a precommitment, and an order directly generates a commitment. To issue an order an agent must have powers that are not required to simply make a request; however, developing an articulated model of power relationships lies beyond the scope of this paper.

5 Discussion

In this paper we have presented a logical model of social commitment embedded in $\text{CTL}^{\pm}$, a logic of discrete time with no start or end points and branching in the future. The logical model of commitment has been completely specified at the level of formal semantics, and this has allowed us to prove some properties of commitment, expressed by valid formulae of our Semantic Language.

Some of the above issues are dealt with also by other authors in this volume. In particular, we would like to discuss the differences and similarities of our approach with respect to the works by Jones and Parent, Mallya *et al.*, and Chopra and Singh.

Jones and Parent

Commitment-based approaches to ACL semantics have recently been criticized by some authors, and in particular by Jones and Parent (this volume).

A basic criticism is that it is not clear what it means for an agent to commit to the truth of a statement. For example, according to Jones and Parent (Section 1), "Should not the propositional content of a commitment be a future act of the speaker? If so, to what action is [an agent] preparing to commit himself, when asserting p?"

It seems to us that Jones and Parent take commitment as essentially equivalent to obligation. However, this is not the intended meaning of the term 'commitment' as used in our proposal. Consider for example a person swearing that something is the case: here we have an example of a (very strong) commitment to the truth of a sentence, which may or may not be the description of a future act of the speaker. Committing to the truth of a sentence, *s*, simply means that the debtor of the commitment will be in a state of fulfillment if *s* is settled true, in a state of violation if *s* is settled false, and in a pending state if the truth value of *s* is still undetermined. This definition does not assume the speaker's obligation, or even the speaker's ability, to defend the content of his or her assertions.

In section 2.4, Jones and Parent suggest that it is not acceptable to assume that an agent commits relative to "everyone to whom he addresses his assertion," because "there may well be members of the audience who do not care whether [the speaker] is sincere, and there may be also others who require [him] to be insincere." Again, there seems to be a misunderstanding here. Commitment has nothing to do with sincerity. When an agent makes an assertion, it commits to its content, in the sense that the agent will enter a state of fulfillment if the content of the assertion is settled true, and a state of violation if the content of the sentence is settled false. This is an objective fact, in that it solely depends on the conventions underlying assertions, and has nothing to do with sincerity and/or the audience' interest in what is asserted.

Let us now analyze the example that Jones and Parent consider problematic for commitment-based semantics. An agent, a, informs a group of agents, say $\{b_0,b_1,...,b_n\}$, that p [2]. However, there is a previous private agreement between a and b_0, unknown to $\{b_1,...,b_n\}$, to the extent that a is going to lie. If we were dealing with human language, the solution to this puzzle would be very simple and straightforward. In human communication, communicative acts are not defined only in terms of static conventions, but depend on the speaker's intentions, and on the recognition of such intentions by the hearers. An utterance with an assertive surface form (i.e., in the indicative mood) is not going to count as an assertive illocutionary act if there is a previous agreement between the speaker and the hearer that bypasses usual conventions. A similar situation occurs, for example, when two actors carry out a dialogue on the stage. As far as artificial agent communication is concerned, however, we agree

---

[2] Indeed, Jones and Parent deal with acts of asserting, and we deal with acts of informing. However, both types of communicative acts belong to the category of assertives, and the difference between them is irrelevant here.

with Jones and Parent that it is advisable to forget about intentions and stick to predefined conventions. The simplest way to deal with Jones and Parent's puzzle, then, would be to assume that agent a actually does enter a state of commitment, relative to b_0, which will be automatically cancelled by the agreement between a and b_0. A slightly more complex but more elegant solution would be to treat the agreement between a and b_0 as setting up a special institutional context, in which a's assertive message that p will not count as making a commitment to p relative to b_0.

Jones and Parent claim (Section 2.4) that "the move towards agent *commitment* [...] is the result of a confusion" between preservative norms (or regulative rules, as we prefer to call them) and constitutive conventions. Well, we hope not, because we also consider this distinction to be fundamental. All the rules connecting the messages to commitments are constitutive conventions: they say that messages of certain forms *count as* certain operations on commitments. We have not yet worked on the regulative component of communication, which in particular will have to include the regulations for the management of violations. Such regulations, contrary to the constitutive conventions we have described in this paper, are likely to be strongly application dependent.

Our comments so far are intended to correct some misunderstandings concerning the commitment-based approach. On the other hand, it is probably too early to establish the relative merits and drawbacks of this approach in comparison with Jones and Parent's optimality-based proposal. Indeed, the two approaches have at least one point in common: they both consider agent communication as fully conventional, and regard a false assertion as a kind of violation. In our approach, a false assertion is the violation of a commitment; in Jones and Parent's approach, it is a violation of the optimality of the signaling system, with respect to its function of facilitating the transmission of reliable information.

Mallya et al.

Mallya *et al.* contribute to this volume with a work that focuses on commitments as a key component of agent interaction. The authors define commitment as including a debtor, a creditor and a content, and also a number of related operations and predicates that present some analogies to what has been presented in our work. Among the six commitment operations that the authors define in Section 2.3, CREATE can be mapped to our *mc* (make commitment), and RELEASE corresponds to our *cc* (cancel commitment). Instead, Mallya at al. define CANCEL as an operation that only the debtor of a commitment can perform, generally compensating that cancellation by making another commitment. From our point of view, as in the case of orders, to perform such a cancellation, agents need special powers that lie beyond the context of an ordinary communication framework. We have not considered the possibility of transferring commitments among agents, and thus the ASSIGN and DELEGATE operations do not find any correspondence in our approach. The DISCHARGE operation raises the most critical issues, as it is related to the fulfillment and the violation of a commitment, which, in our opinion, are not dealt with in a satisfactory way. More specifically, in Section 3.2 the authors define the relevant predicates (*satisfied*(c) and *breached*(c), where c stands for a commitment) in terms of whether a DISCHARGE operation has been performed in the past or not. Still, the authors seem to bypass the problem instead of solving it, as in Section 2.3 they assume that "the DISCHARGE operation brings about p [the relevant commitment's content], and conversely, if p

occurs, the DISCHARGE operation is assumed to have happened". Such an assumption "discharges" the authors from defining the truth conditions of the content of a commitment, which, from our point of view, is one of the key points of the specification of a logical model of commitments.

Chopra and Singh

Chopra and Singh's contribution is also mainly dealing with commitments. In particular, the authors develop a formalism based on commitments to specify interaction protocols. Such formalism relies on the Non-monotonic Causal Logic (NCL) as the authors take into account the fact that protocol specifications often have to deal with defeasible reasoning. We also think that, in general, defeasible reasoning plays an important role in communicative interactions. For example, we assume that an agent has special powers to bring about particular (communicative) events if and only if such condition is explicitly stated. This shows that the definitions dealing with powers rely on a closure assumption, which inevitably requires some form of non-monotonic reasoning. Our main concern about the work by Chopra and Singh is that it does not provide enough evidence for the advantages of choosing NCL instead of other non-monotonic reasoning schemes described in the literature.

6 Future Work

Even if social commitment has already been proposed [2,12] as a basis for the definition of ACL semantics, no full formal account of commitment has been put forward so far. Needless to say, we are just at the beginning of a long way. Below we point out some aspects that need to be further investigated.

Time

A sound and complete formal system for $CTL^{\pm}$ has to be developed. This result should be easy to achieve by extending some known formal system for $CTL^{\cdot}$. It would also be important to develop efficient model checking techniques for at least a sub-language of $CTL^{\pm}$. Moreover, it may be worthwhile to consider an extension of $CTL^{\pm}$ dealing with dense time, in order to give a more flexible account of interactions in a multiagent system.

Another important aspect is the expression of temporal qualifications in content sentences. Indeed, $CTL^{\pm}$ is a powerful but very abstract temporal language. In many practical applications, like for example in the field of e-business, we can expect that temporal qualifications will be expressed with respect to some standard date system, like the Gregorian calendar. The critical point here is to specify a language by which common temporal qualifications can be represented in a natural and transparent way (see for example [10]).

Action

In this paper we have defined a minimal set of logical tools for the treatment of action. We feel, however, that it might be worthwhile to embed our logic of commitment in a richer language, possibly based on some version of dynamic logic.

An important point in our treatment is the association between an action and its results. In the case of commitment, this association has been represented by inserting an event-denoting term as the first argument of the *Comm* and *Prec* predicates. This solution has proved sufficient for our current goals, but may be difficult to extend to more complex situations.

Commitment

The main contribution of this paper is the logical treatment of commitment. Commitment is intrinsically a second-order concept, in that an agent commits to a proposition. Driven by a concern for simplicity, we decided to represent a commitment by a first-order predicate, and its content as a first-order term.

In designing our representation of commitment we have constantly kept in mind the reasons that motivate the development of a logical model in an area of Computer Science. In our opinion, the rigor and precision given by the use of logic is highly valuable, but should never bring us too far from practical applications, lest we give up the hope of influencing actual software practice.

We believe that our model of commitment can easily be translated into the conceptual toolkit and jargon of software designers. More precisely, commitments may be viewed as instances of a "commitment class," whose instance variables contain: a reference to the commitment-inducing event (a message exchange), two references to agents (the debtor and the creditor), and an abstract representation of a CL sentence. In such a context, the commitment manipulation actions can be regarded as methods of the commitment class, with formal specification given by Axioms MC, MP, and AP of Section 3.2. Continuing this line of thought, the definitions of fulfillment and violation can be viewed as the core specification of a "commitment management system," which may be in charge of monitoring communicative exchanges in a multi-agent system. Finally, the examples of Section 4 suggest that a Communicative Act Library may define a communicative act by specifying: (i), the general form of the class of messages by which the act is performed; (ii), relevant contextual conditions for a successful execution of the communicative act; and (iii), the effect of a successful execution of the communicative act, expressed in terms of commitment-manipulation actions. A first proposal in this direction is presented by Fornara and Colombetti in [6] and [7]. However, there are still a number of discrepancies between the logical model presented in this paper and the above-mentioned operational model. Integrating the two levels of our model of agent communication is a major goal for our future research.

Acknowledgments

We are grateful to Alessio Lomuscio and Marek Sergot for commenting on the first draft of this paper and for many interesting discussions, made possible by a British Council/CRUI grant for the year 2002.

References

1. P. R. Cohen and H. J. Levesque. Rational interaction as the basis for communication. In P.R. Cohen, J. Morgan, and M. E. Pollack, editors, *Intentions in communication*, pages 221–256, MIT Press, Cambridge, MA, 1990.

2. M. Colombetti, A commitment-based approach to agent speech acts and conversation. In *Proc. Workshop on Agent Languages and Communication Policies, 4th International Conference on Autonomous Agents (Agents 2000)*, pages 21–29. Barcelona, Spain, 2000.
3. E. A. Emerson and J. Y. Halpern. 'Sometimes' and 'Not Never' revisited: On branching versus linear time temporal logic. *Journal of the ACM*, 33(1):151–178, 1986.
4. T. Finin, Y. Labrou, and J. Mayfield, KQML as an agent communication language. In J. Bradshaw, editor, *Software agents*. MIT Press, Cambridge, MA, 1995
5. FIPA, Agent Communication Language. FIPA 2000 Specification, Foundation for Intelligent Physical Agents, www.fipa.org, 2000.
6. N. Fornara and M. Colombetti. Operational specification of a commitment-based communication language. In *Proceedings of the 1st International Joint Conference on Autonomous Agents and Multi-Agent Systems (AAMAS 02)*, Bologna, Italy, 2002.
7. N. Fornara and M. Colombetti. Defining interaction protocols using a commitment-based agent communication language. In *Proceedings of the 2nd International Joint Conference on Autonomous Agents and Multi-Agent Systems (AAMAS 03)*, Melbourne, Australia, 2003.
8. Y. Labrou and T. Finin, Semantics and conversations for an agent communication language. In *Proceedings of the 15th International Joint Conference on Artificial Intelligence (IJCAI'97)*, Nagoya, Japan, 1997.
9. F. Laroussinie and P. Schnoebelen. A hierarchy of temporal logics with past. *Theoretical Computer Science*, 148(2):303–324, 1995.
10. H. J. Ohlbach and D. Gabbay. Calendar logic. *Journal of Applied Non-classical Logics*, 8(4):291–324, 1998.
11. H. Reichenbach, *Elements of Symbolic Logic*. MacMillan, New York, 1947.
12. M. P. Singh, Agent communication languages: Rethinking the principles. *IEEE Computer*, 31:40–47, 1998.
13. P. Yolum, M. P. Singh. Flexible protocol specification and execution: applying event calculus planning using commitments. In *Proceedings of the 1st International Joint Conference on Autonomous Agents and Multi-Agent Systems (AAMAS 02)*, Bologna, Italy, 2002.

Commitment and Argument Network: A New Formalism for Agent Communication

Jamal Bentahar[1], Bernard Moulin[1,2], and Brahim Chaib-draa[1]

[1] Laval University, Computer Science and Software Engineering Department
Ste Foy, QC, G1K 7P4, Canada
{jamal.bentahar,bernard.moulin,brahim.chaib-draa@ift.ulaval.ca}
[2] Geomatica Research Centre
Ste Foy, QC, G1K 7P4, Canada

Abstract. This paper proposes a formal framework which offers an external representation of conversations between conversational agents. Using this formalism allows us: (1) to represent the dynamics of conversations between agents; (2) to analyze conversations; (3) to help autonomous agents to take part in consistent conversations. The proposed formalism, called "commitment and argument network", uses a combined approach based on commitments and arguments. Commitments are used to capture the social and the public aspect of conversations. Arguments on the other side are used to capture the reasoning aspect. We also propose a layered communication model in which the formalism and the approach take place.

1 Introduction

In the multi-agent domain, it is widely recognized that communication between autonomous agents is a challenging research area that involves several disciplines: philosophy of language, social psychology, artificial intelligence, logics, mathematics, etc. In a multi-agent system, agents may need to interact in order to negotiate, to solve conflicts of interest, to cooperate, etc [16]. All these communication requirements cannot be fulfilled by simply exchanging messages. Agents must be able to take part in coherent conversations which result from the performance of coordinated speech acts [31].

Three main approaches have been proposed to model communication between software agents in general and to define a semantics for agent communication languages (ACLs). These approaches are: the mental approach, the social approach, and the argumentative approach.

In the mental approach, so-called agent's mental structures (e.g. beliefs, desires and intentions) are used to model conversations and to define a formal semantics of speech acts. In the first system that was based on these notions, speech acts were planned like non-communicative actions [10]. It was used by [21] and [22] to define a formal semantics of KQML. However, this semantics has been criticized for not being verifiable because one cannot verify whether the agents' behavior matches their private mental states [13] [5]. This approach is used in the development of a pragmatic for agent communication based on cognitive coherence theory [29].

F. Dignum (Ed.): ACL 2003, LNAI 2922, pp. 146–165, 2004.
© Springer-Verlag Berlin Heidelberg 2004

An alternative to the mental approach was proposed by [33] under the name of social approach. In contrast to the mental approach, this approach emphasizes the importance of conventions as well as the public and social aspects of conversations. It is based on social commitments that are thought of as social and deontic notions. Social commitments are commitments towards the other members of a community. They differ from the agent's internal psychological commitments which capture the persistence of intentions as specified in the rational interaction theory [9]. As a social notion, commitments are a base for a normative framework that makes it possible to model the agents' behaviour. This notion has been used to define a formal semantics that is verifiable [32] [11] [36] [24]. The role of social commitments in modeling and specifying agent interactions is widely recognized. They are used in order to specify ACL protocols [18] and to represent these protocols by capturing interactions that describe new scenarios and by using causal logic [6].

Another approach, called the argumentative approach, was proposed by [2] as a method for modelling dialogue. It also has been used to define a semantics of some communicative acts [1] and to define protocols [26] [28]. It is based upon an argumentation system in which the agents' reasoning capabilities are often linked to their ability to argue. They are mainly based on the agent's ability to establish a link between different facts, to determine if a fact is acceptable, to decide which arguments support which facts, etc. The approach relies upon the formal dialectics introduced by [20] and [23]. Dialectical models are rule-governed structures of organized conversations in which two parties (in the simplest case) speak in turn in an orderly way.

Recently, researchers have begun to address the issues raised by conversation policies. According to [25] two approaches can be distinguished: Commitment-based protocols and dialogue-game based protocols. The first approach uses social commitments to specify the sequences of utterances. The second one considers that protocols are captured within appropriate structures that can be combined in different ways to form the global structure of a dialogue [12].

Despite all this research works focused on modeling dialogue and semantic issues, few researchers have addressed the issue of representing the dynamics and the coherence of conversations. The purpose of this paper is to propose a formal framework that can represent agent actions likely to take place in a conversation. These actions are interpreted in terms of creation and of positioning on social commitments and arguments. The proposed formalism allows us to model the dynamics of conversations and offers an external representation of the conversational activity. This notion of external representation [7] is very useful because it provides conversational agents with a common understanding of the current state of the conversation and its advancement. An example of such an external representation is the conversational model proposed by [30]. Based on our formalism, a model is made available to the agents and they can access it simultaneously. The formalism also allows us to ensure conversational consistency when considering the actions performed by the agents. Called "commitment and argument network" (CAN) our formalism relies on an approach combining commitments and arguments [3]. This approach has the advantage of capturing both the social and public aspects of a conversation, and the reasoning aspect required in order to take part in coherent conversations. The formalism can clearly illustrate the creation steps of new commitments and the positioning steps on these commitments, as well as the argumentation and justification steps. This formalism supposes that conversational agents are able to manipulate commitments and arguments. Therefore, the agents architecture must take into account this aspect.

In Section 2 we present our vision of a communication model. In Section 3 we discuss a model of social commitments which is a part of our communication model, and we show how speech acts can be interpreted as actions on these commitments. In Section 4 we introduce the argumentation aspect and we illustrate the link between commitments and arguments. The foundations of the CAN formalism are presented in Section 5. We also give an example of the analysis of a dialogue and we show how our formalism can be used either to analyze a conversation or as a means that allows agents to take part in conversations.

2   A Communication Model

The model that we propose combines the three approaches discussed in the introduction. It is based on a hybrid approach that we call MSA (Mental-Social-Argumentative). Indeed, if they are taken individually, the three approaches introduced earlier do not allow us to model all the aspects of conversations. For this reason, we suggest to combine them in a unified approach. In addition, the conversation is a cognitive and social activity which requires a mechanism making it possible to reason on mental states, on what other agents say (public aspects) and on the social aspects (conventions, standards, obligations, etc). These three approaches are thus not exclusive but rather complementary.

The MSA approach has the advantage of capturing simultaneously the mental aspect that characterizes the agents participating in a conversation, the social aspect that reflects the context in which these agents communicate and the reasoning aspect which is essential to be able to take part in coherent conversations. The combination of commitments and arguments seems essential to us because agents must be able to justify the facts on which they are committed and to justify their actions on commitments. This justification cannot be made if the agents do not have the necessary argumentation mechanisms. In addition, the combination of commitments and private mental states is necessary because public commitments reflect these mental states. Finally, the combination of argumentation and mental states is significant because agents have to reason on their mental states before committing in a conversation.

The model of communication is composed of three layers: the conversation layer, the commitment/argument layer and the cognitive layer. This stratification in layers is justified by the abstraction levels. The conversation layer is directly observable because it is composed of the speech acts that the agents perform. These acts are not performed in an isolated way, but within a particular conversation. The commitment/argument layer is used to correctly manage the social commitments and the arguments that are related to the conversation. These commitments and arguments are not directly observable, but they should be deduced from the speech acts performed by the agents. Finally, the cognitive layer is used to take into account the private mental states of the agents, the social relations and other elements that the agents use in order to communicate. In this paper we propose a formalism that is used to model the elements composing the second layer.

In order to allow conversational agents to suitably use the communication model, this model must be compatible with the agent architecture. Thus, we propose an architecture of conversational agent which is composed of three models: the mental model, the social model and the reasoning model (Fig. 1). The mental model includes beliefs, desires, goals, etc. The social model captures the social concepts such as conventions, roles, etc. Social commitments constitute a significant component of this model. A social commitment is a participant public attitude relative to a proposition. It defines a particular relationship between a participant and a statement. The commitments that the agent makes public when performing speech acts are different from the private mental states, but these two elements are not independent. Indeed, social commitments reflect mental states. Thus, agents must use their reasoning capabilities to reason on their mental states before producing or manipulating social commitments. The agent's reasoning capabilities are represented by the reasoning model via an argumentation system. The conversational agent model is formed by general knowledge, such as the knowledge on the conversation subject. This knowledge will be used by the agent in order to build the *common ground* that it must share with its partners. The notion of common ground introduced by the philosophers of language Clark and Haviland [8] indicates the set of knowledge, beliefs and presuppositions which the agents believe that they share during their conversations.

The conversational agent architecture

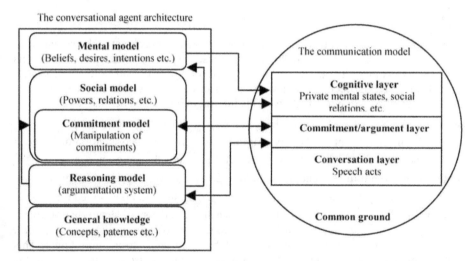

Fig. 1. The links between the conversational agent architecture and the communication model

3 Social Commitment Formulation

A *social commitment* is a commitment made by an agent (called the *debtor*), that some fact is true. This commitment is directed to a set of agents (called *creditors*) [4]. The *commitment content* is characterized by time t_φ, which is different from the utterance time denoted t_u and from the time associated with the commitment and denoted t_{sc}. Time t_{sc} refers to the time during which the commitment is in vigor. It can correspond to a fixed value or an interval. When it is an interval, this time is denoted $[t_{sc}^{\text{inf}}$, $t_{sc}^{\text{sup}}]$. When a temporal bound is instantiated, it takes a numerical value which respects the time unit used by the agents. We denote a social commitment as follows:

Definition 1: $SC(id_n, Ag_1, A*, t_{sc}, \varphi, t_\varphi)$

where id_n is an integer identifying the commitment, Ag_1 the debtor, $A*$ the set of the creditors $(A*=A/\{Ag_1\}$, where A is the set of participants), t_{sc} is the time associated with the commitment, φ its content and t_φ the time associated with the content φ. To simplify the notation, we suppose throughout this paper that $A=\{Ag_1, Ag_2\}$. For example, the utterance:

(Example 1)

> U: "I met agent Ag_3 on MSN one hour ago"

leads to the creation of the commitment:

$$SC(id_n, Ag_1, Ag_2, t_{sc}, Meet(Ag_1, Ag_3, MSN), t_{sc} - 1h).$$

The creation of such a commitment is an *action* denoted:

$$Create(Ag_1, t_u, SC(id_n, Ag_1, Ag_2, t_{sc}, Meet(Ag_1, Ag_3, MSN), t_{sc}-1h)).$$

In general an action ACT performed by an agent Ag_1 on a social commitment SC is denoted:

Definition 2: $Act(Ag_1, t_u, SC(id_n, Ag_1, Ag_2, t_{sc}, \varphi, t_\varphi))$

Example 1 illustrates that there is a mapping between a speech act and a social commitment. Singh [32] and Colombetti [11] propose a social semantics of speech acts using such a mapping. In our approach, we go beyond Singh's and Colombetti's models and interpret a speech act as an action performed on a commitment in order to model the dynamics of conversations. This interpretation can be denoted by :

Definition 3: $SA(i_k, Ag_1, Ag_2, t_u, U) \vdash_{déf} Act(Ag_1, t_u, SC(id_n, Ag_1, Ag_2, t_{sc}, \varphi, t_\varphi))$

where $\vdash_{def}$ means "is interpreted by definition as", SA is the abbreviation of "Speech Act", i_k the identifier of the speech act and Act indicates the action performed by the debtor on the commitment. The definiendum $(SA(i_k, Ag_1, Ag_2, t_u, U))$ is defined by the definiens $(Act(Ag_1, t_u, SC(id_n, Ag_1, Ag_2, t_{sc}, \varphi, t_\varphi)))$ as an action performed on a social commitment. The agent that performs the speech act is the same agent that performs the action Act. Act can take one of four values: *Create*, *Withdraw*, *Violate* and *Fulfill*. These four actions are the actions that the debtor can apply to a commitment. This reflects only the debtor's point of view. However, we must also take into account the creditors when modeling a conversation which is, by definition, a joint activity. We thus propose modeling the creditors' actions which do not apply to the commitment, but to the contents of this commitment This separation between the commitment and its content enables us to remain compatible with the semantics of commitments, i.e. the fact that only the debtor can handle its commitment. The semantics associated with this types of actions is expressed in terms of argumentation (see Section 4.2).

Hence, we must differentiate between the actions applied on a commitment (*Act*) and the actions performed on the content of a commitment (*Act-content*). We denote an action applied on the content of a commitment as follows:

Definition 4: $Act\text{-}content(Ag_k, t_u, SC(id_n, Ag_i, Ag_2, t_{sc}, \varphi, t_\varphi))$

where $i, j \in \{1, 2\}$ and $(k=i$ or $k=j)$. Agent Ag_k can thus act on the content of its own commitment (in this case we get $k=i$) or on the content of the commitment of another agent (in this case we get $k=j$).

In addition, the actions that can be carried out by the debtor on the commitment content are different from the actions that can be carried out by the creditor. The debtor can change the content of its own commitment, can defend it if the debtor refuses it or questions it. The creditor can refuse the content of another agent's commitment, accept it or question it.

Thus, a speech act leads either to an action on a commitment when the speaker is the debtor, or to an action on a commitment content when the speaker is the debtor or the creditor. When an agent acts on the content of a commitment created by another agent we refer to this as "taking a position on a commitment content". However, it should be noted that the same utterance can lead both to taking a position on the content of an existing commitment and to the creation of a new commitment. Generally, a speech act leads to an action on a commitment and/or an action on a commitment content. Formally:

Definition 5: $SA(Ag_1, Ag_2, t_u, U) \vdash_{déf}$

$$\left\{ \begin{array}{l} Act(Ag_1, t_u, SC(id, Ag_1, Ag_2, t_{sc}, \varphi, t_\varphi)) \\ and/or \\ Act\text{-}content(Ag_k, t_u, SC(id, Ag_i, Ag_j, t_{sc}, \varphi, t_\varphi)) \end{array} \right.$$

where i, j $\in \{1, 2\}$ and (k=i or k=j).

3.1 The Notion of State

A commitment can evolve and be transformed as a result of the actions that the debtor performs on it (creation, withdrawal, violation and fulfillment). Its content may also be transformed following the actions that the debtor and the creditors apply to it (change, acceptance, justification, etc.). Therefore, the agents act on their own commitments and on the content of both these commitments and other agents' commitments, which leads to their transformation. Hence the notion of state, which makes it possible to capture the evolution of commitments and their contents. However, we must distinguish between the notion of the commitment state [17] and the notion of the content state relative to this commitment as we propose here. Indeed, whenever an agent acts on its commitment, the commitment state is affected; whereas when the agent acts on the content of a commitment, the content state is transformed. Indeed, the notion of commitment state alone does not reflect the conversation dynamics since it only captures the debtor's actions on its commitment. The two states (the commitment state and the content state of the commitment) reflect this dynamics. This notion is of great importance since it allows us to keep a trace of the dialogue evolution in so far as each speech act leads to an action performed on a commitment or on its content.

Here are the states that we propose to use in our model. Once created, a commitment will take the *active* state and its content the *submitted* state. This expresses the fact that the content is presented for possible negotiation. A commitment can be in one of four states: *active, fulfilled, cancelled,* and *violated.*

A commitment content can take six states: *submitted, changed, refused, accepted, questioned* and *justified.* These states and the operations which trigger them depend on the commitment type. Hence, the commitment state and the content state are two parameters which characterize this commitment at any moment. Thus, we need to revise the definition of a commitment (**Definition 1**) by adding 3 new parameters. So, a social commitment is a 8-uple:

Definition 6: $SC(id_n, Ag_1, Ag_2, t_{sc}, S, S_{content}, \varphi, t_\varphi)$

where S a vector presenting the various commitment states and $S_{content}$ a vector presenting the various content states. Using vectors as parameters for commitment and content states makes it possible to keep track of all the transitions that reflect the evolution of the commitments and their contents.

3.2 Classification

In the literature [38] [17], several commitment types have been proposed. Similarly to the classification suggested by [17] we distinguish *absolute commitments*, *conditional commitments* and *commitment attempts*.

3.2.1 Absolute Commitments

Absolute commitments are commitments whose fulfillment does not depend on any particular condition. Two types can be distinguished: *propositional commitments* and *action commitments*.

Propositional commitments
Propositional commitments are related to the state of the world. They are generally, but not necessarily, expressed by assertives. They can be directed towards the past, the present, or the future. We denote a propositional commitment as follows:

Definition 7: $PC(id_n, Ag_1, Ag_2, t_{pc}, S, S_{content}, p, t_p)$
where p is the proposition on which Ag_1 commits.

Action commitments
Contrary to propositional commitments, *action commitments* (also called *commitments to a course of action*) are always directed towards the future and are related to actions that the debtor is committed to carrying out. The fulfillment and the lack of fulfillment of such commitments depend on the performance of the underlying action and the specified delay. This type of commitment is typically conveyed by promises. We denote an action commitment as follows:

Definition 8: $AC(id_n, Ag_1, Ag_2, t_{ac}, S, S_{content}, \alpha, t_\alpha)$
where α is the action to be carried out.

3.2.2 Conditional Commitments
Absolute commitments do not consider the conditions that may restrain their fulfillment. However, in several cases, agents need to make commitments not in absolute terms but under given conditions. Another commitment type is therefore required. These commitments are said to be *conditional*. The structure of a *conditional commitment* which must reflect the underlying condition, is different from the structure of a social commitment (***Definition 6***). We denote a conditional commitment as follows:

Definition 9: $CC(id_n, Ag_1, Ag_2, t_{cc}, S, S_{content}, (\beta, t_\beta) \Rightarrow (\gamma, t_\gamma))$
where $\Rightarrow$ stands for classical implication. This commitment expresses the fact that if β is true (or carried out) at time t_β, then Ag_1 will be committed towards Ag_2 to making γ or that γ is true at time t_γ. The addition of the symbol $\Rightarrow$ in the formula enables us to better illustrate the implication relation existing between the condition and the action.

3.2.3 Commitment Attempts

The commitments described so far directly concern the debtor who commits either that a certain fact is true or that a certain action will be carried out. For example, these commitments do not allow us to explain the fact that an agent asks another one to be committed to carrying out an action (by a speech act of a directive type). To solve this problem, we propose the concept of *commitment attempt* inspired by the notion of *pre-commitment* proposed in [11]. We consider a commitment attempt as a request made by a debtor to push a creditor to be committed. Thus, when an agent Ag_1 requests another agent Ag_2 to do something, we say that the first agent is trying to induce the other agent to make a commitment. We denote a commitment attempt as follows:

Definition 10: $CT(id_n, Ag_1, Ag_2, t_{ct}, S, S_{content}, \varphi, t_\varphi)$

where φ is the content of the commitment attempt. A commitment attempt is thought of as a type of social commitment because it conveys content which is made public once the attempt is performed. However, in our approach, there is a true commitment only after the creditor agent reacts in response to the commitment attempt. The debtor and the creditor of a commitment attempt can act both on the attempt and on its content. On the one hand, the creditor agent reserves the right to accept a commitment attempt definitively, to accept it conditionally, to refuse it or to suspend it by asking for a period of reflection. It can also question the content of a commitment attempt. On the other hand, the debtor agent can cancel a commitment attempt. It can also change the content of a commitment attempt and defend it. Like a social commitment, a commitment attempt can be related to a proposition, an action or a condition. The evolution of the states of commitments and of their contents as well as the different rules of manipulating the commitment attempts are detailed in [3].

4 Argumentation

In artificial intelligence, argumentation is used in two distinct ways: to structure knowledge or to model dialectical reasoning. The first approach aims at determining how utterances form arguments and how arguments can be decomposed. This approach has been used in Toulmin's model [35]. On the other hand, the second approach deals with argument construction. Models suggested for example in [14] et [15] follow this approach. When considering dialogue modeling, the second approach seems to be more relevant because agents must be able to produce arguments supporting their propositions.

4.1 Formulation

An argumentation system essentially includes a logical language, a definition of the argument concept, a definition of the attack relation between arguments and finally a definition of acceptability. Several definitions were also proposed for the argument concept. In our model, we adopt the following definitions of [15]. Here Γ indicates a possibly inconsistent knowledge base with no deductive closure. $\vdash$ Stands for classical inference and $\equiv$ for logical equivalence.

Definition 11: An argument is a pair (H, h) where h is a formula of L and H a sub-set of Γ such that : i) H is consistent, ii) $H \vdash h$ and iii) H is minimal, so no subset of H satisfying both i and ii exists. H is called the support of the argument and h its conclusion.

Definition 12: Let (H_1, h_1), (H_2, h_2) be two arguments.

(H_1, h_1) attack (H_2, h_2) iff $\exists h \in H_2$ such that $h \equiv \neg h_1$. In other words, an argument is attacked if and only if there exists an argument for the negation of an element of its support.

We can now define the concept of acceptability [14]:

Definition 13: An argument (H, h) is acceptable for a set S of arguments iff for any argument (H', h'): if (H', h') attacks (H, h) then (H', h') is attacked by S.

Intuitively, an argument is acceptable if it is not attacked, if it defends itself against all its attackers, or if it is defended by an acceptable argument.

4.2 Linking Commitments and Arguments

Argumentation is based on the construction of arguments and counter-arguments (arguments attacking other arguments), the comparison of these various arguments and finally the selection of the arguments that are considered to be acceptable. In our approach, agents must reason on their own mental states in order to build arguments in favor of their future commitments, as well as on other agents' commitments in order to be able to take position with regard to the contents of these commitments. The systems proposed in the literature, for example in [14] and [37], do not take into account the arguments which can support actions on commitments. It is these arguments which we define in this section.

In fact, before committing to some fact h being true (i.e. before creating a commitment whose content is h), the speaker agent must use its argumentation system to build an argument (H, h). On the other side, the addressee agent must use its own argumentation system to select the answer it will give (i.e. to decide about the appropriate manipulation of the content of an existing commitment). For example, an agent Ag_1 accepts the commitment content h proposed by another agent Ag_2 if its argumentation system is compatible with h. i.e. if it is able to build an argument which supports this content from its knowledge base. If Ag_1 has an argument $(H', \neg h)$, then it refuses the commitment content proposed by Ag_2. Now, if Ag_1 has an argument neither for h, nor for $\neg h$, then it must ask for an explanation. Surely, an argumentation system is essential to help agents act on commitments and their contents. However, reasoning on other mental and social attitudes (beliefs, intentions, conventions, etc.) should be taken into account in order to explain the agents' decisions in a broader context than the agents interactions [27]. We do not address this issue in this paper.

Thus, we claim that an agent should always use its argumentation system before creating a new commitment or positioning itself on an existing commitment and on its content. Consequently, an argument of an agent Ag_1 must support an action performed by this agent on a given commitment and/or on its content. Formally we denote:

Definition 14: $Arg(Ag_k, H, Act(Ag_k, t_u, SC(id, Ag_i, Ag_j, t_{sc}, S, S_{content}, \varphi, t_{\varphi})))$

Definition 15: $Arg(Ag_k, H, Act\text{-}content(Ag_k, t_u, SC(id, Ag_i, Ag_j, t_{sc}, S, S_{content}, \varphi, t_\varphi)))$
such that H being the support of the argument and the agent identifiers i, j, k verify: $i,$
$j, k \in \{1, 2\}, i \neq j$ and $(k=i$ or $k=j)$. In the first formula, H is the support of the action Act
performed by agent Ag_k on commitment SC. In the second formula, H is the support
of the action $Act\text{-}content$ performed by agent Ag_k. $Act\text{-}content$ is an action on the
content of the commitment SC.

The relation between H and the commitment content φ is defined according to the
value of Act and $Act\text{-}content$. For instance, for an absolute or a conditional commitment we have:
$Act \in \{Create, Discharge\} \Rightarrow H \vdash \varphi$
I.e. if Act takes the value "Create" or "Fulfill", then H defends φ. In the same way:
$Act \in \{Withdraw\} \Rightarrow H \vdash \neg\varphi$
$Act\text{-}contenent \in \{Accept, Change, Defend\} \Rightarrow H \vdash \varphi$
$Act\text{-}content \in \{Refuse\} \Rightarrow H \vdash \neg\varphi$
An agent can question a commitment content φ if it has an argument neither for φ nor
for $\neg\varphi$. Formally we have:
$\nexists H$ such that $H \vdash \varphi$ or $H \vdash \neg\varphi$
For the other types of commitments, this relation is detailed in [3].

A speech act can lead to an action not only on a commitment as explained in Section 3, but also on an argument. An agent can thus accept, refuse, defend or attack an
argument. Thus we have:

Definition 16: $SA(i_l, Ag_i, Ag_j, t_u, U) \vdash_{déf}$
$Act\text{-}arg(Ag_i, t_u, Arg(Ag_k, H, Act(Ag_m, t_u, SC(id, Ag_x, Ag_y, t_{sc}, S, S_{content}, \varphi, t_\varphi)))$

Definition 17: $SA(i_l, Ag_i, Ag_j, t_u, U) \vdash_{déf}$
$Act\text{-}arg(Ag_i, t_u, Arg(Ag_k, H, Act\text{-}content(Ag_m, t_u, SC(id, Ag_x, Ag_y, t_{sc}, S, S_{content}, \varphi, t_\varphi)))$
where : Act-arg $\in \{$Accept, Refuse, Defend or Attack$\}$, i, j, k, m, x, y $\in \{1, 2\}$ and i$\neq$j,
x$\neq$y, (k, m=i or k, m=j).

5 Using the CAN Formalism for Conversation Representation

So far, we presented our framework of commitments and of the relations between
these commitments and arguments. Indeed, our goal is to represent speech acts in a
single approach based on commitments and arguments. This approach aims at offering software agents a flexible means to interact in a coherent way. Thus, agents can
participate in conversations by manipulating commitments and by producing arguments. It is the agents' responsibility (and not the designers' role) to choose, in an
autonomous way, the actions to be performed by using their argumentation systems.
    In this section, we show how a conversation can be modeled using the CAN for-
malism on the basis of this framework. In a conversational activity, agents manage
commitments and arguments whose chaining must be coherent. Our purpose is to
present the dynamics of conversations using our formalism. This representation allows us to ensure conversational consistency in terms of the actions performed by the
agents on the commitments and arguments. Indeed, this formalism has two objectives:

it can be used to analyze conversations, as well as a means to allow agents to take part in coherent conversations.

5.1 Formal Definition of a CAN

A commitment and argument network is a mathematical structure which we define formally as follows:

Definition 18: *A commitment and argument network is a 15-uple:* $<A, E, SC_0, I, \Omega, \Sigma,$
$\Phi, \Delta, \Pi, \alpha, \beta, \delta, \theta, \gamma, \eta>$ *where:*

- *A: a finite and nonempty set of participants.* $A = \{Ag_1, ..., Ag_n\}$
- *E: a finite and nonempty set of social commitments. These commitments can be absolute commitments (C), conditional commitments (CC) or commitment attempts (CT). $E = \{SC_0, ..., SC_n\}$.*
- *SC_0: a distinguished element of E: the initial commitment. This element allows us to define the subject of a conversation.*
- *I : a finite and nonempty set of speech act indices (or identifiers) which can be related to the creation and the positioning actions and to the argumentation relations and to the connection relations.* $I = \{i_0, ..., i_n\}$.
- *Ω: a finite and nonempty set of both creation actions of elements of E and positioning actions on elements of E, of $\Omega \times I$ and of $\Sigma \times I$. $\Omega = \{Create, Accept, Accept conditionally, Refuse, Question, Change, Withdraw, Satisfy\}$*
- *Σ: a finite and possibly empty set of argumentation relations. $\Sigma = \{Defend, Attack\}$.*
- *Φ: a finite and possibly empty set of connection relations that can exist between elements of E or between elements of E and elements of $\Sigma \times I$. $\Phi = \{Satisfy, Not satisfy, Contradict, Explain, etc.\}$*
- *Δ: a partial function relating a commitment to another commitment using one argumentation relation characterized by an identifier i of I.*
  $\Delta: E \times E \rightarrow \Sigma \times I$
- *Π: a partial function relating a commitment to a pair made up of an argumentation relation and an element of I using one argumentation relation (characterized by an identifier i of I).*
  $\Pi: E \times \Sigma \times I \rightarrow \Sigma \times I$
- *α: a partial function relating an agent (a participant) to a commitment using a set of pairs made up of a creation or a positioning action and an element of I.*
  $\alpha: A \times E \rightarrow 2^{\Omega \times I}$
- *β: a partial function relating an agent to an argumentation relation (characterized by an identifier i of I) using a set of pairs made up of a creation or positioning action and of an element of I.*
  $\beta: A \times \Sigma \times I \rightarrow 2^{\Omega - \{Change\} \times I}$
- *δ: a partial function relating an agent to a creation or a positioning action (characterized by an identifier i of I) using a set of pairs made up of a positioning action and an element of I*
  $\delta: A \times \Omega \times I \rightarrow 2^{\Omega - \{Create, Withdraw, Change\} \times I}$

- θ: *a partial function relating a commitment to a creation or a positioning action (characterized by an identifier i of I) using one argumentation relation.*
  θ: $E \times \Omega \times I \rightarrow \Sigma \times I$
- γ: *a partial function relating two commitments using a connection relation (characterized by an identifier i of I).*
  γ: $E \times E \rightarrow \Phi \times I$
- η: *a partial function relating a commitment to an argumentation relation using a connection relation (characterized by an identifier i of I).*
  η: $E \times \Sigma \times I \rightarrow \Phi \times I$

Let us now comment upon these sets and functions. In a conversation, the sets A, E, Ω, Σ, Φ and I must be instantiated. For example, in a given conversation we can have: $A=\{Ag_1, Ag_2\}$, $E=\{PC_0, PC_1, PC_2\}$, $\Omega=\{Create, Accept, Question\}$, $\Sigma=\{Defend\}$ etc.

The function Δ allows us to define the argumentation relation which can exist between two commitment contents, i.e. a defense or an attack relation. For example:

$$\Delta(SC_i, SC_j) = (Defend, i_k).$$

This means that the content of the commitment SC_i (called *source* of the defense relation) defends the content of the commitment SC_j (called *target* of the defense relation). The index i_k associated with the defense relation is the identifier of the speech act whose performance gives rise to this relation. Associating such an index with argumentation relations and with various actions allows us to distinguish a relation from another and an action from another of the same type.

The function Π allows us to define an argumentation relation on another argumentation relation. For example:

$$\Pi(SC_i, Defend, i_k) = (Attack, i_l).$$

This relation points out that the content of the commitment SC_i attacks a defense relation characterized by the index i_k. This defense relation is defined using the function Δ. The attack relation defined by the function Π is characterized by the index i_l.

The function α allows us to define a set of creation and positioning actions (acceptance, refusal, etc.) performed by an agent on a commitment content. For example:

$$\alpha(Ag_1, SC_i)=\{(Accept, i_k)\}$$

This reflects the acceptance of the content related to the commitment SC_i. This acceptance relation is characterized by the index i_k. Ag_1 belongs to the debtors set associated with this commitment.

The function β allows an agent to take position by accepting, accepting conditionally or refusing an argumentation relation. For instance:

$$\beta(Ag_1, Defend, i_k)=\{(Refuse, i_l)\}$$

This means that the agent Ag_1 refuses the defense relation which is defined by the function Δ and characterized by the index i_k. The refusal relation is characterized by the index i_l

The function δ allows an agent to position itself relative to a positioning action characterized by an index i by accepting it, accepting it conditionally, refusing it or questioning it. The positioning action on which an agent can take positions can be defined by the function α or the function β. For instance:

$$\delta(Ag_1, Refuse, i_k) = \{(Question, i_l)\}$$

This example shows the case in which agent Ag_1 questions a refusal action characterized by index i_k. The question action is characterized by the index i_1.

The function θ allows us to define an argumentation relation binding a commitment SC_i to a creation or a positioning action. The action is defined by the function α. For example:

$$\theta(SC_i, Refuse, i_k) = (Defend, i_l)$$

This example highlights the case in which the content of the commitment SC_i defends the refusal action characterized by the index i_k. The refusal action is defined by the function α. The index i_l characterizes the defense action.

The function γ allows us to define the connection relation which can exist between the contents of two commitments. For example:

$$\gamma(SC_i, SC_j) = (Contradict, i_k).$$

This translates the fact that the content of the commitment SC_i contradicts the content of the commitment SC_j. If p is the content of SC_i, then the content of SC_j is $\neg p$. This contradiction relation is characterized by the index i_k.

The function η allows us to define a connection relation between a commitment and an argumentation relation. For instance:

$$\eta(SC_i, Defend, i_k) = (Contradict, i_l).$$

This relation points out that the content of the commitment SC_i contradicts the defense relation characterized by the index i_k. The connection relation thus defined is characterized by the index i_l.

5.2 Example

In this section, we show how to represent a dialogue using the CAN formalism. We use the *conceptual graphs notation* (CG) proposed by Sowa [34] in order to describe the propositional contents of commitments. Conceptual graphs are a system of logic and a knowledge representation language consisting of concepts and relations between these concepts. They are labeled graphs in which concept nodes are connected by relation nodes. With their direct mapping to natural language, CG serve as an intermediate language for translating computer-oriented formalisms to and from natural languages. A concept is represented by a type (ex. PERSON) and a referent (ex. john) and denoted [TYPE: Referent] (ex. [PERSON: John]). A conceptual relation links two concepts and is represented between brackets. When representing natural language sentences, case-relations are usually used. Examples are: AGNT (agent), PTNT (patient), OBJ (object), CHRC (characteristic), PTIM (point in time). The advantage of

CG over predicate calculus is that they can be used to represent the literal meaning of utterances without ambiguities and in a logically precise form.

Let us consider the following dialogue $D1$:

(Example 2: dialogue D1)

$SA(i_0, Ag_1, \{Ag_2\}, t_{u0}, U_0)$: The disease M is not genetic.

$SA(i_1, Ag_2, \{Ag_1\}, t_{u1}, U_1)$: Why?

$SA(i_2, Ag_1, \{Ag_2\}, t_{u2}, U_2)$: Because it does not appear at birth.

$SA(i_3, Ag_2, \{Ag_1\}, t_{u3}, U_3)$: A disease which does not appear at birth can be genetic as well.

$SA(i_4, Ag_1, \{Ag_2\}, t_{u4}, U_4)$: How?

$SA(i_5, Ag_2, \{Ag_1\}, t_{u5}, U_5)$: It can be due to a genetic anomaly in the DNA appearing at a certain age.

$SA(i_6, Ag_1, \{Ag_2\}, t_{u6}, U_6)$: It is true, you are right.

By its speech act identified by i_0, agent Ag_1 creates, as explained in Section 3, a propositional commitment, i.e.:

$SA(i_0, Ag_1, \{Ag_2\}, t_{u0}, U_0) \vdash_{déf}$

$Create(Ag_1, t_{u0}, PC_0(id_0, Ag_1, \{Ag_2\}, t_{pc0}, (active), (submitted), p_0, t_{p0}))$

where PC_0 is the initial commitment of the dialogue, $t_{pc0} = t_{p0}$ and p_0 is the propositional content which can be described by the following CG:

$$\neg[[DISEASE : M] \rightarrow (CHRC) \rightarrow [GENETIC]]$$

In the CAN formalism this speech act results in the function:

$$\alpha(Ag_1, PC_0) = \{(Create, i_0)\}$$

Thereafter, agent Ag_2 performs the speech act identified by i_1 and takes position on the content of PC_0 by questioning it. Thus, "questioned" becomes the current state of PC_0. Hence, we have:

$SA(i_1, Ag_2, \{Ag_1\}, t_{u1}, U_1) \vdash_{déf}$

$Question(Ag_2, t_{u0}, PC_0(id_0, Ag_1, \{Ag_2\}, t_{pc0}, (active), (submitted, questioned), p_0, t_{p0}))$

In the CAN formalism this speech act results in the function:

$$\alpha(Ag_2, PC_0) = \{(Question, i_1)\}$$

Then, agent Ag_1 defends the propositional content p_0 of its commitment PC_0 by performing the speech act identified by i_2. Hence, it creates another commitment PC_1 whose content is p_1. Thus, "justified" becomes the current state of PC_0. We have:

$SA(i_2, Ag_1, \{Ag_2\}, t_{u2}, U_2) \vdash_{déf}$

$Defend(Ag_1, t_{u2}, PC_0(id_0, Ag_1, \{Ag_2\}, t_{pc0}, (active), (submitted, questioned, justified), p_0, t_{p0}))$

$\wedge Create(Ag_1, t_{u2}, PC_1(id_1, Ag_1, \{Ag_2\}, t_{pc1}, (inform, null, null), (active), (submitted), p_1, t_{p1}))$

where $t_{pc1} = t_{p1}$ and p_1 is described by the following CG:

$$\neg[[DISEASE : M] \leftarrow (AGNT) \leftarrow [APPEAR] \rightarrow (PTIM) \rightarrow [BIRTH]]$$

In argumentation terms, agent Ag_1 presents its argument (p_1, p_0) (see Section 4). Thus, we have:

$Arg(Ag_1, p_1, Defend(Ag_1, t_{u0}, PC_0(id_0, Ag_1, \{Ag_2\}, t_{pc0}, (active), (submitted, questioned, justified), p_0, t_{p0}))$

This is represented in the CAN formalism by the functions:

$$\alpha(Ag_1, PC_1) = \{(Create, i_2)\}, \Delta(PC_1, PC_0) = (Defend, i_2)$$

By the speech act identified by i_3, agent Ag_2 refuses the Ag_1's argument. Then, it creates a new commitment PC_2 whose content is p_2. We have:

$SA(i_3, Ag_2, \{Ag_1\}, t_{u3}, U_3) \vdash_{déf}$

$\quad Refuse(Ag2, t_{u3}, Arg(Ag_1, p_1, Defend(Ag_1, t_{u0}, PC_0(id_0, Ag_1, \{Ag_2\}, t_{pc0}, (active), (submitted, questioned, justified), p_0, t_{p0})))$

$\quad \wedge Create(Ag_2, t_{u3}, PC_2(id_2, Ag_2, \{Ag_1\}, t_{pc2}, (active), (submitted), p_2, t_{p2}))$

where $t_{pc2} = t_{p2}$ and the content p_2 is described by the following CG[1] :

$$\neg[\neg[[DISEASE :*x] \leftarrow (AGNT) \leftarrow [APPEAR] \rightarrow (PTIM) \rightarrow BIRTH]]$$
$$\wedge [[*x] \rightarrow (CHRC) \rightarrow [GENETIC]]].$$

This is represented in the CAN formalism by the functions:

$$\beta(Ag_2, Defend, i_2) = \{(Refuse, i_3)\}, \alpha(Ag_2, PC_2) = \{(Create, i_3)\}$$

Agent Ag_1's speech act identified by i_4 questions the content of the commitment PC_2. This allows us to transfer the content to the "questioned" state:

$SA(i_4, Ag_1, \{Ag_2\}, t_{u4}, U_4) \vdash_{déf}$

$\quad Question(Ag_1, t_{u4}, PC_2(id_2, Ag_2, \{Ag_1\}, t_{pc2}, (active), (submitted, questioned), p_2, t_{p2}))$

In the CAN formalism, this results in the function:

$$\alpha(Ag_1, PC_2) = \{(Question, i_4)\}$$

Then, agent Ag_2 defends the content of its commitment PC_2 by performing the speech act identified by i_5. It then creates another commitment PC_3 whose content is p_3. Thus, "Justified" becomes the current state of PC_2. We have:

$SA(i_5, Ag_2, \{Ag_1\}, t_{u5}, U_5) \vdash_{déf}$

$\quad Defend(Ag_2, t_{u5}, PC_2(id_2, Ag_2, \{Ag_1\}, t_{pc2}, (active), (submitted, questioned, justified), p_2, t_{p2}))$

$\quad \wedge Create(Ag_2, t_{u5}, PC_3(id_3, Ag_2, \{Ag_1\}, t_{pc3}, (active), (submitted), p_3, t_{p3}))$

where $t_{pc3} = t_{p3}$ and the content p_3 is described by the following CG:

$$[ANOMALY\text{-}DNA : *x]\text{-}$$

---

[1] To get this graph, we use the rule:
$p \Rightarrow q \equiv \neg(p \wedge \neg q)$, with $p = \neg$("there is a disease that appears at birth") and $q = \neg$("this disease is genetic").

Note that in the formula *x is a mark of coreference which appears in the referent part of a concept.

$$(AGNT)\leftarrow[CAUSE]\rightarrow(PTNT)\rightarrow[DISEASE : y]$$
$$[*x]\leftarrow(AGNT)\leftarrow[APPEAR]\rightarrow(PTIM)\rightarrow[AGE : @certain]$$

In argumentation terms, agent Ag_2 presents its argument (p_3, p_2). Thus, we have:

$Arg(Ag_2, p_3, Defend(Ag_2, t_{u5}, PC_2(id_2, Ag_2, \{Ag_1\}, t_{pc2}, (active),$

$(submitted, questioned, justified), p_2, t_{p2}))$

In the CAN formalism, this results in the following functions:

$\alpha(Ag_2, PC_3)=\{(Create, i_5)\}, \Delta(SC_3, PC_2)=(Defend, i_5)$

Agent Ag_2's speech act identified by i_6 reflects the Ag_2's acceptance of both PC_3's content and the argument defending it. Thus, "Accepted" is the final state of p_3. We have:

$SA(i_6, Ag_1, \{Ag_2\}, t_{u6}, U_6) \models_{déf}$

    $Accept(Ag1, t_{u6}, Arg(Ag_2, p_3, Defend(Ag_2, t_{u5}, PC_2(id_2, Ag_2, \{Ag_1\}, t_{pc2}, (active),$
    $(submitted, questioned, justified), p_2, t_{p2})))$

    $\wedge Accept(Ag_1, t_{u6}, PC_3(id_3, Ag_2, \{Ag_1\}, t_{pc3}, (active), (submitted, accepted), p_3, t_{p3}))$

In the CAN formalism, this is represented by the functions:

$$\beta(Ag_1, Defend, i_5)=\{(Accept, i_6)\}, \alpha(Ag_1, PC_3)=\{(Accept, i_6)\}$$

To summarize, the dialogue $D1$ can be represented by the following CAN: $<A, E, PC_0, I, \Omega, \Sigma, \Phi, \Delta, \Pi, \alpha, \beta, \delta, \theta, \gamma, \eta>$ such that:

$A=\{Ag_1, Ag_2\}$,

$E=\{PC_0, PC_1, PC_2, PC_3\}$,

$\Omega=\{Create, Question, Refuse, Accept, \}$,

$\Sigma=\{Defend\}$,

$\Phi=\varnothing$,

$I=\{i_0, ..., i_6\}$

$\alpha(Ag_1, PC_0)=\{(Create, i_0)\}, \alpha(Ag_2, PC_0)=\{(Question, i_1)\}$

$\alpha(Ag_1, PC_1)=\{(Create, i_2)\}, \Delta(SC_1, PC_0)=(Defend, i_2)$

$\beta(Ag_2, Defend, i_2)=\{(Refuse, i_3)\}, \alpha(Ag_2, PC_2)=\{(Create, i_3)\}$

$\alpha(Ag_1, PC_2)=\{(Question, i_4)\}, \alpha(Ag_2, PC_3)=\{(Create, i_5)\}$

$\Delta(SC_3, PC_2)=(Defend, i_5), \alpha(Ag_1, PC_3)=\{(Accept, i_6)\}$

$\beta(Ag_1, Defend, i_5)=\{(Accept, i_6)\}$

Fig. 2 shows the graphical representation of the network.

5.3   CAN: A Means of Inter-agent Communication

So far, we have shown how the CAN formalism enables us to illustrate the connect-edness of speech acts performed by the agents in a conversation. In the example of the previous section, we started from a pre-established dialogue, we examined it and we modeled it using a CAN. This highlights a process that enables us to analyze a conversation using the CAN formalism. But the formalism also offers a means that enables agents to take part in consistent conversations.

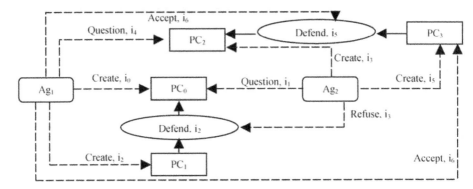

Fig. 2. The network associated with the dialogue *D1*

Agents can jointly build the network that represents their conversation as it progresses. This allows the agents:

1. To make sure at any time that the conversation is consistent;
2. To determine which speech act to perform on the basis of the current state of the conversation, and using an argumentation system and other cognitive elements.

Consistency is ensured by the relationships existing between different commitments, different argumentation relations and different actions (creation, acceptance, fulfillment, etc.). A speech act is consistent with the rest of the conversation if it leads to the creation of a new commitment related to another commitment through a connection or an argumentation relation, or if it makes it possible to take position on a commitment, on an argumentation relation or on an action. Moreover, the agent must know every thing about the current state of the conversation in order to determine its next speech act. For example, when an agent creates a commitment and/or an argumentation relation, one of the other agents may decide to act on what has been created by accepting it, by refusing it or by questioning it, depending on its argumentation system. Similarly, when an agent finds that its commitment, argument or action is being questioned, it must create a commitment in order to defend it. The network is built as the conversation progresses. This process differs from the one used to analyze a conversation. Therefore, agents use a dynamic process in order to build the network while taking part in the conversation.

To illustrate this way of using the CAN formalism, we take the example of Section 5.2 and demonstrate how agents build the final network piece by piece. By doing that, agents are able to continue conversing.

Agent Ag_1 decides to start a conversation (a dialogue) with another agent Ag_2 about a particular topic p_0 that interests it (the underlying mechanism related to this choice belongs to the cognitive layer and thus is not considered here (Figure 1)). Hence, Ag_1 creates a propositional commitment whose content is p_0, i.e.:

$$\alpha(Ag_1, PC_0) = \{(Create, i_0)\}$$

This corresponds to the speech act identified by i_0.

Then, agent Ag_2 decides to take position on the content of PC_0 by questioning it since it does not have any argument in favor or against it. As a matter of fact, Ag_2 wants to know which Ag_1's argument supports the content of PC_0. Therefore, Ag_2 performs the action corresponding to the speech act identified by i_1:

$$\alpha(Ag_2, PC_0)=\{(Question, i_1)\}$$

Now, Ag_1 must defend its proposition: it creates the commitment PC_1 whose content defends the content of PC_0. In doing so, this agent performs the action corresponding to the speech act identified by i_2:

$$\alpha(Ag_1, PC_1)=\{(Create, i_2)\}, \Delta(PC_1, PC_0)=(Defend, i_2)$$

Ag_2 has an argument against the defense relation. It refuses it by creating the commitment PC_2. It performs the action corresponding to the speech act identified by i_3:

$$\beta(Ag_2, Defend, i_2)=\{(Refuse, i_3)\}, \alpha(Ag_2, PC_2)=\{(Create, i_3)\}$$

Agent Ag_1 questions the content of PC_2 using its argumentation system. By doing that, it performs the action corresponding to the speech act identified by i_4:

$$\alpha(Ag_1, PC_2)=\{(Question, i_4)\}$$

The content of Ag_2's commitment PC_2 being questioned. The agent must try to defend it. Thus, it creates the commitment PC_3 and performs the actions corresponding to the speech act identified by i_5:

$$\alpha(Ag_2, PC_3)=\{(Create, i_5)\}, \Delta(SC_3, PC_2)=(Defend, i_5)$$

Thereafter, agent Ag_1 accepts the content of PC_3 and the argumentation relation $(Defend, i_5)$ that are compatible with its argumentation system. It performs the actions corresponding to the speech act identified by i_6:

$$\beta(Ag_1, Defend, i_5)=\{(Accept, i_6)\}, \alpha(Ag_1, PC_3)=\{(Accept, i_6)\}$$

6 Conclusion and Future Work

In this paper, we proposed a formalism to represent the dynamics of conversations. The formalism offers an external representation of the conversational activity. In essence, the formalism has two purposes: on the one hand it helps to analyze conversations, and on the other hand it is a means of helping agents to take part in consistent conversations. This formalism uses an approach based on commitments and arguments to model conversations between autonomous agents. Using this approach, we can capture both the social and public aspects of conversations as well as the reasoning aspect. We also proposed a communication model and an architecture for conversational agents that is compatible with this approach and this formalism.

As an extension to our work, we intend to prove mathematically the existence of one and only one CAN to represent a given coherent conversation (proof of uniqueness) by using a formal way of representing dialogues proposed by [19]. We also intend to use the formalism in order to represent different types of dialogues, for example according to the classification of [38]. On the other hand, we intend to integrate our formalism in dialogue games to provide more flexibility to agent communication. Another key issue for future work is to define a formal semantics for our formalism.

We investigate the idea of using CTL* and dynamic logic to develop a unified semantics for commitments, arguments and existing relations between them. Finally, we want use model checking techniques to prove the validity of this semantics.

References

1. Amgoud, L., Maudet, N., and Parsons, N. An argumentation-based semantics for agent communication languages. 15th European Conference on Artificial Intelligence, 2002.
2. Amgoud, L., Maudet, N., and Parsons, N. Modelling dialogues using argumentation. Proceeding of the 4th International Conference on MAS, 2000, 31-38.
3. Bentahar, J., Moulin, B., and Chaib-draa, B. Vers une approche à base d'engagements et d'arguments pour la modélisation du dialogue. 2ème Journées Francophones des Modèles Formels de l'Interaction, 2003.
4. Castelfranchi, C. Commitments: from individual intentions to groups and organizations. Proceedings of the International Conference on Multi-Agent Systems, 1995, 41-48.
5. Chaib-draa, B., and Dignum, F. Trends in agent communication languages. Computational Intelligence, 2002.
6. Chopra, A., and Singh, M. Nonmonotonic Commitment Machines. Dignum, F. (ed.). Advances in Agent Communication, Springer Verlag, 2003, in this volume.
7. Clark, H.H. Using language. Cambridge University Press, 1996.
8. Clark, H.H., and Haviland, S.E. Psychological processes in linguistic explanation. Cohen, D. (eds.). Explaining Linguistic Phenomena, 1974, 91-124.
9. Cohen, P.R., and Levesque, H.J. Persistence, intentions and commitment. Cohen, P.R., Morgan. J., and Pollack, M.E. (eds.). Intentions in Communication, MIT Press, Cambridge, 1990, 33-69.
10. Cohen, P.R., and Perrault, C.R. Elements of a plan-based theory of speech acts. Cognitive Science, 3, 1979, 177-212.
11. Colombetti, M. A commitment-based approach to agent speech acts and conversations. Proceedings of the Autonomous Agent Workshop on Conversational Policies. 4th International Conference on Autonomous Agent, 2000, 21-29.
12. Dastani, M., Hulstijn, J., and der Torre, L.V. Negotiation protocols and dialogue games. Proceedings of the Belgium/Dutch AI Conference, 2000.
13. Dignum, F., and Greaves, M. Issues in agent communication: an introduction, Dignum. F., and Greaves. M. (eds.). Issues in Agent Communication, 2000, 1-16.
14. Dung, P.M. On the acceptability of arguments and its fundamental role in non-monotonic reasoning, logic programming and n-person games. Artificial Intelligence, 77, 1995, 321-357.
15. Elvang-Goransson, M., Fox, J., and Krause, P. Dialectic reasoning with inconsistent information. Proceedings of the 9th Conference on Uncertainty in Artificial Intelligence, 1993, 114-121.
16. Ferber, J. Les Systèmes Multi-Agents : vers une intelligence collective. InterEditions (eds.), 1995.
17. Fornara, N., and Colombetti, M. Operational specification of a commitment-based agent communication language. The First International Joint Conference in Autonomous Agent and Multi-Agent Systems, 2002, 535-542.
18. Fornara, N., and Colombetti, M. Protocol Specification using a Commitment-based ACL. Dignum, F. (ed.). Advances in Agent Communication, Springer Verlag, 2003, in this volume.
19. Günter, A. Some ways of representing dialogues. Cognitive Constraints on Communication, Vatina, L. and Hintikka, J. (eds.), 1984, 241-250.
20. Hamblin, C.L. Fallacies, Methuen, 1970.

21. Labrou, Y. Semantics for an agent communication language, Ph.D. Thesis, University of Maryland, USA, 1997.
22. Labrou, Y., and Finin, T. Semantics and conversation for an agent communication language. Huhns, M. and Singh, M.P. (eds.). Readings in Agents, Morgan Kaufman Publisher, 1998, 235-242.
23. MacKenzie, J. Question-begging in non-cumulative systems. Journal Of Philosophical Logic, 8, 1979, 117-133.
24. Mallya, A.U., Yolum, P., and Singh, M. Resolving Commitments Among Autonomous Agents. Dignum, F. (ed.). Advances in Agent Communication, Springer Verlag, 2003, in this volume.
25. Maudet, N., and Chaib-draa, B. Commitment-based and dialogue-game based protocols, new trends in agent communication languages. Knowledge Engineering Review, 17(2), Cambridge University Press, 2002, 157-179.
26. McBurney, P., Parsons, S., and Wooldridge, M. Desiderata for agent argumentation protocols. Proceedings of the First International Conference on Autonomous Agent and Multi-Agents Systems, 2002, 402-409.
27. Moulin, B. The social dimension of interactions in multi-agent systems. Wobcke, W., Pagnucco, M., and Zhang, W. (eds.). Agent and Multi-Agent Systems, Formalisms, Methodologies and Applications. Artificial Intelligence, 1441, 1998, 109-122.
28. Parsons, S., Wooldridge, M., and Amgoud, L. An analysis of formal inter-agent dialogues. Proceedings of the First International Joint Conference on Autonomous Agents and Multi-Agent Systems, 2002, 394-401.
29. Pasquier, P., Andrillon, N., Chaib-draa, B., and Labrie, M.A. An Exploration in Using Cognitive Coherence Theory to Automate BDI Agents' Communicational Behavior. Dignum, F. (ed.). Advances in Agent Communication, Springer Verlag, 2003, in this volume.
30. Rousseau, D., Moulin, B., and Lapalme, G. Interpreting communicative acts and building a conversation model. Journal Natural Language Engineering, 2(3), 1996, 253-276.
31. Searle, J.R. Speech acts: an essay in the philosophy of language. Cambridge University Press, England, 1969.
32. Singh, M.P. A social semantics for agent communication language, Dignum. F and Greaves. M. (eds.). Issues in Agent Communication, 2000, 31-45.
33. Singh, M.P. Agent communication languages: rethinking the principles. IEEE Computer, 1998, 40-47.
34. Sowa, J.F. Conceptual structures: information processing in mind and machines. Addison-Wesley, Reading, MA, 1984.
35. Toulmin, S. The uses of argument, Cambridge University Press, England, 1958.
36. Verdicchio, M., and Colombetti, M. A logical model of social commitment for agent communication. Dignum, F. (ed.). Advances in Agent Communication, Springer Verlag, 2003, in this volume.
37. Vreeswijk, G.A.W. Abstract argumentation systems. Artificial Intelligence, 90 (1-2), 1997, 225-279.
38. Walton, D.N., and Krabbe, E.C.W. Commitment in dialogue: basic concepts of interpersonal reasoning. State University of New York Press, NY, 1995.

Resolving Commitments among Autonomous Agents*

Ashok U. Mallya[1], Pınar Yolum[2], and Munindar P. Singh[1]

[1] Department of Computer Science, North Carolina State University
Raleigh NC 27695-7535, USA
[2] Department of Artificial Intelligence, Vrije Universiteit Amsterdam
De Boelelaan 1081a, 1081 HV Amsterdam, The Netherlands

Abstract. Commitments are a powerful representation for modeling multiagent interactions. Previous approaches have considered the semantics of commitments and how to check compliance with them. However, these approaches do not capture some of the subtleties that arise in real-life applications, e.g., e-commerce, where contracts and institutions have implicit temporal references. The present paper develops a rich representation for the temporal content of commitments. This enables us to capture realistic contracts and institutions rigorously, and avoid subtle ambiguities. Consequently, this approach enables us to reason about whether and when exactly a commitment is satisfied or breached and whether it is or ever becomes unenforceable.

1 Introduction and Objectives

Protocols help streamline the complex interactions that can take place between autonomous, heterogeneous agents in a multiagent system. A special application setting is e-commerce, where the agents represent different parties that do business on-line.

The role of commitments in modeling such rich interactions is widely recognized, because they enable the key content of an interaction to be represented and reasoned about, especially in the face of opportunities or exceptions. Commitments are thus more expressive than traditional formalisms such as finite state machines. Yolum and Singh [1] show how to build and execute commitment-based protocols and to reason about such protocols in the event calculus. Fornara and Colombetti [2] capture key aspects of the commitment lifecycle and further advance the idea of commitments as a data structure. Some compliance aspects of commitment protocols in a branching-time temporal logic with potential causality have also been studied by Venkataraman and Singh [3].

Motivation. The above approaches show that commitments provide a viable representational framework for designing, executing, and validating flexible protocols in multiagent systems. However, current approaches take a limited view of the temporal aspects of commitments. This can prove to be a drawback for their use in real systems, since business deals usually involve many clauses and have subtle time periods of reference. The following is an informal list of some properties that are relevant in practice, but not naturally handled by current approaches.

---

* We thank the anonymous referees for their comments and suggestions that helped improve the text. We also thank Mario Verdicchio and Marco Colombetti for their comments. This research was supported by the National Science Foundation under grant DST-0139037.

F. Dignum (Ed.): ACL 2003, LNAI 2922, pp. 166–182, 2004.

- *Time Intervals.* Contracts often involve time bounds, which simplify decisions about the satisfaction or breach of commitments, which is one of the reasons traditional representations (e.g., paper documents) rely on them. Practical commitments often must be satisfied either within a fixed, bounded interval or at a specified instant in the future.
- *Maintenance.* Current work on commitments has concentrated on achievement conditions, whereas real-life commitments are as likely to be about the maintenance of certain conditions. For example, a typical service-level agreement (SLA) may involve committing to maintaining network connectivity during business hours.
- *Temporal anaphora.* A particular variety of time bounds arise in the notion of temporal anaphora, as introduced by Partee [4]. A promise such as "I will send you the goods" or a claim such as "I tried to call you five times" involves an implicit range of salient times within which the specified action occurred or will occur. Although we are not concerned here with commonsense reasoning, our representational framework for commitments should be able to accommodate the results of such reasoning.

Point-based temporal logics, which are commonly used in distributed system specifications, are inadequate to express the above requirements. Accordingly, we develop an extension of the well-known branching-time logic, Computation Tree Logic (CTL) developed by Emerson [5], which can capture the cases of interest here.

Challenges. We use examples from situations that arise in practical applications of web services to motivate our study of temporal aspects of commitments. We consider the example of a travel agent, who wishes to book an airline ticket to a certain destination, a rental car to use while there, and also a hotel room to stay at.

Example 1. The travel agent wants the passenger to be able to fly on one particular day, reserving the right to choose any flight on that day. If the airline is willing to offer such a deal, it becomes committed to maintaining a condition – a booked ticket – over an extended period of time. We need to be able to specify such maintenance conditions in commitments.

Example 2. The car rental company might offer, for some reason, one weeks free rental in the month of January. This is a maintenance condition within another time period. We need to be able to capture such temporal intricacies without bloating the domain language.

Example 3. Some commitments may violate constraints about time that commonsense reasoning would have detected. Such a situation can arise, for example, when a hotel offers an electronic discount coupon that expires today, but the coupon can be used only in some future time period, say, a special spring break offer that expires much before spring break.

Example 4. Another interesting example is when a warranty cannot be verified within the period over which the warranty is valid. Consider a customer who rents a car from a company which guarantees that the car will not break down for at least a two days, and promises a replacement car if it does. However, if the car were rented on a Friday and the company is closed on the weekends, then the customer is at a disadvantage.

Example 1 is solved in Section 4.1, Examples 2 and 3 in Section 4.2, and Example 4 in Section 4.3.

Contribution. Our main contribution is in applying a richer temporal representation to commitments and showing how the satisfaction or breach of a commitment can be detected. Further, the temporal aspects of commitments are independent of the domain-specific semantics of the condition that the commitment is about, so that we can reason about the temporal aspects of commitments in a domain-independent manner.

Organization. Section 2 introduces background concepts, Section 3 develops our technical approach, Sections 4 explains our results on the resolution of commitments that use temporally qualified propositions, and Section 5 summarizes our proposal and identifies directions of further research.

2   Background: Time and Commitments

We next briefly explain our model of time and our temporal logic, and introduce the notion of commitments.

2.1   The Temporal Framework

We use a discrete, branching-time model, as shown in Figure 1. The temporal model has the following features:

F_1 The world is a set of discrete *moments* in time. $\mathbb{M}$ is the set of all possible moments, partially ordered by $\prec$. The past is linear, and the future branches.

F_2 Each moment m is given a timestamp $\tau(m) \in \mathbb{T}$, totally ordered by $<$. If $m_0 \prec m_1$ then $\tau(m_0) < \tau(m_1)$.

F_3 A *scenario* S at a moment is a maximal set of moments containing the given moment and all moments along some branch in the future of the given moment. $\mathbb{S}_m$ denotes the set of all scenarios at a moment m. A scenario $S \in \mathbb{S}_m$ has the following properties:

–S is *rooted*; i.e., $m \in S$.

–S is *linear*; i.e., $(\forall m_1, m_2 \in S : (m_1 = m_2$ or $m_1 \prec m_2$ or $m_2 \prec m_1)$ and $m \preceq m_1)$.

For example, in Figure 1, the path $m_0 m_1 m_5 \ldots \in \mathbb{S}_{m_0}$

We use an extension of Emerson's Computational Tree Logic (CTL) [5]. We now introduce the components of CTL.

1. *Booleans.* $\neg$ and $\vee$ carry their usual meaning. true, false, $\rightarrow$, and $\wedge$ are obvious abbreviations.

2. *Linear time.* These operators apply over a particular scenario.

   U: A proposition $p\mathsf{U}q$, read p *until* q, is true at a moment m_i on a scenario, iff q holds at some moment m_x in the future on the given scenario and p holds at all moments between m_i and m_x.

   F: A proposition $\mathsf{F}p$, read *eventually* p, means that p holds at some point in the future in the given scenario. $\mathsf{F}p$ abbreviates true$\mathsf{U}p$.

   G : A proposition $\mathsf{G}p$, read *always* p, means that p always holds in the future on the given scenario. $\mathsf{G}p$ abbreviates $\neg\mathsf{F}\neg p$

3. *Branching quantifiers.* The operator A denotes *in all scenarios* at the present moment.

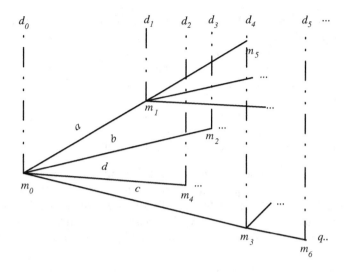

Fig. 1. A schematic representation of our model of time

2.2   Temporal Qualification

The temporal commitment structure specified by Fornara and Colombetti [2] forms the basis for our temporal commitment scheme. Every condition specified in the commitment language has a time interval, a temporal quantifier, and a proposition in the domain language.

We use timestamps to denote endpoints of time intervals. Two timestamps d_l and d_u are used to represent an interval that begins at d_l and ends at d_u, both instants inclusive. For any such time interval, $d_l \leq d_u$. We introduce the following *temporal quantifiers* to quantify over instants in the interval:

1. [ ] is an existential quantifier over a time interval. $[d_1, d_2]p$ means the proposition p has to hold at one or more instants in the interval beginning at d_1 and ending at d_2.
2. $\overline{[\,]}$ is a universal quantifier over a time interval. That is, $\overline{[d_1, d_2]}p$ means the proposition p has to hold at every instant in the interval beginning at d_1 and ending at d_2.

2.3   Commitments

Commitments are obligations that one agent has towards another, as Castelfranchi describes [6]. Formally, a commitment C*(id, x, y, p)*, relates a debtor x, a creditor y, and a condition p in such a way that x becomes responsible to y for satisfying the condition p; the commitment has a unique identifier id. The commitment is said to be satisfied when the condition p holds. There can be at most one commitment with a particular identifier in our entire model.

Commitment Operations. Commitments are created, satisfied, and transformed in certain ways. According to Singh [7], the following operations can be performed on commitments.

1. CREATE(x, c) establishes the commitment c in the system. This can only be performed by c's debtor x.
2. CANCEL(x, c) cancels the commitment c. This can only be performed by c's debtor x. Generally, cancellation is compensated by making another commitment.
3. RELEASE(y, c) releases c's debtor x from commitment c. This only can be performed by the creditor y.
4. ASSIGN(y, z, c) replaces y with z as c's creditor.
5. DELEGATE(x, z, c) replaces x with z as the c's debtor.
6. DISCHARGE(x,c) c's debtor x fulfills the commitment.

We note that a commitment has to be created using the CREATE operation for it to exist. Further, we assume equivalence of the performance of a DISCHARGE operation and the satisfaction of the condition p. That is, we assume that the DISCHARGE operation brings about p, and conversely, if p occurs, the DISCHARGE operation is assumed to have happened. This assumption does not impoverish the theory, and we defer a discussion on it to Section 5.

We also introduce two predicates in Section 3.1 that help us capture the notion of fulfillment of a commitment rigorously.

Commitment Predicates. For every operation on commitments listed above, we introduce a corresponding predicate which has the same name as the operation, but with lowercase letters. The predicates, instantiated with proper parameters, are true at the moment at which the corresponding operation is performed. For example, if an agent x performs a CREATE(x,c) operation at a moment m_i, then the predicate $create(x,c)$ is said to have the truth value true at the moment m_i.

Commitment Identifiers. Every commitment is assumed to have a unique identifier that helps to distinguish it from other commitments that may have the same debtor, the same creditor, and the same condition. For example, if I promise to pay you $5 twice, then a single payment of $5 should not suffice. The predicates in question also apply to specific commitments, i.e., respecting their unique identifiers. For example, I may cancel one of my two commitments to pay $5 without automatically canceling the other commitment. The identifiers come from a domain $\mathbb{D}$, which can be thought of as formed of the natural numbers.

3   Technical Framework

This section introduces the concept of time intervals, describes the formal language for our scheme, and introduces two key predicates dealing with the resolution of commitments.

3.1   The Formal Language

The following is a grammar for our formal language, $\mathcal{T}$, expressed in Backus-Naur Form (BNF). Here, tokens beginning with an uppercase letter denote nonterminals, tokens beginning with a lowercase letter denote lexical items that are not analyzed by this grammar, *agent* stands for any agent symbol, $\longrightarrow$ and $|$ are meta-symbols of the BNF, and all other symbols are terminals. T is the unique starting symbol for the language of $\mathcal{T}$.

G_1 $T \longrightarrow \mathsf{A}Expr \mid \mathsf{E}Expr \mid breached(C) \mid satisfied(C)$
G_2 $Expr \longrightarrow Expr \mathsf{U} Expr \mid Prop$
G_3 $Prop \longrightarrow \neg Prop \mid Prop \vee Prop \mid Tprop \mid Atomic$
G_4 $Tprop \longrightarrow [I,I]Prop \mid \overline{[I,I]}Prop$
G_5 $I \longrightarrow date \mid variable \mid date + duration \mid variable + duration$
G_6 $Atomic \longrightarrow Oper \mid a$
G_7 $Oper \longrightarrow create(agent, C) \mid cancel(agent, C) \mid delegate(agent, agent, C) \mid$
  $assign(agent, agent, C) \mid release(agent, C) \mid discharge(agent, C)$
G_8 $C \longrightarrow \mathsf{C}(identifier, agent, agent, Prop)$

In the grammar, a is an atomic proposition in the domain, *identifier* is a unique commitment identifier, *date* is a timestamp, $date \in \mathbb{T}$, *variable* is a time variable that is bound to a timestamp , and *duration* is a length of time used to construct simple additive expressions with time variables. The terms generated by I in the grammatical rule G_5 are called *temporal terms*. Temporal terms that have no variables are called *ground temporal terms*.

As a convention, we use p and q to denote simple propositions and p_t and q_t to denote temporally qualified propositions.

New Predicates for Resolving Commitments. We propose two predicates, *breached(c)* and *satisfied(c)*, indicating violation and fulfillment of the given commitment, respectively.

3.2 Semantics

We now describe the semantics for the language $\mathcal{T}$. For a proposition p, $M \models_m p$ means that a model M satisfies proposition p at moment m. $M \models_{S,m} p$ means that the model M satisfies p at moment m in the scenario S. When resolving nested interval expressions, $M \models_{S,m,m_l,m_u,\mathrm{E}} p$ means that M satisfies p at a moment m in the scenario S within the interval that begins at m_l and ends at m_u, both m_l and m_u being in the scenario S. Two constants E and U are used as subscripts to denote whether the interval is to be interpreted as existentially or universally quantified, respectively.

An *interpretation* $\mathbb{I}$ labels each moment with the atomic propositions and the ground commitment predicates that are true at that moment. Ground commitment predicates here refer to $create(\cdot, \cdot)$, $assign(\cdot, \cdot, \cdot)$, $delegate(\cdot, \cdot, \cdot)$, $cancel(\cdot, \cdot)$, $release(\cdot, \cdot)$, and $discharge(\cdot, \cdot)$. In a practical system, these elements would be specified in some manner external to the logic. For instance, a create operation might be taken to hold wherever a user submits a form over the Web. Let Φ be a set containing the atomic propositions a and ground commitment predicates. Then $\mathbb{I} : \mathbb{M} \mapsto \varphi(\Phi)$.

Let $M = \langle \mathbb{A}, \mathbb{M}, \prec, \mathbb{I}, \mathbb{T} \rangle$ be a model for the formal language $\mathcal{T}$, where $\mathbb{M}$, $\mathbb{T}$, and $\prec$ have the meaning as explained in Section 2, $\mathbb{A}$ is a set of agent symbols, and $\mathbb{I}$ is an interpretation as defined above.

The semantics uses a *substitution* for time variables that occur in the bounds of intervals. If p is an expression, and $\boldsymbol{x}$ is a vector of all time-variables in the expression, then, $p\,|_{\boldsymbol{d}}^{\boldsymbol{x}}$ is the expression produced by a uniform, concurrent, and element-wise substitution of $\boldsymbol{x}$ by $\boldsymbol{d}$. Such an expression will have only ground temporal terms. A ground temporal term is evaluated through date arithmetic. In the following, if t is a ground temporal term, then $[\![t]\!]$ is the timestamp corresponding to it. For example, if a temporal term t is bound to a timestamp corresponding to January 1, then the temporal term $t + 7days$ will be bound to the ground temporal term $January8$. The details of the arithmetic are not formalized here.

The semantics of $\mathcal{T}$ is given next. Here, c refers to a commitment of the form $\mathsf{C}(id, j, k, p)$, d_i's denote timestamps, and $active(c)$ is an abbreviation for $\neg(cancel(j, c) \lor delegate(j, \cdot, c) \lor assign(k, \cdot, c) \lor release(k, c) \lor discharge(j, c))$.

The semantic rules R_1, R_2, R_4, and R_3 give the meanings of the expressions generated by the grammar rule G_1 and the rules R_5 and R_6 give the meanings for the grammar rule G_2. Rule R_6 uses m_0 to denote the earliest moment on a scenario S and ∞ as a place holder to denote the limit of the scenario.

R_1 $M \models_m \mathsf{A}p$ iff $(\forall S : S \in \mathbb{S}_m \Rightarrow M \models_{S,m} p)$.

R_2 $M \models_m \mathsf{E}p$ iff $(\exists S : S \in \mathbb{S}_m \Rightarrow M \models_{S,m} p)$.

R_3 $M \models_m satisfied(c)$ iff $(\exists m_3 : m_3 \preceq m$ and $m \in S$ and $M \models_{S,m_3} discharge(j, c)$ and $(\exists m_1 \in S : m_1 \prec m_3$ and $M \models_{S,m_1} create(j, c)$ and $(\forall m_2 \in S : m_1 \preceq m_2 \prec m_3 \Rightarrow M \models_{S,m_2} active(c))))$

R_4 $M \models_m breached(c)$ iff $(\exists m_3 \in S : m_3 \preceq m$ and $m \in S$ and $M \models_{S,m_3} \mathsf{AG}\neg discharge(j, c)$ and $\exists m_1 \in S : m_1 \preceq m_3$ and $M \models_{S,m_1} create(j, c)$ and $(\forall m_2 \in S : m_1 \preceq m_2 \preceq m_3 \Rightarrow M \models_{S,m_2} active(c)))$.

R_5 $M \models_{S,m} p\mathsf{U}q$ iff $(\exists m_1 \in S : m \preceq m_1$ and $M \models_{S,m_1} q$ and $(\forall m_2 : m \preceq m_2 \preceq m_1 \Rightarrow M \models_{S,m_2} p))$.

R_6 $M \models_{S,m} p$ iff $\exists \boldsymbol{d} : M \models_{S,m,m_0,\infty,E} p\,|_{\boldsymbol{d}}^{\boldsymbol{x}}$, where $p \notin \Phi$, $\boldsymbol{x}$ is a vector of variables the occur in p, $\boldsymbol{d}$ is a vector of timestamps, and $|\boldsymbol{d}| = |\boldsymbol{x}|$.

The following are the semantics of the grammatical rules G_3 and G_4. Rules R_7 through R_{11} apply to an existentially quantified interval while rules R_{12} through R_{16} apply to a universally quantified interval.

R_7 $M \models_{S,m,m_l,m_u,E} p$ iff $\exists m_x \in S : m_l \preceq m_x \preceq m_u$ and $m_l, m_u \in S$ and $p \in \mathbb{I}(m_x)$.

R_8 $M \models_{S,m,m_l,m_u,E} \neg p$ iff $\exists m_x \in S : m_l \preceq m_x \preceq m_u$ and $m_l, m_u \in S$ and $M \not\models_{m_x} p$.

R_9 $M \models_{S,m,m_l,m_u,E} p \lor q$ iff $\exists m_x, m_y \in S : m_l \preceq m_x, m_y \preceq m_u$ and $m_l, m_u \in S$ and $M \models_{m_x} p$ or $M \models_{m_y} q$

R_{10} $M \models_{S,m,m_l,m_u,E} [d_l', d_u']p$ iff $\tau(m_l') = d_l'$ and $\tau(m_u') = d_u'$ and $m_l, m_u, m_l', m_u' \in S$ and $\exists m_x, m_x' : m_l \preceq m_x \preceq m_u$ and $m_l' \preceq m_x' \preceq m_u'$ and $m_x' \preceq m_x \Rightarrow M \models_{S,m_x} p$

R_{11} $M \models_{S,m,m_l,m_u,E} \overline{[d_l', d_u']}p$ iff $\tau(m_l') = d_l'$ and $\tau(m_u') = d_u'$ and $m_l, m_u, m_l', m_u' \in S$ and $\exists m_x, \forall m_x' : m_l \preceq m_x \preceq m_u$ and $m_l' \preceq m_x' \preceq m_u'$ and $m_x' \preceq m_x \Rightarrow M \models_{S,m_x} p$

R_{12} $M \models_{S,m,m_l,m_u,\mho} p$ iff $\forall m_x \in S : m_l \preceq m_x \preceq m_u$ and $m_l, m_u \in S$ and $p \in \mathbb{I}(m_x)$.

R_{13} $M \models_{S,m,m_l,m_u,\mho} \neg p$ iff $\forall m_x \in S : m_l \preceq m_x \preceq m_u$ and $m_l, m_u \in S$ and $M \not\models_{m_x} p$.

R_{14} $M \models_{S,m,m_l,m_u,\mho} p \vee q$ iff $\forall m_x \in S : m_l \preceq m_x \preceq m_u$ and $m_l, m_u \in S$ and $M \models_{m_x} p$ or $M \models_{m_x} q$.

R_{15} $M \models_{S,m,m_l,m_u,\mho} [d'_l, d'_u]p$ iff $\tau(m'_l) = d'_l$ and $\tau(m'_u) = d'_u$ and $m_l, m_u, m'_l, m'_u \in S$ and $\forall m_x, \exists m'_x : m_l \preceq m_x \preceq m_u$ and $m'_l \preceq m'_x \preceq m'_u$ and $m'_x \preceq m_x \Rightarrow M \models_{S,m_x} p$

R_{16} $M \models_{S,m,m_l,m_u,\mho} \overline{[d'_l, d'_u]}p$ iff $\tau(m'_l) = d'_l$ and $\tau(m'_u) = d'_u$ and $m_l, m_u, m'_l, m'_u \in S$ and $\forall m_x, m'_x : m_l \preceq m_x \preceq m_u$ and $m'_l \preceq m'_x \preceq m'_u$ and $m'_x \preceq m_x \Rightarrow M \models_{S,m_x} p$

Further, we impose the following constraints on the model to capture operations on commitments.

C_1 A commitment cannot be created more than once with a given identifier.
  $M \models_{S,m} create(j, C(id, j, k, p)) \Rightarrow \forall m_1 : m \prec m_1 \Rightarrow (\forall j_1, k_1, p : M \not\models_{S,m_1} create(j_1, C(id, j_1, k_1, p)))$.

C_2 When a commitment is assigned, it is no longer active, but a new commitment with the new creditor is created.
  $M \models_{S,m} (assign(k, z, c) \Rightarrow AG \neg active(c) \wedge create(j, c'))$
  where $c \equiv C(id, j, k, p)$ and $c' \equiv C(id', j, z, p)$.

C_3 When a commitment is delegated, it is no longer active, but a new commitment with a different debtor is created.
  $M \models_{S,m} (delegate(j, z, c) \Rightarrow AG \neg active(c) \wedge create(z, c'))$
  where $c \equiv C(id, j, k, p)$ and $c' \equiv C(id', z, k, p)$.

C_4 When a commitment is first created, it is active and not impossible to discharge.
  $M \models_{S,m} (create(c) \Rightarrow active(c) \wedge \neg AG \neg discharge(c))$

C_5 After a commitment has been breached, no operation can be performed on it.
  $M \models_m breached(c) \Rightarrow M \models_{S,m} AG active(c)$

3.3 Commitment Life Cycle

Using the above semantics, we establish some simple but important lemmas indicating the stability of the $breached(\cdot)$ and $satisfied(\cdot)$ predicates.

When a commitment is first created, it is neither breached nor satisfied. Eventually, it might be breached and thus remain breached forever; or it may be be satisfied and remain satisfied forever. This has the effect of applying a three-valued logic for the satisfaction commitments.

Lemma 1. $M \models_{S,m} create(c) \Rightarrow M \models_m (\neg breached(c) \wedge \neg satisfied(c))$.

Proof. By applying constraint C_4 to the semantic definitions R_4 and R_3.

Lemma 2. $M \models_m breached(c)$ iff $\forall m_x : m \preceq m_x \Rightarrow M \models_{m_x} breached(c)$.

Proof. By semantic definition R_4.

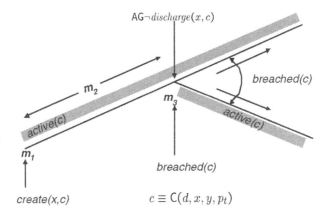

Fig. 2. Temporal behavior of the $breached(\cdot)$ predicate

Lemma 3. $M \models_m satisfied(c)$ iff $\forall m_x : m \preceq m_x \Rightarrow M \models_{m_x} satisfied(c)$.

Proof. By semantic definition R_3.

Lemma 4. $M \models_m (\neg satisfied(c) \not\Rightarrow breached(c))$.

Proof. By Lemma 1.

Lemma 5. $M \models_m (\neg breached(c) \not\Rightarrow satisfied(c))$.

Proof. By Lemma 1.

The Lemmas 2 and 3 are shown in Figures 2 and 3 respectively. The moments m_1, m_2, and m_3 marked in the figures denote moments used in R_3 and R_4. Note that a commitment is active even after it is breached. However, a commitment cannot be active after it is satisfied. These observations follows from the definition of the $active(\cdot)$ predicate and the constraint C_5.

4   Resolving Temporal Commitments

A temporal commitment is resolvable if its satisfaction or breach can be determined at some moment. Under certain conditions, the unresolvability of a temporal commitment can be ascertained even before the specified time interval occurs. We now discuss cases where a temporally quantified proposition is not resolvable, and develop methods to detect such cases. Based on the resolvability of such propositions, we can detect satisfaction or breach of temporal commitments.

4.1   Nested Interval Expressions

The language given in section 3.1 allows for propositions to be nested within multiple levels of time intervals. Although there are many nested intervals whose interpretation

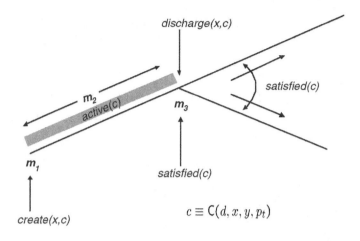

Fig. 3. Temporal behavior of the *satisfied*(·) predicate

in common language does not make sense or induces redundancy, some nested time intervals do make sense in real-life situations. We give examples of both meaningful and meaningless nested interval propositions.

Allen [8] defines 13 possible temporal relationships between any two given time intervals. Figure 4 shows these 13 relationships for the two intervals contained in the proposition $[d_1, d_2]\overline{([d_3, d_4]}q)$; i.e., the intervals $[d_1, d_2]$ and $\overline{[d_3, d_4]}$. Here, time increases from left to right. The shaded portions are intervals of the type $\overline{[d_l, d_u]}$, and the unshaded portions are of the type $[d_l, d_u]$. 13 such cases can be constructed *for each combination* of temporal quantifiers applied to each of the intervals, but we show only one interval-quantifier combination pair as an example; i.e., the quantified intervals $[d_1, d_2]$ and $\overline{[d_3, d_4]}$.

If we consider nested temporally quantified propositions as being conditions of commitments, we can see which kinds of nesting will make the success of the commitment unresolvable. Cases 1.1, 3.1, 4.1, 5.1, and 6.1 are not resolvable, but cases 1.2, 2.1, 3.2, 4.2, 5.2, 6.2, 7.1, and 7.2 can be resolved for reasons listed below. The term *inner proposition* is used to refer to the temporal proposition $\overline{[d_3, d_4]}p$.

In cases 1.1, 3.1, 4.1, 5.1, and 6.1, the inner proposition's time interval does not complete until after the outer time interval completes. The inner interval has references to instants in the future. Since the future cannot be seen in advance, these cases cannot be resolved.

In cases 1.2, 2.1, 3.2, 4.2, 5.2, 6.2, 7.1, and 7.2 the inner proposition's success can be resolved at at least one instant within the interval of the outer proposition. Since the outer proposition has an existentially quantified time interval $[t_1, t_2]$ and we have at least one instant of resolvability, these cases can be resolved.

A temporally quantified proposition can be used to represent events like that in Example 1; i.e., the passenger using one ticket on a particular day, on any flight of her choice.

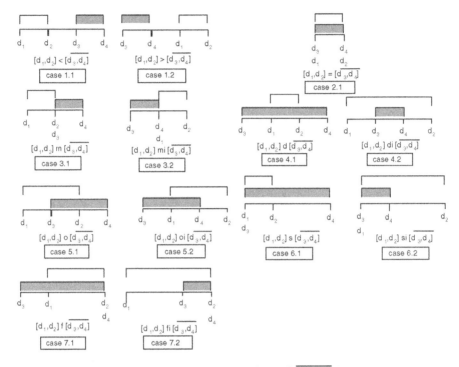

Fig. 4. Allen's intervals for $[d_1, d_2]([\overline{d_3, d_4}]p)$

Solution 1. If p represents the proposition that a ticket is on offer, then $[d_1, d_2]p$ can be used to denote that a ticket will be on offer for the period of time between d_1 and d_2. Hence a ticket valid for an entire day would be represented by $[d_1, d_1 + 24hours]p$.

Nested temporal intervals can be used to denote maintenance conditions like the one in Example 2.

Solution 2. If d_1 denotes January 1 and t denotes a time variable, and p denotes that the company will rent a car for free, then the proposition $[d_1, d_1 + 31days][\overline{t, t + 7days}]p$ denotes one week of free rental in the month of January.

Note that it only requires a simple extension of our language to be able to specify timestamps in relation to one another.

We next formalize the notions of nested intervals and results about their resolution. These results can be used to detect some commitment violations before they occur.

Definition 1. *A temporally quantified proposition is positive-resolvable at an instant if its value is known to be true at that instant; it is negative-resolvable at an instant if its value is known to be false at that instant.*

Definition 2. *A temporal commitment is positive-resolvable at an instant if its satisfaction can be known at that instant; it is negative-resolvable at an instant if its breach can be known at that instant.*

We use the following notation to denote some important instants with respect to an interval. Below, p_t is a temporal proposition, and r denotes resolvability. Given an interval,

$r_\perp^+(p_t)$ represents the earliest instant at which p_t is positive-resolvable;

$r_\top^+(p_t)$ represent the latest instant in that interval at which p_t is positive-resolvable.

$r_\perp^-(p_t)$ represents the earliest instant at which p_t is negative-resolvable;

$r_\top^-(p_t)$ represents the latest instant in that interval at which p_t is negative-resolvable.

The following observations form the base cases for detecting resolvability of propositions that have intervals nested to any arbitrary depth and the resolvability of temporal commitments. Here, p is a proposition.

$$r_\perp^+([d_l, d_u]p) = d_l, \; r_\top^+([d_l, d_u]p) = d_u.$$
$$r_\perp^-([d_l, d_u]p) = d_u, \; r_\top^-([d_l, d_u]p) = d_u.$$
$$r_\perp^+(\overline{[d_l, d_u]}p) = d_u, \; r_\top^+(\overline{[d_l, d_u]}p) = d_u.$$
$$r_\perp^-(\overline{[d_l, d_u]}p) = d_l, \; r_\top^-(\overline{[d_l, d_u]}p) = d_u.$$

These observations imply that p_t is not positive-resolvable at any instant before $r_\perp^+(p_t)$, not negative-resolvable at any instant before $r_\perp^-(p_t)$, positive-resolvable at any instant after $r_\top^+(p_t)$, and negative-resolvable at any instant after $r_\top^-(p_t)$.

4.2 Resolving Nested Interval Expressions

Using the rules in Section 4.1, we can now see why some of the two-level interval nesting cases shown in Figure 4 were determined to be unresolvable.

In cases 1.1, 3.1, 4.1, 5.1, and 6.1, the earliest instant at which the satisfaction of $\overline{[d_3, d_4]}q$ can be determined is d_4, which is beyond d_2, the latest instant for the satisfaction of $[d_1, d_2]p$. As a consequence, the expression $[d_1, d_2](\overline{[d_3, d_4]}q)$ cannot be resolved, which is why commitments whose conditions are propositions of this type are disadvantageous for the creditor.

Solution 3. To model Example 3, the hotel H makes a commitment to a customer c. The commitment is $C(d, H, c, A[d_1, d_1 + 24hrs](\overline{[d_2, d_2 + 7days]}q))$, where $d_1 + 24hrs < d_2$ because it is not spring break yet, $[d_1, d_1 + 24hrs]$ denotes the interval "today" (say, a day in July), $\overline{[d_2, d_2 + 7days]}$ denotes the interval when spring break happens, and q is an atomic proposition that denotes some offer that the coupon offers. In this case, $\overline{[d_2, d_2 + 7days]}q$ cannot be resolved at least until $d_2 + 7days$, and $[d_1, d_1 + 24hrs](\cdot)$ *has* to be resolved at most by $d_1 + 24hrs$. But since $d_1 + 24hrs < d_2 + 7days$, this condition cannot be resolved. Hence the commitment cannot satisfied. Formally, $r_\top^+([d_1, d_1 + 24hrs](\cdot)) < r_\perp^+(\overline{[d_2, d_2 + 7days]}q)$.

To summarize, the following conditions are necessary to ensure resolvability of a temporally quantified proposition:
A temporally quantified proposition of the form $[d_l, d_u]p_t$ must have at least one instant in the interval d_l, d_u, at which p_t is resolvable. A temporally quantified proposition of the form $\overline{[d_l, d_u]}p_t$ must have p_t resolvable at all instants in the interval d_l, d_u.

For a commitment c, the following lemmas indicate the three valued logic of satisfaction due to the *satisfied*($\cdot$) and the *breached*($\cdot$) predicates.

Lemma 6.

$$M \models_{S,m} create(x,c) \Rightarrow (\forall m_x : m \preceq m_x \Rightarrow$$
$$(M \models_{m_x} satisfied(c) \Rightarrow M \models_{S,m_x} \mathsf{AG}\neg active(c))) \ .$$

Proof. By the definition of the predicate $active(\cdot)$ and the semantic rule R_3.

Lemma 7.

$$M \models_{S,m} create(x,c) \Rightarrow (\forall m_x : m \preceq m_x \Rightarrow$$
$$(M \models_{m_x} breached(c) \Rightarrow M \models_{S,m_x} \mathsf{AG} active(c))) \ .$$

Proof. By the constraint C_5 and Lemma 2.

We have shown how unresolvable commitments can be detected. Such resolution results will enable earlier detection of protocol violations, and are of practical importance where an unresolvable commitment is as good (or as bad) as one that is breached.

4.3   Disjunctive Forms

Another important aspect of resolution concerns *disjunctive commitments* whose conditions are disjunctions of temporally-quantified propositions.

Disjunctive commitments regularly arise in common business interactions and can sometimes lead to what we call *the warranty paradox* — a situation where some subtle clauses render the warranty void before the customer can ascertain the quality of the good. This can happen, for instance, if ascertaining the quality of the good takes more time than the life of the warranty.

Intuitively, we reason as follows about the satisfiability of a disjunction of temporal propositions: *A disjunction of temporal propositions can potentially be satisfied if it has not already been satisfied, and at least one of the disjuncts is still resolvable.*

Let $p_1, p_2, \ldots p_n$ be temporally quantified propositions that occur in a disjunctive commitment of the form $\mathsf{C}(id, x, y, \mathsf{A}((p_1 \vee p_2 \ldots \vee p_i) \vee (p_{i+1} \vee p_{i+2} \vee \ldots \vee p_n)))$. Here, $p_1 \vee p_2 \ldots \vee p_i$ represents some quality that the good satisfies, as claimed by the merchant x, and $p_{i+1} \vee p_{i+2} \vee \ldots \vee p_n$ represents the replacement for the good that the merchant promises to the customer y. If the quality assured by the merchant becomes false at some moment, then the replacement proposition should be positive-resolvable at that moment. Otherwise, the warranty is unfavorable for the customer.

Formally, this requirement is stated as

$$M \models_{S,m} \neg(p_1 \vee p_2 \ldots \vee p_i) \Rightarrow (\ M \models_{S,m} (p_{i+1} \vee p_{i+2} \vee \ldots \vee p_n) \vee$$
$$(\tau(m) < r_\top^+(p_{i+1} \vee p_{i+2} \vee \ldots \vee p_n) \wedge$$
$$(M \not\models_{S,m} \neg(p_{i+1} \vee p_{i+2} \vee \ldots \vee p_n)))$$

If none of the warranty disjuncts are resolvable at an instant at which the claim about the quality is false, then the warranty is unfavorable to the customer.

Applying this requirement to Example 4 of Section 1 gives us the following.

Solution 4. Example 4 can be modeled by the commitment $C(id, R, c, A(\overline{[d_1, d_2]}\ good\_car \vee [d_1, d_3]\ replace\_car))$, where "*good_car*" means the the car hasn't broken down, "*replace_car*" represents the warranty that the rental company gives on the quality of the car, R represents the rental company, and c the customer. d_1 represents the time at which the car is rented on Friday, d_2 is the time at which the car should be returned on Monday, and d_3 denotes the closing of the rental company on Friday. Hence $d_3 < d_2$. We see that there exists a moment in between d_1 and d_3, at which the literal $([d_1, d_3]\ replace\_car)$ is beyond the upper bound of its positive-resolution. If the car breaks down on Saturday, then the only proposition that has not yet been resolved at that moment is the guarantee by the renter to replace it. However, the upper bound of positive resolvability of this proposition has passed. Formally, $\exists m : d_1 < d_3 < \tau(m) < d_2$ and $M \models_{S,m} \neg(\overline{[d_1, d_2]}great\_car)$ and $M \not\models_{S,m} ([d_1, d_3]replace\_car)$ and $r_\top^+([d_1, d_3]replace\_car) < \tau(m)$.

Figure 5 shows Example 4.

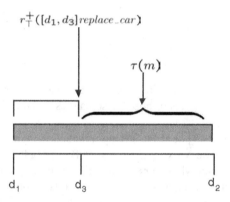

Fig. 5. Unfavorable warranty in Example 4

Thus we have shown how the warranty paradox can be captured in our scheme of temporal commitments.

5 Discussion

The concept of deadlines in commitments is doubtless necessary for practical uses of commitments. Traditionally, deadlines are hidden within the atomic propositions. However, an explicit formulation of temporal commitments, as developed above, is highly desirable. It offers a uniform treatment of operational characteristics across domains. We have shown how such a system of commitments with deadlines can be developed and used to reason about the possibility of satisfaction. Our approach not only allows for the expression of statements that involve deadlines, but also decouples the temporal quantification from the proposition itself, thus allowing us to reason about the temporal aspect without regard to the meaning of the propositions. We now discuss related issues.

In Section 2.3, we assumed that all commitments are fulfilled by the DISCHARGE operation, and not just by the condition p holding. This assumption helps simplify the theory because it excludes a situation where a commitment $C(d_1, x, y, p)$ is satisfied by p being brought about by some agent z rather than by agent x. However, the assumption does not weaken the scope of the commitment operations. We may require that only agent x bring about p. The domain language used to specify p should be rich enough to incorporate such constraints.

For instance, the condition p might be " turn the lights on", in which case any agent could turn the lights on to fulfill the commitment $C(d_1, x, y, p)$. In fact, we might want to allow such a fulfillment. On the other hand, if the condition were subjective, like "teach a graduate course", we might want to make sure that only the intended party brings about the condition. We would therefore have to have a language for specifying p that can express that "x will teach a graduate course".

5.1   Literature

Literature related to our work can be classified according to two main orthogonal fields:

– The semantics of agent interaction protocols.
– The semantics and implementation of business processes.

A middle ground, where our work lies, is the operational aspects of commitments. Our work embodies desirable aspects of both the semantics and the business processes.

Semantics. Dignum *et al.* [9] describe a temporal deontic logic that helps specify obligations and constraints. The work focuses on specifying deadlines, so that a planner can take deadlines into account while generating plans. Their approach, however, is based on the notion of obligations, and no operational methods for obligations are given. Once a deadline has passed, and a certain rule has been violated, the logic has nothing to say about the effects on the system. This work, although semantically rich, has not been designed with an operational framework in mind. Nevertheless, Dignum *et al.*'s approach is detailed in the kinds of deadlines and constraints that it allows to be modeled. For example, deadlines like . . . *as soon as possible*, which cannot be modeled in our grammar, can be modeled using theirs. We have, however, a system that is closer to being operationalized than theirs.

Business Protocols. Grosof *et al.* [10] develop semantics for systems that represent business rules using *Courteous Logic Programs*. Their approach uses explicit rules to use to decide between conflicting rules, and the emphasis is on the implementation and application of CLP to real businesses. The work however does not define the semantics for the grammar they use. Business rules are represented by general if-then clauses. Hence, all concepts beyond the structure of the if-then rules are domain specific, including the temporal references. Their work, however, has been applied to actual business systems, and proves the value of intelligent agents in business processes.

From the standpoint of real-world implementation, the *Business Transaction Protocol* proposed by the OASIS [11] addresses the need for long-lived interactions among web services as opposed to short-lived transactions in the classical sense of the word. This protocol also recognizes that many of the offers made in real-world businesses involve deadlines. For example, an airline participating as a web service provider in a BTP run could specify how long it is willing to hold an offer open when it agrees to take part in a transaction [12].

Commitment Operations. Our scheme for temporal quantification is related to a similar notion presented by Fornara and Colombetti [2]. Their approach seeks to operationalize commitments and define the life cycle of a commitment, but does not pay attention to the issue of deadlines and temporally sensitive commitments, whereas our approach develops interesting results about the resolution of fulfillment of commitments. Although Fornara and Colombetti have taken a good first step towards the operationalization of commitments in agent interaction, they stop short of developing a semantics for temporal commitments as we have done here.

Verdicchio and Colombetti [13] develop a theory of the evolution of commitments over time. Their work is closest to ours among all others discussed in this section. It specifies constraints on the creation and satisfaction of temporal commitments using a variant of CTL*.

McBurney and Parsons [14] define the *Posit Spaces Protocol*, which is an agent interaction protocol. This protocol uses a central repository for storing all the commitments that have been made. The idea is simple and corresponds to the concept of the *Sphere of Commitment* that was proposed by Singh [15]. This work does not relate to our results directly, but is yet another demonstration of the use of commitments in modeling and building multiagent systems.

5.2   Directions

Our work on temporal aspects of commitments is far from complete. One direction for further research is to investigate ways to do away with rigid protocols by having agents commit to each other by taking small risks at a time to finally arrive at a state where both parties are committed so that there is no risk of a loss to one party. This is just an intuitive notion, and further work is required to assess the viability of this approach.

Another direction is to describe agent interaction protocols using the theory of universal causation developed by Giunchiglia *et al.* [16], so that commitment machines that exploit nonmonotonic reasoning can be automatically generated. A commitment machine, proposed by Yolum and Singh [1], is a novel way of representing interaction protocols using commitments. It specifies the states that are allowed in the interaction in terms of the commitments that hold in those states. A commitment machine allows greater flexibility in the enactment of a protocol since interacting agents have many ways of reaching final states. Nonmonotonic reasoning in commitment machines would allow greater flexibility as compared to the incremental inferencing approach used by Yolum and Singh [1]. Chopra and Singh [17] present this idea in greater detail and clarity.

Venkataraman and Singh [3] develop a vector-clock based scheme to verify agents' compliance to a commitment protocol. However, they do not consider rich temporal structures as we have done here. It will be interesting to apply the theory developed here to their scheme of compliance checking.

References

1. Yolum, P., Singh, M.P.: Flexible protocol specification and execution: Applying event calculus planning using commitments. In: Proceedings of the 1st International Joint Conference on Autonomous Agents and MultiAgent Systems (AAMAS), ACM Press (2002)
2. Fornara, N., Colombetti, M.: Operational specification of a commitment- based agent communication language. In: Proceedings of the International Joint Conference on Autonomous Agents and MultiAgent Systems, ACM Press (2002) 535–542
3. Venkatraman, M., Singh, M.P.: Verifying compliance with commitment protocols: Enabling open Web-based multiagent systems. Autonomous Agents and Multi-Agent Systems **2** (1999) 217–236
4. Partee, B.: Nominal and temporal anaphora. Linguistics and Philosophy **7** (1984) 287–324
5. Emerson, E.A.: Temporal and modal logic. In van Leeuwen, J., ed.: Handbook of Theoretical Computer Science. Volume B. North-Holland, Amsterdam (1990) 995–1072
6. Castelfranchi, C.: Commitments: From individual intentions to groups and organizations. In: Proceedings of the AAAI-93 Workshop on AI and Theories of Groups and Organizations: Conceptual and Empirical Research. (1993)
7. Singh, M.P.: An ontology for commitments in multiagent systems: Toward a unification of normative concepts. Artificial Intelligence and Law **7** (1999) 97–113
8. Allen, J.F.: Maintaining knowledge about temporal intervals. Communications of the ACM **26** (1983) 832–843
9. Dignum, F., Weigand, H., Verharen, E.: Meeting the deadline: On the formal specification of temporal deontic constraints. In Ras, Z.W., Michalewicz, M., eds.: Foundations of Intelligent Systems, 9th International Symposium, (ISMIS '96). Volume 1079 of Lecture Notes in Computer Science., Springer (1996) 243–252
10. Grosof, B.N., Labrou, Y., Chan, H.Y.: A declarative approach to business rules in contracts: Courteous logic programs in XML. In Wellman, M.P., ed.: Proceedings 1st Annual ACM Conf. on Electronic Commerce, EC'99, Denver, CO, USA, 3–5 November 1999, ACM Press (1999)
11. OASIS: Business transaction protocol (2002) www.oasis-open.org/committees/business-transactions/ documents/specification/2002-06-03.BTP_cttee_spec_ 1.0.pdf.
12. Dalal, S., Temel, S., Little, M., Potts, M., Webber, J.: Coordinating business transactions on the web. IEEE Internet Computing **7** (2003) 30–39
13. Verdicchio, M., Colombetti, M.: A logical model of social commitment for agent communication. In: Proceedings of the 2nd International Joint Conference on Autonomous Agents and MultiAgent Systems (AAMAS), ACM Press (2003)
14. McBurney, P., Parsons, S.: Posit spaces: A performative model of e-commerce. In: Proceedings of the International Joint Conference on Autonomous Agents and MultiAgent Systems. (2003) To appear.
15. Singh, M.P.: Multiagent systems as spheres of commitment. In: Proceedings of the International Conference on Multiagent Systems (ICMAS) Workshop on Norms, Obligations, and Conventions. (1996)
16. Giunchiglia, E., Lee, J., McCain, N., Lifschitz, V., Turner, H.: Nonmonotonic causal theories. Artificial Intelligence (AIJ) (2003) To Appear.
17. Chopra, A., Singh, M.: Nonmonotonic commitment machines. In Dignum, F., ed.: Advances in Agent Communication. LNAI, Springer Verlag (2003) in this volume

Nonmonotonic Commitment Machines*

Amit Chopra and Munindar P. Singh

Department of Computer Science, North Carolina State University
Raleigh, NC 27695-7535, USA
{akchopra,mpsingh}@ncsu.edu

Abstract. Protocols for multiagent interaction need to be flexible because of the open and dynamic nature of multiagent systems. Such protocols cannot be modeled adequately via finite state machines (FSMs) as FSM representations lead to rigid protocols. We propose a commitment-based formalism called Nonmonotonic Commitment Machines (NCMs) for representing multiagent interaction protocols. In this approach, we give semantics to states and actions in a protocol in terms of commitments. Protocols represented as NCMs afford the agent flexibility in interactions with other agents. In particular, situations in protocols when nonmonotonic reasoning is required can be efficiently represented in NCMs.

1   Introduction

A protocol is a means of achieving meaningful interaction. Agents that constitute a multiagent system use protocols to guide their interactions with each other. Protocols have traditionally been specified as FSMs that specify sequences of states. The protocol designers have certain scenarios in mind that they directly incorporate in an FSM. As a result, agents using a protocol specified as FSMs are limited to behaving in a rigid manner. Such agents cannot handle exceptions or take advantage of opportunities that might arise during interactions with other agents. In this paper, we present an alternative way of specifying protocols that is based on commitments which we formalize below. Our approach is based on the general notion that an agent does not violate a given protocol as long the agent does not violate the commitments prescribed by the protocol. Using commitments makes the protocol flexible and enables the agent to handle exceptions and opportunities without violating the given protocol.

Protocols for interaction in multiagent systems often resemble protocols routinely used by humans in their social interactions. The Contract Net [1] and NetBill [2] are examples of such protocols. Such protocols have traditionally been represented by FSMs that represent sequences of states and transitions. Since FSMs are a low level representation, it becomes cumbersome to capture multiple scenarios in an FSM. Thus FSMs designed by hand tend to be rigid and do not allow scenarios other than the specified "normal" ones. A protocol transitions from state to state as a result of the actions of the interacting agents. A transition is usually labeled with the actions that cause it. In

---

* We are grateful to the anonymous referees for their useful comments. We would like to thank Ashok Mallya and Pinar Yolum for the helpful discussions. This work is supported by the National Science Foundation under grant DST-0139037.

F. Dignum (Ed.): ACL 2003, LNAI 2922, pp. 183–200, 2004.

an FSM, the states and the actions in the protocol are meaningless tokens. The agent is limited to executing one of the sequences of actions hard-coded by its designer. These sequences represent the only legal behaviors of the agent. Anything the agent does outside of this protocol is considered a violation. This makes the protocol inflexible and, therefore, undesirable in open multiagent systems where agents are autonomous and heterogeneous, and opportunities and exceptions need to be handled appropriately.

Acting flexibly presupposes reasoning about the protocols. Reasoning formally presupposes that the protocols have a formal semantics. We base our semantics on the notion of commitments. Protocols can naturally be seen as an exchange and manipulation of commitments. A commitment is a directed obligation from one agent to another for achieving or maintaining a state of affairs. A commitment is social because it involves two parties and is publicly observable by all the agents in the agent society. Since a commitment is public, it is also possible to verify whether an agent has fulfilled its commitment, thereby making it possible to check an agent's compliance with a protocol.

This paper uses the NetBill e-commerce protocol [2] as a running example throughout the paper. Figure 1 shows an FSM representation of a NetBill simplified to focus on the core part. The customer, represented by c, sends a request for offers to the merchant, represented by m. The merchant sends an offer in response. If the customer accepts the offer, the merchant sends the goods. The customer then sends the payment for the goods in return for which the merchant sends a receipt. The only execution scenario possible in the protocol starts with the customer sending a request and ends with the merchant sending a receipt. The FSM in Figure 1 does not accommodate scenarios that would arise naturally in open and dynamic multiagent systems and is, therefore, unnecessarily rigid. Protocols for multiagent interaction should be flexible in the following ways:

- *Autonomy:* A protocol specification should not impinge on the autonomy of an agent beyond the essential nature of the interaction it describes. Consider a scenario where a customer wants to buy goods from a merchant. A desirable specification should not limit the autonomy of an merchant by preventing him from advertising his wares by sending an *offer* message prior to receiving a request for offers.
- *Opportunities:* A protocol should enable an agent to take advantage of opportunities that may arise. For example, if a merchant advertises an attractive deal to a customer, the customer should be able to entertain this offer.
- *Exceptions:* A protocol should enable an agent to deal with exceptions instead of aborting the interaction altogether. For example, a customer who doesn't have enough money might delegate a commitment to pay the merchant to some other agent. This is not allowed in the NetBill protocol as specified above.

The above forms of flexibility can be achieved only if we are able to reason about the content of the states and actions in a protocol. Often, the essential element of content in many protocols is the commitments of the different parties in a protocol. Specifically, we claim that if the protocol representation uses commitments and the criterion for protocol compliance is the satisfaction of commitments, then the above scenarios would be valid behaviors in the protocol.

We propose a formalism for specifying protocols called Nonmonotonic Commitment Machines (NCMs) that uses commitments for representing states and actions.

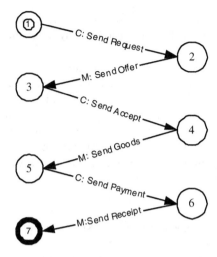

Fig. 1. FSM representation of the simplified NetBill protocol

The meaning of a state is given by the commitments that hold in that state; a state is a description of the world. The meaning of an action is given by how it manipulates commitments. An NCM does not directly specify sequences of states and transitions. Instead, it specifies rules in Nonmonotonic Causal Logic (NCL) [3]. These rules model the changes in the state of a protocol as a result of execution of actions. The inference mechanism of NCL computes new states at runtime. Yolum and Singh [4] first studied commitment machines. They did not consider situations during the execution of a protocol when agents must act with incomplete information. In such situations, the agent would need nonmonotonic or defeasible reasoning. Since NCL supports nonmonotonic reasoning, NCMs can express defaults in a protocol in a natural manner. Protocols represented as NCMs are more elaboration tolerant [5] than those represented using classical logic or FSMs. We develop a causal theory of commitments and represent the NetBill protocol as an NCM using that theory.

The rest of the paper is organized as follows. Section 2 motivates the need for nonmonotonic logic for protocol representation and describes the NCL that we employ for this purpose. Section 3 provides a description of commitments. Section 4 formalizes commitments and NetBill in this logic. Section 5 discusses the relevant literature and section 6 discusses future directions.

2 Nonmonotonic Causal Logic

In logic, the consequence relation $\vdash$ is a relation between sets of propositions and individual propositions. $A \vdash x$, where A is a set of propositions and x is a proposition, means that x is a logical consequence of A. Classical logic is monotonic meaning that if $A \subseteq B$, where $A \vdash x$ and B is a set of propositions, then $B \vdash x$. Informally, monotonicity means that the addition of new information does not invalidate old information. Therefore, making rules defeasible in the face of change poses difficulties. Consider Example 1.

Example 1. A customer may not return goods received and should pay for them. However, if the goods are damaged, then the customer may return the goods and then cancel his commitment to pay.

Example 1 involves defeasible reasoning. The *default* rule is that the commitment to pay cannot be canceled. (A more accurate rule is that the debtor of a commitment cannot cancel his commitment. However, the above simplified version is adequate for this example.) The general rule is defeasible, i.e., if a special condition applies, like when the goods are damaged and they are returned, the commitment can be canceled. The default rule should be applicable when no information about the condition is available. This is the essence of nonmonotonic reasoning. Such defeasible reasoning is beyond the realm of classical logic.

2.1   Introduction

To overcome the aforementioned difficulties in specifying protocols, we use NCL. We choose NCL because it has an intuitive syntax and semantics. The language $C+$ [3], which is based on NCL, has a semantics based on state transition systems which agrees with our intuition about protocols. Further, it has been shown to be elaboration tolerant [6]. NCL is a logic of *universal causation* meaning that every fact that is caused holds and every fact that holds is caused. Universal causation is not so much a philosophical stance as a practical one, as universal causation yields a uniform semantics for causal theories. Taking this stance makes NCL suitable for simulation and planning since everything can be explained. Also, in our domain, a commitment holds or does not hold only because there is a reason for it to hold or not hold. Moreover, as we show below, universal causation can be disabled for selected formulas.

The *signature* of a causal theory is the set α of symbols called *constants*. Each constant c is assigned a nonempty finite domain $Dom(c)$ of symbols. An *atom* is of the form $c = v$ where $v \in Dom(c)$. An *interpretation* of α is an assignment $c = v$ for each $c \in \alpha$ where $v \in Dom(c)$. Since we consider only boolean atoms, either $c = true$ or $c = false$. A *formula* in NCL is a combination of atoms using the connectives of classical logic. A causal rule is of the form $F \Leftarrow G$, where F and G are formulas of classical logic and are called the head and the body of the rule, respectively. This means that there is cause for F to be true if G is true. It does not say that G is the cause for F. This reflects the intuition that it is sufficient to know the conditions under which a fact is caused. As an example, consider a switch S that, when closed, lights two bulbs A and B. Even though A being lit is not the cause for B being lit, it is correct to say that there is a cause for B to be lit when A is lit. A theory in NCL consists of a set of causal rules.

Constants in causal theories are either *fluents* or *actions*. A causal theory describes histories of length $m+1$, $(m \geq 0)$, by creating for all i, $(i \in \{0, \ldots, m\})$, a copy of every fluent and, for all i, $(i \in \{0, \ldots, m-1\})$, a copy of every action. The interpretation of fluents for a particular i represents state s_i and the interpretation of actions in state s_i represent the transition to state s_{i+1}.

2.2   NCL Semantics

Models for formulas in NCL are defined in the same way as classical logic. An interpretation is a model of a set X of formulas iff it satisfies all the formulas in X. If every model of X satisfies a formula F, then X entails F, or symbolically $X \models F$. We can now define models of a causal theory. Let I be an interpretation of the signature α of a theory T. The reduct T^I is the set of all heads whose bodies are satisfied by the interpretation I. If I is also a unique model of T^I, then I is a model of T. If I is not a unique model of the reduct, then some constant is missing from the reduct, and therefore there is no explanation for that constant. But NCL is a logic of universal causation, therefore, no constant should be unexplained.

As an example, consider the following theory T_1 consisting of rules $R1$ and $R2$.

R1. $p \Leftarrow q$
R2. $q \Leftarrow q$

R1 says that there is a cause for p if q is true. R2 says that there is a cause for q. Reasoning informally using the principle of universal causation, we see that there is no cause for $\neg p$ to be true. Therefore, p has to be true. Therefore, p must be caused. The only way p can be caused is if q is true. And, q is caused by R2. Therefore, the only possible interpretation for this theory is $I = \{p = true, q = true\}$.

Intuitively, T^I represents facts that are caused, according to theory T under interpretation I. If a causal theory T has a model I, we say that it is consistent or satisfiable. If all models of T satisfy a formula F, that means T entails F or $T \models F$.

Coming back to our example theory T_1 with rules R1 and R2, we consider all the possible interpretations to see which, if any, is a model of T_1:

1. $I^1 = \{p = true, q = true\}$: $T_1^{I_1} = \{p, q\}$. I_1 is a unique model of $T_1^{I_1}$. Therefore, I_1 is a model of T_1.
2. $I^2 = \{p = false, q = true\}$: $T_1^{I_2} = \{p, q\}$. I_2 is not a model of $T_1^{I_2}$. Therefore, I_2 is not a model of T_1.
3. $I^3 = \{p = true, q = false\}$: $T_1^{I_3} = \{\}$. $T_1^{I_3}$ has no models. Therefore, I_3 is not a model of T_1.
4. $I^4 = \{p = false, q = false\}$: $T_1^{I_4} = \{\}$. $T_1^{I_4}$ has no models. Therefore, I_4 is not a model of T_1.

Note that $I^1 = \{p = true, q = true\}$ is the only model of this theory that matches the result of our informal reasoning.

To see how NCL is nonmonotonic, consider a theory T_2 consisting of the rule $c = 1 \Leftarrow c = 1$. This rule is like a default rule. The only model of T_2 is $I(c) = 1$. Now consider a theory T_3 such that it had two rules, $c = 1 \Leftarrow c = 1$ and $c = 2 \Leftarrow true$. Note that $T_2 \subseteq T_3$. However, the only model of T_3 is $I(c) = 2$.

2.3   Action Descriptions in C+

Recall that C+ is a high level action description language based on NCL. It is easier to specify theories in C+ than directly in NCL because of it's concise notation. Before we describe the syntax and semantics of NCL and C+ formally, we describe informally the meanings of some of C+ rules that we use later. A formula in C+ is a propositional combination of constants which could either be *action* constants or *fluent* constants. Actions in NCL are interpreted to be unit-length. This paper is restricted to boolean constants. An action constant being true represents the execution of the action. The meanings of the rules we use follow.

- *a causes b*, where *a* and *b* are actions.
  This means that action *a* causes action *b* and both happen concurrently.
- *a causes f*, where *a* is an action and *f* is a fluent.
  This means that action *a* causes *f* to hold in the next state.
- *A ∧ F causes b*, where *A* is a conjunction of actions, *b* is an action and *F* is a conjunction of fluents.
  This means that in a state where *F* is true and actions in *A* happen, then action *b* happens concurrently.
- *a causes a*, together with the rule *¬a causes ¬a*, where *a* is an action.
  These two rules mean that there is a cause for *a* and there is a cause for *¬a* respectively. In other words the *a* is exogenous, it simply happens or does not happen. Without these rules, the action is not exogenous. Universal causation is disabled for these rules.
- *a may cause f*, where *a* is an action and *f* is a fluent.
  This means that *f* may hold after *a*'s execution if it does not already hold. Thus, this rule expresses nondeterminism.
- *caused a after f*, where *a* is an action and *f* is a fluent.
  This means that *f* causes *a* in the same state. Notice that this rule uses the *caused* form and not the *causes* form because no suitable formulation in terms of *causes* exists. This rule expresses the causation of an action and differs from the rule *a causes f* above which expresses the causation of a fluent.
- Fluents are declared as *inertialFluents* meaning that their assignment persists from one state to the next unless changed by some other rule.

2.4   Translating C+ to NCL

Let's describe $C+$ formally and show the translation from rules in $C+$ to rules in NCL. $C+$ includes three kinds of rules, namely, static rules, fluent dynamic rules and action dynamic rules. A fluent can be either a *statically determined fluent* or a *simple (dynamic) fluent*. Static fluents can appear in the heads of only static rules. A *fluent formula* consists only of fluents. An *action formula* consists only of actions. A *static rule* is an expression of the form

R3.   *caused F if G*

where *F* and *G* are fluent formulas. Static rules express indirect effects of actions that are instantaneous with respect to the causal fluent formula. A dynamic rule is an expression of the form

R4.   *caused F if G after H*

It is called an *action dynamic rule* if *F* and *G* are both action formulas. It is called a *fluent dynamic rule* if *F* and *G* are both fluent formulas. Action dynamic rules express the causation of an action and fluent dynamic rules the causation of a fluent.

An action description D consisting of such rules is turned into a causal theory D_m where *m* is the length of the history. The signature α of D_m then consists of

1. $i{:}c$ for every fluent $c \in \alpha$ for every $i \in \{0, \ldots, m\}$
2. $i{:}c$ for every action $c \in \alpha$ for every $i \in \{0, \ldots, m{-}1\}$

The domain of $i{:}c$ is the same as $Dom(c)$ and $i{:}F$ means i is inserted in front of every occurrence of every constant in F. The rules of D_m are then:

R5. $i{:}F \Leftarrow i{:}G$, for every static rule R3 in D and every $i \in \{0, \ldots, m\}$;

R6. $i{:}F \Leftarrow i{:}G \land i{:}H$, for every action dynamic rule R4 in D and every $i \in \{0, \ldots, m{-}1\}$;

R7. $i{+}1{:}F \Leftarrow i{+}1{:}G \land i{:}H$, for every fluent dynamic rule R4 in D and every $i \in \{0, \ldots, m{-}1\}$;

R8. $0{:}c = v \Leftarrow 0{:}c = v$, for every simple fluent constant $c \in \alpha$ and every $v \in Dom(c)$. (Notice that every simple fluent has all possible values in the initial state and therefore, they are exogenous in the initial state. Thus, universal causation is disabled for them.)

All examples that follow are in the abbreviated $C{+}$ notation. We list the relevant $C{+}$ abbreviations below, extracted from [3].

A1. A dynamic rule of the form *caused F if true after H* abbreviates to *H causes F*.
A2. An action dynamic rules of the form *caused F if G after H* abbreviates to *G $\land$ H causes F*
A3. The action dynamic rules *caused a if a* and *caused ¬a if ¬a* where *a* is an action, together abbreviate to *exogenous a*. In $C{+}$ such an action is called an *exogenous-Action*.
A4. The fluent dynamic rules *caused p if p after p* and *caused ¬p if ¬p after ¬p* where *p* is a fluent together abbreviate to *inertial p*
A5. The fluent dynamic rule *caused F if F after H* abbreviates to *H may cause F*.

3 Commitments

Commitments among agents have been recognized as a fundamental notion in cooperative problem solving [7–9]. Castelfranchi [10] and Krogh [11] present, respectively, a social and logical perspective on commitments. In our work, we do not reason about the commitments from the point of view of cooperation among agents. We use commitments to specify protocols. As agents interact with each other using some protocol, they create and manipulate commitments. The breach of a commitment represents a violation of a protocol. The agent that is bound to fulfill the commitment is called the debtor of the commitment. The agent that is the beneficiary of the commitment is called the creditor.

Definition 1. *A base-level commitment C(x,y,G,p) binds a debtor x to a creditor y for fulfilling the condition p in context G.*

Definition 2. *A conditional commitment CC(x,y,G,p,q) denotes that if a condition p is brought about, then the commitment C(x,y,G,q) will hold.*

Both commitments and conditional commitments are created in a context G, which can be thought of as an institution or society whose rules are binding on the agents that join it. The context also defines the meanings of the terms used in the context. Henceforth, we omit G to reduce clutter.

Singh[12] lists operations for the creation and manipulation of commitments. These operations cannot be arbitrarily carried out. They are subject to metacommitments that are rules that govern the commitment operations and are part of the context G. The operations are listed below.

- *Create(x,y,p)* creates a new commitment $C(x,y,p)$.
- *Discharge(x,y,p)* discharges the existing commitment $C(x,y,p)$ so that it no longer holds.
- *Cancel(x,y,p)* cancels the existing commitment $C(x,y,p)$ so that it no longer holds.
- *Delegate(x,y,p,z)* delegates the commitment $C(x,y,p)$ to a new debtor z. More specifically, the original commitment $C(x,y,p)$ no longer holds and a new commitment $C(z,y,p)$ is created in its place.
- *Assign(x,y,p,z)* assigns the commitment $C(x,y,p)$ to a new creditor z. More specifically, the original commitment $C(x,y,p)$ no longer holds and a new commitment $C(x,z,p)$ is created in its place.
- *Release(x,y,p)* releases the debtor x from the commitment $C(x,y,p)$ so that the commitment no longer holds.

4   NCM Representation of Protocols

In our approach, we represent protocols as NCMs. An NCM is a causal theory in $C+$ that consists of two parts. The first part is a protocol-independent causal theory of commitments in which we capture the representation of commitments and the operations on them. The second part is protocol specific and includes constants and rules describing the given protocol's domain. The distinction between the two parts is only to separate out the domain independent part, logically they form a complete causal theory as we shall see later. We first present the theory of commitments and then model the NetBill protocol in causal logic. Together they represent the NetBill NCM.

4.1   Commitments in Causal Logic

We represent commitments and operations on them in the causal logic. Commitments in causal logic are declared to be constants of the type inertial fluents.

- $C(x,y,p)$, $CC(x,y,p,q)$ :: *inertialFluents*

where x and y are variables of the sort *agent* and p and q are variables of the sort *condition*. By declaring commitments to be *inertialFluents*, we include rules of the kind A4 for each commitment. Conditional commitments are declared as $CC(x,y,p,q)$ where q is also a variable of sort *condition*. Conditional commitments are also declared as *inertialFluents*. For each of the operations on commitments listed in Section 3, there is a declaration of the form

– ⟨ *Operation* ⟩ :: *action*

Constants of type *action* are not exogenous, that is, rules of the form A3 are not included in the theory. Their execution, therefore, has to be *caused* by other actions or fluents. We add two more operations for handling conditional commitments.

– *CDischarge(x,y,p,q), CCreate(x,y,p,q) :: action*

The following rules capture the meaning of the operations:

R9. *Create(x,y,p) causes C(x,y,p)*
R10. *Discharge(x,y,p) causes ¬C(x,y,p)*
R11. *Cancel(x,y,p) causes ¬C(x,y,p)*
R12. *Delegate(x,y,p,z) causes ¬C(x,y,p) & C(z,y,p)*
R13. *Release(x,y,p) causes ¬C(x,y,p)*
R14. *Assign(x,y,p,z) causes ¬C(x,y,p) & C(x,z,p)*
R15. *CCreate(x,y,p,q) causes CC(x,y,p,q)*
R16. *CDischarge(x,y,p,q) causes ¬CC(x,y,p,q) & C(x,y,q)*

All the variables are grounded such that $x \neq y$ and $p \neq q$. We omit the rules specifying the grounding of the variables. Since we want the operations to be *caused* by other things, then in those states where an operation is not caused, there must be a reason for it to be not caused. In other words, we want the operations to be partially exogenous. So for each of the commitment operations, we include rules of the form

R17. ¬⟨ Operation ⟩ *causes* ¬⟨ Operation ⟩

An example is the rule ¬*Create(x,y,p) causes* ¬*Create(x,y,p)*. The specification also includes rules to capture the restriction that no two commitment operations are concurrent.

4.2   NetBill Specification in Causal Logic

We now represent the NetBill protocol in causal logic. The following rules together with the theory of commitments given above represent the specification of NetBill NCM. We declare

– *m, c* to be of the sort *agent*
– *goodsc, payc, acceptc, receiptc* to be of the sort *condition*
– *request, offer, accept, goods, pay, receipt* to be *inertialFluents*
– *SendRequest, SendOffer, SendAccept, SendGoods, SendPayment, SendReceipt* to be *exogenousActions*.

The meanings of the above constants are as their name indicates. Conditions are an artifact of conditional commitments. We assume that all fluents and actions have unique identifiers. We have the following rules.

R18. *SendRequest causes request*
R19. *SendOffer causes offer*

R20. *SendOffer causes CCreate(m, c, acceptc, goodsc)*

R21. *SendAccept causes accept*

R22. *SendAccept & CC(m,c,acceptc,goodsc)*
     causes CDischarge(m,c,acceptc,goodsc)

R23. *SendAccept causes CCreate(c,m,goodsc,payc)*

R24. *SendGoods causes goods*

R25. *SendGoods causes CCreate(m, c, payc, receiptc)*

R26. *SendGoods & CC(c,m,goodsc,payc) causes CDischarge(c,m,goodsc,payc)*

R27. *SendGoods & C(m,c,goodsc) causes Discharge(m,c,goodsc)*

R28. *SendPayment causes pay*

R29. *SendPayment & CC(m,c,payc,receiptc) causes CDischarge(m,c,payc,receiptc)*

R30. *SendPayment & C(c,m,payc) causes CDischarge(c,m,payc)*

R31. *SendReceipt causes receipt*

R32. *SendReceipt & C(m,c,receiptc) causes Discharge(m,c,receiptc)*

In our representation no two commitment operations are concurrent. Also, no two protocol actions are concurrent. However, when a protocol action causes a commitment operation, they are concurrent. By rule R6, the interpretation of *ActionA causes ActionB* is such that *ActionA* and *ActionB* are concurrent. This ensures that the protocol action is concurrent with the commitment operation it causes is satisfied. There could be other concurrency models possible for NetBill. We choose this one because of its simplicity.

We now add rules for our motivating example, Example 1, to this protocol specification. We introduce *SendReturn* and *SendGoods* as exogenous actions. We introduce a new action *Ab* and a new fluent *damagedGoods* to indicate that the goods are damaged. We also include the nondeterministic rule R34 to say that as a result of the *SendGoods* action, the goods may be damaged. Rule R33 captures the condition that the cancel operation is not allowed for any commitment. Rule R35 however says that a commitment can be canceled under abnormal conditions. Rules R36 and R37 ensure that *Ab* is false, except when *damagedGoods* is true. We add the Rules R35 − R37 to accommodate Example 1. Rules R33 and R34 are already in the theory. *Ab* is an action because it has no meaning in the states. It acts as a qualifier for the exogenous action *SendReturn*.

R33. *¬Cancel(x,y,p) causes ¬Cancel(x,y,p)*

R34. *SendGoods may cause damagedGoods*

R35. *SendReturn ∧ C(c,m,pay) ∧ Ab causes Cancel(c,m,pay)*

R36. *caused Ab if damagedGoods*

R37. *¬Ab causes ¬Ab*   .

The theory also contains rules that place constraints on the actions so that the execution of actions makes sense. For example, we specify that the *SendRequest* action cannot happen after the payment has been made. Rules

4.3   Executing NetBill in CCalc

CCalc (Causal Calculator) is a reasoning tool that implements causal logic. Given a causal theory and a goal in the form of a query, *CCalc* finds paths to the goal. We load the NetBill NCM into *CCalc* and pose queries one after the other. *CCalc* then finds paths to satisfy each query.

```
:- query
label::0;
maxstep:: 3;
0: -offer,
    -accept,
    -returned,
    -goods,
    -C(x,y,p),
    -CC(x,y,p,q),
    -pay,
    -request,
    -receipt,
    -damagedGoods;
maxstep: returned.
```

Fig. 2. Example Query

Figure 2 shows an example query. This query asks for an execution sequence of three of fewer steps, beginning from a state in which all fluents are false, in which the goods have been returned. Running this query in *CCalc* produces the output as shown in Figure 3 (formatted for readability).

The action *SendAccept* is caused which in turn causes the *CCreate* which creates the conditional commitment that if the goods are sent then the customer will pay. The result of these actions is reflected in state 1. *SendGoods* is then caused which reflects the fact that the merchant has sent the goods. *SendGoods* causes the discharge of the conditional commitment created by the customer resulting in the customer's commitment to pay. *SendGoods* also creates a new conditional commitment that if the customer pays then the merchant will send the receipt. This example is interesting as *SendGoods* also causes *damagedGoods*, resulting in state 2. *damagedGoods* causes *Ab* in state 2. So the *SendReturn* action is successful, which in turn causes the cancellation of the commitment to pay. State 3 is the resulting state which also satisfies the goal state of our query.

5   Discussion

Our focus in this work is to develop meaningful representations of agent communication protocols. We do so by using commitments to declaratively represent states and actions. This gives our representation a verifiable semantics [13]. By using commitments to model protocols, we constrain protocols no more than is necessary. We have highlighted the need for a nonmonotonic logic for commonsense reasoning in protocols. We used NCL towards this end and showed how a protocol can be represented in NCL. Like the NCL, there are a few other noteworthy formalisms for reasoning about action and change. Dynamic Logic [14] is a modal logic augmented with an algebra of regular events. However, it is monotonic and therefore not suitable for our purposes. Event Calculus [15] and situation calculus [16] have been extended with circumscription to enable nonmonotonic reasoning.

```
Solution:

State 0:

ACTIONS:    CCreate(c,m,goodsc,payc)
            SendAccept

State 1:    CC(c,m,goodsc,payc) accept

ACTIONS:    CCreate(m,c,payc,receiptc)
            CDischarge(c,m,goodsc,payc)
            SendGoods

State 2:    C(c,m,payc) CC(m,c,payc,receiptc)
            accept goods damagedGoods

ACTIONS:    Cancel(c,m,payc) Ab Return

State 3:    CC(m,c,payc,receiptc) accept
            goods returned damagedGoods
```

Fig. 3. Answer

Both FSMs and NCMs are formal representations of protocols. Both approaches are verifiable and in the case of an FSM, trivially so. An NCM, though, represents meaning. Agents that can reason about commitments take actions accordingly. For example, if, as part of a particular protocol, an agent enters into a commitment, then the agent can plan its actions, even those not directly related to the protocol, so that the commitment is never violated. Alternate paths through the protocol may be selected based on criteria like safety or number of messages exchanged. For example, an agent can adopt an approach where it does not commit unless another agent also commits for some desirable condition. Also it is not convenient to express defaults in FSMs. In fact, the defaults wouldn't be obvious at all in an FSM. FSMs are also not as elaboration tolerant as NCMs.

5.1 Conventional Protocols and Protocol Modeling

Conventional protocols like TCP/IP, RPC, HTTP, and so on have a well-defined environment and scope. Their focus is on the correct delivery of data and they are therefore strict in the sense that they prescribe all paths for correct execution as well as for error recovery. Modeling such protocols as FSMs is usually sufficient. Notable among other formalisms for modeling protocols are Petri Nets [17] and statecharts [18]. Petri Nets have proven to be especially useful in modeling concurrency. Petri nets specify transitions (T-elements) between places (P-elements) which are sets of conditions. Statecharts is a visual formalism that extends state machines by adding support for hierarchy, concurrency and communication. Statecharts provide the designer the power to cluster states into super-states as well as refine states, thereby leading to compact representations for complex behavior. Statecharts can also represent defaults. However, statecharts also specify the transitions between states. As such, neither petri nets nor statecharts afford much flexibility. Statecharts though, are easier to comprehend because of the ability to cluster and refine states unlike NCMs where the specification may become difficult to manage as the number of rules increase.

5.2   Commitments

Commitments have been studied in the context of distributed problem solving and coordination. Bratman [7] argues that for shared cooperative activity, among other things, commitment to joint activity and commitment to mutual support are required. Grosz and Kraus [9] investigate the formulation of shared plans for coordinating group action. In their framework, an agent can adopt two types on intentions, intend-to and intend-that, that commit the agent to an action and state of affairs respectively. Jennings [19] presents commitments as a fundamental notion for efficient coordination in distributed systems. Jennings also mentions conventions which monitor the commitments and state when a commitment may be reassessed. Jennings further reformulates different models of coordination in terms of commitments. A distinguishing feature of all of the above work is that they present commitments as a mentalistic notion, assuming a system of cooperative agents. Shoham's agent oriented computing paradigm [8] introduces obligation as a modality required to describe the mental state of an agent. Sandholm and Lesser [20] study automated negotiation among self-interested agents whose computations are resource bounded. They argue that protocols that have leveled commitments, that is, when commitments vary from breakable to unbreakable in a continuum by assigning a function to evaluate the cost of breach of each commitment, are more suitable for contracts than full commitment protocols. Krogh [11] examines the possibility of using of deontic logic for analyzing multiagent systems. Castelfranchi [10] presents an ontology of commitments with the aim of understanding organizational activity. He defines social commitment as a relation between two or more agents and discusses its various aspects. Singh [13] defends a commitment-based social semantics for agent communication.

We do not study commitments from the point of view of coordination. However as we pointed out earlier in this section, an agent can reason about its future actions depending upon the commitments it already has or ones that the agent might have to make in the future. Also, we do not specify that commitments necessarily have to be represented in an agent's state. We are exploring the possibility of compiling NCMs into FSMs that have no representations of commitments (see section 6 for details). We are also not concerned directly with the economic impact of the breach of a commitment. Though we specify protocols in a logical language using commitments, we do not present a deontic logic. Social commitments, that is, directed obligation from one agent to another, represent the cornerstone of our research. Our scope is limited to the flexible specification of protocols and their verification.

5.3   Protocols

Yolum and Singh [4] proposed commitment machines and also showed how event calculus can be used to represent protocols and generate new paths in the protocols [21]. They do not consider commonsense reasoning situations. Koning and Huget [22] describe a methodology for designing interaction protocols for multiagent systems. In their work, the focus is on reusability and modularity of protocols. They achieve this by composing protocols out of microprotocols using a formal language called *Communication Protocol Description Language* (CPDL). A formula in CPDL corresponds to an edge going from an initial state to a final state. The edge is labeled with a sequence of microprotocols which makes the protocol quite rigid. Koning and Huget also do not consider which microprotocols can be composed. This job is presumably left to the designer. With our commitment-based approach, it is possible for the agent to determine which protocols can be composed by looking at the states in the protocol.

5.4   Agent Communication Languages

An agent communication language (ACL) allows agents of heterogeneous designs to interact. Developing a semantics for agent communication languages (ACLs) that is expressive and verifiable has been a long standing goal of the agent community. To be verifiable, an ACL should have social semantics [23]. Earlier efforts at standardization of ACLs like Arcol [24] and KQML [25] promoted mental agency, that is, they were based on mental concepts like beliefs and intentions, and were therefore, not verifiable. The ongoing efforts at standardizing ACLs are based on communicative acts. The problem with giving a communicative acts based semantics is that it is not clear what the meanings of the communicative acts should be. Also it is not clear how many communicative acts are needed. Another challenge is relating the communicative acts to the conversation in which they occur. By giving semantics to protocols directly we are able to give a simple, operational characterization of protocols without getting bogged down with the above issues.

Dignum and van Linder [26], and Guerin and Pitt [27] define ACLs in term of communicative acts. Dignum and van Linder's framework considers four components, the *information* component, the *action* component, the *motivational* component and the *social* component as constituting an agent framework and formally describes and relates them. The framework is developed in dynamic logic which is monotonic. They postulate a COMMIT communicative act, but other communicative acts have mentalistic preconditions which makes the framework suitable only for a system of cooperative agents.

Guerin and Pitt propose an ACL specification in which declarative ACL specifications are given procedural interpretations. An ACL specification in their approach, consists of three parts: a *Converse Function* that specifies permissions and obligations for subsequent speech acts based on the conversation state, a *Protocol Semantics* that captures protocol dependent meanings of speech acts, and a *Speech-Act Semantics* that give the protocol independent part of the meaning. It is not clear how useful it is to model the protocol-independent part of the meaning, since most meaning comes from the protocol.

6   Future Directions

Our main aim in this work is to come up with protocols that have verifiable semantics and constrain the agent no more than to the extent necessary to carry out legal interactions. To carry our work further, we have identified the following future directions.

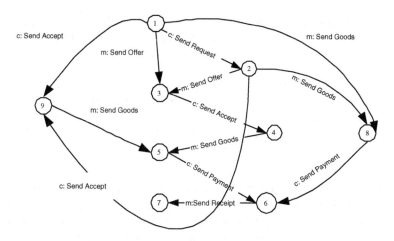

Fig. 4. FSM representation of the extended NetBill protocol

Compiling NCMs into FSMs: The preceding sections present commitment-based semantics for interaction protocols and show how an agent can reason with commitments.
However, it is not necessary that agents be able to reason about commitments to execute a protocol. For some applications efficient execution might be important. It may
also be the case that an agent designer wants to exclude certain risky or lengthy paths
(behaviors) in the protocol. For such agents, it would be useful if we could compile an
NCM into an FSM. The complete NCM need not be compiled into an FSM. A designer
could selectively compile behaviors (sequences of transitions) from an NCM into an
FSM. The FSM can then be executed without an inference engine. Another advantage
of compilation instead of directly designing or extending an FSM is that it is not always clear how to add states and transitions to an FSM. Compilation from an NCM
makes this process automatic. Figure 4 shows an example FSM for NetBill, that may
be compiled from the action description presented in Section 4.2.

Since C+ action descriptions have a transition system semantics, it should be relatively straightforward to compile NCMs into FSMs. An important future direction is to
formally define NCMs in terms of C+ action descriptions and present a procedure for
compiling NCMs into FSMs. It is equally important to prove that the generated FSM
is sound and complete with respect to the NCM it was compiled from. We are also investigating ways to automatically compile FSMs from NCMs. Selective compilation is
also a subject of future research.

Protocol Specification: While our formulation of NCM has some desirable properties
like declarative rules and elaboration tolerance, it lacks other properties desirable in
protocols such as a comprehensible graphical representation, role bindings for agents
and temporal model checking [28]. For example, we cannot prove satisfactorily if the
NetBill NCM is correct and complete. A related piece of work is to compare NCMs
with other formalism like statecharts and Petri Nets in more depth. Another interesting
avenue to explore is the compilation of NCMs into more expressive graphical formalism
like statecharts.

Protocol Distribution: In the NCM representation of NetBill, we did not specify roles in the protocol. However, an agent will be executing the role that it adopts in the protocol. We want to formulate procedures based on symbol manipulation to distribute a centralized protocol among the various roles in the protocol. The result will be roles skeletons that are also NCMs. It is not clear what the specification of a role itself should be. Is a role just a label, or does it specify the required capability of an agent to adopt a role along with normative rules and authorizations that come along with the role? Another technical challenge is proving that a distributed protocol is sound and complete with respect to the centralized protocol.

Creating Role Skeletons from BPEL Flows: BPEL [29], the Business Process Execution Language is a draft standard for specifying and coordinating business processes. Intuitively, it is a process flow graph with nodes as tasks and edges as messages. Business flows, as they are currently specified, are like FSMs in the sense that they have been designed with certain scenarios in mind. As such, they are quite rigid. To make business processes more flexible, we envisage the following design-time methodology.

1. The designers start with an interaction diagram or state machine or some other graphical representation for the protocol that is to be modeled as a BPEL flow.
2. The designers build NCM representation of the protocol with enhancements to make it more flexible and then partition the NCM into the role skeletons.
3. The role skeletons are compiled into FSMs
4. Compile FSMs into a BPEL flow. This should be easier than compiling an NCM into a BPEL flow.

We plan to build a tool which incorporates this methodology. The tool would suggest enhancements to the designer for a given protocol, build an NCM based on the choices of the designer and compile it into an FSM and then, perhaps with annotations from the user, compile it into a BPEL flow.

Verifying Strategies: It will often be the case that an agent is confronted with the problem of selecting between multiple paths that it can take to reach a goal. The agent selects a path based on some strategy. For example, if the customer does not trust a merchant, the customer might adopt a strategy where it never pays before receiving the goods. On the other hand, if it does, it could adopt a strategy where it accepts to buy goods for a certain price without even asking the merchant for offers or pays before getting the goods. It is possible to imagine more complex strategies. An interesting problem is the specification of strategies with respect to commitments and determining which protocols (more specifically, paths in the protocol) satisfy a given strategy. An agent can then inspect a role to check whether it satisfies its strategy.

We conclude by saying that this work represents the first step in the development of a comprehensive methodology for designing flexible multiagent interaction protocols. Development of the protocol design tool that incorporates this methodology is the primary objective of this research.

References

1. Smith, R.G.: The contract net protocol: High-level communication and control in a distributed problem solver. IEEE Transactions on Computers **29** (1980) 1104–1113
2. Cox, B., Tygar, J., Sirbu, M.: Netbill security and transaction protocol. In: Proceedings of the First USENIX Workshop on Electronic Commerce. (1995) 77–88
3. Giunchiglia, E., Lee, J., Lifschitz, V., McCain, N., Turner, H.: Nonmonotonic causal theories. Artificial Intelligence (2003) To appear.
4. Yolum, P., Singh, M.P.: Commitment machines. In: Proceedings of the 8th International Workshop on Agent Theories, Architectures, and Languages (ATAL-01), Springer-Verlag (2002) 235–247
5. McCarthy, J.: Elaboration tolerance. In progress (1999) http://www-formal.stanford.edu/jmc/elaboration.html.
6. Lifschitz, V.: Missionaries and cannibals in the causal calculator. In: Proceedings of the 7th International Conference on Principles of Knowledge Representation and Reasoning. (2000) 85–96
7. Bratman, M.E.: Shared cooperative activity. The Philosophical Review **101** (1992) 327–341
8. Shoham, Y.: Agent-oriented programming. Artificial Intelligence **60** (1993) 51–92
9. Grosz, B.J., Kraus, S.: Collaborative plans for complex group action. Artificial Intelligence **86** (1996) 269–357
10. Castelfranchi, C.: Commitments: From individual intentions to groups and organizations. In: Proceedings of the AAAI-93 Workshop on AI and Theories of Groups and Organizations: Conceptual and Empirical Research. (1993)
11. Krogh, C.: Obligations in multiagent systems. In Åmodt, A., Komorowski, J., eds.: Scandinavian Artificial Intelligence Conference 1995 (SCAI'95), Trondheim (1995) 19–30
12. Singh, M.P.: An ontology for commitments in multiagent systems: Toward a unification of normative concepts. Artificial Intelligence and Law **7** (1999) 97–113
13. Singh, M.P.: A social semantics for agent communication languages. In: Proceedings of the 1999 IJCAI Workshop on Agent Communication Languages, Springer-Verlag (2000)
14. Harel, D., Kozen, D., Tiuryn, J.: Dynamic Logic. MIT Press, Cambridge, MA (2000)
15. Kowalski, R., Sergot, M.: Logic-based calculus of events. New Generation Computing **4** (1986) 67–95
16. McCarthy, J.: Situations, actions and causal laws. TR, Stanford University (1963)
17. Girault, C., Valk, R.: Petri Nets for System Engineering. (2003)
18. Harel, D.: Statecharts: A visual formalism for complex systems. Science of Computer Programming **8** (1987) 231–274
19. Jennings, N.R.: Commitments and conventions: The foundation of coordination in multi-agent systems. Knowledge Engineering Review **2** (1993) 223–250
20. Sandholm, T., Lesser, V.: Issues in automated negotiation and electronic commerce: Extending the contract net framework. In: [?]. (1998) 66–73 (Reprinted from *Proceedings of the International Conference on Multiagent Systems, 1995*).
21. Yolum, P., Singh, M.P.: Flexible protocol specification and execution: Applying event calculus planning using commitments. In: Proceedings of the 1st International Joint Conference on Autonomous Agents and MultiAgent Systems (AAMAS), ACM Press (2002) 527–534
22. Koning, J.L., Huget, M.P.: A semi-formal specification language dedicated to interaction protocols. In Kangassalo, H., Jaakkola, H., Kawaguchi, E., eds.: Information Modeling and Knowledge Bases XII, Frontiers in Artificial Intelligence and Applications. IOS Press (2001)
23. Singh, M.P.: Agent communication languages: Rethinking the principles. IEEE Computer **31** (1998) 40–47
24. Sadek, D.: Compliance in Arcol (1997) Personal communication.

25. Finin, T., Fritzson, R., McKay, D., McEntire, R.: KQML as an agent communication language. In: Proceedings of the International Conference on Information and Knowledge Management, ACM Press (1994) 456–463
26. Dignum, F., van Linder, B.: Modelling social agents: Towards deliberate communication. In: Handbook of Defeasible Reasoning and Uncertainty Management Systems, Kluwer (2002) 357–380
27. Guerin, F., Pitt, J.: Denotational semantics for agent communication languages. In: Proceedings of the Fifth International Conference on Autonomous Agents, ACM Press (2001) 497–504
28. Holzmann, G.J.: Design and Validation of Computer Protocols. Prentice-Hall, London (1991)
29. W3C: Business process execution language for web services, version 1.1. (2003) URL: http://www-106.ibm.com/developerworks/webservices/library/ws-bpel/.

Issues in Multiparty Dialogues

David Traum

Institute for Creative Technologies
University of Southern California
Marina del Rey, CA, USA

Abstract. This article examines some of the issues in representation of, processing, and automated agent participation in natural language dialogue, considering expansion from two-party dialogue to multi-party dialogue. These issues include Some regarding the roles agents play in dialogue, interactive factors, and content management factors.

1 Introduction

Most formal and computational studies of natural language dialogue have considered only the two-party case. E.g., communication between two people, a person and a dialogue system, or a pair of agents. In this article, we consider several issues in dialogue management, and how the nature of the problem changes when considering multiple participants. For many of these issues, we refer to the dialogue models in the *Mission Rehearsal Exercise* (MRE) Project [1, 2]. The MRE project [3] uses virtual humans to help train decision-making in a team context, by allowing a human trainee to rehearse simulated missions, interacting with the virtual humans using spoken and multi-modal communication in an embodied virtual world. Each virtual human maintains its own model of a plan, goals, beliefs, team tasks, dialogue state, negotiation state [4], and emotional state [5]. Virtual humans can understand and talk to the human trainee, as well as other virtual humans (using an agent communication language modelled on the physical performance of speech, indicating the verbal and non-verbal information expressed and the timing of actions). In the initial, Bosnia scenario, the trainee plays the role of an Army Lieutenant platoon leader, facing a dilemma in a peacekeeping situation. The Lieutenant must communicate with a Sergeant, a Medic, and others including platoon members and local citizens as well as more distant units by radio. Since the trainee has considerable flexibility in how he chooses to communicate, and the aim is to immerse the user in a realistic simulation, many issues in multi-party and multi-modal communication must be addressed.

2 Participant Roles

There are a number of different types of participant roles that are important for dialogue interaction. These include both local roles that shift during the

F. Dignum (Ed.): ACL 2003, LNAI 2922, pp. 201–211, 2004.
© Springer-Verlag Berlin Heidelberg 2004

conversation, such as speaker and hearer, roles tied to the activities that the dialogue is a part of, and more permanent social roles that transcend particular dialogues.

2.1   Conversational Roles

At the most immediate level, there are the conversational roles. For two party dialogue, there are the basic roles of speaker and listener/addressee. When we consider multi-party communication, there are two related sub-issues: who can receive (is intended to receive) an utterance, and who is it addressed to. For instance an agent A might want to ask a question of agent B, but might also want C to hear the question as well. Likewise, D might also hear the question even though A had no intention for D to do so. There a number of types of other listener roles, including ratified by the speaker (intended to hear the communication) or not, known to be listening by the speaker, or not. Clark gives a taxonomy of some of these listener roles [6]. An additional consideration is whether the listener is in-context or out of context. An in-context listener (who has heard the previous relevant utterances) may interpret an utterance quite differently from one who comes in without this context (or worse, with a partial or different context). There are also roles that we can use to characterize agents with respect to a whole conversation, as well as a specific utterance. *Active* Participants may take up speaker and addressee roles in a conversation, and generally are engaged and attentive to the conversation. Overhearers (who may be ratified or not) are also part of the conversation, in that they will receive and interpret the constituent utterances, and utterances may be planned with them in mind (either to facilitate or block understanding), but do not play a main part in the conversation. Finally some agents may be un-involved in the conversation.

2.2   Speaker Identification

In two-party dialogue, speaker identification is not a real issue - any speech that does not come from oneself must come from the other participant. In multi-party situations, it may not be so trivial [7]. If just a single audio stream is present, one can use a number of features as evidence for identifying speakers. These include acoustic features of the voice itself, as well as stylistic features, and self-identifications (in the case where one can trust the speaker to provide accurate information). If multi-modal information is available, additional cues can be used. E.g., stereo microphone arrays can localize the position of the speech, and thus give clues as to the speaker's identity. Likewise, visual information (e.g., of lips moving or other speech-related gestures), can help an agent identify the speaker. When multiple agents are involved in dialogue, it can also be important to provide cues to others as to who is speaking. For agent-agent communication, it is easy to put identifying information in the message channel itself. For humans, however, it may be helpful to provide other cues, such as different voices, and visual cues such as lip movement and gestures for the speaking agent's body or avatar.

1. **If** utterance specifies addressee (e.g., a vocative or utterance of just a name when not expecting a short answer or clarification of type person)
   then Addressee = specified addressee
2. **else if** speaker of current utterance is the same as the speaker of the immediately previous utterance
   then Addressee = previous addressee
3. **else if** previous speaker is different from current speaker
   then Addressee = previous speaker
4. **else if** unique other conversational participant
   then Addressee = participant
5. **else** Addressee unknown

Fig. 1. MRE Agent Speech Addressee Identification Algorithm

2.3   Addressee Recognition

In the two party case, like speaker identification, addressee identification is trivial: whoever is not speaking is the intended recipient of an utterance. In the multi-party case, we must consider *hearers* and *addressees* separately, as discussed above. Hearers of a spoken utterance can be computed by properties such as volume-level of speech, ambient noise, and distance and perceptual abilities of other agents. For agent messages delivered through a router, or other network channels, it may be possible to specify the exact set of receivers of the message.

For calculating the addressee(s) of an utterance several types of information can be used. First, the speaker may directly indicate the addressee using a vocative expression (e.g., calling by name or role). One may also use information included in the content of an utterance, if, e.g., it would be clear that that content would only be addressed to a specific individual. Context is also an important clue – e.g., who had previously spoken or been addressed. If multimodal information is available this can also play an important clue: e.g., gaze or body orientation at a particular individual. Likewise, attention getting or deictic gestures are also clues. If one is the only observable hearer, that can also be a reason to assume the hearer is the addressee. The algorithm used for computing addressees in the MRE project is shown in Figure 1.

2.4   Other Participant Roles

In addition to the conversational roles, there are also specific task roles, relating participants to tasks in a variety of ways. In two-party dialogue, typically agents are either performers of a task or those who desire the task to be done, although more complex relationships are possible. For multi-party team situations, such as those in MRE, more complex models are required to support negotiation and team action [4]. We distinguish the agent who will perform a primitive task, from the agent who is *responsible* for a complex task (this agent might perform all of the sub-actions, or might coordinate a team of actors). Also, some tasks have a *authority*, who can authorize the team-members to carry out the task. This might be different both from the responsible party, the performers of the primitive acts, and agents who actually desire the task to be performed. Agents might also be *guards* for a task, e.g., making sure that it is *not* performed.

Some activities involving dialogue have specific roles, each with designated rights and responsibilities concerning participation in dialogue. This is true even for two party dialogue, such as shopkeeper and buyer, or information seeker and information provider, however much more complex relationships are possible with multiple participants and roles. These can include the ability and length and content of turns, right to assign turns, right to set and change the topic of the conversation. Courtroom dialogue is a striking case with many distinct roles, such as judge, clerk, prosecutor, defense counsel, and witness [8]. Roles may be filled by a single individual, or multiple individuals may fulfil the same role. Likewise, a single individual may play multiple roles.

There are also *social roles* that go beyond a single activity, but structure multiple interactions and tasks. Two types of social roles include status roles (e.g., superior, subordinate, equal, incomparable), and closeness (e.g., friend, comrade, colleague, acquaintance, stranger, opponent, antagonist). These roles will influence the kinds of interaction allowed (e.g., only a superior may give an order to a subordinate), to how likely one will be to adopt the attitudes of another, or comply with their perceived desires. There are also *institutional roles*, such as office in a company, or military rank, defined by the institution.

3 Interaction Management

There are a number of aspects of managing the flow of communication, including the issues of who speaks when, what is the topic under discussion (and how it shifts), and what communicative channels are used (for which topics). Each of these are research topics even for two-party conversation, but become more complex with multiple agents.

3.1 Turn Management

There has been a fair amount of work on turn-taking even for two-party dialogue. The basic questions are when to speak and when to stop speaking. Older dialogue systems generally force rigid turn-taking, where one party must wait until the other finishes before speaking. Many more recent systems allow "barge-in", where a human who already understands a system query may provide the answer before the system has finished the utterance. Other systems allow interruptions by both parties, to correct or initiate something new, as well as to respond to the current utterance. Speakers can give verbal and non-verbal signals of continuation or imminent termination of the turn. Speakers use prosody, sentence structure, filled pauses (e.g., "uhhh"), as well as gaze and gesture. Turn-taking can be modelled using these cues as well as timing information to recognize turn-taking acts [9] such as `take-turn release-turn` and `keep-turn`.

In multi-party dialogue turn-taking is more complex, since more agents are available to potentially take the turn. As well as simply more agents competing for the turn, more actions are possible, e.g., assigning the turn to a particular next speaker vs just releasing it to whoever wants to speak next. Likewise, one may need to request the turn in order to be able to take it, especially if one is not already an active participant.

3.2   Channel Management

In uni-modal communication systems, such as simple telephone speech systems, channel management is very similar to turn-management, though differences may arise if the communication channel enforces a single communicator at a time (as with half-duplex circuits, or chat systems which allow only one person to type at a time). In multi-channel systems, however, there is an additional issue of which channel to use for which content, as well as the timing of the contributions. Channels can be using the same modality (e.g., a radio with different frequencies, or a chat system with different chat rooms or different communication commands), or different modalities, e.g., in the MRE system, agents can use verbal communication for face to face or radio communications, and can also use gaze and gesture in the visual mode for face to face communications. One could thus use the speech channel as the main communicative mode, while using the visual mode for *backchannels*, indicating attention and understanding.

For multi-party dialogue, one can simultaneously have multiple "main-channels", e.g., one per topic, one per conversation, or one per set of participants. Thus, one may have simultaneous communication that is not interruption, because of occurring on different channels between different participants.

3.3   Thread/Conversation Management

Turn and channel management concern when and where communication take place. Thread management concerns what is being communicated, specifically which topics are discussed when, and how to organize the progression of topics. Traditional models follow a stack-based topic organization [10], in which one can have hierarchical organization of topics, but not parallel topics under discussion at the same time – when one goes back to a previous topic, one should "pop" the current topic from the stack. Even for two-party conversation, this may be too restrictive [11], especially when multiple channels can be used (e.g., many chat systems, in which two people can type simultaneously without seeing the text until one hits return, and topics often proceed in pairs). With multiple participants, it is also much easier to keep multiple topics open, with different sets of participants.

Another issue is that of multiple conversations. Most current dialogue systems are concerned with only a single conversation with a single user. In contrast, many tasks require different periods of communication separated by periods of task performance or maintenance in which no communication is required. While some of the information that is conveyed during a prior communication episode is maintained by the participants, often the specific dialogue structure such as the turn and topic structure is not preserved. While it maybe be best to model separate conversations even for extended two-party dialogue, it is essential for multi-party dialogue, where multiple groups of participants communicate with different groups, using different media, about different topics. Having multiple conversation models allows each one to have its own structure, which can be simple and independent of the structure of other conversations that might be going on at the same time. For example, in the MRE Bosnia domain, there is usually a main conversation between Lieutenant, Sergeant and sometimes medic, and subordinate conversations between the Lieutenant and other units over the radio, and between the sergeant and troop members on specific tasks. Each conversation has its own starting, body, and ending phases, as well as participant roles. In some circumstances, especially when multiple participants are part of a conversation, participants can dynamically enter and leave a conversation while it is ongoing. In more complex situations, such as cocktail party conversation, conversations can also split and merge dynamically.

Sometimes multiple conversations are not completely independent. This occurs especially when they share a participant, so that different conversations must compete for attention of the participant. Sometimes topics are linked as well. One conversation might be dependent on another, E.g., if agent A asks agent B a question in conversation m, and then B must query agent C in conversation n in order to reply to A. In this case conversation m is dependent on conversation n, at least for that content. Sometimes conversations are not dependent, but influenced by another. E.g., when participants overhear another conversation and take up the same topic (or comment on the other conversation in some way).

When multiple threads are going on at the same time, it can be tricky to determine which thread a particular utterance belongs to. For the two-party, single conversation case, one can usually rely on topical coherence and cue phrases to determine whether the current utterance continues an existing thread, ends a thread, or begins a new one (and at which level of structure). With multiple participants and multiple conversations which may share participants, the problem becomes more difficult. One can use a number of relationships to try to match the utterance to the proper conversation. There may be a connection between a conversation and a channel, in that case observing the utterance on that channel may help determine the conversation. Likewise, there is a relationship between the addressee and the conversation. As in Figure 1, where knowledge of the conversation was used to help predict the addressee, knowledge of the addressee can point to a conversation containing that addressee as a participant. There is also a relationship between topics and conversations. Identifying the topic of an utterance may help determine which conversation it belongs to, and vice versa.

3.4   Initiative Management

Initiative (or control) [12–16], concerns which agent is currently setting the agenda for topics of discussion. If one agent has the initiative, then another agent does take turns, but only to react to what was said, not to start new topics. Two-party dialogue systems are traditionally either user-initiative (such as question answering systems, where a user may pose a query, and the system consults a database and provides an answer) or system-initiative, in which the system asks a series of queries to specify the parameters for a service request. More recently, *mixed-initiative* systems allow user and system to both take the initiative at different points. E.g., system can take the initiative when there are problems in communication, to direct toward possible solutions,and human can take control to more efficiently provide known information.

In multi-party dialogues, initiative is less symmetric than two party dialogues for equivalent tasks [17]. Thus, the more participants in a conversation, the less likely it will be that each participant has an equal amount of initiative. Team leaders tend to develop, either formally, or informally, who structure the interaction. Other kinds of initiative are also possible, e.g., cross-initiative, where a responder does not take initiative herself, but redirects it to a third party (who might not even have been active), or in which a third party interjects. There are also issues of cross-conversation initiative, e.g. in the case of one conversation being dependent on another, the initiative-holder of one conversation is really taking direction from someone else in another conversation.

3.5   Attention Management

Attention is mostly assumed to be always present for most single-user, single-system dialogue systems. Even when attention is explicitly modelled, it is usually a binary decision of either being on the conversation and other participant, or elsewhere. In multi-party, multi-conversation situations, however, a much more detailed model of attention is required. An attention model can be used to summon others into a new or existing conversation, and can model which conversation each participant is attending to.

4   Grounding and Obligations

Much of the local content of dialogue can be modelled using notions like obligations and grounding [9, 18–24]. These models become more complex when considering the multiparty case.

Grounding is the process of adding to the common ground between participants in conversation [24]. The grounding model in [9, 19, 25] consisted of a structure of *Common ground units*, (CGUs) each of which contains material that is added to the common ground together. Each CGU has a unique initiator, responder, contents and state. The state is calculated using a finite state automaton, updated by *grounding acts* performed on the CGU. States include those in which the contents are grounded and ungroundable, as well as intermediate states in which an acknowledgement or repair is needed from one party or another. By recognizing grounding units and the CGUs that they construct and add to, a computational agent is able to model and participate in the grounding process.

In the MRE project, this model has been used in multiparty conversation, but only in cases in which there is a single initiator and responder of a particular CGU. For the more general case, in which there are multiple addressees, it is less clear what the proper grounding model *should* be. One option is to allow any of the addressees to acknowledge for the contents to be considered grounded. The problem is that this may lead to overly optimistic [26] estimations of common ground, where some agents did not in fact understand or possibly receive the communications. The pessimistic extreme is to require evidence of understanding from each addressee. While this is safer, it seems somewhat unrealistic when many of the addressees are human. Some sort of middle-ground is also possible, requiring an amount of evidence that is more than a single acknowledgement from one agent, but less than a separate acknowledgement from each agent.

Another interesting issue is grounding across conversations. E.g., if A asks B a question and observes B asking the same question to C (whether in the same conversation or a different one), A has evidence that B has understood the question, even though B has not yet responded to A.

Multiple addressees also present a challenge for models of obligation. The model of discourse obligations presented in [19–21] takes one of the main effects of utterances like requests and questions to be an obligation to perform some action such as addressing the request (by performing the requested action, accepting or rejecting the request, or other negotiating or explaining move). When there are multiple addressees, however, it is not so clear what the status of these obligations are. Does every addressee have a personal obligation? Is there an indefinite obligation assigned to the group, that can be satisfied by any member performing an obligation-relieving action? In the case of this indefinite obligation, what is it that motivates any particular agent to act?

Also there is the issue of transfer of obligation. To take the example given above, where B redirects A's question to C, if this is done in the presence of A, does B still have the obligation? Whether or not B still holds the obligation, does C's response in A's presence relieve B of this obligation? Can another party, say D relieve the obligation by providing an answer even when not addressed? The answers to some of these questions depend on the particular type of activity. For instance, if the purpose of A's question is to solicit information, and C or D are trustworthy, probably no more action is required of B. On the other hand, if it is a classroom situation, where A is asking the question not so much to find out the answer, but to determine whether B knows it, then B's redirect to C and D's spontaneous reply would be out of place, and perhaps subject to sanctions.

In some cases, multi-party dialogue can actually make the theoretical models of dialogue clearer rather than obscuring them. A case in point is an account of what motivates agents to answer questions. As described above, one model that has been used in some dialogue systems takes obligations as the motivation; the systems are designed to track obligations and then use these to motivate performing answers. An alternate model has been to use dialogue structural considerations, such as *Questions Under Discussion* (QUD), based on work by Ginzburg [27] to model question answering. When a question is asked, it gets added to the QUD, which in turn licenses answers to the question (including elliptical short answers). Both approaches were used in the TRINDI project [28, 29]. The GoDiS system [30] uses a QUD structure, while the EDIS system [31], uses the obligation approach. For simple two-party information-seeking domains such as Autoroute [29], there is little to choose between these two accounts. Both do an adequate job of representing questions, answers, intermediate states, and observation of lack of answers or other responses.

However we can see that there are really some distinct functions, as pointed out in [32]. QUD represents information about what would count as an answer, while obligations represent who should/must answer. Both reflect on the question of when the answer should occur. Obligations may specify time-limits on the answer. QUD, on the other hand will allow one to track when a particular utterance could be understood as an answer to that question. E.g., if an intervening question of a similar type is asked after the original question, a new utterance may be taken as an answer to the second rather than first question. In the MRE dialogue model, we represent both QUD and obligations. The former is part of the conversation structure of a specific conversation, while the latter (if grounded) is a property of the social state between agents. Thus an obligation might be introduced by a question in one conversation, and relieved in another conversation. The form of the answer depends on the QUD structure, however. If a question is not on QUD in the current conversation, then the question must be reintroduced before answering, or at least the answer must be given with sufficient clarity to accommodate the question [33].

5   Conclusions

In this article we have examined a number of issues in dialogue management for how they scale when moving from a two-participant model to a multi-participant model. Two obvious choices are available for multi-party models. One is to treat multiparty conversation as a set of pairs of two-party conversations. While this has the advantage of simplicity and using existing models, it is less than satisfactory in some cases. In the worst case, one will still need to move beyond the two party case in order to arbitrate between the multiple interactions, e.g. A with B and A with C. In some cases this will be more complex than changing the model to allow multiple participants. In some cases, we can see two-party dialogue as a special simple case of multiparty dialogue.

Dialogue system evaluation is also a difficult subject even for two-party dialogue. There are no universally agreed on metrics, due in large part to the very different types of tasks that dialogue systems are used for. Still, there are some general themes for evaluation, including task success, naturalness of interaction, user satisfaction, and efficiency. Some of these can be applied to the multi-party case, but the metrics become more difficult to calculate. E.g., for efficiency does one count real-time, or total agent time? One might count only a human's time, but what if there are multiple humans? Similar issues exist for other issues - how does one count naturalness when some agents communicate fairly naturally but others don't?

We are as yet only in the beginning stages of modelling multi-party dialogue, with few applications and very few implemented systems. The requirements will surely increase, however, as more societies of agents and people interact in more fluid ways.

Acknowledgements

This article was first presented as an invited talk to the 4th Sigdial workshop on discourse and dialogue, July 2003 in Chiba, Japan. The work described in this paper was supported by the Department of the Army under contract number

DAAD 19-99-D-0046. Any opinions, findings and conclusions or recommendations expressed in this paper are those of the authors and do not necessarily reflect the views of the Department of the Army. The author would like to thank many colleagues for helping develop the ideas and intuitions presented in this paper.

References

1. Traum, D.R., Rickel, J.: Embodied agents for multi-party dialogue in immersive virtual worlds. In: Proceedings of the first International Joint conference on Autonomous Agents and Multiagent systems. (2002) 766–773
2. Rickel, J., Marsella, S., Gratch, J., Hill, R., Traum, D., Swartout, W.: Toward a new generation of virtual humans for interactive experiences. IEEE Intelligent Systems **17** (2002)
3. Swartout, W., Hill, R., Gratch, J., Johnson, W., Kyriakakis, C., Labore, K., Lindheim, R., Marsella, S., Miraglia, D., Moore, B., Morie, J., Rickel, J., Thiebaux, M., Tuch, L., Whitney, R., Douglas, J.: Toward the holodeck: Integrating graphics, sound, character and story. In: Proceedings of 5th International Conference on Autonomous Agents. (2001)
4. Traum, D., Rickel, J., Marsella, S., Gratch, J.: Negotiation over tasks in hybrid human-agent teams for simulation-based training. In: In proceedings of AAMAS 2003: Second International Joint Conference on Autonomous Agents and Multi-Agent Systems. (2003) 441–448
5. Marsella, S., Gratch, J.: Modeling coping behavior in virtual humans: Don't worry, be happy. In: In proceedings of AAMAS 2003: Second International Joint Conference on Autonomous Agents and Multi-Agent Systems. (2003)
6. Clark, H.H.: Using Language. Cambridge University Press, Cambridge, England (1996)
7. Brunelli, R., Falavigna, D.: Person identification using multiple cues. IEEE Transactions on Pattern Analysis and Machine Intelligence **17** (1995) 955–966
8. Martinovski, B.: The Role of Repetitions and Reformulations in Court Proceedings – a Comparison of Sweden and Bulgaria. PhD thesis, Göteborg University: Department of Linguistics (2001)
9. Traum, D.R., Hinkelman, E.A.: Conversation acts in task-oriented spoken dialogue. Computational Intelligence **8** (1992) 575–599 Special Issue on Non-literal language.
10. Grosz, B.J., Sidner, C.L.: Attention, intention, and the structure of discourse. Computational Linguistics **12** (1986) 175–204
11. Walker, M.A.: Limited attention and discourse structure. Computational Linguistics **22** (1996) 255–264
12. Whittaker, S., Stenton, P.: Cues and control in expert-client dialogues. In: Proceedings ACL-88. (1988) 123–130
13. Walker, M.A., Whittaker, S.: Mixed initiative in dialogue: An investigation into discourse segmentation. In: Proceedings ACL-90. (1990) 70–78
14. Novick, D.: Control of Mixed-Initiative Discourse Through Meta-Locutionary Acts: A Computational Model. PhD thesis, University of Oregon (1988) also available as U. Oregon Computer and Information Science Tech Report CIS-TR-88-18.
15. Chu-Carroll, J., Brown, M.K.: Tracking initiative in collaborative dialogue interactions. In: Proceedings of the Thirty-Fifth Meeting of the Association for Computational Linguistics, Association for Computational Linguistics (1997) 262–270

16. Ishizaki, M.: Mixed-Initiative natural Language Dialogue with Variable Communicative Modes. PhD thesis, University of Edinburgh (1997)
17. Ishizaki, M., Kato, T.: Exploring the characteristics of multi-party dialogues. In: COLING-ACL. (1998) 583–589
18. Allwood, J.: Obligations and options in dialogue. Think Quarterly **3** (1994) 9–18
19. Traum, D.R.: A Computational Theory of Grounding in Natural Language Conversation. PhD thesis, Department of Computer Science, University of Rochester (1994) Also available as TR 545, Department of Computer Science, University of Rochester.
20. Traum, D.R., Allen, J.F.: Discourse obligations in dialogue processing. In: Proceedings of the 32nd Annual Meeting of the Association for Computational Linguistics. (1994) 1–8
21. Poesio, M., Traum, D.R.: Towards an axiomatization of dialogue acts. In: Proceedings of Twendial'98, 13th Twente Workshop on Language Technology: Formal Semantics and Pragmatics of Dialogue. (1998)
22. Dignum, F., van Linder, B.: Modeling social agents: Communication as action. In Müller, J.P., Wooldridge, M.J., Jennings, N.R., eds.: Intelligent Agents III — Proceedings of the Third International Workshop on Agent Theories, Architectures, and Languages (ATAL-96). Lecture Notes in Artificial Intelligence. Springer-Verlag, Heidelberg (1996)
23. Cahn, J.E., Brennan, S.E.: A psychological model of grounding and repair in dialog. In: Working Notes AAAI Fall Symposium on Psycholiogical Models of Communication in Collaborative Systems. (1999)
24. Clark, H.H., Schaefer, E.F.: Contributing to discourse. Cognitive Science **13** (1989) 259–294
25. Poesio, M., Traum, D.R.: Conversational actions and discourse situations. Computational Intelligence **13** (1997)
26. Poesio, M., Cooper, R., Larsson, S., Matheson, C., Traum., D.: Annotating conversations for information state update. In: Proceedings of Amstelogue'99 workshop on the semantics and pragmatics of dialogue. (1999)
27. Ginzburg, J.: Interrogatives: Questions, facts and dialogue. In Lappin, S., ed.: The Handbook of Contemporary Semantic Theory. Blackwell, Oxford (1996)
28. Larsson, S., Traum, D.: Information state and dialogue management in the TRINDI dialogue move engine toolkit. Natural Language Engineering **6** (2000) 323–340 Special Issue on Spoken Language Dialogue System Engineering.
29. Traum, D., Bos, J., Cooper, R., Larsson, S., Lewin, I., Matheson, C., Poesio, M.: A model of dialogue moves and information state revision. Technical Report Deliverable D2.1, Trindi (1999)
30. Bohlin, P., Cooper, R., Engdahl, E., Larsson, S.: Information states and dialogue move engines. In: Proceedings of the IJCAI99 workshop: Knowledge And Reasoning in Practical Dialogue Systems. (1999) 25–31
31. Matheson, C., Poesio, M., Traum, D.: Modelling grounding and discourse obligations using update rules. In: Proceedings of the First Conference of the North American Chapter of the Association for Computational Linguistics. (2000)
32. Traum, D.: Semantics and pragmatics of questions and answers for dialogue agents. In: proceedings of the International Workshop on Computational Semantics. (2003) 380–394
33. Larsson, S.: Issue-based Dialogue Management. PhD thesis, Göteborg University (2002)

Towards a Testbed for Multi-party Dialogues

Frank P.M. Dignum and Gerard A.W. Vreeswijk

Dept. of Computer Science
Utrecht University
The Netherlands
{dignum,gv}@cs.uu.nl

Abstract. In many situations conversations involve more than two parties. However, most research on communication modelling in e.g. multi-agent systems limits itself to conversations between two parties at a time. Very little research has been done yet on modelling multi-party dialogues. In this paper we first explore the differences between two party and multi-party dialogues and we indicate a number of issues that arise when considering dialogues between more than two parties. Then we take some steps towards creating a testbed in which these issues can be explored and theory on multi-party dialogues can be developed.

1   Introduction

In the past few years quite some research has been done in the area of agent communication (see e.g. [4, 3]). In most of the reported work the dialogues only involve two parties at the time. Even though specifications like the FIPA ACL [6] permit a message to be sent to more than one addressee, the protocols they give are mainly based on two party dialogues. If more parties are involved this is mostly through a broadcast message from one party to all other parties, after which each of these parties reply to the original sender (cf. for instance the Contract Net protocol). A good example of this type of dialogues where more than two agents are present, but conversation is always bi-lateral is [18] in which dialogues for purchase negotiations are modelled. Actually, we do not consider this to be multi-party dialogues but rather a number of parallel two-party dialogues.

The fact that most prior work in argumentation has focused on 2-party dialogues can be explained by the fact that philosophy of argumentation has, for 2300 years, focused mostly on persuasion dialogues, perhaps because philosophers were seeking after truth. Further, the multi-agent negotiation literature has focused on 2-party commercial transactions, perhaps due to the pernicious effects of economic theory (which studies only simplified models of reality, not realistic models) of our field.

The fact that agent communication also focussed on two-party dialogues, in our opinion, stems from the fact that much of the work done on agent conversations, such as [17, 19] draws from the work on dialogue theory in linguistics (e.g. [27] is quite influential in this area). The theory gives a typology and theory for the moves that can be made in the different types of dialogues. However, this

F. Dignum (Ed.): ACL 2003, LNAI 2922, pp. 212–230, 2004.

theory is built for two-party dialogues and there is little or no (usable) research done on multi-party dialogues. Neither in the field of pure linguistics nor in the field of distributed AI did we find much leads to use for constructing theories of multi-party dialogues for agents. The only work we have been able to find treating multi-party dialogues is from Traum [5] which mainly deals with focus of attention and initiative in multi-party conversations.

In practice the need for multi-party dialogues becomes more and more apparent. For instance, several agents have to cooperate in order to find a solution for a problem. Each of the agents might have a part of the solution, but only their interaction might reveal how to combine all the pieces of the puzzle. This might happen when a user agent tries to compose a holiday to a certain town and needs a flight and a hotel and maybe some local entertainment. If each of these components is delivered by a different source maintained by a different agent, it might be beneficial if hotel and flight manager can negotiate dates on which both flights and hotel are available. The user agent could listen in and intervene whenever the dates drift of too much from the preferred dates or the prices get too high. This would be more efficient than the user agent trying to first reserve a flight and afterwards a hotel (or the other way around) and having to go back and forth whenever the hotel is not available on the days between the flights.

In this paper we will explore the field of multi-party dialogues. First, in section 2, we discuss a number of the issues that arise when changing from a two-party situation to a multi-party situation. So, it does not contain a list of all dialogue issues, because many issues exist for both two-party as well as for multi-party dialogues (e.g. whether parties are cooperative or not or are sincere or not). After this exploration of issues, we will present a first implementation of a kind of test-bed in which a number of these issues can be examined in section 3 and 4. We only show the most simple case of an inquiry dialogue. The value of the example shown in section 5 is mainly as a first step of a systematic way of exploring the influence that design choices have on the resulting dialogues. Whereas the proof of interesting properties of two-party dialogues is already quite difficult (see [17]) it will be even harder in multi-party dialogues. The implementation presented in this paper can be seen as the start of a testbed in which such properties can be empirically explored and theory can be developed towards making the right choices for dialogues depending on the environment of the system.

2   Issues in Multi-party Dialogues

Probably one of the few things that does not change when moving from two to multiple parties is the typology of the dialogues. The well-known typology of Walton and Krabbe [27] is based on the goal of the dialogue (synchronization of believes and/or actions) and the starting situation (conflicting believes and/or intentions). Both elements play an equal role in multi-party dialogues.

2.1 Open vs. Closed Systems

The first difference that comes up right away, is whether the system is open or closed. I.e. are all parties present during the whole dialogue or can they join later and/or leave before the end of the dialogue? When we have only two parties there is no choice, both parties are needed to keep the dialogue going. However, when more parties are involved this is no longer necessary. In news groups it probably is more common for parties to join and leave during a dialogue than for parties to stick around during the complete dialogue. Also in situations where the parties consult experts during the dialogue to explain issues or arbitrate on conflicts, the expert is only part of a small slice of the dialogue, although in some dialogues, e.g., legal proceedings, experts and expert witnesses may be excluded by the rules of the interaction from participating in the entire dialogue. There are presumably good reasons for this in legal theory, e.g., so that the expert's testimony is not biased by what has occurred before in the courtroom.

This brings up the first consequence. One has to distinguish between situations in which the participation in the dialogue is formally arranged and situations where participation is left up to the individual agents. In the first case the entrance and exit of a participant in the dialogue is arranged and can only take place at certain points during the dialogue. When the participation is completely left to individual participants the question becomes how we know that a party has left the dialogue or joined it? Are there special speech acts to denote these acts, do participants register? Often entrance and exit are marked by special messages (e.g. a register or "hello" message and a de-register or "bye" message)(For speech acts see [21, 22]). However, if asynchronous communication is used it might happen that a question is directed to an agent that just exited the dialogue. A mechanism should be devised to both detect this situation (preventing agents to wait indefinitely for an answer) and a way to recover from it.

Of course open settings also make it difficult to check whether, for instance, the goal of a dialogue has been reached. Is there general agreement on a course of action, is there mutual believe, is everyone convinced? For each of these questions one should specify which parties (still) count.

2.2 Roles

A following issue is the role of each of the parties in the dialogue. This can be viewed from different perspectives. In the first perspective we look at roles from a linguistic point of view. In a two-party dialogue there is always a speaker and an addressee (or hearer). However, in a multi-party dialogue we can at least distinguish: speaker, addressee, auditor, overhearer and eavesdropper (see e.g. [14]). Although the speaker directs a message to one (or more) other parties there can also be parties that hear the message without being addressed explicitly. The auditor is a party that is supposed to hear the message (this is intended by the speaker). An example is when I cc a mail to my boss to "proof" that I indeed made an inquiry as I had promised to my boss before. The overhearer is allowed to hear the message but the speaker does not intend him to hear it. This happens when I send a message as a response to a question in a news group. All people subscribed to that news group can see the response but are not necessarily the intended audience. Finally, the eavesdropper is a party that happens to hear the message without the speaker wanting him to hear it at all. E.g. I do a "reply-all" while I intended a "reply" to a mail. When determining the effect of a message on the other parties one has to take the role of that party into account. A request to perform an action might lead to an intention in the addressee while leading to a dropping of the same intention in the overhearer.

One can also look at the roles from a dialectic perspective. In a typical two-party persuasive dialogue there is a proponent and an opponent. In two-party dialogues of the inquiry or deliberation-type (in the Walton and Krabbe typology), the pro/con distinction already blurs. Additionally, in a multi-party dialogue we can also have roles such as: neutral party, interested party, interviewer, advocate, respondent, examinator, challenged party, mediator, or arbitrator (to coin a few disciplinary-neutral terms). The role an agent plays influences the type of responses it can give during the dialogue. E.g. a mediator might give an alternative proposal or might ask for additional information from other parties after the first arguments have been exchanged.

A third type of roles that can be distinguished are the social roles within the dialogue. A good example is that of a chairperson. These types of roles can influence the turn taking within the dialogue, but can also determine when parties can join the dialogue and leave it again. Finally, the chairperson might have the power to terminate a dialogue one-sided or through some predetermined protocol.

A last perspective on roles that we mention here are interests. Some parties in a dialogue will have the goal to terminate the dialogue successfully, while other parties might want just to disrupt the dialogue or try to extend it eternally. This might happen in multi-party negotiations. Some parties might want to conclude the negotiations, trying to get the optimum result for themselves, while other parties benefit most when no agreement is reached at all.

For each of the perspectives on roles one can choose whether roles are fixed once or can change during the dialogue. For linguistic roles this seems the most likely choice, but also other roles might change (either explicitly or implicitly) during a dialogue.

2.3   Medium and Addressing

This issue ties in with that of linguistic roles. The main question is how messages are addressed. We can make a distinction between one-to-one distribution, one-to-many distribution and one-to-all distribution. In a two-party dialogue all messages are directed at the "other" party. However, in a multi-party dialogue one can choose whether to address a message to a specific other party or to several (specified) other parties or just broadcast the message to all other parties.

Considering especially open dialogues it is also interesting to know whether the messages are observable throughout the dialogue or only when they are sent. In the first case, latecomers can check the messages that are exchanged so-far, while in the second case they just miss the start of the dialogue.

Independently one can decide whether all communication is "overheard" by all parties or not. I.e. can all parties hear all communication or only the messages that are directed to them? One might even make distinction between observing that a message is exchanged and observing the content of the message. I.e. one might see two persons whispering to each other without hearing the content. One might argue that messages that are only heard by a subgroup are a separate dialogue between that subgroup. In that case all messages should at least be heard by all participants of the dialogue.

2.4   Coordination

The first question on the issue of coordination is whether the parties can all react asynchronously or whether each time only one party can have its turn. Although the asynchronous coordination may seem chaotic, it is the standard for most news groups and mailing lists.

The issue of turn-taking is relatively trivial in two-party dialogues. However, how is the order determined in which the parties take turns in a multi-party dialogue? Is it a round-robbin protocol (the generalization of the strict turn-taking for two parties) or do we use other mechanisms? As said above, one might also have a chairman that explicitly determines the next party that can or should take its turn.

Independently one should decide on which messages each party can react. Can parties react on all messages delivered before, the last messages of all parties delivered before, only to the originator, etc.? Can they react to a message of which they were not the addressee?

Of course, one should also consider *how* all parties can react. A common rule in many two-party argumentation systems is that parties are not allowed to repeat an argument in order to avoid infinite regression of arguments (see e.g. [24]). In multi-party arguments the question arises whether other parties are allowed to repeat an argument. One could argue that this indicates additional support for an argument and it would be useful to strengthen an argument.

2.5   Termination

Although we argued above that the goals of the multi-party dialogues are similar to the two-party dialogues they have to be translated to their multi-party versions. For instance, does a persuasion dialogue end successful if all parties are convinced of an argument, or if most are convinced of it, or if some designated parties are convinced? One might say that the original addressees should be convinced while the auditors and overhearers do not have to be convinced. But many more choices are possible.

In the same vein the termination of the dialogue becomes less obvious. Who determines whether a dialogue is terminated? In case there is a chairman he might decide. However, it might also be that a majority of the parties should agree that the dialogue is terminated. Or the party that started the dialogue can explicitly end it.

Each of these choices influences not only the point of termination but also the strategy and maybe the rules of the dialogue game. In case a majority of the participants has to agree to terminate the dialogue, a party can try to form a coalition with enough other parties to "win" the dialogue. In case only the originator has to be convinced all arguments will be directed to this party.

2.6   Properties of the Dialogue

There are some interesting new properties to be checked for multi-party dialogues. E.g. can we guarantee that an inquiry dialogue protocol will deliver the answer if the union of all the knowledge of the parties in the dialogue would be enough to derive this answer?

Other issues would involve whether a protocol only reveals information to participants that they need to know in order to respond or whether information is released that parties would rather not divulge if not needed.

A typical issue coming up in human conversations is whether all parties have an equal opportunity to reach their part of the goal of the dialogue. I.e. can they put forward all their arguments at the right time to convince some party or the whole group?

Of course the question of guaranteed termination of a protocol is also very relevant for a multi-party dialogue.

2.7   Internal Operation of the Agents

Besides the issues described above on the external properties of a multi-party dialogue one might also want to consider whether the parties should have some extra internal properties to take part in a multi-party dialogue. One obvious candidate is how agents determine when and with what content to respond to which other parties.

2.8   Conclusion

The issues discussed in this section probably do not cover the whole field, but hopefully give a good insight in the landscape of multi-party dialogues and its challenges. Far from trying to answer all of the above questions in the rest of this paper we will sketch a framework in which these questions can be studied and possible answers formulated in an empirical way.

Our hope is that by working on a systematic implementation where all possible choices are made explicit and adjustable we will in the end create a test-bed that reveals all issues and can be used to test which are the consequences for certain combinations of features.

In order to arrive at this test-bed that should register all choices, we will start with a very simple implementation that only contains the core of multi-party dialogues that should be shared by all forms.

3   A Starting System: Blackboard Dialectic

As said before the basis of agent conversations can be found in linguistics and one of the most relevant areas is that of computational dialectics. So, we will take the work from this field as a basis for our own experimental work and discuss the methods of computational dialectic [1990-now] in the next section.

Because multi-party dialogues require different methods of communication than only the one-to-one and one-to-many we decided to use the blackboard system metaphor as a basis for communication. Blackboard systems are probably the most generic form of multi-party communication. More sophisticated communication forms can easily be build on top of these systems. We discuss the methods of blackboard systems [1975-now] in the second subsection below.

Computational dialectic. Influenced by work on nonmonotonic reasoning and argumentation theory, computational dialectic emerged as an area that makes significant progress with the (formal) synthesis and (computational) execution of artificial argument and dispute [12, 26, 1]. As far as we know, however, most if not all work in computational dialectic models disputes in which two parties, named PRO and CON, exchange arguments in such manner that each party is obliged to immediately respond to moves of its (or his, or her) opponent. In his pioneering paper "process and policy," Loui termed this type of dispute as so-called *two-party immediate response dialectic* [13]. An example of a two-party immediate response dispute, adapted from [25], is the following example

Example. Two parties named PRO and CON, have arguments of the most simple sort for and against A, respectively.

Proposition	DOB	Proposition	DOB
B	1.00	$B \dashv(0.97)\mapsto A$	1.00
C	1.00	$C \dashv(0.91)\mapsto \neg A$	1.00

Thus, both believe all four propositions B, C, $B \dashv(0.97)\mapsto A$, and $C \dashv(0.91)\mapsto \neg A$ to be absolutely true. This certainty is expressed as a degree of belief (DOB), of 1.00. The implicational strength with which the two rules imply their conclusion is 0.97 and 0.91, respectively. Accordingly, the dispute evolves as in Table 1.

The first row of numbers in Table 1 are line numbers. Of the second row of numbers (separated by a comma) the first row indicates the *level* of the dispute, i.e., the number of times that the burden of proof has alternated. For example, if PRO starts a dispute on A and, *within* this dispute, CON starts a dispute on B and, within CON's dispute, PRO starts a dispute on C, then the dispute is at level three. The second half of the row of numbers that are separated by a comma indicates the *depth* of the dispute, i.e., the number of times that the defending party justifies his claim via regression through rules.

The point of this sample-dispute is to note that a two-party immediate response protocol forces both parties to enter and explore every part of the search space in a strict depth-first search fashion, something that is not akin to informal dispute. Still, the two-person dispute system presented in [25] provides a

Table 1. Output of a simple two-person immediate response dialogue.

1. 0,0 pro: I claim that A holds.
2. 1,0 con: Why?
3. 0,0 pro: Because it follows from B with strength 0.97, and I claim that B holds.
4. 1,1 con: Why?
5. 0,1 pro: Simply because B is the case with DOB = 1.00
6. 1,1 con: Frankly, I am willing to contest B: I claim that $\neg B$ holds.
7. 2,1 pro: Why?
8. 1,1 con: Um... upon closer inspection I see I have no grounds for $\neg B$.
9. 0,1 pro: That leaves me with B, obviously. And via B my A is supported 0.97
10. 1,0 con: Sure, but now this: I claim that $\neg A$ holds.
11. 2,0 pro: Why?
12. 1,0 con: Because it follows from C with strength 0.91, and I claim that C holds.
13. 2,1 pro: Why?
14. 1,1 con: Simply because C is the case with DOB = 1.00
15. 2,1 pro: Frankly, I am willing to contest C: I claim that $\neg C$ holds.
16. 3,1 con: Why?
17. 2,1 pro: Um... upon closer inspection I see I have no grounds for $\neg C$.
18. 1,1 con: That leaves me with C, obviously. And via C my $\neg A$ is supported 0.91. Nevertheless, I grant that earlier on (line 9), you were able to support A more strongly. Therefore I drop $\neg A$.
19. 0,0 pro: Combining my support (line 1-9) and your counter-support (line 10-18) yields 0.97 for A, which means that I am right on A.

number of clues to multi-party dialogue. Therefore, the example implementation presented in this paper continues to build on the system presented in [25].

Blackboard systems. Another development relevant to multi-agent dispute are so-called blackboard systems [2, 7, 8]. We see blackboard systems as the most basic form of communication medium. Many other systems can be seen as refinements of this system. A blackboard system is an expert system based on the blackboard metaphor. This metaphor says that, to solve a problem, or to answer a question, a number of more or less independent artificial experts, named *knowledge sources* in BB-terminology, should communicate by means of a central medium, *the blackboard* from which all knowledge sources may read and write. Of course, there must be some protocol to arrange who goes to the blackboard if more than one expert "reaches for the chalk", and there must be agreement on a common language that experts use, but these questions are clearly addressed in research on blackboard systems. In the initial stages of research on knowledge based systems, the motivation to work with blackboard was that such systems are less compiled and more modular than conventional expert systems. The idea was that they should be more transparent and easier to maintain than monolithic expert systems. After some time, however, research on blackboard systems lost focus, because it was claimed that they were not fast enough to meet the DARPA criteria at that time [10, p. 350]. (An argument that has now become obsolete.)

In 2003 it is fair to state that research on multi-agent systems has turned the blackboard metaphor into something that does not live up to contemporary standards of agent-communication and geographically distributed expertise. However, research on blackboard systems can be put into new light by elaborating on the idea of a newsgroup expert discussion. For example, if a computer programmer has a question on feature X of the newest release of programming language Y, he or she can post a question to the appropriate newsgroup and may expect an answer within a time range of one to twenty-four hours (depending on the turnover of a particular group). More specifically we propose to convey the idea of cooperating agents from internet metaphor such as the newsgroup metaphor or, in Google terminology the *discussion groups* metaphor, to a simple but new protocol for the exchange of knowledge. Our motivation for this step is that news and discussion groups are the *de facto* standards to let human agents communicate asynchronously in public. The example implementation presented in this paper adopts the blackboard metaphor (rather than adopting its precise architecture) and gives it a dialectic twist.

4   Implementation

In this and the following section we describe the implementation of a dialectic blackboard architecture implemented in Ruby. Ruby is a kind of crossbreed between Perl and Smalltalk created around 1993 by Yukihiro Matsumoto [15]. We choose for Ruby because it is a pure and sober object-oriented scripting language with an intuitive syntax, extremely suited for prototyping. (Some even advocated Ruby as executable pseudo code.) De-facto authority is http://www.ruby-lang.org/[1]. De-facto reference is what afficionado's call "the pickaxe book" [23]. We hope to be able to implement the dialogues on the 3APL platform in the coming year (see [9] for a basic description of 3APL). This will allow us to use "real" agents to implement the knowledge of each agent and also the conversation rules that the agents use can easily and explicitly be represented in 3APL. A second advantage is that the platform is readily available for us and we can change the platform structure to suit our dialogue needs.

Based on two-party disputes in computational dialectic on the one hand, and based on the blackboard metaphor in expert systems on the other hand, we start with a dialectic blackboard architecture with the following multi-party properties:

i. A fixed number of equivalent participants engage in an inquiry dialogue, with the goal to discover how to undertake a particular action. So, in terms of section 2.1 we start with a closed system. We start with inquiry dialogues, because they are the easiest with respect to regulating turn taking.

ii. There are no specific roles for the agents. They are equivalent in all respects.

---

[1] A websearch with keyword "Ruby" should give enough leads.

iii. Agents communicate through a central medium, called the forum, the function of which may be compared to the function of an internet newsgroup. Messages are public. They are not addressed to specific agents.

iv. Agents act (listen, reason, and speak) in turn, for a fixed number of rounds. The current experiment, for instance, involves 3 agents and 7 rounds, which implies the performance of 21 atomic acts.

v. There is no criterion for termination. Cf. point (iv).

The following properties are not typical multi-party issues, but also determine the course of a dialogue.

a. Participants are cooperative. They do not lie about their beliefs. All agents acknowledge and process all messages (in so far these messages are applicable), all agents have ample time to reason, and all agents have the opportunity to post all their messages desired.

b. Agents have logical capabilities. In particular, they do not ask what they already know or can infer. Before asking, an agent tries to infer the desired item itself.

c. The facilitation of information is dialectic: claims are justified with other claims or denied with reasons that support a contradiction. Agents accept claims if and only if they can be resolved to information that they believe to be true.

d. Regression to previous messages is always possible. Agents are allowed to question or justify prior claims. Thus, an immediate response is not required.

e. For simplicities' sake the agents have a shared ontology. One consequence of this assumption is that propositions (internal representations of claims) conveyed through messages are not renamed.

4.1   Notation

We use the following notation as convenient shorthand in our implementation.

Definition 1. *A discussion group $G = \langle \mathcal{A}, F \rangle$ is a (possibly infinite) set of agents $\mathcal{A}$ that communicate by means of a forum F. Individual agents are denoted by a_i.*

A forum $F = \{m_i \mid 1 \leq i \leq n\}$ is an array of messages, where m_n is the last message published. A message $m_i = (q, A)$ is a tuple consisting of a question q, possibly followed by one ore more answers to that question. The set of answers, A, is an ordered list.

The internal structure of agents, questions and answers is left unspecified in the theory, but a possible interpretation is elaborated in the rest of this section. Each agent a_i possesses a name, knowledge, a number of questions to be answered, a bookmark to remember the first unread item, bookmarks per question for the first unread answer of that question, and a hash to remember which questions have already been answered (Figure 1).

```
@name       = 'Pete'
@knowledge = { 'a' => [['f', 'b'], ['c', 'd']],
               'd' => [['e', 'b'], ['c']],
               'p' => TRUE
             }
@questions = { 'a' => nil, # new question
               'd' => 3, # first unread answer
             }
# first unread article:
@fid        = 45 # @fid means "forum identifier"
@bookmark  = { 4 => 2, 56 => 6 }
@answered   = { 4 => TRUE, 8 => TRUE }
```

Fig. 1. Datastructure per agent.

```
N => {
   'owner'    => 'Claude',
   'question' => 'bake a cake',
   'answers'  => [ { 'owner'  => 'Francois',
                     'answer' =>
                        'knead the flower',
                        'bake the paste' } ]
```

Fig. 2. Datastructure per question.

4.2   Data Structures

The agent's knowledge is implemented as a hash, where each atomic action is mapped onto a set of alternative preconditions, or to the value TRUE. The latter indicates that the agent knows how to perform this action.

The scenario consists of a (theoretically unlimited) number of agents which run concurrently. Furthermore, the scenario accommodates a forum that is shared by all agents. The forum is a passive medium, but is otherwise responsible for the management and administration of messages and personalities (agent-id's). In our current model, these bookkeeping activities amount to no more than maintaining a hash that maps questions onto message-id's (a so-called *reverted index*).

Each agent may be in a consumptive mode or in a productive mode. In the consumptive mode an agent takes actions that are supposed to deal with the accumulation of new knowledge. In this case, we have limited this part of the algorithm to two actions, viz. reading the forum and publishing questions to it. In the productive mode an agent does things that are supposed to deal with the dissemination of (private) knowledge. In our case, we have limited this part to answering questions of other agents. In the following paragraphs, we describe how an agent reads a forum, publishes questions, and responds to questions of other agents.

4.3 Consumptive Mode

An agent reads news by cycling through its own (typically short) list of unanswered questions. (Cf. Figure 1.) For each such question, it locates the message-id of this question by means of a reversed index. (Recall our assumption about the administrative responsibilities of the forum-object.) If the question is absent, the agent publishes its question and proceeds with its next (and possibly non-assimilating) activity[2]. Else, if the question is already present in the forum, the agent starts scanning the answers to that question, beginning with the first answer not read (by that agent), and ending with the last answer. The point where the agent left the previous time reading answers to that particular question is called the agent's bookmark for that question. Previous to the first scan of a question, the bookmark is typically set to zero. After scanning all the answers to a question, the bookmark is put behind the last question.

Agent method 1 Reading answers.

Require: index

```
 1: while @bookmark[index] < public.answers(index).length do
 2:    question = public.question(index)
 3:    @bookmark[index] += 1
 4:    answer = public.answer(index, @bookmark[index])
 5:    incorporate_justification(question, answer)
 6:    if elements_of_explanation_suffice?(answer) then
 7:      delete_question(question)
 8:      break
 9:    end if
10: end while
```

When an agent reads an answer it first incorporates the question/answer-combination into its knowledge base. It then verifies whether the answer really suffices as an answer (a process to be explained shortly). If the answer suffices, the agent deletes the question from its private question list and marks it as answered in the forum. It also stops reading further answers to this question. Else, if the answer does not suffice, the agent proceeds reading answers to that particular question. Notice that an answer is incorporated in the knowledge base, irrespective of whether it suffices as an answer or not. This is because an unsatisfactory answer may become useful in a later stage of the process if further knowledge becomes available.

To verify whether a particular answer is satisfactory, an agent verifies whether all elements of that answer can be reduced to its own knowledge. If one such element cannot be resolved, the verification of the other elements is suspended. This is because answers to dependent issues become irrelevant when the original answer cannot be answered either. To verify whether an element can be reduced

---

[2] A published question may roughly be compared to what is called a *knowledge source activation record* (KSAR) in blackboard systems. Cf. [2].

to private knowledge, the agent verifies whether it has marked the element as true in its own knowledge base, or whether its knowledge base contains a rule supporting that element. In the latter case, the algorithm recursively applies the verification process until the agent encounters private facts or, in the negative case, cannot further justify one particular element. When a particular element cannot be further reduced (i.e., justified) it is published as a question to the forum.

The last type of action is crucial to the process as it closes the consumption/production cycle of questions and answers.

4.4   Productive Mode

When in productive mode an agent reads the news chronologically, starting at the first message that was not read by that agent. Thus every agent now possesses two types of bookmarks: one global bookmark for keeping track of questions, and one for each question to keep track of the answers to that question. Since it does not seem to make much sense to try to answer one's own questions, an agent skips its own messages (i.e., questions) if it is in productive mode. A question is also skipped if an agent has given all its answers to that particular question. Else, it publishes an answer to that question. This answer may not already have been published by other agents, including itself. Answers to questions cannot (and need not) be bookmarked, because other agents may have contributed possibly identical answers in the meantime.

After this action, the agent proceeds with its next (and possibly non-productive) activity.

It turns out that the consumer-part of the algorithm is more complex than the producer part, which might seem to reinforce an old adage, namely, that listening is more difficult than speaking.

5   A Sample Dialogue

As an example, suppose we have three equivalent parties, Arie, Bill and Claude. Arie stands next to his bike. He has pulled out the front wheel out of the fork and holds it up. Bill and Claude are two friends of Arie and stand next to him. (Cf. Figure 3-5.) Bill's `neg-knowledge` indicates that pulling out a wheel and standing there are perfect conditions to ensure that you can no longer go to the hardware store. With this information, the dialogue ensues that is shown in Table 2 at the end of this article.

Looking at Figure 3-5), we see that the formulation of line 23-26 is somewhat unfortunate. This is so because the elements of the knowledge-base are actually action descriptions, rather than verifications of the state of an agent. Line 23 actually indicates that the wheel *has* been put out, and lines 25-26 actually indicate that Arie cannot verify (or does not agree) that he looks foolish. Apart from this and similar linguistic glitches (that were to be expected due to inter-

Table 2. Ruby-generated dialogue.

1.	Arie:	asks: "How do I repair a flat tire?"
2.	Bill:	responds: "Arie, if you want to repair a flat tire then you must buy a new tire and apply it"
3.	Claude:	responds: "Arie, if you want to repair a flat tire then you must find the leak and seal it"
4.	Arie:	tries to recall for himself how to buy a new tire ..
5.	Arie:	.. he realizes he does not know how to buy a new tire
6.	Arie:	therefore suspends his attempt to apply it
7.	Arie:	tries to recall for himself how to find the leak ..
8.	Arie:	realizes that he knows how to find the leak
9.	Arie:	knows that find the leak can be done by trying to inspect the tire and then mark the leak
10.	Arie:	tries to find the leak by trying to inspect the tire and then mark the leak
11.	Arie:	tries to recall for himself how to inspect the tire ..
12.	Arie:	.. he realizes he does not know how to inspect the tire
13.	Arie:	therefore suspends his attempt to mark the leak
14.	Arie:	therefore suspends his attempt to seal it
15.	Arie:	asks: "How do I buy a new tire?"
16.	Arie:	asks: "How do I inspect the tire?"
17.	Bill:	responds: "Arie, if you want to buy a new tire then you must go to the hardware store"
18.	Claude:	responds: "Arie, if you want to inspect the tire then you must put the tire in a bucket and watch for bubbles"
19.	Arie:	tries to recall for himself how to go to the hardware store ..
20.	Arie:	.. he realizes he does not know how to go to the hardware store
21.	Arie:	asks: "How do I go to the hardware store?"
22.	Bill:	responds: "Arie, if you want to go to the hardware store then do not pull out wheel from fork and stand there like a looney"
23.	Arie:	knows how to pull out wheel from fork and does so.
24.	Arie:	tries to recall for himself how to stand there like a looney ..
25.	Arie:	.. he realizes he does not know how to stand there like a looney
26.	Arie:	asks: "How do I stand there like a looney?"
27.	Arie:	knows how to put the tire in a bucket and does so.
28.	Arie:	knows how to watch for bubbles and does so.
30.	Arie:	now inspect the tire by put the tire in a bucket, watch for bubbles first and then inspect the tire
31.	Arie:	does mark the leak
32.	Arie:	does seal it

polating[3] agent-specific strings into different template utterances), we maintain that the dialogue otherwise exhibits a surprisingly natural flow of messages and message justifications, so much so, we think, that the algorithm hints at a further and more mature elaboration.

---

[3] Like Perl's string interpolation: if $year is 1984, then "It's $year" evaluates to "It's 1984".

```
Agent.new(
   'name'         => 'Arie',
   'questions' => {
      'repair a flat tire' => TRUE
   },

   'knowledge' => {
      'pull out wheel from fork'    => TRUE,
      'stand there like a looney'   => TRUE,
      'seal it'                     => TRUE,
      'find the leak'               =>
         [['inspect the tire', 'mark the leak']],
      'put the tire in a bucket'    => TRUE,
      'watch for bubbles'           => TRUE })
```

Fig. 3. Creation of Arie.

```
Agent.new(
   'name'         => 'Bill',
   'questions'    => {},

   'knowledge'    => {
      'repair a flat tire' =>
         [['buy a new tire', 'apply it']],
      'buy a new tire' =>
         [['go to the hardware store']] },

   'neg-knowledge' => {
      'go to the hardware store' =>
         [['pull out wheel from fork',
         'stand there like a looney']] })
```

Fig. 4. Creation of Bill.

6   Related Work

First of all we should reiterate that there is not much other work done on multi-party dialogues. Of course it does not mean that there is no related work at all. Much of the work on modelling multi-party dialogues can be based on or be inspired by the two-party dialogue frameworks. In this section we will briefly discuss work of Amgoud et al. on formal inter-agent dialogues [20]. Then, we will discuss some other work on agent communication that is relevant for our work.

In their study on argumentation-based dialogues between agents, Amgoud et al. define a set of locutions by which agents can trade arguments, a set of agent attitudes which relate what arguments an agent can build and what locutions it can make, and a set of protocols by which dialogues can be carried out. They then consider some properties of dialogues under the protocols, in particular termination and complexity, and show how these relate to the agent attitudes.

```
Agent.new(
    'name'      => 'Claude',
    'questions' => {},

    'knowledge' => {
        'know that the hardware store closed' => TRUE,
        'repair a flat tire' =>
            [['find the leak', 'seal it']],
        'inspect the tire' =>
            [['put the tire in a bucket',
            'watch for bubbles']] },

    'neg-knowledge' => {} )
```

Fig. 5. Creation of Claude.

Compared to our work, Amgoud *et al.*'s analysis is more logic-oriented. Rather than being focused on a prototypical implementation, it is more directed towards results (theorems) on the correctness of verification protocols, and the existence of termination conditions. The properties of the dialogue follow completely from the properties of the agents participating in the dialogue plus some other (implicit) assumptions on turn taking etc. This work is certainly usable as a basis for proving properties of multi-party dialogues as well. It will be interesting to implement the agents as modelled logically by Amgoud *et al.* and check whether the properties do indeed hold and whether they would still hold when more than two parties are involved.

Of course, much work from the area of agent communication in general is relevant for this work as well. See [4, 3] for some overview. Of particular interest is the work on the semantics of agent communication. The semantics of the communication determines in large part which messages can be send at which moment in time. The work of Singh [21, 22] is illustrative for this line of research that is geared towrds getting the speech-acts right. In [21], Singh provides a formal semantics for the major kinds of speech acts at a more formal level. In particular, Singh claims that in order for multi-agent systems to be formally and rigorously designed and analyzed, a semantics of speech acts that gives their objective model-theoretic conditions of satisfaction is needed. In [22], this work is more elaborated and results in normative constraints for felicitous communication.

In [11] Kumar *et al.* describe group communication with agents. The work especially deals with the semantics of speech acts when a group of other agents is addressed. I.e. it distinguishes addressees and overhearers and tries to capture this difference in the semantics as well. This work will certainly be used when we extend our framework to take this type of messages into account.

It will also be interesting to check how multi-party communication fits in the framework provided by the FIPA specifications [6]. These specifications are geared towards modelling communications between two agents, even though more parties can be involved in the conversation. First of all it should be examined whether the standard messages contain all components to model the dialogues between multiple parties. Secondly, one should carefully look at the FIPA ACL semantics to check whether they are stil sensible in the context of a multi-party dialogue.

7   Conclusion

In this paper we have scanned the landscape of multi-party dialogues. Some issues have been discussed that surface when changing from two-party dialogues to multi-party dialogues. Many issues come up that have crucial influence on the ensuing dialogues. In order to get some grip on this area, we started of to implement a multi-party dialogue architecture in which we can systematically research these issues.

We emphasize again that the implemented example protocol is extremely simple and is not designed to compete with established and more elaborated protocols for the exchange of knowledge.

What we do hope, however, is that our example has illustrated the possibility to set up a test-bed on the basis of this implementation in which a large number of parameters can be set and in which different ideas on multi-party deferred-response protocols can be tested and improved.

What we have shown already is how two-person immediate response protocols can be generalized and extended to a multi-agent setting by means of a simple blackboard or forum metaphor.

As next steps we have to look at the way turn taking is organized in the system. At the moment this is coded in the system itself and can't be regulated either by the user or the agents. The next point will be to extend the dialogues to include persuasion dialogues. This is a big step because it involves the inclusion in the agents to process inconsistent information and finding counter-arguments for arguments. Also interesting is the issue of linguistic roles. Instead of using a plain blackboard structure we can make sections that are visible for different sets of participants. In this way we can simulate different linguistic roles. Finally, we hope to start looking into properties such as termination of the dialogues depending on these different parameters.

Acknowledgments

We'd like to thank Joris Hulstijn for sharing his knowledge with us on collective addressees and audience roles in multi-party dialogue theory. We also like to thank the two anonymous referees for their valuable comments.

References

1. P. Baroni, M. Giacomin, and G. Guida. Extending abstract argumentation systems theory. *Artificial Intelligence*, 120(2):251–270, 2000.
2. D. Corkill. Blackboard systems. *AI Expert*, 6(9):40–47, 1991.

3. F. Dignum and B. Chaib-Draa. *Computational Intelligence: Special issue on Agent Communication*, 18(2), 2002.
4. F. Dignum and M. Greaves. *Issues in Agent Communication*, volume LNCS(1916). Springer-Verlag, 2002.
5. D.Traum et al. Embodied agents for multi-party dialogue in immersive virtual worlds. In *Proc. of the First Int. Joint Conf. on Autonomous Agents and Multi-Agent Systems*, pages 766–773. ACM Press, July 2002.
6. FIPA. Fipa agent communication specification. http://www.fipa.org/, 2003.
7. B. Hayes-Roth et al. Blackboard architecture for control. *Artificial Intelligence*, 26:251–321, 1985.
8. B. Hayes-Roth et al. Builing systems in the BB* environment. In R. Englemore et al., editors, *Blackboard systems*, chapter 29. Addison-Wesley, 1988.
9. K. V. Hindriks, F. S. D. Boer, W. V. der Hoek, and J.-J. C. Meyer. Agent programming in 3apl. *Autonomous Agents and Multi-Agent Systems*, 2(4):357–401, 1999.
10. P. Jackson. *Expert Systems*. Addison-Wesley, 1999.
11. S. Kumar, M. J. Huber, D. R. McGee, P. R. Cohen, and H. J. Levesque. Semantics of agent communication languages for group interaction. pages pages 42–47, 2000.
12. R. Loui. Defeat among arguments: A system of defeasible inference. *Computational Intelligence*, 3(2):100–106, April 1987.
13. R. Loui. Process and policy: Resource-bounded nondemonstrative reasoning. *Computational Intelligence*, 14(1):1–38, 1998.
14. R. Malouf. Towards an analysis of multi-party discourse. Talk, 1995.
15. Y. Matsumoto. *Ruby in a nutshell*. O'Reilly, 2001.
16. P. McBurney et al. Desiderata for agent argumentation protocols. In *Proc. of the First Int. Joint Conf. on Autonomous Agents and Multiagent Systems*, pages 402–409. ACM Press, 2002.
17. P. McBurney and S. Parsons. Games that agents play: A formal framework for dialogues between autonomous agents. *Journal of Logic, Language and Information*, (to appear).
18. P. McBurney, R. M. van Eijk, S. Parsons, and L. Amgoud. Dialogue-game protocol for agent purchase negotiations. *Journal of Autonomous Agents and Multi-Agent Systems*, 7(1-2), 2003. To appear.
19. C. Reed, T. Norman, and N. Jennings. Negotiating the semantics of agent communication languages. *Computational Intelligence*, 18(2):229–252, 2002.
20. L. A. Simon Parsons, Michael Wooldridge. An analysis of formal inter-agent dialogues. In *Proc. of the 1st Int. Joint Conf. on Autonomous agents and Multi-agent systems (Aamas)*, pages 394–401, Bologna, Italy, 2002.
21. M. P. Singh. Towards a formal theory of communication for multi-agent systems. In J. Mylopoulos and R. Reiter, editors, *Proceedings of the Twelfth International Joint Conference on Artificial Intelligence (IJCAI-91)*, pages 69–74, Sydney, Australia, 1991. Morgan Kaufmann publishers Inc.: San Mateo, CA, USA.
22. M. P. Singh. A semantics for speech acts. In M. N. Huhns and M. P. Singh, editors, *Readings in Agents*, pages 458–470. Morgan Kaufmann, San Francisco, CA, USA, 1997.
23. D. Thomas and A. Hunt. *Programming Ruby: The Pragmatic Programmer's Guide*. Addison-Wesley, 2000. Aka "the Pickaxe book" (because the cover shows a pickaxe mining rubies). Available online at http://www.rubycentral.com/book/.
24. P. Torroni. A study on the termination of negotiation dialogues. In *Proc. of the First Int. Joint Conf. on Autonomous Agents and Multiagent Systems*, pages 1223–1230. ACM Press, 2002.

25. G. Vreeswijk. Eight dialectic benchmark discussed by two artificial localist disputors. *Synthese*, 127:221–253, 2001.
26. G. Vreeswijk and H. Prakken. Credulous and sceptical argument games for preferred semantics. In M. Ojeda-Aciego et al., editors, *Proc. of the European Workshop on Logics in AI*, pages 239–253, Berlin, 2000. Springer-Verlag.
27. D. N. Walton et al. *Commitment in Dialogue: Basic Concepts of Interpersonal Reasoning*. State University of New York Press, Albany, NY, 1995.

Intra-role Coordination
Using Group Communication:
A Preliminary Report

Paolo Busetta[1], Mattia Merzi[1], Silvia Rossi[2,3], and François Legras[4]

[1] ITC-irst – Povo, Trento, Italy
{busetta,merzi}@itc.it
[2] Università di Trento – Povo, Trento, Italy
[3] Istituto di Cibernetica, CNR – Pozzuoli, Napoli, Italy
silvia.rossi@dit.unitn.it
[4] Onera DCSD – Toulouse, France
francois.legras@cert.fr

Abstract. We propose group communication for agent coordination within "active rooms" and other pervasive computing scenarios featuring strict real-time requirements, inherently unreliable communication, and a large but continuously changing set of context-aware autonomous systems. Messages are exchanged over *multicast channels*, which may remind of chat rooms in which everybody hears everything being said. The issues that have to be faced (e.g., changing users' preferences and locations; performance constraints; redundancies of sensors and actuators; agents on mobile devices continuously joining and leaving) require the ability of dynamically selecting the "best" agents for providing a service in a given context. Our approach is based on the idea of *implicit organization*, which refers to the set of all agents willing to play a given role on a given channel. An implicit organization is a special form of team with no explicit formation phase and a single role involved. No middle agent is required. A set of protocols, designed for unreliable group communication, are used to negotiate a coordination policy, and for team coordination. Preconditions and effects of these protocols are formalized by means of the joint intention theory (JIT).

1 Introduction

So-called "active rooms" or "active environments" are pervasive computing scenarios providing some form of "ambient intelligence", i.e. some form of automatic, sophisticated assistance to humans performing physical or cognitive tasks by specialized devices present in the same place. Active environments often feature a large and continuously changing set of context-sensitive, partly mobile autonomous systems; thus, a multi-agent architecture is a natural choice. As an example, our current domain of application[1] is interactive cultural information

---

[1] This work was supported by the PEACH and TICCA projects, funded by the Autonomous Province of Trento (Provincia Autonoma di Trento, Italy).

F. Dignum (Ed.): ACL 2003, LNAI 2922, pp. 231–253, 2004.

delivery within museums or archaeological sites, for which we develop multi-user, multi-media, multi-modal systems. Agents, which are distributed on both static and mobile devices, guide visitors, provide presentations, supervise crowds, and so on, exploiting whatever sensors and actuators are close to the users during their visit. The agents must immediately react to changes in the focus of attention or to movements of the users, in order not to annoy them with irrelevant or unwanted information. To make things even harder, wireless networks (required to support mobility) are intrinsically unreliable for a number of reasons. Consequently, agents have to deal, in a timely and context-dependent way, with a range of problems that include unexpectedly long reaction times by cooperating agents, occasional message losses, and even network partitioning.

We propose a form of group communication, called *channeled multicast* [1], as the main technique for agent coordination in ambient intelligence scenarios. Group communication is an active area of agent research (see [6] in this volume); among its advantages, it often reduces the amount of communication needed when more than two agents are involved in a task, and allows *overhearing* of the activity of other agents[2]. Overhearing, in turn, enables monitoring [11], group formation (see [15] in this volume), and the collection of contextual information; by overhearing, an agent can understand the state of other agents and possibly build models of their information needs (see [24] in this volume), leading to pro-active assistance [3].

This work describes an agent coordination technique based on group communication and provides its initial formal ground. Specifically, we define a set of social conventions, formalized with the Joint Intention Theory [5], for establishing and enforcing a coordination policy among agents playing the *same* role. This approach addresses issues of redundancies and adaptation to the context without the intervention of middle agents. Our communication infrastructure, being based on IP multicast, features almost instantaneous message distribution on a local area network but suffers from occasional message losses. Consequently, protocols have been designed to work under the assumption of unreliable communication.

This paper is organized as follows. Next section presents our reference scenario, while the following (Sec. 3) focuses on our objectives and our current technology. Sec. 4 introduces the concept of *implicit organization*, that is, a team of agents coordinating to play a role on a channel. Sec. 5 describes the interaction between agents and implicit organizations. The behavior of an organization is formally described in Sec. 6. The following three sections discuss how organizations decide their own coordination policies, describe a few ones, and show some examples (Sections 7, 8, and 9 respectively). Sec. 10 compares some works available in the literature with ours.

---

[2] Listeners that are non explicitly addressed are classified as *auditors, overhearers,* or *eavesdroppers* by [6]. They differ because of the attitudes of either speakers or hearers, but are indistinguishable from the perspective of the communication media. For the sake of simplicity, we drop this distinction and call them all overhearers.

2   A Reference Scenario

The PEACH project [20] aims at creating "active museums", i.e. smart environments featuring multimodal I/O where a visitor would be able to interact with her environment via various sensors and effectors, screens, handheld devices, etc. In this challenging application domain, agents can come and go dynamically, visitors move around the museum (potentially carrying handheld devices), communication media are heterogeneous and sometimes unreliable (a mix of wired and wireless networks are likely). An important consideration is that, if the system does not react timely to the movements and interests of the visitors, they will simply ignore it or, worse, will become annoyed.

A typical problem that such a system should be able to solve is the following. A visitor is supposed to receive a multimedia presentation on a particular subject, but (1) several agents are able to produce it with different capabilities (pictures + text or audio + video) and variable availabilities (CPU load or communication possibilities) and (2) the visitor is close to several actuators (screens, speakers) each able to "display" the presentation, and the visitor carries a PDA which is also able to display it, albeit in a more limited way. In addition, several other visitors are nearby potentially using the actuators, and of course if the visitor does not get a presentation within a few seconds she will leave.

3   Settings and Assumptions

We deal here with cooperation with unreliable communication and highly dynamic environment. We do not address the well-known problems of task decomposition or sub-goal negotiation. We assume that once agents are set to execute a task they know how to do it. Rather, we aim at achieving robustness and tolerance to failure in a setting where agents can be redundant, communication is unreliable, hardware can be switched off, and so on. Such an environment can evolve faster than the agents execute their task, so it is not feasible to use "traditional" techniques e.g. guided team selection [22] or shared planning [9]. Our objective is to avoid centralized or static solutions like mediators, facilitators or brokers, but rather to have a fully distributed and flexible system, without looking for optimality.

Our experimental communication infrastructure, used in PEACH, is called LoudVoice and is based on the concept of channeled multicast [1]. LoudVoice uses the fast but inherently unreliable IP multicast – which is not a major limitation when considering that, as said above, our communication media is unreliable by nature. Channels in LoudVoice can be easily discovered by their *themes*, that is, by the main subjects of conversation; a theme is just a string taken from an application-specific taxonomy of subjects, accessible as an XML file via its URL. Having discovered one or more channels, an agent can freely "listen" to and "speak" on them by means of FIPA-like messages, encoded as XML documents. The header of a message includes a performative, its sender and one or more destinations; the latter can be agent identifiers, but any other expression is accepted (for instance, we use role names – see Sec. 5).

4   Implicit Organizations

Following a common convention in multi-agent systems, we define a *role* as a communication based API, or abstract agent interface (AAI), i.e. one or more protocols aimed at obtaining a cohesive set of functions from an agent. A simple example is mentioned in [1], an auction system with two main roles: the auctioneer (which calls for bids, collects them and declares the winner) and the bidder (which answers to calls for bids and commits to perform whatever transaction is requested when winning an auction). An agent may play more than one role, simultaneously or at different times depending on its capabilities and the context.

We adopt the term *organization* from Tidhar [23], to refer to teams where explicit *command*, *control*, and *communication* relationships (concerning team goals, team intentions, and team beliefs respectively) are established among sub-teams.

We call *implicit organization* a set of agents tuned on the same channel to play the same role and willing to coordinate their actions. The term "implicit" highlights the facts that there is no group formation phase (joining an organization is just a matter of tuning on a channel), and no name for it – the role and the channel uniquely identify the group, indeed. It is important to highlight that all agents of an implicit organizations play the same role but they may do it in different ways – redundancy (as in traditional fault tolerant or high capacity, load-balanced systems) is just a particular case where agents are perfectly interchangeable. This situation is commonly managed by putting a broker or some other form of middle agent supervising the organization. By contrast, our objective is to explore advantages and disadvantages of an approach based on unreliable group communication, in a situation where agents can come and go fairly quickly, their capabilities can change or evolve over time, and it is not necessarily known a-priori which agent can achieve a specific goal without first trying it out.

An implicit organization is a special case of team. Generally speaking, a team includes different roles, and is formed in order to achieve a specific goal; as said above, an implicit organization includes all agents playing a given role on a channel at any given time. Goals for an implicit organization are automatically established by requests to achieve something and queries addressed to its role. In Tidhar's terms, this is to say that a command relationship is established between any agent performing a goal-establishing communicative action (the "commanding agent") and the implicit organization, whose consequence is that the latter is committed to achieving the goal. Section 5 below discusses the corresponding protocol.

An implicit organization is in charge of defining its own control policy, which means: (1) how a sub-team is formed within the organization in order to achieve a specific goal; and, (2) how the intentions of this sub-team are established. For this initial work, a goal-specific sub-team is fixed to be simply *all agents that are willing to commit immediately at achieving the organizational goal at the time this is established*; i.e., there is no explicit sub-team formation, rather

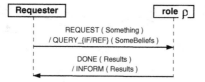

Fig. 1. A role-based interaction

introspection by each agent to decide whether or not it has enough resources immediately available. A *coordination policy* established for the organization is then used within a sub-team to decide who actually works towards achieving its goal, and possibly to coordinate the agents if more than one is involved.

We assume that policies are well-known to agents; Section 8 describes some of those used in our domain. We assume the existence of a library of application-independent policies. Thus, it is possible to refer to a policy simply by its name. A policy, however, may have parameters that need to be negotiated before use – for instance, the currency used for auctions, or the master agent in a master-slave environment. We call *policy instance* a tuple composed of a policy name and ground values for its parameters.

Note that a goal-specific sub-team may well be empty, e.g. when all agents of the implicit organization are busy or simply no agent is part of the organization. With unreliable communication, this case is effectively indistinguishable from the loss of the goal-establishing message (unless overhearing is applied; this is left to future work) or even from a very slow reaction; consequently, it must be properly managed by the commanding agent. These considerations have an important impact on the protocol between commanding agents and implicit organizations, as discussed below.

5   Role-Based Communication

In this initial work, we assume that any request – by which we mean any RE-QUEST and QUERY, using the FIPA performatives [8] – generates a commitment by an implicit organization to perform the necessary actions and answer appropriately (strategic thinking by the organization is not considered for now). Thus, in principle the interactions between commanding agents and implicit organizations are straightforward, and can be summarized in the simple UML sequence diagram of Fig. 1. A generic *Requester* agent addresses its request to a role ρ on a channel; the corresponding implicit organization replies appropriately.

As mentioned above, however, unreliable channels, continuous changes in the number of agents in the organization, and strict real-time constraint, substantially complicate the picture. Fig. 2 is a finite state machine that captures, with some simplifications, the possible evolutions of the protocol. The events on top half represent the normal case - no message loss, a goal-specific subteam achieves the goal. The events in brackets on the lower half represent degraded cases.

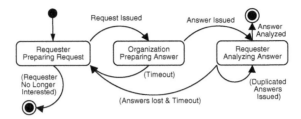

Fig. 2. Interacting with unreliable communication – a simplified protocol machine

Consider, for instance, the cases where a request or its answer are lost, or no goal-specific sub-team can be formed. A timeout forces the commanding agent to reconsider whether its request is still relevant – e.g., the user's context has not changed – and, if so, whether to resend the original message. It follows that an implicit organization must be able to deal with message repetitions. This implies that agents should discard repeated messages or re-issue any answer already sent; also, the coordination policies should contain mechanisms that prevent confusion in the cases of partial deliveries or new agents joining the organization between two repetitions.

Similarly, the commanding agent has to deal with repeated answers, possibly caused by its own repeated requests. In the worse case, these repeated answers may even be different – e.g., because something has changed in the environment, a new agent has joined the organization, and so on. Rather than introducing middle-agents or making the organizational coordination protocols overly complicated to prevent this to happen (which is likely to be something impossible to achieve anyway, according to [10]), our current choice is to have the requester to consider whatever answer it receives first as the valid one, and ignore all others.

Of course, the protocol presented above can be used only in non-safety critical applications or in situations where some level of uncertainty can be tolerated. This is definitely the case in our multi-media environments, where quality of communications is fairly high and the objective is nothing more critical than providing some guidance and context-sensitive cultural information to visitors of museums.

Observe that third parties overhearing a channel, in accordance to [3], may help in making the interaction with implicit organizations much more robust – for instance, by detecting some message losses, or whether a goal-specific sub-team has been established. Exploring these possibilities is left to future work.

6   Formalization

This section provides a high-level formalization of the coordination within an implicit organization. This is done by means of a logic specifically designed for conversation policies, the Joint Intention Theory (JIT) [5, 17]. JIT was born as a follow-up of a formalization of the theory of speech acts [18]. Recently, it has been applied to group communication [12], and a particular form of diagram, composed of *landmark expressions*, has been introduced. This diagram "resembles state machines but instead of specifying the state transitions, it specifies a partially ordered set of states" [14] called *landmarks* and corresponding to JIT formulas.

Strictly speaking, JIT is not applicable to our domain because we adopt unreliable communication, however it is very convenient for capturing certain aspects of teamwork; we return on this point in Sec. 6.1 below.

JIT is expressed as a modal language with connectives of the first order logic and operators for propositional attitudes. Greek letters are used for groups, and lowercase variables for agents. We use the definitions from the mentioned papers [17, 12, 14], to which we add a few new ones in order to simplify the formulas introduced later. We identify an implicit organization with the role it plays, and indicate it with ρ; $\rho(x)$ is true if x is member of ρ, which means that x is playing the role ρ on a given channel. We simplify the definition of group mutual belief given in [12] – that is: $(MB\ \tau_1\ \tau_2\ p) \equiv (BMB\ \tau_1\ \tau_2\ p) \wedge (BMB\ \tau_2\ \tau_1\ p)$ – for the special case of "all agents of a group towards their group and viceversa":

$$(MB\ \rho\ p) \equiv \forall x\ \rho(x) \supset (BMB\ x\ \rho\ p) \wedge (BMB\ \rho\ x\ p)$$

Analogously, we extend the definitions of mutual goal (MG), joint persistent goal (JPG), and introduce group extensions of some others from [18], as follows. For simplicity, we consider the relativizing condition q always true, thus it will be omitted in all the following formulas. A *mutual goal* is defined as:

$$(MG\ \rho\ p) \equiv (MB\ \rho\ (GOAL\ \rho\ \Diamond p))$$

A *weak achievement goal* is:

$$(WAG\ x\ \rho\ p) \equiv [(BEL\ x\ \neg p) \wedge (GOAL\ x\ \Diamond p)] \vee$$
$$[(BEL\ x\ p) \wedge (GOAL\ x\ \Diamond(MB\ \rho\ p))] \vee$$
$$[(BEL\ x\ \Box\neg p) \wedge (GOAL\ x\ \Diamond(MB\ \rho\ \Box\neg p))]$$

i.e., x has a WAG toward ρ when it believes that p is not currently true, in which case it has a goal to achieve p, or if it believes p to be either true or impossible, in which case it has a goal to bring about the corresponding mutual beliefs. A *weak mutual goal* is:

$$(WMG\ \rho\ p) \equiv \forall x\ \rho(x) \supset (MB\ \rho\ (WAG\ x\ \rho\ p) \wedge (WAG\ \rho\ x\ p))$$

where: $(WAG\ \rho\ y\ p) \equiv \forall x\ \rho(x) \supset (WAG\ x\ y\ p)$. A weak mutual goal is a mutual belief that each agent has a weak achievement goal towards its group for achieving p, and conversely the group has the goal towards its members. A *joint persistent goal* is:

$$(JPG\ \rho\ p) \equiv (MB\ \rho\ \neg p) \wedge (MG\ \rho\ p) \wedge$$
$$(UNTIL\ [(MB\ \rho\ p) \vee (MB\ \rho\ \Box\neg p)]\ (WMG\ \rho\ p))$$

that is, ρ has a joint persistent goal p when there is a mutual belief that p is not currently true, there is a mutual goal to bring about p, and p will remain a weak mutual goal until there is a mutual belief that p is either true, or will never be true.

The expression $(DONE \, \rho \, p)$, used in the following, is a group-extension of the definition of DONE given in [4], i.e. any agent in the group ρ believes that p happened immediately before the present time.

Finally, we define $Coord(P_i \, \sigma \, r \, p)$, where P_i is a coordination policy, σ is a group of agents, r is another agent, and p is a goal, as a function that computes the sequence of actions that must be performed by σ under policy P_i in order to achieve p and notify r when done. This sequence is composed of coordination actions and sub-goals assigned to individual agents, and must terminate with a DONE or INFORM message to r on the results. Recall that, by using a channeled multicast infrastructure such as LoudVoice, everybody listening to a channel receives everything sent on it; thus, the action of sending the results to r also establishes – via overhearing – a belief in the listeners that the goal has been reached (or is not reachable).

With the definitions given above, we can now formalize how an implicit organization must behave to achieve a goal p commanded by a request from agent r to the role ρ (Section 5). In the following, $CurrentPolicyDecided$ represents whether or not a coordination policy has already been established, i.e. $CurrentPolicyDecided \equiv \exists P_i \, (CurrentPolicy \, P_i)$, where P_i is a *policy instance* (Sec. 4). σ represents the goal-specific sub-team instantiated to achieve p. The behaviour of the implicit organization is represented by the landmark diagram of Figure 3, where the landmarks correspond to the following JIT expressions:

L1: $\neg(DONE \, \rho \, p) \, \wedge \, (JPG \, \rho \, ((DONE \, \rho \, p) \wedge (BEL \, r \, p)))$
L2: $(MB \, \rho \, CurrentPolicyDecided) \wedge (INTEND \, \sigma \, Coord(P_i \, \sigma \, r \, p))$
L3: $(MB \, \rho \, ((DONE \, \rho \, p) \vee \Box\neg(DONE \, \rho \, p)))$
L4: $(MB \, \rho \, \neg CurrentPolicyDecided) \wedge (JPG \, \rho \, CurrentPolicyDecided)$
$\wedge (JPG \, \rho \, ((DONE \, \rho \, p) \wedge (BEL \, r \, p)))$

The machine starts executing (i.e. landmark L1 is entered) when a request for p from r arrives to an implicit organization ρ, and concludes (i.e., L3 is reached) when the request is satisfied. In other words, Fig. 3 is an expansion of the state **Organization Preparing Answer** of the diagram of Fig. 2. Landmark L1 says that the requested goal has not been achieved yet, and that ρ has a joint persistent goal to achieve it and notify r.

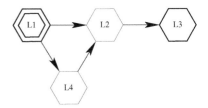

Fig. 3. Coordination in an implicit organization

However, achieving p is possible only if the organization knows how to coordinate. If this is the case, i.e. a coordination policy has already been established, then it moves to landmark L2, otherwise to L4. The transition from L4 to L2 is called *policy negotiation*, and is discussed in Sec. 7 below.

In the transitions from L1 to L2 and from L4 to L2, a sub-team σ is formed and given an intention to achieve p on behalf of ρ. As stated in Sec. 4, in this work we assume that σ are all agents able to achieve p at the time the request arrives (i.e., when L1 is entered). In a policy-specific way, σ does whatever is required to achieve p. The notification of the results to r is overheard by everybody in ρ, thus it establishes the mutual belief within the organization that satisfies its joint goal (landmark L3).

6.1   Common Knowledge, JIT, and LoudVoice

As mentioned in Sec. 3, our communication infrastructure LoudVoice privileges speed over reliability. In our settings (typically a standard LAN extended with a wireless infrastructure), we can assume practically instantaneous transport of messages on a channel with respect to the evolution of the environment, and a certain probability that – for whatever reason, including network jams and inherent unreliability of wireless links – messages can be occasionally lost and temporary network partitions happen (typically when mobile devices move through areas not covered by any signal). Apparently, this goes against using JIT for formalization, because JIT assumes the possibility of establishing *mutual beliefs* within a team.

In a simplistic interpretation, a mutual belief is a form of *common knowledge* [10], e.g. an agent i believes that an agent j believes b, j believes that i believes that j believes b, i believes that j believes that i believes that j believes b, and so on forever. "Perfect" common knowledge cannot be attained with either unreliable group communication or reliable but non-instantaneous delivery of messages. Specifically, Halpern and Moses in [10] formalize well-known results in distributed systems theories, i.e. that synchronized action based on perfect common knowledge is not possible.

By applying game theory, Morris and Shin reached an important result on *probabilistic coordination* [16]. In short, they show that, in *non-strategic games* – i.e. where all agents play by rules determined a-priori independently of their individual objectives and preferences – and a reasonably small probability of losing messages, it is possible to design protocols which achieve coordination (in game theory-speak, maximize payoff) with a probability arbitrarily close to the desired one. Non-strategic behavior, pre-defined rules, and small probability of loss, are all characteristics of our domain. We designed our protocols to be robust against single message losses or the occasional network partitioning, thus giving a high level of confidence on their outcomes. Some mechanisms, such as the periodic reminders sent on the control channel about the current policy adopted by an implicit organization (Sec. 7.3), have the specific purpose of increasing that confidence by detecting problems as soon as possible.

Contrary to the interpretation given above, Kumar et al. argue [13] that a mutual belief does *not* imply common knowledge – indeed, agents may be wrong about their beliefs, including their mutual ones. Kumar mentions a number of works on the establishment of mutual beliefs by default rules, and introduces a set of defeasible rules of communication that cause belief revision when an agent realizes that some assumptions on others' beliefs were wrong. Observe that our periodic reminders mentioned above serve exactly this purpose, i.e. triggering a belief revision when necessary.

Our conclusion is that we can adopt JIT for a high-level formalization in spite of using unreliable communication. However, the protocols described in this work were not directly derived from landmark expressions (as done by [14]) – this would have left fixing failures to the rules mentioned above. Rather, we decided to deal directly with message losses in order to reach our required level of confidence. Automatic protocol derivation from JIT in our setting may be the objective of future work.

7   Negotiating a Policy

This section formalizes the negotiation protocol for the organizational coordination policy, and describes an algorithm to be applied with unreliable group communication. In summary, the negotiation protocol works in two phases: first, the set of *policy instances* common to all agents is computed; then, one is selected.

7.1   Defining Policy Instances

Recall, from Sec. 4, that a policy instance is a tuple with the name of a policy and ground values for all its parameters; e.g.: <auction, Euro>, represents an "auction" policy whose first parameter (presumably the currency) is "Euro". A potential issue with our two-phase protocol is that an agent may support a very large (even infinite) or undetermined number of policy instances: this happens, for instance, when a parameter may take any integer value, or has to be set to the name of one of the agents of the organization. To this end, we have designed a language for expressing sets of policy instances in a compact way by means of constraints on parameters [2]. These are currently limited to be integers or strings, but this is enough for our purposes. An expression in this language describes a (possibly infinite) *set* of policy instances. *Reducing* two expressions means to generate zero or more expressions that describe the intersection of the sets in input. The intersection of policies performed during negotiation (see the algorithm later) is thus the reduction of all expressions exchanged during the protocol. Simple examples of expressions are:

```
name = MulticastContractNet
    param = Currency costraint = (one of Dollar, Euro) suggested = (Euro)
    param = WinningCriteria value = lowest
    param = BidTimeout constraint = (in 100..2000 ) suggested = (1000)
name = MasterSlave
    param = Master constraint = (not one of Agent1, Agent2)
                suggested = (Agent3, Agent4)
name = any
```

The last expression represents *all* possible policy instances, and is used by agents leaving an organization or external to it when triggering a negotiation, as shown later.

7.2   Formalization

From the perspective of an individual member x, the coordination policy of an organization, independently from its specific value, goes through three different states: "unknown", "negotiating", and "decided". The policy is unknown when the agent joins the organization, i.e. when it tunes on a channel to play the organization's role; the first goal of x is to negotiate it with the other members. At that point, the following applies:

$$(\nexists P_i \; (BEL \; x \; (CurrentPolicy \; P_i)))\wedge$$
$$(INTEND \; x \; SEND(\rho, REQUEST(CurrentPolicy \; ?)))$$

that is, the agent does not hold any belief on the current policy, and asks to the other members about it. This request is interpreted by the organization as a notification that a new member has joined. In turn, this triggers the negotiation protocol, modeled by the landmark diagram of Fig. 4, whose landmarks are the following:

L1: $(JPG \; \rho \; CurrentPolicyDecided)$
L2: $(JPG \; \rho \; CurrentPolicyDecided) \; \wedge \; (MB \; \rho \; (CommonPolicies \; \Pi))$
$\quad \wedge (GOAL \; o \; (MB \; \rho \; (CurrentPolicy \; selectFrom(o, \Pi))))$
L3: $(MB \; \rho \; (CommonPolicies \; \Pi)) \; \wedge \; (MB \; \rho \; (CurrentPolicy \; P_i))$

L1 represents the state of the implicit organization when negotiation is started. There is a mutual belief that no policy has been currently decided within the organization. This happens, for instance, when a new

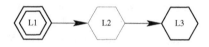

Fig. 4. Policy negotiation protocol

agent joins - the REQUEST it sends makes the organization aware that the mutual belief on the current policy, if it had ever held before, does no longer hold and must be re-established. Thus, ρ sets for itself a joint persistent goal of agreeing on the current policy.

As mentioned earlier, this is done in two steps. In the first, corresponding to the transition from L1 to L2, a mutual belief about the policy instances common to the entire group is established. This can be easily achieved by exchanging reciprocal INFORMs on what each agent is able to support, and intersecting their contents; the resulting set of policy instances is the mutual belief $(CommonPolicies \; \Pi)$.

At this stage (landmark L2), a special agent o, called the *oracle*, assumes the goal of establishing the $CurrentPolicy$ of the role; the function $selectFrom(o, \Pi)$ is evaluated by o and returns a member of its input set. Thus, the second step of the protocol (the transition from L2 to L3) consists of the decision-making by the oracle and the establishment of the current policy, which can be done by o sending an ASSERT to ρ about the value returned by $selectFrom(o, \Pi)$. This assertion, in turn, causes the agents to know that $CurrentPolicyDecided$ is now true, and thus the related joint goal is automatically satisfied.

The oracle can be anybody, a member of the organization as well as an external agent (the latter can overhear the negotiation protocol, thus it knows the common policies). It can apply whatever decision criteria it deems more appropriate – from a random choice, to a configuration rule, to inferring on previous policies based on machine learning, and so on. In this work, we do not elaborate on how the oracle is chosen, nor on its logic (but examples are given in Sec. 9). The algorithm presented below: (1) allows for any external agent (such as a network monitor or an application agent interested in enforcing certain policies) to intervene just after the common policies have been established; (2) provides a default oracle election mechanism if an external one is not present; and, (3) handles conflicting oracles by forcing a re-negotiation.

7.3   From Theory to Practice

As discussed in Sec. 6.1, JIT does not work with unreliable communication. A practical protocol for the decision of a policy has to take this issue into account, as well as the problem of a highly dynamic environment where agents can join and leave very quickly. To this end, the protocol implemented by the algorithm described below adds one information and a few more messages to the formal model given above.

All messages concerning policy negotiation are marked with a *Negotiation Sequence Number* (NSN). A NSN is the identifier of a negotiation process, and is unique during the lifetime of an organization. NSNs form an ordered set; an `increment(nsn)` function returns a NSN that is strictly greater than its input nsn. In our current implementation, a NSN is simply an integer; the first agent joining an organization sets the NSN of the first negotiation to zero.

Goal of the NSN is to help in guaranteeing coherence of protocols and integrity of mutual beliefs in the cases of message losses, network partitioning, and new agents joining mid-way a negotiation. As described in the algorithm below, messages related to policy negotiation are interpreted by an agent depending on their NSN. Messages containing an obsolete NSN are simply discarded, possibly after informing the sender that it is out of date. Messages that have a NSN newer than the one known to the agent are also ignored but cause the agent to enter into a negotiating state. Only messages whose NSN is equal to the known one are actually handled.

The protocol is made robust in two other ways. First, during the transition from L1 to L2, rather than exchanging simple INFORMs on the policies they support, agents send repeated INFORMs on the known common policies and participating agents. Second, a *policy reminder* message, consisting of an INFORM on what is believed to be the current policy, is periodically sent by each agent after the end of the negotiation, allowing recovery from the loss of the oracle announcement and consistency checking against other problems.

Note that a network partitioning may cause two sub-organizations, each living on its own partition, to increment their NSN independently; when the partitions are rejoined, the integrity checks on the NSNs described above cause the organization to re-negotiate the policy.

A member of an organization can be modeled as having three main beliefs directly related to policies: the supported policies, the common policies, and the current policy. As its name suggests, the first belief consists of all the policy instances that an agents supports: $SupportedPolicies(\rho, \{P_1 \ldots P_k\})$, where ρ is the role and $\{P_i\}$ is a set of policy instances, typically defined by the agent developer. The common policies belief contains a set of agents participating to a negotiation (identified by its NSN) and the policies supported by everybody, i.e. the intersection of their supported policies: $CommonPolicies(\rho, NSN, \{P_1 \ldots P_k\}$, $\{A_1 \ldots A_i\})$, where ρ is the role and $\{P_i\}$ is the intersection of all the policy instances supported by agents $\{A_1 \ldots A_i\}$. Finally, the current policy is the policy instance decided by the oracle for a given negotiation (identified by its NSN): $CurrentPolicy(\rho, NSN, P_k)$.

7.4   The Algorithm

This section describes, as pseudo-code, the negotiation algorithm performed by each agent of an implicit organization.

In the following, we assume that an agent is a simple event-driven rule engine. We adopt some obvious syntactical conventions, a mixture of generic event-action rules, C (for code structuring, $==$ for testing equality and $! =$ for diversity) and Pascal (variable declarations as **name: type**). The **suspend** primitive blocks the execution of the calling rule until its input condition (typically a timeout) is satisfied; during the time of suspension, other rules can be invoked as events unfold. A few primitives are used to send messages (INFORM, ASSERT, REQUEST) to the role for which the policy is being negotiated; for simplicity, we assume that the beliefs being transmitted or queried are expressed in a Prolog-like language. For readability, the role is never explicitly mentioned in the following, since the algorithm works for a single role at the time.

The three main beliefs described above and the state of the negotiation are represented by the following variables:

```
myself: Agent_Identifier;
myNSN: Negotiation_Sequence_Number;
negotiationState: {UNKNOWN, NEGOTIATING, DECIDED};
supportedPolicies: set of Policy;
commonPolicies: set of Policy;
negotiatingAgents: set of Agent_Identifier;
currentPolicy: Policy;
```

When the agent starts playing a role, it needs to discover the current situation of the organization, in particular its current NSN. This is done by sending a query to the role about the current policy. If nothing happens, after a while the agent assumes to be alone, and starts a negotiation – message losses are recovered by the rest of the algorithm.

```
on_Start() {
  set negotiationState = UNKNOWN;
  set myNSN = MIN_VALUE;
  set myself = getOwnAgentIdentifier();
  REQUEST (CURRENT_POLICY(?,?));
  suspend until timeout;
  if ((currentPolicy == nil) AND (negotiationState == UNKNOWN))
    negotiate (increment(myNSN), supportedPolicies, set_of (myself));
}

on_Request ( CURRENT_POLICY (input_NSN, input_policy) ) {
  if ((input_NSN == ?) AND (input_policy == ?) AND (currentPolicy != nil))
      INFORM ( CURRENT_POLICY(myNSN,currentPolicy) );
  else ...... }
```

The negotiation process mainly consists of an iterative intersection of the policies
supported by all agents, which any agent can start by sending an INFORM with
its own supported policies and a NSN higher than the one of the last negotiation
(see **negotiate()** later on). Conversely, if the agent receives an INFORM on
the common policies whose NSN is greater than the one known to the agent, it
infers that a new negotiation has started, and joins it.

The contents of the INFORMs on the common policies that are received
during a negotiation are intersected as shown in the following. If the resulting
common policies set is empty, i.e. no policy can be agreed upon, the agent notifies
a failure condition, waits for some time to allow network re-configurations or
agents to leave, and then restart the negotiation again.

```
on_Inform ( COMMON_POLICIES (input_NSN, input_policies, input_agents) ) {
  if (input_NSN > myNSN)
    negotiate ( input_NSN,
                intersect (supportedPolicies, input_policies),
                union (input_agents, set_of(myself)) );
  else
  if ((input_NSN == myNSN) AND (negotiationState == NEGOTIATING)) {
    commonPolicies = intersect (commonPolicies, input_policies);
    negotiatingAgents = union (negotiatingAgents, input_agents);
    if (commonPolicies == {empty set}) {
        {notify failure to user};
        suspend until timeout;
        negotiate(increment(myNSN), supportedPolicies, set_of (myself));
    }
  }
  else
  if (negotiationState == DECIDED)
    INFORM (CURRENT_POLICY (myNSN,currentPolicy));
  else
  if (negotiationState == NEGOTIATING)
    INFORM(COMMON_POLICIES (myNSN, commonPolicies, negotiatingAgents));
}
```

A negotiation is either started by the agent, which sets the initial value of the common policies to those it supports, or joined when receiving information on the common policies (see the code above). As described earlier, during the first phase of a negotiation the agent informs the channel about the policies it knows as common, then waits for a period, during which it collects INFORMs from the other members of the organization. This process is repeated for (at most) `max_repeats` times, to allow the synchronization of the mutual beliefs on the common policies and the recovery of any lost message. It follows that `max_repeats` is a sensitive parameters, whose value mainly depends on the reliability of the transport media in use for the channels: if this is very reliable, then `max_repeats` can be low (two or three). The set of negotiating agents, which is not exploited by this algorithm, may be used by a more sophisticated algorithm for a better recovery (e.g., by comparing this set with the set of those agents from which messages have been actually received).

After `max_repeats` repetitions, the set of common policies should correspond to the intersection of all policies accepted by all negotiating agents. It is now time to choose a policy from this set. As mentioned in the previous section, this is done either by an external oracle, or – if none is present – by an agent chosen with an arbitrary heuristic. Below, we choose the agent with the lowest identifier (after checking the NSN, to prevent confusion when `negotiate()` is called recursively by a new negotiation starting in the middle of another). The self-nominated oracle can apply whatever criteria it prefers to pick a policy; here, we use a simple random choice.

```
procedure negotiate (negotiation_NSN: NSN,
                     initial_policies: set of Policy,
                     initial_agents: set of Agent_Identifier ) {
  set negotiationState = NEGOTIATING;
  set myNSN = negotiation_NSN;
  set commonPolicies = initial_policies;
  set negotiatingAgents = initial_agents;
  currentPolicy = nil;
  INFORM (COMMON_POLICIES (myNSN, commonPolicies, negotiatingAgents));
  repeat max_repeats times {
    suspend until timeout;
    if (currentPolicy != nil)
        break;    /// out of the 'repeat' block
    INFORM (COMMON_POLICIES (myNSN, commonPolicies, negotiatingAgents));
  }
  suspend until (timeout OR currentPolicy != nil);
  if ((currentPolicy == nil) AND (myNSN == negotiation_NSN) AND
      (LowestId (negotiatingAgents) == myself)) {
    set currentPolicy = random_choice(commonPolicies);
    ASSERT (CURRENT_POLICY(myNSN,currentPolicy));
  }
  while (currentPolicy == nil)
    suspend until (timeout OR currentPolicy != nil);
  set negotiationState = DECIDED;
}
```

When an ASSERT of the current policy is received, the agent does a few checks to detect inconsistencies – for instance, that the NSN does not refer to a different negotiation, or that two oracles have not attempted to set the policy independently. If everything is fine, the assertion is accepted, causing `negotiate()` to finish (see the code above). Otherwise, the assertion is either refused, or triggers a new negotiation.

```
on_Assert( CURRENT_POLICY ( input_NSN, input_policy ) ) {
  if (input_NSN == myNSN) {
    if (((currentPolicy == nil) AND
         commonPolicies.contains(input_policy)) OR
        (currentPolicy == input_policy))
      set currentPolicy = input_policy;
    else
      negotiate (increment(myNSN), supportedPolicies, set_of (myself));
  }
  else
  if (myNSN < input_NSN)
    negotiate (increment (input_NSN), supportedPolicies, set_of (myself));
}
```

Since the assertion of the current policy can be lost, and to prevent inconsistencies caused for instance by network partitioning and rejoining, periodically each agent reminds to the group what it believes to be the current policy. The frequency of the reminders may change depending on the reliability of the transport media. When an agent receives a remainder, it checks for consistency with what it believes – i.e., that the NSN and the policy are the same. If not, depending on the situation it may either react with an inform (to let the sender know of a likely problem and possibly re-negotiate) or by triggering a negotiation itself.

```
on_PolicyReminder_Timeout() {
  INFORM (CURRENT_POLICY (myNSN,currentPolicy));
  set policy_reminder_timeout = getPolicyReminder_Timeout();
}


on_Inform ( CURRENT_POLICY (input_NSN, input_policy) ) {
  if (input_NSN > myNSN)
    negotiate (increment(input_NSN), supportedPolicies, set_of(myself));
  else
  if (input_NSN < myNSN) {
    if (negotiationState == DECIDED)
      INFORM (CURRENT_POLICY (myNSN, currentPolicy));
  }
  else   /** that is, input_NSN == myNSN **/
  if ((currentPolicy == nil) AND commonPolicies.contains(input_policy))
      set currentPolicy = input_policy;
  else
  if (input_policy != currentPolicy)
      negotiate (increment(myNSN), supportedPolicies, set_of(myself));
}
```

Finally, when an agent leaves the channel, it has a social obligation to start a new negotiation to allow the others to adapt to the changed situation. This is done by triggering the negotiation process with an INFORM about the common policies, with an incremented NSN and the policies set to a special value `any` which means "anything is acceptable" (Sec. 7.1).

```
on_Leave() {
  INFORM ( COMMON_POLICIES (increment(myNSN), set_of("any"), nil) );
}
```

8   Coordination Protocols

Recall, from Sec. 4, that when an implicit organization receives a request (i.e., the state `Organization Preparing Answer` of Fig. 2 is entered), its members with available resources form a sub-team. This happens silently, i.e. there is no explicit group formation message. As described in Sec. 7, if an organizational coordination policy has not been established yet, then one is negotiated among all members of the organization (these are the transitions from L1 to L4 and then to L2 in Fig. 3). Once the policy has been decided, the goal-specific subteam can start working.

All policies have to follow a straightforward, abstract three-phase schema, summarized in Fig. 5. Before doing anything, the sub-team coordinates to form a joint intention on how to achieve the goal (`Pre-Work Coordination`). The agents in charge perform whatever action is required, including any necessary on-going coordination (`Working`). When finally everybody finishes, a `Post-Work Coordination` phase collects results and replies to the requester (which corresponds to the `Answer Issued` event of Fig. 2).

We describe in the following four basic organizational coordination policies that we use in our domain; examples of their application are in next section. Many other variants and alternatives can be designed to meet different requirements, such as Quality of Service objectives, efficiency, and so on.

The *Plain Competition* policy is nothing more than "everybody races against everybody else, and the first to finish wins". It is by far the easiest policy of all: no pre-work nor post-work coordination is required, while the on-going coordination consists in overhearing the reply sent by who finishes first. In summary, *Plain Competition* works as follows: when a role receives a request, any agent able to react starts working on the job immediately. When an agent finishes, it sends back its results (as an INFORM or DONE to the requester, in accordance to Fig. 1). The other agents overhear this answer and stop working on the same job.

Fig. 5. Abstract coordination policy, UML state diagram

A race condition is possible: two or more agents finish at the same time and send their answers. This is not a problem, as explained in Sec. 5, since the requester accepts whatever answer comes first and ignores the others.

The **Simple Collaboration** policy consists of a collaboration among all participants for synthesizing a common answer from the results obtained by each agent independently. This policy does not require any pre-work coordination; the on-going coordination consists in declaring what results have been achieved, or that work is still on-going; finally, the post-work coordination consists in having one agent (the first to finish) collecting answers from everybody else and sending a synthesis to the requester.

Simple Collaboration works as follows. As in *Plain Competition*, all agents able to react start working on the job as soon as the request is received. The first agent that finishes advertises his results with an INFORM to the role, and moves to the post-work phase. Within a short timeout (a parameter negotiated with the policy, usually around half a second), all other members of the subteam must react by sending, to the role again, either an INFORM with their own results, or an INFORM that says that they are still working followed by an INFORM with the results when finally done. The first agent collects all these messages and synthesizes the common result, in a goal-dependent way. Let us stress that, to support this policy, an agent must have the capabilities both to achieve the requested goal, and to synthesize the results.

As in the previous case, a race condition is possible among agents finishing at the same time, so more than one may be collecting the same results; as always, multiple answers are not a problem for the requester, and generally imply a minor waste of computational resources because of the synthesis by multiple agents.

The **Multicast Contract Net** policy is a simplification of the well-known Contract Net protocol [19], where the Manager is the agent sending a request to a role, and the award is determined by the bidder themselves, since everybody knows everybody else's bid. Thus, effectively this policy contemplates coordination only in the pre-work phase, while neither on-going nor post-work are required. This policy has three parameters: the winning criteria (lowest or highest bid), a currency for the bid (which can be any string), and a timeout within which bids must be sent.

Multicast Contract Net works as follows. As soon as a request arrives to the role, all participating agents send their bid to the role. Since everybody receives everybody else's offer, each agent can easily compute which one is the winner. At the expiration of the timeout for the bid, the winning agent declares its victory to the role with an INFORM repeating its successful bid, and starts working.

Some degraded cases must be handled. The first happens when two or more agents send the same winning bid; to solve this issue, as in the policy negotiation protocol, we arbitrarily chose a heuristics, which consists in taking as winner the agent with the lowest communication identifier. The second case happens because of a race condition when the timeout for the bid expires, or because of the loss of messages; as a consequence, it may happen that two or more agents believe to be winners. This is solved by an additional, very short wait after declaring victory, during which each agent believing to be the winner listens for contradictory declarations from others.

In spite of these precautions, it may happen that two or more agents believe to be the winners and attempt to achieve the goal independently. The winner declaration mechanism, however, reduces its probability to the square of the probability of losing a single messages, since at least two consecutive messages (the bid from the real winner and its victory declaration) must be lost by the others.

The **Master-Slave** policy has many similarities with the Multicast Contract Net; the essential difference is that, in place of a bidding phase, a master decides which agent is delegated to achieve a goal. The master is elected by the policy negotiation protocol. Typically, agents that support this policy either propose themselves as masters, or accept any other agent but refuse to be master themselves; this is because the master must react to all requests in order to select a slave delegated to achieve a goal, and must have an appropriate selection logic.

Master-Slave works as follows. When a request arrives, all agents willing to work send an INFORM to the role to declare their availability. The master (which may or may not among those available to work) collects all declarations, and issues an INFORM to the role nominating the slave, which acknowledges by repeating the same INFORM. Message loss is recovered by the master handling a simple timeout between its nomination and the reply, and repeating the IN-FORM if necessary. Thus, it is not possible for two agents to believe to be slaves for the same request.

9   Practical Examples

We elaborate on three examples, which have been chosen to show some practical implicit organizations and the usage of the policies discussed in Sec. 8. Interactions will be illustrated with a simplified, FIPA-like syntax.

Our first example is of *collaboration among search engines*. A CitationFinder accepts requests to look for a text in its knowledge base and returns extracts as XML documents. For the sake of illustration, we model searching as an action (e.g., as in scanning a database) rather than a query on the internal beliefs of the agent. An example of interaction is:

```
REQUEST                      DONE
   From: UserAssistant033       To: UserAssistant033
   To: CitationFinder           Content: done ( find (Michelangelo),
   Content:                         results (<doc1>born in Italy</doc1>,
      find ( Michelangelo )         <doc2>...</doc2>, <doc3>...</doct3>) )
```

Typically, different CitationFinders work on different databases. Any coordination policy of those presented above seems to be acceptable for this simple role. Particularly interesting is Simple Collaboration, where an agent, when done with searching, accepts to be the merger of the results; indeed, in this case, synthesizing is just concatenating all results by all agents. Consider, for instance, the situation where CitationFinders are on board of PDAs or notebooks. A user entering a smart office causes its agent to tune into the local channel for its role; consequently, in a typical peer-to-peer fashion, a new user adds her knowledge base to those of the others in the same room. This could be easily exploited to develop a collaborative work (CSCW) system. In this case, collaboration may be enforced by the CSCW agent by acting as the oracle during policy negotiation.

The second example is of *competition among presentation planners*. The interactive museum we are developing need PresentationPlanners (PP for short) for generating multi-media presentations on specific topics relevant to the context where a user, or a group of users, is. For instance, a user getting close to an art object should receive – depending on her interests, profile, previous presentations she received, etc. – a personalized presentation of the object itself, of its author, possibly of related objects in the same environment or other rooms. A typical interaction looks like the following:

```
REQUEST                              DONE
  From: UserAssistant033               To: UserAssistant033
  To: PresentationPlanner              Content: done (
  Content:                               buildPresentationForUser (621),
    buildPresentationForUser (621)       results (
                                           file (http://srv/pres1377.ram),
                                           bestResolution ( 800, 600 ),
                                           includeVideo ( true ),
                                           includeAudio ( true ) ) )
```

Typically, a PP works on a knowledge base containing text, audio and video tracks. When a request arrives, the PP collects data on the user and her contexts, e.g. by querying roles as UserProfiler, RoomLayout. Then, it queries its own knowledge base and, if information is available, it builds a multimedia presentation, by connecting audio and video tracks, generating audio via text-to-speech systems, and so on.

A PP is often the leader of its own team, formed by highly specialized agents. By contrast, it is unlikely that different PPs collaborate – sensibly merging multi-media presentations is a hard task even for a human. Observe that, in realistic situations, redundancy of PPs is a necessity, e.g. to handle the workload imposed by hundredth of simultaneous visitors. Redundancy can be obtained in various ways, for instance by putting identical PPs working on the same knowledge bases, or by specializing them by objects, or by rooms, or by user profiles.

Given the variety of possible configuration choices, the best policies for a PP are *Plain Competition* and *Multicast Contract Net* based on some quality parameter; it may also be that, in well controlled situations, a *Master* can be elected (or imposed by an oracle). Thus, the developer of a PP should enable a number of non-collaborative policies, which means specifying criteria for bidding in a Multicast Contract Net, accepting a Master-Slave policy but preventing its own PP from becoming a master, and so on.

Our third and last example is about *choosing among multiple screens*. Smart rooms may contain multiple places where to show things to users, e.g. large screens on different walls, the users' own PDAs, computers scattered in the room. Location, but also quality and logical congruence with the tasks being performed by the user, are all important factors. Also, it is not necessarily the case that a single screen is a good choice – for example, a presentation to a group of people may be better shown in multiple locations simultaneously.

For our interactive museum, we are working on SmartBrowsers (*SB* for short). A *SB* is an agent able to show a multi-media presentation (video and audio) and aware of its position (which may be static, if its display is a wall screen, or mobile, if on board of a PDA). A typical interaction looks like the following:

```
REQUEST                              DONE
  From: UserAssistant033               To: UserAssistant033
  To: SmartBrowser                     Content:
  Content:                               done (
    showMultiMedia (                       showMultiMedia (),
      user (621),                          results ( completed ) )
      file (http://server/pres1377.ram),
        bestResolution ( 800, 600 ),
        includeVideo ( true ),
        includeAudio ( true )
    )
```

SBs should accept a policy that allows a clear selection of one, or (better) a fixed number of agents at request time. Thus, *Plain Competition* and *Simple Collaboration* are not suitable; *Master-Slave* works, but seems unduly restrictive in a situation where *SBs* are context aware. We are working on a *Multicast Contract Net* policy where bids are a function of screen resolution, distance from user, impact on other people in the same room (e.g. when audio is involved). Only *SBs* visible to the user from her current position, having all required capabilities, and not busy showing something else, can participate to the sub-team bidding for a multi media presentation.

10   Related Works

Team programming based on joint intentions has been explored by various authors, in addition to those already mentioned in Sections 4 and 6. For instance, STEAM [21] combines Joint Intentions Theory and SharedPlans [9], and adds decision theoretic communication selectivity in order to adapt type and amount of communication to the context, by taking in account its costs and its benefits with respect to the team's goals.

Dignum et al. [7] deal with team formation via communication, something that is clearly related to our work. Our primary objective is not team formation, since this is solved by the very definitions of implicit organization and goal-specific sub-team – however, as mentioned in Sec. 4, the way the latter is formed may become more sophisticated in future. Moreover, with respect to the decomposition in steps required to form a team proposed by the model in [7], we can draw a parallel between their "potential recognition" step, where an agent takes the initiative to find a team, and the situations where a new agent joins an organization, or takes the initiative of renegotiating the coordination policy (and consequently how tasks are allocated among agents) because, for instance, of the poor performance of the current policy.

11   Conclusions and Future Directions

We proposed *implicit organizations* for the coordination of agents able to play the same role, possibly in different ways, exploiting group communication and over-hearing in environments where messages may be occasionally lost and agents can join and leave very frequently. We presented a protocol for negotiating a common coordination policy, outlined a general organizational coordination protocol, and discussed a few examples.

Current work is focusing on practical experimentation and application to our domain, i.e. multi-media, multi-modal cultural information delivery in smart rooms ("active museums"). Preliminary performance results on the negotiation algorithm show that, on a real, busy LAN, 20 agents can negotiate their own common policy in less than a second, without any external oracle intervention.

Longer term research objectives include more investigation on overhearing. We envision the creation of overhearing agents, helping in achieving robustness by catching and recovering partial message losses, supervising the behavior of implicit organizations, and applying machine learning techniques for deciding the "best" policy for a role in a given environment.

References

1. P. Busetta, A. Doná, and M. Nori. Channeled multicast for group communications. In *Proceedings of the first international joint conference on Autonomous agents and multiagent systems*, pages 1280–1287. ACM Press, 2002.
2. P. Busetta, M. Merzi, S. Rossi, and F. Legras. Intra-role coordination using channeled multicast. Technical Report 0303-02, ITC-IRST, Trento, Italy, 2003.
3. P. Busetta, L. Serafini, D. Singh, and F. Zini. Extending Multi-Agent Cooperation by Overhearing. In *Proceedings of the Sixth Int. Conf. on Cooperative Information Systems (CoopIS 2001)*, Trento, Italy, 2001.
4. P. R. Cohen and H. J. Levesque. Intention is choice with commitment. *Artificial Intelligence*, 42(2-3):213–261, 1990.
5. P. R. Cohen and H. J. Levesque. Teamwork. Technical Report 504, AI Center, SRI International, Menlo Park, CA, 1991.
6. F. Dignum and G.A.W. Vreeswijk. Towards a test bed for multi-party dialogues. In F. Dignum, editor, *Advances in Agent Communication*, LNAI, page in this volume. Springer Verlag.
7. Frank Dignum, Barbara Dunin-Kęplicz, and Rineke Verbrugge. Agent theory for team formation by dialogue. *Lecture Notes in Computer Science*, 1986, 2001.
8. Foundation for Intelligent Physical Agents. FIPA Communicative Act Library Specification. http://www.fipa.org/repository/cas.html.

9. Barbara J. Grosz and Sarit Kraus. Collaborative plans for complex group action. *Artificial Intelligence*, 86(2):269–357, 1996.
10. J. Y. Halpern and Y. O. Moses. Knowledge and common knowledge in a distributed environment. *Journal of the Association for Computing Machinery*, 37:549–587, 1990.
11. A. Kaminka, D. Pynadath, and M. Tambe. Monitoring Teams by Overhearing: A Multi-Agent Plan-Recognition Approach. *Journal of Artificial Intelligence Research*, 17:83–135, 2002.
12. S. Kumar, M. J. Huber, D. McGee, P. R. Cohen, and H. J. Levesque. Semantics of agent communication languages for group interaction. In *Proceedings of the 17 th Int. Conf. on Artificial Intelligence*, pages 42–47, Austin, Texas, 2000.
13. S. Kumar, Marcus J. Huber, Philip R. Cohen, and David R. McGee. Toward a formalism for conversation protocols using joint intention theory. *Computational Intelligence Journal (Special Issue on Agent Communication Language)*, 18(2):174–228, 2002.
14. Sanjeev Kumar, Marcus J. Huber, and Philip R. Cohen. Representing and executing protocols as joint actions. In *Proceedings of the first international joint conference on Autonomous agents and multiagent systems*, pages 543–550. ACM Press, 2002.
15. F. Legras and C. Tessier. Lotto: Group formation by overhearing in large teams. In F. Dignum, editor, *Advances in Agent Communication*, LNAI, page in this volume. Springer Verlag.
16. Stephen Morris and Hyun Song Shin. Approximate common knowledge and coordination: Recent lessons from game theory. *Journal of Logic, Language and Information*, 6(2):171–190, 1997.
17. I. Smith, P. Cohen, J. Bradshaw, M. Greaves, and H. Holmback. Designing conversation policies using joint intention theory. In *Proceedings of Third International Conference on Multi-Agent Systems (ICMAS98)*, 1998.
18. Ira A. Smith and Philip R. Cohen. Toward a semantics for an agent communication language based on speech acts. In Howard Shrobe and Ted Senator, editors, *Proc. of the 13th National Conference on A.I. and the 8th Innovative Applications of A. I. Conference, Vol. 2*, pages 24–31, Menlo Park, California, 1996. AAAI Press.
19. R. G. Smith. The contract net protocol: High level communication and control in a distributed problem solver. *IEEE Transactions on Computers*, C-29(12):1104–1113, 1980.
20. O. Stock and M. Zancanaro. Intelligent Interactive Information Presentation for Cultural Tourism. In *Proc. of the International CLASS Workshop on Natural Intelligent and Effective Interaction in Multimodal Dialogue Systems*, Copenhagen, Denmark, 28-29 June 2002.
21. M. Tambe. Towards flexible teamwork. *Journal of Artificial Intelligence Research*, 7:83–124, 1997.
22. G. Tidhar, A. S. Rao, and E. A. Sonenberg. Guided team selection. In *Proceedings of the Second International Conference on Multi-Agent Systems*, Kyoto, Japan, December 1996. AAAI Press.
23. Gil Tidhar. *Organization-Oriented Systems: Theory and Practice*. PhD thesis, Department of Computer Science and Software Engineering, The University of Melbourne, Australia, 1999.
24. J. Yen, X. Fan, and R.A. Volz. Proactive communications in agent teamwork. In F. Dignum, editor, *Advances in Agent Communication*, LNAI, page in this volume. Springer Verlag.

LOTTO: Group Formation by Overhearing in Large Teams

François Legras and Catherine Tessier

Onera DCSD – Toulouse, France
{legras,tessier}@cert.fr

Abstract. We present in this paper an extension to our overhearing-based group formation framework OTTO (Organizing Teams Through Overhearing). This framework allows a team to dynamically re-organize itself in accordance to the evolution of the communication possibilities between agents. In OTTO, each agent overhears some of the messages exchanged within the team and uses them to incrementally update a map of the organization of the team. One of the key points of OTTO is that only few resources are used - a small data structure is used to track each team member and there is no need to store the overheard messages. With LOTTO (OTTO for Large numbers of agents) we address the problem of large teams in which using OTTO "as is" would be costly in terms of memory and therefore contrary to OTTO's philosophy of low resource usage. Therefore, we have implemented a strategy that allows an agent with a limited memory to track only a part of the team. We have run a series of experiments in order to evaluate the impact of this limitation and present some results.

1 Introduction

In this paper, we present an extension to an overhearing-based group formation framework called OTTO (Organizing Teams Through Overhearing). OTTO deals with cooperation between non-selfish agents in communication-limited and dynamic environments. More precisely, the focus is on cooperation with local communication. The property of locality is classically induced by the discrepancy between the range of communication and the distance between the agents, but we generalize this to encompass situations in which (1) every agent cannot communicate with every other team member at will, and (2) the communication possibilities between agents remain the same during (short) time intervals. In such conditions, a solution to achieve cooperation consists in creating local groups of agents that are able to interact during a certain period. Thus, OTTO allows the dynamic evolution of groups (subteams) within a team of agents accomplishing a collaborative task. Each group accomplishes the task with no (or little) coordination with other groups. OTTO is task-independent, its objective is to allow the formation of groups despite very adverse communication conditions. The responsibility for the adequacy between the agents' skills and the needs of the group is left to the agents and particularly the *leaders* (the agents at the

F. Dignum (Ed.): ACL 2003, LNAI 2922, pp. 254–270, 2004.

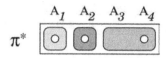

Fig. 1. Organization map.

origin of groups). Considering the dynamic nature of the environment, we avoid over-long negotiations: agents decide to petition the *leader* for acceptance in the group and the leader accepts or rejects them, both basing their decisions on task-dependent information.

Initially, OTTO was designed (see [13, 14]) for small teams, experiments were run with at most 16 team-mates. Given the lightweight nature of OTTO, it was natural to try to use it within large teams of (simple) agents. But the size of the data that each agent has to store within the first implementation of OTTO grows with the square of the size of the team and each agent is supposed to know beforehand the composition of the team. These limitations become serious when one moves from a few agents to several dozens or hundreds of simple agents with low processing power, like for example micro-aerial vehicles (MAV). Therefore, we have extended OTTO to LOTTO. In LOTTO, agents can discover the existence of their team-mates by overhearing and can limit their memory usage by "forgetting" the team-mates they are not directly interacting with and whose information is the oldest. The point of LOTTO is that forgetting some of the information that should be kept within OTTO brings few additional incoherence in the team and allows to scale up the framework to large teams while maintaining low resource usage.

This paper is organized as follows: Section 2 describes the components and concepts supporting OTTO and therefore LOTTO as well, it can be safely skipped by the reader already familiar with this material. The results of a series of experiments conducted on LOTTO are described and discussed in Section 4 and finally some related work is discussed in Section 5.

2   The Group Formation Framework OTTO

Let $\Gamma = \{A_1, A_2, \ldots, A_N\}$ represent the team, composed of agents A_i. The set of groups forms a partition[1] of the team *i.e.* at any moment an agent belongs to a group, even if the agent is alone. At any moment, it is theorically possible to draw a *map* $\pi^* \in \overline{\Gamma}$ of the team's organization as in the example of Figure 1 which shows the state of a four-member team Γ. The gray boxes correspond to the different groups while the ○'s indicate the leaders of the groups.

But such a global information is not readily accessible. Each agent has its own beliefs about the state of the team, *i.e.* its own map, which can be incomplete

---

[1] We denote $\overline{E}$ the set of the partitions of E. By definition we have $X \in \overline{E}$ if and only if: (i) $\varnothing \notin X$; (ii) $E = \bigcup_{x \in X} x$; (iii) $\forall(x, y) \in X^2 : x \neq y \to x \cap y = \varnothing$.

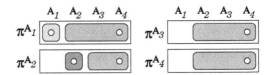

Fig. 2. Organization maps.

or even erroneous. So, for each task, an agent A_i has only a semi-partition[2] of the team in groups. If we denote π^{A_i} A_i's map of the team's organization, we have $\pi^{A_i} \in \tilde{\Gamma}^{A_i}$.

Rather than striving to construct a global π^* from the various π^{A_i}, the objective of the framework is to obtain a set of π^{A_i} as coherent as possible. In Figure 2, we can see two types of incoherences. First, no-one except A_1 itself knows that it has created its own group, this has no serious consequence as no-one expects cooperation from A_1. Second, we can see that A_2 seems to have left A_4's group and to have created its own, but neither A_4 nor A_3 are informed about that. This incoherence is serious as A_3 and A_4 might expect some cooperation from A_2. In short: inter-group incoherence is considered harmless as opposed to intra-group incoherence.

2.1   Propositional Attitudes

In order to allow the creation and evolution of the groups, we have identified three classes of Propositional Attitudes (PAs) [8]: positive (creating a group or expressing its desire to join one), negative (dissolving a group or quitting one) and informative (asking the other agents for information about the groups or giving such information). By combining these classes with the status of the sender (being a leader or not) we have determined six types of PAs for the framework:

AFF (positive and informative PA, leader) is used by an agent to assert the creation a group, thereby becoming *publicly* its leader and sole member *i.e.* that agent becomes liable to receive requests from other agents to join this group. Consecutively, the leader also uses AFFs to express its beliefs about the evolving composition of its group. Note: a group is entirely identified by its leader and its creation date.

BEL (informative PA, non-leader) is used by an agent to express its beliefs about a group while not being its leader.

JOIN (positive PA, non-leader) is used by an agent to express its desire to join a pre-existing group. It implies that the agent is *alone i.e.* sole member and *implicit* leader of its own non-public group.

---

[2] For a given set E and an element $a \in E$, we define $\tilde{E}^a$ the set of the semi-partitions of E covering a. By definition, we have $X \in \tilde{E}^a$ if and only if: (i) $\varnothing \notin X$; (ii) $\bigcup_{x \in X} x \subset E$; (iii) $\forall(x, y) \in X^2 : x \neq y \rightarrow x \cap y = \varnothing$; (iv) $\exists x \in X, a \in x$.

CHK (informative PA) is used by an agent to request information from the other
agents about a particular group. A belief is expressed and the other agents
are expected to confirm or infirm it with BELs/AFFs.

BRK (negative PA, leader) is used by a leader to signify the dissolution of its
group. All the members (including the leader) are immediately considered
to be alone.

QUIT (negative PA, non-leader) is used by a non-leader member of a group to
quit it. This agent is immediately considered to be alone.

These PAs are instantiated in the form:

$$PA(A_e, T_e, (A_L, T_L), \{(A_i, d_i), \ldots\})$$

where A_e is the sender and T_e is the date of emission. (A_L, T_L) identifies the
group, A_L is the leader and T_L is the date of creation. If the PA deals with
lone agents, it is instantiated with $\varnothing$ instead of (A_L, T_L). $\{(A_i, d_i), \ldots\}$ is the
set of the members with the latest dates at which they were acknowledged as
being members (these can only correspond to the emission date of a previous
PA, see Section 2.3). These instantiated PAs are the only kind of message that
the agents use to communicate about groups within the team.

2.2   Overhearing

According to Kraus [12], *"In non-structured and unpredictable environments,
heuristics for cooperation and coordination among automated agents, based on
successful human cooperation and interaction techniques, may be useful."* Therefore let us consider *overhearing*. This phenomenon is studied in ergonomy [10]
and corresponds to the fact that human subjects working in a common environment have a tendency to intercept messages that are not clearly directed to
them and to use this information to facilitate group work.

The framework that we propose uses broadcast communication, so each message (an instantiated PA) is potentially received by every other team member.
When receiving (or intercepting) a message, an agent A_i uses it to update its
knowledge π^{A_i} about the organization of the team even if A_i is not directly
concerned by this message. This mechanism is described in Section 2.3. This is
how we mirror overhearing in teams of artificial agents. The agent A_i monitors
the activity and organization of the whole team though it may have no direct
use for this information in its current activity. This information can have three
different uses: (1) it may effectively concern the current activity of A_i; (2) it
may be used in the future by A_i if it wishes to move from its current group to
another; (3) it may be transferred to other agents if these agents seem to have
inexact beliefs.

In this paper, we present overhearing in the light of the group formation
framework, but this framework is designed to be part of a complete cooperation
architecture in which the agents overhear task information in addition to cooperation information. For example, information obtained through overhearing
may motivate an agent to quit its group to join another in which it may be more
useful to the team.

2.3   Group Tracking

In order to build a representation π^{A_i} of the organization of the team at time t, an agent A_i has potentially at its disposal all the messages (instantiated PAs) it has received up to time t. Rather than storing all these messages we have implemented a mechanism that updates a map with each message received. This is the reason why the dates d_j are present in the instantiated PAs: $\mathsf{PA}(A_e, T_e, (A_L, T_L), \{(A_j, d_j), \ldots\})$. Updating the map π^{A_i} with a message is based on the semantics of the PA and dates comparisons in order to determine whether the information in the message about a given agent A_j is relevant or not. For each agent A_j, the latest date D_j at which A_j was known to be part of a group (or to be alone) is stored, updated with the d_j present in the messages (when greater than the current value of D_j) and used to instantiate the messages further emitted by A_i.

In addition, for each agent A_j and for each known group γ, the latest date $\bar{D}_j^\gamma$ at which A_j was *not* a member of γ is stored. $\bar{D}_j^\gamma$ is useful for example if a message indicates that A_j is member of γ at d_j and if $\bar{D}_j^\gamma > d_j > D_j$. In this situation, A_j is not considered a member of γ even though $d_j > D_j$.

The d_j present in the instantiated PAs mean that there exists an objective evidence that at the date d_j, agent A_j was a member of the group concerned by the message. The d_j correspond to the emission date of previous messages emitted by A_j or its leader. When the leader emits a message stating that A_j is in its group, uses the emission date of A_j's latest message saying so, and conversely for A_j which uses the emission date of its leader's latest AFF. For a given group and a member A_j, the first d_j is present in the AFF that acknowledges A_j as a member and is equal to the emission date of A_j's JOIN. See Figure 3 for an example.

$$\mathsf{JOIN}(A_2, 11, (A_1, 6), \{(A_1, 7), (A_3, 8)\})$$

$$\mathsf{AFF}(A_1, 12, (A_1, 6), \{(A_1, 7), (A_2, 11), (A_3, 8)\})$$

$$\mathsf{BEL}(A_3, 13, (A_1, 6), \{(A_1, 12), (A_2, 11), (A_3, 12)\})$$

$$\mathsf{BEL}(A_2, 14, (A_1, 6), \{(A_1, 12), (A_2, 12), (A_3, 12)\})$$

Fig. 3. Example of evolution of the dates d_j. The emission date of A_2's JOIN is used by A_1 as a "certainty date" of A_2 membership.

An incremental mechanism based on dates comparison allows to forget the messages previously received and to get the correct membership for any agent A_j, given the messages received in the past. The crucial hypotheses are that the groups form a semi-partition of the team (and particularly that an agent cannot be in two groups at the same time) and that the agents are rational: they cannot emit simultaneously two incoherent messages.

Under these hypotheses, we do not need to store the messages received up to time t to deduct to which group A_j belongs. It is sufficient to store and incrementally update information of the form: $(\gamma_j, D_j, \{\bar{D}_j^1 \ldots\})$ even if the messages are received in a "wrong" order (γ_j is the current group of A_j and the dates $D_j, \{\bar{D}_j^1 \ldots\}$ were explained earlier). For more details and a proof, please refer to [14].

3   LOTTO: OTTO for Large Teams

The key idea behind LOTTO is that an agent A_i can "forget" information about another agent A_j if it has been a long time since it last received information about A_j. That is: the less often one interacts with someone the less you need to keep track of its whereabouts. So, as we consider that our agents have limited resources available to track the organization of the team, they must "make room" in their memory in order to accommodate the most recent and relevant information. The basic information units that we consider are the structures $S_j = (\gamma_j, D_j, \{\bar{D}_j^1 \ldots\})$. In order to compare the relative interest of two structures S_{j_1}, S_{j_2}, we define four classes by order of importance:

1. $\{S_i\}$ the information concerning the agent A_i itself!
2. $\{S_j | \gamma_j = \gamma_i\}$ the agents belonging to the same group as A_i. This is crucial in order to preserve intra-group coherence. One can note that therefore, the size of the memory sets a bound to the maximal size of a group.
3. $\{S_j | lead(\gamma_j) = A_j\}$ the agents leading their own group. These are the agents that A_i petitions if it must join another group.
4. The rest of the team.

Within a given class, S_{j_1} is preferred to S_{j_2} if $D_{j_1} > D_{j_2}$. Therefore one can sort the structures present in memory and keep only a limited number of structures.

We have seen in the preceding section that OTTO allows an agent to track a given team-mate A_j by updating a structure $S_j = (\gamma_j, D_j, \{\bar{D}_j^1 \ldots\})$ where the dates $\bar{D}_j^i$ correspond to the latest date at which A_j was known not to be part of the group led by A_i (if such a group exists). In OTTO the dates D_j are kept for all potential leaders (which is the reason behind the memory usage growing with the square of the size of the team). As LOTTO keeps track of a limited number of agents, the number of potential leaders is bounded. Therefore, by limiting the number of the structures S_j, one can bound the memory used by an agent to track the organization of the team.

4   Experiments

We have conducted a series of experiments on LOTTO in order to validate our hypothesis that memory-bounded agents can use this extension of OTTO in large teams with only a small effect on overall team coherence.

4.1   Experimental Setup

As in [13, 14], the decision processes of several agents are simulated with stochastic Finite State Machines (FSMs) driven by Poisson laws that enable them to periodically create, join, quit or check groups. In order to obtain "realistic" communication conditions, agents are simulated as moving randomly in a 2-dimensional space and having a limited range of communication. The agents have a constant speed of $5m.s^{-1}$, change heading following a Poisson law with a time constant of $10s$ and they evolve within a square $1km \times 1km$ area. Figure 4 illustrates this.

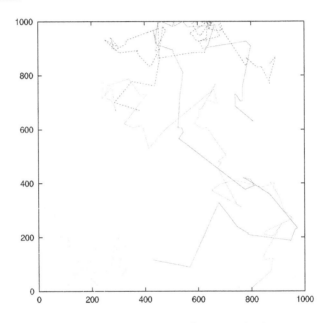

Fig. 4. Trajectories of four agents during a 10 minutes run.

The main parameters of the simulations are:

- *range*: the communication range of the agents – within $\{50m, 200m, 350m, 500m\}$.
- N: the number of agents present in the simulation, within $\{30, 60, 90, 120\}$.
- $Tchk$: the average time interval between two CHKs emitted by an agent – within $\{12.5s, 25s, 37.5s, 50s\}$.
- *memory*: the ratio between the numbers of structures S_j stored in memory and N – within $\{0.125, 0.25, 0.375, 0.5, 0.625, 0.75, 0.875, 1.0\}$.

We average two values to evaluate the behavior of LOTTO during 10-minute simulation runs:

- *cohesion* is the ratio between the number of agents that are members of a group (while not being its leaders) and N. To be considered member of a group γ, the agent *and* the leader of γ must believe so.

Table 1. Correspondence *range* – density.

range	density
100m	3%
300m	22%
500m	49%

- *incoherence* is calculated at a given moment by counting the number of cases where a leader wrongly believes that an agent is a member of its group or where an agent wrongly believes to a member of a group. This number is then divided by N to obtain an average number of actual incoherences per agent.

For the sake of comparison with previous experiments [13, 14] table 1 presents the correspondence between the range of communication and the average reliability of the communication (noted α in our previous work). This correspond to the average *density* of the communication graph *i.e.* the ratio between the number of pairs of agents that can communicate and the number of edges of the complete graph of size N *i.e.* $N(N-1)/2$. In our previous experiments, the default density was 50%, we del here with much lower values.

4.2   Results and Analysis

Here are some of the results of the numerous simulation we have run. These results are presented as 3-dimensional plots representing the effects of the variation of N, *range* and T_{CHK}, and this for several values of *memory* so as to show whether using LOTTO degrades team performance compared to OTTO (which is equivalent to LOTTO with *memory* = 1).

Variations of *range*

Figures 5 and 6 show the evolution of cohesion and incoherence for different values of *range* and *memory*. On one hand, we can note that globally, *range* has a small impact on cohesion except when CHKs are emitted very often and with a very small memory (figure 5), which is due to a kind of saturation of the agents: information flows very quickly and they only have a small memory, so the more information they get (the greater the *range*) the more "confused" they are. On the other hand we can say that *range* has an important impact on incoherence, as more communication possibilities reduce the occurrence of "misunderstandings" within the team.

Concerning the effect of *memory* we observe that reducing the size of the memory has an impact on the capability of the team to form (large) groups, as it reduces cohesion. But we must note also that it has little to no impact on incoherence.

Variations of *N*

Figure 7 illustrate the evolution of cohesion and incoherence for different values of N and *memory* with *range* = 100m and T_{CHK} = 50s. We can note that *memory*

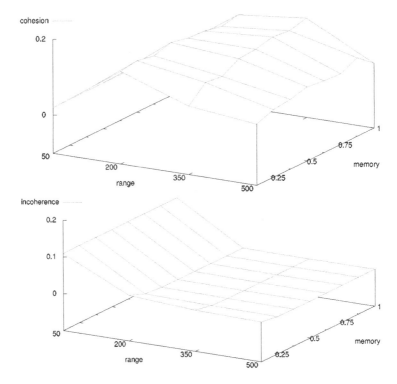

Fig. 5. Cohesion and incoherence variations for $N = 120$ and $T_{CHK} = 5s$.

has no effect here, neither on cohesion nor on incoherence. The only observable variation is the increase of cohesion with N. As we have $range = 100m$, with bigger values of N comes more possibilities of communication for the agents, and therefore a better cohesion.

Figure 8 illustrate the evolution of cohesion and incoherence for different values of N and $memory$ with $range = 500m$ and $T_{CHK} = 50s$. On one hand, the increased $range$ gives very good communication possibilities to the agents, therefore the variations N have not the effect on cohesion seen on figure 7. On the other hand, with such good communication possibilities, the agents can make good use of their memory to increase cohesion within the team. Though, we can observe that small values of $memory$ lead to an increase of incoherence. This phenomenon can be explained by the fact that each agent can interact with a large number of their teammates, and when this number is larger than their memory capacity, important information is lost, which leads to incoherence.

Variations of T_{CHK}

Figures 9 and 10 illustrate the evolution of cohesion and incoherence for different values of T_{CHK} and $memory$. Here we can observe that in general T_{CHK} has no notable impact neither on cohesion nor on incoherence. This corresponds to the results already obtained in [13, 14] and is in accordance with one of the

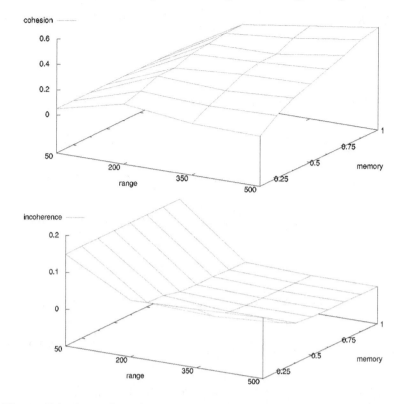

Fig. 6. Cohesion and incoherence variations for $N = 120$ and $T_{CHK} = 30s$.

central idea behind OTTO (and therefore LOTTO) *i.e.* that by using overhearing it is possible to obtain a good coherence in the team without having the agents constantly checking each other for membership.

As in preceding section dealing with the variation of N, the effect of the variation of *memory* are only observable for very good communication possibilities, in which case a large memory allows a good cohesion while a small memory brings some incoherence.

4.3 Discussion

We can make two global conclusions on the behavior of LOTTO out of these experimental results: (1) limiting the size of the memory has no impact on the global incoherence of the team except in extreme cases; (2) this limitation of memory seems to affect the cohesion of the team by preventing the agents to form large groups. This second point seems to be a serious drawback for LOTTO, but we must notice that the group-formation behavior of the agents in these simulations is *very* rudimentary (based on very simple FSMs). Therefore, we believe that it is possible to design group-formation behaviors for the agents that would alleviate this limitation of LOTTO.

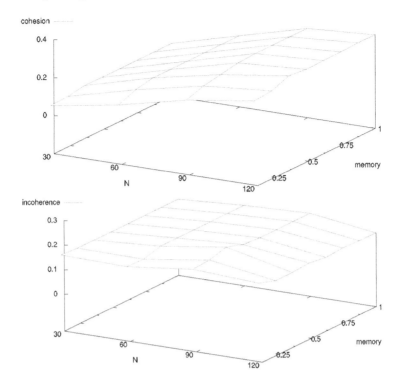

Fig. 7. Cohesion and incoherence variations for $range = 100m$ and $T_{CHK} = 50s$.

5   Related Work

The problem of team or group formation has been widely dealt with from several points of view. Among others, game theory has been used by Sheory and Kraus [15] to evaluate and divide the payoff of cooperation. Cohen *et al.* [5] stress the importance of the joint mental state or commitment of the participants to differentiate collaborative or joint action from mere coordination. Tidhar *et al.* [19] propose that a team leader makes a selection among pre-compiled teams, using the commitment of the potential team members to guide its choice. Dignum *et al.* [6] use formal structured dialogues as opposed to fixed protocols like contract nets [16]. This allows them to prove that a certain dialogue has a specific outcome. Let us focus on recent literature relative to group formation and overhearing. These study seldom take into account communication possibilities between agents either static or fully dynamic as in OTTO/LOTTO. Furthermore, a majority of research in the field consider only 1-to-1 communication between agents, while we focus on broadcast communication.

5.1   Group Formation

Group and coalition formation has been recently studied in dynamic contexts, i.e. contexts where agents, tasks, and the environement may change over time.

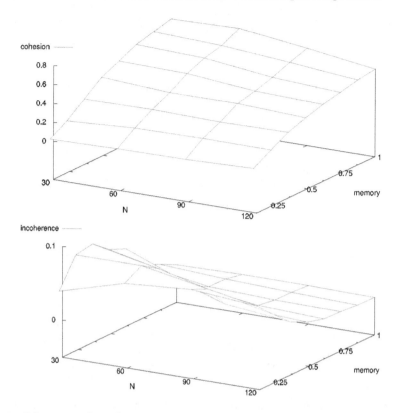

Fig. 8. Cohesion and incoherence variations for $range = 500m$ and $T_{CHK} = 50s$.

[11] deals with coalition formation in dynamic environments. The DCF (Dynamic Coalition Formation) problem is such that: agents may enter or leave the coalition formation process at any moment; the set of tasks to be accomplished and the resources may change dynamically; the information, network and environment of each agent may change dynamically.

DCF-S, a simulation dedicated to DCF, is proposed. In this framework, each agent can adapt its own decision-making to changes in the environment through a learning process. Special agents, the World Utility Agents, maintain information about their registered agents. Each coalition is represented by a coalition leading agent (CLA) and each agent is a CLA for the coalition it has formed for one of its goals.

Once the CLA has determined the set of goals to be accomplished, it simulates the formation of coalitions: possible candidates are determined, then coalitions of limited sizes are simulated by randomly adding or removing candidates and assessing both the contribution and risk of each possible member. The simulation goes on when changes in the environment occur. Then, the negotiation phase determines binding agreements between the agents within the coalitions.

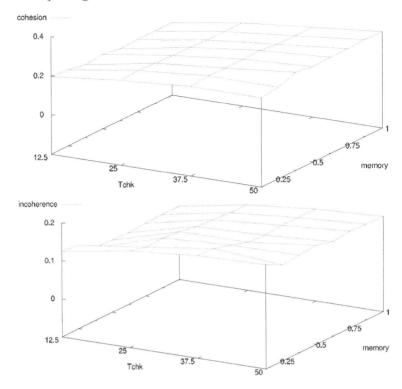

Fig. 9. Cohesion and incoherence variations for $range = 100m$ and $N = 120$.

The problem of coalition formation in time and resource - constrained and partially known environments is dealt with in [17,18]. Sub-optimal coalitions are searched for, through a two-step process: (1) initial coalition formation is performed by the initiating agent on the basis of its knowledge about its neighbours' (numerical) utilities for the task to achieve, which represent their skills for the task and their past and current relationships with the initiating agent. Negotiation is started only with top-ranked candidates; (2) coalition refinement is based on 1-to-1 negotiations to know which agent is actually willing to help and to make constraints and commitments clear. The application is multisensor target tracking, where each sensor is controlled by an agent. Several algorithms have been tested for resource allocation, to search for a good compromise between speed of coalition formation with incomplete information, robustness and flexibility of coalition.

[4] build coalitions with the assumption that the agents' utilities are not comparable nor have to be aggregated, and use dynamic reconfiguration to update coalitions when changes occur. The aim of the protocol is to find a Pareto-optimal solution, i.e. a solution where an agent's utility cannot be increased without decreasing another agent's. The algorithm is based on the fact that the agents involved in the negotiation pass possible sets of coalitions round, each

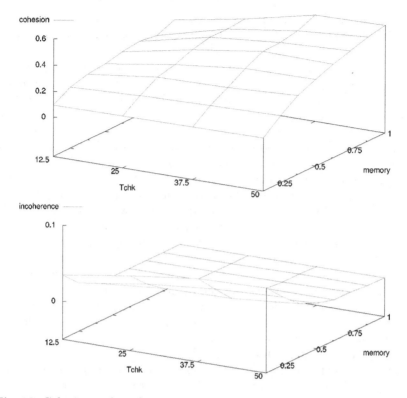

Fig. 10. Cohesion and incoherence variations for $range = 500m$ and $N = 120$.

agent sorting the sets according to its preferences, if they are at least equivalent to a reference situation (the modified previous optimal situation in case of dynamic reconfiguration). Implementation is performed on a class allocation problem with preferences set on agents (teachers and students). Results (number and sizes of messages, number of coalition sets evaluated) are given for a small number of agents (4) and tasks (4 to 8) with different heuristics for improving the computational complexity of the protocol.

5.2   Overhearing

Multi-party communication (as opposed to dyadic communication) and specifically overhearing is quite new in the agent literature [7]. Most often, overhearing agents are special agents whose role is to track dialogues between a group of agents and provide information either to some agents inside the group who have subscribed to the service, or to external agents. An overhearing agent has to classify and assess the overheard communication according to criteria that are useful to the end-users.

   The possibility of broadcasting messages to a wide audience including *overhearing agents* unknown to the sender is studied by Busetta *et al.* [3, 1, 2]. In [1], communication is based on *channeled multicast*, with the following characteristics: many channels can co-exist; each channel is dedicated to one *theme*; each message has a specific destination (one agent or one group of agents); each agent can tune into any channel. Therefore messages are not necessarily routed to their best destination (they can be heard by everybody — *overhearing*) and delivery is not guaranteed. Overhearing enables unplanned cooperation. The communication architecture implements *overhearers*, e.g. agents whose role is to listen to several channel and forward relevant messages to subscriber agents (event if they are not intented to receive the messages). Communication between overhearers and their subscribers is point-to-point. The implementation (*LoudVoice*) focuses more on real-time than on reliability of message delivery. Channeled multicast improves such protocols as the English Auction Interaction Protocol (reduction of the number of messages, increase of the social awareness of the auction's progress through updating of a group belief — all listeners can update their data about the other agents). Only four types of messages are required and the states of the agents (auctioneer and participants) are described by simple finite state machines. Overhearing agents monitor several parameters on the auction and on the participants and may provide the auctioneer or bidders with private reports and suggestions. Therefore overhearing is based on communication observation and situation monitoring (or "spying"), and is deliberately dedicated to information delivery to specific agents.

The monitoring system OVERSEER ([9]) focuses on a non-intrusive approach to agent team monitoring by *overhearing*. Overhearing (or *key-hole* plan recognition) is performed by specific agents which are dedicated to monitoring, through listening the messages (routine communication) exchanged by the team agents with each other. This avoids team agents regularly communicating their states to the monitoring agents. Monitored agents are assumed to be truthful in their communication to their teammates and not to deceive the monitoring agent nor to prevent it from overhearing. When agents are monitored as independent entities (a separate plan recognition is maintained for each agent), the belief about an agent's actual state is represented as a probability distribution over variables $\{X_t\}$, $\{X_t\}$ being true when the agent is executing plan X at time t. Evidence for belief updating comes with messages identifying either plan initiation or termination. When no messages are observed at time t, updating is performed thanks to a probabilistic model of plan execution. A markovian assumption is made both for incorporating evidence and for reasoning forward to time $t + 1$ (both only based on beliefs at time t).The state of the team at time t is the combination of the most likely state of the individual agents at time t, but this approach gives very poor results. When agents are monitored as a team, the relationships between the agents are used, especially the fact that a message changes the beliefs on the state of the sender *and* of the listeners. The coherence heuristic is used, i.e. evidence for one team member is used to infer the other members' states, and to predict communications.

6   Conclusions and Future Work

We have presented LOTTO, an extension to our dynamic overhearing-based group formation framework OTTO. LOTTO distinguishes itself from OTTO by allowing the agents to track only the fraction of the team's organization that is the most useful to them and correspond to their memory capabilities. We have run a series of experiments on LOTTO and have observed that by using the same principles than in OTTO but with a bounded memory no additional incoherence appears within the team. Nevertheless rudimentary FSM-based mechanisms are not sufficient in order to form *large* groups within the team.

LOTTO will be at the heart of a fully-fledged subsumption-inspired cooperation architecture in which the team can be viewed as a multi-bodied entity functioning with a *distributed architecture* which continuously adapts its organization within each layer to allow its components to be ready when a particular layer gets in control.

References

1. P. Busetta, A. Doná, and M. Nori. Channeled multicast for group communications. In *Proceedings of the First International Joint Conference on Autonomous Agents and Multi-Agent Systems (AAMAS)*, pages 1280–1287, Bologna, Italy, 2002.
2. P. Busetta, M. Merzi, S. Rossi, and F. Legras. Intra-role coordination using group communication: A preliminary report. In F. Dignum, editor, *Advances in Agent Communication*, LNAI, page in this volume. Springer Verlag.
3. P. Busetta, L. Serafini, D. Singh, and F. Zini. Extending multi-agent cooperation by overhearing. *Lecture Notes in Computer Science*, 2172:40–52, 2001.
4. P. Caillou, S. Aknine, and S. Pinson. A multi-agent method for forming and dynamic restructuring of Pareto optimal coalitions. In *Proceedings of AAMAS'02*, pages 1074–1081, 2002.
5. P. Cohen and H. Levesque. Teamwork. *Nous*, 25(4):487–512, 1991.
6. F. Dignum, B. Dunin-Kęplicz, and R. Verbrugge. Dialogue in team formation: a formal approach. In W. van der Hoek, J.-J. Meyer, and C. Witteveen, editors, *Proceedings of the ESSLLI99 Workshop on the Foundations and Applications of Collective Agent-Based Systems (CABS)*, 1999.
7. F. Dignum and G. Vreeswijk. Towards a test bed for multi-party dialogues. In F. Dignum, editor, *Advances in Agent Communication*, LNAI, page in this volume. Springer Verlag.
8. J. Fodor. *Psychosemantics*. The MIT Press, 1987.
9. G. Kaminka, D. Pynadath, and M. Tambe. Monitoring teams by overhearing: a multi-agent plan-recognition approach. *Journal of Artificial Intelligence Research (JAIR)*, 17:83–135, 2002.
10. L. Karsenty and B. Pavard. Various levels of context analysis in the ergonomic study of cooperative work. *Reseaux: The French journal of communication*, 6(2):167–193, 1998.
11. M. Klusch and A. Gerber. DCF-S: a dynamic coalition formation scheme for rational agents. In *AAMAS02 Workshop 7 "Teamwork and coalition formation"*, pages 1–7, 2002.

12. S. Kraus. Negotiation and cooperation in multi-agent environments. *Artificial Intelligence*, 94(1-2):79–98, 1997.
13. F. Legras. Group formation through overhearing and local communication. In *Proceedings of STAIRS*, pages 23–32, Lyon, France, 2002.
14. F. Legras. Using overhearing for local group formation. In *AAMAS02 Workshop 7 "Teamwork and Coalition Formation"*, pages 8–15, 2002.
15. O. Shehory and S. Kraus. Coalition formation among autonomous agents: strategies and complexity. In *From reaction to cognition – MAAMAW-93 (LNAI Volume 957)*, pages 56–72. Springer, 1995.
16. R. Smith. The contract net protocol: high-level communication and control in a distributed problem solver. *IEEE Transaction on computers*, 29(12):1104–1113, 1980.
17. L.-K. Soh and C. Tsatsoulis. Allocation algorithms in dynamic negotiation-based coalition formation. In *AAMAS02 Workshop 7 "Teamwork and coalition formation"*, pages 16–23, 2002.
18. L.-K. Soh and C. Tsatsoulis. Satisficing coalition formation among agents. In *Proceedings of AAMAS'02*, pages 1062–1063, 2002.
19. G. Tidhar, A. Rao, M. Ljungberg, D. Kinny, and E. Sonenberg. Skills and capabilities in real-time team formation. Technical Report 27, Australian Artificial Intelligence Institute, Melbourne, Australia, 1992.

Proactive Communications in Agent Teamwork

John Yen[1], Xiaocong Fan[1], and Richard A. Volz[2]

[1] School of Information Sciences and Technology
The Pennsylvania State University
University Park, PA 16802
{jyen,zfan}@ist.psu.edu
[2] Department of Computer Science
Texas A&M University
College Station, TX 77843
volz@cs.tamu.edu

Abstract. The capabilities for agents in a team to anticipate information-needs of teammates and proactively offer relevant information are highly desirable. However, such behaviors have not been fully prescribed by existing agent theories. To establish a theory about proactive information exchanges, we first introduces the concept of "information-needs", then identify and formally define the intentional semantics of two proactive communicative acts, which highly depend on the speaker's awareness of others' information-needs. It is shown that communications using these proactive performatives can be derived as helping behaviors. Conversation policies involving these proactive performatives are also discussed. The work in this paper may serve as a guide for the specification and design of agent architectures, algorithms, and applications that support proactive communications in agent teamwork.

1 Introduction

Passive communications (i.e., ask/reply) are prevalently used in existing distributed systems. Although the ask/reply approach is useful and necessary in many cases, it exposes several limitations, where proactive approach may come into play. For instance, an information consumer may not realize certain information it has is already out of date. If this agent needs to verify the validity of every piece of information before they are used (e.g., for decision-making), the team can be easily overwhelmed by the amount of communications entailed by these verification messages. Proactive information delivery by the information source agents offers an alternative, and it shifts the burden of updating information from the information consumer to the information provider, who has direct knowledge about the changes of information. In addition, an agent itself may not realize it needs certain information due to its limited knowledge (e.g., distributed expertise). For instance, a piece of information may be obtained only through a chain of inferences (e.g., being fused according to certain domain-related rules). If the agent does not have all the knowledge needed to make such a chain of inferences, it will not be able to know it needs the information, not to mention

F. Dignum (Ed.): ACL 2003, LNAI 2922, pp. 271–290, 2004.
© Springer-Verlag Berlin Heidelberg 2004

requesting for it. Proactive information delivery can allow teammates to assist the agent under such a circumstance.

In fact, to overcome the abovementioned limitations of "ask", many human teams incorporate proactive information delivery in their planning. In particular, psychological studies about human teamwork have shown that members of an effective team can often anticipate needs of other teammates and choose to assist them proactively based on a shared mental model [1]. We believe this type of approaches developed by human teams provides critical evidence for software agents to be also equipped with proactive information delivery capabilities.

Even though several formal theories on agent teamwork have been proposed, they do not directly address issues regarding proactive information exchange among agents in a team. To do this, "information-needs" should be treated as first-class objects, the intentional semantics of acts used in proactive communications need to be formally defined, and agents should be committed to these acts as helping behaviors under appropriate contexts.

The rest of this paper is organized as follows. In section 2 we make some preparations and define the semantics of elementary performatives in the Shared-Plan framework. In section 3 we identify two types of information-needs, and propose axioms for agents to anticipate these two types of information-needs for their teammates. In section 4 we give the semantics of two proactive performatives based on the speaker's awareness of information-needs, and show how agents, driven by information-needs of teammates, could potentially commit to these communicative actions to provide help. Potential conversation policies for ProInform and third-party subscribe are discussed in section 5. Section 6 devotes to comparison and section 7 concludes the paper.

2   Preparation

We use $\alpha, \beta, \gamma \cdots$ to refer to actions. An action is either primitive or complex. The execution of a complex action relies on some recipe, i.e., the *know-how* information regarding the action. A recipe is composed of an action expression and a set of constraints on the action expression. Action expressions can be built from primitive actions by using the constructs of dynamic logic: $\alpha; \beta$ for sequential composition, $\alpha|\beta$ for nondeterministic choice, $p?$ for testing (where p is a logical formula), and α^* for repetition. Thus, a recipe for a complex action γ is actually a specification of a group of subsidiary actions at different levels of abstraction, the doing of which under certain constraints constitutes the performance of γ.

Appropriate functions are defined to return certain properties associated with an action. In particular, $pre(\alpha)$ and $post(\alpha)$ return a conjunction of predicates that describe the preconditions and effects of α, respectively. By $I \in pre(\alpha)$ we mean I is a conjunct of $pre(\alpha)$.

We adopt the SharedPlan theory [2,3] as the cornerstone of our framework. Thus, all actions will be intended, committed and performed in some specific context. By convention, C_α is used to refer to the context in which α is being done, and $Constr(C_\alpha)$ refers to the constraints component of C_α.

Bel and MB are standard modal operators for belief and mutual belief, respectively. Three modal operators in the SharedPlan theory are used to relate agents and actions: $Do(G, \alpha, t, \Theta)$ is used to denote that G (a group of agents or a single agent) performs action α at t under constraints Θ; $Commit(A, \alpha, t_1, t_2, C_\alpha)$ represents the commitment of agent A at t_1 to perform the basic-level action α at t_2 under the context C_α; and $Exec(A, \alpha, t, \Theta)$ is used to represent the fact that agent A has the ability to perform basic-level action α at time t under constraints Θ. Four types of intentional attitudes were defined. $Int.To(A, \alpha, t, t_\alpha, C_\alpha)$ means agent A at t intends to do α at t_α in the context C_α; $Int.Th(A, p, t, t', C_p)$ means agent A at t intends that p hold at t' under the context C_p. $Pot.Int.To$ and $Pot.Int.Th$ are used for *potential* intentions. They are similar to normal intentions (i.e., $Int.To$ and $Int.Th$) except that before really adopting them, the agent has to reconcile the potential conflicts that may be introduced by the potential intentions to the existing intentions. Meta-predicate $CBA(A, \alpha, R_\alpha, t_\alpha, \Theta)$ means agent A at t_α can bring about action α by following recipe R_α under constraints Θ.

Grosz and Kraus proposed several axioms for deriving helpful behaviors [2, 3]. The following one simplifies the axiom in [3] without considering the case of multiple-agent actions (we assume communicative acts to be examined are single-agent actions) and the case of action-intention conflicts.

Axiom 1 $\forall A, p, t, \beta, t_\beta, t' > t_\beta, C_p.$
$Int.th(A, p, t, t', C_p) \wedge \neg Bel(A, p, t) \wedge lead(A, \beta, p, t, t_\beta, \Theta_\beta) \Rightarrow$
$\quad Pot.Int.To(A, \beta, t, t_\beta, \Theta_\beta \wedge C_p),$ where
$lead(A, \beta, p, t, t_\beta, \Theta_\beta) \triangleq Bel(A, \exists R_\beta \cdot CBA(A, \beta, R_\beta, t_\beta, \Theta_\beta)), t) \wedge$
$\quad [Bel(A, (Do(A, \beta, t_\beta, \Theta_\beta) \Rightarrow p), t) \vee Bel(A, Do(A, \beta, t_\beta, \Theta_\beta) \Rightarrow$
$\quad\quad [\exists B, \alpha, R_\alpha, t_\alpha, t'' \cdot (t_\alpha > t_\beta) \wedge (t_\alpha > t'') \wedge CBA(B, \alpha, R_\alpha, t_\alpha, \Theta_\alpha) \wedge$
$\quad\quad\quad Pot.Int.To(B, \alpha, t'', t_\alpha, \Theta_\alpha) \wedge (Do(B, \alpha, t_\alpha, \Theta_\alpha) \Rightarrow p)], t)].$

Axiom 1 says that if an agent does not believe p is true now, but has an intention that p be true at some future time, it will consider doing some action β if it believes the performance of β could contribute to making p true either directly or indirectly through the performance of another action by another agent.

$Hold(p, t)$ is used to represent the fact that p is true at time t. Note that $Hold$ is external to any rational agents. It presupposes an omniscient perspective from which to evaluate p. On the other hand, assume there exists an omniscient agent G, then $Hold(p, t) = Bel(G, p, t)$. $Hold$ will be used only within belief contexts, say $Bel(A, Hold(p, t), t)$, which means agent A believes from the omniscient's perspective p is true. Since omniscient is always trustable, $Bel(A, Hold(p, t), t) \Rightarrow Bel(A, p, t)$, but not vice versa.

We define some abbreviations needed later. Awareness $(aware)$[1], belief contradiction $(CBel)$ between two agents (from one agent's point of view), and wrong beliefs $(WBel)$ are given as:

---

[1] We assume belief bases allow three truth values for propositions.

$$aware(A, p, t) \triangleq Bel(A, p, t) \vee Bel(A, \neg p, t),$$
$$unaware(A, p, t) \triangleq \neg aware(A, p, t),$$
$$CBel(A, B, p, t) \triangleq (Bel(A, p, t) \wedge Bel(A, Bel(B, \neg p, t), t)) \vee$$
$$(Bel(A, \neg p, t) \wedge Bel(A, Bel(B, p, t), t)),$$
$$WBel(A, p, t) \triangleq (Hold(p, t) \wedge Bel(A, \neg p, t)) \vee (Hold(\neg p, t) \wedge Bel(A, p, t)).$$

In the following, let TA be an agent team with finite members. The proposal put forward in the SharedPlans theory is to identify potential choices of action (ultimately represented in terms of a $Pot.Int.To$) as those which would reduce the cost or the resources required to perform actions intended by a teammate. For the purpose of this paper, we will only focus on barriers to actions rooted in lack of information regarding the preconditions of the actions.

2.1   Reformulate Performative-as-Attempt

Following the idea of "performative-as-attempt" [4, 5], we will model the intentional semantics of proactive performatives as attempts to establish certain mutual beliefs between the speaker and the addressee (or addressees). In order to do that, we first need to reformulate the concept of *Attempt* within the framework of the SharedPlan theory. Then, the semantics of *Inform* and *Request* are given in terms of attempts, which serves partially to validate our approach of encoding "performative-as-attempt" in the SharedPlan framework.

Definition 1. $Attempt(A, \epsilon, P, Q, C_n, t, t_1) \triangleq [\neg Bel(A, P, t) \wedge$
$Pot.Int.Th(A, P, t, t_1, C_n) \wedge Int.Th(A, Q, t, t_1, \neg Bel(A, P, t) \wedge C_n) \wedge$
$Int.To(A, \epsilon, t, t, Bel(A, post(\epsilon) \Rightarrow Q, t) \wedge Pot.Int.Th(A, P, t, t_1, C_n)))]?; \epsilon.$

Here, P represents some ultimate goal that may or may not be achieved by the attempt, while Q represents what it takes to make an honest effort. The agent has only a limited commitment (potential intention) to the ultimate goal P, while it has a full-fledged intention to achieve Q. More specifically, if the attempt does not achieve the goal P, the agent may retry the attempt, or try some other strategy or even drop the goal. However, if the attempt does not succeed in achieving the honest effort Q, the agent is committed to retrying (e.g., performing ϵ again) until either it is achieved (A comes to believe P) or it becomes unachievable (t' comes) or irrelevant (the escape condition C_n no longer holds)[4, 6]. Thus, the *Attempt* would actually be an intent to achieve Q by performing ϵ while the underlying intent was to achieve P. Of course, P and Q may refer to the same formula.

For example, agent A may desire that $Bel(B, I, t)$ under conditions that agent A does not believe that B believes I. While $Bel(B, I, t)$ (P in this case) may be unachievable for A, $MB(\{A, B\}, Bel(B, Bel(A, I, t), t'))$ (Q in this case) can be achieved by exchanging appropriate messages with B. In case of communication failure in establishing the mutual belief, A will retry until either the mutual belief is achieved or C_n no longer holds or the deadline t_1 comes. Here ϵ may refer to a sequence of *send*, the act of wrapping the message in a wire language and physically sending it. When communication is reliable and sincerity is assumed, one *send* may suffice.

According to the *speech act* theory [7], every speech act has an utterance event associated with it. For the purpose of this paper, we simply assume all the utterance events are single-agent complex actions, for which each agent has full individual recipes. For instance, when the honest goal of a performative is to establish certain mutual beliefs, the recipe for the corresponding ϵ may involve negotiations, persuasions, failure-handling, etc.

The semantics of elementary performatives are given by choosing appropriate formulas (involving mutual beliefs) to substitute for P and Q in the definition of *Attempt*. As in [8], the semantics of *Inform* is defined as an attempt of the speaker to establish a mutual belief with the addressee about the speaker's goal to let the addressee know what the speaker knows.

Definition 2. $Inform(A, B, \epsilon, p, t, t_a) \triangleq (t < t_a)?; Attempt(A, \epsilon,$
$MB(\{A, B\}, p, t_a), \exists t'' \cdot (t \leq t'' < t_a) \wedge MB(\{A, B\}, \psi, t''), C_p, t, t_a),$ *where*
$\psi = \exists t_b \cdot (t'' \leq t_b < t_a) \wedge Int.Th(A, Bel(B, Bel(A, p, t), t_b), t, t_b, C_p),$
$C_p = Bel(A, p, t) \wedge Bel(A, unaware(B, p, t), t).$

When communication is reliable and agents trust each other, it's easy to establish the mutual belief about ψ required in the honest goal of *Inform*: agent B believes ψ upon receiving a message with content ψ from agent A; and A knows this, and B knows A knows this, and so on.

A request with respect to action α is defined as an attempt of the speaker to make both the speaker and the addressee believe that the speaker intends that the addressee commit to performing the action α [5].

Definition 3. $Request(A, B, \epsilon, \alpha, t, t_a, \Theta_\alpha) \triangleq (t < t_a)?; Attempt(A, \epsilon,$
$Do(B, \alpha, t_a, \Theta_\alpha), \exists t'' \cdot (t \leq t'' < t_a) \wedge MB(\{A, B\}, \psi, t''), C_p, t, t_a),$ *where*
$\psi = \exists t_b < t_a \cdot Int.Th(A, Int.To(B, \alpha, t_b, t_a, C_p), t, t_b, C_p),$
$C_p = Bel(A, \exists R_\alpha \cdot CBA(B, \alpha, R_\alpha, t_a, \Theta_\alpha), t) \wedge$
$\quad Int.Th(A, Do(B, \alpha, t_a, \Theta_\alpha), t, t_a, \Theta_\alpha).$

The *Request* means that agent A at t has an attempt where (1) the ultimate goal is for B to perform α at t_a, and (2) the honest goal is to establish a mutual belief that agent A has an intention that agent B commit to performing α, all of the above being in appropriate contexts.

According to the definition, agent A would be under no obligation to inform B that its request is no longer valid when A discovers that C_n on longer holds. In [9] Smith and Cohen defined another version of *Request* in terms of a *PWAG* (persistent weak achievement goal) rather than an intention. That means, upon discovering that the goal has been achieved or become impossible, or that C_p is on longer true, agent A will be left with a persistent goal to reach mutual belief with B, which will free B from the commitment towards A regarding α. Rather than introducing a counterpart of *PWAG* into the SharedPlan framework, we prefer to encode such team-level obligations using an axiomization approach by introducing an axiom stating that any agent intending others to be involved in a team activity should also adopt an intention to release those agents from the obligations whenever the intentional context no longer holds. The axiom is omitted here for space limit.

The semantics associated with the receipt of a *Request* is a bit involved. In addition to realizing that the sender wishes him/her to commit to the action, the receiver can make certain deductions based upon knowledge of the semantics of *Request*. In particular, the receiver can deduce that the sender believes that there is a recipe the receiver could be following that would lead the receiver to bring about α. Note that the *Request* does not indicate which recipe the receiver should follow, only that the sender believes there exists one. This is sufficient, though it does not guarantee that the receiver will actually perform α. If the receiver is not directly aware of such a recipe, it could lead the receiver to initiate a search for an appropriate recipe. If the receiver cannot find one as the sender expected, the receiver can discharge himself from the obligation and letting the sender know the reason.

3   Information Needs

For any predicate symbol p with arity n, it will be written in the form $p(?x, c)$, where $?x$ is a set of variables, c is a set of constants in appropriate domains, and the sum of the sizes of the two sets is n. We start with the identifying reference expression (IRE), which is used to identify objects in appropriate domain of discourse[10]. IRE is written using one of three referential operators defined in FIPA specification. $(iota \ ?x \ p(?x, c))$ refers to "the collection of objects, which maps one-to-one to $?x$ and there is no other solution, such that p is true of the objects"; it is undefined if for any variable in $?x$ no object or more than one object can satisfy p (together with substitutions for other variables). $(all \ ?x \ p(?x, c))$ refers to "the collection of sets of all objects that satisfy p, each set (could be an empty set) corresponds one-to-one to a variable in $?x$". $(any \ ?x \ p(?x, c))$ refers to "any collection of objects, which maps one-to-one to $?x$, such that p is true of the objects"; it is undefined if for any variable in $?x$ no object can satisfies p (together with substitutions for other variables). We will omit operator any if possible. Hence, expressions of form $(any \ ?x \ p(?x, c))$ can be simplified as $p(?x, c)$.

Information is defined in WordNet Dictionary as a message received and understood that reduces the recipient's uncertainty. We adopt the definition prescribed in the Open Archival Information System (OAIS) [11]: information is "any type of knowledge that can be exchanged, and it is always represented by some type of data". Throughout this paper, we deal with two types of information: factual information and referential information. Factual information is represented as a proposition (predicate with constant arguments), and referential information is represented in terms of a special predicate $Refer(ire, obj)$, where ire is an identifying reference expression, and obj is the result of the reference expression ire evaluated with respect to a certain theory.

In the following we will use I to represent the information to be communicated: when I refers to a proposition, the sender is informing the receivers that the predicate is true; when I refers to $Refer(ire, obj)$, the sender is informing the receivers that those objects in obj are what satisfy ire evaluated with respect to the sender's belief base.

Now we come to the concept of information-needs. An information-need may state that the agent needs to know the truth value of a proposition. For instance, suppose a person sends a query $Weather(Cloudy, Today)$ to a weather station. The weather station will realize that the person want to know, at least literally, whether today is cloudy [2]. More often than not, an agent wants to know the values of some arguments of a predicate, where the values could trusify the predicate. For example, a person may send a query $Weather(?x, Today)$ to a weather station, this will trigger the weather station, if it's benevolent, to inform the person about the (change of) weather conditions whenever necessary.

Thus, corresponding to information, an expression for information-needs may also be in one of two forms: described either as a proposition, or as a reference expression. In what follows N is used to refer to a (information) need-expression, $pos(N)$ $(ref(N))$ is true if N is a proposition (reference expression). An information-need consists of a need-expression, an information consumer (needer), an expiry time after which the needs is no longer applicable, and a context only under which the needs is valid. To combine them together, we introduce a modal operator $InfoNeed(A, N, t, C_n)$ to denote information-needs. In case that N is a proposition, it means that agent A needs to know the truth value of N by t under the context C_n [3]; in case that N is a reference expression, it means agent A needs to know those objects satisfying the reference expression N. Making the context of information-needs explicit not only facilitates the conversion from information-needs of teammates to intentions to assist them, but also enables the context to be included in need-driven communicative actions. The properties of $InfoNeed$ are omitted here.

The most challenging issue in enabling agents to proactively deliver information to teammates is for them to know the information-needs of teammates. Agents can subscribe their information-needs from other teammates. In this paper however, we will focus on how to *anticipate* potential information-needs based on the SharedPlans theory.

3.1   Anticipate Information-Needs of Teammates

We distinguish two types of information-needs. The first type of information-need enables an agent to perform certain (complex) actions, which contributes to an agent's individual commitments to the whole team. We call this type of information-need *action-performing information-need*. The second type of information-need allows an agent to discharge itself from a chosen goal. Knowing such information will help an agent to give up achieving an impossible or irrel-

---

[2] Refer to [12] for indirect speech acts.
[3] In such cases, $InfoNeed(A, p, t, C_n)$ is equivalent to $InfoNeed(A, \neg p, t, C_n)$.

evant goal. Thus, we call this type of information-need *goal-escape information-need*. We first define a generated set. For any action α, let $Needs(\alpha)$ be a set of need-expressions generated from $pre(\alpha)$:

1. $p \in Needs(\alpha)$, if $p \in pre(\alpha)$ is a proposition;
2. $(any\ ?x\ p(?x)) \in Needs(\alpha)$, if $p \in pre(\alpha)$ is of form $p(?x)$ [4].

Axiom 2 (Action-performing Information-Need)

$\forall A, B \in TA, \alpha, C_\alpha, t, t' \geq t \forall N \in Needs(\alpha)\cdot$
$Bel(A, Pot.Int.To(B, \alpha, t, t', C_\alpha), t) \Rightarrow Bel(A, InfoNeed(B, N, t', C_n), t)$, where $C_n = C_\alpha \wedge Pot.Int.To(B, \alpha, t, t', C_\alpha)$.

Axiom 2 characterizes action performing information-needs, which states that agent A believes that agent B will need information described by N by t' under the context C_n, if A believes that B is potentially intending to perform action α at time t'. The context C_n of the information-need consists of C_α and B's potential intention to perform α.

Lemma 1. $\forall A, B \in TA, \phi, \alpha, C_\phi, \Theta_\alpha, t, t' \geq t, t'' \geq t' \forall N \in Needs(\alpha)\cdot$
$Bel(A, Int.Th(B, \phi, t, t'', C_\phi), t) \wedge\ Bel(A, \neg Bel(B, \phi, t), t) \wedge$
$Bel(A, Lead(B, \alpha, \phi, t', t, \Theta_\alpha), t) \Rightarrow \exists C_n \cdot Bel(A, InfoNeed(B, N, t', C_n), t)$.

Proof. Follows directly from axiom 1 and 2.

Similarly, let $Needs(C)$ be the generated set of need-expressions from a set C of predicates. Axiom 3 specifies goal-escape information-needs.

Axiom 3 (Goal-escape Information-Need)

$\forall A, B \in TA, \phi, C_\phi, t, t' \geq t \forall N \in Needs(C_\phi)\cdot$
$Bel(A, Int.Th(B, \phi, t, t', C_\phi), t) \Rightarrow Bel(A, InfoNeed(B, N, t', C_n), t)$, where $C_n = C_\phi \wedge Int.Th(B, \phi, t, t', C_\phi)$.

Axiom 3 states that if agent A believes that agent B has a goal towards ϕ, it will assume B will need information described by N, which is generated from the context of B's intention. The context of the information-need consists of C_ϕ and B's intention.

By reflection, a rational agent should be able to know its own information-needs when it intends to do some action but lacks the pre-requisite information. In case that A and B in Axiom 2 and 3 refer to the same agent, they state how an agent can anticipate its own information-needs. Being aware of its own information-needs, an agent could subscribe its information-needs from an information provider.

---

[4] Depending on domains, need-expressions of the form $(iota\ ?x\ p(?x))$ or $(all\ ?x\ p(?x))$ can also be generated. For instance, if α is a joint action where some doer should be exclusively identified, *iota* expression is preferred. *all* expression is suitable if all objects substitutable for variables in $?x$ will be needed in the performance of α.

3.2   Assist Others' Information Needs

When an agent knows the information-needs of its teammates by being informed or by anticipating, it will consider providing help.

Let B_A be the belief base of agent A, and $B_A \models p$ means p is a logical consequence of B_A. For any agent A and need-expression N, function $info(A, N)$ returns the information with respect to N evaluated by A:

$$info(A, N) \triangleq \begin{cases} N & \text{if } B_A \models N, \text{ and } N \text{ is a proposition,} \\ \neg N & \text{if } B_A \models \neg N, \text{ and } N \text{ is a proposition,} \\ Refer(N, Q) & \text{if } N = (iota \ ?x \ p(?x)), \\ & Q \in \Sigma = \{\theta \cdot ?x : B_A \models \theta \cdot p, \theta \text{ is most general} \\ & \quad \text{substitution (mgs)}\}, \text{ and } \Sigma \text{ is singleton,} \\ Refer(N, Q) & \text{if } N = (any \ ?x \ p(?x)), \\ & Q \in \Sigma = \{\theta \cdot ?x : B_A \models \theta \cdot p, \theta \text{ is mgs}\} \neq \emptyset, \\ Refer(N, \Sigma) & \text{if } N = (all \ ?x \ p(?x)), \\ & \Sigma = \{\theta \cdot ?x : B_A \models \theta \cdot p, \theta \text{ is mgs}\}, \end{cases}$$

$info(A, N)$ is undefined in case that N is a proposition, but neither $B_A \models N$ nor $B_A \models \neg N$; or in case that $N = (any \ ?x \ p(?x))$ but $\Sigma = \emptyset$; or in case that $N = (iota \ ?x \ p(?x))$ but Σ is not a singleton. In case that $N = (any \ ?x \ p(?x))$ and $|\Sigma| > 1$, a randomly selected element of Σ is returned. We use $defined(info(A, N))$ to denote $info(A, N)$ is defined.

The following axiom says that, when an agent comes to know another agent's information needs, it will adopt an attitude of intention-that towards "the other's belief about the needed information".

Axiom 4 (ProAssist) $\forall A, B \in T \ A, N, C_n, t, t' > t$.
$Bel(A, InfoNeed(B, N, t', C_n), t) \Rightarrow$
$\quad [defined(info(A, N)) \Rightarrow Int.Th(A, Bel(B, info(A, N), t'), t, t', C_n) \lor$
$\quad (\neg defined(info(A, N)) \land pos(N)) \Rightarrow Int.Th(A, aware(B, N, t'), t, t', C_n)]$.

We use $Int.Th$ rather than $Int.To$ in the axiom because $Int.To$ requires the agent adopt a specific action to help the needer, while $Int.Th$ offers the agent with the flexibility in choosing whether to help (e.g., when A is too busy), and how to help. This axiom relates information-needs with appropriate intentions-that. Thus, Axiom 1 and the Axiom 4 together enable an agent to choose appropriate actions to satisfy its own or other's information-needs. Note that A and B could refer to the same agent, that means agent A will try to help itself by adopting appropriate intentions.

4   Proactive Communication Acts

4.1   Proactive-Inform

ProInform (Proactive Inform) is defined by extending the semantics of *Inform* with additional requirements on the speaker's awareness of the addressee's information needs. More specifically, we explicitly include the speaker's belief about the addressee's need of the information as a part of the mental states being communicated. Hence, the meaning of $ProInform$ is an attempt for the speaker to establish a mutual belief (with the addressee) about the speaker's goal to let the addressee know that (1) the speaker knows the information being communicated, and (2) the speaker knows the addressee needs the information.

Definition 4. $ProInform(A, B, \epsilon, I, N, t, t_a, t', C_n) \triangleq [(t_a < t') \wedge (I = info(A, N))]?;$
$Attempt(A, \epsilon, Bel(B, I, t'), \exists t'' \cdot (t \le t'' < t_a) \wedge MB(\{A, B\}, \psi, t''), C_p, t, t_a),$ where
$\psi = \exists t_b \cdot (t'' \le t_b < t_a) \wedge Int.Th(A, Bel(B, Bel(A, I, t) \wedge$
$\quad Bel(A, InfoNeed(B, N, t', C_n), t), t_b), t, t_b, C_p),$
$C_p = C_n \wedge Bel(A, I, t) \wedge (I = info(A, N)) \wedge Bel(A, InfoNeed(B, N, t', C_n), t) \wedge$
$\quad [pos(N) \Rightarrow Bel(A, unaware(B, I, t), t) \vee CBel(A, B, I, t)].$

Notice that $t_a < t'$, which ensures the $ProInform$ is adopted to satisfy other's information needs in the future. Also, the context of information-need is included as an argument of $ProInform$. This context serves in the context (C_p) of the speaker's goal (i.e., intention) to let the addressee know the information. C_p justifies the behavior of an agent who uses the communicative action. For instance, suppose $ProInform$ is implemented in a multi-agent system using a component that reasons about the information-needs of teammates and a communication plan involving sending, receiving confirmation, and resending if confirmation is not received. During the execution of such a plan, if the agent realizes the context of the addressee's information-need is no longer true, the agent can choose to abandon the communication plan. This use of context in the definition of $ProInform$ supports our choice of explicitly including the context of information-needs in $InfoNeed$.

The semantics of $ProInform$ has direct impacts on the receivers. By accepting $ProInform$, the addressee attempts to confirm the informing agent that it believed the information being communicated at the beginning of the attempt:
$$Accept(B, A, \epsilon, I, N, t, t_a, t', C_n) \triangleq Attempt(B, \epsilon, \psi, \phi, C_n, t, t_a),$$
where $\psi = MB(\{A, B\}, Bel(B, I, t'), t'),$ $\phi = MB(\{A, B\}, Bel(B, I, t), t_a).$

Since the ultimate goal of $ProInform$ is to let the addressee believe I at t', the ultimate goal of $Accept$ is also set to establish a mutual belief about I at t'. Neither may be achievable, because I may change between t and t' for both $ProInform$ and $Accept$ (In such a case, another $ProInform$ may be adopted). In case that I persists until t', the assumption of persistent beliefs will guarantee the addressee's information-need be satisfied.

The addressee may reject a $ProInform$ because (1) it knows something different from the information received, or (2) it does not think the information is needed. We define the first rejection as $RefuseInfo$, and the second as $RefuseNeed$.
$$RefuseInfo(B, A, \epsilon, I, N, t, t_a, t', C_n) \triangleq Attempt(B, \epsilon, \psi, \psi, C_n, t, t_a),$$
$$RefuseNeed(B, A, \epsilon, I, N, t, t_a, t', C_n) \triangleq Attempt(B, \epsilon, \phi, \phi, C_n, t, t_a),$$ where
$\psi = MB(\{A, B\}, \neg Bel(B, I, t), t_a),$
$\phi = MB(\{A, B\}, \neg Bel(B, InfoNeed(B, N, t', C_n), t), t_a).$

Upon receiving *RefuseNeed*, the performer of *ProInform* might revise its belief about the addressee's information-needs.

The following properties are obvious.

Proposition 1. *For any t_0, t_1, t_2, t_3, t', where $t_0 < t_1 < t'$, $t_0 < t_2 < t_3 < t'$,*

(1)$ProInform(A, B, \epsilon, I, N, t_0, t_1, t', C_1) \wedge Accept(B, A, \epsilon', I, N, t_2, t_3, t', C_2) \Rightarrow Bel(A, Bel(B, I, t_2), t_3)$.

(2)$ProInform(A, B, \epsilon, I, N, t_0, t_1, t', C_1) \wedge RefuseInfo(B, A, \epsilon', I, N, t_2, t_3, t', C_2) \Rightarrow Bel(A, \neg Bel(B, I, t_2), t_3)$.

(3)$ProInform(A, B, \epsilon, I, N, t_0, t_1, t', C_1) \wedge RefuseNeed(B, A, \epsilon', I, N, t_2, t_3, t', C_2) \Rightarrow Bel(A, \neg Bel(B, InfoNeed(B, N, t', C_n), t_2), t_3)$.

The following theorem can be proved using Axiom 1, 4 and Proposition 1.

Theorem 1. $\forall A, B \in TA, N, C_n, t, t' > t,$

$Bel(A, InfoNeed(B, N, t', C_n), t) \wedge (I = info(A, N)) \wedge Bel(A, I, t) \wedge$
$\neg Bel(A, Bel(B, I, t'), t) \Rightarrow$
$(\exists t_1, t_2, C_p \cdot Pot.Int.To(A, ProInform(A, B, \epsilon, I, N, t_1, t_2, t', C_n), t, t_1, C_p))$.

It states that if agent A believes I, which agent B will need by t', it will consider proactively sending I to B by *ProInform*.

4.2 Proactive-Subscribe

While an agent in a team can anticipate certain information-needs of teammates, it may not always be able to predict all of their information-needs, especially if the team interacts with a dynamic environment. Under such circumstances, an agent in a team needs to let teammates know about its information-needs so that they can provide help. There exists at least two ways to achieve this. An agent might merely inform teammates about its information-needs, believing that they will consider helping if possible, but not expecting a firm commitment from them for providing the needed information. Alternatively, the speaker not only wants to inform teammates about its information-needs, but also wishes to receive a firm commitment from teammates that they will provide the needed information whenever the information is available. For instance, let us suppose that agent B provides weather forecast information to multiple teams in some areas of a battle space, and agent A is in one of these teams. If agent A needs weather forecast information of a particular area in the battle space for certain time period, A needs to know whether agent B can commit to deliver such information to it. If agent B can not confirm the request, agent A can request another weather information agent or consider alternative means (such as using a broker agent).

An agent's choice between these two kinds of communicative actions obviously depends on many factors including the level of trust between the speaker and the addressee, the criticality and the utility of the information-need, the sensing capability of the addressee, and the strength of the cooperative relationship between them. However, here we focus on capturing the semantics of communicative actions without considering such factors, and leave the issue of choosing communication actions to agent designers.

The first kind of communication actions can be modeled as $Inform(A, B, \epsilon,$ $InfoNeed(A, N, t'', C_n), t, t')$. That is, A informs B at time t so that B will know at time t' that "A will need information described by N by t'' under the context C_n". If agent B's reply to such an $Inform$ action is $Accept$, B will consider (i.e., have a "potential intention") to proactively deliver the needed information to A when relevant information is available to B.

The second type of communication actions mentioned above is similar to subscription in the agent literature. In fact, subscription between two agents is a special case of subscription involving a "broker" agent. As the size of a team or the complexity of its task increases, the mental model about information-needs of teammates may vary significantly among members of the team. For instance, as the team scales up in size or task complexity, the team is often organized into subteams, which may be further divided into smaller subteams. Because (top-level) team knowledge might be distributed among several sub-teams, agents in one sub-team might not be able to know the team process (the plans, task assignments, etc.) of other subteams, and hence can not anticipate information-needs of agents in these subteams. To facilitate proactive information flows between these subteams, an agent in a subteam can be the designated point of contacts with other subteams. These broker agents play a key role in informing agents external to the subteam about information-needs of agents in the subteam. Situations such as these motivate us to formally define the semantics of third-party subscribe (called $3PTSubscribe$). Conceptually, $3PTSubscribe$, issued by a broker agent A to information provider C, forwards the information-needs of B to C and requests C to meet B's needs whenever possible. When A and B are the same agent, it reduces to "subscribe".

It seems the semantics of $3PTSubscribe$ involves a $Request$, since the speaker expects the addressee to perform the information delivery action to the needer. We might be attempted to model the communicative action as "A requests C to $Inform$ B regarding B's information need". However, defined as such, C is demanded to reply based on C's current belief (like a request to a database server). What we want to model is that if C accepts the request, C will commit to deliver relevant information whenever it becomes available. Neither can we model it as "A requests C to proactively inform B regarding B's information need", because it requires that agent C already know about B's needs, which is not the case here.

Failed to capture the semantics of $3PTSubscribe$ in our mind by composing existing communicative actions, we introduce it as a new performative. Thus, by $3PTSubscribe(A, B, C, \epsilon, N, t_1, t_2, t_3, C_n)$ we mean the action that A subscribes information-need N (as a broker) on behalf of agent B from agent C until time t_3 under the context C_n. The ultimate intent of the action is that A could hold the information relevant to N at time t_3. The intermediate effect is to establish a mutual belief between A and C that (1) B has an information-need N by t_3 under the context C_n, and (2) whenever C acquires new information about N, C intends to inform the information proactively to B as long as B still needs it. We formally define the semantics of $3PTSubscribe$ below.

Definition 5. $3PTSubscribe(A, B, C, \epsilon, N, t_1, t_2, t_3, C_n) \triangleq (t_1 < t_2 < t_3)?; Attempt$
$(A, \epsilon, Bel(B, info(B, N), t_3), \exists t'' \cdot (t_1 \leq t'' < t_2) \wedge MB(\{A, C\}, \rho, t''), C_p, t_1, t_2),$ where
$\rho = \exists t_b \cdot (t'' \leq t_b < t_2) \wedge Int.Th(A, \psi \wedge \phi, t_1, t_b, C_n),$
$\psi = Bel(C, Bel(A, InfoNeed(B, N, t_3, C_n), t_1), t_b),$
$\phi = Int.Th(C, [\forall t' \leq t_3 \cdot BChange(C, N, t') \Rightarrow \exists t_a, t_c \cdot Int.To(C,$
$\qquad ProInform(C, B, \epsilon', info(C, N), N, t_a, t_c, t_3, C_n), t', t_a, C_n)], t_b, t_b, C_n),$
$BChange(C, N, t) \triangleq info_t(C, N) \neq info_{t-1}(C, N)\ ^5,$
$C_p = Bel(A, InfoNeed(B, N, t_3, C_n), t_1) \wedge Bel(A, defined(info(C, N)), t_1) \wedge$
$\qquad \neg defined(info_{t_1}(A, N)) \wedge \neg Bel(A, Bel(C, InfoNeed(B, N, t_3, C_n), t_1), t_1).$

Notice that this definition requires the context of the information-need to be known to the addressee (agent C), since it is part of the mutual belief. This enables the information provider (agent C) to avoid delivering unneeded information when the context no longer holds.

A special case of "third-party subscribe" is the case in which the information needer acts as the broker agent to issue a subscription request on behalf of itself to an information service provider. Hence, a two party subscription action can be modeled as $3PTSubscribe(A, A, C, \epsilon, N, t_1, t_2, t_3, C_n)$.

Upon receiving a $3PTSubscribe$ request, the service provider (agent C in Definition 5) can reply in at least three ways. It can accept the request and commit to proactively delivering the needed information to agent B whenever the information changes. Alternatively, it can reject the request by letting A know that it has no intention to deliver information to B. Finally, it can accept to believe the information-need of B, but choose not to make a strong commitment to proactively informing B. This option still allows agent C to consider (i.e., potentially intend to) to $ProInform$ B later based on Theorem 1, yet it gives agent C the flexibility to decide whether to commit to $ProInform$ based on the current situation (e.g., take into account of C's current cognitive load level). We call these three replies $AcceptSub$, $RejectSub$, and $WeakAcceptSub$ respectively. They are formally defined below.

Let $Q = (\forall t' \leq t_3 \cdot BChange(C, N, t') \Rightarrow \exists t_a, t_c \cdot Int.To(C, ProInform(C, B, \epsilon', info(C, N), N, t_a, t_c, t_3, C_n), t', t_a, C_n)).$

$\qquad AcceptSub(C, B, A, \epsilon, N, t_1, t_2, t_3, C_n) \triangleq Attempt(C, \epsilon, \psi, \psi, C_n, t_1, t_2),$
$\qquad RejectSub(C, B, A, \epsilon, N, t_1, t_2, t_3, C_n) \triangleq Attempt(C, \epsilon, \phi, \phi, C_n, t_1, t_2),$
$\qquad WeakAcceptSub(C, B, A, \epsilon, N, t_1, t_2, t_3, C_n) \triangleq Attempt(C, \epsilon, \rho, \rho, C_n, t_1, t_2),$ where
$\psi = MB(\{A, C\}, Bel(C, InfoNeed(B, N, t_3, C_n), t_2) \wedge Bel(C, Q, t_2), t_2),$
$\phi = MB(\{A, C\}, \neg Bel(C, Q, t_2), t_2),$
$\rho = MB(\{A, C\}, Bel(C, InfoNeed(B, N, t_3, C_n), t_2), t_2).$

Similar to Theorem 1, an agent could assist its teammates by performing $3PTSubscribe$. The proof is based on the indirect effect of $3PTSubscribe$, which can LEAD to $Bel(B, info(B, N), t')$.

Theorem 2. $\forall A, B, C \in TA, N, C_n, t, t' > t,$
$Bel(A, InfoNeed(B, N, t', C_n), t) \wedge \neg defined(info_t(A, N)) \wedge$
$Bel(A, defined(info(C, N)), t) \wedge \neg Bel(A, Bel(B, info(B, N), t'), t) \Rightarrow$
$(\exists t_1, t_2, C_p \cdot Pot.Int.To(A, 3PTSubscribe(A, B, C, \epsilon, N, t_1, t_2, t', C_n), t, t_1, C_p)).$

---

^{5} $info_t(C, N)$ means C evaluates N at t.

In addition to *3PTSubscribe*, there are at least two other ways a third-party agent can assist a team member with its information-needs: (1) *Ask-ProInform*: agent *A* asks agent *C*, then pro-informs agent *B* upon receiving replies from *C*, (2) *request-inform*: agent *A* requests agent *C* to *Inform* agent *B* directly (by composing *request* and *inform* together) [6].

In the *Ask-ProInform* approach, agent *A* needs to perform two communicative actions. The benefit is that *A* can also obtain the information as a by-product during the process. While in the second approach, agent *A* only needs to perform one communicative action. The drawback is that agent *A* cannot obtain the information.

An agent's choice between these two approaches and the acts mentioned earlier (i.e., *Inform-InfoNeed* and *3PTSubscribe*) could depend on the nature of the information-needs. For instance, if the information needed is static, *request-inform* is better than *3PTSubscribe*, because the former relieves the information providing agent from monitoring a need for detecting changes.

5   Conversation Policies with Proactiveness

Intentional semantics of performatives is desirable because human's choice of commitments to communicative acts really involves reasoning about the beliefs, intentions, and abilities of other agents. However, reliable logical reasoning about the private beliefs and goals of others is technically difficult. Practical agent systems typically employ various assumptions to simply this issue. One promising approach is to frame the semantics of performatives using protocols or conversation policies. As publicly shared, abstract, combinatorial, and normative constraints on the potentially unbounded universe of semantically coherent message sequences [14], conversation policies make it easier for the agents involved in a conversation to model and reason about each other, and restrict agents' attention to a smaller (otherwise maybe larger) set of possible responses.

Conversation protocols are traditionally specified as finite state machines [6, 15]. Enhanced Dooley graphs[16], Colored Petri Nets [17], and Landmark-based representation [18] were proposed to specify richer semantics of protocols. For instance, in Landmark-based representation, a protocol (family) is specified as a sequence of waypoints (landmarks) that must be followed in order to accomplish the goal associated with that protocol, while concrete protocols are realized by specifying action expressions for each landmark transition such that performing the action expressions provably results in the landmark transitions [18]. Here we only consider concrete protocols, which are viewed as patterns of communicative acts, and their semantics tie to those of the involved individual acts.

One of our design criteria for conversation protocols is that it should be able to enhance team intelligence concerning about others' information-needs by considering the flow of information-needs as well as information itself. Figure 1 shows

---

[6] It's different from PROXY with INFORM as the embedded act [13], which, like *forward*, requires the originating agent *A* already believes the information to be delivered.

the Petri-Net representation of a conversation protocol regarding *ProInform*, where the applicable contexts and goal (let *B* know *I*) are encoded as predicates and kept in the *start* node and main *end* node (i.e., *e*1), respectively. The protocol covers all the acceptable end points possibly occurring in conversations between agents *A* and *B*: terminate when *B* accepts, *B* keeps silent or refuses the pro-informed information, or when *A* accepts *B*'s refusal of information needs.

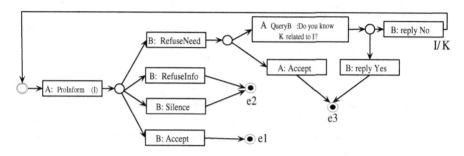

Fig. 1. A conversation policy involving *ProInform* regarding information *I*

One case is a bit involved, wherein agent *A* keeps trying to help *B* figure out his related information needs derived from *I* and appropriate inference knowledge. Suppose agent *A* initiates *ProInform* to agent *B* about information *I* that *A* believes *B* will need, but *B* responds with *RefuseNeed*. *A* has two choices at this point: either accepts *B*'s refusal and revises his beliefs regarding *B*'s information needs; or assuming *B* could not recognize her own information needs regarding *I* (e.g., due to lack of inference knowledge), *A* will take *K* as *B*'s information-need that is closer than *I* to *B*'s purpose (e.g., action performing), and adopts another instance of *ProInform* with *K* this time instead of *I*. Such recursive process may end when *A* chooses to accept *B*'s refusal, or *B* clarifies to *A* that her refusal is not due to lack of certain inference knowledge (e.g., *B* regards *A*'s anticipation of her needs as wrong).

It's easy to show that the protocol is complete in the sense that no undischarged commitments are left behind [18]. The protocol is also correct in the sense that successful execution of the protocol can achieve the goal of the protocol (refer to Property 1).

Conforming to the abovementioned criterion, we also designed a protocol involving communicative act *3PTSubscribe* as shown in Figure 2. There are three end points: either agent *C* accepts agent *A*'s subscription regarding agent *B*'s information needs, or *C* weakly accepts agent *A*'s subscription (i.e., *C* comes to believe *B*'s information needs, but not makes an commitment) and agent *A* chooses to end this helping behavior by keeping silent, or *C* rejects *A*'s subscription, and *A* comes to take *C*'s view regarding *B*'s needs [7] after being informed by *C* that *C* does not believe *B* will need *I*.

---

[7] That is, at state *S*1, agent *A* believes that agent *C* does not think *B* has a need regarding *I*. At the end state *e*3, *A* will revise his mental model about *B*'s needs.

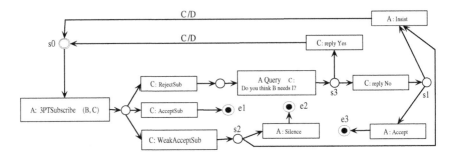

Fig. 2. A conversation policy involving $3PTSubscribe$

Likewise, this protocol allows recursive invocations (with different third-party service providers): (1) at state $s2$ agent A chooses to continue helping B (Insist) by finding another potential information provider (D) and attempting to subscribe B's needs from D; (2) at state $s3$ agent C replies "Yes" to A's query (i.e., C rejects A's subscription under the situation that C himself is already aware of B's needs [8]); (3) at state $s1$, instead of accepting C's view on B's needs, agent A insists on his/her own viewpoint of B's needs and attempts to subscribe B's needs from another known teammates.

6   Comparison

The reasoning of speech acts can be traced to the work of Austin [19], which was extended by Searle in [20]. In [5], Cohen and Levesque modeled speech acts as actions of rational agents in their framework of intentions. Henceforward, several agent communication languages were proposed, such as Arcol [21], KQML [22], and FIPA's ACL (<http://www.fipa. org/>). The formal semantics of the performatives in these languages are all framed in terms of mental attitudes.

The way of defining semantics for performatives in this paper shares the same origin with those adopted in the abovementioned languages. A common element lies in the strictly declarative semantics of performatives. For example, Arcol uses performance conditions to specify the semantics of communicative acts. KQML adopts a more operational approach by using preconditions, postconditions and completion conditions. FIPA ACL is heavily influenced by Arcol, wherein the semantics of performatives are specified by feasibility preconditions and rational effect, both of which are formulas of a semantic language SL. The semantics of proactive performatives defined in this paper draws heavily on Cohen's work on performative-as-attempt.

---

[8] Most likely, C cannot help B with B's needs because C is not an information provider of I. In such a case, C's reply is actually an indirect speech act, from which A can infer that C does not have (the observability regarding) I. However, there may exist other reasons, say, C is simply too busy. But anyway, at state $s0$ agent A needs to revise his/her model of C appropriately.

The main difference is not in the way of defining semantics, but in the requirement of proactive performatives that prior to delivering information to an agent, the speaker needs to know (either by anticipating or being informed) that agent's information-needs, which guarantees the information delivered is relevant to what the receiver should hold in order to participate team activities smoothly. To fully support such proactive communications, we also established a framework for reasoning other's information needs. Needs-driven communication is also allowed partially in Arcol. For instance, in Arcol if agent A is informed that agent B needs some information, A would supply that information as if B had requested it by reducing the explicit *inform* to implicit *request*. However, in essence, agent A acts in a reactive rather than a proactive way, because Arcol lacks a mechanism for anticipating information needs as presented in this paper.

ProInform (proactive inform) defined in this paper is comparable with *tell* in KQML, although they are not equivalent *per se*. Both *tell* and *ProInform* require that an agent cannot offer unsolicited information to another agent. The modal operator $WANT$ in KQML, which stands for the psychological states of desire, plays the same role as $InfoNeed$. However, the semantics of $WANT$ is left open for generality. $InfoNeed$ can be viewed as an explicit way to expressing information-needs under certain context.

Both *3PTSubscribe* and *broker_one* in KQML involve three parties (they have different semantics, though). However, *3PTSubscribe* is initiated by a broker agent, while *broker_one* is not. Consequently, the speaker of *3PTSubscribe* needs to know the other two parties, while the speaker of *broker_one* only needs to know the broker agent. Such difference results from the fact that we are focusing on proactive information delivery by anticipating information-needs of teammates, while KQML does not. In our approach, if an agent does not know any information provider of information I, it could choose not to offer help. Of course, the needer itself could alternatively *publish* its needs to certain facilitator agent in its team, who then might initiate a *request* (involving three parties) to some known provider. In such a sense, $broker\_one(A, B, ask\_if\ (A, -, X))$ [22] can be simulated by *publish* and *request*. However, *3PTSubscribe* cannot be easily simulated in KQML.

Proxy is defined in FIPA [10] as an Inform between the originating agent and the middle agent, which captures rather weaker third-party semantics. Stronger third-party semantics as we have introduced in this paper has independently defined for PROXY and PROXY-WEAK in [13]. Both PROXY and PROXY-WEAK are based on REQUEST. PROXY imposes significant commitments upon the intermediate agent, while PROXY-WEAK reduces the burden placed upon the intermediate agent. "PROXY of an INFORM" and "PROXY-WEAK of an INFORM" are different from *3PTSubscribe*. PROXY of an INFORM requires the middle agent believe the information that the speaker wants him/her to forward to the target agent. Even though PROXY-WEAK of an INFORM loosens this requirement, both still require the speaker already hold the information to be delivered. *3PTSubscribe*, focusing on information-needs, applies to situations when the speaker does not have the information needed by others.

To fully understand the ties between the semantics of communicative acts and patterns of these acts, conversation policies or protocols have been studied heavily in ACL field [23, 24, 6, 18, 25, 26]. The protocols proposed in this paper are rather simple, but they are helpful in understanding proactive communications enabled by proactive communicative acts and how information-needs flow.

More recently, social agency is emphasized as a complement to mental agency due to the fact that communication is inherently public [27], which requires the social construction of communication be treated as a first-class notion rather than as a derivative of the mentalist concepts. For instance, in [15] speech acts are defined as social commitments, which are obligations relativized to both the beneficiary agent and the whole team as the social context. Kumar [18] argued that joint commitments may simulate social commitments, because PWAG entails a social commitment provided that it is made public. We agree on this point. In our definition, the context argument of $ProInform$ and $3PTSubscribe$ includes the context of the information-need under concern. Thus, an information providing agent could terminate the information delivery service once the context is no longer valid. The contexts can be enriched to include protocols in force, as suggested in [6], and even social relations.

To summarize, we are not proposing a complete ACL that covers various categories of communicative acts (assertives, directives, commissives, permissives, prohibitives, declaratives, expressives) [27], nor are we focusing on the semantics of performatives alone. We are more concerned about information-needs and how to enable proactive information flows among teammates by reasoning about information-needs. The semantics of the performatives presented in this paper are motivated by our study about team proactivity driven by information-needs, and they rely on the speaker's awareness of information-needs.

7   Concluding Remarks

In this paper we established a theory about proactive information exchanges by introducing the concept of "information-needs", providing axioms for anticipating the information-needs of teammates based on shared team knowledge such as shared team process and joint goals, and defining the semantics of $ProInform$ and $3PTSubscribe$ based on the speaker's awareness of the information-needs of teammates. It is shown that communications using these proactive performatives can be derived as helping behaviors. Conversation policies involving these proactive performatives are also discussed.

Agent infrastructures like Grid [28] aim to enable trans-architecture teams of agents (a team consisting of subteams of agents with different architectures like TEAMCORE [29], D'Agents [30], CAST [31]) to support joint activities by providing mechanisms for accessing shared ontologies, and for publishing and subscribing agents' services. $3PTSubscribe$ plays an important role in sharing information among hierarchical teams, but there is still a long way to go to fully support proactive communications among teams with heterogeneous agents.

The work in this paper not only serves as a formal specification for designing agent architectures, algorithms, and applications that support proactive information exchanges among agents in a team, it also offers opportunities for extending existing agent communication protocols to support proactive teamwork, and for further studying proactive information delivery among teams involving both human and software agents.

Acknowledgments

This research is supported by a DOD MURI grant F49620-00-1-0326 administered through AFOSR.

References

1. Rouse, W., Cannon-Bowers, J., Salas, E.: The role of mental models in team performance in complex systems. IEEE Trans. on Sys., man, and Cyber **22** (1992) 1296–1308
2. Grosz, B., Kraus, S.: Collaborative plans for complex group actions. Artificial Intelligence **86** (1996) 269–358
3. Grosz, B., Kraus, S.: The evolution of sharedplans. In Rao, A., Wooldridge, M., eds.: Foundations and Theories of Rational Agencies. (1999) 227–262
4. Cohen, P.R., Levesque, H.J.: Performatives in a rationally based speech act theory. In: Proceedings of the 28th Annual Meeting of the Association for Computational Linguistics. (1990) 79–88
5. Cohen, P.R., Levesque, H.J.: Rational interaction as a basis for communication. In: Intentions in Communication, MIT Press (1990) 221–255
6. Smith, I., Cohen, P., Bradshaw, J., Greaves, M., Holmback, H.: Designing conversation policies using joint intention theory. In: Proceedings of the Third International Conference on Multi-Agent Systems (ICMAS98). (1998) 269–276
7. Searle, J.R.: How performatives work. Linguistics and Philosophy **12** (1989) 535–558
8. Cohen, P.R., Levesque, H.J.: Communicative actions for artificial agents. In: Proceedings of the International Conference on Multi-Agent Systems, AAAI Press (1995)
9. Smith, I.A., Cohen, P.R.: Toward a semantics for an agent communications language based on speech-acts. In: Proceedings of the Annual Meeting of the American Association for Artificial Intelligence (AAAI-96), AAAI Press (1996) 24–31
10. FIPA: Agent communication language specification (2002)
11. OAIS: Reference model for an open archival information system. In: http://www.ccsds.org/documents/pdf/CCSDS-650.0-R-1.pdf. (1999)
12. Searle, J.: Indirect speech acts. In Cole, P., Morgan, J., eds.: Syntax and semantics. III. Speech acts. NY: Academic Press (1975) 59–82
13. Huber, M.J., Kumar, S., Cohen, P.R., McGee, D.R.: A formal semantics for proxycommunicative acts. In Meyer, J.J.C., Tambe, M., eds.: Intelligent Agents VIII (ATAL 2001). Volume 2333 of Lecture Notes in Computer Science., Springer (2002)
14. Greaves, M., Holmback, H., Bradshaw, J.: What is a conversation policy? In: Proceedings of the Workshop on Specifying and Implementing Conversation Policies at Autonomous Agents'99. (1999)

15. Singh, M.P.: A social semantics for agent communication languages. In Dignum, F., Greaves, M., eds.: Issues in Agent Communication. Springer-Verlag: Heidelberg, Germany (2000) 31–45
16. Parunak, C.: Visualizing agent conversations: Using enhanced dooley graphs for agent design and analysis. In: Proceedings of 2nd International Conference on Multi-Agent Syatems (ICMAS-96). (1996) 275–282
17. Cost, R., Chen, Y., Finin, T., Labrou, Y., Peng, Y.: Modeling agent conversations with colored petri nets. In: Proceedings of workshop on Agent Conversation Policies at Agents-99, Seattle, WA (1999)
18. Kumar, S., Huber, M.J., Cohen, P.R., McGee, D.R.: Toward a formalism for conversation protocols using joint intention theory. Computational Intelligence **18** (2002) 174–228
19. Austin, J.: How to Do Things with Words. Oxford University Press: Oxford, England (1962)
20. Searle, J.: Speech Acts: An Essay in the Philosophy of Language. Cambridge University Press (1969)
21. Breiter, P., Sadek, M.: A rational agent as a kernel of a cooperative dialogue system: Implementing a logical theory of interaction. In: Proceedings of ECAI-96 workshop on Agent Theories, architectures, and Languages, Springer-Verlag, Berlin (1996) 261–276
22. Labrou, Y., Finin, T.: Semantics and conversations for an agent communication language. In Huhns, M., Singh, M., eds.: Readings in Agents, Morgan Kaufmann, San Mateo, Calif. (1998) 235–242
23. Pitt, J., Mamdani, A.: A protocol-based semantics for an agent communication language. In: Proceedings of IJCAI-99. (1999) 486–491
24. Labrou, Y.: Standardizing agent communication. In Marik, V., Stepankova, O., eds.: Multi-Agent Systems and Applications (Advanced Course on Artificial Intelligence). (2001)
25. Vitteau, B., Huget, M.P.: Modularity in interaction protocols. In Dignum, F., ed.: Advances in Agent Communication. LNAI, (Springer Verlag) in this volume
26. Chopra, A., Singh, M.: Nonmonotonic commitment machines. In Dignum, F., ed.: Advances in Agent Communication. LNAI, (Springer Verlag) in this volume
27. Singh, M.P.: Agent communication languages: Rethinking the principles. IEEE Computer **31** (1998) 40–47
28. Kahn, M., Cicalese, C.: The CoABS Grid. In: JPL Workshop on Rational Agent Concepts, Tysons Corner, VA. (2002)
29. Tambe, M.: Towards flexible teamwork. Journal of Artificial Intelligence Research **7** (1997) 83–124
30. Gray, R., Cybenko, G., Kotz, D., Peterson, R., Rus, D.: D'agents: Applications and performance of a mobile-agent system. Software, Practices and Experience **32** (2002) 543–573
31. Yen, J., Yin, J., Ioerger, T., Miller, M., Xu, D., Volz, R.: CAST: Collaborative agents for simulating teamworks. In: Proceedings of IJCAI'2001. (2001) 1135–1142

Modularity in Interaction Protocols

Benjamin Vitteau[1] and Marc-Philippe Huget[2]

[1] Départment SMA, Centre SIMMO
Ecole Nationale Supérieure des Mines de Saint-Etienne
158, Cours Fauriel, 42023 Saint-Etienne, France
vitteau@csc.liv.ac.uk
[2] Department of Computer Science
University of Liverpool
Liverpool L69 7ZF, United Kingdom
mph@csc.liv.ac.uk

Abstract. Protocols or part of protocols are frequently reused through projects if they are sufficiently generic. For instance, the Contract Net protocol can be used verbatim or in other protocols such as the supply chain management. This reusability might be difficult to do due to the lack of reusability in current interaction protocol formalisms. In this paper, we present a new approach based on a modular architecture. A protocol is no longer monolithic but a composition of modules called micro-protocols. This approach improves modularity and reusability in interaction protocol engineering. We apply this idea to the example of supply chain management.

1 Introduction

Communication represents one of the main components in multiagent systems as stated in the Vowels approach [6] [7] under the letter I, which stands for Interaction. Traditionally, communication is described through protocols. Even if these protocols are as old as multiagent systems, designers are still facing challenges when designing communication. One of the main challenges is the lack of flexibility requiring designers to design protocols from scratch each time [22]. Designers cannot make profit of previous protocols to define new ones. This problem is due to the lack of flexibility in formal description techniques as stated in [16]. Formal description techniques do not consider that a protocol can be made of components (or modules) that represent a part of the interaction. For instance, one would like to represent that the interaction in supply chain problem exhibits a first phase where customers express what they want to purchase, a second phase where customers and companies negotiate price and delay and finally, a third phase where the different tasks for the production are processed: from task allocation to shipping. Above all, one would like to express that it is possible to replace a specific part of the protocol by another one because the current one no longer fits needs. A component-based approach for protocols would allow this flexibility and reusability.

F. Dignum (Ed.): ACL 2003, LNAI 2922, pp. 291–309, 2004.
© Springer-Verlag Berlin Heidelberg 2004

A first attempt to make interaction protocols more flexible was done in [16]. Protocols are composed of micro-protocols that represent part of the interaction. This proposal exists and is, in the best of our knowledge, the only one which is in use in applications [23]. However, this approach remains simple and will not be of any help when designers will consider negotiation or protocols that belong to a same class: Contract Net protocol and Iterated Contract Net, that is to say, when expressiveness is at stake.

The aim of this paper is to present a revision of the current approach to tackle a broader range of interaction and negotiation protocols. This revision passes by the addition of several new fields to increase the expressiveness of micro-protocols. Such fields are, for instance, the participant cardinality, the agent communication language, the ontology and the norms to name a few. A second refinement is the possibility that a micro-protocol contains micro-protocols; thus offering a hierarchy of decomposition. Finally, the last enhancement is the micro-protocol description as a XML file; although it is not presented here due to lack of space. It is then easier to read and retrieve information for both agents and designers. Moreover, documents can be generated from XML file.

The paper is organized as follows. Section 2 justifies the aim of using micro-protocols in interaction protocols and the advantages. This section summarizes what was said in [16]. As stated above, the current version of micro-protocols is insufficient to represent negotiation protocols or a broad range of protocols; Section 3 explains why the current proposal missed its objectives. Section 4 describes the new approach for micro-protocols. Section 5 considers the protocol level that binds micro-protocols together. Section 6 presents the example of supply chain management. Due to lack of space, we will focus here on only one micro-protocol that defines the negotiation between customers and companies. Section 7 concludes the paper and give future directions of work.

2   Modularity in Interaction Protocols

Traditionally, designers either use formal description techniques coming from distributed systems [11] to represent interaction protocols or define new ones to encompass agent features such as COOL [1], temporal logic [10] or Agent UML [20]. These approaches lack of flexibility as stated in [16]. It is then difficult to easily modify a protocol as soon as a part of it no longer fits designer needs. To cope with this problem, we proposed to consider a modular architecture to describe interaction protocols [16]. The aim of such approach is to allow designers to combine these modules into a protocol to generate a specific need. Moreover, designers can easily replace a module by another if it no longer satisfies the needs. These modules are called *micro-protocols* to remind that they convey a part of the interaction usually carried by protocols. The language CPDL (*Communication Protocol Description Language*) combines these micro-protocols to form a protocol.

Several contributions are provided by a modular approach in interaction protocols:

1. It should allow for the definition of *reusable* protocols. With the current formalisms, one cannot consider replacing a piece of protocol by another. This necessitates to look for the beginning and the end of such pieces. Furthermore, it appears it is difficult to identify the exact semantics of these protocol pieces.

   By representing a protocol as a combination of micro-protocols and providing a semantics for each of them, they can be reused in other protocols. In a modular approach, a protocol becomes more flexible since one just has to remove the micro-protocol that does not suit and replace it by another one. The only constraint is to correctly connect the new micro-protocol to the others already in place.

2. It should allow for *abstraction* capabilities. Following a modular-based approach introduces a meta-level. A basic level corresponds to elements pertaining to a micro-protocol. A higher level conveys the global protocol in a more abstract fashion, i.e. a plan. With the current approaches, a protocol's global view cannot easily be perceived. The use of micro-protocols hides implementation details which are useless for a protocol's understanding.

3. It should *facilitate* the *validation* process, We agree with the following idea [11]: *"A well, structured protocol can be built from a small number of well-designed and well-understood pieces. Each piece performs one function and performs it well. To understand the working of the pieces from which it is constructed and the way in which they interact. Protocols that are designed in this way are easier to understand and easier to implement efficiently, and they are more likely to be verifiable and maintainable."* With components, it becomes easier to validate a protocol because (1) each component is less complex that a whole protocol and can be separately verified, (2) a global protocol is then verified by checking that its micro-protocols are correctly connected together.

The notion of modularity is not really addressed in interaction protocols, we can only quote work done around COSY [3] and AgenTalk [18]. Work on communication and cooperation in COSY have led to view a protocol as a combination of primitive protocols. Each primitive protocol can be represented by a tree where each node corresponds to a particular situation and transitions correspond to a possible message an agent can either receive or send. The main weakness of COSY is the semantic expression. Semantics is based on the first communicative act in the primitive protocol. As a consequence, it is difficult to distinguish two primitive protocols with the same prefix.

Work in AgenTalk is different since there is the notion of inheritance. Such approach is interesting to derive protocols to specific tasks. Each protocol is represented as a finite state machine. Unfortunately, designers in AgenTalk need to link transitions from the composite protocol to the transitions within the component protocol. This approach reduces the reuse since designers need to study the component protocols before linking states.

In the best of our knowledge, our approach seems to be the only one proposed in the literature and the only one in use [23].

3   Drawbacks of Current Micro-protocols

In this section, we first describe the current version of micro-protocols before addressing the drawbacks of the current version.

3.1   Current Version of Micro-protocols

Micro-protocols in our approach represent the basic component in a protocol [17]. It contains an ordered set of communicative acts. Some programmatic notions are added to this set to improve the power of expression such as loops, decisions, time management, conditions and exceptions. Micro-protocols must be seen as functions in programming. Micro-protocols have parameters which are used within the micro-protocol. It is then possible to reuse several times the same micro-protocol in the same protocol but with different parameters. Usually, the parameters correspond to the sender, the receiver and the content of the message. The content corresponds frequently to the content of the first communicative act, next contents are computed according the interaction.

Current micro-protocols are defined through four fields:

- a name
- a semantics
- a definition
- the semantics of the parameters

The *name* is the name of the micro-protocol. Micro-protocols are distinguished by their name; as a consequence, names must be unique. The *semantics* gives the semantics of the micro-protocol. This field is a free-format text. Designers can use either a natural language description or a set of logical formulae. The *definition* is the main part of micro-protocols. It contains the set of communicative acts. We add conditions, decisions, loops, time management and exceptions to increase micro-protocols' expressiveness. Each communicative act has usually three parameters: the sender, the receiver and the content of the message. The *semantics of the parameters* gives the semantics associated to these parameters. It helps agents to fill the messages correctly.

Thanks to its expressibility, it is possible to represent the Contract Net protocol [5] as a micro-protocol. The micro-protocol is given on Figure 1.

We do not explain in detail this micro-protocol, readers are urge to read [12]. The important elements in the definition field are the synchronization mechanism, the time management, alternatives and the exception. The keyword *token* is used for the synchronization between agents. The number inserted into parentheses corresponds to the number of messages the receiver expects before resuming the interaction. If a star is used instead of a number, it corresponds to a number of agents which is known at run time. Not giving the number of messages expected offers more flexibility to designers, they are not obliged to hardwire this piece of information into the micro-protocol. The synchronization is realized on the next message. The time management is performed with the keyword *time*.

Name: ContractNet
Parameters' semantics:
A: sender
B: receiver
T: task
P: proposal
R: refuse
Definition:
cfp(A,B,T).token(*).time(10).(not-understood(B,A,T).exit |

refuse(B,A,R).exit | propose(B,A,P)).

(reject-proposal(A,B,R) |

accept-proposal(A,B,P).

exception{cancel=exit}.(failure(B,A,R) | inform(B,A,T)))

Semantics: ContractNet

Fig. 1. The Contract Net Protocol as a Micro-Protocol

The number within the parentheses means that the receiver is waiting answers from senders during 10 time units. Putting *token* and *time* together has a different semantics, it means that the receiver expects several answers but it waits at most 10 time units. When the deadline is passed, it follows the interaction even if it does not receive all the messages. This approach prevents from deadlocks in interaction. The main novelty of this micro-protocol is the exception management. This notion is barely proposed in agent communication. Moore seems to be the only one to consider it [19]. Exceptions are interesting to unlock situations, for instance if a receiver is waiting for n answers and only gets m ($m < n$); or if an agent receives an unexpected message. The exception is given within curly brackets as well as the action to do for this exception. For instance, on the Contract Net example on Figure 1, as soon as the task manager receives a *cancel* message, it triggers an exception and do the action *exit* corresponding to stop the interaction with this agent. Finally, alternatives represent different paths in the interaction. They are written within parentheses and separated by a vertical bar. An example is given on the first line of the definition where agents can answer either with a *not-understood* message, a *refuse* message or a *propose* message. We let readers consult [13] to find other examples.

3.2   Critics against the Current Version

Even if micro-protocols were successfully applied to the Baghera project [23], they remain simple and several critics can be formulated. This section summarizes them.

Micro-protocol Distinction. One of our critics on COSY's approach is that it is not possible to describe a broad range of primitives due to the way to distinguish them. The distinction is made on the first communicative act. Even if micro-protocols allow more possibilities, the problem of distinction is still present. Micro-protocols are distinguished by their name. Such an approach allows, *a priori*, an infinite number of micro-protocols but this approach falls down due to a lack of readability. Let us suppose that we want to express the Contract Net protocol as stated in Section 3, we straightly name the micro-protocol Contract Net. Now, let us suppose that we want two Contract Net protocols: the current one and an iterated version [9]. We naturally extend the name of the micro-protocol to express the different Contract Nets. This approach is quickly intractable as soon as micro-protocols only differ on some features such as the number of agents, the way to interact (broadcast, multicast), the negotiation phase, etc.

To increase the power of distinction between micro-protocols, it seems reasonable to consider as many fields as necessary to well characterize micro-protocols. For instance, a field on the cardinality is interesting to distinguish micro-protocols dealing with one-to-one communication or one-to-many communication. Several new fields are added to the current version of micro-protocols to increase the expressiveness as Section 4 demonstrates it.

Semantic Weaknesses. The *semantics* field in the current version of micro-protocols is a free-format text. It means that designers are free to use either a natural language description, a set of logical formulae or whatsoever they want. The absence of a well-structured field for the semantics decreases the ability to describe accurately the micro-protocol. Designers can delay writing a formal description and as a consequence providing a micro-protocol without clear semantics. The example shown on Figure 1 clearly demonstrates this point since the semantics is reduced to *ContractNet*.

In the new proposal, we advocate to increase the semantics definition by adding several fields. The semantics field is helped with fields such as prerequisite, termination or type (see Section 4).

Conditions on Execution. Conditions on execution are missing in the current version of micro-protocols. It is thus not possible to describe the conditions allowing or preventing such execution. Designers have no other choice that to describe this information outside micro-protocols. It is important that micro-protocols contain the conditions which are required. These conditions refer to the mental states of the agent which wants to use this micro-protocol, the conditions on the environment, etc.

The current version has some conditions via CPDL [17]. CPDL is the language responsible to link the different micro-protocols. However, these conditions are not sufficiently fine grained to be worthwhile. Conditions are applied to a set of micro-protocols and not for each micro-protocol.

Agent Communication Languages and Ontologies. Even if micro-protocols are using communicative acts, the agent communication language and the ontology used are not written. The piece of information *agent communication language* is important in the context of interoperability; particularly if agents are heterogeneous. Writing the agent communication language used helps agents to know if they have to translate messages to other agents. The notion of ontologies allows agents to share a same meaning on terms used.

Micro-protocols Defined for Agents. The first version of micro-protocols is directed to agents and not to designers. Designers give a name to the micro-protocol, describe the parameters and the semantics and finally insert the definition. Agents use them during their interactions. As soon as the domain of applications of such micro-protocols augments, it is important to increase the quality and the documentation of micro-protocols. At this moment, designers have to write a documentation separately since there is no way to store this information in the micro-protocol. The principle of reuse is transgressed since it is not possible to have both documentation and definition in the same element.

The new version of micro-protocols attempts to fix this problem by inserting several new fields in the micro-protocol. Moreover, we propose to store the micro-protocol as a XML document [25]. Thus, the micro-protocol is readable by both designers and agents and it is possible for designers to document micro-protocols. Finally, another advantage of XML is XSLT which allows designers to generate documentation automatically. This point is in favour of reuse.

Absence of Hierarchical Decomposition. In the current version of micro-protocols, there are three levels: the communicative act level, the micro-protocol level and the protocol level. Communicative acts are contained in micro-protocols. Micro-protocols are contained in protocols. Even if this decomposition offers large possibilities, it is better if the decomposition can be more important. In the new proposal, we still have the communicative level and the protocol level but it is now possible to have as many levels as we want between these two levels. Hence, a micro-protocol can be composed of micro-protocols. And consequently, the notion of micro-protocol itself must be thought differently and more broadly than the smallest piece of a protocol.

4   Proposal for New Micro-protocols

As stated in Section 3, the current version of micro-protocols is insufficient to represent negotiation protocols and protocols that differ a little bit. In this section, we present a new proposal based on the drawbacks found in Section 3. Concerns about the hierarchical decomposition are treated in Section 5. We only focus here on the micro-protocol content.

Micro-protocols are still organized as a document with fields. However, several new fields were added to the previous version of micro-protocols. The micro-protocol fields are the following:

- Name/Type
- Synonyms
- Participant cardinality
- Other attributes
- Agent communication language
- Ontology
- Semantics
- Function
- Behavior
- Roles
- Initiator
- Norms
- Constraints
- Prerequisite
- Termination
- Input/Output
- Code sample

The remaining of this section describes the different fields in the micro-protocols and which fields are used by designers and those used by agents.

Name/Type: *Name* identifies the micro-protocol. The field *Name* should be unique to ease the selection of micro-protocols. However, in case of several micro-protocols sharing the same name, designers have to study the micro-protocols and particularly, the fields *Function*, *Semantics* and *Other attributes* to distinguish the different micro-protocols. *Type* refers to the ability to categorize micro-protocols to help designers to select the correct micro-protocol. For instance, an example of *Type* could be *Auction*. Thus, this micro-protocol belongs to auction protocols. Designers can be as accurate as they want to express the type of the micro-protocol. *Name* is defined as a natural language term. The usual way to represent *Type* is to use a natural language term but it is also possible to describe the *Type* as a path description referring to an object-oriented approach: $Name_1 : Name_2 : \ldots : Name_n$. It means that the type of this micro-protocol is composed of several subtypes separated by colons. Types are ordered from left to right. As a consequence, $Name_2$ is considered as a subtype of $Name_1$ and so on. *Type* is separated from the *Name* by a slash. Several examples are given below:

```
Contract Net
English/Auction
Dutch/Auction
Vickrey/Auction
Iterated/Contract Net
Iterated/Contract Net:1 to 5
Iterated/Contract Net:1 to n
```

Synonyms: English auction is one of the name used to represent this protocol, we can also use open outcry auction or ascending price auction. *Synonyms* gives the list of synonyms to help designers to browse list of micro-protocols. *Synonyms* are represented as a list of terms.

Participant cardinality: In case protocols are described through Petri nets, considering a protocol for m participants is not the same than considering a protocol for n participants where $m \neq n$. Two formats are possible for this field: $m - n$ and m. In the first case, it means that m refers to the sender cardinality and that n refers to the recipient cardinality. Usual values are $1 - 1$, $1 - n$, $n - 1$, $n - n$ refering to one-to-one communication, one-to-many communication, many-to-one communication and many-to-many communication respectively. In the second case, m refers to the participant cardinality without addressing the sender cardinality and the recipient cardinality. In both cases, m and n must correspond to non-zero positive integers.

Other attributes: The field *Other attributes* depicts keywords that characterize the micro-protocols. It might be, for instance, that the interaction is only between authenticated agents, messages are encrypted, secured, or anonymous. Obviously, this list is not exhaustive and greatly depends on the context of the micro-protocol. *Other attributes* are denoted by a list of terms.

Agent Communication Language: This field refers to the language used by the agents in this micro-protocol. Usual values are KQML or FIPA ACL. It is thus possible to describe the same protocol with two micro-protocols, each one for a specific agent communication language.

Ontology: This field indicates the ontology used in this micro-protocol.

Semantics: Representing the semantics of a micro-protocol is important to help designers to understand the meaning of such a micro-protocol. The *behavior* field describes informally what the intention of the micro-protocol is. This field is insufficient to describe the micro-protocol due to ambiguities and misunderstandings of the natural language. It is important to describe formally the micro-protocol. The *semantics* field is defined to this purpose.

Function: The *Function* field gives a summary of the intention of the micro-protocol. Actually, the *Behavior* field may be too long to read in the context of reuse. It is better if designers can read an abstract. That is the aim of this field.

Behavior: The *Behavior* field is the main field in the micro-protocol since it provides a detailed description of the micro-protocol (the communicative acts, the message sequence and the message content). BDI modalities [24] and agent actions are also stored in this field. It is then possible for designers to know what is the impact of the interaction on agents. This is the field that designers will use to generate code for this micro-protocol. The *Behavior* field can be completed by a diagram that represents graphically the micro-protocol. Due to space restriction, we only give one example in Section 6.

Roles: Agents involved in interactions and interaction protocols are involved for a particular role. For instance in auctions, there are usually two roles *auctioneer* and *participant*. This piece of information is used at several levels: first knowing agents' roles allow designers to know how agents will behave in the interaction. Knowing agents' roles, designers know the responsibilities of each agent in the interaction and what they are expected to do. Second, this criterion can make a distinction between different micro-protocols. Two micro-protocols could have the same set of communicative acts but two different set of agents' roles. For instance, in the Baghera project [23], the same micro-protocol *request-information* will not have the same meaning if it is applied between a pupil and his/her companion and between a pupil's companion and the pupil's tutor. In the first case, pupil asks whether his/her proof is correct, the companion answers yes or no. In the second case, companion and tutor can exchange several messages if they need more information about the proof. Finally, agents' roles are used when defining norms for this micro-protocol. Norms are linked to agents' roles and as a consequence to their roles in this interaction. Agents will be "punished" differently according to their roles and their responsibilities.

The agents' cardinality that defines the number of agents per roles is added to agents' roles. For instance, for an auction there is one and only one auctioneer but at least two participants. This piece of information prevents from jeopardizing the system if this is an open system thus too many agents enter the system and consume the resources. Agents' cardinality format is $m - n$ where both m and n represent respectively the lower and the upper bound. There is at least m agents of this role and at most n agents. Lower and upper bounds are positive numbers.

Initiator: This field gives which role is initiator for this interaction. The role must be a role defined in the *Roles* field.

Norms: Norms were first considered in electronic institutions [8] to enforce agents to do some actions or to conform to some behaviors. Norms define what is permitted, what is obliged and what is forbidden. Norms have also a meaning in open systems to prevent actions that will jeopardize the system. Norms can be defined formally (see [8] to this purpose) or informally. Such an example of norms is: "The participant of an auction that gets the higher bid at the end of the auction must pay the amount corresponding to the bid except if the highest bid is less than the reserved price."

Constraints: *Constraints* correspond to constraints that must hold during the execution of the micro-protocol. These constraints are important when designers will check properties on micro-protocols. *Constraints* correspond to safety properties (nothing bad happens) and liveness properties (something good eventually happens). *Constraints* are defined formally via temporal logic or informally. Such examples of constraints are for instance mutual exclusion, deadlock but constraints can be also oriented to the goal of the micro-protocol, for instance, bids less than the current price are forbidden.

Prerequisite: The *Prerequisite* field describes the conditions that must be satisfied before executing the micro-protocol. Prerequisite can be defined formally through temporal logic or informally. Such example of prerequisites is agents must be authenticated before requesting information.

Termination: The *Termination* field gives the valid exits for this micro-protocol. The exit of a micro-protocol is considered valid if the exit matches one defined in the *Termination* field. For the NetBill protocol [4], a valid exit is "the customer has the good and no longer the money, the seller has the money and no longer the good."

Input/Output: Micro-protocols can be linked to express that a protocol is a composition of micro-protocols. To this aim and to add reuse, it is worthwhile if micro-protocols can exhibit entry points and exit points. These points are data (called input and output respectively) that will be used in the current micro-protocol or in the next micro-protocol. Discussion on inputs and outputs is given in Section 5.

Sample Code: Previous fields are more oriented to the definition and the documentation of micro-protocols. This one is directed to the use of the micro-protocol in agents. Two kinds of information can be found in this field, either a sample code that gives the behavior of the micro-protocol in a programming language or an ordered set of communicative acts and micro-protocols that could be directly used by agents as defined in [12]. The former proposal corresponds to the usual approach for protocol synthesis as described in [11]. The latter is related to our interaction module where definition is directly executed [14].

Table 1 describes the use of these fields by designers and agents.

Table 1. Use of Micro-Protocol Fields

Field	Designers	Agents
Name/Type	√	√
Synonyms	√	
Participant cardinality	√	√
Other attributes	√	
Agent communication language	√	√
Semantics	√	
Ontology	√	√
Function	√	
Behavior	√	
Roles	√	√
Initiator	√	√
Norms	√	√
Constraints	√	√
Prerequisite	√	√
Termination	√	√
Input/Output	√	√
Sample code	√	√

We briefly explain this table. All fields are useful for designers. Some of the fields are written in natural language. As a consequence, agents are unable to process them. Such fields are *Other attributes*, *Function* and *Behavior*. The field *Semantics* is written as a formal description but it will be really difficult for agents to figure it out. The field *Synonyms* cannot be applied to agents since we define it as a field for designers. The other fields can be used by agents providing that the description is structured to be understandable by agents.

5   Protocol Level

In Section 4, we described the micro-protocols. These micro-protocols can be decomposed into micro-protocols giving several levels of micro-protocols. At the lower end of this decomposition, there is the communicative act level containing the communicative acts exchanged in the messages. At the upper end of the decomposition, there is the protocol level that seizes all the micro-protocols used in the interaction protocol as shown on Figure 2.

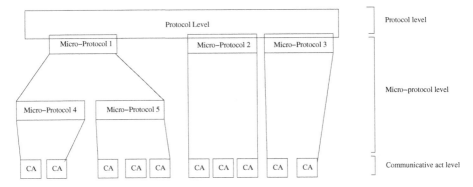

Fig. 2. Decomposition of Interaction Protocols in our Model

For instance on Figure 2, there are four levels: one protocol level, two micro-protocol levels and one communicative act level. The protocol level is different from the micro-protocol level as it can be seen as a meta-level addressing the aim of the interaction protocol and the structuration of the interaction. The distinction between protocols and micro-protocols is similar to the one existing between goals and plans in planning.

Protocols are rendered graphically as diagrams as shown on Figure 3. A diagram contains the protocol name in the left upper corner in a "snippet" pentagon as UML 2 proposes it. Constraints on protocols are written in the right upper corner either formally (via OCL [21] for instance) or informally. The remaining of the diagram contains the different micro-protocols and the flow between them.

Micro-protocols are rendered as rectangles with the name of the micro-protocol inside. Micro-protocols are linked together via transitions. Transitions are directed arrows with open arrowhead. Two kinds of information are written

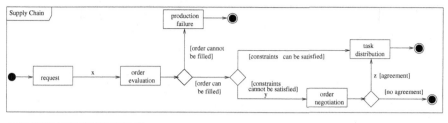

x = [car, model X, red, 10,000 per unit, quantity = 7]
y = [car, model X, red, 11,000 per unit, quantity = 7, delay = 4 weeks]
z = [car, model X, red, 10,000 per unit, quantity = 7, delay = 3 weeks]

Fig. 3. Supply Chain Protocol Representation

Fig. 4. Protocol Level Connector

on transitions: (1) values used by a micro-protocol and (2) constraints on the execution of the micro-protocol. Values can be supplied by previous micro-protocols or by agent knowledge base. Values can be represented textually on diagrams if there is enough space else designers can use variables and give the content of the variables below the diagram as shown on Figure 3. Constraints are nested into square brackets. Paths in protocols can be splitted or merged. Designers have connectors to this purpose as shown on Figure 4. The diamond connector represents the OR connector meaning that several alternatives are possible. One and only one alternative will be chosen. Parallel executions of micro-protocols are depicted through vertical bars with outgoing arrows. Each arrow corresponds to a parallel execution. Synchronization of these parallel executions are done via incoming arrows on vertical bars. The beginning of the protocol is depicted as a solid circle and an arrow pointing the initial micro-protocol or connector. The end of the protocol is denoted as a solid circle with a hollow circle around. There must be one and only one initial beginning but several endings are possible.

6   The Example of Supply Chain Management

To illustrate our matter, we have chosen to present here the example of Supply Chain Management. At first, we describe succinctly and in a simplistic view what Supply Chain Management is. Then we show the different phases of the process and how they can be matched with micro-protocols. And finally we give the complete depiction of one of the micro-protocols, as the limitations of this paper do not allow us to depict them all.

In its global view, supply chain management renders the material, the information and the finance flows between customers, suppliers and manufacturers. It describes how materials are passing from suppliers to customers and how suppliers and manufacturers attempt to reduce stock. The information flow defines

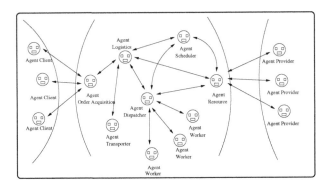

Fig. 5. Agents in Supply Chain Management

the ordering and the update of orders. Finally, the finance flow presents how and when payments will be made and under what conditions. Pragmatically speaking, the management of supply chain describes how customers pass orders and how suppliers process these orders.

In this paper, we limit the view of supply chain management to the order of customers, the negotiation between customers and companies to fill the order and finally, the task allocation and distribution to process the order.

We follow the idea of Barbuceanu and Fox [2] to agentify the management of supply chain as shown on Figure 5. The list of agents is given below:

- Client
- Order acquisition
- Logistics
- Scheduler
- Dispatcher
- Resource
- Transporter
- Provider
- Worker

Several agents are involved in this application as shown on Figure 5:

- a client agent who places, modifies and deletes orders.
- an order acquisition agent who receives the orders and negotiates the price and the delay with the logistics agent. It is responsible for the connection between clients and the company. It informs clients as soon as deliveries are postponed or delivered.
- a logistics agent who negotiates the delay and the price with the order acquisition agent. As soon as orders are accepted, it asks the scheduler agent to generate a plan for this order. This plan is sent to the agents transporter, resource and dispatcher. It asks for a new plan as soon as some modifications appear either if the client wants to modify the order or if some delays arise on the production.

- a scheduler agent who generates a plan according to the order, the delay and the allocation of workers and resources.
- a transporter agent who is responsible for the delivery of raw materials for the production and for the delivery of the final product to the client.
- a resource agent who manages the allocation of materials in order to realize the order. If the materials are not available, it places an order to provider agents.
- a dispatcher agent who manages worker agents. It allocates work to worker agents. The dispatcher agent informs the logistics agent if some problems arise occurring a delay for the delivery.
- several worker agents who realize the work. If they are unable to complete their tasks at time, they inform the dispatcher agent.
- several provider agents who provide raw materials if the company has not enough materials for the order. In fact, a provider agent is an order acquisition agent from another company.

As stated above, there are several phases in supply chain management: request, evaluation, negotiation and finally task allocation. The request phase involves customers and order acquisition agents to define orders. Then, the companies evaluate if this order can be processed in terms of products to be manufactured and constraints on company production and scheduling. If this evaluation fails, companies enter in a negotiation loop with customers to relax constraints such as prices, delays or features. Finally, companies allocate tasks to workers to fill the order. The production is finished when the order is delivered to the customer.

All these different phases defined above are good candidates to be shaped in micro-protocols. Moreover, such phases are relatively reusable through projects. For instance, the request and negotiation micro-protocols can be used as soon as designers have to deal multiagent systems for commerce. It would be the same for task allocation used either in cooperation systems or in meeting scheduling.

Several micro-protocols are proposed to represent the management of supply chain:

1. **Request micro-protocol**, used by the client agents to contact the order acquisition agent of the company and send an order.
2. **Order evaluation micro-protocol**, composed of several micro-protocols not detailed here which involve every agent of the company and whose function is to evaluate if the order is achievable or not.
3. **Production failure micro-protocol**, to inform the client that the company is unable to process the order.
4. **Order negotiation micro-protocol** used by clients and order acquisition agents to negotiate price, delay and whichever elements of importance.
5. **Tasks distribution micro-protocol**, which implies the scheduler and the dispatcher agents to distribute the different tasks among the worker and the transporter agents in order to achieve the order. A Contract Net is performed prior to distribution to define which workers and transporters have to be involved.

The composition of these micro-protocols is depicted on Figure 3. This figure shows the data flow between micro-protocols.

Due to lack of space, we only give here the order negotiation micro-protocol.

Name/type: Order Negotiation / Negotiation
Synonyms: none
Participant Cardinality: 1-1
Other Attributes: none
Agent Communication Language: FIPA ACL
Ontology: Negotiation, Sale
Function: this protocol is employed when the order acquisition agent cannot satisfy the order, and needs to negotiate some points with the clients, most of the time, points refer to the delay or the price. The negotiation stage is based on proposals and counter-proposals and should reach an agreement else the negotiation fails.
Behavior: The order acquisition agent first sends the new proposal to the client by issuing a proposal via the *propose* message. The content of the message is the new conditions proposed by the company. The client agent receives the proposal and has three choices: (1) accepting it (via the *accept* message), (2) rejecting it (via the *reject* message) and finally, (3) countering it (via the *counter* message). In the first case, the negotiation ends since an agreement is reached. In the second case, the negotiation fails since the client gave up. In the third case, the client modifies the proposal and sends its counter-proposal to the order acquisition agent. Proposals and counter-proposals can continue as long as the client does not answer either by the *accept* message or the *reject* message. The automaton corresponding to this micro-protocol is in Figure 6.

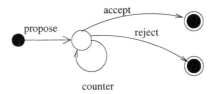

Fig. 6. Order Negotiation Example

Roles: Client, cardinality = 1
    Order Acquisition, cardinality = 1
Initiator: Order Acquisition
Constraints: agents are benevolent and do not try to stuck into a loop where no solution will appear.
Prerequisite: Such criteria for the order to fill are not possible to satisfy. The order acquisition must have a counter-proposal which is processable by the company.

Termination: Three situations are possible for the termination:
1. Client accepts the counter-proposal
2. Order Acquisition rearranges the production to fill this order and satisfy the constraints
3. Order cannot be processed since no agreement was found

Input/Output: Input: counter-proposal
   Output: order with a set of agreed constraints or no order

7   Conclusion

Modularity and reusability are now two terms frequently in use in multiagent system design, particularly in agent design. Unfortunately, reuse is barely considered when designing interaction protocols. As Singh [22] quoted it, designers need to start from scratch each time. A first proposal for reusability was made in [15]. This approach is based on micro-protocols and the CPDL language. Micro-protocols represent part of the interaction. They are composed through the CPDL language. This proposal allows flexibility, modularity and reusability but remains simple and in a certain way, missed its objectives. Actually, reusability is not properly addressed in this proposal since two protocols relatively similar will be difficult to represent and to distinguish. This paper attempts to fix this problem through the addition of several fields to increase the micro-protocol expressiveness. Moreover, micro-protocols can now be used by both agents and designers where previous version of micro-protocols are dedicated to agents.

Several directions of work are already considered. First, we will generate micro-protocols for the protocols defined in the FIPA library [9] in order to exemplify this approach. Then, we will provide a library that will be accessible by both agents and designers. Designers can add, delete and modify micro-protocols through a Web interface. Agents can search and retrieve micro-protocols. The final step of our work on this approach will be to update the interaction module [14] and define an application that emphasizes the use of micro-protocols and their reuse.

Acknowledgments

This work was supported by the EC under project IST-1999-10948 (SLIE) and by the EPSRC under project GR/R27518.

References

1. M. Barbuceanu and M. S. Fox. COOL : A language for describing coordination in multiagent system. In *First International Conference on Multi-Agent Systems (ICMAS-95)*, pages 17–24, San Francisco, USA, June 1995. AAAI Press.
2. M. Barbuceanu and M. S. Fox. Coordinating multiple agents in the supply chain. In *Proceedings of the Workshops on Enabling Technologies: Infrastructure for Collaborative Enterprises (WET ICE 96)*, Stanford University, USA, june 1996.

3. B. Burmeister, A. Haddadi, and K. Sundermeyer. Generic, configurable, cooperation protocols for multi-agent systems. In C. Castelfranchi and J.-P. Muller, editors, *From Reaction to Cognition*, volume 957 of *Lecture notes in AI*, pages 157–171, Berlin, Germany, 1995. Springer Verlag. Appeared also in MAAMAW-93, Neuchatel.

4. B. Cox, J. Tygar, and M. Sirbu. Netbill security and transaction protocol. In *Proceedings of the First USENIX Workshop in Electronic Commerce*, july 1995.

5. R. Davis and R. G. Smith. Negotiation as a metaphor for distributed problem-solving. *Artificial Intelligence*, 20:63–109, 1983.

6. Y. Demazeau. From interactions to collective behaviour in agent-based systems. In *First European Conference on Cognitive Science*, Saint-Malo, France, April 1995.

7. Y. Demazeau. Steps towards multi-agent oriented programming. slides Workshop, 1st International Workshop on Multi-Agent Systems, IWMAS '97, October 1997.

8. M. Esteva, J. A. Rodriguez, C. Sierra, P. Garcia, and J. L. Arcos. *On the formal specifications of electronic institutions*, pages 126–147. Number 1991 in Lecture Notes in Artificial Intelligence. Springer-Verlag, 2001.

9. FIPA. *Specification*. Foundation for Intelligent Physical Agents, http://www.fipa.org/repository/fipa2000.html, 2000.

10. M. Fisher and M. Wooldridge. Specifying and executing protocols for cooperative action. In *International Working Conference on Cooperating Knowledge-Based Systems (CKBS-94)*, Keele, 1994.

11. G. J. Holzmann. *Design and Validation of Computer Protocols*. Prentice-Hall, 1991.

12. M.-P. Huget and J.-L. Koning. Interaction protocol engineering in multiagent systems. In M.-P. Huget, editor, *Communication in Multiagent Systems: Background, Current Trends and Future*, number 2650 in LNCS/LNAI State of the Art Survey. Springer-Verlag, 2003.

13. M.-P. Huget. *Une ingénierie des protocoles d'interaction pour les systèmes multi-agents*. PhD thesis, Université Paris 9 Dauphine, June 2001.

14. M.-P. Huget. Design agent interaction as a service to agents. In M.-P. Huget, F. Dignum, and J.-L. Koning, editors, *AAMAS Workshop on Agent Communication Languages and Conversation Policies (ACL2002)*, Bologna, Italy, July 2002.

15. J.-L. Koning and M.-P. Huget. A component-based approach for modeling interaction protocols. In *10th European-Japanese Conference on Information Modelling and Knowledge Bases*, Finland, May 2000.

16. J.-L. Koning and M.-P. Huget. Validating reusable interaction protocols. In H. Arabnia, editor, *The 2000 International Conference on Artificial Intelligence (ICAI-00)*, Las Vegas, NV, June 2000. CSREA Press.

17. J.-L. Koning and M.-P. Huget. A semi-formal specification language dedicated to interaction protocols. In H. Kangassalo, H. Jaakkola, and E. Kawaguchi, editors, *Information Modelling and Knowledge Bases XII*, Frontiers in Artificial Intelligence and Applications. IOS Press, Amsterdam, 2001.

18. K. Kuwabara, T. Ishida, and N. Osato. AgenTalk: Coordination protocol description for multiagent systems. In *First International Conference on MultiAgent Systems (ICMAS-95)*, San Francisco, June 1995. AAAI Press. Poster.

19. S. A. Moore. On conversation policies and the need for exceptions. In *Autonomous Agents'99 Special Workshop on Conversation Policies*, 1999.

20. J. Odell, H. V. D. Parunak, and B. Bauer. Representing agent interaction protocols in UML. In P. Ciancarini and M. Wooldridge, editors, *Proceedings of First International Workshop on Agent-Oriented Software Engineering*, Limerick, Ireland, june, 10 2000. Springer-Verlag.

21. OMG. UML 1.4. Technical report, OMG, 2001.
22. M. P. Singh. On the semantics of protocols among distributed intelligent agents. In *IEEE Conference on Computers and Communication*, pages 1–14, Phoenix, USA, 1992.
23. C. Webber, L. Bergia, S. Pesty, and N. Balacheff. The baghera project: a multi-agent architecture for human learning. In *Proceedings of the Workshop Multi-Agent Architectures for Distributed Learning Environments, AIED2001*, pages 12–17, San Antonio, TX, 2001.
24. M. Wooldridge. *Reasoning about Rational Agents*. MIT Press, 2000.
25. XML. The xtensible markup language. See `http://www.xml.org/`.

Concepts of Optimal Utterance in Dialogue: Selection and Complexity

Paul E. Dunne and Peter McBurney

Dept. of Computer Science
University of Liverpool
Liverpool L69 7ZF, UK
{ped,p.j.mcburney}@csc.liv.ac.uk

Abstract. Dialogue protocols have been the subject of considerable attention with respect to their potential applications in multiagent system environments. Formalisations of such protocols define classes of dialogue *locutions*, concepts of a dialogue *state*, and *rules* under which a dialogue proceeds. One important consideration in implementing a protocol concerns the criteria an agent should apply in choosing which utterance will constitute its next contribution: ideally, an agent should select a locution that (by some measure) *optimises* the outcome. The precise interpretation of optimise may vary greatly depending on the nature and intent of a dialogue area. One option is to choose the locution that results in a *minimal length* debate. We present a formal setting for considering the problem of deciding if a particular utterance is optimal in this sense and show that this decision problem is *both* NP–hard *and* CO-NP–hard.

1   Introduction

Methods for modeling discussion and dialogue processes have proved to be of great importance in describing multiagent interactions. The study of *dialogue protocols* ranges from perspectives such as argumentation theory, e.g., [26, 30], taxonomies of types of dialogue such as [30, 33], and formalisms for describing and reasoning about protocols, e.g. [17, 23, 25]. Among the many applications that have been considered are bargaining and negotiation processes, e.g. [18, 26, 21]; legal reasoning, e.g. [15, 20, 2, 3, 29], persuasion in argumentation and other systems, e.g. [32, 12, 4, 9], and inquiry and information-discovery, e.g. [22, 24]. The collections of articles presented in [8, 16] give an overview of various perspectives relating to multiagent discourse.

While we present a general formal model for dialogue protocols below, informally we may view the core elements of such as comprising a description of the 'locution types' for the protocol ("what participants can *say*"); the topics of discussion ("what participants talk *about*"); and how discussions may start, evolve, and finish.

Despite the divers demands of protocols imposing special considerations of interest with particular applications, there are some properties that might be considered desirable irrespective of the protocol's specific domain, cf. [25]. Among such properties are *termination*; the capability to *validate* that a discussion is being conducted according to the protocol; and the ability for participants to determine "sensible" contributions. In [17] frameworks for uniform comparison of protocols are proposed that are defined

F. Dignum (Ed.): ACL 2003, LNAI 2922, pp. 310–328, 2004.
© Springer-Verlag Berlin Heidelberg 2004

independently of the application domain. In principle, if two distinct protocols can be shown 'equivalent' in the senses defined by [17], then termination and other properties need only be proved for one of them.

In this paper our concern is with the following problem: in realising a particular discussion protocol within a multiagent environment, one problem that must be addressed by each participant can, informally, be phrased as *"what do/should I say next?"* In other words, each agent must "be aware of" its permitted (under the protocol rules) *utterances* given the progress of the discussion so far, and following specific criteria, either choose to say nothing or contribute one of these. While the extent to which a protocol admits a 'reasonable' decision-making process is, of course, a property that is of domain-independent interest, one crucial feature distinguishing different types of discussion protocol is the criteria that apply when an agent makes its choice. More precisely, in making a contribution an agent may be seen as "optimising" the outcome. A clear distinction between protocol applications is that the sense of "optimality" in one protocol may be quite different from "optimality" in another. For example, in multiagent bidding and bargaining protocols, a widely-used concept of "optimal utterance" is based on the view that any utterance has the force of affording a particular "utility value" to the agent invoking it that may affect the utility enjoyed by other agents. In such settings, the *policy* (often modeled as a probability distribution) is "optimal" if no agent can improve its (expected) utility by unilaterally deviating. This – Nash equilibrium – has been the subject of intensive research and there is strong evidence of its computational intractability [5]. While valid as a criterion for utterances in multiagent bargaining protocols, such a model of "optimality" is less well-suited to fields such as persuasion, information-gathering, etc. We may treat a "persuasion protocol" as one in which an agent seeks to convince others of the validity of a given proposition, and interpreting such persuasion protocols as proof mechanisms – a view used in, among others, [32, 12] – we contend that a more appropriate sense of an utterance being "optimal", is that it *allows* the discussion to be *concluded* "as quickly as possible"[1]. There are several reasons why such a measure is appropriate with respect to persuasion protocols. In practice, discussions in which one agent attempts to persuade another to carry out some action cannot (reasonably) be allowed to continue indefinitely; an agent may be unable to continue with other tasks which are time-constrained in some sense until other agents in the system have been persuaded through some reasoned discussion to accept particular propositions. It is, of course, the case that describing optimality in terms of length of discussion provides only one measure. We discuss alternative notions of optimality in the concluding sections.

Concentrating on persuasion protocols we formulate the "optimal utterance problem" and establish lower bounds on its complexity. In the next section we outline an abstract computational framework for dialogue protocols and introduce two variants of the optimal utterance decision problem. In Section 3 we present a setting in which this problem is proved to be both NP–hard *and* CO-NP–hard. Conclusions and further work are presented in the final section.

---

[1] An alternative view is proposed in [11], where it is argued that utterances which *prolong* discussions can, in certain settings, be seen as "optimal".

2   Definitions

Definition 1 *Let $\mathcal{F}$ be the (infinite) set of all well-formed formulae (wff) in some propositional language (where we assume an enumerable set of propositional variables x_1, $x_2, \ldots$).*

A dialogue arena, *denoted $\mathcal{A}$, is a (typically infinite) set of* finite *subsets of $\mathcal{F}$. For a dialogue arena,*

$$\mathcal{A} = \{\Phi_1, \Phi_2, \ldots, \Phi_k, \ldots, \} \quad \Phi_i \subset \mathcal{F}$$

the set of wff in $\Phi_i = \{\psi_1, \psi_2, \ldots, \psi_q\}$ is called a dialogue context *from the dialogue arena $\mathcal{A}$.*

Definition 2 *A* dialogue schema *is a triple $\langle \mathcal{L}, \mathcal{D}, \Phi \rangle$, where $\mathcal{L} = \{L_j | 1 \leq j \leq l\}$ is a finite set of* locution types, *$\mathcal{D}$ is a* dialogue protocol *as defined below, and Φ is a dialogue context.*

We are interested in reasoning about properties of protocols operating in given dialogue arenas. In the following, $\mathcal{A} = \{\Phi_1, \Phi_2, \ldots, \}$ is a dialogue arena, with $\Phi = \{\psi_1, \ldots, \psi_q\}$ a (recall, finite) set of wff constituting a single dialogue context of this arena.

Definition 3 *Let $\mathcal{L} = \{L_j | 1 \leq j \leq l\}$ be a set of* locution types. *A* dialogue fragment *over the dialogue context Φ is a (finite) sequence,*

$$\mu_1 \cdot \mu_2 \cdots \mu_k$$

where $\mu_t = L_{j,t}(\theta_t)$ is the instantiated locution *or* utterance *(with $\theta_t \in \Phi$) at time t. The* commitment *represented by a dialogue fragment δ – denoted $\Sigma(\delta)$ – is a subset of the context Φ.*

The notation $M^*_{\mathcal{L}, \Phi}$ is used to denote the set of all dialogue fragments involving instantiated locutions from $\mathcal{L}$; δ to denote an arbitrary member of this set, and $|\delta|$ to indicate the length (number of utterances) in δ.

In order to represent dialogues of interest we need to describe mechanisms by which dialogue fragments and their associated commitments evolve.

Definition 4 *A* dialogue protocol *for the discussion of the context Φ using locution set $\mathcal{L}$ – is a pair $\mathcal{D} = \langle \Pi, \Sigma \rangle$ defined by:*

a. A possible dialogue continuation *function –*

$$\Pi : M^*_{\mathcal{L}, \Phi} \to \wp(\mathcal{L} \times \Phi) \cup \{\bot\}$$

The subset of dialogue fragments δ in $M^*_{\mathcal{L}, \Phi}$ having $\Pi(\delta) \neq \bot$ is called the set of legal dialogues *over $\langle \mathcal{L}, \Phi \rangle$ in the protocol $\mathcal{D}$, this subset being denoted $T_\mathcal{D}$. It is required that the empty dialogue fragment, ϵ containing no locutions is a legal dialogue, i.e. $\Pi(\epsilon) \neq \bot$, and we call the set $\Pi(\epsilon)$ the* legal commencement locutions[2]. *We further require that Π satisfies the following condition:*

---

[2] Note that we allow $\Pi(\epsilon) = \emptyset$, although the dialogues that result from this case are unlikely to be of significant interest.

$$\forall \delta \in M^*_{\mathcal{L},\Phi} \ (\Pi(\delta) = \bot) \Rightarrow (\forall \, \mu = \mathcal{L}_j(\theta) \ \Pi(\delta \cdot \mu) = \bot)$$

i.e. if δ is not a legal dialogue then no dialogue fragment starting with δ is a legal dialogue.

b. *A commitment function* $-\ \Sigma : T_{\mathcal{D}} \to \wp(\Phi)$ *associating each legal dialogue with a subset of the dialogue context Φ.*

This definition abstracts away ideas concerning commencement, combination and termination rules into the pair $\langle \Pi, \Sigma \rangle$ through which the possible dialogues of a protocol and the associated states (subsets of Φ) are defined. Informally, given a legal dialogue, δ, $\Pi(\delta)$ delineates all of the utterances that may be used to continue the discussion.

A dialogue, δ, is *terminated* if $\Pi(\delta) = \emptyset$ and *partial* if $\Pi(\delta) \neq \emptyset$.

We now describe mechanisms for assessing dialogue protocols in terms of the *length* of a dialogue. The following notation is used.

$$\Delta = \{\Delta_k\} = \{\langle \mathcal{L}, \mathcal{D} = \langle \Pi, \Sigma \rangle, \Phi_k \rangle\}$$

is a (sequence of) dialogue schemata for an arena

$$\mathcal{A} = \{\Phi_1, \ldots, \Phi_k, \ldots\}$$

Although one can introduce concepts of dialogue length predicated on the number of utterances needed to attain a particular state Θ, the decision problem we consider will focus on the concept of "minimal length terminated *continuation* of a dialogue fragment δ". Formally

Definition 5 *Let $\langle \mathcal{L}, \mathcal{D} = \langle \Pi, \Sigma \rangle, \Phi_k \rangle$ be a dialogue schema Δ_k instantiated with the context Φ_k of $\mathcal{A}$. Let $\delta \in M^*_{\langle \mathcal{L}, \Phi_k \rangle}$ be a dialogue fragment. The* completion length *of δ under $\mathcal{D}$ for the context Φ_k, denoted $\chi(\delta, \mathcal{D}, \Phi_k)$, is,*

$$\min\{|\eta| : \eta \in T_{\mathcal{D}}, \ \eta = \delta \cdot \zeta, \ \Pi(\eta) = \emptyset\}$$

if such a dialogue fragment exists, and undefined otherwise.

Thus the completion length of a (legal) dialogue, δ, is the least number of utterances in a terminated dialogue that *starts* with δ. We note that if δ is *not* a legal dialogue then $\chi(\delta, \mathcal{D}, \Phi_k)$ is always undefined.

The decision problem whose properties we are concerned with is called the *Generic Optimal Utterance Problem*.

Definition 6 *An instance of the* Generic Optimal Utterance Problem (GOUP) *comprises,*

$$\mathcal{U} = \langle \Delta, \delta, \mu \rangle$$

where $\Delta = \langle \mathcal{L}, \mathcal{D}, \Phi \rangle$ is a dialogue schema with locution set $\mathcal{L}$, protocol $\mathcal{D} = \langle \Pi, \Sigma \rangle$, and dialogue context Φ; $\delta \in M^*_{\langle \mathcal{L}, \Phi \rangle}$ is a dialogue fragment, and $\mu \in \mathcal{L} \times \Phi$ is an utterance.

An instance $\mathcal{U}$ is accepted if there exists a dialogue fragment $\eta \in M^*_{\langle \mathcal{L}, \Phi \rangle}$ for which all of the following hold

1. $\eta = \delta \cdot \mu \cdot \zeta \in T_{\mathcal{D}}$.
2. $\Pi(\eta) = \emptyset$.
3. $|\eta| = \chi(\delta, \mathcal{D}, \Phi)$.

If any of these fail to hold, the instance is rejected.

Thus, given representations of a dialogue schema together with a *partial* dialogue, δ and utterance μ, an instance is accepted if there is a terminated dialogue (η) which commences with the dialogue fragment $\delta \cdot \mu$ and whose length is the completion length of δ under $\mathcal{D}$ for the context Φ. In other words, the utterance μ is such that it *is* a legal continuation of δ leading to a shortest length terminated dialogue.

Our formulation of GOUP, as given in Definition 6, raises a number of questions. The most immediate of these concerns how the schema Δ is to be represented, specifically the protocol $\langle \Pi, \Sigma \rangle$. Noting that we have (so far) viewed $\langle \Pi, \Sigma \rangle$ in abstract terms as mappings from dialogue fragments to sets of utterances (subsets of the context), one potential difficulty is that in "most" cases these will not be *computable*[3]. We can go some way to addressing this problem by representing $\langle \Pi, \Sigma \rangle$ through (encodings of) Turing machine programs $\langle M_\Pi, M_\Sigma \rangle$ with the following characteristics: M_Π takes as its input a *pair* $\langle \delta, \mu \rangle$, where $\delta \in M^*_{\langle \mathcal{L}, \Phi \rangle}$ and $\mu \in \mathcal{L} \times \Phi$, accepting if $\delta \cdot \mu$ is a legal dialogue and rejecting otherwise; similarly M_Σ takes as its input a pair $\langle \delta, \Psi \rangle$ with $\Psi \in \Phi$ accepting if δ is a legal dialogue having $\Psi \in \Sigma(\delta)$, rejecting otherwise. There remain, however, problems with this approach: it is *not* possible, in general, to validate that a given input *is* an instance of GOUP, cf. Rice's Theorem for Recursive Index Sets in e.g., [10, Chapter 5, pp. 58–61]; secondly, even in those cases where one can interpret the encoding of $\langle \Pi, \Sigma \rangle$ "appropriately" the definition places no time-bound on how long the computation of these programs need take. There are two methods we can use to overcome these difficulties: one is to employ 'clocked' Turing machine programs, so that, for example, if no decision has been reached for an instance $\langle \delta, \mu \rangle$ on M_Π after, say $|\delta \cdot \mu|$ steps, then the instance is rejected. The second is to consider *specific* instantiations of GOUP with protocols that can be established "independently" to have desirable efficient decision procedures. More formally,

Definition 7 *Instances of the* Optimal Utterance Problem *in* Δ – OUP$^{(\Delta)}$ – *where* $\{\Delta\} = \{\langle \mathcal{L}, \mathcal{D} = \langle \Pi, \Sigma \rangle, \Phi_k \rangle\}$ *is a sequence of dialogue schema over the arena* $\mathcal{A} = \{\Phi_k : k \geq 1\}$, *comprise*

$$\mathcal{U} = \langle \Phi_k, \delta, \mu \rangle$$

where $\delta \in M^*_{\langle \mathcal{L}, \Phi_k \rangle}$ *is a dialogue fragment, and* $\mu \in \mathcal{L} \times \Phi_k$ *is an utterance.*

An instance $\mathcal{U}$ *is accepted if there exists a dialogue fragment* $\eta \in M^*_{\langle \mathcal{L}, \Phi_k \rangle}$ *for which all of the following hold*

1. $\eta = \delta \cdot \mu \cdot \zeta \in T_{\mathcal{D}}$.
2. $\Pi(\eta) = \emptyset$.
3. $|\eta| = \chi(\delta, \mathcal{D}, \Phi_k)$.

If any of these fail to hold, the instance is rejected.

---

[3] For example, it is easy to show that the set of distinct protocols that could be defined using only *two* locutions and a *single element* context is not enumerable.

The crucial difference between the problems GOUP and OUP$^{(\Delta)}$ is that we can consider the latter in the context of *specific* protocols without being concerned about *how* these are represented – the protocol description does *not* form part of an instance of OUP$^{(\Delta)}$ (only the specific context Φ_k). In particular, should we wish to consider some 'sense of complexity' for a given schema, we could use the device of employing an 'oracle' Turing machine, M_Δ, to report (at unit-cost) whether properties (1–2) hold of any given η. With such an approach, should Δ be such that the set of legal dialogues for a specific context is *finite*, then the decision problem OUP$^{(\Delta)}$ is *decidable* (relative to the oracle machine M_Δ). A further advantage is that any *lower* bound that can be demonstrated for a specific incarnation of OUP$^{(\Delta)}$ gives a lower bound on the "computable fragment" of GOUP. In the next section, we describe a (sequence of) dialogue schemata, $\{\Delta_k^{DPLL}\}$ for which the following computational properties are provable.

1. The set of legal dialogues for Δ_k^{DPLL} is finite: thus every continuation of any legal partial dialogue will result in a legal terminated dialogue.
2. Given $\langle \delta, \mu, \Phi_k \rangle$ with δ a dialogue fragment, μ an utterance, and Φ_k the dialogue context for Δ_k^{DPLL}, there is a deterministic algorithm that decides if $\delta \cdot \mu$ is a legal dialogue using time linear in the number of bits needed to encode the instance.
3. Given $\langle \delta, \Psi, \Phi_k \rangle$ with δ a legal dialogue and Ψ an element of the context Φ_k, there is a deterministic algorithm deciding if $\Psi \in \Sigma(\delta)$ using time linear in the number of bits needed to encode the instance.

We will show that the Optimal Utterance Problem for Δ_k^{DPLL} is both NP–hard and CO–NP–hard.

3   The Optimal Utterance Problem

Prior to defining the schema used as the basis of our results, we introduce the dialogue arena, $\mathcal{A}_{CNF}$ upon which it operates.

Let $\Theta(n)$ $(n \geq 1)$ denote the set of all CNF formulae formed from propositional variables $\{x_1, \ldots, x_n\}$ (so that $|\Theta(n)| = 2^{3^n}$). For $\Psi \in \Theta(n)$ with

$$\Psi = \bigwedge_{i=1}^{m} \bigvee_{j=1}^{i_r} y_{i,j} \quad y_{i,j} \in \{x_k, \neg x_k \ : \ 1 \leq k \leq n\}$$

we use C_i to denote the clause $\vee_{j=1}^{i_r} y_{i,j}$. Let Ψ_{rep} be the set of wff given by,

$$\Psi_{rep} = \{\Psi, C_1, \ldots, C_m, x_1, \ldots, x_n, \neg x_1, \ldots, \neg x_n\}$$

The *dialogue arena of formulae in* CNF is

$$\mathcal{A}_{CNF} = \bigcup_{n=1}^{\infty} \bigcup_{\Psi \in \Theta(n)} \{\{\Psi_{rep}\}\}$$

Thus, each different CNF, Ψ gives rise to the dialogue context whose elements are defined by Ψ_{rep}.

We note that $\Phi \in \mathcal{A}_{CNF}$ may be encoded as a word, $\beta(\Phi)$, over alphabet $\{-1,0,1\}$

$$\beta(\Phi) = 1^n 0\alpha \quad \text{with } \alpha \in \{-1,0,1\}^{nm}$$

where the i'th clause is described by the sub-word

$$\alpha_{(i-1)*n+1} \cdots \alpha_{i*n}$$

so that

$$\alpha_{(i-1)n+k} = -1 \text{ if } \neg x_k \in C_i$$
$$\alpha_{(i-1)n+k} = 1 \quad \text{if } x_k \in C_i$$
$$\alpha_{(i-1)n+k} = 0 \quad \text{if } \neg x_k \notin C_i \text{ and } x_k \notin C_i$$

It is thus immediate that given any word $w \in \{-1,0,1\}^*$ there is an algorithm that accepts w if and only if $w = \beta(\Phi)$ for some CNF Φ and this algorithm runs in $O(|w|)$ steps.

The basis for the dialogue schema we now define is found in the classic DPLL procedure for determining whether a well-formed propositional formula is satisfiable or not [6, 7]. Our protocol – the DPLL-dialogue protocol – is derived from the realisation of the DPLL-procedure on CNF formulae.

In describing this we assume some ordering

$$\langle \Phi_1, \Phi_2, \ldots, \Phi_k, \ldots \rangle$$

of the contexts in the arena $\mathcal{A}_{CNF}$.

DPLL-**Dialogue Schema.** The sequence of DPLL-*Dialogue Schema* – $\Delta_{DPLL} = \{\Delta_k^{DPLL}\}$ – is defined with contexts from the arena $\mathcal{A}_{CNF}$ as

$$\Delta_k^{DPLL} = \langle \mathcal{L}_{DPLL}, \mathcal{D}_{DPLL} = \langle \Pi_{DPLL}, \Sigma_{DPLL} \rangle, \Phi_k \rangle$$

where

$$\mathcal{L}_{DPLL} = \{\text{ASSERT,REBUT,PROPOSE,DENY,MONO,UNIT}\}$$

and the set Φ_k from $\mathcal{A}_{CNF}$ is,

$$\{\bigwedge_{i=1}^{m} C_i, C_1, \ldots, C_m, x_1, \ldots, x_n, \neg x_1, \ldots, \neg x_n\}$$

Recall that Ψ_k denotes the formula $\bigwedge_{i=1}^{m} C_i$, and C_i is the clause $\bigvee_{j=1}^{i_r} y_{i,j}$ from the context Φ_k. It will be convenient to regard a clause C both as a disjunction of literals and as a *set* of literals, so that we write $y \in C$ when C has the form $y \vee B$.

The protocol $\langle \Pi_{DPLL}, \Sigma_{DPLL} \rangle$ is defined through the following cases.

At any stage the commitment state – $\Sigma_{DPLL}(\delta)$ consists of a (possibly empty) subset of the clauses of Ψ_k and a (possibly empty) subset of the literals, subject to the condition that y and $\neg y$ are never simultaneously members of $\Sigma_{DPLL}(\delta)$. With the exception of $\{\text{ASSERT,REBUT}\}$ the instantiated form of any locution involves a literal y.

Case 1: $\delta = \epsilon$ the empty dialogue fragment.

$$
\begin{aligned}
\Pi_{DPLL}(\epsilon) &= \{\text{ASSERT}(\Psi_k)\} \\
\Sigma_{DPLL}(\epsilon) &= \emptyset \\
\Sigma_{DPLL}(\text{ASSERT}(\Psi_k)) &= \{C_i : 1 \le i \le m\}
\end{aligned}
$$

In the subsequent development, y is a literal and

$$
\begin{aligned}
Open(\delta) &= \{C_i : C_i \in \Sigma_{DPLL}(\delta)\} \\
Lits(\delta) &= \{y : y \in \Sigma_{DPLL}(\delta)\} \\
Single(\delta) &= \{y : \neg y \notin Lits(\delta) \text{ and } \exists C \in Open(\delta) \text{ s.t.} \\
&\quad y \in C \text{ and } \forall z \in C/\{y\} \; \neg z \in Lits(\delta)\} \\
Unary(\delta) &= \{y : \neg y \notin Lits(\delta) \text{ and} \\
&\quad \forall C \in Open(\delta) \; \neg y \notin C \text{ and} \\
&\quad \exists C \in Open(\delta) \text{ with } y \in C\} \\
Bad(\delta) &= \{C_i : C_i \in Open(\delta) \text{ and} \\
&\quad \forall y \in C \; \neg y \in Lits(\delta)\}
\end{aligned}
$$

Informally, $Open(\delta)$ indicates clauses of Ψ_k that have yet to be satisfied and $Lits(\delta)$ the set of literals that have been committed to in trying to construct a satisfying assignment to Ψ_k. Over the progress of a dialogue the literals in $Lits(\delta)$ may, if instantiated to **true**, result in some clauses being reduced to a *single* literal – $Single(\delta)$ is the set of such literals. Similarly, either initially or following an instantiation of the literals in $Lits(\delta)$ to **true**, the set of clauses in $Open(\delta)$ may be such that some variables occurs only positively among these clauses or only negated. The corresponding literals form the set $Unary(\delta)$. Finally, the course of committing to various literals may result in a set that contradicts all of the literals in some clause: thus this set cannot constitute a satisfying instantiation: the set of clauses in $Bad(\delta)$ if non-empty indicate that this has occurred. Notice that the definition of $Single(\delta)$ admits the possibility of a literal y and its negation being in this set: a case which cannot lead to the set of literals in $Lits(\delta)$ being extended to a satisfying set. Thus we say that the literal set $Lits(\delta)$ is a *failing set* if either $Bad(\delta) \ne \emptyset$ or for some y, $\{y, \neg y\} \subseteq Single(\delta)$.

Recognising that $\Sigma_{DPLL}(\delta) = Open(\delta) \cup Lits(\delta)$ it suffices to describe changes to $\Sigma_{DPLL}(\delta)$ in terms of changes to $Open(\delta)$ and $Lits(\delta)$.

Case 2: $\delta \ne \epsilon$, $Open(\delta) = \emptyset$

$$\Pi(\delta) = \emptyset$$

Case 3: $\delta \ne \epsilon$, $Open(\delta) \ne \emptyset$, $Lits(\delta)$ is *not a failing set*.
There are a number of sub-cases depending on $\Sigma_{DPLL}(\delta)$

Case 3.1: $Single(\delta) \ne \emptyset$.

$$
\begin{aligned}
\Pi_{DPLL}(\delta) &= \{\text{UNIT}(y) : y \in Single(\delta)\} \\
Open(\delta \cdot \text{UNIT}(y)) &= Open(\delta)/\{C : y \in C\} \\
Lits(\delta \cdot \text{UNIT}(y)) &= Lits(\delta) \cup \{y\}
\end{aligned}
$$

Case 3.2: $Single(\delta) = \emptyset$, $Unary(\delta) \ne \emptyset$

$$
\begin{aligned}
\Pi_{DPLL}(\delta) &= \{\text{MONO}(y) : y \in Unary(\delta)\} \\
Open(\delta \cdot \text{MONO}(y)) &= Open(\delta)/\{C : y \in C\} \\
Lits(\delta \cdot \text{MONO}(y)) &= Lits(\delta) \cup \{y\}
\end{aligned}
$$

Case 3.3: $Single(\delta) = Unary(\delta) = \emptyset$
Since $Bad(\delta) = \emptyset$ and $Open(\delta) \neq \emptyset$, instantiating the literals in $Lits(\delta)$ will neither falsify nor satisfy Ψ_k. It follows that the set

$$Poss(\delta) = \{y : y \notin Lits(\delta), \neg y \notin Lits(\delta) \text{ and}$$
$$\exists C \in Open(\delta) \text{ with } y \in C\}$$

is non-empty. We note that since $Unary(\delta) = \emptyset$, $y \in Poss(\delta)$ if and only if $\neg y \in Poss(\delta)$. This gives,

$$\begin{aligned}
\Pi_{DPLL}(\delta) &= \{\text{PROPOSE}(y) : y \in Poss(\delta)\} \\
Open(\delta \cdot \text{PROPOSE}(y)) &= Open(\delta)/\{C : y \in C\} \\
Lits(\delta \cdot \text{PROPOSE}(y)) &= Lits(\delta) \cup \{y\}
\end{aligned}$$

This completes the possibilities for Case 3. We are left with,
Case 4: $\delta \neq \epsilon$, $Lits(\delta)$ is *a failing set*.
Let $\delta = \text{ASSERT}(\Psi_k) \cdots \mu_t$
    Given the cases above, there are only three utterances that μ_t could be:

$$\mu_t \in \{\text{ASSERT}(\Psi_k), \text{PROPOSE}(y), \text{DENY}(y)\}$$

Case 4.1: $\mu_t = \mu_1 = \text{ASSERT}(\Psi_k)$
Sinces $Lits(\text{ASSERT}(\Psi_k)) = \emptyset$, Ψ_k either contains an *empty clause* (one containing no literals), or for some x both (x) and $(\neg x)$ are clauses in Ψ_k[4]. In either case Ψ_k is "trivially" unsatisfiable, giving

$$\begin{aligned}
\Pi_{DPLL}(\text{ASSERT}(\Psi_k)) &= \{\text{REBUT}(\Psi_k)\} \\
\Sigma_{DPLL}(\text{ASSERT}(\Psi_k) \cdot \text{REBUT}(\Psi_k)) &= \emptyset \\
\Pi_{DPLL}(\text{ASSERT}(\Psi_k) \cdot \text{REBUT}(\Psi_k)) &= \emptyset
\end{aligned}$$

Case 4.2: $\mu_t = \text{PROPOSE}(y)$

$$\begin{aligned}
\Pi_{DPLL}(\delta) &= \{\text{DENY}(y)\} \\
Open(\delta \cdot \text{DENY}(y)) &= Open(\mu_1 \cdots \mu_{t-1})/\{C : \neg y \in C\} \\
Lits(\delta \cdot \text{DENY}(y)) &= Lits(\mu_1 \cdots \mu_{t-1}) \cup \{\neg y\}
\end{aligned}$$

Notice this corresponds to a 'back-tracking' move under which having failed to complete a satisfying set by employing the literal y, its negation $\neg y$ is tried instead.
Case 4.3: $\mu_t = \text{DENY}(y)$
Consider the sequence of utterances given by

$$\eta = \mu_2 \cdot \mu_3 \cdots \mu_{t-1} \cdot \mu_t = \text{DENY}(y)$$

We say that η is *unbalanced* if there is a position p such that $\mu_p = \text{PROPOSE}(z)$ with $\text{DENY}(z) \notin \mu_{p+1} \cdots \mu_t$ and *balanced* otherwise. If η is unbalanced let $index(\eta)$ be the *highest* such position for which this holds (so that $p < t$).
    We now obtain the final cases in our description.

---

[4] Note that we distinguish the wff y (a *literal* used in Ψ_k) and (y) (a *clause* containing the *single* literal y) within the context Φ_k.

Case 4.3(a): η is unbalanced with $index(\eta)$ equal to p.

$$
\begin{aligned}
\Pi_{DPLL}(\delta) &= \{\text{DENY}(y) : \mu_p = \text{PROPOSE}(y)\} \\
Open(\delta \cdot \text{DENY}(y)) &= Open(\mu_1 \cdots \mu_{p-1})/\{C : \neg y \in C\} \\
Lits(\delta \cdot \text{DENY}(y)) &= Lits(\mu_1 \cdots \mu_{p-1}) \cup \{\neg y\}
\end{aligned}
$$

Thus this case corresponds to a 'back-tracking' move continuing from the "most recent" position at which a literal $\neg y$ instead of y can be tested.

Finally,

Case 4.3(b): η is balanced.

$$
\begin{aligned}
\Pi_{DPLL}(\delta) &= \{\text{REBUT}(\Psi_k)\} \\
\Sigma_{DPLL}(\delta \cdot \text{REBUT}(\Psi_k)) &= \emptyset \\
\Pi_{DPLL}(\delta \cdot \text{REBUT}(\Psi_k)) &= \emptyset
\end{aligned}
$$

We state the following without proof.

Theorem 1 *In the following, δ is a dialogue fragment from $M^*_{\langle \mathcal{L}_{DPLL}, \Phi_k \rangle}$; Φ_k is a context from $\mathcal{A}_{CNF}$, and $N(\delta, \Phi_k)$ is the number of bits used to encode δ and Φ_k under some reasonable encoding scheme.*

1. *The problem of determining whether δ is a legal dialogue for the protocol $\mathcal{D}_{DPLL}$ in context Φ_k can be decided in $O(N(\delta, \Phi_k))$ steps.*
2. *The problem of determining whether δ is a terminated legal dialogue for the protocol $\mathcal{D}_{DPLL}$ in context Φ_k is decidable in $O(N(\delta, \Phi_k))$ steps.*
3. *For any $\psi \in \Phi_k$, the problem of determining whether $\psi \in \Sigma_{DPLL}(\delta)$ is decidable in $O(N(\delta, \Phi_k))$ steps.*
4. *For all contexts $\Phi_k \in \mathcal{A}_{CNF}$, the set of legal dialogues over Φ_k in the protocol $\mathcal{D}_{DPLL}$ is finite.*
5. *If δ is a terminated dialogue of $\mathcal{D}_{DPLL}$ in context Φ_k then $\Sigma_{DPLL}(\delta) \neq \emptyset$ if and only if Ψ_k is satisfiable. Furthermore, instantiating the set of literals in $Lits(\delta)$ to **true**, yields a satisfying assignment for Ψ_k.*

Before analysing this protocol we review how it derives from the basic DPLL-procedure. Consider the description of this below.

DPLL-**Procedure.**

Input: Set of clauses C
        Set of Literals L

if $C = \emptyset$ **return true.** (SAT)
if any clause of C is empty
    or C contains clauses (y) and $(\neg y)$ (for some literal y)
            return false. (UNSAT)
if C contains a clause containing a single literal y
            return DPLL($C^{|y}, L \cup \{y\}$)   (U)
if there is a literal y such that $\neg y$ does not occur in any

clause (and y occurs in some clause)

$\qquad$**return** DPLL$(C^{|y}, L \cup \{y\})$ $\qquad$ (M)

choose a literal y. $\qquad\qquad\qquad\qquad\qquad\qquad$ (B)

if DPLL$(C^{|y}, L \cup \{y\})$

then $\quad$ **return true**

else $\quad$ **return** DPLL$(C^{|\neg y}, L \cup \{\neg y\})$ $\qquad$ (FAIL).

For a set of clauses and literal, y, the set of clauses $C^{|y}$ is formed by removing all clauses, C_i for which $y \in C_i$ and deleting the literal $\neg y$ from all clauses C_j having $\neg y \in C_j$.

To test if $\Psi = \wedge_{i=1}^{m} C_i$ is satisfiable, the procedure is called with input $C = \{C_1, \ldots, C_m\}$ and $L = \emptyset$.

Lines (U) and (M) are the "unit-clause" and "monotone literal" rules which improve the run-time of the procedure: these are simulated by the UNIT and MONO locutions. Otherwise a literal is selected – at line (B) – to "branch" on: the PROPOSE locution; should the choice of branching literal FAIL to lead to a satisfying assignment, its negation is tested – the DENY locution. Each time a literal is set to **true**, clauses containing it can be deleted from the current set – the $Open(\delta)$ of the protocol; clauses containing its negation contain one fewer literal. Either all clauses will be eliminated (C is satisfiable) or an empty clause will result (the current set of literals chosen is not a satisfying assignment). When all choices have been exhausted the method will conclude that C is unsatisfiable.

The motivation for the form of the dialogue protocol Δ_k^{DPLL} is the connection between terminated dialogues in T_{DPLL} and *search trees* in the DPLL-procedure above.

Definition 8 *Given a set of clauses C, a* DPLL*–search tree for C is a binary tree, S, recursively defined as follows: if $C = \emptyset$ or C conforms to the condition specified by* UNSAT *in the* DPLL*-procedure, then S is the empty tree, i.e. S contains no nodes. If y is a monotone literal or defines a unit-clause in C, then S comprises a root labelled y whose sole child is a* DPLL*-search tree for the set $C^{|y}$. If none of these four cases apply, S consists of a root labelled with the branching literal y chosen in line (B) with at most two children – one comprising a* DPLL*-search tree for the set $C^{|y}$, the other child – if the case (FAIL) arises – a* DPLL*-search tree for the set $C^{|\neg y}$.*

A DPLL*-search tree is* full *if no further expansion of it can take place (under the procedure above).*

The size *of a* DPLL*-search tree, $S - \nu(S)$ – is the total number of edges[5] in S. A full* DPLL*-search tree, S, is* minimum *for the set of clauses C, if given any full* DPLL*-search tree, R for C, $\nu(S) \leq \nu(R)$. Finally, a literal y is an* optimal branching literal *for a clause set C, if there is a minimum* DPLL*-search tree for C whose root is labelled y.*

We say a set of clauses, C, is *non-trivial* if $C \neq \emptyset$. Without loss of generality we consider only CNF-formulae, Ψ, whose clause set is non-trivial. Of course, during the evolution of the DPLL-procedure and the dialogue protocol $\mathcal{D}_{DPLL}$ sets of clauses which are trivial may result (this will certainly be the case is Ψ is satisfiable): our assumption refers *only* to the initial instance set.

---

[5] The usual definition of *size* is as the number of *nodes* in S, however, since S is a tree this value is exactly $\nu(S) + 1$.

Theorem 2 *Let* $\Psi = \bigwedge_{i=1}^{m} C_i$ *be a* CNF-*formula over propositional variables* $\langle x_1, ..., x_n \rangle$. *Let* $C(\Psi)$ *and* Φ_k *be respectively the set of clauses in* Ψ *and the dialogue context from the arena* $\mathcal{A}_{CNF}$ *corresponding to* Ψ, *i.e. the set* Ψ_{rep} *above.*

1. *Given any full* DPLL-*search tree*, S, *for* $C(\Psi)$ *there is a legal terminated dialogue*, $\delta_S \in T_{DPLL}$ *for which,*

$$\delta_S = \text{ASSERT}(\Psi_k) \cdot \eta_S \cdot \mu$$

   and $|\eta_S| = \nu(S)$, *with* μ *being one of the locution types in*

$$\{\text{PROPOSE}, \text{UNIT}, \text{MONO}, \text{REBUT}\}.$$

2. *Given any legal terminated dialogue* $\delta = \text{ASSERT}(\Psi_k) \cdot \eta \cdot \mu$, *with*

$$\mu \in \{\text{REBUT}(\Psi_k), \text{PROPOSE}(y), \text{MONO}(y), \text{UNIT}(y)\}$$

   there is a full DPLL-*search tree*, S_δ *having* $\nu(S_\delta) = |\eta|$.

Proof. Let Ψ, $C(\Psi)$, and Φ_k be as in the Theorem statement. For Part 1, let S be any full DPLL-search tree for the clause set $C(\Psi)$. We obtain the result by induction on $\nu(S) \geq 0$.

For the inductive base, $\nu(S) = 0$, either S is the empty tree or S contains a single node labelled y. In the former instance, since Ψ is non-trivial it must be the case that Ψ is unsatisfiable (by reason of containing an empty clause or opposite polarity unit clauses). Choosing

$$\delta_S = \text{ASSERT}(\Psi_k) \cdot \eta_S \cdot \text{REBUT}(\Psi_k)$$

with $\eta_S = \epsilon$ is a legal terminated dialogue (Case 4.1) and $|\eta_S| = 0 = \nu(S)$.

When S contains a single node, so that $\nu(S) = 0$, let y be the literal labelling this. It must be the case that $C(\Psi)$ is *satisfiable* – it cannot hold that $C(\Psi)^{|y}$ and $C(\Psi)^{|\neg y}$ *both* yield empty search trees, since this would imply the presence of unit-clauses (y) and $(\neg y)$ in $C(\Psi)$[6]. Thus the literal y occurs in every clause of $C(\Psi)$. If y is a unit-clause, the dialogue fragment,

$$\delta_S = \text{ASSERT}(\Psi_k) \cdot \text{UNIT}(y)$$

is legal (Case 3.1) and terminated (Case 2). Fixing $\eta_S = \epsilon$ and $\mu = \text{UNIT}(y)$ gives $|\eta_S| = 0 = \nu(S)$ and $\delta = \text{ASSERT}(\Psi_k) \cdot \eta_S \cdot \mu$ a legal terminated dialogue. If y is not a unit clause, we obtain an identical conclusion using $\eta_S = \epsilon$ and $\mu = \text{MONO}(y)$ via Case 3.2 and Case 2.

Now, inductively assume, for some M, that if S_M is a DPLL-search tree for a set of clauses $C(\Psi)$, with $\nu(S_M) < M$ then there is a legal terminated dialogue, δ_{S_M}, over the corresponding context, Φ, with $\delta_{S_M} = \text{ASSERT}(\Psi) \cdot \eta_{S_M} \cdot \mu$ and $|\eta_{S_M}| = \nu(S_M)$.

Let S be a DPLL-search tree for $C(\Psi)$ with $\nu(S) = M \geq 1$. Consider the literal, y, labelling the root of S. Since $\nu(S) \geq 1$, the set $C(\Psi)^{|y}$ is non-empty. If $C(\Psi_k)$ contains a unit-clause, then (y) must be one such, thus S comprises the root labelled y and a single child, $S^{|y}$ forming a full DPLL-search tree for the (non-empty) clause

---

[6] It should be remembered that *at most one* of $\{y, \neg y\}$ occurs in any clause.

set $C(\Psi)^{|y}$. It is obvious that $\nu(S^{|y}) < \nu(S) \leq M$, so from the Inductive Hypothesis, there is a legal terminated dialogue, $\delta^{|y}$ in the context formed by the CNF $\Psi_k^{|y}$. Hence,

$$\delta^{|y} = \text{ASSERT}(\Psi_k^{|y}) \cdot \eta^{|y} \cdot \mu$$

and $|\eta^{|y}| = \nu(S^{|y})$. From Case(3.1), the dialogue fragment

$$\delta_S = \text{ASSERT}(\Psi_k) \cdot \text{UNIT}(y) \cdot \eta^{|y} \cdot \mu$$

is legal and is terminated. Setting $\eta_S = \text{UNIT}(y) \cdot \eta^{|y}$, we obtain

$$|\eta_S| = 1 + |\eta^{|y}| = 1 + \nu(S^{|y}) = \nu(S)$$

A similar construction applies in those cases where y is a monotone literal – substituting the utterance $\text{MONO}(y)$ for $\text{UNIT}(y)$ – and when y is a branching literal with exactly one child $S^{|y}$ – in this case, substituting the utterance $\text{PROPOSE}(y)$ for $\text{UNIT}(y)$.

The remaining case is when S comprises a root node labelled y with *two* children – $S^{|y}$ and $S^{|\neg y}$ – the former a full DPLL-search tree for the clause set $C(\Psi)^{|y}$, the latter a full DPLL-search tree for the set $C(\Psi)^{|\neg y}$. We use $\Phi^{|y}$ and $\Phi^{|\neg y}$ to denote the contexts in $\mathcal{A}_{CNF}$ corresponding to these CNF-formulae. As in the previous case, $\nu(S^{|y}) < \nu(S) = M$ and $\nu(S^{|\neg y}) < \nu(S) = M$. Invoking the Inductive Hypothesis, we identify legal terminated dialogues, over the respective contexts $\Phi^{|y}$ and $\Phi^{|\neg y}$

$$\delta^{|y} = \text{ASSERT}(\Psi^{|y}) \cdot \eta^{|y} \cdot \mu^{|y}$$
$$\delta^{|\neg y} = \text{ASSERT}(\Psi^{|\neg y}) \cdot \eta^{|\neg y} \cdot \mu^{|\neg y}$$

with $|\eta^{|y}| = \nu(S^{|y})$ and $|\eta^{|\neg y}| = \nu(S^{|\neg y})$.

We first note that the set $C(\Psi)^{|y}$ cannot be satisfiable – if it were the search-tree $S^{|\neg y}$ would not occur. We can thus deduce that $\mu^{|y} = \text{REBUT}(\Psi^{|y})$. Now consider the dialogue fragment, δ_S, from the context Φ_k

$$\text{ASSERT}(\Psi_k) \cdot \text{PROPOSE}(y) \cdot \eta^{|y} \cdot \text{DENY}(y) \cdot \eta^{|\neg y} \cdot \mu^{|\neg y}$$

Certainly this is a legal terminated dialogue via the Inductive hypothesis and Cases 4.2, 4.3(a–b). In addition, with

$$\eta_S = \text{PROPOSE}(y) \cdot \eta^{|y} \cdot \text{DENY}(y) \cdot \eta^{|\neg y}$$

we have

$$|\eta_S| = 2 + |\eta^{|y}| + |\eta^{|\neg y}| = 2 + \nu(S^{|y}) + \nu(S^{|\neg y}) = \nu(S)$$

so completing the Inductive proof of Part 1.

For Part 2 we use an inductive argument on $|\eta| \geq 0$. Let $\delta = \text{ASSERT}(\Psi_k) \cdot \eta \cdot \mu$ be a legal terminated dialogue in T_{DPLL} as above, with

$$\mu \in \{\text{REBUT}(\Psi_k), \text{PROPOSE}(y), \text{MONO}(y), \text{UNIT}(y)\}$$

For the inductive base, we have $|\eta| = 0$, in which event it must hold that

$$\delta \in \{\text{ASSERT}(\Psi_k) \cdot \text{REBUT}(\Psi_k),\ \text{ASSERT}(\Psi_k) \cdot \text{MONO}(y),\ \text{ASSERT}(\Psi_k) \cdot \text{UNIT}(y)\}$$

In the first of these, via Case 4.1, Ψ_k is unsatisfiable by virtue of it containing an empty clause or having both (x) and $(\neg x)$ as clauses. Thus, choosing S as the *empty tree* gives $\nu(S) = |\eta| = 0$. In the remaining two possibilities, Ψ_k must be satisfied by the instantiation that sets the literal y to **true** and now choosing S as the tree consisting of a single node labelled y gives a full DPLL search tree for Ψ_k with $\nu(S) = |\eta| = 0$.

For the inductive step, assume that given any

$$\delta' = \text{ASSERT}(\Psi') \cdot \eta' \cdot \mu$$

a legal terminated dialogue in T_{DPLL} in which $|\eta'| < r + 1$ for some $r \geq 0$, there is a full DPLL search tree S' for Ψ' with $\nu(S') = |\eta'|$. We show that if

$$\delta = \text{ASSERT}(\Psi) \cdot \eta \cdot \mu$$

is a legal terminated dialogue in T_{DPLL} in which $|\eta| = r + 1$ then we can construct a full DPLL search tree, S for Ψ with $\nu(S) = r + 1$. Noting that $|\eta| \geq 1$, let μ_1 be the first locution occuring in η, so that

$$\delta = \text{ASSERT}(\Psi) \cdot \mu_1 \cdot \eta' \cdot \mu$$

It must be the case that

$$\mu_1 \in \{\text{MONO}(y),\ \text{UNIT}(y),\ \text{PROPOSE}(y)\}$$

For the first two,

$$\delta' = \text{ASSERT}(\Psi^{|y}) \cdot \eta' \cdot \mu$$

is a legal terminated dialogue for the set of clauses $C(\Psi)^{|y}$, thus by the inductive hypothesis there is a full DPLL search tree $S^{|y}$ for this set with $\nu(S^{|y}) = |\eta'| = r$. Defining the tree S by taking a single node labelled y whose only child is the root of $S^{|y}$ provides a full DPLL search tree for Ψ whose size is exactly $|\eta| = r + 1$.

The remaining possibility is $\mu_1 = \text{PROPOSE}(y)$. First suppose that the locution $\text{DENY}(y)$ does not occur in η': then, exactly as our previous two cases

$$\delta' = \text{ASSERT}(\Psi^{|y}) \cdot \eta' \cdot \mu$$

is a legal terminated dialogue for the set of clauses $C(\Psi)^{|y}$ and we form a full DPLL search tree S for Ψ from $S^{|y}$ – a full DPLL search tree for the set of clauses $C(\Psi)^{|y}$ which has size $|\eta'|$ via the inductive hypothesis – by adding a single node labelled y whose sole child is the root of $S^{|y}$. The resulting tree has size $|\eta|$ as required.

Finally, we have the case in which $\text{DENY}(y)$ does occur in η'. For such,

$$\delta = \text{ASSERT}(\Psi) \cdot \text{PROPOSE}(y) \cdot \eta_1 \cdot \text{DENY}(y) \cdot \eta_2 \cdot \mu$$

Consider the two dialogues

$$\begin{aligned}
\delta_y &= \text{ASSERT}(\Psi^{|y}) \cdot \eta_1 \text{REBUT}(\Psi^{|y}) \\
\delta_{\neg y} &= \text{ASSERT}(\Psi^{|\neg y}) \cdot \eta_2 \cdot \mu
\end{aligned}$$

Clearly δ_y is a legal terminated dialogue for the set of clauses $C(\Psi)^{|y}$ and, similarly, $\delta_{\neg y}$ one for the set of clauses $C(\Psi)^{|\neg y}$. Hence, by the inductive hypothesis we find full DPLL search trees – $S^{|y}$ and $S^{|\neg y}$ – of sizes $|\eta_1|$ and $|\eta_2|$ respectively for these clause sets. Consider the DPLL search tree, S, formed by adding a single node labelled y whose left child is the root of $S^{|y}$ and whose right child that of $S^{|\neg y}$. Then

$$\nu(S) = \nu(S^{|y}) + \nu(S^{|\neg y}) + 2 \;=\; |\eta_1| + |\eta_2| + 2 = |\eta|$$

Thus completing the inductive argument.

Corollary 1. *An instance,*

$$U = \langle \Phi_k, \text{ASSERT}(\Psi_k), \text{PROPOSE}(y) \rangle$$

of the Optimal Utterance Problem for Δ_{DPLL} is accepted if and only if y is neither a unit-clause nor a monotone literal and y is an optimal branching literal for the clause set $C(\Psi_k)$.

Proof. If y defines a unit-clause or monotone literal in Ψ_k then PROPOSE(y) is not a legal continuation of ASSERT(Ψ_k). The corollary is now an easy consequence of Theorem 2: suppose that

$$\delta \;=\; \text{ASSERT}(\Psi_k) \cdot \text{PROPOSE}(y) \cdot \eta \cdot \mu_y$$

is a minimum length completion of ASSERT(Ψ_k), then Part 2 of Theorem 2 yields a full DPLL-search tree, R, for $C(\Psi_k)$ of size $1 + |\eta|$ whose root is labelled y. If R is not minimum then there is smaller full DPLL-search tree, S. From Part 1 of Theorem 2 this yields a legal terminated dialogue

$$\text{ASSERT}(\Psi_k) \cdot \mu_S \cdot \eta_S \cdot \mu$$

with

$$\nu(S) \;=\; |\mu_S \cdot \eta_S \cdot \mu| - 1 \;<\; |\text{PROPOSE}(y) \cdot \eta \cdot \mu_y| - 1 \;=\; \nu(R)$$

which contradicts the assumption that δ is a minimum length completion.

We now obtain a lower bound on the complexity of OUP$^{(\Delta)}$ via the following result of Liberatore [19].

Fact 1 Liberatore ([19]) *Given an instance $\langle C, y \rangle$ where C is a set of clauses and y a literal in these, the problem of deciding whether y is an optimal branching literal for the set C is NP–hard and CO-NP–hard.*

Theorem 3 *The Optimal Utterance in Δ Problem is NP–hard and CO-NP–hard.*

Proof. Choose Δ as the sequence of schema $\{\Delta_k^{DPLL}\}$. From Corollary 1 an instance $\langle \Phi_k, \text{ASSERT}(\Psi_k), \text{PROPOSE}(y) \rangle$ is accepted in OUP$^{(\Delta)}$ if and only if y does not form a unit-clause of Ψ_k, is not a monotone literal, and is an optimal branching literal for the clause set $C(\Psi_k)$. We may assume, (since these are easily tested) that the first two conditions do not hold, whence it follows that decision methods for such instances of OUP$^{(\Delta)}$ yield decision methods for determining if y is an optimal branching literal for $C(\Psi_k)$. The complexity lower bounds now follow directly from Liberatore's results stated in Fact 1.

4 Conclusion

The principal contentions of this paper are three-fold: firstly, in order for a dialogue protocol to be realised effectively in a multiagent setting, each agent must have the capability to determine what contribution(s) it must or should or can make to the discussion as it develops; secondly, in deciding which (if any) utterance to make, an agent should (ideally) take cognisance of the extent to which its utterance is 'optimal'; and, finally, the criteria by which an utterance is judged to be 'optimal' are *application dependent*. In effect, the factors that contributors take into consideration when participating in one style of dialogue, e.g. bargaining protocols, are *not* necessarily those that would be relevant in another style, e.g. persuasion protocols.

We have proposed one possible interpretation of "optimal utterance in persuasion protocols": that which leads to the debate terminating 'as quickly as possible'. There are, however, a number of "length-related" alternatives that may merit further study. We have already mentioned in passing the view explored in [11]. One drawback to the concept of "optimal utterance" as we have considered it, is that it presumes the protocol is "well-behaved" in a rather special sense: taking the aim of an agent in a persuasion process as "to convince others that a particular proposition is valid", the extent to which an agent is successful may depend on the 'final' commitment state attained. In the DPLL-protocol this final state is either *always* empty (if Ψ_k is not satisfiable) or *always* non-empty: the protocol is "sound" in the sense that conflicting interpretations of the final state are not possible. Suppose we consider persuasion protocols where there is an 'external' interpretation of final state, e.g. using a method of defining some (sequence) of mappings $\tau : \wp(\Phi_k) \rightarrow \{\mathbf{true}, \mathbf{false}, \bot\}$, so that a terminated dialogue, δ, with $\tau(\Sigma(\delta)) = \mathbf{true}$ indicates that the persuading agent has successful demonstrated its desired hypothesis; $\tau(\Sigma(\delta)) = \mathbf{false}$ indicates that its hypothesis is *not* valid; $\tau(\Sigma(\delta)) = \bot$ indicates that no conclusion can be drawn[7]. There are good reasons why we may wish to implement 'seemingly contradictory' protocols, i.e. in which the persuasion process for a given context Φ can terminate in any (or all) of **true**, **false** or $\bot$ states, e.g. to model concepts of cautious, credulous, and sceptical agent belief, cf. [27]. In such cases defining "optimal utterance" as that which can lead to a shortest terminated dialogue may not be ideal: the persuading agent's view of "optimal" is not simply to terminate discussion but to terminate in a **true** state; in contrast, "sceptical" agents may seek utterances that (at worst) terminate in the inconclusive $\bot$ state. We note that, in such settings, there is potentially an "asymmetry" in the objectives of individual agents – we conjecture that in suitably defined protocols and contexts with appropriately defined concepts of "optimal utterance" the decision problems arising are likely to prove at least as intractable as those for the basic variant we consider in Theorem 3.

A natural objection to the use of length-related measures to assess persuasion processes is that these do not provide any sense of how convincing a given discourse might be, i.e. that an argument can be presented concisely does not necessarily render it effective in persuading those to whom it is addressed. One problem with trying formally to capture concepts of persuasiveness is that, unlike measures based on length, this is

---

[7] For example, game theorists in economics have considered the situation where two advocates try to convince an impartial judge of the truth or otherwise of some claim, e.g. [14, 31].

a subjective measure: a reasoning process felt to be extremely convincing by one party may fail to move another. One interesting problem in this respect concerns modeling the following scenario. Suppose we have a collection of agents with differing knowledge and 'prejudices' each of whom an external agent wishes to persuade to accept some proposition, e.g. election candidates seeking to persuade a cross-section of voters to vote in their favour. In such settings one might typically expect contributions by the persuading party to affect the degree of conviction felt by members of the audience in different ways. As such the concept of an 'optimal' utterance might be better assessed in terms of proportionate increase in acceptance that the individual audience members hold after the utterance is made. Recent work in multi-agent argumentation has considered dialogues between agents having different knowledge, different prejudices or different attitudes to the utterance and acceptance of uncertain claims, e.g. [1, 28].

We conclude by mentioning two open questions of interest within the context of persuasion protocols and the optimal utterance problem in these. In practical terms, one problem of interest is, informally, phrased as follows: can one define "non-trivial" persuasion protocols for a "broad" collection of dialogue contexts within which the optimal utterance problem is tractable? We note that, it is unlikely that dialogue arenas encompassing the totality of all propositional formulae will admit such protocols, however, for those subsets which have efficient decision procedures e.g. Horn clauses, 2-CNF formulae, appropriate methods may be available. A second issue is to consider complexity-bounds for other persuasion protocols: e.g. one may develop schema for the arena $\mathcal{A}_{CNF}$ defined via the TPI–dispute mechanism of [32], the complexity (lower and upper bounds) of the optimal utterance problem in this setting is open, although in view of our results concerning $\mathcal{D}_{DPLL}$ it is plausible to conjecture that the optimal utterance problem for $\mathcal{D}_{TPI}$ will also prove intractable.

Acknowledgement

A preliminary version of this article appeared in [13]. We thank the anonymous referees and the AAMAS 2003 audience for their comments.

References

1. L. Amgoud and S. Parsons. Agent dialogues with conflicting preferences. In J. J. Meyer and M. Tambe, editors, *Pre-Proc. Eighth Intern. Workshop on Agent Theories, Architectures, and Languages (ATAL 2001)*, pages 1–14, 2001.
2. T. J. M. Bench-Capon. Specification and implementation of Toulmin dialogue game. In J. C. Hage *et al.*, editor, *Legal Knowledge Based Systems*, pages 5–20. GNI, 1998.
3. T. J. M. Bench-Capon, P. E. Dunne, and P. H. Leng. A dialogue game for dialectical interaction with expert systems. In *Proc. 12th Annual Conf. Expert Systems and their Applications*, pages 105–113, 1992.
4. C. Cayrol, S. Doutre, and J. Mengin. Dialectical proof theories for the credulous preferred semantics of argumentation frameworks. In *Sixth European Conference on Symbolic and Quantitative Approaches to Reasoning with Uncertainty (ECSQARU-2001)*, pages 668–679. Lecture Notes in A.I., 2143, Springer, 2001.

5. V. Conitzer and T. Sandholm. Complexity results about Nash equilibria. Technical Report CMU-CS-02-135, School of Computer Science, Carnegie-Mellon University, May 2002.

6. M. Davis, G. Logemann, and D. Loveland. A machine program for theorem proving. *Communications of the ACM*, 5:394–397, 1962.

7. M. Davis and H. Putnam. A computing procedure for quantification theory. *Journal of the ACM*, 7:201–215, 1960.

8. F Dignum and M. Greaves (editors). *Issues in Agent Communication*. Springer-Verlag, 2000.

9. S. Doutre and J. Mengin. Preferred extensions of argumentation frameworks: Query answering and computation. In *First Intern. Joint Conf. Automated Reasoning (IJCAR 2001)*, pages 272–288. Lecture Notes in A.I., 2083, Springer, June 2001.

10. P.E. Dunne. *Computability Theory - Concepts and Applications*. Ellis-Horwood, 1991.

11. P.E. Dunne. Prevarication in dispute protocols. *Proc. Ninth International Conference on A.I. and Law*, (ICAIL' 03), Edinburgh, June 2003, ACM Press, pages 12–21

12. P.E. Dunne and T.J.M. Bench-Capon. Two party immediate response disputes: Properties and efficiency. *Artificial Intelligence*, 149(2):221–250, 2003.

13. P.E. Dunne and P.J. McBurney Optimal Utterances in Dialogue Protocols *Proc. Second International joint Conference on Autonomous Agents and Multiagent Systems* (AAMAS'03), July 2003, ACM Press, pages 608-615

14. J. Glazer and A. Rubinstein. Debates and decisions: on a rationale of argumentation rules. *Games and Economic Behavior*, 36(2):158–173, 2001.

15. T. F. Gordon. *The Pleadings Game: An Artificial Intelligence Model of Procedural Justice*. Kluwer Academic, Dordrecht, 1995.

16. M. P. Huget, editor, *Communication in Multiagent Systems: Agent Communication Languages and Conversation Policies*. Lecture Notes in A.I., 2650, Springer, 2003.

17. M. W. Johnson, P. McBurney, and S. Parsons. When are two protocols the same? In M. P. Huget, editor, *Communication in Multiagent Systems: Agent Communication Languages and Conversation Policies*, pages 253–268. Lecture Notes in A.I., 2650, Springer, 2003.

18. S. Kraus. *Strategic negotiation in multiagent environments*. MIT Press, 2001.

19. P. Liberatore. On the complexity of choosing the branching literal in DPLL. *Artificial Intelligence*, 116:315–326, 2000.

20. A. R. Lodder. *Dialaw: On legal justification and Dialogue Games*. PhD thesis, Univ.of Maastricht, 1998.

21. P. McBurney, R. van Eijk, S. Parsons, and L. Amgoud. A dialogue-game protocol for agent purchase negotiations. *J. Autonomous Agents and Multiagent Systems*, 7(3): 235–273, 2003.

22. P. McBurney and S. Parsons. Representing epistemic uncertainty by means of dialectical argumentation. *Annals of Mathematics and AI*, 32(1–4):125–169, 2001.

23. P. McBurney and S. Parsons. Games that agents play: A formal framework for dialogues between autonomous agents. *J. Logic, Language and Information*, 11:315–334, 2002.

24. P. McBurney and S. Parsons. Chance Discovery using dialectical argumentation. In T. Terano *et al.*, editors, *New Frontiers in Artificial Intelligence*, pages 414–424. Lecture Notes in A.I., 2253, Springer, 2001.

25. P. McBurney, S. Parsons, and M. J. Wooldridge. Desiderata for agent argumentation protocols. In *Proc. First Intern. Joint Conf. on Autonomous Agents and Multiagent Systems*, pages 402–409. ACM Press, 2002.

26. S. Parsons, C. A. Sierra, and N. R. Jennings. Agents that reason and negotiate by arguing. *J. Logic and Computation*, 8(3):261–292, 1998.

27. S. Parsons, M. J. Wooldridge, and L. Amgoud. An analysis of formal inter-agent dialogues. In *Proc. First Intern. Joint Conf. Autonomous Agents and Multiagent Systems*, pages 394–401. ACM Press, 2002.

28. S. Parsons, M. J. Wooldridge, and L. Amgoud. Properties and complexity of some formal inter-agent dialogues. *J. Logic and Computation*, 13(3):347–376, 2003.

29. H. Prakken. *Logical Tools for Modelling Legal Argument.* Kluwer, Dordrecht, 1997.
30. C. Reed. Dialogue frames in agent communications. In Y. Demazeau, editor, *Proc. 3rd Intern. Conf. Multiagent Systems (ICMAS-98)*, pages 246–253. IEEE Press, 1998.
31. A. Rubinstein. Strategic considerations in pragmatics. In *Economics and Language: Five essays*, pages 37–52. Cambridge Univ. Press, 2000.
32. G. Vreeswijk and H. Prakken. Credulous and sceptical argument games for preferred semantics. In *Proc. JELIA'2000, The 7th European Workshop on Logic for Artificial Intelligence.*, pages 224–238, Berlin, 2000. Lecture Notes in A.I., 1919, Springer.
33. D. N. Walton and E. C. W. Krabbe. *Committment in Dialogue: Basic Concepts of Interpersonal Reasoning.* SUNY Press, Albany, 1995.

The Mechanics
of Some Formal Inter-agent Dialogues

Simon Parsons[1,2], Peter McBurney[2], and Michael Wooldridge[2]

[1] Department of Computer and Information Science, Brooklyn College
City University of New York, 2900 Bedford Avenue, Brooklyn
New York, NY 11210, USA
parsons@sci.brooklyn.cuny.edu
[2] Department of Computer Science, University of Liverpool
Chadwick Building, Liverpool L69 7ZF, UK
{p.j.mcburney,m.j.wooldridge}@csc.liv.ac.uk

Abstract. This paper studies argumentation-based dialogues between agents. It takes a previously defined system by which agents can trade arguments and examines in detail what locutions are passed between agents. This makes it possible to identify finer-grained protocols than has been previously possible, exposing the relationships between different kinds of dialogue, and giving a deeper understanding of how such dialogues could be automated.

1 Introduction

When building multi-agent systems, we take for granted the fact that the agents which make up the system will need to communicate: to resolve differences of opinion and conflicts of interest; to work together to resolve dilemmas or find proofs; or simply to inform each other of pertinent facts. Many of these communication requirements cannot be fulfilled by the exchange of single messages. Instead, the agents concerned need to be able to exchange a sequence of messages which all bear upon the same subject. In other words they need the ability to engage in dialogues. As a result of this requirement, there has been much work on providing agents with the ability to hold such dialogues. Recently some of this work has considered argument-based approaches to dialogue, for example the work by Dignum *et al.* [5], Parsons and Jennings [17], Reed [24], Schroeder *et al.* [25] and Sycara [26].

Reed's work built on an influential model of human dialogues due to argumentation theorists Doug Walton and Erik Krabbe [27], and we also take their dialogue typology as our starting point. Walton and Krabbe set out to analyse the concept of commitment in dialogue, so as to "provide conceptual tools for the theory of argumentation" [27, page ix]. This led to a focus on persuasion dialogues, and their work presents formal models for such dialogues. In attempting this task, Walton and Krabbe recognised the need for a characterisation of dialogues, and so they present a broad typology for inter-personal dialogue. They make no claims for its comprehensiveness.

F. Dignum (Ed.): ACL 2003, LNAI 2922, pp. 329–348, 2004.

Their categorisation identifies six primary types of dialogues and three mixed types. The categorisation is based upon: what information the participants each have at the commencement of the dialogue (with regard to the topic of discussion); what goals the individual participants have; and what goals are shared by the participants, goals we may view as those of the dialogue itself. This *dialogue game* view of dialogues, revived by Hamblin [12] and extending back to Aristotle, overlaps with work on conversational policies (see, for example, [4, 7]), but differs in considering the entire dialogue rather than dialogue segments.

As defined by Walton and Krabbe, the three types of dialogue we consider here are:

Information-Seeking Dialogues: One participant seeks the answer to some question(s) from another participant, who is believed by the first to know the answer(s).

Inquiry Dialogues: The participants collaborate to answer some question or questions whose answers are not known to any one participant.

Persuasion Dialogues: One party seeks to persuade another party to adopt a belief or point-of-view he or she does not currently hold. These dialogues begin with one party supporting a particular statement which the other party to the dialogue does not, and the first seeks to convince the second to adopt the proposition. The second party may not share this objective.

Our previous work investigated capturing these types of dialogue using a formal model of argumentation [2], the protocols behind these types of dialogue, and properties and complexity the dialogues [20, 22], and the range of possible outcomes from the dialogues [21]. Here we extend this investigation, turning to consider the internal detail of the dialogues, detail that we have previously skated over.

There are two reasons why we do this. First, we want to make sure that the protocols we introduced in [20] are fully specified. From our previous work, we already know that they capture the essence of information seeking, inquiry and persuasion – here we aim to ensure that all the necessary mechanics are in place as well. Second, our previous analysis suggests some deep connections between the different protocols – they seem to be variations on a theme rather than separate themes – and looking at their internal detail is one way to find out if these connections exist.

Note that, despite the fact that the types of dialogue we are considering are drawn from the analysis of human dialogues, we are only concerned here with dialogues between artificial agents. Unlike Grosz and Sidner [11] for example, we choose to focus in this way in order to simplify our task – dealing with artificial languages avoids much of the complexity inherent in natural language dialogues.

2   Background

In this section we briefly introduce the formal system of argumentation, due to Amgoud [1], that forms the backbone of our approach. This is inspired by the work of Dung [6] but goes further in dealing with preferences between arguments. Further details are available in [1]. We start with a possibly inconsistent knowledge base Σ with no deductive closure. We assume Σ contains formulas of a propositional language $\mathcal{L}$. $\vdash$ stands for classical inference, $\rightarrow$ for material implication, and $\equiv$ for logical equivalence. An argument is a proposition and the set of formulae from which it can be inferred:

Definition 1. *An* argument *is a pair $A = (H, h)$ where h is a formula of $\mathcal{L}$ and H a subset of Σ such that:*

1. *H is consistent;*
2. *$H \vdash h$; and*
3. *H is minimal, so no proper subset of H satisfying both 1. and 2. exists.*

H is called the support *of A, written $H = Support(A)$ and h is the* conclusion *of A written $h = Conclusion(A)$.*

We talk of h being *supported* by the argument (H, h)

In general, since Σ is inconsistent, arguments in $\mathcal{A}(\Sigma)$, the set of all arguments which can be made from Σ, will conflict, and we make this idea precise with the notion of undercutting:

Definition 2. *Let A_1 and A_2 be two arguments of $\mathcal{A}(\Sigma)$. A_1 undercuts A_2 iff $\exists h \in Support(A_2)$ such that $h \equiv \neg Conclusion(A_1)$.*

In other words, an argument is undercut if and only if there is another argument which has as its conclusion the negation of an element of the support for the first argument.

To capture the fact that some facts are more strongly believed[1] we assume that any set of facts has a preference order over it. We suppose that this ordering derives from the fact that the knowledge base Σ is stratified into non-overlapping sets $\Sigma_1, \ldots, \Sigma_n$ such that facts in Σ_i are all equally preferred and are more preferred than those in Σ_j where $j > i$. The preference level of a nonempty subset H of Σ, $level(H)$, is the number of the highest numbered layer which has a member in H.

Definition 3. *Let A_1 and A_2 be two arguments in $\mathcal{A}(\Sigma)$. A_1 is* preferred *to A_2 according to Pref, $Pref(A_1, A_2)$, iff $level(Support(A_1)) \leq level(Support(A_2))$.*

By $\gg^{Pref}$ we denote the strict pre-order associated with *Pref*. If A_1 is preferred to A_2, we say that A_1 is *stronger* than A_2[2]. We can now define the argumentation system we will use:

Definition 4. *An* argumentation system *(AS) is a triple $\langle \mathcal{A}(\Sigma), Undercut, Pref \rangle$ such that:*

---

[1] Here we only deal with beliefs, though the approach can also handle desires and intentions as in [19] and could be extended to cope with other mental attitudes.

[2] We acknowledge that this model of preferences is rather restrictive and in the future intend to work to relax it.

- $\mathcal{A}(\Sigma)$ is a set of the arguments built from Σ,
- Undercut is a binary relation representing the defeat relationship between arguments, $Undercut \subseteq \mathcal{A}(\Sigma) \times \mathcal{A}(\Sigma)$, and
- Pref is a (partial or complete) preordering on $\mathcal{A}(\Sigma) \times \mathcal{A}(\Sigma)$.

The preference order makes it possible to distinguish different types of relation between arguments:

Definition 5. Let A_1, A_2 be two arguments of $\mathcal{A}(\Sigma)$.

- If A_2 undercuts A_1 then A_1 defends itself against A_2 iff $A_1 \gg^{Pref} A_2$. Otherwise, A_1 does not defend itself.
- A set of arguments $\mathcal{S}$ defends A iff: $\forall\, B$ undercuts A and A does not defend itself against B then $\exists\, C \in \mathcal{S}$ such that C undercuts B and B does not defend itself against C.

Henceforth, $C_{Undercut,Pref}$ will gather all non-undercut arguments and arguments defending themselves against all their undercutting arguments. In [1], Amgoud showed that the set $\underline{\mathcal{S}}$ of acceptable arguments of the argumentation system $\langle \mathcal{A}(\Sigma), Undercut, Pref \rangle$ is the least fixpoint of a function $\mathcal{F}$:

$$\mathcal{S} \subseteq \mathcal{A}(\Sigma)$$
$$\mathcal{F}(\mathcal{S}) = \{(H, h) \in \mathcal{A}(\Sigma) | (H, h) \text{ is defended by } \mathcal{S}\}$$

Definition 6. The set of acceptable arguments for an argumentation system $\langle \mathcal{A}(\Sigma), Undercut, Pref \rangle$ is:

$$\underline{\mathcal{S}} = \bigcup \mathcal{F}_{i \geq 0}(\emptyset)$$
$$\underline{\mathcal{S}} = C_{Undercut,Pref} \cup \left[\bigcup \mathcal{F}_{i \geq 1}(C_{Undercut,Pref}) \right]$$

An argument is acceptable if it is a member of the acceptable set.

An acceptable argument is one which is, in some sense, proven since all the arguments which might undermine it are themselves undermined. However, this status can be revoked following the discovery of a new argument (possibly as the result of the communication of some new information from another agent).

3   Locutions and Attitudes

As in our previous work, agents decide what they know by determining which propositions they have acceptable arguments for. They assert propositions for which they have acceptable arguments, and accept propositions put forward by other agents if they find that the arguments are acceptable to them. The exact locutions and the way that they are exchanged define a formal dialogue game which agents engage in.

Dialogues are assumed to take place between two agents, for example called P and C. Each agent has a knowledge base, Σ_P and Σ_C respectively, containing their beliefs. In addition, each agent has a further knowledge base, accessible to both agents, containing commitments made in the dialogue[3]. These commitment stores are denoted $CS(P)$ and $CS(C)$ respectively, and in this dialogue system an agent's commitment store is just a subset of its knowledge base. Note that the union of the commitment stores can be viewed as the state of the dialogue at a given time. Each agent has access to their own private knowledge base and both commitment stores. Thus P can make use of $\langle \mathcal{A}(\Sigma_P \cup CS(C)), Undercut, Pref \rangle$[4] and C can make use of $\langle \mathcal{A}(\Sigma_C \cup CS(P)), Undercut, Pref \rangle$.

All the knowledge bases contain propositional formulas, are not closed under deduction, and all are stratified by degree of belief as discussed above. Here we assume that these degrees of belief are static and that both the players agree on them, though it is possible [3] to combine different sets of preferences, and it is also possible to have agents modify their beliefs on the basis of the reliability of their acquaintances [16].

With this background, we can present the set of dialogue moves first introduced in [20]. Each locution has a rule describing how to update commitment stores after the move, and groups of moves have conditions under which the move can be made – these are given in terms of the agents' assertion and acceptance attitudes (defined below). For all moves, player P addresses the ith move of the dialogue to player C.

assert(p) where p is a propositional formula.

$$CS_i(P) = CS_{i-1}(P) \cup \{p\} \text{ and } CS_i(C) = CS_{i-1}(C)$$

Here p can be any propositional formula, as well as the special character $\mathcal{U}$, discussed below.

assert(S) where S is a set of formulas representing the support of an argument.

$$CS_i(P) = CS(P)_{i-1} \cup S \text{ and } CS_i(C) = CS_{i-1}(C)$$

The counterpart of these moves are the acceptance moves. They can be used whenever the protocol and the agent's acceptance attitude allow.

accept(p) p is a propositional formula.

$$CS_i(P) = CS_{i-1}(P) \cup \{p\} \text{ and } CS_i(C) = CS_{i-1}(C)$$

accept(S) S is a set of propositional formulas.

$$CS_i(P) = CS_{i-1}(P) \cup S \text{ and } CS_i(C) = CS_{i-1}(C)$$

There are also moves which allow questions to be posed.

---

[3] Following Hamblin [12] commitments here are propositions that an agent is prepared to defend.

[4] Which, of course, is exactly the same thing as $\langle \mathcal{A}(\Sigma_P \cup CS(P) \cup CS(C)), Undercut, Pref \rangle$.

challenge(p) where p is a propositional formula.

$$CS_i(P) = CS_{i-1}(P) \text{ and } CS_i(C) = CS_{i-1}(C)$$

A challenge is a means of making the other player explicitly state the argument supporting a proposition. In contrast, a question can be used to query the other player about any proposition.

question(p) where p is a propositional formula.

$$CS_i(P) = CS_{i-1}(P) \text{ and } CS_i(C) = CS_{i-1}(C)$$

We refer to this set of moves as the set $\mathcal{M}'_{DC}$. The locutions in $\mathcal{M}'_{DC}$ are similar to those discussed in models of legal reasoning [8, 23] and it should be noted that there is no *retract* locution. Note that these locutions are ones used within dialogues – locutions such as those discussed in [15] would be required to frame dialogues.

We also need to define the attitudes which control the assertion and acceptance of propositions.

Definition 7. *An agent may have one of two assertion attitudes.*

- *a confident agent can assert any proposition p for which it can construct an argument (S, p).*
- *a careful agent can assert any proposition p for which it can construct an argument, if it is unable to construct a stronger argument for $\neg p$.*
- *a thoughtful agent can assert any proposition p for which it can construct an acceptable argument (S, p).*

Definition 8. *An agent may have one of three acceptance attitudes.*

- *a credulous agent can accept any proposition p if it is backed by an argument.*
- *a cautious agent can accept any proposition p that is backed by an argument if it is unable to construct a stronger argument for $\neg p$.*
- *a skeptical agent can accept any proposition p if it is backed by an acceptable argument.*

Since agents are typically involved in both asserting and accepting propositions, we denote the combination of an agent's two attitudes as

$$\langle assertion\ attitude \rangle / \langle acceptance\ attitude \rangle$$

The effects of this range of agent attitudes on dialogue outcomes is studied in [22], and for the rest of this paper we will largely ignore agents' attitudes, though the distinction between agents that are credulous and those that are not becomes important in a couple of places.

4   Types of Dialogue

Previously [20] we defined three protocols for information seeking, inquiry and persuasion dialogues. These protocols are deliberately simple, the simplest we can imagine that can satisfy the definitions given by [27], since we believe that we need to understand the behaviour of these simple protocols before we are to able to understand more complex protocols.

4.1   Information-Seeking

In an information seeking dialogue, one participant seeks the answer to some question from another participant. If the information seeker is agent A, the other agent is B, and the proposition that the dialogue is concerned with is p, then the dialogue starts with A having no argument for p or $\neg p$, and one possible protocol for conducting an information-seeking dialogue about p is the following protocol we denote as $\mathcal{IS}$:

1. A asks $question(p)$.
2. B replies with either $assert(p)$, $assert(\neg p)$, or $assert(\mathcal{U})$. Which will depend upon the contents of its knowledge-base and its assertion attitude. $\mathcal{U}$ indicates that, for whatever reason B cannot give an answer.
3. A either $accepts$ B's response, if its acceptance attitude allows, or $challenges$. $\mathcal{U}$ cannot be $challenged$ and as soon as it is asserted, the dialogue terminates without the question being resolved.
4. B replies to a $challenge$ with an $assert(S)$, where S is the support of an argument for the last proposition challenged by A.
5. Go to 3 for each proposition in S in turn.

Note that A accepts whenever possible, only being able to challenge when unable to accept – "only" in the sense of only being able to challenge then and $challenge$ being the only locution other than $accept$ that it is allowed to make. More flexible dialogue protocols are allowed, as in [2], but at the cost of possibly running forever[5].

4.2   Inquiry

In an inquiry dialogue, the participants collaborate to answer some question whose answer is not known to either. There are a number of ways in which one might construct an inquiry dialogue (for example see [14]). Here we present one simple possibility. We assume that two agents A and B have already agreed to engage in an inquiry about some proposition p by some control dialogue as suggested in [15], and from this point can adopt the following protocol $\mathcal{I}$:

1. A asserts $q \rightarrow p$ for some q or $\mathcal{U}$.
2. B accepts $q \rightarrow p$ if its acceptance attitude allows, or challenges it.
3. A replies to a $challenge$ with an $assert(S)$, where S is the support of an argument for the last proposition challenged by B.
4. Goto 2 for each proposition $s \in S$ in turn, replacing $q \rightarrow p$ by s.
5. B asserts q, or $r \rightarrow q$ for some r, or $\mathcal{U}$.
6. If $\mathcal{A}(CS(A) \cup CS(B))$ includes an argument for p which is acceptable to both agents, then first A and then B accept it and the dialogue terminates successfully.

---

[5] The protocol in [2] allows an agent to interject with $question(p)$ for any p at several points, making it possible for a dialogue between two agents to continue indefinitely.

7. Go to 5, reversing the roles of A and B and substituting r for q and some t for r.

Here the initial conditions of the dialogue are that neither agent has an argument for p.

This protocol[6] is basically a series of implied $\mathcal{IS}$ dialogues. First A asks "do you know of anything which would imply p were it known?". B replies with one, or the dialogue terminates with $\mathcal{U}$. If A accepts the implication, B asks "now, do you know q, or any r which would imply q were it known?", and the process repeats until either the process bottoms out in a proposition which both agents agree on, or there is no new implication to add to the chain.

4.3   Persuasion

In a persuasion dialogue, one party seeks to persuade another party to adopt a belief or point-of-view he or she does not currently hold. In other words, the dialogue starts with one agent having an argument for a proposition p, and the other either having no argument for p, or having an argument for $\neg p$[7]. The dialogue game DC, on which the moves in [2] are based, is fundamentally a persuasion game, so the protocol below results in games which are very like those described in [2]. This protocol, $\mathcal{P}$, is as follows, where agent A is trying to persuade agent B to accept p.

1. A asserts p.
2. B accepts p if its acceptance attitude allows, if not B asserts $\neg p$ if it is allowed to, or otherwise challenges p.
3. If B asserts $\neg p$, then goto 2 with the roles of the agents reversed and $\neg p$ in place of p.
4. If B has challenged, then:
   (a) A asserts S, the support for p;
   (b) Goto 2 for each $s \in S$ in turn.

If at any point an agent cannot make the indicated move, it has to concede the dialogue game. If A concedes, it fails to persuade B that p is true. If B concedes, then A has succeeded in persuading it. An agent also concedes the game if at any point if there are no propositions made by the other agent that it hasn't accepted.

We should point out that this kind of persuasion dialogue does not assume that agents necessarily start from opposite positions, one believing p and one believing $\neg p$. Instead one agent believes p and the other may believe $\neg p$, but also may believe neither p nor $\neg p$. This is perfectly consistent with the notion of persuasion suggested by Walton and Krabbe [27].

---

[6] Which differs from the inquiry dialogue in [20] in the *accept* moves in step 6.

[7] This second condition is better stated as having an argument for $\neg p$ that is acceptable according to its acceptability attitude, and no argument for p that is acceptable in this way.

Note that all three of these protocols have the same core steps. One agent *asserts* something, the other *accepts* if it can, otherwise it *challenges*. A *challenge* provokes the *assert*ion of the grounds, which are in turn either *accept*ed or *challenge*d. The proposition p that is the first assertion, and the central proposition of the dialogue, is said to be the *subject* of the dialogue. This basic framework has been shown [18, 20] to be capable of capturing a range of dialogue types, and we have studied a number of the properties of these dialogues including termination and complexity [22] and what their possible outcomes are [21]. Our purpose here is to look in more detail at the structure of these dialogues, in particular the core steps.

5   Dialogue Mechanics

As already mentioned, the dialogue protocols given above have the same core steps, and it is interesting to consider these steps as forming *atomic protocols* from which other protocols are constructed. Are these truly atomic, in the sense that they cannot be broken down into combinations of simpler protocols? What combinations of atomic protocols make sense (in other words, are there protocols that we have not yet identified which can be made from the atomic protocols)? Indeed, we haven't as yet even answered the most basic question – what atomic protocols are there?

5.1   Identifying Atomic Protocols

To identify what atomic protocols there are, we will start by writing out a complete $\mathcal{IS}$ dialogue. We imagine a dialogue between agent A and agent B about a proposition p. A typical $\mathcal{IS}$ dialogue might proceed as follows, where the dialogue has an acceptance outcome of p for B (so that B *asserts* p, and A later accepts it[8]). This dialogue is in what we will call *extensive form*, by which we denote the fact that every choice of locution is such that it tends to extend the dialogue as much as possible, so what we have here is the longest possible dialogue that can arise. Clearly any of A's *accepts* could equally well be a *reject*, and the dialogue would stop after at most two more *rejects* (and, indeed, after one *reject*, *reject* would be the only locution that could possibly be uttered).

> A: *question*(p)
> B: *assert*(p)
>> A: *challenge*(p)
>> B: *assert* $\left(\bigcup_i \{s_i\}_{i=1...n}\right)$
>>> A: *challenge*(s_1)
>>> B: *assert*($\{s_1\}$)
>>> A: *accept*(s_1)
>>> A: *challenge*(s_2)
>>> B: *assert*($\{s_2\}$)

---

[8] The notion of an acceptance outcome is formally defined in [21].

> A: $accept(s_2)$
>
> $\vdots$
>
> A: $challenge(s_n)$
> B: $assert(\{s_n\})$
> A: $accept(s_n)$
> A: $accept\ (\bigcup_i \{s_i\}_{i=1...n})$
> A: $accept(p)$

If we consider this dialogue to be made up of a series of (indented) *sub-dialogues* – each of which is an instantiation of an atomic protocol – we can easily identify two distinct atomic protocols. We first have Q (for "question") protocol:

> A: $question(x)$
> B: $assert(y)$
> A: $accept(y)$ or $reject(y)$

where y is either x or $\neg x$. In the example above, the outermost sub-dialogue is built according to this protocol, and every other sub-dialogue is embedded in this sub-dialogue.

This Q protocol is too simple to even describes simplest possible kind of $\mathcal{IS}$ dialogue on its own, since the only kind of dialogue it covers is one in which A asks the question, B replies, and A immediately accepts.

Proposition 1. *A dialogue under $\mathcal{IS}$ with subject p between agents A and B will never only involve a dialogue under the Q atomic protocol.*

Looking again at the example dialogue above, we can identify instantiations of a second atomic protocol, which we will call A. This is the protocol responsible for the "core steps" mentioned at the end of the last section (though without the initial *assert* that at first seems to be an obvious part of those steps). In other words A is:

> A: $challenge(x)$
> B: $assert(y)$
> A: $accept(x)$ or $reject(x)$

In the outermost instantiation of this protocol in the example, x is the last proposition to be *assert*ed and y is the set of propositions that form the grounds of p. The dialogue generated by this instantiation of the atomic protocol is embedded within the dialogue generated by the Q protocol[9], and then has n A dialogues nested within it. All the other instantiations of the A protocol are nested within the first A dialogue, follow each other in sequence, and all have the same form. x is one of the propositions s_i in the set *assert*ed in the first A dialogue, and y is the set $\{s_i\}$ which is the only possible set of grounds supporting the assertion s_i.

---

[9] From here on, we will refer to "the dialogue generated by the X sub-protocol" as the "X dialogue", where this usage is not ambiguous and in Section 5.2 we will develop this idea formally.

Before preceding any further, it is clear from this exposition of a dialogue under $\mathcal{IS}$ that any such dialogue will terminate provided that the set of grounds S_i is finite, and that it will terminate in time proportional to $|S_i|$. In other words:

Proposition 2. *A dialogue under $\mathcal{IS}$ with subject p between agents A and B, in which will A utters the first illocution, will terminate in at most $O(|S_i|)$ steps, where B has an argument (S_i, p) or $(S_i, \neg p)$.*

This is an even tighter bound on the length of the dialogue than we obtained in [22], and doesn't depend upon the knowledge base Σ_B of the agent making the initial assertion being finite.

Having identified the atomic protocols underlying $\mathcal{IS}$, we can turn to look at $\mathcal{I}$. As described above, a full-fledged $\mathcal{I}$ dialogue would look as follows:

A: $assert(q \rightarrow p)$
   B: $challenge(q \rightarrow p)$
   A: $assert\left(\bigcup_i \{s_i\}_{i=1...n}\right)$
      B: $challenge(s_2)$
      A: $assert(\{s_2\})$
      B: $accept(s_2)$
           ⋮
      B: $challenge(s_n)$
      A: $assert(\{s_n\})$
      B: $accept(s_n)$
   B: $accept\left(\bigcup_i \{s_i\}_{i=1...n}\right)$
B: $accept(q \rightarrow p)$
B: $assert(r \rightarrow q)$
     ⋮
A: $accept(r \rightarrow q)$
     ⋮
A: $assert(v \rightarrow w)$
     ⋮
B: $accept(v \rightarrow w)$
B: $assert(v)$
     ⋮
A: $accept(v)$
A: $accept(p)$
B: $accept(p)$

In other words, $\mathcal{I}$ start with an agent asserting a formula $q \rightarrow p$ that provides a means to infer p, the subject of the dialogue. The agents then engage in the same kind of nested A dialogue we saw above to determine if this formula is an acceptance outcome for the first agent. Then the second agent asserts a formula from which provides the means to infer q (and so is another step in the proof of p). This process continues until one agent accepts the latest step in this chain, $v \rightarrow w$, and then can get the other agent to accept v.

This analysis exposes a number of weaknesses with the $\mathcal{I}$ protocol, which we have already noted [22][10]. One such weakness is the rigidity of the protocol – it relies on strict turn taking by the agents, they have to supply sequential pieces of the proof, and it only explores one possible proof of the subject[11]. Another weakness is the fact that it assumes the agents have already agreed to engage in an inquiry dialogue – unlike the information seeking dialogue, there is no initial illocution to specify "let's start trying to prove p".

Without such an utterance, the structure of an $\mathcal{I}$ dialogue isn't a combination of clearly identifiable atomic dialogues. It is perhaps more elegant to consider adding an utterance $prove(p)$ which has exactly the sense of "let's start trying to prove p" and imagine a P (for "proof") atomic dialogue which runs as either of

<table>
<tr><td>B: $prove(x)$</td><td></td><td>B: $prove(x)$</td></tr>
<tr><td>A: $assert(x)$</td><td>or</td><td>A: $assert(y \rightarrow x)$</td></tr>
<tr><td>B: $accept(y)$ or $reject(y)$</td><td></td><td>B: $accept(y \rightarrow x)$ or $reject(y \rightarrow x)$</td></tr>
</table>

Such a dialogue could produce a version of the $\mathcal{I}$ example above when iterated as:

B: $prove(p)$
A: $assert(q \rightarrow p)$
    nested A dialogues about $q \rightarrow p$
B: $accept(q \rightarrow p)$
A: $prove(q)$

    $\vdots$

B: $assert(v)$
    nested A dialogues about v
A: $accept(v)$
B: $accept(p)$
A: $accept(p)$

Although such a dialogue is an extension of $\mathcal{I}$ as we have previously defined it (and requires an extension of the set of locutions to $\mathcal{M}'_{DC} \cup \{prove(p)\}$), this is what we will consider to be a prototypical inquiry dialogue, $\mathcal{I}''$, for the remainder of this paper[12]. Defining P in this way gives us analogous results to those for Q, for instance:

Proposition 3. *A dialogue under $\mathcal{I}''$ with subject p between agents A and B will never only involve a dialogue under the P atomic protocol.*

---

[10] Another weakness that we have not mentioned before is that as it stands the $\mathcal{I}$ protocol only allows the construction of proofs that are chains of material implications. A more general formulation would require each assertion to be any formula which would help in the proof of p.

[11] [22] also provides some solutions to these particular problems.

[12] And we should point out that modifying $\mathcal{I}$ in this way will not change any of the properties already proved for it.

Finally, we can look for the atomic protocols that make up the $\mathcal{P}$ protocol for persuasion dialogues. As defined above, there are two ways that a persuasion dialogue may, in general, be played out. The simplest is as follows:

A: $assert(p)$
   B: $challenge(p)$
   A: $assert\left(\bigcup_i\{s_i\}_{i=1...n}\right)$
      B: $challenge(s_1)$
      A: $assert(\{s_1\})$
      B: $accept(s_1)$
      B: $challenge(s_2)$
      A: $assert(\{s_2\})$
      B: $accept(s_2)$

          ⋮

      B: $challenge(s_n)$
      A: $assert(\{s_n\})$
      B: $accept(s_n)$
   B: $accept\left(\bigcup_i\{s_i\}_{i=1...n}\right)$
B: $accept(p)$

This kind of dialogue, which we might call $persuasion_1$, is the kind which arises for example when B does not initially have an opinion about whether p is true or not. As a result, $\mathcal{P}$ generates a dialogue that has the same form as a $\mathcal{IS}$ dialogue though without the initial $question$. Just as in the case for the inquiry dialogue without the $prove$ locution, the fact that this is a persuasion dialogue is implicit – any assertion can be the start of a $\mathcal{P}$ dialogue. To make the start of the dialogue explicit, we could insist that before A makes its initial $assert$, it signals the start of a persuasion dialogue by using a locution $know(p)$, which has the intended meaning "do you know that p is the case?". (Again we will have to extend the set of locutions, this time to $\mathcal{M}'_{DC} \cup \{prove(p), know(p)\}$, a set we will call $\mathcal{M}^{PK}_{DC}$.)

The other way that $\mathcal{P}$ (well, in fact it is a new protocol $\mathcal{P}'$ which includes the $know$ locution) can play out is when B replies to the initial assertion of p with its own assertion of $\neg p$ in which case we get a $persuasion_2$ dialogue that looks like:

A: $know(p)$
A: $assert(p)$
   B: $know(\neg p)$
   B: $assert(\neg p)$
      A: $challenge(\neg p)$
      B: $assert\left(\bigcup_i\{s_i\}_{i=1...n}\right)$
         A: $challenge(s_1)$
         B: $assert(\{s_1\})$
         A: $accept(s_1)$
         A: $challenge(s_2)$

> B: $assert(\{s_2\})$
> A: $accept(s_2)$
> $\vdots$
> A: $challenge(s_n)$
> B: $assert(\{s_n\})$
> A: $accept(s_n)$
> A: $accept\ (\bigcup_i\{s_i\}_{i=1...n})$
> A: $accept(\neg p)$
> B: $reject(p)$

From this we can identify a new atomic protocol:

> A: $know(x)$
> A: $assert(x)$
> B: $reject(x)$ or $accept(x)$

which we will call K after its first locution. It is then clear that $persuasion_1$ is just the usual set of nested A dialogues within a K dialogue, and that $persuasion_2$ is a $persuasion_1$ nested within a further K. Exactly as for the A and Q protocols, the P protocol cannot generate a $\mathcal{P}'$ dialogue on its own:

Proposition 4. *A dialogue under $\mathcal{P}'$ with subject p between agents A and B will never only involve a dialogue under the Q atomic protocol.*

5.2　Combinations of Atomic Protocols

We can formally describe how dialogues under $\mathcal{IS}$ $\mathcal{I}''$, and $\mathcal{P}'$ are constructed from the atomic protocols using the notation we developed in [15]. In that paper we defined:

Iteration: If G is a dialogue, then G^n is also a dialogue, being that dialogue which consists of the n-fold repetition of G, each occurrence being undertaken until closure, and then being followed immediately by the next occurrence.

Sequencing: If G and H are both dialogues, then $G; H$ is also a dialogue, representing that dialogue which consists of undertaking G until its closure and then immediately undertaking H.

Parallelization: If G and H are both dialogues, then $G \cap H$ is also a dialogue, representing that dialogue which consists of undertaking both G and H simultaneously, until each are closed.

Embedding: If G and H are both dialogues, and $\Phi \subseteq M^1 \times M^2 \ldots \subseteq \Theta^G \times \Theta^G \ldots$ is a finite set of legal locution sequences in G, then $G[H|\Phi]$ is also a dialogue, representing that dialogue which consists of undertaking G until a sequence in Φ has been executed, and then switching immediately to dialogue H which is undertaken until its closure, whereupon dialogue G resumes from immediately after the point where it was interrupted and continues until closure. Dialogue H is said to be embedded in G, at one level lower than G. In the time between when H opens and closes, dialogue G remains open, no matter how many embedded dialogues H itself may contain.

Testing: If p is a wff in $\mathcal{L}$, then $\langle p \rangle$ is a dialogue to assess the truth-status of p. We assume such a dialogue returns a truth-value for p to whichever was the lowest-level dialogue open at the time of commencement of the testing dialogue.

Up to this point it has sufficed to talk informally about dialogues generated by protocols, but for the remainder of the paper we need to be a bit more formal. We start by defining what a dialogue is:

Definition 9. *A* dialogue *is an ordered sequence of valid locutions.*

A given protocol can clearly generate many different dialogues, with the exact dialogue being dependent upon what agents are involved (the important aspect being what the agents know), what order the agents generate locutions in (which is specified by which agent makes the first locution), and what the subject of the dialogue. We can therefore fully specify a dialogue by identifying the protocol and these features. For instance, we write:

$$Q^{B \to A}(\Sigma_B, \Sigma_A)(p)$$

to denote the dialogue generated by protocol Q, with subject p, between agents A and B, with knowledge bases Σ_A and Σ_B, where the first locution is uttered by B. If any of these specifiers have no bearing on a particular dialogue, we omit them.

With this notation, we can describe our first dialogue example as:

$$Q^{A \to B}(p) \left[A^{A \to B}(p) \left[\left(A^{A \to B}(s_i) \right)^n | \{ assert(S) \} \right] | \{ assert(p) \} \right]$$

where (S, p) is an argument in $\mathcal{A}(\Sigma_B \cup CS(A))$, $S = \{ s_1, \ldots, s_n \}$.

Now, while any information seeking dialogue won't necessarily be exactly the same as this, it will have exactly this form. To be able to express what "exactly this form" is, we need the following notion:

Definition 10. *A* protocol G sequence includes *a protocol H if, for any two agents A and B, with knowledge bases Σ_A and Σ_B, G can generate all the dialogues that H can generate.*

Thus $\mathcal{IS}$ sequence includes Q, but Q does not sequence include $\mathcal{IS}$ (because, for example, Q cannot generate dialogues like our first example on its own). Sequence inclusion gives us a notion of equivalence between protocols:

Definition 11. *Two protocols G and H are* sequence equivalent *if G sequence includes H and H sequence includes G.*

In other words two protocols are sequence equivalent if they generate exactly the same sets of dialogues. This is a new notion of equivalence between protocols, one that we didn't identify in [13], but it is close to the notion of bisimulation equivalence from that paper.

With these ideas, we can show a more precise version of Proposition 1:

Proposition 5. $Q^{A\to B}(p)$ *does not sequence include* $\mathcal{IS}^{A\to B}(p)$.

In fact we can even drop the specifier p, since any dialogue that opens with a *question* will play out in the same way. This sets a lower limit on the complexity of a $\mathcal{IS}$ dialogue, in the sense that it must contain more than the locutions that can be generated by a single atomic protocol. In fact, it must contain at least two atomic protocols:

Proposition 6. *If A is credulous, then:*

$$Q^{A\to B}(p)\left[\mathsf{A}^{A\to B}(p)|\{assert(p)\}\right]$$

where (S,p) is an argument in $\mathcal{A}(\Sigma_B \cup CS(A))$, will be sequence equivalent to $\mathcal{I}''^{A\to B}(p)$.

This dialogue is the simplest kind of information seeking dialogue that is possible under the $\mathcal{IS}$ protocol. If A isn't credulous, we need the full kind of dialogue in our first example to capture the $\mathcal{IS}$ protocol:

Proposition 7. *If A is not credulous, then:*

$$Q^{A\to B}(p)\left[\mathsf{A}^{A\to B}(p)\left[\left(\mathsf{A}^{A\to B}(s_i)\right)^n|\{assert(S)\}\right]|\{assert(p)\}\right]$$

where (S,p) is an argument in $\mathcal{A}(\Sigma_B \cup CS(A))$, $S = \{s_1,\ldots,s_n\}$, will be sequence equivalent to $\mathcal{IS}^{A\to B}(p)$

We can obtain similar results for the other kinds of dialogue. For inquiry dialogues we have a similar lower limit on the complexity of a dialogue:

Proposition 8. $P^{A\to B}(p)$ *does not sequence include* $\mathcal{I}''^{A\to B}(p)$.

If A is credulous, then we get the simplest kind of $\mathcal{I}''$ dialogue:

Proposition 9. *If A is credulous, then:*

$$P^{A\to B}(p)\left[\mathsf{A}^{A\to B}(p)|\{assert(p)\}\right]$$

where (S,p) is an argument in $\mathcal{A}(\Sigma_B \cup CS(A))$, will be sequence equivalent to $\mathcal{I}''^{A\to B}(p)$.

If A is not credulous, then the dialogue gets more complex. Exactly how complex is determined by the length of the proof assembled by the two agents.

Proposition 10. *If A is not credulous, then:*

$$P^{A\to B}(p)\left[\mathsf{A}^{A\to B}(p)\left[\left(\mathsf{A}^{A\to B}(s_{i_j})\right)^n|\{assert(S_1)\}\right]|\{assert(p)\}\right];$$
$$P^{B\to A}(v_1)\left[\mathsf{A}^{B\to A}(v_1)\left[\left(\mathsf{A}^{B\to A}(s_{i_j})\right)^n|\{assert(S_2)\}\right]|\{assert(v_1)\}\right];$$
$$\vdots$$
$$P^{A\to B}(v_n)\left[\mathsf{A}^{A\to B}(v_n)\left[\left(\mathsf{A}^{A\to B}(s_{i_j})\right)^n|\{assert(S_n)\}\right]|\{assert(v_n)\}\right];$$

where (S_i,v_i) is an argument in $\mathcal{A}(\Sigma_B \cup CS(A))$, $S_i = \{s_{i_1},\ldots,s_{i_n}\}$ for odd i, and (S_k,v_k) is an argument in $\mathcal{A}(\Sigma_A \cup CS(B))$, $S_k = \{s_{k_1},\ldots,s_{k_n}\}$ for even k, such that $\{v_1,\ldots,v_n\} \vdash p$, will be sequence equivalent to $\mathcal{IS}^{A\to B}(p)$

This makes the iterative structure of inquiry dialogues clear, as well as the similarity between a single iteration and an $\mathcal{IS}$ dialogue.

For persuasion dialogues we have to consider two cases, $persuasion_1$ and $persuasion_2$, but the first two results hold for both kinds:

Proposition 11. $\mathsf{K}^{A \to B}(p)$ *does not sequence include* $\mathcal{P'}^{A \to B}(p)$.

The second result depends on B (since it is the agent to whom the assertion is made) rather than A as in the previous dialogues.

Proposition 12. *If B is credulous, then:*

$$\mathsf{K}^{A \to B}(p) \left[\mathsf{A}^{B \to A}(p) | \{ assert(p) \} \right]$$

where (S, p) is an argument in $\mathcal{A}(\Sigma_A \cup CS(B))$, will be sequence equivalent to $\mathcal{P'}^{A \to B}(p)$.

It seems odd that this should hold for a $persuasion_2$ dialogue, since we know that in a $persuasion_2$ dialogue which starts with A uttering a *know*, B has an argument for $\neg p$. However, that is the nature of credulous agents – they accept anything backed by an argument. When the persuadee is not credulous, then we have to consider $persuasion_1$ and $persuasion_2$ dialogues separately. For a $persuasion_1$ dialogue we get a result just like that for $\mathcal{IS}$:

Proposition 13. *If B is not credulous, and $(S', \neg p) \notin \mathcal{A}(\Sigma_B \cup CS(A))$ then:*

$$\mathsf{K}^{A \to B}(p) \left[\mathsf{A}^{B \to A}(p) \left[\left(\mathsf{A}^{B \to A}(s_i) \right)^n | \{ assert(S) \} \right] | \{ assert(p) \} \right]$$

where (S, p) is an argument in $\mathcal{A}(\Sigma_A \cup CS(B))$, $S = \{s_1, \ldots, s_n\}$, will be sequence equivalent to $\mathcal{P'}^{A \to B}(p)$

However, it is easy to see that there is an important difference between this kind of dialogue and a $\mathcal{IS}$ dialogue, other than the first atomic dialogue, which which is that the order in which the agents utter locutions is different. For a $persuasion_2$ dialogue we have:

Proposition 14. *If B is not credulous, and $(S', \neg p) \in \mathcal{A}(\Sigma_B \cup CS(A))$, then*

$$\mathsf{K}^{A \to B}(p) \left[\mathsf{K}^{B \to A}(\neg p) \right.$$
$$\left. \left[\mathsf{A}^{A \to B}(p) \left[\left(\mathsf{A}^{A \to B}(s_i) \right)^n | \{ assert(S') \} \right] | \{ assert(\neg p) \} \right] | \{ assert(p) \} \right]$$

where $S' = \{s_1, \ldots, s_n\}$, will be sequence equivalent to $\mathcal{P'}^{A \to B}(p)$

These results, then, guarantee that the atomic protocols exactly capture, in a strong sense, the protocols we first identified in [20]. There is more that we have done concerning atomic protocols, for example examining legal combinations of them other than those given above, which we do not have room to include here, and making use of the specifications of the types of dialogue given above (for example to make formal comparisons of them). We will report these results in a later paper.

6   Conclusions

This paper has extended the analysis of formal inter-agent dialogues that we began in [20, 21]. The main contribution of this paper is to identify a set of atomic protocols which can be combined (in the ways that we described in [15]) to give exactly the protocols introduced in [20, 21]. In this way we have done what we said we would in the introduction, putting the protocols from our previous work under the microscope to find out exactly how they work. As a result of this work, we now have a precise formal characterisation of our protocols, and are now in a position to start to compare protocols in some of the ways we suggested in [13].

One thing that has emerged, rather to our surprise, is a link between our work and conversation policies (for example [9]). Though we have yet to look at the matter in detail, it seems to us that the atomic protocols we have identified here are rather like conversation policies as we understand them – rules about short sequences of locutions which assemble sections of an overall conversation between agents. We intend to look at this matter more in the near future, however, it seems that we can think of the kinds of protocol we have been studying as composed of combinations of conversation policies, something that suggests it will be particularly important to establish the full range of sensible combinations of atomic protocols.

More work, of course, remains to be done in this area in addition to that outlined above. Particularly important are: determining the relationship between the locutions we use in these dialogues and those of agent communication languages such as the FIPA ACL; examining the effect of adding new locutions (such as *retract*) to the language; extending the system with a more detailed model of preferences; and providing an implementation. We are currently investigating these matters along with further dialogue types, such as planning dialogues [10].

Acknowledgments

This work was partially supported by NSF REC-02-19347.

References

1. L. Amgoud and C. Cayrol. On the acceptability of arguments in preference-based argumentation framework. In *Proceedings of the 14th Conference on Uncertainty in Artificial Intelligence*, pages 1–7, 1998.
2. L. Amgoud, N. Maudet, and S. Parsons. Modelling dialogues using argumentation. In E. Durfee, editor, *Proceedings of the Fourth International Conference on Multi-Agent Systems*, pages 31–38, Boston, MA, USA, 2000. IEEE Press.
3. L. Amgoud and S. Parsons. Agent dialogues with conflicting preferences. In J.-J. Meyer and M. Tambe, editors, *Proceedings of the 8th International Workshop on Agent Theories, Architectures and Languages*, pages 1–15, 2001.

4. B. Chaib-Draa and F. Dignum. Trends in agent communication language. *Computational Intelligence*, 18(2):89–101, 2002.
5. F. Dignum, B. Dunin-Kęplicz, and R. Verbrugge. Agent theory for team formation by dialogue. In C. Castelfranchi and Y. Lespérance, editors, *Seventh Workshop on Agent Theories, Architectures, and Languages*, pages 141–156, Boston, USA, 2000.
6. P. M. Dung. On the acceptability of arguments and its fundamental role in nonmonotonic reasoning, logic programming and n-person games. *Artificial Intelligence*, 77:321–357, 1995.
7. R. A. Flores and R. C. Kremer. To commit or not to commit. *Computational Intelligence*, 18(2):120–173, 2002.
8. T. F. Gordon. The pleadings game. *Artificial Intelligence and Law*, 2:239–292, 1993.
9. M. Greaves, H. Holmback, and J. Bradshaw. What is a conversation policy? In F. Dignum and M. Greaves, editors, *Issues in Agent Communication*, Lecture Notes in Artificial Intelligence 1916, pages 118–131. Springer, Berlin, Germany, 2000.
10. B. J. Grosz and S. Kraus. The evolution of sharedplans. In M. J. Wooldridge and A. Rao, editors, *Foundations of Rational Agency*, volume 14 of *Applied Logic*. Kluwer, The Netherlands, 1999.
11. B. J. Grosz and C. L. Sidner. Attention, intentions, and the structure of discourse. *Computational Linguistics*, 12(3):175–204, 1986.
12. C. L. Hamblin. *Fallacies*. Methuen and Co Ltd, London, UK, 1970.
13. M. W. Johnson, P. McBurney, and S. Parsons. When are two protocols the same? In M-P Huget, editor, *Communication in Multi-Agent Systems: Agent Communication Languages and Conversation Policies*, Lecture Notes in Artificial Intelligence 2650, pages 253–268. Springer Verlag, Berlin, 2003.
14. P. McBurney and S. Parsons. Representing epistemic uncertainty by means of dialectical argumentation. *Annals of Mathematics and Artificial Intelligence*, 32(1–4):125–169, 2001.
15. P. McBurney and S. Parsons. Games that agents play: A formal framework for dialogues between autonomous agents. *Journal of Logic, Language, and Information*, 11(3):315–334, 2002.
16. S. Parsons and P. Giorgini. An approach to using degrees of belief in BDI agents. In B. Bouchon-Meunier, R. R. Yager, and L. A. Zadeh, editors, *Information, Uncertainty, Fusion*. Kluwer, Dordrecht, 1999.
17. S. Parsons and N. R. Jennings. Negotiation through argumentation – a preliminary report. In *Proceedings of Second International Conference on Multi-Agent Systems*, pages 267–274, 1996.
18. S. Parsons and P. McBurney. Argumentation-based communication between agents. In M.-P. Huget, editor, *Communication in Multi-Agent Systems: Agent Communication Languages and Conversation Policies*, pages 164–178. Springer Verlag, Berlin, 2003.
19. S. Parsons, C. Sierra, and N. R. Jennings. Agents that reason and negotiate by arguing. *Journal of Logic and Computation*, 8(3):261–292, 1998.
20. S. Parsons, M. Wooldridge, and L. Amgoud. An analysis of formal inter-agent dialogues. In *1st International Conference on Autonomous Agents and Multi-Agent Systems*. ACM Press, 2002.
21. S. Parsons, M. Wooldridge, and L. Amgoud. On the outcomes of formal inter-agent dialogues. In *2nd International Conference on Autonomous Agents and Multi-Agent Systems*. ACM Press, 2003.
22. S. Parsons, M. Wooldridge, and L. Amgoud. Properties and complexity of formal inter-agent dialogues. *Journal of Logic and Computation*, 13(3):347–376, 2003.

23. H. Prakken. Relating protocols for dynamic dispute with logics for defeasible argumentation. *Synthese*, 127:187–219, 2001.
24. C. Reed. Dialogue frames in agent communications. In Y. Demazeau, editor, *Proceedings of the Third International Conference on Multi-Agent Systems*, pages 246–253. IEEE Press, 1998.
25. M. Schroeder, D. A. Plewe, and A. Raab. Ultima ratio: should Hamlet kill Claudius. In *Proceedings of the 2nd International Conference on Autonomous Agents*, pages 467–468, 1998.
26. K. Sycara. Argumentation: Planning other agents' plans. In *Proceedings of the Eleventh Joint Conference on Artificial Intelligence*, pages 517–523, 1989.
27. D. N. Walton and E. C. W. Krabbe. *Commitment in Dialogue: Basic Concepts of Interpersonal Reasoning*. State University of New York Press, Albany, NY, 1995.

A Cooperative Dialogue Game
for Resolving Ontological Discrepancies

Robbert-Jan Beun and Rogier M. van Eijk

Institute of Information and Computing Sciences
Utrecht University, P.O. Box 80.089
3508 TB Utrecht, The Netherlands
{rj,rogier}@cs.uu.nl

Abstract. The goal of this paper is to present a computational framework that enables us to generate elementary speech act sequences in a dialogue between an electronic assistant and a computer user. Since naive users of complex systems often do not think and communicate in terms of domain characteristics, we will concentrate on the conversational process of the understanding of the meaning of a vocabulary shared by two dialogue participants. In order to give meaning to their vocabulary, agents need to translate terms into their private domain ontologies. We consider a dialogue game in which agents produce speech acts or 'moves' to transfer relevant information with respect to a particular agreement about the meaning of the words in the vocabulary. Describing the properties and the dynamics of the cognitive states or cognitive constructs in relation to the various dialogue contributions is an essential part of this work. In particular, we address the following basic questions: What type of cognitive constructs should be included to model the dialogue's basic structural properties? How do the various dialogue contributions change the existing cognitive constructs? How do these changes influence the generation of new contributions?

1 Introduction

When we interact with computers, we often want them to be endowed with characteristics that closely mimic human communication. One of these characteristics is the ability of humans to react in a cooperative manner to the communicative actions of the dialogue partner. In everyday conversation, people effortlessly answer questions, accept or deny assertions, confirm the receipt of a message and provide relevant feedback in case of communication problems. Since the cognitive and communicative abilities of humans are so well adapted to the real-time processing of these various interaction structures, we expect that including natural conversational skills in interfaces may contribute to a more efficient and satisfactory human-computer interaction.

It was only twenty years ago that interaction with computers was for the most part only possible through symbols that could be understood exclusively by expert users. Today we can hardly imagine that the interface once did not include the graphical apparatus of icons, buttons, pictures and diagrams that we have become so accustomed to. Clearly, the visual interactive qualities of interfaces have improved a lot, but they are still unable to generate the basic communication structures in a similarly powerful and

F. Dignum (Ed.): ACL 2003, LNAI 2922, pp. 349–363, 2004.
© Springer-Verlag Berlin Heidelberg 2004

cooperative way as we find in human-human communication. Today's commercially available systems hardly ever answer questions in a proper way, are unable to argue about particular information and rarely provide relevant or even truthful feedback in case of communication errors.

An important reason for this shortcoming is the lack of fundamental knowledge about the basic concepts and the theoretical principles that drive a conversation. The goal of this paper is to present some of these theoretical principles and a computational framework that enables us to generate elementary speech act sequences in a dialogue between an electronic assistant and a computer user. Since naive users of complex systems often do not think and communicate in terms of domain characteristics, we will concentrate on the conversational process of the understanding of the meaning of a vocabulary shared by two dialogue participants. Users of cars, for instance, often speak in terms of 'safety' or 'comfort', while domain characteristics are, for instance, expressed in terms of 'power brakes', 'presence of airbags' and 'suspension system'. In order to give meaning to the user's vocabulary, his or her vocabulary has to be translated into the domain ontology. In the framework discussed in this paper, we will try to show how parts of the translation process can be simulated in a computational dialogue framework.

In our approach, two electronic agents play a dialogue game (see also [7]) in which speech acts or 'moves' are produced to transfer relevant information with respect to a particular agreement about the meaning of the words in the vocabulary. We will distance ourselves from the idea that conversation can be modelled by a concatenation of speech acts regulated by a set of sequencing rules or a grammar (see also [14] and [9]). In line with [5], agents and their behaviour are modelled, respectively, by cognitive states in terms of various types of beliefs and the rules that generate adequate speech acts and that determine the change of the cognitive states as a result of a particular speech act.

In what follows, a dialogue game and its underlying communication model will be described that enable us to generate cooperative speech act sequences. A particular instance of the model will be chosen in which the agent that simulates the user's behaviour - the user-agent - has no access to the outside world and only receives information based on the exchange of conversational units. On the other hand, the agent that simulates the computer system - the computer-agent - may receive information by both conversational exchanges and domain observations. Describing the properties and the dynamics of the cognitive states or cognitive constructs in relation to the various dialogue contributions is an essential part of this work. In order to develop such a framework, the following questions will be addressed: What type of *cognitive constructs* should be included to model the dialogue's basic structural properties (see [17])? How do the various dialogue contributions *change* the existing cognitive constructs (see e.g. [8] and [6])? How do these changes influence the *generation* of new contributions?

2   Natural Dialogue

In its basic form, a dialogue can be conceived as a linear alternating sequence of symbolic elements between two participants [12]. The various contributions in the dialogue have a meaning and a purpose, i.e. there is a relation between the symbolic elements and particular cognitive constructs that result from the interpretation process of the dialogue contributions, and the sender intends to accomplish through them a particular effect on the cognitive state of the addressee. In general the utterances do not form independent segments of speech, but show a coherent structure of conversational units like words in a single sentence. A criterion for the acceptability of a dialogue is usually hard to give and heavily depends on its contextual characteristics such as the goals and knowledge of the dialogue participants.

In our case the main goal will be determined by an initial question asked by the user-agent. Given a limited number of belief constructs, a restricted number of initial states can be distinguished from which the dialogue may start. For instance, the user-agent by mistake assumes that the meaning of the predicate is a shared belief by both partners, but the computer-agent has no knowledge about the meaning. Or worse, both dialogue partners initially assume a different shared meaning of the predicate, but the discrepancy remains unnoticed. The latter case appears probably quite often in dialogue and may cause serious communication problems.

Before we start the description of the dialogue game, we will first discuss some examples. In all example dialogues the user-agent U asks the first question to the computer-agent C whether the predicate 'safe' is applicable to a particular car.

Dialogue 1:
U: Is it a safe car?
C: Yes, it is.
U: OK

Dialogue 2:
U: Is it a safe car?
C: Yes, it has air bags and a good crash test.
U: OK

In these two cases both participants know the term 'safe' and may believe that they have shared knowledge about its meaning, although discrepancies may exist between the two belief states. In dialogue 2, the reason for the extra information given by C may be that he is aware of possible misunderstandings and therefore the meaning of the term is verified by explicitly stating the definition in the response.

In Dialogue 3 neither of the two participants accepts the other as an expert on the meaning of the term and neither contributes extra information on which a decision may be forced, therefore the dialogue ends in an infinite loop of disagreement.

Dialogue 3:
U: Is it a safe car?
C: Yes, it has air bags and a good crash test.
U: To my opinion, a safe car also has automatic screen wipers.
C: To my opinion, a safe car does not need automatic screen wipers.
U: Well, it does.
C: No, it doesn't. ....

Clearly, the property of infinity has to be avoided in the framework. C's strategy could be, for instance, to accept temporarily the definition stated by U and drop it after the answer has been given (Dialogue 4). This implies that C has to make a distinction between his own private beliefs and his beliefs about U's private beliefs.

Dialogue 4:
U: Is it a safe car?
C: Yes, it has air bags and a good crash test.
U: To my opinion, a safe car also has automatic screen wipers.
C: It is my opinion that a safe car does not need automatic screen wipers, but this car has them, so in your terms, it would be safe.
U: OK

Agent C also has various strategies in the second turn. If a common understanding is doubted, he may simply ask for the meaning without manifesting his own interpretation.

Dialogue 5:
U: Is it a safe car?
C: What do you mean by 'safe'?
U: A safe car is a car that has air bags and a good crash test.
C: In that case, it is safe.

A problem in Dialogue 5 is that, depending on C's tenacity, U may incorrectly come to believe that U's interpretation of the term is a shared belief and the dialogue suggests that C has no interpretation. Not giving an interpretation in these cases will be considered as a violation of the Gricean quantity maxim, which roughly states: 'Say enough, but not too much' [10]. A possible solution is given in Dialogue 6 where C immediately provides the extra information after U has manifested her translation of the term:

Dialogue 6:
U: Is it a safe car?
C: What do you mean by safe?
U: To my opinion, a safe car is a car that has air bags and a good crash test.
C: Well, I think that a safe car also has automatic screen wipers.
U: I don't care whether the car has automatic screen wipers.
C: In that case, it is safe.

In Dialogue 6, C gives another cue by stressing the pronomen 'you', which already implicates that there may be other translations as well, in particular C's translation. In the framework below, we will avoid the extra turns and in case of doubt of a shared translation, C will explicitly state his translation of the term.

A rather bizarre case is given in Dialogue 7 where both participants do not know a translation of term.

Dialogue 7
U: Is it a safe car?
C: What do you mean by safe?
U: I don't know what it means.
C: In that case I cannot say whether it is a safe car.

In practice we do not expect these cases, since it implies that U does not really know what she is talking about. As we will see, however, the dialogue rules enable C to give the responses that are provided in this dialogue.

From the previous discussion we conclude that there may be four basic initial settings:

a. both agents have the same interpretation and so agree about the meaning of the term (Dialogue 1 and 2),
b. both agents have different interpretations (Dialogue 3, 4 and 6),
c. only one of the agents has an interpretation (Dialogue 5),
d. none of the agents has an interpretation (Dialogue 7).

So, in general, in response to the question "$P(c)$?" by U, where P refers to the term that has to be translated and which is applicable to the object c, C has three basic moves in the second turn:

a. C may simply answer the question (e.g. "Yes, it is", "No, it is not")
b. C may give information about his translation (e.g. "Do you mean that it has?", "No, because it has no ...")
c. C may simply ask a counter-question (e.g. "What do you mean by 'safe'?")

Note that, depending on C's knowledge state, the initial setting in b. may lead to different responses by C. For instance, suppose that C incorrectly believes that a particular interpretation is shared, then he may simply answer the question without providing extra information. As a result, a possible deviation in U's and C's interpretation will not be manifested in the dialogue. If, on the other hand, C does not believe that U shares the information, C may add extra information about his interpretation of the term. In conclusion, the content of C's turn not only depends on his knowledge about the answer to the question, but also on his knowledge about his dialogue partner.

Another important observation is that C's response in b. enables the participants to initiate an *argumentation* about the interpretation of the term, since his interpretation or a part of the interpretation is manifested in the dialogue and U may notice inconsistencies with her own interpretation. Examples were already given in Dialogue 3 and Dialogue 6. Below we will assume, however, that the computer-agent gives priority to the translation of the user-agent.

3 The Basic Model

The dialogue framework presented in this paper is based on a simple model employed in human-computer interaction [13, 1, 15]. Underlying this model is the recognition that humans interact naturally with their environment in two ways: symbolically and physically. On the one hand, if there is an intermediary interpreter, humans can interact symbolically and use language to give commands, ask for or provide information, etcetera. On the other hand, physically, one manipulates objects, for instance, by moving or fastening them, or observes them by seeing, feeling, hearing, tasting or smelling. The essential difference between the two types of interaction is that actions of the first type (e.g. illocutionary acts and their semantic content [4, 16]) need an interpreter who can bridge the gap between the symbols and their actual meaning and purpose, while actions of the second type are related in a more direct manner to human perception and action.

Domain of Discourse

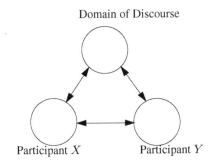

Participant X Participant Y

Fig. 1. The triangle metaphor

In parallel with the distinction symbolical vs. physical, humans engaged in dialogues can perform two types of *external* actions: a. *communicative actions* intended to cause some cognitive effect in the recipient, and b. *non-communicative* actions to observe or change particular properties of the domain. Obviously, the two types of action can be considerably interrelated (c.f. [11, 2]). In addition, we will include an action type that is neither communicative nor external, namely *inference* – i.e. the process of adjusting the cognitive states of participants solely based on their previous states. In short, the basic model includes perception, action, communication and thinking in an extremely rudimentary form.

The distinctive interaction channels are represented in the so-called triangle metaphor (Figure 1), where the corners represent the domain of discourse (or the external world) and the two participants, and the arrows the flow of information between the participants themselves and between the participants and the domain. The external actions can be expressed in terms of the flow of information between the corners of the triangle. A communicative act performed by participant X towards participant Y is a flow of information from X to Y; observation of the domain is a flow of information from the domain towards the observer and an action carried out in the domain is a flow of information from the actor to the domain. Below, the term *communication* will be used exclusively in reference to an information flow between the participants; *interaction* will be conceived in a broader sense and includes flows of information between the participants and the domain.

In practice, the communication channel between the two participants may cause messages to be delayed (as in letters) or disturbed by, for instance, noise. Also, the channel can be duplex, where both participants can speak at a time, or half-duplex, where only one participant can speak at the time. Here, we will consider the channel between the participants and between the participants and the domain of discourse as an ideal half-duplex channel, which means that no information is delayed or lost during transfer and that information can flow only in one direction at a time. Time is unimportant, but the order of communicative and non-communicative acts is important, since the acts change the cognitive states of the dialogue agents.

In the model, we clearly distinguish between the world and knowledge (or beliefs) about the world. The world is represented by a set of concrete objects (cars, clothes, buildings, . . .) that have particular characteristics (colour, weight, . . .) with a particular value (green, red, heavy, ...). Also, the objects may have particular relations between them (next, heavier, ...). The knowledge about the world is a *representation* of the objects with their characteristics and their relations. In the latter case we will also use the term *ontology*. In general, the ontology abstracts the essence of the domain of discourse and helps to catalogue and distinguish various types of objects in the domain, their properties and relationships. To indicate the subjective nature of the agents' information state, we will often use the term 'belief' instead of knowledge.

Agents may assign characteristics to certain aspects of the world that are not directly perceivable. A particular agent may find the colour red ugly, but ugliness is not a direct perceivable feature or does not even have to exist in the actual world. Red will therefore be called a *perceivable* feature, while ugliness represents a *non-perceivable* feature. We will assume that non-perceivable features are always based on or expressible in one or more perceivable features. So, ugliness may be a combination of, for instance, the features red and big.

4   A Cooperative Dialogue Game

In the dialogue game described in this paper, we will make some simplifications with respect to the model described in the previous section. Firstly, we assume that the user-agent U of the question has no access to the domain of discourse and that her partner C can observe the perceivable features whenever necessary. This implies that C is always able to answer the question whenever a translation of the term is available. Secondly, it will be assumed that both agents know the meaning of perceivable predicates; in other words, the predicates are part of the agents' shared beliefs, have the same interpretation for both agents and, consequently, the meaning of perceivable predicates is never part of the discussion. Thirdly, it will be assumed that the communication channel is ideal, i.e. the partner will always receive correctly the information sent by one of the participants. Also, observations made by C will always be in agreement with the actual state of the world.

Facts about the world will be described as one-place predicates, such as $Red(car1)$ or $Big(car2)$. It will be assumed that all facts in the world are static and perceivable. The first assumption implies that facts in the world do not change during the interaction and therefore do not become false. The second assumption implies that all facts may become part of the belief state of the computer-agent.

We will distinguish the following sets:

1. Ω, i.e. a set of perceivable features in the world common to both U and C,
2. Ψ, i.e. a set of non-perceivable features, and
3. $\Psi \leftrightarrow \Omega$, i.e. a set of translations from non-perceivable features to perceivable features.

Since non-perceivable features and their translations are subjective by their very nature, we will add the agent's cognitive state in the description. The agents' cognitive state consists of the following constructs:

-- Private information of an agent m about the domain of discourse (B_m)
-- Private information of an agent m about what the other agent believes ($B_m B_n$)

- Private information of an agent m about shared beliefs of both agents m and n ($B_m MB$)
- A pending stack that contains in order of appearance the speech acts that have to be processed.

Furthermore, we will introduce some abbreviations:

- Below we use capital letters for predicates $P, Q, R, \ldots$ and small letters for the accompanying propositions, $p, q, r, \ldots$ For instance, P applied to a particular object c, notated as $P(c)$, is abbreviated to the proposition p.
- $P(c) \leftrightarrow Q(c)$: The translation of the non-perceivable predicate P is Q, where Q is a single perceivable predicate or a conjunction of perceivable predicates. Below we will also write $p \leftrightarrow q$ in case of propositions.
- $B_m z$: The proposition or translation z is part of the private beliefs of agent m; if z is a proposition, the predicate Z can either be a perceivable predicate or a non-perceivable predicate.
- $B_m MB z$: The proposition or translation z is part of the shared beliefs of agent m; if z is a proposition, the predicate Z can either be a perceivable predicate or a non-perceivable predicate.
- $\neg \exists q B_m(p \leftrightarrow q)$: Agent m has no translation of the non-perceivable predicate P in his private belief .
- $\neg \exists q B_m MB(p \leftrightarrow q)$: Agent m has no translation of the non-perceivable predicate P in his shared belief.

Note that an agent's cognitive state not only contains propositions, but also translations, which can be considered as a special type of propositions.

We assume that the agents can reason about beliefs by Modus Ponens and that the following dependencies exist between the cognitive constructs of an agent:

$$(R1)\ B_m MB z \rightarrow B_m z\ \&\ B_m B_n z$$

Hence, if a proposition or a translation is part of the mutual belief of agent m, it is also part of the private belief and of the beliefs about the other. It is important to note that the opposite does not hold.

In R2 it is expressed that the user-agent takes over the perceivable propositions of the computer-agent.

$$(R2)\ B_m B_n p\ \&\ p \in \Omega \rightarrow B_m p,$$

provided that m denotes the user-agent.

In fact, the rule establishes particular roles in the dialogue, since the computer-agent is considered as an expert on perceivable propositions. A problem could be that the information state of the user-agent becomes inconsistent. This has to be prevented by an update function, which will not be discussed in this paper.

5   Rules of the Dialogue

Moves are fully determined by the cognitive state of the participant who performs the move and the rules that are applicable to this state. A double arrow '$\Rightarrow$' links the preconditions of the move to the move itself. The left side of the arrow is of type proposition and represents the preconditions in terms of the cognitive state of an agent; the right side is of type action and represents the generated move. We will use the expression TOP_m to indicate the speech act that is on top of the stack of agent m. The following speech acts are part of the framework.

We let m denote the performing agent and z and z' range over (negated) propositions and translations. Agent m tells that z holds: $tell(m, z)$, it asks whether z holds: $tell(m, z?)$, it tells that is does not know whether z holds: $tell(m, z*)$, it tells that z holds under condition that z' holds: $tell(m, z \mid z')$ and it tells that it stops the dialogue: $stop(m)$.

The precise meaning of the speech acts is determined by the generation and update rules given below.

We will assume that the initial question by the user-agent has been asked in the first turn. For reasons of legibility, we will describe the rules in the order of the various turns. It should be stressed, however, that the applicability of the rules depends on the preconditions of a particular move and is not determined by the turn. So, the variables m and n below may refer to the user-agent or the computer-agent.

5.1 The Second Turn

After the user-agent has asked the initial question, the computer-agent has three possibilities to continue the dialogue:

1. The computer-agent knows that a translation is shared by his partner and so gives the answer.
2. The computer-agent has a translation, but he believes that A does not share it.
3. The computer-agent has no translation.

Generation rules G1a and G1b express that if m believes that if p has previously been asked by the partner n - i.e. n's question is on top of the m's stack - and m believes that there is a shared translation of p and m does not believe the partner has a different translation and m believes p (G1a) or m believes not p (G1b), then an answer will be provided without extra information:

$$(G1a) \; TOP_m = tell(n, p?) \; \& \; \exists q B_m MB(p \leftrightarrow q) \; \& \; B_m p$$

$$\Rightarrow tell(m, p)$$

$$(G1b) \; TOP_m = tell(n, p?) \; \& \; \exists q B_m MB(p \leftrightarrow q) \; \&$$

$$B_m(\neg p) \Rightarrow tell(m, \neg p)$$

Note that we do not consider the case where m does not know the answer, since we have assumed that m was always able to find an answer to the question as long as the proposition is build up from perceivable predicates and a translation is available.

In the rules G2a and G2b, m does not believe that his partner shares the meaning of the term, but a translation is available. As a result, a conditional answer is generated and extra information about the translation is added:

$$(G2a)\ TOP_m = tell(n, p?)\ \&\ \neg\exists q(B_m MB(p \leftrightarrow q)\lor$$

$$B_m B_n(p \leftrightarrow q))\ \&\ B_m(p \leftrightarrow r)\ \&\ B_m(p)$$

$$\Rightarrow tell(m, p \mid p \leftrightarrow r)$$

$$(G2b)\ TOP_m = tell(n, p?)\ \&\ \neg\exists q(B_m MB(p \leftrightarrow q)\lor$$

$$B_m B_n(p \leftrightarrow q))\ \&\ B_m(p \leftrightarrow r)\ \&\ B_m(\neg p)$$

$$\Rightarrow tell(m, \neg p \mid p \leftrightarrow r)$$

In both rules we have added the extra precondition that m may have no belief about the belief of the other with reference to the translation $(\neg\exists q B_m B_n(p \leftrightarrow q))$. In those cases, m should give priority to n's belief (G2c and G2d; see also the fourth turn):

$$(G2c)\ TOP_m = tell(n, p?)\ \&\ B_m B_n(p \leftrightarrow q))\ \&\ B_m(q)$$

$$\Rightarrow tell(m, p \mid p \leftrightarrow q)$$

$$(G2d)\ TOP_m = tell(n, p?)\ \&\ B_m B_n(p \leftrightarrow q))\ \&\ B_m(\neg q)$$

$$\Rightarrow tell(m, \neg p \mid p \leftrightarrow q)$$

Rule G3 expresses that if no translation is available, m asks for a translation to her partner:

$$(G3)\ TOP_m = tell(n, p?)\ \&\ \neg\exists q B_m(p \leftrightarrow q)$$

$$\Rightarrow tell(m, p \leftrightarrow r?)$$

In rule G3 the question by m refers to the perceivable predicates, not the whole translation. In natural language this can be expressed by a WH-question, indicating that the variable r has to be instantiated (e.g. 'What is the translation of p?').

5.2   The Third Turn

So far we have described the rules that regulate the second turn in the dialogue. In the third turn, the response of the computer-agent is on top of the stack of the user-agent. Depending on this response and the cognitive state of the user-agent, the user-agent has four possible reactions:

4. the computer-agent's response may be accepted,
5. the response may be rejected and a translation may be provided,
6. the user-agent may indicate that he has a translation available or
7. the computer-agent may indicate that he does not have a translation.

As we already discussed, the last of these cases is rather bizarre.

In G4a and G4b, n accepts the statement by m that p or that $\neg p$ as long as there is no proof for the contrary and stops the dialogue.

$$(G4a)\ TOP_n = tell(m, p)\ \&\ \neg B_n(\neg p) \Rightarrow stop(n)$$

$$(G4b)\ TOP_n = tell(m, \neg p)\ \&\ \neg B_n(p) \Rightarrow stop(n)$$

In G4c, n accepts a translation if there is no other translation available, and therefore also accepts the truth value of p:

$$(G4c)\ TOP_n = tell(m, p \mid p \leftrightarrow q)\ \&\ \neg \exists r B_n(p \leftrightarrow r\ \&$$

$$r \neq q) \Rightarrow stop(n)$$

In G5 the translation is rejected because n has found a translation that does not correspond to his own translation. In a rejection, the agent tells the grounds for his rejection $(p \leftrightarrow r)$, so that m has knowledge about the reason of the discrepancy.

$$(G5)\ TOP_n = tell(m, p \mid p \leftrightarrow q)\ \&\ B_n(p \leftrightarrow r)$$

$$\Rightarrow tell(n, p \leftrightarrow r)$$

G6 expresses that if a question has been asked by m about the translation, n will manifest his translation if he has one.

$$(G6)\ TOP_n = tell(m, p \leftrightarrow q?)\ \&\ B_n(p \leftrightarrow q)$$

$$\Rightarrow tell(n, p \leftrightarrow q)$$

If there is no translation, the agent will say so (G7).

$$(G7)\ TOP_n = tell(m, p \leftrightarrow q?)\ \&\ \neg \exists r B_n(p \leftrightarrow r)$$

$$\Rightarrow tell(n, p \leftrightarrow q*))$$

5.3 The Fourth Turn

Depending on the cognitive state of the computer-agent, he may apply one of the previous rules, or a rule that stops the dialogue. If, for instance, the user-agent has manifested a translation and the computer-agent had no translation available, the translation will be used by m to provide an answer to the initial question. This is expressed in rules G2c and G2d.

If n has manifested that he does not know a translation, the dialogue ends, as expressed by rule G8:

$$(G8)\ TOP_m = tell(n, p \leftrightarrow q*) \Rightarrow stop(m)$$

6 The Update of Cognitive States

The update function yields a new cognitive state depending on the old state and the move just performed. To represent the consequences (or postconditions) of a particular move, we introduce '$\gg$'. The left side is of type action and represents the performed move; the right side represents the postconditions and denotes how the cognitive states should be updated. POP_m means that the top of the stack of m will be removed, $PUSH_m$ indicates that the just performed speech act has to be put on top of m's stack .

We will not be concerned with the full details of the update mechanism and assume that the cognitive states will be updated in accordance with the principles expressed in the rules R1 and R2. In the postconditions we will represent always the weakest conditions. For instance, if the shared beliefs are represented in the postcondition, the private beliefs and beliefs about the other are automatically updated in accordance with rule R1.

U1a and U1b express that a question is pushed on top of the stack of the recipient. The speech act has no further consequences for the cognitive state of the dialogue partners.

$$(U1a) \; tell(m, p?) \gg PUSH_n$$

$$(U1b) \; tell(m, p \leftrightarrow q?) \gg PUSH_n$$

U2 expresses that a proposition is simply added to the mutual beliefs of the dialogue participants and pushed on the stack of the partner:

$$(U2) \; tell(m, z) \gg B_n MBz \; \& \; B_m MBz \; \&$$

$$PUSH_n \; \& \; POP_m$$

where z denotes a (negated) proposition.

In case the statement contains a translation, the translation is added to the belief state of the partner about the other and the stack of the performer of the speech act is popped.

$$(U3) \; tell(n, p \leftrightarrow q) \gg B_m B_n(p \leftrightarrow q) \; \& \; POP_n$$

$$(U4) \; tell(m, p \mid p \leftrightarrow q) \gg PUSH_n \; \& \; B_n B_m q$$

$$(U5) \; tell(m, \neg p \mid p \leftrightarrow q) \gg PUSH_n \; \& \; B_n B_m \neg q$$

$$(U6) \; tell(n, p \leftrightarrow q*) \gg POP_n \; \& \; POP_m$$

We will now turn to an example where the computer agent C and the user-agent U play the co-operative dialogue game based on the previously introduced cognitive constructs and the generation and update rules.

In Figure 2 we have depicted the game-board, i.e. the cognitive states of C and U, the communicative acts (MOVE) that occur as a result of the dialogue rules, and, in addition, a reference to the applied update and generation rules (RULE); empty states are indicated by 'ϵ'. We have only depicted the content of a cognitive state in case of a change. We have omitted beliefs on mutual beliefs because we assume them to be initially empty and moreover, in this particular dialogue they do not change.

In this example, the computer-agent has a translation that does not correspond to the user-agent's translation. It can be observed how the various dialogue rules regulate the behaviour so that the computer-agent uses the translation of his partner to provide an answer, but does not transfer the translation to his own beliefs.

In natural language, this dialogue looks as follows:

B_C	$B_C B_U$	Stack$_C$	MOVE	B_U	$B_U B_C$	Stack$_U$	RULE
$p \leftrightarrow q_1 \wedge q_2$ $q_1, \neg q_2, q_3, \neg p$	ϵ	ϵ		$p \leftrightarrow q_1 \wedge q_3$	ϵ	ϵ	
			$tell(U, p?)$				
		$tell(U, p?)$					U1a
			$tell(C, \neg p \mid$ $p \leftrightarrow q_1 \wedge q_2)$				G2b
				$p \leftrightarrow q_1 \wedge q_3$ $\neg(q_1 \wedge q_2)$	$\neg(q_1 \wedge q_2)$	$tell(C,$ $\neg p \mid \ldots)$	U5 R2
			$tell(U, p \leftrightarrow$ $q_1 \wedge q_3)$				G5
	$p \leftrightarrow q_1 \wedge q_3$					ϵ	U3
			$tell(C, p \mid$ $p \leftrightarrow q_1 \wedge q_3)$				G2c
				$p \leftrightarrow q_1 \wedge q_3$ $\neg(q_1 \wedge q_2)$ q_1, q_3, p	$\neg(q_1 \wedge q_2)$ q_1, q_3	$tell(C,$ $p \mid \ldots)$	U4 R2
			$stop(U)$				G4c

Fig. 2. Dialogue in which there is no shared understanding of a non-perceivable predicate

U: Is this car a safe car?
C: No, it is not safe in case you mean that it has air bags and a good crash test.
U: Well, with 'safe' I mean: does it have airbags and automatic screen wipers?
C: Oh, well, in that case the car is safe.
U: Thank you.

7 Discussion

In the previous sections, we have sketched a dialogue framework that enables a computer system to generate particular feedback sequences in interaction with a user of the system. The framework is comparable to approaches in dialogue game theory (see also [7]) and consists mainly of two parts: a. a game-board that contains information about a particular state of the game (i.e. the mental states of the participants) and b. the dialogue rules that control the behavior of the participants (generation rules) and that prescribe how the game-board changes (update rules). The framework is based on an explicit modeling of mental states in terms of the beliefs of the dialogue participants and their goals. Parts of these mental states function as preconditions for the generation of feedback contributions. In this paper we have applied the dialogue game to problems that may arise as a result of conceptual disparities about a particular domain of discourse between a user-agent and a computer-agent and we have shown how the framework enables the system to generate feedback either to resolve the disparity or to accept it and respond in an adequate manner.

In the dialogue model that we presented, the computer interface is considered to be a cooperative agent. This view has important consequences for the design of the interface, because the designer has to include the mechanisms that drive a natural human dialogue. In this paper, we have tried to show a small part of the machinery needed for modeling such a dialogue. In order to behave cooperatively, the agent has to be equipped with various mental constructs so that information about a particular domain of discourse (private beliefs) and about its dialogue partner (beliefs about beliefs) can be separated. Moreover, we distinguished between beliefs about the dialogue partner in 'beliefs about the partners private beliefs' and 'beliefs about shared beliefs' (the propositions and interpretations that were already agreed on). Including these types of mental constructs enables the computer agent to adapt its feedback in a number of ways. Information that is part of the shared beliefs can be considered as presupposed and should not be stated explicitly; this can be viewed in rule $G1$, where shared information is not discussed. Beliefs by the agent about private beliefs of the user influence feedback contributions in another way. In rule $G2$, extra information is added because the computer agent has no knowledge about the beliefs of the user (c and d) or because the agent believes that the user has a distinct belief (a and b).

Evidently, the framework is still rudimentary and extensions can be developed along many different lines. One of these lines is, for instance, the use of more complex ontologies. Concepts in real life can be defined in an almost infinite number of different terms and subterms with complex interrelationships and constraints, with different degrees of certainty and relevance. Since the dialogue rules in this paper are based on the structure of the ontology, adapting the rules to the meta-properties of the ontology (e.g. structure, complexity) seems inevitable.

Another simplification is the treatment of goals. Here we have presented goals as a simple stack with the operations 'push' and 'pop'. In these simple cases, it seems that neither a planning approach (see e.g. [3]), nor a speech act grammar approach is needed (or wanted) to build coherent structures of conversation and that feedback generation can be based on the immediately preceding conversational unit. Note that in general the consequences of the speech act ask is that goals are added to the stack of the receiver and that the speech act tell deletes goals from the stack of the sender. An important shortcoming of this approach is that, once the goals are deleted, the agents 'forget' what has been discussed before, so a 'rule designer' has to be careful in popping goals from the stack. An advantage is that the framework does not suffer from the same computational complexity as in most planning approaches where agents are not only able to reason about the discourse domain in the future, but also about their own and their partner's beliefs and intentions. We do not expect, however, that nested beliefs have to be modeled beyond the third level (A believes that B believes that A believes), since they simply seem to be unnecessary to model the basic properties of a cooperative dialogue (see also [17]).

It seems that the general framework of a dialogue game, in terms of the defined mental states and the generation and update rules applicable to these states, is an interesting and fundamental framework for adequate feedback generation. The framework does not suffer from the problems that we have in speech act grammars, such as a lack of situational dependency, and those that we have in planning approaches, such as computational complexity. In the long run, a planning approach is inevitable, but it remains to be seen which dialogue phenomena have to be modeled with a planning approach and which phenomena can be modeled without planning. It seems reasonable not to include complex methods as long as we can solve the same problems in a computational more simple and, therefore, more attractive way.

References

1. R.M.C. Ahn, R.J. Beun, T. Borghuis, H.C. Bunt, and C.W.A.M. van Overveld. The DenK-architecture: A fundamental approach to user-interfaces. *Artificial Intelligence Review*, 8:431–445, 1995.
2. G. Airenti, B.G. Bara, and M. Colombetti. Failures, exploitations and deceits in communication. *Journal of Pragmatics*, 20:303–326, 1993.
3. J.F. Allen and C.R. Perrault. Analyzing intention in utterances. *Artificial Intelligence*, 15:143–178, 1980.
4. J.L. Austin. *How to do Things with Words*. Oxford University Press, Oxford, 1962.
5. R.J. Beun. On the generation of coherent dialogue: A computational approach. *Pragmatics and Cognition*, 9(1):37–68, 2001.
6. H.C. Bunt. Information dialogues as communicative action in relation to partner modelling and information processing. In Taylor et al. [18], pages 47–73.
7. L. Carlson. *Dialogue Games. An Approach to Discourse Analysis*. D. Reidel Publishing Company, Dordrecht, 1985.
8. G. Gazdar. Elements of discourse understanding. In A.K. Joshi, B.L. Webber, and I.A. Sag, editors, *Speech act assignment*. Cambridge University Press, Cambridge, 1981.
9. D.A. Good. The viability of conversational grammars. In Taylor et al. [18], pages 135–144.
10. H.P. Grice. Logic and conversation. In P. Cole and J.L. Morgan, editors, *Speech Acts. Syntax and Semantics, Vol. 11*, pages 41–58. Academic Press, New York, 1975.
11. B.J. Grosz and C.L. Sidner. Attention, intentions and the structure of discourse. *Computational Linguistics*, 12(3):175–204, 1986.
12. C.L. Hamblin. Mathematical models of dialogue. *Theoria*, 37:130–155, 1971.
13. E. Hutchins. Metaphors for interface design. In Taylor et al. [18], pages 11–28.
14. S.C. Levinson. *Pragmatics*. Cambridge University Press, Cambridge, 1983.
15. C. Rich, N. Lesh, J. Rickel, and G. Garland. A plug-in architecture for generating collaborative agent responses. In C. Castelfranchi and W. Lewis Johnson, editors, *Proceedings of the First International Joint Conference on Autonomous Agents and Multi-Agent Systems*, pages 782–789, New York, New York, 2002. ACM Press.
16. J.R. Searle. *Speech acts: An essay in the philosophy of language*. Cambridge University Press, Cambridge, 1969.
17. J.A. Taylor, J. Carletta, and C. Mellisch. Requirements for belief models in co-operative dialogue. *User Modelling and User-Adapted Interaction*, 6:23–68, 1996.
18. M.M. Taylor, F. Néel, and D.G. Bouwhuis, editors. *The structure of multimodal dialogue*, Amsterdam, 1989. Elsevier Science Publishers.

The Posit Spaces Protocol for Multi-agent Negotiation

Peter McBurney[1] and Simon Parsons[2]

[1] Department of Computer Science
University of Liverpool
Liverpool L69 7ZF UK
p.j.mcburney@csc.liv.ac.uk
[2] Department of Computer and Information Science
Brooklyn College
City University of New York
Brooklyn NY 11210 USA
parsons@sci.brooklyn.cuny.edu

Abstract. We present the syntax and an axiomatic semantics for a protocol for multi-agent negotiation, the Posit Spaces Protocol or *PSP*. This protocol enables participants in a multi-agent commercial interaction to propose, accept, modify and revoke joint commitments. Our work integrates three strands of prior research: the theory of Tuple Spaces in distributed computation; formal dialogue games from argumentation theory; and the study of commitments in multi-agent systems.

1 Introduction

Despite the success of e-commerce on the Internet, we know of no formal theory of e-commerce. In what way, if at all, does e-commerce differ from other forms of commerce? In what way, if at all, does it differ from parallel or distributed computing? In what way, if at all, do e-commerce systems differ from multi-agent systems? A theory of e-commerce should provide answers to these questions, in order to distinguish, if this is possible, e-commerce from these other activities. In other words a theory of e-commerce should describe activities we would recognize as e-commerce and should describe *all* such activities, from online auctions to complex multi-party commercial negotiations. In this paper, we outline initial steps towards such a theory, drawing on speech act theory, the philosophy of argumentation, distributed computation and the study of commitments in multi-agent systems.

The paper is structured as follows: In Section 2 we present our theory of e-commerce, and distinguish it from other forms of commerce. In Section 3, we present a list of requirements for a computational model for our theory, and review the three main antecedents of our work: Tuple Space theory as a model of distributed computation; dialogic commitment stores in formal dialogue games; and Singh's treatment of commitments in multi-agent systems. In Section 4 we present the syntax and semantics of our Posit Spaces Protocol (PSP) and give a brief example of its use. In Section 5 we compare our protocol with Tuple Space theory and with Singh's framework. Section 6 concludes the paper with a discussion of related and future work.

F. Dignum (Ed.): ACL 2003, LNAI 2922, pp. 364–382, 2004.

2   What Is e-Commerce?

Can e-commerce be distinguished from other forms of commerce? To answer this we begin by discussing commerce. In accordance with standard approaches in economics, we define a **good** as a product or service, either of which may be material or intangible. We define a **legal person** as a human person, a legally-constituted company, society or charity, or a Government agency. We define a **commercial transaction** as the exchange, between two or more legal persons, of two or more goods for one another. In the simplest such transactions, both goods are material products, as when two subsistence farmers barter their agricultural outputs, e.g., maize for cotton. In modern societies, however, most commercial transactions involve the exchange of one good for money or a money-equivalent. Initially, money comprised coins made of rare heavy metals, such as gold and silver; paper money, when it was introduced, expressed a promise by the issuer to exchange the paper for a designated amount of some rare metal upon demand. Even today, monetary equivalents such as cheques and credit card vouchers express promises to exchange them for money upon demand. In other words, we may view financial instruments from paper money onwards as encoding commitments by a legal person to undertake some future action or to bring about some future state.

Of course, all the goods in an exchange may encode such commitments, as when one currency is exchanged for another, or when a customer uses a cheque to purchase a sofa from a furniture store for later delivery; Here, the store is committing to undertake a future action – delivery of a specific sofa to the customer's home – in exchange for the customer also committing to instruct his bank, via the message on his signed cheque, to transfer money to the store's account. So what are the *goods* in this transaction? They are both promises of future actions, and one can readily see that a given customer may view particular promises more favorably than others: a sofa delivered the next day may be preferred to the very same sofa delivered in a year's time.

So what is distinctive about e-commerce? Commercial transactions executed over the Internet do not, with only a few exceptions permit the actual exchange there and then of the goods in question[1]. Accordingly, what is exchanged electronically are normally commitments of the sort just described, i.e., promises of future action by one or more persons involved in the transaction. In executing a transaction involving the exchange of such commitments, the persons involved are making utterances of the following sort:

- Buyer: *I agree to give you payment of monetary amount p, to be paid by means w, in exchange for the good g, under conditions a, b, c, . . .*
- Seller: *I agree to give you the good g in exchange for payment of monetary amount p, to be paid by means w, under conditions a, b, c, . . .*

These expressions change the world external to the electronic domain where they are uttered, and thus become true by virtue of their utterance: they are *performatives* in the terminology of speech act theory [3, 36]. Their utterance implies, as with the exchange of cheques or promises of sofa delivery, commitments to future action or achievement of some future state, namely the actual exchange between the parties of the goods to which they refer.

---

[1] The exceptions are products and services capable of digitization, such as music, medical advice, or access to networked resources.

The implied commitments of such utterances share a number of characteristics. Firstly, they are made by persons (or their electronic agents) who are, at least for the purposes of the transaction concerned, autonomous. The persons making the commitments cannot be ordered to make them or not to make them by the other parties involved in the transaction; at best, those others can attempt to *persuade* an agent to adopt a particular commitment. There is a subtle consequence of agent autonomy involved here. Since each agent is autonomous, no commitment binds an agent unless that agent first agrees to it. But, once so bound, an agent cannot normally unilaterally modify or revoke the commitment without the prior agreement of all other agents party to the original commitment; *their* autonomy requires this. Thus, the commitments are made jointly by the parties to the transaction.

Secondly, the commitments made in an electronic transaction are promises to establish or maintain a specified real-world state, as a result of executing, incurring or maintaining an action or course of action[2]. They are not commitments in the sense of the persistence of an agent's beliefs or intentions [43, p. 205], although they may reflect the existence of such internal commitments. Nor are they merely an expression of a willingness to defend a particular statement in a dialogue [14, p. 257], although again such a defense may be required in the interaction. In other words, these commitments have a semantics in the real world external to the electronic interaction in which the performative statements expressing them are uttered.

Thirdly, the external meaning is determined by the context of the interaction in which the performatives are uttered, and this context includes both the agreed rules of the interaction, such as the procedural rules of an auction, and the prior statements of the parties to the interaction. Thus, the real-world meaning of any deal achieved is potentially constructed incrementally, in the course of the negotiation, rather than existing – whether in the real-world or in the minds of the agents – prior to commencement. As the external meaning of the dialogue evolves along with it, so too may the beliefs, desires and intentions of the participants; a consumer's preferences between products, for example, may alter radically depending on how many and which alternatives the consumer believes are available [17].

In asserting that e-commerce commitments have meanings which are constructed incrementally, we are saying that the meaning of utterances may depend on the sequence of interactions which lead to them. We can view the communication and negotiation process prior to a transaction as a joint search by the participants through a space of possible deals [15], in which each party may only know at the outset its own subspace of acceptable deals. As proposed deals and responses are communicated by the parties to one another, each gains a better understanding of the overlap between its subspace and those of others. Each may also gain a better understanding of its own subspace, since the other party may propose possible deals of which it previously was not aware, and of its own preferences across the elements of this sub-space. The process of negotiation incrementally creates the space of possible deals and the subspaces of acceptable and feasible deals. This semantics is thus a semantics for the interaction itself, not merely of the statements expressed in it. It is thus analogous to the possible-

---

[2] In viewing commitments as specifying a future world-state rather than actions, we follow the treatment of [39, 41].

worlds semantics for human language dialogues studied by linguists under the name of Discourse Representation Theory [16], in which participants to a conversation jointly and incrementally construct the meaning of the utterances and of the dialogue itself.

Following these comments we now define e-commerce transactions:

> An *e-commerce transaction* is an exchange via electronic media of perfor- mative statements by two or more persons, or software agents acting on their behalf, in which commitments to achievement of future states involving the ex- change of goods with one another are expressed. The real-world meanings of these commitments are constructed jointly and incrementally by the partici- pants in the course of the electronic interaction leading to the utterance of the performatives. Their meaning will depend on the context of the exchange, including any rules governing the interaction and the prior dialogue itself.

Thus, according to this definition, the two features distinguishing e-commerce from or- dinary commerce is the use of electronic media for communications and the explicit presence of performative statements with a jointly- and incrementally-created seman- tics. Of course, any commercial transaction may involve the utterance of performatives prior to, or coincident with, the exchange of goods, but in e-commerce, under our for- mulation, this exchange of performatives is always present explicitly.

3   e-Commerce and Computation

We desire a computational model for our notion of e-commerce. We may define, in broad outline, the requirments of such a model as follows. The model must:

- Support all forms of electronic commercial transactions, including auctions, listing boards, structured negotiations, and unstructured argumentation-based interactions.
- Support multi-agent negotiations and transactions.
- Support a joint and incremental search for deals, and the joint making and changing of commitments.
- Support a notion of commitments as performatives.
- Allow for agent autonomy in the making, modifying and revoking of commitments.
- Permit spatial and temporal de-coupling of the communications between the agents involved, so as to allow for trade listing boards, market aggregators, etc.

Some of these requirements may be met by existing models and approaches, and so we begin by considering three broad strands of prior research on which we have drawn: Tuple Spaces; formal dialogue games; and models of multi-agent commitments.

3.1   Tuple Spaces

David Gelernter's theory of tuple spaces [5, 13] was proposed as a model of commu- nication between distributed computational entities[3]. This theory, and the associated

---

[3] See [27] for a review of tuple-space models.

programming language *Linda*, have formed the basis of SUN's popular *Javaspaces*[4] technology [12] and IBM's *TSpaces*[5]. The essential idea is that computational agents connected together may create named object stores, called *tuples*, which persist, even beyond the lifetimes of their creators, until explicitly deleted. In their Javaspaces manifestation, tuples may contain data, data structures, programs, objects or devices. They are stored in tuple-spaces, which are blackboard-like shared data stores, and are normally accessed by other agents by associative pattern matching. The use of shared stores means that communication between multiple agents can be spatially and temporally decoupled. There are three basic operations on tuple spaces:

– *out*, with which an agent creates a tuple with the specified contents and name in a shared space accessible to all agents in the system.
– *read*, with which an agent makes a copy of the contents of the specified tuple from the shared space to some private store.
– *in*, with which an agent makes a copy of the contents of the specified tuple from the shared space to some private store, and then deletes it from the shared space.

Tuple spaces are public-write, public-read spaces: any entity in the system may create a new tuple, and any entity may delete an existing one. A refinement of Linda, Law-Governed Linda [25], established an administrative layer which authorizes all attempts to execute *out, in* and *read* commands according to pre-defined security and privacy policies. Although this adds some security features, tuples are still entities created or modified individually, not jointly.

3.2 Dialogue Games

Because commercial deals are typically reached after a process of interaction between the agents concerned, it is appropriate to consider the interaction between them as a form of dialogue. Thus, the second strand of research we will draw on are the formal dialogue games of the philosophy of argumentation. Although studied since the time of Aristotle [2], this subject was revived by philosopher Charles Hamblin's use of dialogue games to study non-deductive reasoning [14]. These games have recently become important for the design of protocols for agent interactions, e.g. [20, 24, 30, 31]. A key concept, formalized initially by Hamblin, is that of an agent's Commitment Store, associated to each participant in an interaction [14, p. 257]. These stores keep track, through the course of a dialogue, of the dialogical commitments incurred by each agent, i.e., the claims which each agent is willing to defend if challenged by others. Commitment stores are different to tuple spaces: firstly, there is not a central store, but one for each participant; secondly, entries are made to the store as a result of specific utterances made by the associated agent [21]. All agents may see the contents of each others' stores, but only the associated agent may delete its contents, and only then if the rules of the dialogue game provide a locution enabling this. Thus, commitment stores are private-write, public-read spaces.

---

[4] See: http://java.sun.com/products/javaspaces/.
[5] See: http://www.alphaworks.ibm.com/tech/tspaces/.

3.3   Commitments

An influential treatment of agent commitments has been presented by Munindar Singh and his colleagues [39, 41, 46]. In this account, commitments are promises made by a *debtor* to a *creditor* to establish or maintain a certain world-state. Formally, a commitment c is an denoted by $c = C(P_1, P_2, \mathcal{I}, p)$ where debtor agent P_1 promises creditor agent P_2 in the context of multi-agent system $\mathcal{I}$ to achieve the world-state described by proposition p (which may include temporal references). Conditional commitments [46], where an agent promises to achieve the world-state identified in one proposition provided another proposition is true, can be notated similarly.

Singh's framework also permits meta-commitments, which are commitments about commitments, and rules or norms in the context of the interaction between the agents. Both meta-commitments and contextual rules may govern the invoking, modifying or revoking of commitments. One norm may be, for example, that a commitment is not delegated without prior agreement of the delegatee. Singh defines six primary operations on commitments, which we summarize here:

Create: This action creates a commitment, and is typically undertaken by the debtor.

Discharge: This action satisfies a commitment, and is performed by the debtor of the commitment when the final state condition of the commitment is satisfied.

Cancel: This action revokes a commitment, and may be performed by the debtor. Depending on the meta-commitments obtaining, a cancellation of one commitment may create another.

Release: This action eliminates a commitment, and may be undertaken by the creditor or arise from the context.

Delegate: This actions shifts the role of debtor to another agent within the same multi-agent system and may be performed by the old debtor or by the context. The creditor is informed of an act of delegation.

Assign: This action transfers a commitment to another creditor within the same multi-agent system, and can be performed by the old creditor or the institution. The debtor is informed of an act of assignation.

Although commitments are understood as joint promises, the formalisation of Singh does not make this explicit. In particular, the rules governing modification or revocation of commitments allow the debtor to discharge, cancel or delegate a commitment, or the creditor to assign a commitment, without the prior approval of the other parties concerned, unless these are required by the context or by any meta-commitments. Thus, the default position is unilateral amendment, discharge or revocation, with meta-commitments and the context covering special cases. In e-commerce, by contrast, the default position should be, we believe, that all parties to a commitment need to give their approval for its amendment, discharge or revocation. It is easy to imagine a debtor, for example, claiming to have discharged a prior commitment on the basis of the achievement of some world-state, and a creditor to that commitment contesting that the world-state has in fact been realized.

A second comment about Singh's framework is important, since it reveals a lack of generality. The framework is applied in [41] to an auction marketplace (the fish market of [34]), a domain where the rules of the auction (the context) treat bids as proposed commitments which are then accepted or rejected by the auctioneer at each round. Thus calls-for-bids and bids-in-response-to-a-call are made using the *Create* locution, with conditional commitments as the contents: the auctioneer promises to provide fish at a certain price if he receives money; the bidders promise to buy fish, if the price is a certain level. These statements are conditional promises, and the rules of the interaction context (the auction) turn them into commitments once certain other locutions are uttered. So, effectively the *Create* locution is being used here for proposing commitments, not for their creation, because the framework has no locution for proposing a commitment[6].

That this is possible in the fish-market domain is because the rules of the auction institution are sufficiently constraining, and because the commitments concerned can be expressed as conditional commitments, each to be undertaken upon achievement of some defined world state. However, if the commitments were to involve simultaneous achievement of different world states, or simultaneous execution of actions, by different parties, then they could not be expressed as conditional commitments. They could only be expressed as conjunctions, e.g., $c = C(P_1, P_2, \mathcal{I}, p)$ & $d = D(P_2, P_1, \mathcal{I}, q)$. If such a joint commitment were proposed inside a *Create* locution, which agent, P_1 or P_2, would utter it? Agent autonomy means neither can make commitments on behalf of the other, so neither could create it. How could it then be proposed by one agent, and how accepted or refused by the other? The problem here lies in the absence in Singh's framework of a locution with the sole effect of proposing a commitment, an action distinct from creating it.

4   Posit Spaces

We now propose a computational formalism to represent our performative theory of e-commerce, drawing on these three strands of prior research. Our formalism is intended to be general and to achieve the requirements specified at the start of Section 3.

4.1   Syntax of PSP

We suppose we have multi-agent system comprising n autonomous agents, denoted $P_1, \ldots, P_n$, each with the goal of exploring the possibility of executing an e-commerce transaction. Following [26], we call the electronic space in which they interact an *institution*; we assume that it has explicit rules of interaction, and that these become known to each participant upon entry to it. We will denote the institution under which a particular interaction is conducted by $\mathcal{I}$, and call it the *governing* institution for that interaction. An auction-space is an example of such an institution, and the rules of the auction define the rules of interaction.

We assume further there are $n + 1$ stores which the n agents in the interaction may have read-access, depending on the rules of $\mathcal{I}$. Associated to each agent P_i is a **Proposal Store**, denoted $PS(P_i)$, to which only that agent has write-access. Thus, each Proposal

---

[6] This conflation of the act of proposing a commitment with its creation, it should be noted, is contrary to the stated definition of the locution *Create*.

Store is private-write and public-read. In addition, there is a **Deal Store** to which no agent has direct write-access, but to which all may have read-access. The Deal Store will hold the commitments entered into by the participants in their interaction. We denote the Deal Store by $DS(P_1, \ldots, P_n, \mathcal{I})$, or simply DS when this causes no confusion. Depending on the rules of the institution, the Deal Store may also be partitioned, so that only particular agents have read-access to its partition elements; for example, in a multi-party negotiation, the Deal Store may be partitioned into sub-spaces to each of which only 2 parties have read-access; this would facilitate private bilateral side deals within the public space. Likewise, each agent may partition its own Proposal Store, so as to allow private read-access to sub-spaces for other particular agents[7]. For simplicity, from here on we assume that no Store is partitioned in this way.

The contents of the Proposal Stores and Deal Store are persistent entities called **posits**, which are essentially one or more proposed commitments. We denote posits by lower-case greek letters, $\alpha, \beta, \ldots$ Once such proposals are accepted, in accordance to the rules of the governing institution, they enter the Deal Store. We assume that commitments are represented in a suitable formal language, such as that of Singh mentioned above. For e-commerce domains, we assume all proposed deals involve exchanges, that is two or more joint commitments. A buyer commits to transfer money to the seller if and only if the seller agrees to transfer a certain good to the buyer. Thus, a posit α could consist of two (or more) such commitments, of the form $c = C(P_1, P_2, \mathcal{I}, p)$ & $d = D(P_2, P_1, \mathcal{I}, q)$. If the seller only agrees to supply the good upon first receiving the money, the proposition q in the second commitment may refer to a world-state where the first commitment – to achievement of proposition p – has already been fulfilled. Because we allow any notation for commitments, we do not define a specific notation for posits.

We next define a set of locutions which enable participants to create and delete posits from their own Proposal Stores.

- **PROPOSE(P_i, α)**, which creates a new posit α, with specified name and contents, in the Proposal Store $PS(P_i)$ of the speaker P_i.
- **ACCEPT($P_j, PS(P_i), \alpha$)**, which copies an existing posit α and its contents from the Proposal Store $PS(P_i)$ in which it is currently held to the Proposal Store $PS(P_j)$ of the speaker P_j.
- **DELETE(P_i, α)**, which deletes an existing posit α from the Proposal Store $PS(P_i)$ of the speaker P_i.

As mentioned, we assume the rules of the electronic institution $\mathcal{I}$ define when a proposed commitment becomes binding on the participants. In an auction with many potential buyers and one potential seller, for example, a commitment may only come into force when accepted by the seller and by one of the buyers. In a multi-party negotiation, such as the aircraft supply-chain domain of [10, Section 8.5], a commitment may require acceptance from all parties to the interaction before coming into force. We also

---

[7] One could imagine such access privileges being policed by designated support agents not themselves engaged in the e-commerce interaction, similar to the space-administration objects in [7].

assume the rules of $\mathcal{I}$ also specify which agents are required to agree before a commitment can be cancelled or modified in any way. Our model is general across any such set of defined rules, by means of the following two conditions:

- A posit α enters the Deal Store $DS(P_1, \ldots, P_n, \mathcal{I})$ when and only when the rules of the governing institution $\mathcal{I}$ have been satisfied to turn a proposed exchange of commitments into a firm agreement between the parties. Such a posit is said to have become binding, and a deal is said to have been struck.
- A posit α is deleted from the Deal Store $DS(P_1, \ldots, P_n, \mathcal{I})$ when and only when the rules of the governing institution $\mathcal{I}$ have been satisfied to permit its revocation. Such a posit is said to be revoked.

We also define two locutions allowing agents to express their desires regarding posits in the Deal Store:

- **SUGGEST_REVOKE**(P_i, α), an utterance which expresses that participant P_i desires the deletion of posit α from the Deal Store DS, and that P_i desires that other participants agree to its deletion from the Deal Store.
- **RATIFY_REVOKE**(P_j, α), an utterance which expresses that participant P_j desires the deletion of posit α from the Deal Store DS.

Because the rules governing the creation of firm agreements may not require all participants to accept a posit in order that it become a deal, we also allow participants to accede to proposals which have already become deals, with an utterance of:

- **RATIFY_DEAL**(P_j, DS, α), which copies an existing posit α and its contents from the Deal Store $DS(P_1, \ldots, P_n, \mathcal{I})$ in which it is currently held to the Proposal Store $PS(P_j)$ of the speaker P_j.

These six locutions and the two rules together comprise an interaction protocol, called the **Posit Spaces Protocol (PSP)**, which is a parsimonious formalization of the multi-agent performative theory of e-commerce of Section 2. The protocol draws from Tuple Space theory the notion of shared, persistent stores, decoupled spatially and temporally from the agents in the institution. So, for example, posits may be entered by an agent into its Proposal Space and then read at a later time by other agents, just as potential buyers may read a listing of goods for sale on a bulletin board [28]. PSP adds to Tuple Space theory the notion of private-write, public-read spaces, a concept taken from the Commitment Stores of formal dialogue games. The rules governing insertion and deletion of posits from the Deal Store are also motivated by the rules of formal dialogue games, where particular combinations of utterances may have effects on the Commitment Stores of dialogue participants. In addition, the requirements of joint creation and joint revocation imposed by the protocol rules make as default the conditions which appear as exceptions in Singh's framework.

PSP ensures the requirements arising from agent autonomy are met: No proposed commitment becomes binding until all those required to agree to it do so; and once it becomes binding, it can only be revoked with the agreement of every relevant party. In each case the specification of which agents are required is given by the rules of the governing institution. Moreover, in another reflection of agent autonomy, there is nothing in the PSP which precludes posits being entered in the Deal Store which express conflicting commitments. If agents wish to propose or accept mutually-incompatible commitments, then they are free to do so. Of course, other agents recognizing a conflict in the commitments made by a first agent may refuse to accept such posits from it, thus preventing these posits becoming binding.

4.2 Semantics of PSP

Having defined an abstract language in our theory of posit spaces, we now consider its semantics. An **axiomatic semantics** for a programming language [40] defines the pre-conditions and post-conditions for each locution. We give a formal, axiomatic semantics for the locutions of PSP in terms of the beliefs, desires, and intentions of the participating agents, in a manner similar to the modal semantics SL of the FIPA Agent Communications Language, FIPA ACL [11]. Because these pre- and post-conditions specify internal states of each agent concerned, they will generally not be verifiable by other agents involved [42]. Our semantics is specified in terms of three classes of modal operators, $\{B_i, D_i, I_i\}$, where i is an agent identifier. Other symbols have the same definitions as in Section 4.1. These classes have the following intended interpretations:

- $B_i\alpha$: "Agent i believes that α is true."
- $D_i\alpha$: "Agent i desires that α be true."
- $I_i\alpha$: "Agent i intends that α be true."

Accordingly, we can now define the six locutions of PSP in terms of these modal operators, presenting pre- and post-conditions for each instantiated locution.

- **PROPOSE**(P_i, α)
  Pre-conditions: Speaker P_i intends that each participant P_j, $j \neq i$, believe that P_i desires to transact the deal described by the commitments contained in α.

  $$(\alpha \notin DS(P_1, \dots, P_n, \mathcal{I})) \wedge (\alpha \notin PS(P_i)) \wedge (\forall j \neq i)(I_i B_j D_i \alpha).$$

  Post-conditions: Each participant P_k, $k \neq i$, believes that participant P_i intends that each participant P_j, $j \neq i$, believe that P_i desires to transact the deal described by the commitments contained in α.

  $$(\alpha \notin DS(P_1, \dots, P_n, \mathcal{I})) \wedge (\alpha \in PS(P_i)) \wedge (\forall k \neq i)(\forall j \neq i)(B_k I_i B_j D_i \alpha).$$

  Posit Stores: Posit α is added to $PS(P_i)$, the Proposal Store of speaker P_i.

- **ACCEPT**$(P_j, PS(P_i), \alpha)$
  Pre-conditions: Following an utterance of **PROPOSE**(P_i, α) by some participant P_i, Speaker P_j intends that each listener P_k, $k \neq j$, believe that P_j desires to transact the proposed deal described by the commitments contained in α.

  $$(\alpha \notin DS(P_1, \dots, P_n, \mathcal{I})) \wedge (\exists i)(\alpha \in PS(P_i)) \wedge (\alpha \notin PS(P_j)) \wedge (\forall k \neq j)(I_j B_k D_j \alpha).$$

Post-conditions: Each participant P_k, $k \neq j$, believes that participant P_j intends that each participant P_l, $l \neq j$, believe that P_j desires to transact the deal described by the commitments contained in α.

$$(\alpha \in PS(P_j)) \wedge (\forall k \neq j)(\forall l \neq j)(B_k I_j B_l D_j \alpha).$$

Posit Stores: Posit α is added to $PS(P_j)$, the Proposal Store of speaker P_j. In addition, when the particular participants or the requisite number of participants specified by the rules of the governing institution $\mathcal{I}$ have uttered this locution, the posit α is added to the Deal Store, $DS(P_1, \ldots, P_n, \mathcal{I})$.

– **DELETE**(P_i, α)
Pre-conditions: Speaker P_i intends that each participant P_j, $j \neq i$, believe that P_i no longer desires to transact the deal described by the commitments contained in α.

$$(\alpha \in PS(P_i)) \wedge (\alpha \notin DS(P_1, \ldots, P_n, \mathcal{I})) \wedge (\forall j \neq i)(I_i B_j \neg (D_i \alpha)).$$

Post-conditions: Each participant P_k, $k \neq i$, believes that participant P_i intends that each participant P_j, $j \neq i$, believe that P_i no longer desires to transact the deal described by the commitments contained in α.

$$(\alpha \notin PS(P_i)) \wedge (\alpha \notin DS(P_1, \ldots, P_n, \mathcal{I})) \wedge (\forall k \neq i)(\forall j \neq i)(B_k I_i B_j \neg (D_i \alpha)).$$

Posit Stores: Posit α is deleted from $PS(P_i)$, the Proposal Store of speaker P_i.

– **SUGGEST_REVOKE**(P_i, α)
Pre-conditions: Speaker P_i intends that each participant P_j, $j \neq i$, believe that P_i no longer desires that the commitments contained in α be fulfilled.

$$(\alpha \in DS(P_1, \ldots, P_n, \mathcal{I})) \wedge (\forall j \neq i)(I_i B_j \neg (D_i \alpha)).$$

Post-conditions: Each participant P_k, $k \neq i$, believes that participant P_i intends that each participant P_j, $j \neq i$, believe that P_i no longer desires that the commitments contained in α be fulfilled.

$$(\alpha \in DS(P_1, \ldots, P_n, \mathcal{I})) \wedge (\forall k \neq i)(\forall j \neq i)(B_k I_i B_j \neg (D_i \alpha)).$$

Posit Stores: No effect.

– **RATIFY_REVOKE**(P_j, α)
Pre-conditions: Speaker P_i has uttered a **SUGGEST_REVOKE**(P_i, α) locution, and Speaker P_j intends that each participant P_i, $i \neq j$, believe that P_j no longer desires that the commitments contained in α be fulfilled.

$$(\alpha \in DS(P_1, \ldots, P_n, \mathcal{I})) \wedge (\exists i)(\forall k \neq i)(\forall j \neq i)(B_k I_i B_j \neg (D_i \alpha)) \wedge (\forall k \neq j)(I_j B_k \neg (D_j \alpha)).$$

Post-conditions: Each participant P_k, $k \neq j$, believes that participant P_j intends that each participant P_l, $l \neq j$, believe that P_j no longer desires that the commitments contained in α be fulfilled.

$$(\forall k \neq j)(\forall l \neq j)(B_k I_j B_l \neg (D_j \alpha)).$$

Posit Stores: When the particular participants or the requisite number of participants specified by the rules of the governing institution $\mathcal{I}$ have uttered this locution, the posit α is deleted from the Deal Store, $DS(P_1, \ldots, P_n, \mathcal{I})$.

- **RATIFY_DEAL**(P_j, DS, α)
  Pre-conditions: Following the addition of posit α to the Deal Store $DS(P_1, \ldots, P_n, \mathcal{I})$, a posit which is not yet contained in the Proposal Store $PS(P_j)$ of Speaker P_j, then P_j intends that each listener P_k, $k \neq j$, believe that P_j desires to transact the deal described by the commitments contained in α.

  $(\alpha \in DS(P_1, \ldots, P_n, \mathcal{I})) \wedge (\alpha \notin PS(P_j)) \wedge (\forall k \neq j)(I_j B_k D_j \alpha)$.

  Post-conditions: Each participant P_k, $k \neq j$, believes that participant P_j intends that each participant P_l, $l \neq j$, believe that P_j desires to transact the deal described by the commitments contained in α.

  $(\alpha \in DS(P_1, \ldots, P_n, \mathcal{I})) \wedge (\alpha \in PS(P_j)) \wedge (\forall k \neq j)(\forall l \neq j)(B_k I_j B_l D_j \alpha)$.

  Posit Stores: Posit α is added to $PS(P_j)$, the Proposal Store of speaker P_j.

As mentioned above, because this axiomatic semantics is defined in terms of the mental states of the participating agents, it is not directly verifiable [42]. However, it could form the basis of a **social semantics**, in which an agent's utterances can be assessed for consistency by the other participants in the dialogue [37]. For example, if the B, D and I operators are interpreted as separate contexts in a multi-context system within each agent, as in [29], the pre- and post-conditions defined for each locution above could be tied to the internal architectures of the participating agents. While these internal structures would also not be verifiable by other agents, the consistency of utterances generated by them in any one agent could be assessed by other agents through argument and dialogue [1, 22].

In addition to an axiomatic semantics, we also considered defining an operational semantics. An **operational semantics** treats the entire multi-agent system as a single virtual machine [40]. Here, the locutions of the protocol are viewed as commands in a programming language which executes on the machine, each locution acting to alter the machine's state. Given specific internal architectures for the agents in the system (such as a BDI architecture) it would be straightforward to define an operational semantics for the locutions of PSP, in the same way as has been done for social commitments in [45], or for a multi-agent purchase negotiation protocol in [20]. Because we desire PSP to be applicable regardless of the internal architecture of the participating agents, we have not developed an operational semantics for the protocol.

4.3 Example

We present a simple example of a dialogue between agents using PSP to propose, accept and modify joint commitments. Assume three agents, labelled P_1, P_2 and P_3, are engaged in a negotiation, and agent P_1 proposes a set of commitments described in a posit α. Suppose this posit is accepted by the other two agents, and thus becomes binding.

Assume further that agent P_2 subsequently wishes to modify one of the commitments contained in α, with the modified posit denoted as β. Agent P_2 therefore suggests the revocation of α and the adoption of β. The interaction under PSP between these agents could proceed as follows. Here we have numbered the utterances in order, and indicated in italics any effects on the contents of spaces.

1: **PROPOSE**(P_1, α)
   Posit α enters $PS(P_1)$.
2: **ACCEPT**$(P_2, PS(P_1), \alpha)$
   Posit α enters $PS(P_2)$.
3: **ACCEPT**$(P_3, PS(P_1), \alpha)$
   Posit α enters $PS(P_3)$, and then also the Deal Space.
4: **SUGGEST_REVOKE**(P_2, α)
5: **PROPOSE**(P_2, β)
   Posit β enters $PS(P_2)$.
6: **RATIFY_REVOKE**(P_1, α)
7: **ACCEPT**$(P_1, PS(P_2), \beta)$
   Posit β enters $PS(P_1)$.
8: **PROPOSE**(P_3, γ)
   Posit γ enters $PS(P_3)$.
   . . .

In interactions involving proposed amendment or cancellation of binding posits, the generality of the Posit Spaces Protocol permits great representational flexibility. For instance, in this example, once the deal regarding α is struck, each agent has complete freedom regarding the order in which they utter subsequent locutions. At utterance 6, we see agent P_1 signal its acceptance for the revocation of α. However, this posit will not be revoked until agent P_3 also signals acceptance. But in utterance 8, agent P_3 has decided to propose an alternative posit, γ, instead; perhaps P_3 does not wish to revoke α until agreement has been reached on an alternative. Agents may have tactical or strategic reasons to prefer some sequences of locutions over others when modifying or revoking posits, and the flexibility of the protocol permits agents to select the most appropriate sequence according to circumstances.

5   Comparison of PSP

We now consider the relationships between PSP and Tuple Spaces, and between PSP and Singh's commitments framework.

5.1   PSP and Tuple Spaces

One could ask whether Tuple Space theory could provide a computational model for e-commerce. Indeed, it has previously been proposed for this domain [28]. How could this be achieved? Agents could use the *out* locution to propose commitments, the *read* locution to consider them, and the *in* locution to accept them. The only drawback is that, for any tuple, the tuple space has only two states: the tuple is either present or it is absent. Thus, for commitments involving actions by only two agents, this is fine: one agent proposes a commitment and another agent from a group of agents either accepts it or does not. In the electronic bulletin board of [28], for example, potential sales are proposed by sellers and potential buyers, acting individually, either accept these or do not: all transactions involve just two agents. However, many real-world transactions involve more than two autonomous entities. Home purchases in modern capitalist economies, for example, typically involve a seller, a buyer, and a financial institution providing funds to the buyer: all three entities must agree to the deal before it goes ahead. Multiple joint agreements are also characteristic of sophisticated financial products, such as exotic options where several parties may be involved, and many large corporate transactions, where the organizations involved may number in the scores or hundreds[8].

If the commitments involve promises by more than two agents, say by n agents, then there are 2^{n-1} possible outcomes to any one proposal, since every agent involved other than the proposer may accept or reject it. Since, for any given tuple, a tuple space has only 2 states, Tuple Space theory cannot express all 2^{n-1} possible outcomes, whenever $n > 2$. A clumsy alternative would be for the proposing agent to use the *out* locution $n - 1$ times, with each utterance containing almost the same tuple, the only difference being some field indicating which of the $n - 1$ other agents was to consider the tuple. In this approach, the space has 2^{n-1} possible states, and so could express the 2^{n-1} possible possible responses to the proposal. But what is to stop an agent – malevolent or badly-coded – using the *in* locution to remove from the space one or more of the tuples which are intended by the proposer for consideration by other agents. Here, the 2^{n-1} possible states of the space have more than 2^{n-1} meanings, since the absence of a tuple following its insertion into the space could mean that the designated agent accepts it, or it could just mean that another agent has deleted it. Rules permitting only the designated agent to delete a tuple, as in Law-Governed Linda, would thus be required.

Suppose that a commitment involving n agents is agreed in this way. Thus, all $n-1$ versions of the tuple have been legitimately removed from the tuple space, thereby indicating the agreement of the designated agents to the proposed commitment. Suppose, in the fullness of time, that one agent wishes to amend or revoke the commitment. How is this to be done? There is no publicly-accessible record of the commitment, since the tuple is no longer present in the shared space; so the agent would need to utter $n - 1$ *out* locutions, each with a version of a tuple which contained a proposal to amend or revoke the original commitment. Thus, for a proposed commitment which was accepted by all agents, and then revoked by all, Tuple Space theory would require $4 * (n - 1)$ utterances. To achieve the same effect, PSP, by contrast, would require one only *PROPOSE* locution, and $n - 1$ *ACCEPT* locutions, one *SUGGEST_REVOKE* and $n - 1$ *RATIFY_REVOKE* locutions, i.e., $2n$ utterances in all. If there are three or more agents, i.e., if $n > 2$, then PSP is more efficient than tuple spaces used in the way described here. Of course, a more efficient use of Tuple Spaces would be for the proposer to insert just one tuple, and for every other agent to indicate its acceptance by inserting another tuple, marked uniquely with that agent's identifier. This would require only n utterances

---

[8] In 1990, for instance, Rupert Murdoch's News Limited negotiated a debt rescheduling deal which required joint approval from 146 banks and financial institutions [6, p. 71].

to create a joint commitment. However, if agents are precluded from impersonating others, this would be equivalent to partitioning the Tuple Space into n components, one for each participant, in the same way as Proposal Spaces.

The application of Tuple Spaces to the design of an e-commerce listing board described in [28] requires agents to share their private message ports with one another to finalize a negotiation that begins in the public interaction space. PSP, through the use of partitioned Proposal and Deal Spaces and explicit rules regarding the making, modification and revocation of commitments, can ensure both privacy and compliance with the rules of the governing institution. This may be important if other agents, such as regulatory authorities, require oversight of any transactions completed.

5.2 PSP and Commitments

We also consider the relationship between PSP and the framework of Singh *et. al* for commitments, which we summarized in Section 3.3. Commitments are created when they enter the Deal Store, which occurs when they are placed inside the Proposal Stores of each agent required to indicate acceptance. This corresponds to the creation of a commitment, equivalent to the definition of Singh's *Create* locution. For the other five operations: *Discharge, Cancel, Release, Delegate* and *Assign*, PSP enables each of these via the removal and/or amendment of commitments in the Deal Store. Such actions need the agreement of all parties required under the rules of the governing institution; in e-commerce applications this would include all parties to the original commitment, and all new parties in any amended version (such as a new assignee or delegatee). In Singh's framework, by contrast, as mentioned in Section 3.3, the default position is unilateral amendment, discharge or revocation, with meta-commitments and the institutional context covering special cases.

Another difference is that PSP makes no explicit distinction between delegating, assigning or amending a commitment. These involve syntactical differences between commitments (and hence posits) with semantic consequences, and each is achievable through a succession of utterances proposing a new posit and revoking a prior one, as shown in Section 4.3. PSP also makes no distinction between discharging, cancelling and releasing a commitment, actions which involve semantic but not syntactical differences between posits in PSP. Each is achievable through revocation. The importance of such semantic distinctions will differ by Institution, by occasion (such as the dialogical context of the utterances) and by posit, and so we believe a model aimed at generality needs to abstract away from these distinctions. In any particular case, the agents engaged in an interaction will bring to bear whatever considerations they deem relevant to their decision to accept particular posits or particular revocations.

6 Conclusion

In this paper, we have defined e-commerce in a manner which distinguishes it from traditional commercial activities not mediated electronically. Our definition emphasizes the performative nature of the utterances between the participants in an electronic marketplace: these utterances express statements about future action-commitments by the participants, and become true by virtue of being uttered. Their external meaning depends on the institutional and dialogical context in which they are uttered, and is created jointly and incrementally by the participants in the course of their interaction. We then proposed a novel conceptual model for e-commerce activities, which we call Posit Spaces theory. Defining the locutions and the syntactical rules for their use in this model gave us a multi-agent interaction protocol, the Posit Spaces Protocol (PSP). In this paper we also articulated an axiomatic semantics for PSP.

PSP draws on three strands of prior research: (a) Gelernter's Tuple Spaces theory of distributed computation, from which we took the concept of spatially- and temporally-decoupled persistent data stores as a model for distributed computation; (b) the use of Commitment Stores in the formal dialogue games of philosophy; this notion provided us with private-write, public-read stores, thereby enabling commitments to be proposed and accepted, and with the motivation for rules which lead to commitments becoming binding once certain utterances are made; and (c) Singh's treatment of commitments in multi-agent systems as promises to maintain or achieve specified world states, a treatment which provided a formal framework for their representation and a defined set of operations over them.

The PSP framework meets the criteria we presented in Section 3 for a computational model of e-commerce. It is clearly sufficiently general to support all forms of electronic commercial transaction, from auctions to unstructured argumentation-based negotiations. By using shared spaces in a manner which extends Tuple Space theory, PSP permits the spatial and temporal decoupling of communications between the agents involved. It supports multi-agent interactions and, for commitments involving three or more agents, does so at least as efficiently as Tuple Space theory. Moreover, the inclusion of a specific locution for proposing commitments enables the incremental search for deals. Similarly, the incorporation of specific protocol procedures for the creation and revocation of commitments tied to the rules of the electronic institution governing the agent interaction makes explicit the permissions required for commitments to be made and unmade. Thus, the protocol supports a notion of e-commerce commitments as performatives, complementing Singh's model of multi-agent commitments. It clearly supports an incremental and joint search for deals.

In e-commerce research considerable attention has focused on design of electronic marketplaces and institutions, and some of this is formal, e.g. [18, 26, 29, 44]. However, this research typically aims to model a particular type of interaction, such as auctions or argumentation-based dialogues, and not to capture all types of electronic commercial transactions under the one formalism. The Posit Spaces model is sufficiently general to capture any type of commercial interaction. Moreover, some formal work, such as [18], appears to conflate locutions uttered in an electronic interaction with the actions in the real-world which are promised to follow subsequently. Because we treat statements in the electronic interaction as speech-act performatives, our approach does not do this.

A key feature of the Posit Space approach is the view that a multi-agent interaction which aims to achieve a commercial transaction involves the joint search through a deal space whose dimensions and contents are constructed incrementally. The only similar work in agent communications theory is by Chris Reed and colleagues [33], in which agents in an open agent system jointly agree an axiomatic semantics for the agent communications language utterances they will use to communicate. This work assumes that the agents involved all start with a common semantic space, and then together assign particular locutions to specific points in this space. Such a structure would not appear to permit an incremental construction of the semantic space itself. In contrast, Singh's *spheres of commitment* [38], assumes a shared space accessible by all agents to store the commitments they enter into, and does allow the incremental construction of joint commitments. However, this space is unstructured, unlike in our proposal, and there is no association between the creation and manipulation of commitments and specific dialogue utterances, as in PSP.

There are several directions we wish to take this work. Firstly, we aim to use the Posit Space theory to represent existing auction and argumentation protocols for electronic negotiation. This would provide a test of the practical usefulness of the model. The negotiation middleware developed by Bratu and colleagues [4], for example, would be readily represented in PSP. Secondly, we aim to develop a denotational semantics for PSP, perhaps using category theory [19], so as to gain a better understanding of the formal properties of the protocol, particularly when compared with other protocols. Thirdly, we aim to study the possible strategies for agents using the Posit Spaces Protocol, so as to provide guidance in negotiation contexts. Recent work in multi-agent systems [8, 9, 31, 32] and in argumentation theory [35] has begun to address questions of strategy in agent dialogues.

Acknowledgments

An earlier version of this paper was presented at AAMAS 2003 in Melbourne, Australia [23], and we are grateful to the anonymous referees and to the conference audience for their comments.

References

1. L. Amgoud, N. Maudet, and S. Parsons. An argumentation-based semantics for agent communications languages. In F. van Harmelen, editor, *Proceedings of the Fifteenth European Conference on Artificial Intelligence (ECAI 2002)*, Toulouse, France, 2002.

2. Aristotle. *Topics*. Clarendon Press, Oxford, UK, 1928. (W. D. Ross, Editor).

3. J. L. Austin. *How To Do Things with Words*. Oxford University Press, Oxford, UK, 1962.

4. M. Bratu, J. M. Andreoli, O. Boissier, and S. Castellani. A software infrastructure for negotiation within inter-organisational alliances. In J. Padget, D. C. Parkes, N. M. Sadeh, O. Shehory, and W. E. Walsh, editors, *Agent-Mediated Electronic Commerce IV*, Lecture Notes in Artificial Intelligence 2531, pages 161–179. Springer, Berlin, 2002.

5. N. Carriero and D. Gelernter. Linda in context. *Communications of the ACM*, 32(4):444–458, 1989.

6. N. Chenoweth. *Virtual Murdoch: Reality Wars on the Information Superhighway*. Secker and Warburg, London, UK, 2001.

7. S. Ducasse, T. Hofmann, and O. Nierstrasz. OpenSpaces: an object-oriented framework for reconfigurable coordination spaces. In A. Porto and G-C. Roman, editors, *Coordination Languages and Models*, Lecture Notes in Computer Science 1906, pages 1–19. Springer, Berlin, 2000.

8. P. E. Dunne. Prevarication in dispute protocols. In G. Sartor, editor, *Proceedings of the Ninth International Conference on AI and Law (ICAIL-03)*, pages 12–21, New York, NY, USA, 2003. ACM Press.

9. P. E. Dunne and P. McBurney. Concepts of optimal utterance in dialogue: selection and complexity. In F. Dignum, editor, *Advances in Agent Communication*, Lecture Notes in Artificial Intelligence. Springer, Berlin, Germany, 2003. *This volume*.

10. R. M. van Eijk. *Programming Languages for Agent Communications*. PhD thesis, Department of Computer Science, Utrecht University, The Netherlands, 2000.

11. FIPA. Communicative Act Library Specification. Technical Report XC00037H, Foundation for Intelligent Physical Agents, 10 August 2001.

12. E. Freeman, S. Hupfer, and K. Arnold. *JavaSpaces: Principles, Patterns and Practice*. Addison-Wesley, USA, 1999.

13. D. Gelernter. Generative communication in Linda. *ACM Transactions on Programming Languages and Systems*, 7(1):80–112, 1985.

14. C. L. Hamblin. *Fallacies*. Methuen, London, UK, 1970.

15. N. R. Jennings, P. Faratin, A. R. Lomuscio, S. Parsons, M. Wooldridge, and C. Sierra. Automated negotiation: prospects, methods and challenges. *Group Decision and Negotiation*, 10(2):199–215, 2001.

16. H. Kamp and U. Reyle. *From Discourse to Logic: Introduction to Modeltheoretic Semantics of Natural Language, Formal Logic and Discourse Representation Theory*. Kluwer, Dordrecht, The Netherlands, 1993.

17. G. L. Lilien, P. Kotler, and K. S. Moorthy. *Marketing Models*. Prentice-Hall, Englewood Cliffs, NJ, 1992.

18. N. López, M. Núñez, I. Rodríguez, and F. Rubio. A formal framework for e-barter based on microeconomic theory and process algebras. In H. Unger, T. Böhme, and A. Mikler, editors, *Innovative Internet Computing Systems (IICS-2002)*, Lecture Notes in Computer Science 2346, pages 217–228. Springer, Berlin, Germany, 2002.

19. S. Mac Lane. *Categories for the Working Mathematician*. Graduate Texts in Mathematics 5. Springer, New York, NY, USA, second edition, 1998.

20. P. McBurney, R. M. van Eijk, S. Parsons, and L. Amgoud. A dialogue-game protocol for agent purchase negotiations. *Journal of Autonomous Agents and Multi-Agent Systems*, 7(3):235–273, 2003.

21. P. McBurney and S. Parsons. Games that agents play: A formal framework for dialogues between autonomous agents. *Journal of Logic, Language and Information*, 11(3):315–334, 2002.

22. P. McBurney and S. Parsons. Engineering democracy in open agent systems. In A. Omicini, P. Petta, and J. Pitt, editors, *Engineering Societies in the Agents World (ESAW-2003)*, Lecture Notes in Artificial Intelligence, Berlin, Germany, 2003. Springer. *In press*.

23. P. McBurney and S. Parsons. Posit spaces: a performative theory of e-commerce. In M. Wooldridge J. S. Rosenschein, T. Sandholm and M. Yokoo, editors, *Proceedings of the Second International Joint Conference on Autonomous Agents and Multi-Agent Systems (AAMAS 2003)*, pages 624–631, New York City, NY, USA, 2003. ACM Press.

24. P. McBurney, S. Parsons, and M. Wooldridge. Desiderata for agent argumentation protocols. In C. Castelfranchi and W. L. Johnson, editors, *Proceedings of the First International Joint Conference on Autonomous Agents and Multi-Agent Systems (AAMAS 2002)*, pages 402–409, New York, 2002. ACM Press.

25. N. H. Minsky and J. Leichter. Law-governed Linda communication model. In P. Ciancarini, O. Nierstrasz, and A. Yonezawa, editors, *Object-based Models and Languages for Concurrent Systems*, Lecture Notes in Computer Science 924, pages 125–146. Springer, Berlin, Germany, 1995.

26. P. Noriega and C. Sierra. Towards layered dialogical agents. In J. P. Müller, M. J. Wooldridge, and N. R. Jennings, editors, *Intelligent Agents III: Proceedings of the Third ATAL Workshop*, Lecture Notes in Artificial Intelligence 1193, pages 173–188, Berlin, Germany, 1997. Springer.

27. G. A. Papadopoulos and F. Arbab. Coordination models and languages. In M. V. Zelkowitz, editor, *Advances in Computers: The Engineering of Large Systems*, volume 46. Academic Press, The Netherlands, 1998.

28. G. A. Papadopoulos and F. Arbab. Coordinating electronic commerce activities in MANI-FOLD. *Netnomics*, 2:101–116, 2000.

29. S. Parsons, C. Sierra, and N. R. Jennings. Agents that reason and negotiate by arguing. *Journal of Logic and Computation*, 8(3):261–292, 1998.

30. S. Parsons, M. Wooldridge, and L. Amgoud. An analysis of formal interagent dialogues. In C. Castelfranchi and W. L. Johnson, editors, *Proceedings of the First International Joint Conference on Autonomous Agents and Multi-Agent Systems (AAMAS 2002)*, pages 394–401, New York, 2002. ACM Press.

31. S. Parsons, M. Wooldridge, and L. Amgoud. Properties and complexity of some formal inter-agent dialogues. *Journal of Logic and Computation*, 13(3):347–376, 2002.

32. I. Rahwan, P. McBurney, and E. Sonenberg. Towards a theory of negotiation strategy (a preliminary report). In S. Parsons and P. Gmytrasiewicz, editors, *Fifth Workshop on Decision-Theoretic and Game-Theoretic Agents*, pages 73–80, Melbourne, Australia, 2003. AAMAS 2003.

33. C. Reed, T. J. Norman, and N. R. Jennings. Negotiating the semantics of agent communications languages. *Computational Intelligence*, 18(2):229–252, 2002.

34. J. A. Rodríguez, F. J. Martin, P. Noriega, P. Garcia, and C. Sierra. Towards a test-bed for trading agents in electronic auction markets. *AI Communications*, 11(1):5–19, 1998.

35. A. Rubinstein. Strategic considerations in pragmatics. In *Economics and Language: Five Essays*, pages 37–52. Cambridge University Press, Cambridge, UK, 2000.

36. J. Searle. *Speech Acts: An Essay in the Philosophy of Language*. Cambridge University Press, UK, 1969.

37. M. P. Singh. A social semantics for agent communications languages. In F. Dignum, B. Chaib-draa, and H. Weigand, editors, *Proceedings of the Workshop on Agent Communication Languages, International Joint Conference on Artificial Intelligence (IJCAI-99)*.

38. M. P. Singh. Multiagent systems as spheres of commitment. In R. Falcone and E. Conte, editors, *Proceedings of the ICMAS Workshop on Norms, Obligations, and Commitments*, Kyoto, Japan, December 1996.

39. M. P. Singh. An ontology for commitments in multiagent systems: toward a unification of normative concepts. *Artificial Intelligence and Law*, 7:97–113, 1999.

40. R. D. Tennent. *Semantics of Programming Languages*. Prentice-Hall, Hemel Hempstead, UK, 1991.

41. M. Venkatraman and M. P. Singh. Verifying compliance with commitment protocols. *Journal of Autonomous Agents and Multi-Agent Systems*, 2(3):217–236, 1999.

42. M. J. Wooldridge. Semantic issues in the verification of agent communication languages. *Journal of Autonomous Agents and Multi-Agent Systems*, 3(1):9–31, 2000.

43. M. J. Wooldridge. *Introduction to Multiagent Systems*. John Wiley and Sons, New York, NY, 2002.

44. P. R. Wurman, M. P. Wellman, and W. E. Walsh. A parametrization of the auction design space. *Games and Economic Behavior*, 35(1–2):304–338, 2001.

45. P. Yolum and M. P. Singh. Commitment machines. In J-J. Meyer and M. Tambe, editors, *Intelligent Agents VIII: Proceedings of the Eighth International Workshop on Agent Theories, Architectures, and Languages (ATAL 2001)*, Lecture Notes in Artificial Intelligence 2333, pages 235–247, Seattle, WA, USA, 2002. Springer.

46. P. Yolum and M. P. Singh. Flexible protocol specification and execution: applying event calculus planning using commitments. In C. Castelfranchi and W. L. Johnson, editors, *Proceedings of the First International Joint Conference on Autonomous Agents and Multi-Agent Systems (AAMAS 2002)*, pages 527–534, New York, 2002. ACM Press.

On Interest-Based Negotiation

Iyad Rahwan[1], Liz Sonenberg[1], and Frank P.M. Dignum[2]

[1] Department of Information Systems, University of Melbourne
Parkville, VIC 3010, Australia
i.rahwan@pgrad.unimelb.edu.au, l.sonenberg@unimelb.edu.au
http://www.dis.unimelb.edu.au/agent/
[2] Intelligent Systems Group
Institute of Information and Computing Sciences
Utrecht University
3508 TB Utrecht, The Netherlands
dignum@cs.uu.nl

Abstract. Negotiation is essential in settings where computational agents have conflicting interests and a desire to cooperate. Mechanisms in which agents exchange potential agreements according to various rules of interaction have become very popular in recent years as evident, for example, in the auction and mechanism design community. These can be seen as models of negotiation in which participants focus on their *positions*. It is argued, however, that if agents focus instead on the *interests* behind their positions, they may increase the likelihood and quality of an agreement. In order to achieve that, agents need to *argue* over each others' goals and beliefs during the process of negotiation. In this paper, we identify concepts that seem essential for supporting this type of dialogue. In particular we investigate the types of arguments agents may exchange about each others' interests, and we begin an analysis of dialogue moves involving goals.

1 Introduction

In multi-agent systems, agents often need to interact in order to fulfill their objectives or improve their performance. Therefore, agents need mechanisms that facilitate information exchange [8], coordination [9,3], collaboration [25], and so on. One type of interaction that is gaining increasing prominence in the agent community is *negotiation*. We offer the following definition of negotiation, adapted from [24]:

> *Negotiation is a form of interaction in which a group of agents, with conflicting interests and a desire to cooperate, try to come to a mutually acceptable agreement on the division of scarce resources.*

The use of the word "resources" here is to be taken in the broadest possible sense. Thus, resources can be commodities, services, time, money, etc. In short, anything that is needed to achieve something. Resources are "scarce" in the sense that competing claims over them cannot be simultaneously satisfied.

In the multi-agent systems literature, various interaction and decision mechanisms for automated negotiation have been proposed and studied. Frameworks

F. Dignum (Ed.): ACL 2003, LNAI 2922, pp. 383–401, 2004.
© Springer-Verlag Berlin Heidelberg 2004

for automated negotiation have been studied analytically using game-theoretic techniques [21, 22] as well as experimentally by programming and testing actual systems [11, 12]. These frameworks usually assume that agents have complete, pre-set and fixed utilities and preferences, as well as complete awareness of the space of possible agreements (or deals). However, such strong conditions are often not satisfied. Agents may have limited, uncertain, or false information, preventing them from making optimal decisions about the fulfillment of their individual goals. In human negotiations, acquiring and modifying preferences often takes place during the process of negotiation itself. By conducting richer forms of interaction, involving discussions over participant's interests, humans are likely to increase both the likelihood and quality of agreement [13]. Our objective is to realise a similar benefit by equipping computational agents with the ability to conduct dialogues over interests during negotiation. This paper describes our first steps towards this objective.

In this paper, we make two contributions towards automated interest-based negotiation. Firstly, we show that interest-based negotiation requires explicit representation of the relationships between agents' goals and beliefs. We present a model that captures various relationships between goals, sub-goals, super-goals and beliefs. Secondly, we describe a variety of arguments that can be presented against a particular goal and show how these arguments may influence the agent's adopted goals, and consequently its preferences over possible agreements. We introduce a set of dialogue moves that facilitate this type of interaction and demonstrate these moves through an example discourse.

The remainder of the paper is organised as follows. In the next section, we argue, in detail, for the advantages of interest-based negotiation compared to proposal-based approaches. In section 3, we discuss the different reasons that motivate an agent to adopt a particular goal, and sketch an agent model in section 4. Then, in section 5, we show a variety of attacks that can be made against the adoption of a goal. We provide a set of locutions and an example dialogue in 6. The paper concludes in section 7.

2   Positional vs. Interest-Based Negotiation

In this section, we discuss, informally, some of the disadvantages of negotiation dialogues in which participants focus on positions. We then argue for the advantages (and need) for approaches to negotiation that focus on the interests of participants. Throughout the paper, we demonstrate various points using a hypothetical dialogue between a customer (or buyer) and a booking agent (or seller)[1].

2.1   Drawbacks of Positional Negotiation

A *negotiation position* of an agent is informally defined in terms of the resource(s) that agent wants to acquire from its negotiation counterpart. For example, a

---

[1] To avoid ambiguity, we shall use "he/his" to refer to the customer and "she/her" to refer to the booking agent.

customer might approach a travel agent because he wants to hire a car, subject to budget constraints. On the other hand, an agent's *negotiation interests* reflect the underlying goals it wants to achieve using these resources. For example, the customer might need the car in order to drive from Melbourne to Sydney.

We define *positional negotiation* as a negotiation dialogue in which the dialogue between participants is focused on their negotiation positions. Examples of positional negotiations include bargaining, where participants alternately exchange of potential agreements. Auctions are another form of positional negotiation in which bids are submitted or declared according to some protocol, such as the English auction protocol (ascending price open cry) and the Vickery auction protocol (second price sealed bid).

Consider the following dialogue between the buyer **B** and seller **S**. Suppose that **B** wants to pay no more than $200 and that **S** wants to charge no less than $400.

Example 1. Positional negotiation leading to no deal.

B: *I would like to rent a car for 4 days please.*
S: *I offer you one for $400.*
B: *I reject! How about $200?*
S: *I reject!*

This dialogue ended with *no deal*. This happened because the negotiation positions of participants did not overlap, i.e., there was no agreement possible that would simultaneously satisfy the positions of both negotiators.

Let us consider a variant of the above example. Suppose, this time, that the buyer might concede and pay $300, but would be less satisfied. Suppose also that the seller could concede to $300.

Example 2. Positional negotiation leading to sub-optimal deal.

B: *I would like to rent a car for 4 days please.*
S: *I offer you one for $400.*
B: *I reject! How about $200?*
S: *I reject! How about we meet in the middle with $300?*
B: *I guess that's the best I can do! I accept!*

In this case, the negotiation ended with a *sub-optimal deal* from the points of view of both participants. This happened because each agent had to concede into a different, less satisfactory position in order to enable an agreement.

The deficiencies of positional negotiation lie mainly in the assumptions they have about agents' preferences over possible agreements. In particular, positional negotiation assumes each participant's preferences are:

1. **complete** in the sense that the negotiator is able to compare any two offers, and
2. **proper** in the sense that these preferences reflect the actual benefit the negotiator obtains by satisfying them.

However, there are many situations in which agents' preferences are incomplete and improper. Firstly, an agent's preferences may be incomplete for a number of reasons. A consumer, for example, may not have preferences over new products, or products he is not familiar with. During negotiation with potential sellers, the buyer may acquire the information necessary to establish such preferences. Secondly, an agent's preferences may be improper if they are based on false information. For example, a car buyer might prefer a VOLVO over a BMW based on false perception about the safety records of VOLVOs. Suppose that BMWs are in fact safer according to the latest accident statistics. By purchasing the VOLVO, the buyer's actual gain (in terms of safety) is not achieved.

2.2   A Solution: Interest-Based Negotiation

Consider the following alternative to the dialogues presented in examples 1 and 2. Let us assume that the seller makes as much money by renting out cars for $400 as she would make by selling Melbourne to Sydney airline tickets for $200.

Example 3. Interest-based negotiation leading to optimal deal.

B: *I would like to rent a car for 4 days please.*
S: *I offer you one for $400.*
B: *I reject! How about $200?*
S: *I reject! Why do you need the car?*
B: *Because I want to drive to Sydney to attend a conference.*
S: *You can also go to Sydney by flying there! I can book you a ticket with Qantas airlines for $200.*
B: *Great, I didn't know flights were so cheap! I accept!*

In this example, it was possible to reach an agreement that satisfies both the buyer and seller. This happened because participants discussed the underlying interests (the buyer's interests in this particular case).

The interest-based approach to negotiation is advocated extensively in the literature on human negotiation. This is illustrated in the following excerpts from the authoritative book *'Getting to Yes'* by the founders of the Harvard Program on Negotiation [13, pp. 40–42]:

> "The basic problem in a negotiation lies not in conflicting positions, but in the conflict between each side's . . . interests. Interests motivate people; . . . Your position is something you have decided upon. Your interests are what caused you to decide. . . .
> Behind opposed positions lie shared and compatible interests, as well as conflicting ones. . . . In many negotiations, however, a close examination of the underlying interests will reveal the existence of many more interests that are shared or compatible than ones that are opposed."

It is argued that by understanding the reasons behind positions, we can redefine the problem in terms of the underlying interests. By discussing these interests, we are more likely to reach a mutually acceptable agreement.

We hence informally define the *negotiation interests* of an agent as the set of motivational attitudes (e.g., desires, goals, preferences, etc.) that cause the agent to negotiate, and to take a particular negotiation position.

In addition to allowing for the reconciliation of interests, interest-based negotiation allows negotiators to exchange additional information and correct misconceptions during interaction. In other words, agents may *argue* about each other's beliefs and other mental attitudes in order to (i) *justify* their negotiation positions, and (ii) *influence* each other's negotiation positions [19]. This may be useful, for example, in consumer commerce. Current theories of consumer behaviour modelling [17] view consumer perception of products in terms of several attributes. Individual consumers vary as to which attributes they consider most relevant. Moreover, consumers' beliefs or perceptions may vary from the "true" attributes because of consumers' particular experiences and the way they gather and process information. This means that consumers may make uninformed decisions based on false or incomplete information. It also means that different consumers might choose the same product for different reasons. Consequently, consumer preferences are shaped and changed as a result of the interaction with potential sellers, and perhaps with other people of potential influence such as family members or other consumers. Game-theoretic and traditional economic mechanisms have no way to represent such interaction.

3   Reasons for Adopting a Goal

Our aim in this paper is to introduce some essential concepts needed to automate interest-based negotiation among computational agents. Since interest-based negotiation requires, by definition, some form of dialogue about agents' interests, we need to capture the dependencies between agents' goals and negotiation positions. More precisely, we need to capture the elements of the agent's decision model that cause that agent to adopt a particular goal (which may be a goal to acquire some resources through negotiating with others). Defining such goal information would then allow us to systematically examine the types of arguments that could be put, by negotiators, for and against the adoption of different goals. In this section, we discuss the elements that support the adoption of a goal. We leave the discussion about how exactly they can be attacked or defended to section 5.

The justification of a goal comes from different sources. We follow Habermas [15] to distinguish three spheres of justification: the subjective, the objective and the normative one. In the *subjective* sphere the justification of a goal comes from the fact that the agent believes that it can achieve the goal (i.e., it has a plan that it believes is achievable), and the fact that the goal is instrumental towards achieving a higher-level goal (or that the goal corresponds to an intrinsic desire [2]). In the *objective* sphere the justification comes from beliefs that justify the existence of the goal. So, the agent believes that the world is in a state that warrants the existence of this goal. Finally, justifications from the *normative* sphere come from the social position and relations of the agent. For example, a director of a company, an agent is responsible for increasing profits, and also for the well-being of his/her employees. The reason behind the adoption of these goals can be extracted from the reasons behind the adoption of the role.

3.1   Goals and Beliefs

Consumer goals are often linked to their beliefs. For example, a person with the goal of travelling to Sydney might base that on a belief that an important conference will be held there. The beliefs can be seen as the *context* in which the goal holds, and we can say that the beliefs *justify* the goal. If the context turns out to be unsatisfied, the agent would no longer have a reason to keep its goal. We denote the relation between a goal g and a (possibly empty) set of beliefs B that form its justification or context by $justify(B, g)$.

This relation between beliefs and goals is related to the notion of conditional goals as introduced by Cohen and Levesque [5]. However, the notion of justification is stronger than that of conditions for goals. The latter are only effective when a goal already exists. The goal will be dropped when the condition is no longer valid. Simplistically (but illustratively) this could be modelled as: $\neg b \implies \neg g$. Justifying beliefs, however, have a causal link to the goal to the effect that they influence the adoption of the goal. This could be modelled as: $b \implies g$.

Definition 1. Belief Justification
$justify(B, g)$ if and only if whenever B holds, the agent adopts goal g

3.2   Goals and Subgoals

Another important factor that influences the adoption of a goal is the set of resources (or subgoals) that are needed to achieve that goal. For example, in order to achieve the goal of going to Sydney, an agent might have to hire a car and sort out accommodation. If, after checking his account balance, the agent discovers he does not have sufficient funds, he might not be able to afford accommodation anymore and must drop the goal of going to Sydney unless an alternative plan is found, say by borrowing from a friend. We use $achieve(SubG, g)$ to denote the relation between a goal g and the set $SubG$ of resources (or subgoals) that need to be acquired (or achieved) in order for g to be achieved. If $SubG$ is defeated, g is no longer achievable and might be dropped.

Definition 2. Achievability
$achieve(SubG, g)$ if and only if whenever the goals in $SubG$ hold, so does g

3.3   Goals and Supergoals

Agents often adopt certain goals because they believe these help them achieve their more basic, superior goals. For example, an academic might adopt the goal of going to Sydney in order to fulfill the more fundamental goal of attending a conference. If the goal of attending the conference is dropped, its subgoal of travelling to Sydney must also be dropped. Note that the goal of going to Sydney is not assumed to be neither necessary nor sufficient, but rather only *instrumental* to achieving the supergoal (which is a weaker statement). To attend a conference, one also needs to pay the registration fee, delegate lecturing responsibilities, and so on.

We use the relation $instr(g, g')$ to capture the fact that the achievement of goal g is instrumental towards the achievement of a superior goal g'. Instrumentality means that the goal belongs to (or belongs to a sub-plan of) a plan that achieves the supergoal[2].

Definition 3. Instrumentality
$instr(g, sg)$ if and only if there is a set of goals X such that $achieve(X, sg)$ and either (1) $g \in X$; or (2) $\exists g' \in X$ such that $instr(g, g')$ (which means instr is transitive).

3.4   Goals and Roles

Finally, justification of a goal can follow from the role an agent plays. Some goals are intrinsic to certain roles and therefore performing the role is in itself a justification for adopting the goal. For example, a travel agent has an intrinsic goal of selling flights to customers.

Sometimes the justification does not follow from the role itself, but rather from the combination/relation of the role with some other roles. For example, a parent might justify behaviour (like telling the child to shut up) towards a child just by stating that he/she is the parent. The same behaviour could not be justified like that towards a partner.

We will not get into a formal definition of roles but suffice to say that roles can be defined by their goals, norms, interaction rules and relationships to other roles. We only use $RoleG(r)$ here to denote the set of intrinsic goals of the role r. See [7] for more on agents and roles.

4   Agents and Goal Support

In the previous section, we outlined the different concepts that constitute reasons for goal adoption. In this section, we provide a sketch of an agent model that uses these concepts in order to build arguments for goals. Following is the definition of an agent.

Definition 4. *We define an agent i to be a tuple:*

$$\langle KB_i, IG_i, AG_i, Cap_i, Role_i \rangle$$

where KB_i stands for the beliefs of the agent, IG_i stands for the set of intrinsic goals of the agent (it's desires), AG_i stands for the set of adopted goals of the agent (or it's intentions), Cap_i is the set of the capabilities of the agent and $Role_i$ is the role that agent i enacts.

---

[2] Note that "*instr*" relation is weaker than "*achieve*". The latter denotes a sufficient plan for fulfilling a goal, while the former denotes a (possibly partial) contribution to the goal.

We assume that an agent is introspective and therefore the knowledge base contains beliefs about it's own goals, capabilities, role and the relations between them.

Definition 5. *The* knowledge base *for agent i, denoted KB_i, consists of the following:*

1. *A minimal (possibly inconsistent) set $Bels_i$ of belief formulae defined using Bels (the set of all possible beliefs). These are called* basic beliefs *to distinguish them from other types of beliefs involving relations among beliefs and goals.*
2. *A set $IGoals_i \subseteq Goals$ of intrinsic goals the agent is aware of. (where Goals is the set of all possible goals).*
3. *A set of statements of the form $justify(B, g)$ where $B \subseteq Bels_i$ and $g \in Goals$.*
4. *A set of statements of the form $achieve(SubG, g)$ where $SubG \subseteq Goals \cup Cap$ and $g \in Goals$.*
5. *A set of statements of the form $instr(g, g')$ where $g, g' \in Goals$.*
6. *A set of statements of the form $conflict(g, g')$ that explicitly denote pairs of conflicting goals, i.e. goals that cannot be achieved simultaneously[3].*
7. *A set of statements of the form $altGoal(g', g'')$ such that g' and g'' are top level intrinsic goals (i.e. $\nexists x$ where $instr(g', x)$ or $instr(g'', x)$). g' and g'' are viable alternatives (i.e. either of them suffices).*
8. *A role $Role_i$ that the agent plays.*

We can now define the argument for adopting a particular goal as follows:

Definition 6. $H = (SuperG, r, B, SubG)$ *supports goal g, denoted as $support(H, g)$ for agent i if*

- *$SuperG$ is a set of goals such that $\forall x \in SuperG$, $instr(g, x) \in KB_i$,*
- *$g \in AG_i$,*
- *B is a set of beliefs such that $justify(B, g) \in KB_i$*
- *$SubG$ is a set of goals such that $achieve(SubG, g) \in KB_i$.*

A goal argument *is a tuple $\langle H : g \rangle$ where g is a goal and $support(H, g)$.*

Note that, contrary to an argument for a belief, the goal does not "logically" follow from the support! To make this distinction between a goal argument and a belief argument clear we shall use $\Vdash$ (rather than the logical inference relation $\vdash$) to represent the support relation. So we shall write the above relation as:

$$(SuperG, r, B, SubG) \Vdash g$$

Although roles play an important part in justifying goals in more complicated dialogues, we will not use them in this paper. First, because adequate formalisation would need more accurate formalisation of the basic social concepts involved

---

[3] Note that conflicts between goals might involve more subtle dependencies, and may not in fact be represented using an explicit relation. We therefore assume that conflicts can be detected through a separate mechanism (e.g., [23]).

like power, rights, etc. Secondly, the dialogues in which these concepts play a role are very complicated and do not occur in the simple examples explored so far. Consequently, in the remainder of this paper, we shall not consider the use of roles in goal-supporting arguments. Arguments will therefore take the form $\langle (SuperG, B, SubG) : g \rangle$.

We demonstrate the idea of goal support by discussing the adopted goals of the consumer described in section 2. The left hand side of Fig. 4 shows a sketch of the goals selected by the consumer[4]. The consumer can construct arguments for the following adopted goals.

The buyer adopts the goal of attending a conference because it is an intrinsic goal (hence does not have a supergoal), justified by the beliefs that he received a research grant and obtained his supervisor's approval, and achievable by registering for the conference and going to Sydney.

$$\langle (\{\cdot\}, \{supervisorOK, grantReceived\}, \{register, goSyd\}) : attendConf \rangle$$

In turn, the buyer adopts the goal of going to Sydney because it is instrumental towards attending a conference, and because it is achievable by hiring a car and arranging accommodation.

$$\langle (\{attendConf\}, \{\cdot\}, \{hireCar, arrangeAccomm\}) : goSyd \rangle$$

The customer can also construct an argument for the goal of arranging accommodation, which can be achieved individually through the agent's own capabilities (since $arrangeAccomm \in Cap_{buyer}$), and so does not have any subgoal.

$$\langle (\{goSyd\}, \{\cdot\}, \{\cdot\}) : arrangeAccomm \rangle$$

The agent similarly adopts the goal of hiring a car because it is instrumental for going to Sydney, and because the agent believes it is achievable through negotiation (the customer cannot achieve it on his own since $hireCar \notin Cap_{buyer}$). This argument can be expressed using the following argument:

$$\langle (\{goSyd\}, \{\cdot\}, \{negotiate\}) : hireCar \rangle$$

where goal $negotiate$ is a special type of goal which is achieved if and only if a deal with the negotiation counterpart is reached.

Conflicts among Goals

In cases of conflict, the agent must be able to choose between conflicting goals. Moreover, the agent needs to be able to choose among alternative plans towards achieving the same goal (or set of goals). The fact that two alternative plans exist for the same goal can be represented by having two statements $achieve(SubG_1, g)$ and $achieve(SubG_2, g)$. So, the agent needs a mechanism that allows it to generate, from its knowledge base, the set of goals AG that it attempts to achieve.

---

[4] This figure is only illustrative and does not represent a full formal model. The triangles informally represent the hierarchies of goals relating to the intrinsic goals at their tips (e.g., the intrinsic goal of attending a conference).

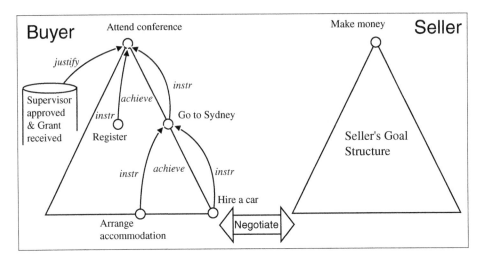

Fig. 1. An abstract view of negotiation

The details of such mechanism are outside the scope of our discussion, so we view it as a black box. However, we assume that the agent attempts to maximise its utility (given what it knows) by considering the costs of adopting different plans as well as the utilities of the goals achieved. One way such a mechanism might be realised is by using influence diagrams [16] to model the different types of support for a goal as probabilistic influences. The goal(s) selected are those that have the "strongest" support according to some appropriate criteria:

Definition 7. *A goal selection mechanism for agent i takes the agent's knowledge base KB_i and returns a set AG_i of adopted goals such that $\forall g \in AG_i, \exists H : support(H, g) \land \forall g' \notin AG_i, \forall H' : support(H', g') : H \geq H'$*

where $H \geq H'$ indicates that the support for g is stronger than the support for g'.

Now that we have defined the different supports of the agent's goals and how the networks of support for goals determine the preferred (and thus adopted) goals, we turn to the ways that the preferred goals can be changed by attacking their supports.

5 How to Attack a Goal

Recall from Fig. 4 that there are multiple components supporting each adopted goal. Agents usually begin negotiation without (or with limited) information about each others' underlying interests. As agents interact, more information about each others' goal structures is revealed. This creates an opportunity for agents to interactively influence these goal structures in order to influence their negotiation positions. Such influences are composed of a primitive set of *attacks* that an agent can exercise upon another agent's goal structure. In this section, we show the different ways in which one can attack a goal, causing it to be dropped, replaced, or even causing additional goals to be adopted.

In this section, we will concentrate on the goal arguments for going to Sydney and attending the conference only, since they are sufficient for our purpose.

$$\langle(\{attendConf\}, \{\cdot\}, \{hireCar, arrangeAccomm\}) : goSyd\rangle \tag{1}$$

$$\langle(\{\cdot\}, \{supervisorOK, grantReceived\}, \{register, goSyd\}) : attendConf\rangle \tag{2}$$

We shall refer to these goal arguments in the remainder of this section as 'goal argument 1' and 'goal argument 2'.

5.1 Attacks on Justifying Beliefs

There are a number of attacks an agent might pose on the beliefs in a goal argument of another agent. An agent might state any of the following:

1. **Attack:** $\neg b$ where $b \in B$

   An agent can attempt to disqualify a goal by attacking its context condition. This is usually an assertion of the negation followed by an argument (i.e. a tentative proof) supporting that assertion. Following our example, another agent might attempt to disqualify the goal argument 2 for attending the conference by arguing that the conference was not refereed, and so the supervisor's approval could not be obtained, written $confNotRef \vdash \neg supervisorOK$.

   Effect: This type of attack triggers an argumentation dialogue that is purely belief based, since agents argue about whether proposition b holds. An existing model such as [1] might be used to facilitate that. If the attack succeeds, then $Bels_i = Bels_i - \{b\}$ and link $justify(B, g)$ ceases to exist. Consequently, the goal must be dropped unless it has another justification.

2. **Attack:** $\neg justify(B, g)$

   An agent might attempt to attack the link between the belief and the goal. The opponent might attack the goal argument 2 by stating that getting grant money and obtaining the supervisor's approval are not sufficient to justify conference attendance, written:
   $$\neg justify(\{supervisorOK, grantReceived\}, attendConf)$$
   The justification relation between a belief and a goal is not one that can be objectively tested. Whether such argument is accepted should be therefore based on the social relations in the agent society. For example, the head of department usually has the authority to refuse such justification. It might be that the head of department also requires a paper to be accepted in the conference in order to agree that $attendConf$ is justified, written:
   $$justify(\{supervisorOK, grantReceived, paperAccepted\}, attendConf)$$

   Effect: $justify(B, g)$ is removed from KB_i, and the goal gets dropped unless it has a different justification.

3. **Attack:** $justify(B', g')$ where $B' \subseteq B$ and $conflict(g, g')$
   An agent might present another goal that is also justified by the same set
   of beliefs, where the two goals are conflicting. In our example, the opponent might argue against the goal argument 2 by stating that receiving the
   grant also justifies the goal of doing administrative work for fund allocation.
   Spending time away at a conference might conflict with these administrative
   duties.

   $$justify(\{grantReceived\}, adminWork)$$
   $$conflict(attendConf, adminWork)$$

   Note that this type of attack requires the opponent to know about what other
   goals the set of beliefs justify. This information might have been acquired
   from the other agent in an earlier stage in the dialogue, from previous encounters, or be part of the domain knowledge. It might instead be something
   that the agent can impose by using its social authority.

   Effect: The success of this attack adds $justify(B', g')$ (and $conflict(g, g')$ if
   it is not already in) to KB_i and hence requires the agent to make a decision
   about which goal is more important, g or g'. If g' is more preferred, then g
   must be dropped.

5.2 Attacks Relating to Subgoals

Similarly, an agent might attack the subgoals that are thought to achieve g. This
might be done in a number of ways:

1. **Attack:** $\neg p$ where $p \in SubG$:
   The opponent attacks an element of the subgoals by arguing that it is unachievable. This might be because the associated resources are not available
   or that there are no successful plans for achieving the subgoal. In our example, the opponent might attempt to disqualify goal argument 1 by arguing
   that the agent cannot arrange accommodation due to lack of funding.

   Effect: Attacking subgoals means that the achievability is undermined. As
   long as some subgoals remain, which together can achieve the goal, it is still
   potentially adopted. So to defend against this attack, the agent is required
   to provide an alternative plan for achieving p, or else drop the goal[5]. If all of
   these plans were defeated eventually, the goal must be dropped. This would
   cause all $achieve(X, p)$ statements to be removed from KB_i.

2. **Attack:** $\neg achieve(SubG, g)$
   Here, the opponent attacks the relation between the subgoals and the goal
   in question. In our example, the opponent might attack goal argument 1 by
   arguing that hiring a car and arranging accommodation are not sufficient
   for going to Sydney (say one must also sort out insurance).

---

[5] Note that even in the case where an alternative plan is found, the preference can be
weakened, and therefore an alternative goal might become preferred.

Effect: $achieve(SubG, g)$ is removed from the knowledge base. If no alternative plan is found, the goal must be dropped.

3. **Attack:** $achieve(P, g')$ where $P \subseteq SubG$ and $g'' \in IG \cup AG \wedge conflict(g', g'')$
   In this case, the opponent argues that by executing (part of) the support, another adopted goal becomes unachievable. The opponent might argue that by hiring a car, the agent would spend too much money and would no longer be able to, say, buy the proceedings. If buying the proceedings is a goal of the opponent, then there is conflict.

   Effect: $achieve(P, g')$ is added to KB_i. This attack again triggers a comparison between the conflicting goals and the more preferred would be chosen. Another possibility is to find an alternative plan that does not clash with the other goal, formally, $SubG'$ such that $P \not\subseteq SubG'$ and $achieve(SubG', g)$.

5.3   Attacks Relating to Supergoals

These attacks can be as follows:

1. **Attack:** $\neg instr(g, g')$ where $g' \in SuperG$:
   A goal argument might be attacked by arguing against the instrumentality link between it and the supergoals. In our example, the opponent might argue against going to Sydney (i.e., against argument 1) by stating that going to Sydney is in fact not instrumental to attending the conference, written

   $\neg instr(goSyd, attendConf)$

   Effect: In defense, the agent might either present a plan P where $g \in P$ and $achieve(P, g')$, i.e. to show a plan involving this goal that achieves the supergoal. Otherwise, if authority does not suffice to win, the agent must remove $instr(g, g')$ from KB_i, which might weaken the goal and cause it to be dropped.

2. **Attack:** Show set of goals P such that $achieve(P, g')$ where $g' \in SuperG$ and $g \notin P$:
   Here, we show an alternative plan which achieves the supergoal but does not include g. In the example, the opponent might say that going to Perth (instead of Sydney) is also instrumental towards attending a conference, written

   $achieve(\{register, goPerth\}, attendConf)$

   This, again, attacks the goal argument 1 for going to Sydney.

   Effect: $achieve(P, g')$ is added to KB_i. The agent compares the plan P with the existing plan for achieving g', and based on the outcome of this comparison, g might be dropped (with the whole plan to which it belongs).

6   Dialogues about Goals

As discussed above, while beliefs are supported by sets of other beliefs, goals are supported by different elements. An important consequence of this difference is that the dialogue games also get more complicated. When arguing about beliefs the arguments are more or less symmetric. Both agents can attack and defend their beliefs by putting forth other beliefs, which in their turn can be attacked in the same way. This leads to a kind of recursive definition of dialogue games, which is always terminated at the level of the knowledge bases of the agents. In the case of dialogues over goals, this does not always hold. However, some similarities arise within the different types of justifications. The existence of a goal can be justified by the existence of another (super)goal. The same attacks can be made to the supergoal as were tried on the original goal. In this way one might traverse the whole tree of goals upwards until an intrinsic goal of the agent is reached. The same can be done downwards for tracing subgoals. On the other hand, when beliefs that justify a goal are attacked one might get into a "classical" argumentation dialogue over those beliefs. What remains different, however, are the possible ways an agent can defend itself against an attack. Studying the intricate details of such complex dialogues is outside the scope of this paper. However, in this section, we begin a discussion of the locutions required to capture interest-based negotiation dialogue, and provide an example dialogue as a proof of concept.

6.1   Locutions and Dialogue Rules

We now define a number of locutions that agents can use in the dialogue. Due to space limitations, we do not provide a complete account of these locutions and the rules that govern them. Instead, we present each locution with an informal description of its meaning. We also do not include locutions that are less relevant, such as those used in opening, closing and withdrawing from the dialogue.

1. REQUEST(G) The agent explicitly requests another agent to achieve a set of goals G. The goals might denote actions to be performed or resources to be provided. This locution can be followed by acceptance, rejection or request of the support elements of g. It also can be followed by a proposal for an exchange.
2. PROPOSE(G_1, G_2) is a locution that allows an agent to propose an exchange of goal achievements. The speaker proposes to take on the achievement of goals in G_1 for the counterpart in exchange for the counterpart achieving G_2.
3. ASSERT(B) The agent asserts a set of beliefs B which might be either propositional belief formulae or relational statements such as *justify*(.), *achieve*(.) and so on. The agent must believe the statement uttered. The other agent can respond with ACCEPT(B), ASSERT$(\neg b)$ or with CHALLENGE(b), where $b \in B$. In the case of attacks on relational statements, the other agent's response depends on the different methods of attack as described in section 5. For example, the opponent can provide an alternative plan for achieving a goal to the counterpart only if the counterpart has previously denoted that it adopts that goal.

4. REJECT(X) where X denotes either a set of goals G or a pair of goal sets (G_1, G_2). This allows an agent to reject a request or a proposal previously made by the counterpart.

5. ACCEPT(X), where X denotes either a set of goals G or a pair of goal sets (G_1, G_2) or a set of beliefs B. This allows an agent to accept requests, proposals, or assertions previously made by the counterpart.

6. CHALLENGE(b) One party may not agree with an assertion made by another party. By uttering this locution, an agent asks another for the reasons behind making a belief assertion b. This must be followed by an assertion of a (possibly empty) set of beliefs H denoting b's support such that $H \vdash b$. In case b is a relational statement (which we assume for the moment not to have a justification itself) or is a basic belief it can only be answered by asserting social authority.

7. REQ-JUST(g) allows one agent to ask for the justification of a goal proposed by another agent. This must be followed by an assertion involving a $justify(B, g)$ statement.

8. REQ-ACHIEVE(g) allows one agent to ask another about how it believes it can achieve the goal g. This must be followed by an assertion involving an $achieve(G, g)$ statement.

9. REQ-PURPOSE(g) allows an agent to ask for what supergoal (if any) the goal g is thought to be instrumental towards. This must be followed by an assertion involving an $instr(g, g')$ statement.

10. PASS allows an agent to pass a turn by saying nothing.

The inclusion of the PASS locution makes it possible to avoid strict turn taking in the dialogue. Especially after a rejection, a party may wish to continue to ask for the reasons or supports of a proposal.

6.2 An Example

In this subsection, we present a more complex example which involves using some of the above locutions. This demonstrates how they may be used to capture interest-based negotiation dialogues.

Example 4. Consider the following extended dialogue between a customer B and a booking agent S based on the dialogue presented in section 2:

1. B: REQUEST($\{hireCar\}$)
2. S: PROPOSE($\{hireCar\}, \{pay\$400\}$)
3. B: REJECT($\{hireCar\}, \{pay\$400\}$)
4. S: PASS
5. B: PROPOSE($\{hireCar\}, \{pay\$200\}$)
6. S: REJECT($\{hireCar\}, \{pay\$200\}$)
7. B: PASS
8. S: REQ-PURPOSE($hireCar$)
9. B: ASSERT($instr(hireCar, goSyd)$)
10. S: ASSERT($instr(flyQantas, goSyd)$)
11. B: ACCEPT($instr(flyQantas, goSyd)$)

12. S: PROPOSE($\{flyQantas\}, \{pay\$200\}$)
13. B: ACCEPT($\{flyQantas\}, \{pay\$200\}$)

After the exchange of two rejected offers by the buyer and seller, the seller asks the buyer for the supergoal that motivates the need for hiring a car. The buyer asserts that he wants the car in order to travel to Sydney. The seller provides an alternative means for travelling to Sydney via flight and offers a cheaper alternative based on that. A deal was facilitated that would not have been possible without arguing about the supergoal.

Example 5. An alternative strategy the seller could adopt after locution 9 would be to challenge the adoption of the supergoal *goSyd* itself, then ask for the justification of the intrinsic goal.

10. S: REQ-PURPOSE($goSyd$)
11. B: ASSERT($instr(goSyd, attendConf)$)
12. S: REQ-JUST($attendConf$)
13. B: ASSERT($justify(\{supervisorOK, grantReceived\}, attendConf)$)
14. S: ASSERT($holidaySeason$)
15. B: ACCEPT($holidaySeason$)
16. S: ASSERT($justify(holidaySeason, goHawaii)$)
17. B: PASS
18. S: PROPOSE($\{goHawaii\}, \{pay\$600\}$)
19. etc...

Here, the seller asks for the belief that justifies the supergoal *attendConf*. She finds out that the buyer bases this on the belief that he obtained supervisor approval and received a grant. The seller does not know much about academic processes, and so it is difficult for her to argue about them. So the seller chooses a different route, stating that the fact that it is a holiday season justifies travelling to an even further destination to Hawaii. The seller then makes an offer for a ticket to Hawaii in exchange of $600. Now, if the buyer agrees on all these statements and finds the justification for going to Hawaii stronger than that for attending the conference, he might consider changing his plans, and the seller would make more money.

7   Conclusions and Related Work

In this paper, we sought to work with negotiation scenarios in which agent preferences are not predetermined or fixed. We argued that since preferences are adopted to pursue particular goals, one agent might influence another agent's preferences by discussing the underlying motivations for adopting the associated goals. We described key concepts that support the selection of a particular goal and used it to show various ways in which goal selection might be attacked. We then presented a set of dialogue moves to support this type of interaction and demonstrated an example discourse that makes use of them.

Throughout the paper, we presented scenarios between buyers and sellers. However, we believe our framework would also be applicable to a wide range of distributive bargaining problems, such as resource allocation and labour union negotiations. We also believe our framework can be extended to deal with more than two agents.

It is important to note that in situations where agents are familiar with the domain and have complete and fixed utilities, there is less incentive to share the underlying reasons behind their choices. In fact, it may be that hiding information (or the true valuation of outcomes) from the opponent can give the agent an advantage. This is often the case in auctions, for example. Our work, on the other hand, concentrates on situations where the agents' limited knowledge of the domain and each other makes it essential for them to be, in a sense, cooperative. In other words, there appears to be some kind of tension between the willingness to provide information about the underlying motives (which can potentially help improve the outcome), and the tendency to hide such information for strategic reasons. We take the position that in some settings where agents have incomplete information, sharing the available information may be more beneficial than hiding it.

One related body of work is that on merging plans belonging to multiple individual agents [14, 10, 6] and resolving potential conflicts between these plans [4]. These models assume that agents are *cooperative* in the sense that they delegate the process of producing a merged plan to a trusted external mechanism, namely the plan merging algorithm. This means that individual agents cannot influence the resulting joint plan through *strategic* interaction. Our work can be seen as a *competitive* version of plan merging in which the plan merging algorithm *emerges* as a result of the negotiation strategies of different participants.

Much work remains to be done. Due to space limitations, the framework presented in this paper is a bit sketchy. To complete the picture, we need to specify argument comparison mechanisms, a complete specification of dialogue locutions, etc. We also intend to explore the different strategies that an agent can adopt in an interest-based negotiation dialogue (See [18] for a preliminary discussion of negotiation dialogue strategies). For example, one agent might prefer to explore the instrumentality of a goal, while another might attempt to argue about its achievability. Another important question is how strategy selection can be guided by the agent's beliefs about the opponent or the domain. For example, an agent that has a strong belief that a certain goal cannot be achieved would rather attack the subgoals instead of the supergoals.

Acknowledgments

Iyad Rahwan is partially supported by a Ph.D. top-up scholarship from CMIS, CSIRO. The authors acknowledge the support of a University of Melbourne International Collaborative Research Grant in the development of this work. A preliminary version of this paper appeared in [20]. The first author is very grateful for motivating discussions with Peter McBurney.

References

1. L. Amgoud and C. Cayrol. A reasoning model based on the production of acceptable arguments. *Annals of Mathematics and Artificial Intelligence*, 34(1–3):197–215, 2002.
2. M. E. Bratman. *Intentions, Plans, and Practical Reason*. Harvard University Press, Cambridge MA, USA, 1987.
3. P. Busetta, M. Merzi, S. Rossi, and F. Legras. Intra-role coordination using group communication: A preliminary report. In F. Dignum, editor, *Advances in Agent Communication*, LNAI, page in this volume. Springer Verlag.
4. B. J. Clement and E. H. Durfee. Identifying and resolving conflicts among agents with hierarchical plans. In *AAAI Workshop on Negotiation: Settling Conflicts and Identifying Opportunities*, number WS-99-12 in Technical Report, pages 6–11. AAAI Press, 1999.
5. P. Cohen and H. Levesque. Intention is choice with commitment. *Artificial Intelligence*, 42:213–261, 1990.
6. J. S. Cox and E. Durfee. Discovering and exploiting synergy between hierarchical planning agents. In J. Rosenschein, T. Sandholm, M. Wooldridge, and M. Yokoo, editors, *Proceedings of the 2nd International Joint Conference on Autonomous Agents and Multiagent Systems (AAMAS-2003)*, pages 281–288. ACM Press, 2003.
7. M. Dastani, V. Dignum, and F. Dignum. Organizations and normative agents. In *Proceedings of 1st EurAsia conference on advances in ICT*, Berlin, Germany, 2002. Springer Verlag.
8. F. de Boer, R. M. van Eijk, W. van der Hoek, and J.-J. Meyer. A fully abstract model for the exchange of information in multi-agent systems. *Theoretical Computer Science*, 290(3):1753–1773, 2003.
9. E. H. Durfee. Practically coordinating. *Artificial Intelligence Magazine*, 20(1):99–116, Spring 1999.
10. E. Ephrati and J. Rosenschein. Divide and conquer in multiagent planning. In *Proceedings of the 12th National Conference on Artificial Intelligence*, pages 375–380. AAAI Press, 1994.
11. P. Faratin. *Automated Service Negotiation Between Autonomous Computational Agents*. PhD thesis, University of London, Queen Mary and Westfield College, Department of Electronic Engineering, 2000.
12. S. Fatima, M. Wooldridge, and N. R. Jennings. Multi-issue negotiation under time constraints. In C. Castelfranchi and L. Johnson, editors, *Proceedings of the 1st International Joint Conference on Autonomous Agents and Multiagent Systems (AAMAS-2002)*, pages 143–150, New York, USA, 2002. ACM Press.
13. R. Fisher, W. Ury, and B. Patton. *Getting to Yes: Negotiating Agreement Without Giving In*. Penguin Books, New York, USA, second edition, 1991.
14. M. Georgeff. Communication and interaction in multiagent planning. In M. R. Genesereth, editor, *Proceedings of the 3rd National Conference on Artificial Intelligence*, pages 125–129. AAAI Press, 1983.
15. J. Habermas. *The Theory of Communicative Action, Volume 1 : Reason and the Rationalization of Society*. Beacon Press, Boston MA, USA, 1984.
16. F. V. Jensen. *Bayesian Networks and Decision Graphs*. Springer Verlag, New York, USA, 2001.
17. G. L. Lilien, P. Kotler, and S. K. Moorthy. *Marketing Models*. Prentice-Hall Press, USA, 1992.

18. I. Rahwan, P. McBurney, and L. Sonenberg. Towards a theory of negotiation strategy (a preliminary report). In S. Parsons and P. Gmytrasiewicz, editors, *Proceedings of the 5th Workshop on Game Theoretic and Decision Theoretic Agents (GTDT-2003)*, 2003.

19. I. Rahwan, S. D. Ramchurn, N. R. Jennings, P. McBurney, S. Parsons, and L. Sonenberg. Argumentation based negotiation. *Knowledge Engineering Review*, (to appear), 2004.

20. I. Rahwan, L. Sonenberg, and F. Dignum. Towards interest-based negotiation. In J. Rosenschein, T. Sandholm, M. Wooldridge, and M. Yokoo, editors, *Proceedings of the 2nd International Joint Conference on Autonomous Agents and Multiagent Systems (AAMAS-2003)*, pages 773–780. ACM Press, 2003.

21. J. Rosenschein and G. Zlotkin. *Rules of Encounter: Designing Conventions for Automated Negotiation among Computers*. MIT Press, Cambridge MA, USA, 1994.

22. T. Sandholm. eMediator: A next generation electronic commerce server. *Computational Intelligence, Special issue on Agent Technology for Electronic Commerce*, 18(4):656–676, 2002.

23. J. Thangarajah, L. Padghgam, and M. Winikoff. Detecting and avoiding interference between goals in intelligent agents. In G. Gottlob and T. Walsh, editors, *Proceedings of the International Joint Conference on Artificial Intelligence (IJCAI 2003)*. Academic Press, 2003.

24. D. N. Walton and E. C. W. Krabbe. *Commitment in Dialogue: Basic Concepts of Interpersonal Reasoning*. SUNY Press, Albany NY, USA, 1995.

25. J. Yen, X. Fan, and R. Volz. Proactive communications in agent teamwork. In F. Dignum, editor, *Advances in Agent Communication*, LNAI, page in this volume. Springer Verlag.

Author Index

Lecture Notes in Artificial Intelligence (LNAI)

Vol. 2715: T. Bilgiç, B. De Baets, O. Kaynak (Eds.), Fuzzy Sets and Systems – IFSA 2003. Proceedings, 2003. XV, 735 pages. 2003.

Vol. 2718: P. W. H. Chung, C. Hinde, M. Ali (Eds.), Developments in Applied Artificial Intelligence. Proceedings, 2003. XIV, 817 pages. 2003.

Vol. 2721: N.J. Mamede, J. Baptista, I. Trancoso, M. das Graças Volpe Nunes (Eds.), Computational Processing of the Portuguese Language. Proceedings, 2003. XIV, 268 pages. 2003.

Vol. 2734: P. Perner, A. Rosenfeld (Eds.), Machine Learning and Data Mining in Pattern Recognition. Proceedings, 2003. XII, 440 pages. 2003.

Vol. 2741: F. Baader (Ed.), Automated Deduction – CADE-19. Proceedings, 2003. XII, 503 pages. 2003.

Vol. 2744: V. Mařík, D. McFarlane, P. Valckenaers (Eds.), Holonic and Multi-Agent Systems for Manufacturing. Proceedings, 2003. XI, 322 pages. 2003.

Vol. 2746: A. de Moor, W. Lex, B. Ganter (Eds.), Conceptual Structures for Knowledge Creation and Communication. Proceedings, 2003. XI, 405 pages. 2003.

Vol. 2752: G.A. Kaminka, P.U. Lima, R. Rojas (Eds.), RoboCup 2002: Robot Soccer World Cup VI. XVI, 498 pages. 2003.

Vol. 2773: V. Palade, R.J. Howlett, L. Jain (Eds.), Knowledge-Based Intelligent Information and Engineering Systems. Proceedings, Part I, 2003. LI, 1473 pages. 2003.

Vol. 2774: V. Palade, R.J. Howlett, L. Jain (Eds.), Knowledge-Based Intelligent Information and Engineering Systems. Proceedings, Part II, 2003. LI, 1443 pages. 2003.

Vol. 2777: B. Schölkopf, M.K. Warmuth (Eds.), Learning Theory and Kernel Machines. Proceedings, 2003. XIV, 746 pages. 2003.

Vol. 2780: M. Dojat, E. Keravnou, P. Barahona (Eds.), Artificial Intelligence in Medicine. Proceedings, 2003. XIII, 388 pages. 2003.

Vol. 2782: M. Klusch, A. Omicini, S. Ossowski, H. Laamanen (Eds.), Cooperative Information Agents VII. Proceedings, 2003. XI, 345 pages. 2003.

Vol. 2792: T. Rist, R. Aylett, D. Ballin, J. Rickel (Eds.), Intelligent Virtual Agents. Proceedings, 2003. XV, 364 pages. 2003.

Vol. 2796: M. Cialdea Mayer, F. Pirri (Eds.), Automated Reasoning with Analytic Tableaux and Related Methods. Proceedings, 2003. X, 271 pages. 2003.

Vol. 2797: O.R. Zaïane, S.J. Simoff, C. Djeraba (Eds.), Mining Multimedia and Complex Data. Proceedings, 2002. XII, 281 pages. 2003.

Vol. 2801: W. Banzhaf, T. Christaller, P. Dittrich, J.T. Kim, J. Ziegler (Eds.), Advances in Artificial Life. Proceedings, 2003. XVI, 905 pages. 2003.

Vol. 2807: V. Matoušek, P. Mautner (Eds.), Text, Speech and Dialogue. Proceedings, 2003. XIII, 426 pages. 2003.

Vol. 2821: A. Günter, R. Kruse, B. Neumann (Eds.), KI 2003: Advances in Artificial Intelligence. Proceedings, 2003. XII, 662 pages. 2003.

Vol. 2829: A. Cappelli, F. Turini (Eds.), AI*IA 2003: Advances in Artificial Intelligence. Proceedings, 2003. XIV, 552 pages. 2003.

Vol. 2831: M. Schillo, M. Klusch, J. Müller, H. Tianfield (Eds.), Multiagent System Technologies. Proceedings, 2003. X, 229 pages. 2003.

Vol. 2835: T. Horváth, A. Yamamoto (Eds.), Inductive Logic Programming. Proceedings, 2003. X, 401 pages. 2003.

Vol. 2837: N. Lavrač, D. Gamberger, H. Blockeel, L. Todorovski (Eds.), Machine Learning: ECML 2003. Proceedings, 2003. XVI. 504 pages. 2003.

Vol. 2838: N. Lavrač, D. Gamberger, L. Todorovski, H. Blockeel (Eds.), Knowledge Discovery in Databases: PKDD 2003. Proceedings, 2003. XVI. 508 pages. 2003.

Vol. 2842: R. Gavaldà, K.P. Jantke, E. Takimoto (Eds.), Algorithmic Learning Theory. Proceedings, 2003. XI, 313 pages. 2003.

Vol. 2843: G. Grieser, Y. Tanaka, A. Yamamoto (Eds.), Discovery Science. Proceedings, 2003. XII, 504 pages. 2003.

Vol. 2850: M.Y. Vardi, A. Voronkov (Eds.), Logic for Programming, Artificial Intelligence, and Reasoning. Proceedings, 2003. XIII, 437 pages. 2003.

Vol. 2854: J. Hoffmann, Utilizing Problem Structure in Planning. XIII, 251 pages. 2003.

Vol. 2871: N. Zhong, Z.W. Raś, S. Tsumoto, E. Suzuki (Eds.), Foundations of Intelligent Systems. Proceedings, 2003. XV, 697 pages. 2003.

Vol. 2873: J. Lawry, J. Shanahan, A. Ralescu (Eds.), Modelling with Words. XIII, 229 pages. 2003.

Vol. 2882: D. Veit, Matchmaking in Electronic Markets. XV, 180 pages. 2003.

Vol. 2891: J. Lee, M. Barley (Eds.), Intelligent Agents and Multi-Agent Systems. Proceedings, 2003. X, 215 pages. 2003.

Vol. 2892: F. Dau, The Logic System of Concept Graphs with Negation. XI, 213 pages. 2003.

Vol. 2902: F. Moura Pires, S. Abreu (Eds.), Progress in Artificial Intelligence. Proceedings, 2003. XV, 504 pages. 2003.

Vol. 2903: T.D. Gedeon, L.C.C. Fung (Eds.), AI 2003: Advances in Artificial Intelligence. Proceedings, 2003. XVI, 1075 pages. 2003.

Vol. 2922: F. Dignum (Ed.), Advances in Agent Communication. Proceedings, 2003. X, 403 pages. 2004.

Vol. 2923: V. Lifschitz, I. Niemelä (Eds.), Logic Programming and Nonmonotonic Reasoning. Proceedings, 2004. IX, 365 pages. 2004.

Vol. 2927: D. Hales, B. Edmonds, E. Norling, J. Rouchier (Eds.), Multi-Agent-Based Simulation III. Proceedings, 2003. X, 209 pages. 2003.

Lecture Notes in Computer Science